COPYRIGHT LAW

RESEARCH HANDBOOKS IN INTELLECTUAL PROPERTY

Series Editor: Jeremy Phillips, *Intellectual Property Consultant, Olswang, Research Director, Intellectual Property Institute and co-founder, IPKat weblog*

Under the general editorship and direction of Jeremy Phillips comes this important new *Handbook* series of high quality, original reference works that cover the broad pillars of intellectual property law: trademark law, patent law and copyright law – as well as less developed areas, such as geographical indications, and the increasing intersection of intellectual property with other fields. Taking an international and comparative approach, these *Handbooks*, each edited by leading scholars in the respective field, will comprise specially commissioned contributions from a select cast of authors, bringing together renowned figures with up-and-coming younger authors. Each will offer a wide-ranging examination of current issues in intellectual property that is unrivalled in its blend of critical, innovative thinking and substantive analysis, and in its synthesis of contemporary research.

Each *Handbook* will stand alone as an invaluable source of reference for all scholars of intellectual property, as well as for practising lawyers who wish to engage with the discussion of ideas within the field. Whether used as an information resource on key topics, or as a platform for advanced study, these *Handbooks* will become definitive scholarly reference works in intellectual property law.

Copyright Law

A Handbook of Contemporary Research

Edited by

Paul Torremans

School of Law, University of Nottingham, UK and Faculty of Law, University of Ghent, Belgium

RESEARCH HANDBOOKS IN INTELLECTUAL PROPERTY

Edward Elgar

Cheltenham, UK • Northampton, MA, USA

Published by
Edward Elgar Publishing Limited
Glensanda House
Montpellier Parade
Cheltenham
Glos GL50 1UA
UK

Edward Elgar Publishing, Inc.
William Pratt House
9 Dewey Court
Northampton
Massachusetts 01060
USA

A catalogue record for this book
is available from the British Library

Library of Congress Control Number: 2007904571

ISBN 978 1 84542 487 9 (cased)

Typeset by Cambrian Typesetters, Camberley, Surrey
Printed and bound in Great Britain by MPG Books Ltd, Bodmin, Cornwall

Contents

Contributors

Professor John Adams, Barrister, University of Notre Dame, London Law Centre and School of Law, University of Sheffield (emeritus)

Professor Valérie-Laure Benabou, University of Versailles-Saint-Quentin-en-Yvelines

Dr Estelle Derclaye, School of Law, University of Nottingham

Professor Thomas Dreier, Institute for Information Law, University of Karlsruhe

Professor Josef Drexl, Max Planck Institute for Intellectual Property, Competition and Tax Law, Munich and University of Munich

Professor Séverine Dusollier, University of Namur

Professor Daniel Gervais, Faculty of Law, University of Ottawa

Professor Jane Ginsburg, Columbia University School of Law, New York

Professor Reto Hilty, Max Planck Institute for Intellectual Property, Competition and Tax Law, Munich and Universities of Zurich and Munich

Brigitte Lindner, Registered European Lawyer, London

Professor Ida Madieha bt. Abdul Ghani Azmi, International Islamic University Malaysia, Kuala Lumpur

Professor Antoon Quaedvlieg, Faculty of Law, Radboud University, Nijmegen

Professor Marco Ricolfi, Faculty of Law, University of Turin

Tom Rivers, Intellectual Property Consultant, London

Professor Jan Rosén, Faculty of Law, University of Stockholm

Dr Irini Stamatoudi, Director of the Greek National Copyright Organisation, Athens

Professor Paul Torremans, School of Law, University of Nottingham and Faculty of Law, University of Ghent

Dr Silke von Lewinski, Max Planck Institute for Intellectual Property, Competition and Tax Law, Munich

Dr Charlotte Waelde, School of Law, University of Edinburgh

Dra Raquel Xalabarder, Universitat Oberta de Catalunya, Barcelona

Foreword

Copyright is in constant evolution and so is research in this field. This *Research Handbook* on copyright law is an attempt to bring together a group of eminent scholars in the field of copyright and to think about the fundamental research questions in this area. Each contributor is at the cutting edge in his or her area of specialisation and his or her chapter aims to share that expertise with the reader.

Some authors deal with fundamental concepts such as originality, the public domain and the various types of works. There are also contributions that focus on the interaction of copyright with competition law and human rights law. Internal mechanisms to regulate the use of copyright and mechanisms to manage copyright exploitation are also covered. Multimedia, on-line teaching, broadcasters' rights, copyright and scientific research, piracy and dispute resolution complete the list of burning issues that are addressed.

It is hoped that this *Handbook* will be a useful research tool for students, academics and practitioners alike in this constantly changing field of copyright in a broad sense.

Paul Torremans
Nottingham, 5 March 2007

1 Originality in copyright: a solution to the database problem?

John Adams[1]

Introduction

This chapter examines the concept of originality in copyright law in the US, the UK and civil law systems. For reasons of convenience, it is proposed to start with US law. Then the historical derivation of both systems will be traced. It will be argued that UK and US law, being derived from a common source, share a common concept of 'originality' which, unlike authors' rights systems, can be supported by a rigorous philosophical analysis. This concept of 'originality' means that copyright attaches to many databases. The requirements will be examined, but certainly had copyright protection been argued, it is possible that the database involved in *British Horseracing Board v William Hill*[2] might have been held to be covered.

Originality in US law

The source of Congress's power to enact copyright laws is Article 1(8)8 of the Constitution. This authorises Congress to 'secure for limited Times to Authors ... the exclusive Right to their respective Writings'. In *The Trade Mark Cases*[3] and *Burrow-Giles Lithograph Co v Sarony*[4] the Court defined the key terms 'authors' and 'writings' in terms which presupposed a degree of originality. These cases were relied on in the well-known case of *Feist Publications Inc v Rural Telephone Service*.[5]

Because readers may be unfamiliar with the Constitutional aspects of these cases, I propose first to deal with them. Congress relies on Article 1(8) of the US Constitution for its powers to make various Federal laws. Before dealing with *Feist*, we need to understand this. In *The Trade Mark Cases*[6] the provision involved was Article 1(8)8. This confers on Congress the power 'To

---

[1] Barrister (Hogarth Chambers); Professor Emeritus, University of Sheffield; Adjunct Professor University of Notre Dame London Law Centre.
[2] Case C-203/02 [2005] RPC 31.
[3] 100 US 82 (1879).
[4] 111 US 53 (1884).
[5] 499 US 340 (1991).
[6] *US v Steffens, US v Witteman, US v Johnson* 100 US 82 (1879).

promote the progress of science and useful arts, by securing for limited terms, to authors and inventors, the exclusive right to their respective writings and discoveries'. These cases involved the defendants counterfeiting well-known trade marks. The Court observed: '. . . neither originality, science or art is in any way essential to the right [*purportedly*] conferred by the Act' (*providing for the registration of trade marks in the Patent Office*).

The Court continued:

> And while the word *writings* may be liberally construed . . . it is only such as are *original*, and are founded on the creative powers of the mind. The writings which are to be protected, are *the fruits of intellectual labor*, embodied in the form of books, prints, engravings and the like. (Emphasis added)

Having concluded that the protection of trade marks could not be justified under Article 1(8)8, the Court went on to consider whether it could be justified under the commerce clause, Article 1(8)3. It held that that provision of the Act was *ultra vires* also, because it was not by its terms limited to the regulation of commerce with foreign nations, among the several States, or with the Indian tribes. In the second case, *Burrow-Giles Lithograph Company v Napoleon Savony*[7] the plaintiff, Savony, a professional photographer, charged the defendant with violating his copyright in a photograph of Oscar Wilde. The findings in the case left no doubt that the plaintiff had taken all steps required by the Act of Congress to obtain copyright in the photograph in question. The principal question for the court was whether Congress had a constitutional right to protect photographs. The Court said:

> It is insisted in argument that a photograph, being a reproduction on paper of the exact features of some natural object or of some person, is not a writing of which the producer is the author.
>
> Unless therefore, photographs can be distinguished in classification on this point from maps, charts, designs, engravings, cuts and other prints, it is difficult to see why Congress cannot make them the subject of copyright as well as the others.[8]

The Court went on to observe that the first and second Constitutional Congresses had enacted statutes to protect the categories of works enumerated above.[9]

> The construction placed on the Constitution by first the Act of 1790 and the Act of 1802 by men who were contemporary with its formation, many of whom were members of the Convention which framed it, is itself entitled to a very great weight.

---

7   111 US 53 (1884).
8   Ibid., pp. 56–7.
9   1 Statutes at Large 124 s. 1; 2 Statutes at Large 171.

We entertain no doubt that the Constitution is broad enough to cover an Act authorizing copyright of photographs, so far as they are representative of original intellectual conceptions of the authors.[10]

The Court went on to point out that, unlike patents, in the case of copyrights there was no examination for novelty.

It is therefore much more important that when the supposed author sues for violation of his copyright, the existence of those facts of originality, of intellectual production, of thought and conception on the part of the author should be proved, than is the case of patent-right.
In the case before us we think this has been done.[11]

The Court then referred to the third finding of facts by the Court of First Instance, that the photograph in question was a

... useful, new, harmonious, characteristic and graceful picture, and that the plaintiff made the same ... entirely from his own mental conception, to which he gave visible form by posing the said Oscar Wilde in front of the camera, selecting and arranging the costume, draperies, and other various accessories in the said photograph, arranging the subject so as to present graceful outlines, arranging and disposing the light and shade, suggesting and evoking the desired expression, and from such disposition, arrangement and representation, made entirely by the plaintiff, he produced that picture in suit.
These findings, we think, show this photograph to be an original work of art, the product of the plaintiff's intellectual inventions.[12]

The Court cited in passing the English case of *Nottage v Jackson*[13] where the issue was whether the owner of the copyright was the photographer, or the person making copies from the negative, in which Bowen MR said, 'The nearest I can come to it, is that [*the author*] is the person who effectively is as near as he can be, the cause of the picture that is produced'. He concluded therefore, that the copyright owner was the photographer.

With these important points in mind, we can now go on to consider the *Feist* case. Rural, the plaintiff in these proceedings, as a condition of its monopoly franchise for telephone services in northwest Kansas, published a white pages telephone directory listing its subscribers alphabetically. Feist published area-wide directories, and for these purposes approached 11 telephone companies in northwest Kansas and requested their permission to use

---

[10]   111 US 53, 57–8 (1884).
[11]   Ibid., pp. 59–60.
[12]   Ibid., p. 60.
[13]   (1833) 11 QB Div. 627.

their white pages listings in return for a fee. Only Rural refused, but Feist went ahead and used their listings without their consent. Rural sued for copyright infringement, and at first instance was given summary judgment, which was affirmed by the Court of Appeals for the Tenth Circuit. The Supreme Court granted *certiorari* to determine whether copyright subsisted in Rural's white pages listings. The judgment of the Supreme Court was delivered by O'Connor J. He started from two well-established propositions: that facts are not copyrightable, but that compilations of facts generally are. He continued by pointing out that the primary objective of copyright is not to reward the labour of authors, but 'to promote the Progress of Science and the useful Arts'.[14] It assures authors the right to their original expression, but encourages others to build freely upon the ideas and information conveyed by a work. This principle, known as the idea/expression dichotomy, applies to all works of authorship. In enacting the 1976 Copyright Act[15] Congress dropped the reference to 'all the writings of an author' and replaced it with the phrase 'original works of authorship'.[16] The Act also made it clear that:

> In no case does copyright protection for an original work of authorship extend to any idea, procedure, process, system, method of operation, concept, principle, or discovery, regardless of the form in which it is described, explained, illustrated, or embodied in such work.[17]

This provision is understood to prohibit the copyrighting of facts.[18] The Copyright Act §103 identifies three requirements which must be met for a work to qualify as a copyrightable compilation: (1) the collection and assembly of pre-existing material, facts, or data; (2) the selection, coordination, or arrangement of those materials; and (3) the creation, by virtue of the particular selection, coordination, or arrangement, of an 'original' work of authorship. The key is the second requirement. It instructs the courts that in determining whether a fact-based work is an orginal work of authorship, they should focus on the manner in which the collected facts have been selected, coordinated and arranged. The originality requirement is not particularly stringent; it requires only that the author make the selection or arrangement independently. §103 makes it clear that copyright is not a tool by which a

---

14   Constitution Article 1(8).8.
15   §101 (which defines 'compilation'), §§102 and 103.
16   Ibid., §102(a).
17   Ibid., §102(b).
18   *Harper & Row Publishers Inc v Nation Enterprises* 471 US 539 (1985). In this case the Court pointed out that the First Amendment to the US Constitution is embodied in the distinction between copyrightable expression, and uncopyrightable facts and ideas.

compilation author may keep others from using the facts or data he or she has collected. He went on to ask '. . . did Feist, by taking 1,309 names, towns and telephone numbers from Rural's white pages, copy anything that was "original" to Rural?' He concluded that the selection, coordination and arrangement of Rural's white pages did not satisfy the minimum constitutional standards for copyright protection. In preparing its white pages Rural simply took the data provided by its subscribers and listed it alphabetically by surname. The end product was a garden-variety white pages directory, devoid of even the slightest trace of creativity. Furthermore, since Rural was required by Kansas Corporation Commission, as part of its monopoly franchise, to produce the listing of its subscribers, it could plausibly be argued that this selection was dictated by state law, not by Rural. Accordingly, there was no copyright in the materials reproduced by Feist.

In passing, O'Connor J dealt with the so-called 'sweat of the brow' or 'industrious collection' doctrine adopted by some courts. The fallacy upon which this doctrine was based was that because §5 of the 1909 Act listed compilations as copyrightable material, all compilations were copyrightable.[19] The logical fallacy of this was that it was equivalent to saying that because stationery items are listed in Class 16 of the Nice Agreement, all stationery trade marks are registrable. 'Sweat of the brow' courts eschewed the most fundamental axiom of copyright law: that no one may copyright facts.

This decision was on the whole welcomed. As *Goldstein on Copyright*[20] points out, it eliminates the economic waste of requiring competitors to reinvent the wheel.[21] The emphasis on the requirement of collection and assembly of pre-existing material, facts or data in the Act should be noted.

The United Kingdom

Historical perspective[22]
Because readers may be unfamiliar with the development of UK copyright law, it is proposed to begin with a brief history. To a substantial extent, the copyright law of the United Kingdom (which formed the basis of US law) grew up as an accidental by-product of censorship. The invention of the printing press was of concern to all European governments. Most took steps to

---

[19]   See *Jeweler's Circular Publishing Co v Keystone Publishing Co* 281 F 83 (CA2 1922).

[20]   Wolters Kluwer (looseleaf).

[21]   §8.4.1.

[22]   For an authoritative account of the history of copyright see R. Deazley, *On the Origin of the Right to Copy*, Oxford and Oregon: Hart Publishing, 2004.

control the dissemination of printed texts. In England and Wales[23] this took two forms: the creation of criminal offences for publishing blasphemous and seditious material, and the introduction of a registration system. The latter was run by a guild called the Stationers' Company. In 1556 the Stationers were granted their original charter by Philip and Mary. It was the declared object of the Crown at the time to prevent the dissemination of the reformed religion.[24] The Stationers thereby in return operated the registration system. Copies of every published work had to be registered at Stationers' Hall in London. This had the effect of conferring on the Stationers' Company an extremely valuable monopoly, and from the Stationers' point of view the registration system fulfilled the useful role of evidencing ownership of the copy. This is the origin of the term 'copyright', i.e. the right to the copy: it is not derived from the right to stop others copying an author's work. In 1695, however, Parliament failed to renew the registration requirement. Thereafter the book trade made a number of attempts to try to get back their monopoly, but never succeeded.[25]

An important influence on the politics that led to the Statute of Anne was the well-known author and journalist Daniel Defoe. He published an influential journal, *A Weekly Review of the Affairs of France*. He used this journal to mount a campaign against what he termed the 'scandalous and unjust Invasions of Property' perpetrated upon the writers of the day, in the absence of any rights protecting them.[26] He had, in an earlier work, argued that the law should prevent 'a certain sort of Thieving which is now in full practice in England . . . Press-piracy'. This he considered an abuse upon authors 'every jot as unjust as lying with their wives, and breaking up their Houses'.[27] In the *Review* of 8 November 1705 he argued that the problem of what we would now call the piracy of unprotected works called for an Act of Parliament '. . . so Property in Copies may be secur'd to Laborious Students, to the Encouragement of Letters and all useful Studies'.

> For the first time in this debate, he drew an explicit link between the benefit to society as a whole that comes with the encouragement of learning, and the provision of some form of statutory protection for books as a way to achieve this end.[28]

---

[23]   The United Kingdom of England, Wales and Scotland was not formed until the Act of Union 1706.

[24]   In addition to exercising control through the Stationers' Company, the control of printing was exercised through various decrees of the Star Chamber.

[25]   See Deazley, op. cit., ch. 1.

[26]   *A Review*, 3 December 1709.

[27]   *An Essay on the Regulation of the Press*, reprinted by the Luttrell Society, Oxford: Blackwell, 1958, p. 27.

[28]   Deazley, op. cit., p. 32.

This argument was eagerly adopted by the book trade itself, which saw it as a means of achieving an indirect security through the recognition of authors' rights in the Act of Anne 1709–10.[29] Accordingly, 13 of the most influential London booksellers and printers on 26 February 1707 laid a petition before the House of Commons in the following terms:

> [M]any learned Men have spent much Time, and been at great Charges in compos-ing Books, who used to dispose of their Copies upon valuable Considerations, to be printed by the Purchasers . . . but of late Years such Properties have been much invaded by other Persons printing the same Books, either here in England, or beyond the Seas . . . to the great Discouragement of Persons from writing Matters, that might be of great Use to the Publick, and to the great Damage of the Proprietors; And praying, that Leave may be given to bring in a Bill for the secur-ing of Property in such Books, as may have been, or shall be, purchased from or reserved to, the Authors thereof.[30]

On the same day as the petition was presented, it was ordered that leave to prepare a Bill be given. Two days later, the Bill for the Better Securing of the Rights of Copies of Printed Books received its first reading. Unfortunately, this Bill remained in committee until the end of the Parliamentary session, and so was lost. Defoe, however, continued his campaign and on 12 December 1709 the booksellers presented a further petition. Leave was given to bring in a Bill 'for securing to [the petitioners] the Property in Books'.

On 11 January 1710 a Bill for the Encouragement of Learning and for Securing the Property of Copies of Books to the Rightful Owners thereof was presented.[31] It was this, subject to various amendments, that passed into law as the Statute of Anne, the modern world's first copyright statute.

In the great case of *Donaldson v Beckett*[32] the House of Lords held by a narrow majority that this statutory scheme abrogated perpetual common law copyright in published (but not unpublished) works. This view was adopted in the US in *Wheaton v Peters*.[33] However, in the US it has been held that common law copyright can still subsist under state law following publica-tion.[34] Consequently, a published sound recording unprotected by Federal law because it was created prior to 15 February 1972, can enjoy state copyright.[35]

---

[29]   The legislative year at the time ran from March to March, as does the British tax year still. The reason the tax year runs from 6 April to 5 April is the adoption of the modern calendar in 1752.

[30]   CJ 15: 313.

[31]   CJ 16: 300.

[32]   (1774) 4 Burr 2408.

[33]   33 US 591 (1834).

[34]   *Capitol Records Inc v Naxos of America* 2005 WL 756591.

[35]   Ibid.

The Copyright Act of 1709–10 recognised the rights of authors, a condition of such recognition being the deposit of their works in Stationers' Hall. The Statute is significant as the earliest statutory recognition of authors' rights in the modern world. It was to form the basis of the United States Copyright Act 1790, and the mandatory system registration system which operated there until 1989. Its philosophy is clearly stated in its long title: An Act for the encouragement of learning, by vesting the copies of printed books in the authors or purchasers[36] of such copies, during the times therein mentioned. The social and economic purposes of the Act stated here should be emphasised. No natural rights theory is involved here.

The so-called Imperial system based on the UK Copyright Act 1911, which constituted (and to some extent still constitutes) the laws of a large number of countries belonging to the British Commonwealth and Empire is also descended from it. In accordance with the 1908 Berlin Act of Berne, this system protected authors' works without formality, i.e. there was no registration or other requirement.

In spite of some eighteenth century dicta favouring an authors' rights basis,[37] it is important to note that copyright in Great Britain was, as noted above, at its inception above, a social and economic right, and this fact results in certain distinctive features of the laws descended from it. Unlike *droit d'auteur*, it was not conceived of in terms of the natural right of authors to the creations of their mind. This was also true of US law. Thomas Jefferson, the third President of the US, like the other American revolutionaries, had an instinctive aversion to monopolies (it was a monopoly on tea which after all had sparked the American War of Independence). At first he opposed even limited monopolies to promote ingenuity.[38] However, later he stated after the drafting of the Bill of Rights that he would be pleased by a provision in the following form:

---

[36]   These would generally be the booksellers who bought the author's copy outright.

[37]   See especially Lord Mansfield's judgment in *Millar v Taylor* (1769) 4 Burr. 2303, 2398: 'From what source, then, is the common law drawn, which is admitted to be so clear, in respect of the copy before publication?

'From this argument – because it is just, that an author should reap the pecuniary profits of his own ingenuity and labour. It is just, that another should not use his name, without his consent. It is fit that he should judge when to publish, or whether he will ever publish. It is fit he should not only choose the time, but the manner of publication; how many; what volume; what print. It is fit, he should choose to whose care he will trust the accuracy and correctness of the impression; in whose honesty he will confide, not to foist in additions: with other reasonings of the same effect'.

An early statement of the moral rights of attribution and paternity – see Berne Convention Article 6*bis*.

[38]   P.L. Ford (ed.), *The Writings of Thomas Jefferson*, New York: Putnam's, 1985.

Art. 9 Monopolies may be allowed to persons for their own productions in literature & their own inventions in the arts, for a term not exceeding – years but for no longer term & no other purpose.[39]

In a letter to Isaac McPherson of August 1813 he rejected a natural-rights theory of intellectual property rights, and clearly recognised their social and economic rationale.

The formulation of Article 1(8)8 of the US Constitution – 'To promote the progress of science and useful arts, by securing for limited terms, to authors and inventors, the exclusive right to their respective writings and discoveries.' – seems to echo the formulation in the Preamble to the Statute of Anne, quoted above (we must bear in mind that the word 'science' at the time meant 'knowledge').

The basic principle of common law jurisdictions is that anything which has involved labour is worth protecting,[40] and the amount of labour involved need not be great. As Megarry J said in *British Northrop Ltd v Texteam Blackburn Ltd*[41] in relation to drawings (to which the same basic principle applies as to literary works):

> It may indeed be that something may be drawn which cannot fairly be called . . . a drawing of any kind: a single straight line drawn with the aid of a ruler would not seem to me a very promising subject for copyright. But apart from cases of such barren and naked simplicity as that, I should be slow to exclude drawings from copyright on the mere score of simplicity.[42]

Over the two centuries following the 1709–10 Act, other works were afforded copyright protection either through case law, as in the case of music[43] and telegram codes,[44] or through Acts of Parliament protecting sculptures, engravings, paintings, drawings and photographs. The law was finally tidied up by the Copyright Act 1911 which, as noted above, also provided for the protection of authors' works without formality. It also introduced copyright protection[45] for phonogram recordings of musical works.[46]

---

[39]   Ibid., p. 113.

[40]   This is not to restate a 'sweat of the brow' doctrine, which was a US peculiar based on an interpretation of §5 of the US Copyright Act – see *Feist Publication Inc v Rural Telephone Service* 499 US 340 (1991) discussed above.

[41]   [1974] RPC 57, at 68.

[42]   And, of course, some 'minimalist' paintings have been close to Megarry J's description, yet no one seems to doubt that they are works of art enjoying copyright.

[43]   *Bach v Longman* (1777) 2 Cowper 623.

[44]   *Anderson & Co Ltd v Lieber Code Co* [1917] 2 KB 469.

[45]   Copyright, i.e., in the medium, as opposed to the traditional copyright in the message.

[46]   Copyright Act 1911, s.19(1).

The principal subsequent UK Acts are the 1956 Act and the Copyright Designs and Patents Act 1988. The minimum protection under the Paris (1971) text of the Berne Convention is the life of the author plus 50 years, but, as a result of the EC's Duration Regulation, this is now increased to the life of the author plus 70 years[47] for literary, dramatic, musical and artistic works under UK legislation. Films enjoy a similar term based on the life of the principal director, and others involved in the production of the film. Sound recordings, broadcasts and cable programmes enjoy protection for a basic term of 50 years. The typographical arrangements of published editions enjoy a term of 25 years from the year of publication.

Types of work protected

As noted above, traditionally, for UK copyright law purposes, a distinction is drawn between original works and productions not requiring 'originality' as a condition of protection. This broadly works out as a distinction between 'the message' and 'the medium'. Works which must be 'original' to be protected are authors' works such as literary works, musical works, drama, art, computer programs (bizarrely protected as literary works). Copyright subsists in such things as records, tapes, films, broadcasts, cable programmes and editions of books without the requirement of 'originality'.[48] In the 1956 Act this distinction was recognised by the fact that the relevant provisions protecting the two kinds of work were contained in different Parts of the Act, and lawyers were in the habit of referring to 'Part I' and 'Part II' subject matter. Under the 1988 Act this formal distinction has gone, but its substance remains. In most legal systems, it is the old Part I works which are considered the proper subjects of copyright, and it is on these that I intend to focus on, as these have a requirement of 'originality'.

Usually the two kinds of copyright are vested in different persons. Thus when an author writes a book he or she owns the literary copyright in the text of it. This copyright is licensed to a publisher for the purposes of reproducing this text in the form of a book (or whatever), but the copyright in the book's typography[49] will belong to the publisher not to the author. The publisher is

---

47   See below.

48   This type of copyright is unknown in the US. 'Derivative works' as defined in §101 of the US Act are works based on original works, and because of Article 1(8)8 of the Constitution, they themselves must exhibit originality.

49   I.e., the typographical arrangement of the 'published edition'. Section 8 of the Copyright Designs and Patents Act 1988 defines 'published edition' as the whole or any part of one or more literary dramatic or musical works. In the language of the publishing trade, 'published edition' is the product, generally between covers, which the publisher offers to the public. In the case of a newspaper, it is the edition of the

reimbursed by the profits he makes on selling the book, and the author by a royalty paid by the publisher on the sales.[50] When a page of a book is photocopied without permission (subject to the availability of any defence[51]), both the author's copyright and the publisher's will be infringed.[52]

It may be noted in passing that in addition to copyright proper, UK law also recognises a number of other rights in this field. These are such things as protection of authors and other rights owners through breach of confidence, passing off and malicious falsehood, moral rights, performers' and recording rights.[53] In addition, there is the *droit de suite*.[54] There are various criminal sanctions against the manufacturers, distributors and users of devices designed to circumvent copy-protection and the fraudulent reception of transmissions. There is also the public lending right scheme by which authors receive payments from a Government fund by reference to the volume of the borrowing of their books from libraries. In addition to providing for the registration of industrial designs, UK law also provides protection for such designs through copyright law (though the period of protection may be reduced to 25 years from the first marketing of objects bearing the design).[55] Designs for products other than artistic works are now protected by a novel right, design right, which like copyright comes into existence automatically,[56] but which is not copyright and enjoys a shorter period of protection.[57]

Section 1 of the 1988 Act provides that:

> Copyright is a property right which subsists . . . in the following descriptions of work –

---

newspaper. As Lord Hoffmann observed in *Newspaper Licensing Agency Ltd v Marks & Spencer Plc* [2001] UKHL 38 it is difficult to think of the skill and labour which has gone into the typographical arrangement of a newspaper being expressed in anything less than a full page. Thus it is in general the facsimile reproduction of a page of a newspaper that infringes this type of copyright, not reproduction of individual articles – s.17(5) and ibid.

   [50]   Sometimes paid in advance.

   [51]   See below.

   [52]   It should be noted that photocopying in universities is governed by the terms of the licence arrangement granted by the Copyright Licensing Agency, a collecting society which acts on behalf of both authors and publishers.

   [53]   I.e. a performer's rights in respect of live performances. Consent is required for recording, broadcasting etc. a live performance (s. 182), use of a recording to show, play in public etc. (s. 173) or importing or dealing in a recording of a live performance (s. 184) In addition, performers enjoy the exclusive right of reproduction (s. 182A), distribution (s. 182B) and rental (s. 182C).

   [54]   See below.

   [55]   Ibid., s. 52(2).

   [56]   Ibid., ss. 213 and 51.

   [57]   Ibid., s. 216.

(a)   *original [emphasis supplied]* literary, dramatic, musical or artistic works,
(b)   sound recordings, films, broadcasts or cable programmes, and
(c)   the typographical arrangement of published editions.

The meaning of these terms is defined in sections 3 to 8. Thus 'literary work' includes a table or compilation, and a computer program,[58] and 'artistic work' means a graphic work, sculpture or collage, irrespective of artistic quality.[59]

Original literary, musical and dramatic works

Introduction   These must be created by an author, or by a computer (e.g. a weather map created by satellite). Because the foundations of UK copyright law are economic considerations, rather than the natural rights of authors in the creations of their mind, it has no problem with the concept of a copyright in computer-generated works. Time and money have been expended in setting up the system, and its products should therefore be accorded protection.[60] Indeed, so far as coming to terms with the computer generally, the 1988 UK Act is arguably the most advanced in the world. The owner of copyright in a computer-generated work is the person by whom the arrangements necessary for the creation of the work were undertaken.[61] Although purists might argue that at the present stage of computer technology there is, strictly speaking, no such thing as 'a computer-generated' work, the basis of the new concept is the pragmatic consideration that the search for an ultimate human author is pointless in relation to this kind of work. The new concept meets the needs of business.

The work must be qualified for protection in the UK by a 'connecting factor'.[62] This may exist by virtue of the author being a British citizen,[63] being domiciled or resident in the United Kingdom or other Berne Convention country, or being a body incorporated under the law of a part of the United Kingdom or other Berne Convention country. Alternatively, it may exist by virtue of the work being published in the United Kingdom or another Berne Convention country.[64] The UK is also a party to the Universal Copyright

---

[58]   Ibid., s. 3.

[59]   Ibid., s. 4(1)(a).

[60]   See *HM Stationery Office Ordnance Survey v Automobile Association* [2001] ECC 272 – Crown copyright in maps generated by satellite with additions and amendments from ground surveys.

[61]   Copyright Designs and Patents Act 1988, s. 9(3).

[62]   Ibid., ss. 1(3) and 153.

[63]   Or a British Dependent Territories citizen, a British National (Overseas), a British Overseas Citizen, a British subject or a British Protected person within the meaning of the British Nationality Act 1981.

[64]   Ibid., s. 155.

Convention (UCC), but the situation in relation to countries where the Universal Copyright Convention is the operative convention is a little more complicated than in the case of Berne Convention countries. A work published in such a country before its accession to the Convention will not be protected by virtue of such accession, because, unlike the Berne Convention, the UCC does not operate retrospectively as regards works in the public domain.

It follows from the UK concept of copyright that a work must be original in the sense that it must not have been directly or indirectly copied from anyone else, and it must result from a certain amount of labour.[65] It certainly does not need to be 'novel'. For example, if you take a photograph of Nelson's column in Trafalgar Square standing in the place where several thousand people have stood before and taken exactly the same photograph, you will acquire copyright in your own photograph, if you have invested the necessary skill and labour. The fundamental requirement is that the work must be recorded in writing or otherwise.[66] If you whistle a new tune, you have no copyright, but if someone switches on a tape recorder and records you whistling it, you will acquire copyright in the tune, though they will acquire copyright in the recording.[67]

1. Literary works[68]   This heading covers the texts of books, poems, codes and ciphers, computer programs and electronic databases.[69] A short poem or advertising jingle is a literary work, but a single word in general cannot be.[70] The work can be written, spoken or sung, but in the latter two cases no copyright will come into existence until the work is recorded in writing or in some other way.[71] If, for example, a lecture is delivered extempore and recorded by a student, two copyrights will come into existence: the lecturer's in the lecture as a literary work, and the student's in the recording. Naturally, the student would be unable to exploit this recording without permission from the lecturer.

2. Dramatic works[72]   This heading covers plays, ballets and mimes which have been choreographed. Again there must be some record of the dance or

---

65   *Cramp & Sons Ltd v Smythson (Frank) Ltd* [1944] AC 329.
66   1988 Act s. 3(2).
67   ss. 3(1) and (2), and s. 9(2).
68   Ibid., s. 3.
69   Since the coming into force of the Copyright and Rights in Databases Regulations 1997, SI 1997 No. 3032 there have been important changes to the protection of databases. This is dealt with later.
70   *Exxon Corporation v Exxon Insurance Consultants* [1982] Ch 119.
71   Ibid., s. 3(2).
72   Ibid., s. 3(1).

mime. Plays are excluded from section 3(1)'s definition of 'literary work', but films can be dramatic works which is important in the case of films which are not recordings of dramatic works.[73]

3. Musical works[74]   The words of a song are protected as a literary work, but the music is protected as a musical work. A theme which is borrowed from a work still in copyright would infringe that copyright though e.g. a variation developed from it would acquire its own copyright as an original work.

4. Artistic works[75]   This heading includes pictures, sculptures, photographs, etc. irrespective of artistic quality. It is problematic whether holograms are protected as films[76] or photographs.[77] This matters because the term of protection is, as noted above, a life plus 70 years for an artistic work,[78] but for films made before the Duration Regulations came into force, it was 50 years from the 1 August 1989 if the film was unpublished at that date (most films were unpublished for these purposes). Otherwise, it was 50 years from publication.[79] For films to which the term provided by the Regulations applies, it is 70 years from the death of the last to die of the principal director, the author of the screenplay, the author of the dialogue and the composer of music specifically written for the film.

Buildings and models for buildings are protected as artistic works,[80] but it is not clear whether this is irrespective of artistic quality as this is not specifically mentioned by the Act in this context.[81] Finally, works of artistic craftsmanship such as furniture and jewellery are protected as a separate category.[82] An ordinary commercial suite of furniture might not qualify under this head.[83]

---

[73]   *Norowzian v Arks Ltd and Guinness Brewing Worldwide Ltd* [1999] FSR 79.
[74]   Ibid., s. 3(1).
[75]   Ibid., s. 4.
[76]   Ibid., s. 5(1).
[77]   Ibid., s. 4(2).
[78]   Ibid., s. 12(1).
[79]   Ibid., Sched 1, para 12(5)(b).
[80]   The correct approach in determining whether there has been infringement of copyright in the plans for a building is to take each drawing in turn and consider whether the respective alleged infringing buildings are copies of the whole or a substantial part of the drawing – *Jones v London Borough of Tower Hamlets*, 10 October 2000 applying *Cala Homes (South) Ltd v Alfred McAlpine Homes East Ltd* [1995] FSR 818.
[81]   Ibid., s. 4(1)(b).
[82]   Ibid., s. 4(1)(c).
[83]   *Hensher v Restawhile* [1976] AC 64; *Merlet v Mothercare* [1986] RPC 126.

The 'originality' requirement   Unless a literary, dramatic or musical work is original it cannot enjoy copyright protection.[84] However, as noted above, the amount of skill, knowledge, mental labour, taste or judgment involved in creating the work need not be large.[85] In the recent case of *Sawkins v Hyperion Records*[86] the claimant had prepared an edition of a work by the baroque composer Michel-Richard de Lalande which the defendants proposed to record, but without paying a royalty. The primary issue before the court was whether the production of a new performing edition of the score of an existing composition was capable of vesting in the editor copyright in the musical work as recorded in the edited score. The court held that it did, and that it was no answer to say that the corrections and additions could or would have been made by players in rehearsal: the claimant had spared them that effort by the use of his own skill and labour.

In fact, the issue as to whether or not a work is original comes most usually to be addressed in infringement actions when deciding whether or not what the defendant has reproduced is a 'substantial part' of the claimant's work. As Laddie, Prescott and Vitoria point out[87] there is little point in trying to defend on the basis that the claimant's work is not original, and therefore not subject to copyright.

> Rather, the defendant should be seeking to show that, insofar as his own work derives from the claimant's work at all, that material was not originated by the author of the claimant's work or that, to the extent that it was, its degree of originality is too modest to count as 'substantial', or arises from being embedded in the context of the claimant's work as a whole.[88]

In fact, it is rather that the onus is on the claimant to show the opposite. So a book about Oscar Wilde contained lengthy extracts from various trials. These had been copied from an earlier work. The defendant's film made extensive use of these materials without the plaintiff's permission. It was held that whilst the book was an original work, what the defendant's film had copied was the trial extracts, not the contribution made by the plaintiff.[89]

---

[84]   Copyright Designs and Patents Act 1988, s. 1(1)(a).
[85]   *Redwood Music Ltd v Chappell & Co Ltd* [1982] RPC 109, 115.
[86]   [2004] EWHC 1530 (Ch).
[87]   H. Laddie, P. Prescott and M. Vitoria, *The Modern Law of Copyright and Designs*, 3rd edn., London: Butterworths, 2000, §3.58.
[88]   Ibid., §84. See *Key Publications Inc v Chinatown Today Pub. Enters. Inc.* 945 F 2d 509 (2d Cir. 1991).
[89]   *Warwick Film Productions Ltd v Eisinger* [1969] 1 Ch 508.

Copyright in databases after Feist

At around the same time that the Supreme Court was deciding *Feist*, the High Court in London was deciding *Waterlow Directories Ltd v Reed Information Services Ltd.*[90] Both the plaintiff and the defendant in this case published legal directories containing the names and addresses of solicitors and barristers. In 1990, the defendant decided to update its directory. It did this by comparing it with the plaintiff's, highlighting those names which appeared in the plaintiff's directory but not the defendant's. It also decided to include, as did the plaintiff's, a section listing solicitors and barristers in public authorities and industry. For the purpose of updating the defendant's directory, the names and addresses not appearing in the defendant's directory were loaded onto a word processor, so that the relevant solicitors and barristers could be written to, inviting them to appear in the defendant's directory. Aldous J held that it was clear that a person could not copy entries from the plaintiff's directory and use them to compile its own directory. The defendant did not deny that the plaintiff had copyright in its directory, but denied infringement. The judge, however, had little difficulty in deciding that what was taken was a substantial part. The quality of what is taken is usually more important than the quantity, but in the present case the parts reproduced were important in that they enabled the defendant to carry out a comprehensive mailing. He cited with approval Lord Cransworth's dictum in *Jefferys v Boosey*[91] that the true definition of 'copyright' is the sole right of multiplying copies.[92] In the circumstances, he granted the plaintiffs an interlocutory injunction.

Before returning to *Feist* it is worth mentioning that *Waterlow Directories* is consistent with two US cases. In *Schroeder v William Morrow & Co*[93] the defendant had copied 27 out of 63 pages of the plaintiff's catalogue of gardening suppliers. It was held that this infringed copyright. In *Adventures in Good Eating v Best Places to Eat*[94] it was held that the defendant had infringed the copyright in the plaintiff's restaurant guide by copying entries from it. It is also to be noted that the *Feist* court approved the earlier 'yellow pages' case of *Bellsworth Advertising and Pub. Corp. v Donnelly Info. Pub. Corp.*[95]

Even bearing in mind that *Waterlow Directories* is an interlocutory decision, in which the judge is weighing the balance of convenience,[96] the facts of

---

90   [1992] FSR 409.
91   (1854) 4 HLC 815.
92   As we saw above, this is historically an inaccurate formulation.
93   566 F 2d 3 (7th Cir. 1977).
94   131 F 2d 809 (7th Cir. 1942).
95   719 F Supp 1551 (SD Fla. 1988).
96   *American Cyanamid Co v Ethicon Ltd* [1975] AC 396.

the case do seem to have more in common with the American cases mentioned above, than with *Feist*. There have also been several US decisions since *Feist*. *Victor Lalli Enterprises Inc. v Big Red Apple Inc.*[97] held that there was no copyright in a chart of horse racing statistics that offered no opportunity for variation in that it was arranged according to a purely functional grid. In *Engineering Dynamics Inc. v Structural Software Inc.*[98] on the other hand, it was held that a compilation of facts for a user interface was copyrightable. Similarly, a guide to state tariffs charged on operating pay telephone companies,[99] and a Red Book listing of used car values based on the professional judgment and expertise of the authors.[100]

In short, *Feist* is quite a narrow decision which does not stop copyright applying to databases which display a minimum of creativity in their selection or arrangement.

The Database Directive
Article 3(1) of the Directive[101] is implemented by section 3A(2) of the Copyright Designs and Patents Act 1988. This provides that a database is original if, and only if, by reason of the selection or arrangement of the contents of the database, the database constitutes the author's own intellectual creation.[102] It is believed that in reaching this formulation, the Commission was influenced by the then recent *Feist* decision. The learned authors of *Copinger on Copyright*[103] write '. . . the definition of originality here would seem to require that the author's time, skill and labour be directed to the selection and arrangement of the database, and not the mere gathering of information. To this extent the law has been altered.'[104]

Whether or not this last point is correct, it is submitted that this is a reasonable summary of the position reached in the US cases discussed above. Moreover, notwithstanding the fact that they were driven by the Constitutional imperative, the position reached as a result of them seems to be similar to that obtaining in the UK.

---

[97] 936 F 2d 851 (6th Cir. 1991).
[98] 26 F 3d 1335 (5th Cir. 1994).
[99] 18 USPQ 2d 2049 (4th Cir. 1991).
[100] *CCC Info. Servs. Inc. v Maclean Hunter Market Reports* 44 F 3d 61 (2d Cir. 1994).
[101] 96/9.
[102] Similar wording is to be found in Art. 5 of the 1996 WIPO Copyright Treaty.
[103] K. Garnett, G. Davies et al., *Copinger on Copyright*, London: Sweet & Maxwell, 2005.
[104] Ibid., §§3–146.

The limitations of database right

As well as purporting to raise the copyright threshold, the Database Directive introduced a new right called 'database right' that was generally supposed to fill the gap so created. This so-called *sui generis* right is contained in Article 7 of the Directive:

> 1. Member states shall provide for a right for the maker of a database which shows that there has been qualitatively and/or quantitatively a substantial investment in either the obtaining, verification or presentation of the contents to prevent extraction and/or re-utilisation of the whole or a substantial part, evaluated qualitatively and/or quantitatively, of the contents of that database.

In *British Horseracing Board v William Hill*[105] the database in question comprised the British Horseracing Board's (BHB) fixture list for each year's racing, weight adding and handicapping, supervision of race programmes, producing various racing and stakes books and compiling data related to horseracing. The database was constantly updated. There was no challenge to the assertion by the BHB that the establishment of the database, and the selection and verification of data for inclusion in the database and the insertion and arrangement of selected data in the database, cost annually around £4,000,000 and occupied about 80 employees. When the declared horses for each race had been finalised, normally by about 12 noon on the day before the race, a list was published of the official runners. Generally, William Hill took its information from this list, but for some popular races such as the Derby, for which bets are accepted earlier, it would use the list of entries, that is the list of horses before the horses were finally declared. The European Court of Justice (ECJ) ruled, *inter alia*, that:

> [38] . . . investment in the selection, for the purpose of organising horse racing, of the horses admitted to run in the race concerned relates to the creation of the data which make up the lists for those races which appear in the BHB database. It does not constitute investment in obtaining the contents of the database. It cannot, therefore, be taken into account in assessing whether the investment in the creation of the database was substantial.
> [40] . . . such prior checks are made at the stage of creating the list for the race in question. They thus constitute investment in the creation of data and not in the verification of the contents of the database.
> [41] It follows that the resources used to draw up a list of horses in a race and to carry out checks in that connection do not represent investment in obtaining and verification of the contents of the database in which the list appears.[106]

---

[105]   Case C-203/02 [2005] RPC 31.
[106]   For the subsequent Court of Appeal decision following the ECJ's ruling see [2005] EWCA Civ 863.

Now whatever we may think of this decision, and the damage it does to the utility of the *sui generis* right for the compilers of databases, it should be carefully noted that it is limited to database right; it says nothing about the availability of copyright.

Could there have been copyright in the BHB database?
The BHB case was argued entirely on the basis of database right, presumably because those advising BHB thought that the provisions noted above, supposedly lifting the copyright threshold, made copyright protection inapplicable. But is this correct? As demonstrated above, the *Feist* decision, upon which that lifting of the threshold was supposed to be based, is a very narrow one. The entire thrust of the ECJ (and subsequent Court of Appeal decision) in BHB was the procedure followed to create the information. But the copyright issue is not concerned with this, but rather only the *presentation* of the information. As noted above, 'sweat of the brow' doctrine has never been part of UK copyright law, because there is no equivalent provision to §5 US Copyright Act upon which that doctrine was based. The operators of the database, Weatherbys, had often to make a decision which horses could be authorised to run in a race (because obviously there is a limitation on the number of horses that can be started in a given race). To this extent there appears to have been an exercise of skill and judgment on the part of the operators. Although this was not considered because it is not relevant to database right, it is relevant to copyright. On the basis of the US case law, and indeed the *Waterlow* case, it is submitted that the exercise of such skill and judgment would be sufficient to attract copyright.

The US Constitution echoes the original purpose of the Act of Anne, which we will recall was the encouragement of learning. This is still, it is submitted, the basis of the common law of copyright. In purporting to raise the copyright threshold, no doubt the European Commission was much influenced by the majority authors' rights jurisdictions of the EU. What at no point seems to have been asked is whether or not the authors' rights position is coherent.

France
The French revolutionary laws of 13–19 January 1791 and 19 July 1793 were the first clear recognition in Continental Europe of the rights of authors, dramatists, composers and artists. The philosophical underpinning of these laws was natural law.[107] This French view was to be highly influential all over

---

[107]   See S. Newman, 'Rights, Freedoms and Phonograms: The Philosophy of Copyright in the Digital Age', Ph.D. thesis, University of Sheffield, 2002, which exhaustively examines this.

Continental Europe. The current French statute of 1957 includes the following provisions:

Article 1   The author of a work shall, by the mere fact of its creation, enjoy an exclusive incorporeal property right in that work as against all persons.

   This right includes attributes of an intellectual and moral nature, as well as attributes of an economic nature, both of which are determined by this law.[108]

Article 2   The provisions of this law shall protect the rights of authors in all intellectual works, regardless of the kind, form of expression, merit or purpose of such works.

Article 6   The author shall enjoy the right to respect for his name, his authorship of the work. . . .

Article 7   A work shall be deemed to be created, independently of any public disclosure, by the mere fact of the author's conception being implemented, even incompletely.

Article 19   The author alone determines the manner and conditions of publication.

Article 32   The author has the right to correct or retract . . .

These last four provisions are, of course, moral rights. These rights cannot be sold or transferred, and are separate from the economic rights. This is not copyright law, it is *author's* law. If an author thinks his or her work has been changed or presented in a way of which he or she subjectively disapproves, the author has a right to take action.[109] This is a subjective, not an objective 'reasonable man' test.

Simon Newman has examined the philosophical basis of the French *droit d'auteur*, and other laws founded on it, in detail,[110] and I am grateful to him for much of the following analysis.

The French *droit d'auteur* emphasises the fact that a work must show 'a trace of the author's personality'.[111] This developed into the highly formalistic German approach, which requiring a high degree of creativity, created problems particularly in relation to computer related works.[112] Thus, it can be

---

[108]   Note the primacy of 'intellectual and moral' as against 'economic'.

[109]   The usual remedy is an injunction; substantial awards of damages are not common.

[110]   Ph.D. University of Sheffield, 2002. See also S. Newman, 'Rights, Freedoms and Phonograms', Computer Law and Security Report (1997) 13.

[111]   Vivant, 'Protection of Raw Data and Databanks in France', in Dommering and Hugenholz (eds.), *Protecting Works of Fact*, Boston: Kluwer, 1990.

[112]   See *Inkasso-Programm*: judgment of 9 May 1985, Bundesgerichtshof, 87 GRUR 1041 (1985).

difficult for a scientific work to attract protection under *urheberecht* no matter how competently it is written, unless it stands out for its individuality.

It is possible that the link between the French and German systems is the Roman law concept of *dominium* in the ownership of physical objects, essentially an absolute right over property.[113] English law has no equivalent, being a relative title system.[114] Although modern civil law systems such as those of France and Germany have abandoned the Roman law concept of *dominium* it is arguable that it still exists in relation to works of the mind: 'The absoluteness of the Roman ownership can [*be seen in*] its inviolability – in the principle that a man cannot lose ownership without his consent . . .'.[115] The transfer of rights in authors' rights systems is strictly regulated, and in certain cases may be impossible. An historically humanist spirit underlies these systems. In *droit d'auteur* systems rights are *personal*.

Under French law, moral rights are perpetual.

> Perhaps it is assumed that the author's spirit in some sense lives on after death (a natural conclusion from Cartesian dualism and Christian theology), though why [*an author*] should object to alterations of his works, but not to direct attacks on his reputation, is not clear. Metaphysics aside, it is strange that the *post mortem* reputations of authors alone should be protected, and in such an indirect manner.[116]

The philosophical underpinning of *droit d'auteur* may thus derive from Cartesian philosophy which separates mind and body, and tends to the view that works of the mind are different from, and superior to, works of the body. This would suggest that works of the mind deserve different and superior protection. The English approach by contrast is reflected in the Lockean view that labours of the mind and body are equivalent, so that workers and creators should have similar rights. Whether a work is a work of the mind, or the product of manual labour, I can alienate it freely.

> Though the earth and all inferior creatures be common to all men, yet every man has a 'property' in his own person. This nobody has any right to but himself. The 'labour' of his body and the 'work' of his hands, we may say, are properly his. Whatsoever, then, he removes out of the state that Nature hath provided and left it in, he hath mixed his labour with it, and joined to it something that is his own, and thereby makes it his property. It being by him removed from the common state Nature placed it in, it hath by this labour something annexed to it that excludes the

---

[113]   See A.M. Honoré, in A.G. Guest (ed.), *Oxford Essays on Jurisprudence* (First Series), Oxford: Clarendon Press, 1968, p. 107.

[114]   Ibid.

[115]   Barry Nicholas, *An Introduction to Roman Law*, Clarendon Law Series, Oxford: Oxford University Press, 1962, p. 157.

[116]   Newman, op. cit., n. 107, p. 68.

common right of other men. For this 'labour' being the unquestionable property of the labourer, no man but he can have a right to what that is once joined to, at least where there is enough, and as good left in common for others.[117]

The philosophy of Locke, Hume and their successors in the history of British thought is essentially inductive.

It relies on empirical method and is sceptical of the tradition that relies on *a priori* positions which are accepted as being true regardless of the underlying experience. It sees all knowledge as derived from experience, so that broad principles can only be developed on the basis of inductive observation.[118]

By contrast, Jean Jacques Rousseau, who was to be influential in French Revolutionary thinking, drew upon the philosophy of Descartes, according to which true knowledge can only come through reasoning from first principles, not through observation.[119]

As noted above, the civilian position has been highly influential in the development of Continental European law in this field. In *Magill*[120] both the Court of First Instance and the Advocate-General stated that 'the essential function of copyright is to protect *moral rights* and reward creative effort'.

So we have the well-known contrast between Continental idealism and Anglo-Saxon pragmatism. However, it should be noted that Anglo-Saxon philosophy has developed since the eighteenth century! In particular, the work of the American philosopher, Alan Gewirth, should be noted. Gewirth's 'principle of generic consistency' (PGC) is essentially a revisiting of Kant's *Moral Law*[121]. Kant's 'categorical imperative' states: 'Act only on that maxim through which you can at the same time will that it should become a universal law'. Under this principle, as long as all persons are treated equally, they can be treated in any manner whatsoever. No substantive rights or duties are specified, only formal rights and duties.[122] Gewirth, by contrast, developed an

---

[117]   John Locke, *Second Treatise on Government*, s. 26, Cambridge: Cambridge University Press, 1960.

[118]   Newman, op. cit., p. 106.

[119]   This is metaphysics, and it can be objected that 'To try to go beyond experience, to what Kant calls things-in-themselves, as metaphysicians do by appealing to what reason can tell them, is to involve oneself in contradiction and paradox'. D.W. Hamlyn, *The Theory of Knowledge*, London: Macmillan Press Ltd, 1977, p. 266.

[120]   *Magill TV Guide/ITP, BBC and RTE* EC Decision 89/205, OJ L78, 21.3.89, p. 43; [1989] 4 CMLR 757; on appeal [1989] 4 CMLR 749.

[121]   E. Kant, *Foundations of Metaphysics of Morals*, New York: Macmillan, 1988.

[122]   Brownsword, R. and D. Beyleveld, *Law as a Moral Judgment*, London: Sweet & Maxwell, London, 1986.

argument which, while it has a superficial resemblance to Kant's categorical imperative, is arrived at by a very different route. Beyleveld summarises it as follows.[123]

> Gewirth argues from the claim of an agent to be an agent within the first-person perspective of that agent. It is appropriate for any one considering the argument to imagine that he or she is that agent ('I').

By claiming to be an agent, I claim (by definition)

(1) 'I do (or intend to do) X voluntarily for a purpose E that I have chosen'.

Because E is my freely chosen purpose, I must accept

(2) 'E is good',

meaning only that *I* attach sufficient value to E to motivate me to pursue it. If I do not accept (2) then I deny that I am an agent – which is to say that it is *dialectically necessary* for me to accept (2).

(3) 'There are generic features of agency.'

Therefore I must accept

(4) 'My having the generic features is good *for* my achieving E *whatever E might be*' = 'My have the generic features is categorically instrumentally good'. Because I value my purposes proactively, this is equivalent to my having to accept

(5) 'I categorically instrumentally ought to pursue my having the generic features'.

Because my having the generic features is necessary for me to pursue my have the generic features, I must hold

(6) 'Other agents categorically ought not to interfere with my having the generic features *against my will*, and ought to aid me to secure the generic features when I cannot do so by my own unaided efforts *if I so wish*',

which is to say

(7) 'I have both negative and positive claim rights to have the generic features' + 'I have the generic rights'.

It follows (purely logically) that I must hold, not only (7), but also

---

[123] 'Moral Status of the Human Embryo and Fetus', in D. Beyleveld and H. Hakers (eds.), *Ethics of Genetics in Human Procreation*, Aldershot: Ashgate, 1999.

(8)   'I am an agent, I have generic rights'.

Consequently it also follows (purely logically) that I must hold

(9)   'All agents have generic rights'.

Since I deny that I am an agent by denying (8), every agent denies that it is an agent by denying (8). Thus, (8) is dialectically necessary for every agent.

Gewirth himself states:

Since the agent regards as necessary goods the freedom and well-being that constitute the generic features of his successful action, he logically must also hold that he has rights (*qua* agent) to these generic features.[124]
. . . to avoid contradicting himself the agent must admit that other persons (*qua* agents) have the same rights to freedom and well-being against himself as he here claims against them.[125]
In saying that freedom and well-being are necessary goods for him, the agent is not merely saying that if he is to act, he must have freedom and well-being: in addition, because of the goodness he attaches to all his purposive actions, he is *opposed* to whatever interferes with his having freedom and well-being and he advocates *his* having these features, so that his statement is prescriptive and not merely descriptive.[126]
If . . . he accepts that it is permissible that other persons interfere with or remove his freedom and well-being . . . He shows that he regards his freedom and well-being with indifference or at least as disposable, so that he accepts 'it is not the case that my freedom and well-being are necessary goods' where 'necessary' has a *prescriptive* force not only a means-end sense.
Therefore, if the agent were to deny that he has rights to freedom and well-being, he would again be caught in a contradiction: he would be in the position of both affirming and denying that his freedom and well-being are necessary goods, that is, goods that he values as the necessary conditions of all his actions and that must hence not be interfered with or removed from him by other persons.[127]

Gewirth states the PGC as follows 'Act in accordance with the generic rights of your recipients as well as yourself'.[128]

Although, at first sight as noted above, this may seem simply to be a restatement of Kant's categorical imperative, 'Act only on that maxim through which you can will at the same time that it should be a universal law',[129] it is different:

---

[124]   A. Gewirth, *Reason and Morality*, Chicago: University of Chicago Press, 1978, p. 61.
[125]   Ibid., p. 75.
[126]   Ibid., p. 79.
[127]   Ibid., p. 80.
[128]   Ibid., p. 139.
[129]   Kant, op. cit.

substantive rights and duties can in theory be derived from it. 'The PGC is an egalitarian universalist moral principle since it requires an equal distribution[130] of the most general rights of action.'[131]

The PGC owes its derivation in turn from the conceptual/normative structure of action, and specifies rights to freedom, and well-being, the content of the latter being specified and provided with an ordering according to three ranks of importance: basic goods, non-subtractive goods, and additive goods.[132] Within these goods there is a hierarchy of importance. Basic goods are headed by life. There is a general logical principle for dealing with conflicts between different rights derived from this normative structure of action.[133]

The hierarchy is derived as follows. One cannot be an agent without having freedom and well-being. The rational agent recognises that in order to have freedom and well-being the agent must uphold certain limits or requirements on the part of all other persons: that they ought at least to refrain from interfering with his freedom and well-being. These limits or requirement that the rational agent upholds with regard to the actions of all other persons constitute his or her claim that he or she has the generic rights.[134] He goes on to argue that such a concept of rights is not restricted to a modern doctrine of the worth of all individuals. He suggests it is to be found in Roman law, feudalism, the Greek concept of *isonomia* and in primitive societies.[135] Obviously, the extent to which a given society conforms to the principle is a matter of historical fact. It does not affect the principle itself which is a metewand against which to test this.

The hierarchy of goods starts with goods which are a precondition because they are not directly constitutive of purposive action or, for the most part of the purposes themselves, but are rather parts of its causal background or prerequisites.[136] Life, physical integrity, health and its various contributing factors are basic goods. Additive goods, by contrast, are part of a prospective agent's well-being when they are viewed generically-dispositionally. They consist in the means or conditions that enable any person to increase his or her capabilities of purpose-fulfilling action and hence to achieve more of his or her goals. They enable an agent to gain and utilise opportunities for improving his or her lot by his or her own productive work.[137] Concepts like 'efficiency' and 'maximising' are therefore especially pertinent in this context of additive goods. Each

---

130   This must not be understood as a crude assertion of egalitarianism, which is incoherent – see D. Miller, *Social Justice*, Oxford: Oxford University Press, 1976.
131   Gewirth, op. cit., p. 140.
132   Ibid., pp. 53 *et seq.*
133   Brownsword and Beyleveld, op. cit., p. 141. Gewirth, op. cit., chs. 4 and 5.
134   Gewirth, op. cit., p. 88.
135   Ibid., pp. 100–101.
136   Ibid., p. 211.
137   Ibid., p. 240.

agent must grant, on pain of contradiction, that all other prospective agents also have these additive rights and that he or she has a correlative obligation to refrain from interfering with their having such conditions.[138]

The conclusion to which this points is that far from according primacy to moral rights, as does French law, we should accord primacy to economic rights. Recognition of an individual's economic rights is necessary in order to enable him or her to earn a living and therefore buy the necessities of life. It falls, therefore, into the category of a basic right, on Gewirth's argument. By contrast, moral rights seem to fall into the category of additive goods. Central to all additive goods viewed as disposition of abilities is the agent's sense of his own worth.[139] Persons must not be insulted, belittled or patronised.[140]

It would also follow from this analysis that the 'inalienability' of moral rights, or their 'unwaivability', cannot be supported to the extent that such waivers do not affect an agent's sense of his own worth, and to the extent that there may be economic advantage in alienation or waiver (it is assumed for present purposes that such alienations or waivers are freely entered into; if they are not, that is an unfair contract issue, and nothing to do with copyright).

Droit d'auteur and copyright systems share a common approach in placing the individual creator at the centre. Where they differ fundamentally, is that copyright reflects the empiricist philosophical tradition, whereas *droit d'auteur* systems reflect a rationalist tradition descended from Descartes. This tends to the creation of self-contained logical systems that do not require experience of the real world. But, in fact, as Kant showed in the *Critique of Pure Reason*[141], concepts do not exist as abstract entities divorced from reality; ultimately it is our perceptions of the world which give content to concepts. To give a very simple example, in mathematics $1 + 1 = 2$, and this could be said to be a self-contained logical truth.[142] But it is not; it depends on our concept of '1'. If the formula is 1 (drop of water) + 1 (drop of water) the answer is 1 (drop of water), therefore $1 + 1 = 1$. In short, the philosophical underpinnings of *droit d'auteur* are incoherent.

Conclusion

The Anglo-US concept of originality derives from the stated purposes of the Copyright Act of 1709–10 and that of 1790. The 1709–10 Act was 'An Act for

---

138   Ibid., p. 241.
139   Ibid., p. 241.
140   Ibid., p. 242.
141   New York: Palgrave Macmillan, 2003.
142   This was certainly a fallacy which underlay the analytic/verifiability dichotomy in logical positivism, of which the best-known exposition was A.J. Ayer, *Language, Truth and Logic*, reprinted, Middlesex: Pelican Books, 1971.

the encouragement of learning . . .', and the US Act of 1790 had a preamble in identical terms. It is clear that the purpose of both Acts was economic and social. This purpose can today be justified in rigorous philosophical terms, which is not the case with the philosophical underpinnings of *droit d'auteur*. In both cases the requirement of 'originality' which a compilation work is required to display is low, as explained above in relation to the *Feist* decision (which killed off the unsupportable 'sweat of the brow' theory). Provided a compilation has involved a certain amount of skill and labour, it should enjoy copyright, because even works involving only such *minima* fulfil the objectives stated in the original Anglo-US legislation of 'encouraging learning', and additionally in US terms of furthering the Constitutional objective of the promotion of science (i.e. knowledge).

It is unclear whether the European Commission really understood this when they formulated the Database Directive Article 3 – 'In accordance with this Directive, databases which, by reason of the selection or arrangement of their contents, constitute the author's own intellectual creation shall be protected as such by copyright'.

It is certainly arguable that a database of the sort that fell for consideration in the *British Horseracing Board v William Hill* should enjoy copyright both in the UK and in the US, because the compilation of the field for each race was not purely mechanical, but involved, for example when there were too many entries, a certain amount of skill and judgment.

It must be conceded, however, that there seems to be a certain hostility to the common law concept of copyright in the European Court of Justice.[143] However, that hostility has to be based on a view that the majority of Member States are right, and that authors' rights systems have a coherent philosophical basis. As I hope I have shown above, it is common law systems which have a coherent philosophical underpinning, not authors' rights systems. Authors' rights systems can be supported in terms of ideas that were current in the eighteenth century, but philosophical thought has progressed since then! It is time to claim the moral high ground for common law systems.

---

[143]   See *Radio Telefis Eireann v Commission* Case C-241/91 [1995] 4 CMLR 718, although this was an Article 82 case, i.e. it was decided on competition law grounds. As Sir Hugh Laddie has written, 'Many believe that part, at least, of the ECJ's motivation in effectively emasculating the right was the belief that in this respect British and Irish law was unreasonably out of line with the law of our Continental neighbours. Put another way, if all Member States of the European Union accorded copyright protection to television . . . schedules, would the ECJ gave felt able to emasculate it as it did in *Magill*? I doubt it' [2001] EIPR 402, 405.

2 Legal issues pertaining to the restoration and reconstitution of manuscripts, sheet music, paintings and films for marketing purposes

Paul Torremans[1]

Introduction

I must admit that I was somewhat taken aback when I started to think about this topic. It seemed so broad and yet very specific at the same time. Very soon though I came to the conclusion that the legal issues to which the topic refers are anything but special issues that relate only to restoration and reconstitution. Instead, it seems to me that the main focus should be on the central concepts of copyright. There are by definition at least two creators involved when one talks about restoration and reconstitution. And they did undertake their creative activity at different times. This raises questions about originality. Is the work of the person restoring or reconstituting a work making an original contribution for the purposes of copyright law? In order to answer the question we need to be very clear about the requirements of originality. We need to define the concept very clearly. A second question that arises is whether there is a separate copyright work resulting from the restoration or reconstitution. In answering both questions the concept of authorship and the way we define it may be of crucial importance.

As a result of this initial realisation, I concluded that it was not a wise idea to try and analyse these issues one by one in an abstract way. That would amount to writing a copyright treatise in order to cover all aspects of all possible factual situations. Instead, I will take the recent decision of the Court of Appeal in the UK case *Hyperion Records v Lionel Sawkins*[2] as a starting point. In a second stage we will then have to see whether any general conclusions can be drawn from that case.

---

[1]   Professor of Intellectual Property Law, School of Law, University of Nottingham and Professor of Intellectual Property Law, Faculty of Law, University of Ghent.

[2]   *Hyperion Records v Lionel Sawkins* [2005] 3 All ER 636 (CA). See also A. Robinson, 'Hyperion Records Ltd v Dr Lionel Sawkins: It's like that and that's the way it is', [2005] *Entertainment Law Review* 191.

The *Hyperion* case

What was it all about?

Let me start immediately by drawing attention to the fact that this is by no means an easy case. A lot depends on understanding the fact correctly, as many of the conclusions arguably depend on small factual details. But this should not come as a surprise to copyright lawyers.

Lord Justice Mummery delivered the main judgment and in his words the overall question before the Court was: 'Does copyright subsist in modern performing editions of the out-of-copyright music of Michel-Richard de Lalande, the principal court composer at the courts of Louis XIV and Louis XV?'[3]

It is important to keep in mind that Dr Lionel Sawkins, who is probably the most eminent Lalande expert, has composed these performing editions of Lalande's music, which itself is of course by now out of copyright. Sawkins claimed copyright in the performing editions, whilst Hyperion did not recognise the existence of copyright in them. One should add that Sawkins had provided the performing editions which the Ex Cathedra choral and orchestral ensemble used in their performance of Lalande's works, which in turn featured on the Hyperion CD. However, the parties never sorted out their differences on the copyright issue and when Hyperion nevertheless released the CD Sawkins sued for copyright infringement. On top of that he argued that his paternity right had been infringed.

But what exactly was it that Sawkins claimed copyright in? Lord Justice Mummery summarised the legal issues in the case as follows:

> As there has been some misunderstanding about the legal issues in the case, I should first make clear what the case is not about. Dr Sawkins has not made any claim in this action to any copyright in (a) the music composed by Lalande; or (b) an arrangement, transcription or interpretation of Lalande's music; or, (c) a compilation of Lalande's music; or (d) a typographical arrangement of Lalande's music. The claim made by Dr Sawkins is confined to copyright in the particular works originated by him. They take the material form of musical scores embodying performing editions of 3 pieces of music by Lalande. Dr Sawkins originated the performing editions in the copyright sense: that is, he used his own substantial and independent effort, skill and time to create them. They did not exist as such before he produced them. He is the author (again in the copyright sense) of each of the [performing] editions.[4]

Sawkins wanted to stay as closely as possible to Lalande's original work. His dealings with the works do not involve a re-composition or Lalande's

---

3   Ibid., at paragraph 1 of the judgment.
4   Ibid., at paragraphs 15 and 16 of the judgment.

music and nor does he make an arrangement of it in the copyright sense of the term. The Court accepts that Lalande's music did not exist in a format that allowed it to be played or performed at a recording session. What Sawkins did was to make the music playable. He transposed the source material into conventional modern notation, he corrected the material where this was necessary and he made a couple of additions. It is crucial to understand though that only in one work were notes added, i.e. new notes were composed by Sawkins. Sawkins' dealings with the works at issue were summarised as follows by the Court of Appeal:

A. Te Deum Laudamus (1684)

Dr Sawkins made necessary corrections and additions to the notation to make the music playable (see paragraph 65). The corrections and re-compositions totalled 141. He added figuring to the bass line. The construction of a figured bass accounted for 672 of 1,139 corrections to the score, either by correcting mistakes or enhancing the performers' comprehension of the chords to be played by adding extra figures. 319 of these were his own interventions. They were not derived from other source materials. Ornamentation in the form of trills on notes was also added.

B. La Grande Piece Royale (1695–Paillard edition 1964)

This orchestral suite in 6 linked movements was derived from 4 sources. Dr Sawkins re-created viola parts for passages of it that were missing. This took up 153 bars of the work's 268 bars. It was the bulk of the work done by Dr Sawkins. There were also 34 editorial interventions. Patten J found (paragraph 64) that Dr Sawkins had made the music playable by transposing from the source material the common notation and, where necessary, had corrected it. Hyperion now accepts that the viola part is a significant re-composition and that it is music in which copyright can subsist, but submits that it was copied from the Paillard edition and that Dr Sawkins has no copyright in it. The judge held, however, that Dr Sawkins did not consciously or unconsciously copy from the Paillard edition (paragraph 31). I shall return to this point later in the judgment.

C. Venite Exultemus (1701)

This is a large scale choral and orchestral piece in 8 movements. It lasts for 26 minutes. Dr Sawkins derived it from various scores and from editions by Cauvin in 1715 and Hue 1729–34. Most of the work done by Dr Sawkins was in adding the figured bass. The changes and additions also included the correction of 27 wrong notes and re-composition of the text. There were 659 corrections to figured bass. 134 of them were not derived from any of the sources, such as Hue. He made a total of 747 interventions.[5]

In order for there to be copyright infringement as Sawkins suggested, he needed to have copyright in these performing editions in the first place. This

---

[5]   Ibid., at paragraph 26 of the judgment.

discussion hinged in the view of the Court on the issues of originality and subsistence.

Originality

A lot has been made in relation to this case of the public policy issue that granting copyright in a restored out of copyright work would hinder access to the work itself. The underlying argument seems to be that the real originality and the real work are out of copyright one and on that line of thought granting a new copyright would clash with public policy. The *Hyperion* case offers a unique opportunity to dispel that myth. Copyright only protects a particular expression of a certain idea and not the idea itself. Copyright in a restored or reconstituted version of an out of copyright work will only protect the expression of the restored or reconstituted version. Everyone remains free to use the out of copyright material itself. Or to use the facts of *Hyperion*, granting Lionel Sawkins copyright in his performing editions will not protect anyone from copying Lalande's music or from making their own performing editions. All they cannot do is use the short cut offered by the existence of the Sawkins performing editions by copying these without his consent. The latter point is the most basic expression of the public policy of copyright, i.e. to prevent the unauthorised copying of certain material forms of expression. One should therefore be very careful in using the public policy argument in this type of case.

The key point is rather found in the fact that only certain material forms of expression are from a public policy point of view worth protecting by copyright. Only original forms of expression are to be protected. Let us look at this for a second from a broad perspective. Originality should not be taken in the normal sense here. Novelty or innovation are not required; the starting point is that the work is not copied and originates from the author, as the House of Lords made clear in *Ladbroke v William Hill*.[6] The author must produce his or her own expression of the idea, but the test to establish whether the work originates indeed from the author is only a minimum effort standard. It is not required that the idea is new, because the idea is not covered by copyright at all. The author must only have expended 'skill, judgment and labour' or 'selection, judgment and experience' or 'labour, skill and capital' in creating the work. In reality two cumulative requirements are involved. First, the work must originate from the author. Second, there must have been a minimum investment by the author of 'skill, judgment and labour'. Both requirements

---

  [6] *Ladbroke (Football) Ltd v William Hill (Football) Ltd* [1964] 1 All ER 465 [1964] 1 WLR 273, at 479 and 291, per Lord Pearce and *University of London Press Ltd v University Tutorial Press Ltd* [1916] 2 Ch 601 at 609, per Peterson J.

have to be met. The investment of 'skill, judgment and labour' merely in the process of copying someone else's work cannot confer originality. This was confirmed by the Court of Appeal in *Biotrading v Biohit*, with reference to Lord Oliver's famous dictum in *Interlego v Tyco*.[7]

But even if the threshold is low, works that do not meet this minimum standard will not attract copyright protection. The question whether an item that is similar to a copyright work was in its own right an original copyright work is a difficult question. The Court of Appeal provided some guidance in *Guild v Eskander Ltd*.[8] A piecemeal approach should be guarded against. The question was instead whether all and not just any one or more of the additional features gave rise to the requisite quality of originality. The need to look at the work as a whole is crucial and this is also emphasised by the Court of Appeal in *Hyperion*. Despite that, some consideration of individual features would be unavoidable in answering that question.

A copy which incorporates some minor alterations of a work which is no longer protected under copyright will not attract copyright.[9] The principle is clearly stated in the *Interlego* case and is widely accepted. Its exact coverage though and the question whether it can be reconciled with the judgment of the House of Lords in *Walter v Lane*[10] are less clear. The *Hyperion* case obliged the Court of Appeal to rule on these points and we will return to that ruling shortly. Suffice it to mention here that copyright infringement in a performing edition of a fourth work was ruled out, as there had been only a very limited editorial input by Dr Sawkins. And even if the content of a work may be nothing else than a compilation of existing elements, some skill and labour must have been invested in the way in which they are organised and expressed.[11] That skill and labour must not be so trivial that it could be characterised as a purely mechanical exercise. On the other hand, creativity as such is not required either, as can be seen from the decision of the Supreme Court of Canada in *The Law Society of Upper Canada v CCH Canadian Ltd, Thomson Canada Ltd and Canada Law Book Inc*.[12]

There is no better way to conclude this overview of the general approach to originality in English law than to quote Dr Dietz, who wrote that there must

[7]   This was reconfirmed by the Court of Appeal in *Biotrading & Financing OY v Biohit Ltd* [1998] FSR 109 at 116; see also Lord Oliver's opinion in *Interlego AG v Tyco Industries Inc* [1989] AC 217 at 258.

[8]   *Guild v Eskander Ltd* [2003] FSR 23.

[9]   See *Interlego AG v Tyco Industries Inc* [1989] AC 217, [1988] 3 All ER 949.

[10]   *Walter v Lane* [1900] AC 539 (HL).

[11]   See *Cramp (GA) & Sons Ltd v Smythson* [1944] AC 329, [1944] 2 All ER 92.

[12]   *The Law Society of Upper Canada v CCH Canadian Ltd, Thomson Canada Ltd and Canada Law Book Inc* [2004] SCC 13.

be 'a relation of creation between the work and the author whatever this act of creation (sometimes only presentation) means'.[13] With hindsight these wise words almost sound prophetic in a *Hyperion* context. What amounts to a sufficient amount of independent 'skill, labour and judgment' is not capable of definition in advance. It has to be determined on the facts of each case.[14]

It is now time to return to the somewhat narrower perspective of the *Hyperion* case and to apply these principles in detail. Lord Justice Mummery looks at this from the following angle:

> The first question is whether the performing editions are incapable of being regarded as 'original' works because Lalande composed the music and Dr Sawkins made his editions of that music with the intention that they should be as close as possible to the Lalande originals.[15]

The Court of Appeal answers that question by relying very strongly on the dictum of the House of Lords over a century ago in *Walter v Lane*.[16] The Court of Appeal suggests that that decision is still good law as a result of the confirmation it received in *Express Newspapers plc v News (UK) Ltd*.[17] In *Walter v Lane* the House of Lords held that copyright subsisted in shorthand writers' reports of public speeches as 'original literary' works. The speeches had been made by the Earl of Rosebery in public with the reporters present. The reporters had made notes in shorthand, they had later transcribed them, corrected, revised and punctuated them and then published them in newspapers as verbatim reports of the speeches. From the copyright point of view adopted by the House of Lords a speech and a report of a speech are two different things. Lord Rosebery was the author of his speeches. The shorthand writers were the authors of their reports of his speeches. They spent effort, skill and time in writing up reports of speeches that they themselves had not written.

For our current purposes it is very important to note that the reports were held to be 'original' literary works, even though the intention of the reporters was to produce as accurate a report as possible of a work of which they were not the authors.

This analysis led Lord Justice Mummery to the following conclusion in the *Hyperion* case:

---

13   Dietz, 'The Artist's Right of Integrity Under Copyright Law – A Comparative Approach' (1994) 25 *IIC* 177 at 182.

14   *Biotrading & Financing OY v Biohit Ltd* [1998] FSR 109 at 116.

15   *Hyperion Records v Lionel Sawkins* [2005] 3 All ER 636 (CA), at paragraph 32 of the judgment.

16   *Walter v Lane* [1900] AC 539 (HL), a decision on the Copyright Act 1842 which used a different kind of wording when compared to the Copyright Designs and Patents Act 1988.

17   *Express Newspapers plc v News (UK) Ltd* [1990] FSR 359 at 365–6.

In my judgment, on the application of Walter v Lane to this case, the effort, skill and time which the judge found Dr Sawkins spent in making the 3 performing editions were sufficient to satisfy the requirement that they should be 'original' works in the copyright sense. This is so even though (a) Dr Sawkins worked on the scores of existing musical works composed by another person (Lalande); (b) Lalande's works are out of copyright; and (c) Dr Sawkins had no intention of adding any new notes of music of his own.[18]

This reliance on *Walter v Lane* cannot be accepted though without considering the dictum in the *Interlego* case that seems at odds with it. One has indeed in the past derived a *de minimis* rule from the words of Lord Oliver in that case,[19] i.e. a copy which incorporates some minor alterations of a work which is no longer protected under copyright will not attract copyright. But the question must be asked whether the impact of the following words does not go further:

Take the simplest case of artistic copyright, a painting or photograph. It takes great skill, judgment and labour to produce a good copy by painting or to produce an enlarged photograph from a positive print, but no one would reasonably contend that the copy painting or enlargement was an 'original' artistic work in which the copier is entitled to claim copyright. Skill, labour or judgment merely in the process of copying cannot confer originality.[20]

In other words, does this dictum in any way reverse what was said in *Walter v Lane* in the context of a somewhat differently worded statutory provision? It is submitted that the two provisions are not incompatible and that the dictum in *Interlego* needs to be interpreted restrictively. The Court was after all dealing with drawings of plastic toy blocks that had barely been touched and the attempt of the producer of the blocks to effectively prolong the term of protection for them was all too obvious. Lord Justice Jacob makes this point very clearly in the second (concurring) judgment in *Hyperion*.[21] Like him I would like to refer to the authors of the *Modern Law of Copyright* who interpret the dictum in *Interlego* as follows:

However, whilst the remarks made in Interlego may be valid if confined to the subject matter then before the Privy Council, they are stated too widely. The Privy Council was there considering fairly simple technical drawings. This is a rather special subject-matter. While the drawing of such a work is more laborious than it looks, it is a fact that any competent draftsman (perhaps, any conscientious amateur) who sets out to reproduce it exactly will almost certainly succeed in the end, because

---

18   *Hyperion Records v Lionel Sawkins* [2005] 3 All ER 636 (CA), at paragraph 36 of the judgment.
19   See e.g. P. Torremans, *Holyoak and Torremans Intellectual Property Law*, Oxford: Oxford University Press (4th edn, 2005), p. 175.
20   *Interlego v Tyco* [1988] RPC 343, per Lord Oliver at 371.
21   At paragraphs 79–82 of the judgment.

of the mathematical precision of the lines and measurements. This should be contrasted with, eg a painting by Vermeer, where it will be obvious that very few persons, if any, are capable of making an exact replica. Now, assume a number of persons do set out to copy such a painting, each according to his own personal skill. Most will only succeed in making something which all too obviously differs from the original – some of them embarrassingly so. They will get a copyright seeing that in each instance the end result does not differ from the original yet it took a measure of skill and labour to produce. If, however, one of these renders the original with all the skill and precision of a Salvador Dali, is he to be denied a copyright where a mere dauber is not? The difference between the two cases (technical drawing and old master painting) is that in the latter there is room for individual interpretation even where faithful replication is sought to be attempted while in the former there is not. Further, a photographer who carefully took a photograph of an original painting might get a copyright and, if this is so, it is rather hard to see why a copy of the same degree of fidelity, if rendered by an artist of the calibre aforementioned, would not be copyright. These considerations suggest that the proposition under discussion is suspect. It is therefore submitted that, for example, a picture restorer may get a copyright for the result of his efforts. Be that as it may, it is submitted that the Interlego proposition is anyway distinguishable where the replicator succeeds in preserving for posterity an original to which access is difficult.[22]

Or to quote Jane Ginsburg:

Reproductions requiring great talent and technical skill may qualify as protectable works of authorship, even if they are *copies* of pre-existing works. This would be the case for photographic and other high quality replicas of works of art.[23]

In conclusion, the two dicta are not incompatible. *Walter v Lane* sets out the rule, but presupposes some creative input. *Interlego* deals with the other end of the spectrum where there is only mere copying. In the words of Lord Justice Jacob:

I think the true position is that one has to consider the extent to which the 'copyist' is a mere copyist – merely performing an easy mechanical function. The more that is so the less is his contribution likely to be taken as 'original.'[24]

One should not underestimate the importance for English copyright law of the fact that the Court of Appeal has now in *Hyperion* clarified the approach that is to be taken to originality by re-confirming the dictum in *Walter v Lane* and by ruling out any conflict with *Interlego*, which is confined to its particular mere

---

[22]   H. Laddie, P. Prescott and M. Vitoria, *The Modern Law of Copyright and Designs*, Butterworths (2nd edn, 1995), at paragraph 4.39.
[23]   Ginsberg, 'The Concept of Authorship in Comparative Copyright Law', 52 *DePaul Law Review* 1063 (2003).
[24]   *Hyperion Records v Lionel Sawkins* [2005] 3 All ER 636 (CA), at paragraph 82 of the judgment.

copying scenario. Crucial as it may have been to reach the conclusion that Dr Sawkins' work was original in nature, its impact goes well beyond any cases of restoration or reconstitution of out of copyright works.

But originality is not the only issue that arises in relation to Dr Sawkins' work. Subsistence is also a very real issue.

Subsistence

Original as it may be, Dr Sawkins' work will only be protected if it is a literary and dramatic work, which under English law means that it has to fit within one of the categories of works set out in the Copyright Designs and Patents Act 1988. The obvious candidate in terms of category is the category of musical works. The main problem here is that the Act does not offer a workable definition of a musical work. The Court therefore had to step in and fill the gap.

Hyperion had argued that no new musical work had been created. In its view the performing edition has no impact on the sound that is produced and perceived by the audience. That sound is essentially the result of Lalande's musical work and has nothing to do with Sawkins' work. The fact that Sawkins wanted to stay as close as possible to Lalande's original work provides a further argument for denying the existence of a new copyright work. The Court summarised that argument as follows:

> The effect of the editorial interventions of Dr Sawkins was, as he asserted was his intention, only to produce more faithful and better copies of Lalande's original music and to make it playable, rather than to create new music of his own. The kind of effort and skill expended by Dr Sawkins was not appropriate or relevant to the creation of a fresh musical copyright, such as might be achieved by changes to the melody and harmony of the underlying work.[25]

At first instance Patten J had summarised Hyperion's position on subsistence as follows:

> [U]nless the edition includes the composition of new music in the form of the notes on the score (and not merely the correction of wrong or unsatisfactory notes in the scores used) then no copyright would exist in the edition as a musical work.[26]

Both Patten J and the Court of Appeal refused to follow this unduly narrow approach. It seems indeed that there is more to music than notes on a score.

---

25   Ibid., at paragraph 41 of the judgment.
26   At paragraph 50 of his judgment which the Court of Appeal praised unanimously and which is reported at [2004] 4 All ER 418. See also V. Jones, 'Musical Works: Out with the Old and in with the New' [2005] *Entertainment Law Review* 89; P. Groves, 'Better than it Sounds: Originality of Musical Works' [2005] *Entertainment Law Review* 20 and V. Jones, 'What Constitutes a Copyright Work – Does it Really Matter' [2005] *Entertainment Law Review* 129.

Any plain language definition will, for example, also refer to sound and rhythm and the impact on the ear in general. By focussing narrowly on notes only Hyperion's argument is also inconsistent with the approach of assessing the work as a whole that the House of Lords laid down in *Ladbroke v William Hill*.[27] The Court of Appeal summarised the two points on the basis of which it rejected Hyperion's argument and held the performing editions to amount to a musical work as follows:

> In my judgment, the fallacies in Hyperion's arguments are that (a) they only treat the actual notes in the score as music and (b) they approach the issue of subsistence from the wrong direction by dividing the whole of the performing edition into separate segments and by then discarding particular segments on the basis that they are not music and not therefore covered by copyright. That is contrary to the correct approach to subsistence of copyright laid down by the House of Lords in Ladbroke (Football) Ltd v William Hill (Football) Ltd. ... The subsistence of copyright involves an assessment of the whole work in which copyright is claimed. It is wrong to make that assessment by dissecting the whole into separate parts and then submitting that there is no copyright in the parts. Hyperion's arguments ignore the fact that the totality of the sounds produced by the musicians are affected, or potentially affected, by the information inserted in the performing editions produced by Dr Sawkins. The sound on the CD is not just that of the musicians playing music composed by Lalande. In order to produce the sounds the musicians played from Dr Sawkins' scores of his edition. Without them Ex Cathedra would not have produced the combination of sounds of *Te Deum*, *La Grande Piece Royale* or *Venite Exultemus* for recording on the CD.[28]

There is indeed no reason for restricting the coverage of musical copyright to the actual notes of the music only. After all a dramatic work is not limited to the words that are to be spoken by the actors either. It is thus common sense that a recording of a person's spontaneous singing or any form of improvisation also amounts to music for copyright purposes.

Sawkins' work was required for the musician to play Lalande's work in the way they did and more importantly it produced aural effects. It did change what people heard. From a subsistence point of view a separate musical work had therefore been created.

Infringement and moral rights
There is for our current purposes no need to go into detail on these points. Suffice it to say that the Court of Appeal went on to hold that in using the

---

[27] *Ladbroke (Football) Ltd v William Hill (Football) Ltd* [1964] 1 WLR 273, at 277–91 (HL).
[28] *Hyperion Records v Lionel Sawkins* [2005] 3 All ER 636 (CA), at paragraph 49 of the judgment.

performing editions without permission for the recording of the CD and by not mentioning Lionel Sawkins as the author of the performing editions on the sleeve of that CD Hyperion had infringed Sawkins' copyright in the performing editions, as well as his paternity right.[29]

The *Dead Sea Scrolls* case

Hyperion was not the first case to draw attention to issues surrounding the restoration and reconstitution of out of copyright works. A couple of years earlier the Supreme Court of Israel had already rendered its judgment in the *Dead Sea Scrolls* case.[30] Rather than the reconstitution of musical works, this case was concerned with the reconstitution and decipherment of ancient texts or literary works. When the 2000 year old Dead Sea Scrolls were discovered many of them consisted essentially of fragments and even when these fragments had been puzzled out and put together mechanically about one third of the text was missing. In relation to one of the most significant scrolls, Professor Qimron spent several years reconstituting those missing bits of text. In the context of the unauthorised use of his work, the question arose whether he had acquired a separate copyright in his work. The Supreme Court of Israel came to a conclusion that runs along the same lines as the one in *Hyperion*. Of course, Professor Qimron did not acquire copyright in the original text, but his reconstitution, or as the Court put it his deciphered text, though reflecting the original text written 2000 years ago, was an original work for the purposes of copyright.[31] Qimron therefore had a copyright in the deciphered text as a literary work in the same way Sawkins had a musical copyright in the performing editions.

Private International Law Considerations

The *Dead Sea Scrolls* case had one additional element to it though. The alleged infringing publication had taken place in a third country. This transnational element is not at all uncommon in restoration and reconstitution of out of copyright works and brings with it a whole range of private international law considerations to which I now turn.[32]

I would indeed like to pick up the fact that the alleged infringement of the

---

29   Ibid., at paragraphs 57–69 of the judgment.
30   *Eisenmann v Qimron* 54(3) PD 817.
31   See M. Birnhack, 'The Dead Sea Scrolls Case: Who is an Author?' (2001) *EIPR* 128 and T. Lim, H. MacQueen and C. Carmichael (eds), *On Scrolls, Artefacts and Intellectual Property*, Sheffield: Sheffield Academic Press (2001).
32   This part of the chapter has been reproduced from my essay on 'Choice of Law Regarding Copyright and the Dead Sea Scrolls: The Basic Principles', which was originally published in Lim et al., op. cit., 116–27.

work of Professor Qimron and the International Team concerning the Dead Sea Scrolls seems to have happened in more than one jurisdiction. This necessarily raises the issue of which copyright law applies. Quite apart from the infringement question, there is the even more fundamental question of copyrightability. Do some of these works attract copyright protection in the first place? Once more the choice of law issue arises, for example because not all national laws use the same originality criterion and the answer may therefore differ depending on the applicable national copyright law.

We will turn first to the questions related to copyrightability. In a second stage we will address the infringement-related questions. The approach taken to the subject is very much based on the Berne Convention and the basic framework should therefore apply in all Member States of the Berne Union. Whenever necessary, American and British copyright laws have been used as examples.

Copyrightability
The Copyright, Designs and Patents Act 1988 and the US Copyright Act 1976 do not contain any detailed guidance on the issue of the applicable law. The national treatment obligation in the Berne Convention may oblige Member States to grant protection to foreign works, but the Convention does not specify the exact modalities of that protection. No indication is to be found that would address the issue of which law should govern protection.

The issue has not yet been addressed directly by the courts in the UK. It can be said though that the creation of copyright leads to an exclusive right that restricts competition. It would therefore seem to follow that the UK's public policy dictates that the creation of a copyright that will be exercisable in the UK will be governed by the provisions of the Copyright, Designs and Patents Act 1988. Protection will be sought in the UK; therefore, the 1988 Act should apply as the law of the protecting country.

In the US the issue has also been virtually ignored for many years, but recently the courts have had to address it head-on in two cases. The *Itar-Tass* case[33] was concerned with Russian news articles which were copied in the US and incorporated in a New York publication by Russian Kurier. The *Corel* case[34] was concerned with the alleged copying in Britain and the US of

---

[33]   *Itar-Tass Russian News Agency; Itar-Tass USA and Fromer & Associates, Inc (Plaintiffs-Counter-Defendants-Appellees), Argumenty I Fakty; Moskowskie Novosti Komsomol-Skaya Pravda; Union of Journalists of Russia; Ekho Planety; Megapolis Express; Balagan Israeli Comic Magazine; Moskowsky Komsomolets: AR Publishing Co., Inc and Yevgen I. Fromer (Plaintiffs-Appellees) v Russian Kurier, Inc (Defendant-Counter-Claimant-Appellant) and Oleg Pogrebnoy (Defendant-Appellant)* 153 F 3d 82, 47 USPQ 2D 1810 (2nd Cir. 1998).

[34]   *Bridgeman Art Library v Corel* 36 F Supp 2d 191 and 25 F Supp 2d 421.

photographs. In both cases issues of choice of law arose. Both cases deal with the law applicable to copyright infringement, but they also address the scope of copyright and copyrightability. The *Corel* case is particularly informative in this respect. The *Itar-Tass* case also deals with the issue of the law applicable to the ownership of copyright, but a full discussion of this point would lead too far.[35]

For our current purposes we turn first to the issue of copyrightability and the scope of copyright. The second circuit held in *Itar-Tass* that the national treatment rule in the Berne Convention does not provide a full answer to all choice of law questions that arise in a copyright context and specifically not to the question whether a work attracts copyright protection or not or to the question of the scope of such copyright protection. The Court then went on to consider copyright as a form of property to which they felt they had to apply the standard Second Restatement rule that the interests of the parties in property are determined by the law of the state with the most significant relationship to the property and the parties.[36] In a copyright context that seemed to mean the law of the country of origin, as the law of the country where the works had been created and published. This led the Court to choose Russian law as the applicable law. The Court was on this basis happy to conclude that the law that determines whether or not a work attracts copyright also determines the scope of the right that is granted in appropriate cases.

In the *Corel* case the United States District Court for the southern district of New York[37] first went down a very similar path, but was later forced to reconsider its position. In its second judgment, dated 18 February 1999, the Court looked at the Constitutional provisions concerning copyright before turning its attention to the Berne Convention Implementation Act (BCIA) 1988. In particular sections 3(a) and 4(c) of that Act attracted its attention. Section 3(a) states that:

---

[35]   For further details see Torremans, 'Jurisdiction and Choice of Law Issues in United States Intellectual Property Cases: From Dodging the Bullet to Biting it' (1999) *Intellectual Property Quarterly* 372.

[36]   *Itar-Tass Russian News Agency; Itar-Tass USA and Fromer & Associates, Inc (Plaintiffs-Counter-Defendants-Appellees), Argumenty I Fakty; Moskowskie Novosti Komsomol-Skaya Pravda; Union of Journalists of Russia; Ekho Planety; Megapolis Express; Balagan Israeli Comic Magazine; Moskowsky Komsomolets: AR Publishing Co., Inc and Yevgen I. Fromer (Plaintiffs-Appellees) v Russian Kurier, Inc (Defendant-Counter-Claimant-Appellant) and Oleg Pogrebnoy (Defendant-Appellant)* 153 F 3d 82, 47 USPQ 2D 1810 (2nd Cir. 1998), at 90.

[37]   The first case was reported as *The Bridgeman Art Library Ltd. v Corel Corp.* 25 F Supp 2d 421 (SDNY 1998). The second judgment in this case was delivered on 18 February 1999.

The provisions of the Berne Convention –
(1)   shall be given effect under title 17, as amended by this Act, and any other relevant provision of Federal or State law, including the common law, and
(2)   shall not be enforceable in any action brought pursuant to the provisions of the
Berne Convention itself.

Section 4(c)[38] adds that '[n]o right or interest in a work eligible for protection under this title may be claimed by virtue of, or in reliance upon, the provisions of the Berne Convention or the adherence of the United States thereto'.

The Court derives from these provisions that Congress cannot have had the
intention to consider any law other than the US Copyright Act on the issue of
copyrightability. This interpretation places particular emphasis on the wording
of section 4(c) of the BCIA 1988. The application of any foreign law would in
this view necessarily occur 'in reliance upon the provisions of the Berne
Convention or the adherence of the United States thereto' and is therefore
excluded in the same way as the solution that would give any direct effect to
the provisions of the Berne Convention itself.

The *Corel* court arrives at a very different solution than the *Itar-Tass* court.
It is submitted that the outcome in the *Corel* case is the better one, since it
leads indirectly to the application of the law of the protecting country. This is
not simply so though because English or Scottish private international law
does not have the equivalent of the rule that property issues are governed by
the law with which the property and the parties have the most significant relationship. The British approach is indeed based more on the *lex situs*. We have
pointed out elsewhere that such an approach, when taken in combination with
the limited guidelines provided by the national treatment rule in the Berne
Convention, leads to the applicability of the law of the protecting country. The
Itar-Tass court's approach is in our view incompatible with the national treatment rule in that it applies the law of the country of origin, which means that
in one country different right holders will receive different rights in similar
works. National treatment then means that the same private international
choice of law rules apply to all authors. It is our view that national treatment
should go further and that also the same substantive rules should apply to all
authors and right holders within the territory. This view leads inevitably to the
application of the law of the protecting country. The approach taken by the
Corel court seems therefore to lead to the right conclusion, even though the
reasoning is not properly based on the correct interpretation of the Berne
Convention and the application of the rules of private international law, but
rather on domestic US law.

The next issue must of course be the determination of what kinds of issues

---

38   Now codified at 17 USC §104(c).

are treated as issues of copyrightability for the purposes of private international law. For our current purposes we can restrict our discussion first to the question of whether or not the scrolls and the work of Professor Qimron and the International Team are works that meet the requirements for copyrightability and especially whether these works are original, before turning secondly to the scope of copyright protection and the related issue of copyright infringement in a second stage.

(a) The types of works that will be protected   Article 2 of the Berne Convention restricts itself to stating the principle that 'literary and artistic works', which include 'every production in the literary, scientific and artistic domain', will be protected and Article 2*bis* allows for certain limitations without obliging Member States to introduce them. The precise definition of the types of works that will be protected and the decision whether or not to introduce any limitation is left to the Member States and their domestic legislation.[39] Even if they are not large, differences exist between the laws of the Member States. Whether a work comes within a category of works to be protected and, if so, in which category of works, will be determined by the law of the protecting country. In practice there is no doubt that all the works involved in the *Dead Sea Scrolls* case are literary works, with the exception of the photographs, which are artistic works. All these works will be works that can be protected, irrespective of whether US, UK or Israeli copyright law applies. Originality seems to be much more of an issue.

(b) Originality   Works are not simply granted copyright protection because they come within the scope of one of the categories of works that are protected or within the general definition of literary and artistic works. Copyright protection also requires that the works are original. The issue of applicable law is particularly relevant here, because there is no uniform legal definition of the concept of originality that is used by all national copyright systems. In other words, depending on which law applies, certain works may either be granted copyright protection or refused copyright protection for lack of originality. The chapters in this book that deal with substantive copyright have made it very clear that whilst British copyright law will probably view all works involved as original works, this may not necessarily be the case under US copyright law.

Since originality is a core factor in the decision as to whether or not a work will attract copyright protection, it seems logical to apply the law of the

---

[39]   Compare in this respect Berne Convention, Article 2(1) and Copyright, Designs and Patents Act 1988, ss. 1–5B.

protecting country to this issue. The originality criterion of the law of the protecting country will therefore be used to determine whether any of the works produced by Professor Qimron and the International Team will attract copyright protection, i.e. Israeli copyright law if the question is whether they will attract copyright protection in Israel, US copyright law if the question is whether they will attract copyright protection in the US, etc.[40]

Infringement

(a) The scope of the right   Once copyright has been created it is important to know what the content of the exclusive right will be. How far will the protection and the restriction of competition extend? Logically speaking, this issue is inextricably linked with the decision to grant copyright, as it determines what exactly is being granted. The issue should therefore be decided under the same applicable law. The law of the protecting country should apply.[41] The law of the place where the right is used has to decide whether the right exists and what its content is.[42] There is, however, no specific provision in any national copyright legislation that deals directly with this issue.

This choice of law point is important in practice as the Berne Convention does not define the scope of protection in a rigid way. It rather sets minimum standards. While it is generally accepted that the copyright holder has the exclusive right to reproduce the work and make public representations of the work, certain national legislations add to this the exclusive right of the copyright holder to distribute copies of the work.[43]

The issue of the scope of an immaterial right such as copyright is inextricably linked with the concept of infringement. The beneficiary of an immaterial right only receives those rights which can be enforced whenever they are infringed. In the light of the fact that the national treatment principle leads to the application of copyright laws on a territorial basis as far as the scope of

---

[40]   *The Bridgeman Art Library Ltd v Corel Corp.* United States District Court for the Southern District of New York, judgment of 18 February 1999. This judgment explicitly confirmed and applied this rule.

[41]   See *Novello & Co LD v Hinrichsen Edition LD and Another* [1951] 1 Ch 595 and see also Article 34, paragraph 1 of the Austrian Private International Law Statute that contains the same rule and H. Schack 108 (1988) *UFITA* 51.

[42]   See M. Walter (1976) 89 *RIDA* 45, at 51 and, for an example, see the judgment of 1 March 1989 of the Arrondissementsrechtbank (Dutch court of first instance) in Leewarden, *United Feature Syndicate Inc v Van der Meulen Sneek BV*, [1990] *Bijblad Indutriële Eigendom* 329. The scope of copyright in the Garfield dolls in the Netherlands was determined by Dutch law (law of the protecting country), rather than under US law.

[43]   E. Ulmer, *Intellectual Property Rights and the Conflict of Laws*, Deventer: Kluwer (1978), at 36.

protection is concerned, it seems logical to assume that in cases of infringement the law of the protecting country will also be the *lex loci delicti*. The
courts in the UK have recently dealt with an international copyright infringement case in *Pearce v Ove Arup*,[44] and although this was primarily a jurisdiction case it seemed clear that the courts would eventually apply the *lex loci
delicti* to the infringement issue.

The US court in the *Itar-Tass* case dealt with the real copyright infringement choice of law issue and the point was also considered in the first *Corel*
judgment. Both courts consider infringement to be a separate matter, for which
there is a separate choice of law rule. They classified copyright infringement
as a tortuous issue and this led them to the application of the *lex loci delicti*.
In the *Itar-Tass* case, the copying of the news articles had taken place in the
US. The Second Circuit therefore applied US law to the infringement issue.[45]
It must be clear though that only those rights that had come into existence
under Russian law, as the law governing copyrightability, could be infringed
in the first place. US law simply governed the issues as to whether or not
certain acts amounted to an infringement and what the consequences of the
infringing activity was. Similarly it was said in the first *Corel* judgment[46] that
the alleged copying had mainly taken place in England and that English law
was therefore applicable to the infringement issue.

The solution to apply the *lex loci delicti* to the issue of copyright infringement must therefore be supported. We have argued elsewhere that copyright
infringement is tortuous in nature and that the normal tort choice of law rules
should be applied.[47] As the outcome of the *Itar-Tass* case shows, this is a most
sensible approach which leads to results that are acceptable and even desirable. The synergy between the *lex loci delicti* and the territoriality principle
means that in practice it is the law of the country where protection is sought,
i.e. the law of the protecting country, that determines the scope of the protection offered by copyright.

Moral rights give rise to a few delicate issues though and need to be considered separately. Whether one sees moral rights as an integral part of copyright
or as separate rights, the precise content of the moral rights that are granted is
also determined by the law of the protecting country.[48] Either they are just part

---

[44]   *Pearce v Ove Arup Partnership Ltd* [1997] 2 WLR 779, [1997] 3 All ER 31.
[45]   Ulmer, op. cit., at pp. 91–2.
[46]   *Bridgeman Art Library v Corel* 36 F Supp 2d 191 and 25 F Supp 2d 421.
[47]   J. Fawcett and P. Torremans, *Intellectual Property and Private International
Law*, Clarendon Press (1998), chapter 11.
[48]   The term 'rights' in the Berne Convention includes both pecuniary and moral
rights; see J. Ginsburg 17 (1993) *Columbia-VLA Journal of Law and the Arts* 395, at
405 and see also the analysis of the *John Huston* case below.

of the scope of the copyright that has been granted, or, if they are seen as independent rights, they come into being automatically through the creation of the copyright. It is logical in these circumstances to accept that they are governed by the same rule, for reasons of uniformity. The applicability of the law of the protecting country is confirmed by Article 6*bis*(3) of the Berne Convention which explicitly states that the means of redress in relation to moral rights are governed by the law of the protecting country. The specific means of redress for each moral right are linked so strongly to the moral right concerned that it would make no sense to separate them in terms of the applicable law.

Moral rights could also be seen as personality rights that are linked to the person of the author of the work. From a choice of law point of view, they could then be classified as forming part of the personal law of the author. An alternative in copyright terms could be the law of the country of origin, because the latter is closely linked to the author. The common law approach to substantive copyright and moral rights, which is based on the commercial exploitation of the work rather than on the author, has never gone down this path. It is, therefore, submitted that this choice of law approach is to be rejected.

We have argued elsewhere that moral rights should be seen as fundamental rights that protect the author against the abuse of his work.[49] From that point of view the UK's approach to moral rights should form part of its public policy. This would have important implications in a situation where the case is litigated in the UK, but where the law of the protecting country is not the Copyright, Designs and Patents Act 1988. Rather than applying the law of the protecting country, the court would be obliged to apply the UK's provisions on moral rights, if the standard of moral rights protection in the law of the protecting country would otherwise be lower than that in the Copyright, Designs and Patents Act 1988. It needs to be stressed that this approach does not replace the choice of law rules and the law of the protecting country altogether. Public policy considerations, and eventually the application of the law of the forum, can only be considered at a later stage.[50] It is doubtful whether this point could also apply to US copyright law. The absence of strong and explicit moral rights protection under the provisions of the US Copyright Act rather seems to lead to the conclusion that the US does not regard this as an issue that touches upon its public policy.

Mandatory rules, however, operate in a slightly different way. These rules

---

[49]   J. Holyoak and P. Torremans, *Holyoak and Torremans Intellectual Property Law*, Butterworths (2nd edn, 1998), chapter 13; see also Stamatoudi (1997) *Intellectual Property Quarterly* 478.

[50]   See Ginsburg and Sirinelli, 15 (1991) *Columbia-VLA Journal of Law and the Arts* 135, at 139.

are directly applicable[51] and the choice of law process is not followed at all. The provisions on moral rights of the forum are directly applicable, irrespective of the content of the law of the protecting country, if they are mandatory rules. This is the approach that was taken by the French Cour de Cassation[52] in the *John Huston* case.[53] It is submitted that the nature of moral rights, as rights that come into operation only when the copyright work is used abusively, does not justify the latter approach. The traditional law of the protecting country, plus public policy of the forum in exceptional cases, is far more suitable.[54] The same law would then also be applied to all issues that form part of the scope of copyright.

(b) Exceptions to the rights   Restrictions placed on the exclusive right of the copyright owner modify the content of the latter. So, if all issues relating to the content of the exclusive right granted by copyright are to be governed by the law of the protecting country, exceptions to the rights granted to the copyright holder form the next issue in this category. The precise scope of the rights granted is, indeed, only to be determined when these exceptions are also taken into account. For example, the right holder's exclusive right to make copies of the work is restricted by the exceptional right of the user to make a copy for personal use. Further exceptions might exist for reporting current events, research and private study, etc.[55] The same exceptions obviously also play a role as defences against copyright infringement.

When all this is applied to the *Dead Sea Scrolls* case it becomes clear that

---

51   In French legal terminology these rules are referred to as 'règles d'application immédiate', which characterises them very well.

52   Different decisions were reached at first instance and upon appeal; see judgment of 23 November 1988 of the Tribunal de Grande Instance de Paris [1989] Recueil Dalloz Sirey 342 (Jurisprudence), annotated by Audit and [1989] Revue Critique de Droit International Privé 372, annotated by Gautier; judgment of 6 July 1989 of the Cour d'Appel de Paris [1990] Recueil Dalloz Sirey 152 (Jurisprudence), annotated by Audit and [1989] Revue Critique de Droit International Privé 706, annotated by Gautier; judgment of 28 May 1991 of the Cour de Cassation [1991] Revue Critique de Droit International Privé 752, annotated by Gautier. In this case French law was both the law of the protecting country and the law of the forum, but that does not influence our conclusions.

53   For an in-depth analysis of the case see Ginsburg and Sirinelli, 15 (1991) *Columbia-VLA Journal of Law and the Arts* 135 (an English translation of the judgment is attached as an appendix); Ginsburg and Sirinelli (1991) 150 *RIDA* 3; see also Ginsburg 36 (1988–9) *Journal of the Copyright Society of the USA* 81 and Ginsburg 17 (1993) *Columbia-VLA Journal of Law and the Arts* 395.

54   See Ginsburg and Sirinelli (1991) 150 *RIDA* 3, at 21.

55   For a full catalogue of these exceptions e.g. under UK law see Copyright, Designs and Patents Act 1988, chapter 3 (ss 28–76).

the whole infringement question in relation to any of the works produced by Professor Qimron and the International Team that attract copyright protection will be answered by Israeli copyright law if the alleged infringement took place in Israel, by US copyright law if the alleged infringement took place in the US, etc.

(c) Civil remedies   Civil remedies are the final issue in this category. The availability of damages and injunctions restraining further encroachments on the exclusive rights of the right holder make the rights effective. This includes the issue of who can sue, for example whether a licensee can sue independently for copyright infringement or whether he needs to rely on the copyright owner to do so. They determine the real scope of the right involved and should therefore come under the law of the protecting country.[56] The parties cannot use the law of contract to change the rights to sue which each of them has, in so far as that change is to have effect against third parties.[57] The traditional procedural restrictions apply though in the situation where the law of the protecting country is not equally the law of the forum. For example, the quantification of damages issue will be governed by the law of the forum.[58]

Conclusion on the private international law considerations
The law of the protecting country governs issues of copyrightability. In other words, whether or not the works of Professor Qimron and the International Team attract copyright protection and especially whether they are original works for the purposes of copyright are matters that will be decided by Israeli copyright law as far as copyright protection in Israel is concerned, by US copyright law as far as copyright protection in the US is concerned, by the British copyright law as far as copyright protection in Britain is concerned, etc.

Once the works attract copyright protection, the issue of infringement of copyright can arise. Here the law of the protecting country becomes *de facto* the *lex loci delicti*. The question as to whether there has been copyright infringement in Israel will therefore be decided under Israeli copyright law and similarly the question whether there has been copyright infringement in the US or Britain will be decided under US and British copyright laws respectively.

---

56   See, for an example in the case law, the judgment of 17 June 1992 of the German Bundesgerichtshof (Supreme Court) [1993] GRUR Int. 257 and see Ulmer, op. cit., at 35.
57   See the judgment of 17 June 1992 of the German Bundesgerichtshof (Supreme Court) [1993] GRUR Int. 257.
58   See Cheshire and North, *Private International Law*, Butterworths (13th edn, 1999), chapter 6 and more specifically at pp. 87–8.

Needless to say, in the light of the differences in substantive copyright law on points such as originality and defences to copyright infringement, to name only the most important, the outcome will differ depending on the jurisdiction concerned.

Conclusion

Leaving aside the impact of the choice of law considerations that have been highlighted above, it seems clear that the conclusion that is to be drawn from the *Hyperion* and *Dead Sea Scrolls* cases is that at least under a UK common law copyright approach there may well be copyright in the restored or reconstituted version of an out of copyright work.

It is submitted that subsistence is not the main issue in these cases. *Hyperion* was a peculiar case and the argument was allowed to take centre stage only because the Copyright Designs and Patents Act 1988 does not offer a definition of a musical work. In most normal cases the subsistence point will be overcome almost automatically once originality has been demonstrated.

Originality though is the main issue. Mere copying will not suffice. In as far as restoration or reconstitution only involves copying there will not be a separate copyright. A personal input or creation by the person restoring or reconstituting the work is required. That link of creation between the author and the work is crucial, but does not involve art, innovation or invention. It may be nothing more than presentation, even if it is presentation of what the author thinks was exactly what the original author created back in time. It is therefore easy to see that a reconstitution effort in the proper sense of the word will more easily and more often give rise to a separate copyright than a mere restoration effort.

That leaves us with one more question. In the title to this chapter, the restoration and reconstitution of paintings and films was also envisaged. *Hyperion* dealt with musical copyright and the *Dead Sea Scrolls* case dealt with literary works. But as we have seen, originality is the crucial point and on that point the same rules apply to paintings, other artistic works and films too. There is therefore no reason to assume that the conclusion which we have reached in relation to musical copyright and literary works would not also apply to paintings, artistic works in general and films.

3   A Canadian copyright narrative
Daniel Gervais[1]

Introduction

Copyright policy, like other major areas of public policy, requires a solid anchoring in fundamental principles. That anchor can only be found through a clear understanding of the purpose of copyright.

One could rely on public choice theory and posit that by allowing various stakeholders to push their issues the end-result will be balanced. From a pragmatist's perspective, the theory rests on three key assumptions. First, that all interested parties are represented by (equally) well-equipped experts. Second, that these experts have correctly analyzed not only the current state of play but also the predictable future and correctly devised measures (including, but not limited to, legislative amendments) that will adequately align the regulatory framework with their objectives. Third, the end-result of blending the various 'adequate' and well-formulated proposals in a single politically acceptable package will maintain the (correct) analysis of each (equally well-equipped) lobby and not produce unintended or negative consequences. If one accepts that these assumptions are well founded, then by all means the government and Parliament should limit themselves to a clearinghouse function whose main objective is to keep everyone equally happy (or as minimally unhappy as possible).

One may also disagree with one or more of the above assumptions. I will declare myself to be one of those sceptics, one who believes that proper policy is made when the policy objective is identified from a national interest perspective, not just by mosaicing sectoral interest groups, and then an objective analysis of the measures designed to implement the objective is made that takes into account possible unintended consequences. I suggest that the first step is to develop a coherent discourse, a narrative. This is what I suggest is needed in the copyright

---

[1]   Osler Professor of Intellectual Property and Technology Law and Vice-Dean (Research), Faculty of Law (Common Law), University of Ottawa. The author wishes to thank Talitha Nabbali, (LL.B. University of Ottawa) for her research assistance; Tanya Woods (LL.B. candidate) for her assistance in editing this chapter, and my University of Ottawa colleague Professor Elizabeth Judge for her useful comments on the first draft. The author is grateful to the Ontario Ministry of Innovation (PREA/ERA) for financial support.

domain. The power of a narrative is at least three-fold: it guides policy-making; it assists courts in interpreting copyright laws; and, with proper education, it increases understanding and, hopefully, internalization of copyright norms.

To develop a copyright narrative, one probably should begin by looking at the roots of the current system. One of the problems of copyright policy in North America is that it is a house built on someone else's foundations, though at times we are not exactly sure whose foundations. This is nothing new. After all, Canada and, in a different way of course, the United States have 'imported' the common law, the French Civil Code (Louisiana, Quebec) and several other parts of their legal edifice, state, provincial and federal, from other countries. There are differences, however, between copyright and, for example, the common law. The volume of contract, property and tort cases, as well as doctrinal debates, restatements etc. – interspersed with numerous statutory interventions of course – have allowed us both to understand the origins of common law rules and to transform, and adapt, many of the underlying common law concepts. Can the same be said of copyright? Seventeenth century debates in Britain, and elsewhere in Europe, from which the first copyright statutes emerged, had the great merit of forcing the courts in those jurisdictions to examine the whys and wherefores of copyright law with much greater depth than was the case in North America, until recently.

The perceived need to anchor copyright debates in a solid policy context and, hence, to develop a coherent (and hopefully convincing) narrative has been the subject of excellent contemporary research. We are indebted to a number of scholars for their work in this area.[2] The attempt to find normative applications from a historically derived model for copyright is not new either. However, the

---

2   See *inter alia*, Rose, Mark (1993), *Authors and Owners*, Cambridge, MA: Harvard University Press; Patterson, L. Ray (1968), *Copyright in Historical Perspective*, Nashville: Vanderbilt University Press; Kaplan, B., Nimmer, Melville B. and David Nimmer (looseleaf), *Nimmer on Copyright*, New York: Matthew Bender [hereinafter 'Nimmer on Copyright']; Bently, Lionel and Brad Sherman (2001), *Intellectual Property Law*, Oxford: Oxford University Press; Seville, Catherine (1999), *Literary Copyright Reform in Early Victorian England*, Cambridge: Cambridge University Press; Feather, John (1994), *Publishing, Piracy, and Politics: A Historical Study of Copyright in Britain*, London: Mansell; Ginsburg, Jane C. (1990), 'A Tale of Two Copyrights: Literary Property in Revolutionary France and America', *Tulsa Law Review* **64**, 991–1032; Hughes, Justin (2006), 'Copyright and Incomplete Historiographies: Of Piracy, Propertization, and Thomas Jefferson', *Southern California Law Review* **79**, 993–1083; Woodmansee, Martha (1984), 'The Genius and the Copyright: Economic and Legal Conditions of the Emergence of the "Author"', *Eighteenth-Century Studies* **17**, 425–48; Hesse, Carla (1990), 'Enlightenment Epistemology and the Law of Authorship in Revolutionary France 1777–1793' (1990), *Representations* **30**, 109–37; Jaszi, Peter (1991), 'Toward a Theory of Copyright: The Metamorphoses of 'Authorship', *Duke Law Journal* 1991, 455–502.

research thus far tends to provide a blurred picture, by espousing justificatory theories based on one or many of the following: commercial and personal interests of authors, understood as property and/or liability rules; commercial interests of publishers and other 'rights holders'; and/or the social costs of overprotection and the related economic-driven search for an optimal point of protection.

In Section 2 of this chapter, I will look at the Canadian narrative and try to present a faithful picture of its current stage of evolution. To do so, however, a detour via England is required, because that is whence the soil from which the Canadian narrative comes. This historical detour will be the focus of Section 1. Section 3 will suggest a path for the next stages of the Canadian narrative that is both consistent with international norms and hopefully useful in moving the debate forward. That section ends with a brief look at the impact that the linkage with trade rules may have on copyright.

1. The British narrative

A look at British copyright history is useful to understand Canadian copyright history.[3] The history of copyright in Britain did not start in 1709 with the Statute of Anne. Early in the sixteenth century, the 'Stationers' (the forefathers of modern publishers) had organized themselves in a guild known as the Stationers' Company, and guild membership insisted upon exclusivity of publication. In other words, no guild member could publish, without authorization, a book already published by another member. Naturally questions emerged rather quickly concerning the enforcement of the exclusivity stemming from guild membership against non-members, i.e., 'outsiders'.[4] This objective was achieved by combining a ban on the importation of foreign books (in 1534[5]) and the grant by Queen Mary of a Charter (enforceable *erga omnes*) to the Stationers' Company (in 1556). The Charter allowed the Stationers to search out and destroy any book printed in contravention of the Statute of Proclamation.[6] As a result, only books licensed by the Stationers could be registered and legally printed in the UK, as entries in the register

---

[3]   See Garon, Jon M. (2003), 'A Conceptual Framework for Copyright Philosophy and Ethics', *Cornell Law Review* **88**, 1278–15 ('Beginning in 1709, England singled out intellectual property from other areas of law, distinctly from the other forms of labor. The United States and even France took similar approaches. The underlying basis was a recognition that intellectual enterprise serves the public in a manner fundamentally different from other forms of labor, and thus needs to be clothed with sufficient reward for the most capable to serve society in this capacity.')

[4]   See Cornish, William and David Llewelyn (2003), *Intellectual Property*, 5th edn, London: Sweet & Maxwell, 345–6.

[5]   As a point of reference, Caxton introduced the printing press into England in 1476, 26 years after its invention by Gutenberg.

[6]   See Cornish and Llewelyn, *supra* note 4.

were restricted to Company members. This served the interests both of publishers and of the Crown, which could maintain a degree of control over new publications. Interestingly, the system was enforced both through the Star Chamber and, for Elizabeth and her Stuart successors, through the Church, no doubt a reflection of the deep religious struggles of that period.[7]

The Stationers' privileges 'outlived the ignominy into which the Star Chamber fell, being kept up by the Long Parliament and confirmed in 1662 after Charles II's restoration. But he allowed it to lapse in 1679; and, while James II revived it for seven years in 1685, it could not last long in the political climate of his dethronement. Parliament finally refused to renew it in 1694. The stationers, who had argued forcefully against their loss of protection, were left with such claim to "copy-right" as they could make out of their own customary practices surrounding registration.'[8]

John Milton[9] and John Locke were instrumental in the fight to put an end to this 'licensing' regime, which they (rightfully) considered as a form of pre-publication censorship.[10] Milton became famous in copyright history for another reason: his contract with printer Samuel Simmons, by which Milton gave over to Simmons 'all that booke copy or manuscript . . . with the full benefit profitt & advantage thereof or which shall or may arise thereby'[11] in *Paradise Lost* for the sum of £20, was used as evidence both that authors were entitled to proprietorship in their work (as far back as the 1660s), and that publishers were (and are) treating authors unfairly.[12]

John Locke's name is of course central to the debate. His name was used to justify extensive copyright protection as a natural property right flowing from an author's labours. Locke's most famous words in this context are:

Every man has Property in his own Person. This no Body has any Right to but himself. The Labour of his Body, and the Work of his Hands, we may say, are properly his.

---

[7]   James I also issued 'printing patents', in the same form as letters patent concerning 'inventions' to certain publishers, but most were issued to Company members. But those patents were limited in time and thus much less important than the unlimited Stationers 'copyright'. The censorship element was reinforced by various decrees of the Star Chamber issued in 1566, 1586 and 1637. See Patterson, *supra* note 2, 6.

[8]   Ibid., 346.

[9]   See his *Areopagitica*, published in 1644.

[10]   Rose, *supra* note 28–32.

[11]   See Lindenbaum, Peter (1992), 'Milton's Contract', *Cardozo Arts & Entertainment Law Journal* **10**, 439, 441.

[12]   See ibid., 452–4.

The various eighteenth-century editors and writers who attacked Simmons . . . and booksellers generally were plainly appropriating Milton in their own struggle for respectability (and cash), a struggle they viewed themselves as carrying on in part with their needed representatives in the marketplace. (ibid., 454)

Whatsoever then he removes out of the State that nature hath provided, and left it in, he hath mixed his Labour with, and joined to it something that is his own, and thereby makes it his Property. It being by him removed from the common state nature placed it in, that excludes the common right of other Men.[13]

Three remarks are in order. First, while this statement justifies a property right derived from labour, the context here is clearly *manual* not intellectual labour. Consequently, the property that Lockean theory justifies is first and foremost *tangible* property because that type of property is rivalrous. One thus needs to be able to exclude all others from using one's property. Not so with literary or artistic works. They are non-rivalrous, and exclusion of others is not required for me to enjoy my copy. What *is* rivalrous, however, is profit. It is much harder for two publishers to profit from the same book in the same market at the same time than if one of them has a monopoly on the book.

Second, authors do not work from what 'nature hath provided', but rather from what other men and women have created before, standing, as it were, on the shoulders of giants.[14]

Third, Locke's theory assumes continuing labour to continue to enjoy exclusivity.[15] It is not surprising, then, to read from his own hand that, whilst he favoured a temporary exclusive right for authors in literary works for the life of the author plus 50 or 70 years[16] – Locke seems to have been less sympathetic toward the publishers' monopoly[17] – he was also aware of the need for the material to enrich the public domain:

---

[13]   Locke, John, *Two Treatises of Government*, bk II, para. 26, Cambridge: Cambridge University Press, 1960.

[14]   The attribution of this to Newton as the first to use this phrase may be erroneous. See Merton, Robert K. (1993), *On the Shoulders of Giants: The Post-Italianate Edition*, Chicago: University of Chicago Press. Merton traced the aphorism to Bernard de Chartres (12th century).

[15]   Locke, *supra*, bk II, para. 51.

[16]   Locke, John, *Memorandum*, King, 203, 208–9.

[17]   In a letter to a Member of Parliament (B. Rand (ed.), *Correspondence of John Locke and Edward Clarke*, Cambridge, MA: Harvard University Press, at 39 (org. 1927, rep. 1975)), he wrote:

By this monopoly also of those ancient authors, nobody here, that would publish any of them anew with comments, or any other advantage, can do it without the leave of the learned, judicious stationers. For if they will not print it themselves nor let any other, by your labour about it never so useful, and you have permission to print it from the Archbishop and all the other licencers, it is to no purpose. If the company of stationers so please it must not be printed. An instance you have of this in Æsop's Fables. Pray talk with A. Churchill concerning this who I believe will be able to show you other great inconveniences of that act, and if they can possibly, I wish they could be remedied. And particularly, I think, that clause, where printing and importation of any books, to which any have a right by patent is prohibited, should be at least thus far restrained that it should be lawful for anyone to print or import any Latin book whose author lived above a thousand years since.

I know not why a man should not have liberty to print whatever he would speak . . .

That any person or company should have patents for the sole printing of ancient authors is very unreasonable and injurious to learning; and for those who purchase copies from authors that now live and write, it may be reasonable to limit their property to a certain number of years after the death of the author, or the first printing of the book, as, suppose, fifty or seventy years. This I am sure, it is very absurd and ridiculous that any one now living should pretend to have a propriety in, or power to dispose of the propriety of any copy or writings of authors who lived before printing was known or used in Europe

Leaving Locke's theory aside for a moment,[18] we see that after approximately a century and a half of exclusive privileges, amounting to indirect censorship granted to the Stationers and in a political climate where those privileges could not be renewed (thus leaving the Stationers with no protection *erga omnes*), debates concerning a statute focusing on the rights of both authors and publishers started in earnest in England in the closing years of the seventeenth century. [19] A Bill eventually passed in 1709, the Statute of Anne, granted 'authors and their assigns' the sole right and liberty of printing books for a period of 14 years from first publication.[20] However, enforcement of the right (still) depended upon registering the book's title with the Stationers' Company.

Why do authors enter the picture at that point in the story? The fact that the *Statute* granted the right first not to the Stationers but to the author – a major difference from the Stationers' monopoly that was in place until 1694 – was the direct result of the *Stationers' reliance* in their petition to Parliament on the natural right of the authors in their works. This was in fact a pan-European strategy of publishers.[21] Focussing the attention on authors allowed booksellers

---

[18]   It is the source of fascinating and continuing academic debates. See Epstein, Richard (2003), 'Liberty versus Property? Cracks in the Foundations of Copyright Law', Olin Working Paper No. 204. Available at SSRN: http://ssrn.com/abstract= 529943 or DOI: 10.2139/ssrn.529943; and Bell, Tom (2001), 'Escape from Copyright: Market Success vs. Statutory Failure in the Protection of Expressive Works', *University of Cincinnati Law Review* **69**, 741, 762–3 ('That facially plausible extension of Locke's theory does not, however, withstand close scrutiny. His labor-desert justification of property gives an author clear title only to the particular tangible copy in which she fixes her expression – not to some intangible plat in the noumenal realm of ideas. Locke himself did not try to justify intangible property. Modern commentators who would venture so far beyond the boundaries of Locke's thought and into the abstractions of intellectual property thus ought to leave his name behind.').

[19]   Patterson, *supra*, at 20.

[20]   A second term of 14 years was possible if the author was still alive.

[21]   See Chartier, Roger (1994) 'Figures of the Author', in Sherman, Brad and Alain Strowel (eds), *Of Authors and Origins: Essays on Copyright Law,* Oxford: Oxford University Press.

to achieve their aims, while avoiding the problem of defending their unpopular trade monopoly.[22] That said, to see the author merely as an excuse to grant an exclusive right would be an oversimplification.[23] Authors did want rights they could enforce themselves, even though most of them were happy to work with publishers. There was, in other words, a timely convergence of interests. On the one hand, authors were basking in the sun of the Enlightenment, stroked by the rays of individualism.[24] On the other, the Stationers were in favour of a right for authors of which they would be the assignees, through the then-prevailing patronage arrangements. They understood that they needed a justificatory theory other than greed or, indeed, their desire to survive, to convince both Parliament and the public.

The Statute was not the first right accorded authors in Europe. The role of the author as 'right-holder' had emerged in France in the early days of the sixteenth century. A French court granted the equivalent of an injunction to prevent an almanac from being sold without the consent of its author.[25] The court's reasoning was close to modern trade-mark/passing off principles in that it was afraid the author's reputation might suffer if a book with his name

---

[22]   See Patterson, *supra*, at 169. As Jon Garon noted:

Transfer of the copyright allowed the parties to effect by two steps what had been prohibited by one [namely the Stationers' monopoly]. Had the House of Lords come to an opposite conclusion in Donaldson [see *infra*], the practical result would have been to re-establish the Stationers' Company Act' Garon, Jon M. (2002), 'Normative Copyright: A Conceptual Framework for Copyright Philosophy and Ethics', *Cornell Law Review* **88**, 1278, 1298.

[23]   As Professor Bently cautioned:

. . . it is often said that a natural-rights-based justification for copyright inevitably produces a different conception of copyright than is produced by an incentive argument. More specifically, it is argued that a natural rights conception of copyright leads to longer and stronger protection for authors (and copyright owners) than an incentive based conception. This is because a natural rights argument for copyright is assumed to result in a form of property that is perpetual and unqualified. In contrast, an incentive-based argument only justifies the grant of the minimum level of protection necessary to induce the right-holder to create and release the work. . . . While it is understandable that lobby groups use (or abuse) the various justifications to further their ends, more problems arise when people begin to believe the rhetoric . . .

Bently, Lionel and Brad Sherman (2001), *Intellectual Property Law*, Oxford: Oxford University Press, 33–4.

[24]   Michel Foucault commented that the modern concept of author 'constitutes a privileged moment of individualism in the history of ideas' Foucault, Michel (1979), 'What is an Author?', in Harari J. (ed.), *Textual Strategies: Perspectives in Post-Structuralist Criticism* Ithaca, NY: Cornell University Press, p. 141. See also Jaszi, Peter (1992), 'On the Author Effect: Contemporary Copyright and Collective Creativity', *Cardozo Arts and Entertainment Law Journal* **10**, 293.

[25]   Mark Rose, *supra*, 17–19.

on it was published without his consent. Yet this case, and the many cases that would follow, support Mark Rose's observation that:

> [In] the early modern period, in connection with the individualization of authorship . . ., there developed a general sense that it was improper to publish an author's text without permission. The acknowledgement of an author's interest in controlling the publication of his texts is not necessarily the same as the acknowledgment of a property right in the sense of an economic interest in an alienable commodity.[26]

One might speak more of *propriety* than *property* in such a context.[27]

A parallel set of arguments in England at the time was that, if authors had an *obligation* not to write libellous, defamatory or otherwise unacceptable content (which they had), then authors should have a coextensive *right* in their writings. Following in the footsteps of Milton and Locke, satirist Daniel Defoe argued that pre-publication control was unnecessary; that a copyright should be granted to all authors and that their content could be controlled by prosecuting 'offenders' after publication.[28] *Ex post* control as opposed to *ex ante* licensing, in other words. Examples of his diatribes include: 'Twould be unaccountably severe to make a Man answerable for the Miscarriages of a thing which he shall not reap the benefit of it well perform'd',[29] and '[w]hy have we laws against House-breakers, High-way Robbers, Pick-Pockets, Ravishers of Women, and all kinds of open violence and yet no protection for an author?'.[30]

Contrary to Lockean arguments based on the author's labour,[31] Defoe's argument seems to rest more on the complementarity of punishment and reward. According to Professor Rose:

> Defoe's agitation on behalf of authorial rights seems to have influenced the London stationers, who perhaps saw in his call for a law to protect authorial property a new

---

[26]   Ibid., 18.

[27]   Professor Hughes commented on this point recently: 'Our modern word "propriety" comes from the Middle English word "propriete," which comes from the Old French word "propriété," which means – in old and modern French – both "property" and "correctness" or "suitability."' Hughes, *supra* note 2, 1011.

[28]   Rose, *supra*, 34–5.

[29]   Quoted in ibid., 35.

[30]   Ibid., 37.

[31]   See Gordon, Wendy (1993), 'A Property Right in Self-Expression: Equality and Individualism in the Natural Law of Intellectual Property', *Yale Law Journal* **102**, 1533; and Locke, John (1967), *Two Treatises of Government,* 2nd edn, Peter Laslett ed., Cambridge: Cambridge University Press, 269–78 (Bk II, para 4–15). William Enfield explained it as follows: 'Labour gives a man a natural right of property in that in which he produces: literary compositions are the effect of labour; authors have therefore a natural right of property in their works'. W. Enfield (1774), *Observations on Literary Property*, London: Johnston, 21 (quoted in Rose, *supra*, 85).

strategy for pursuing their own interests . . . in 1707 the stationers submitted a new petition to Parliament for a bill to secure property in books. Making for the first time no reference to the revival of licensing, the stationers' petition emphasized the negative effect that the disorder in the trade was having on authors.[32]

The entry into force of the Statute in 1710 raised the question whether it abolished or superseded common law copyright. Common law copyright had been chiefly concerned with preventing the first publication of a work without the author's consent, as were several courts in civil law jurisdictions. Only after its first publication, did the book enter the (different) realm of commercial exploitation. Authors and publishers tried to convince various courts that the Statute had not superseded the pre-existing, perpetual common law copyright. Booksellers, on the other hand, including a number of Scottish booksellers who were happy to reprint 'public domain' English titles,[33] argued that if common law copyright ever existed, it could not be enforced after the expiry of the new statutory monopoly. The Stationers thus decided to support Defoe's parliamentary lobbying efforts. Simply put, they were happy to see perpetual property rights vested in authors, provided those rights would be assigned to them.

Alexander Pope was one of most active members of the English author community at the time. His famous case against Edmund Curll[34] is considered a major precedent still today.[35] Curll had published a series of letters on various subjects written by several authors, including Pope. This publication was unauthorized although many commentators believed that Pope – who, as a gentleman, could not seek 'media exposure' directly – was not wholly unhappy that someone else generated that exposure on his behalf[36] (which reminds one of 'scandalous' photos and stories leaked by fading Hollywood stars to the tabloids). More importantly for our purposes, it was probably the first case that clearly separated the tangible property in the letter (belonging to the recipient) and the author's property in the (intangible) content, an important abstraction that would prove important for the rest of the story. The Court was able to rule in Pope's favour:

> I am of the opinion that it is only a special property in the receiver, possibly the property of the paper may belong to him; but this does not give a licence to any person whatsoever to publish them to the world, for at most the receiver has only joint property with the writer.[37]

---

[32] Ibid., 35–6.
[33] See *Millar v Kinkaid* (1750), 4 Burr. 2319, 98 ER 210.
[34] *Pope v Curll* (1741) 1 Ark. 341.
[35] See Pat Rogers (1972) 'The Case Pope v Curll', *The Library: Transactions of the Bibliographical Society* 27, 326–31.
[36] See e.g. Rose, *supra*, 60.
[37] ER 26:608.

The case foreshadowed the debate, and highlighted the divide, between those who advocated authorial rights in the broadest sense and those who preferred to limit common law rights to unpublished content.[38] A number of injunctions had been issued in the Chancery to stop unpublished manuscripts from being published.[39] But could the common law judges be convinced to go in the same direction?

In *Tonson v Collins*,[40] Benjamin Collins, a Salisbury bookseller, was accused of reprinting copies of *The Spectator*. The plaintiff had purchased all rights to the book. The case was heard *en banc* by all common law judges.[41] There was agreement among the parties that authors were protected at common law from the unauthorized first publication of their work. The disagreement focused squarely on whether common law copyright in published works survived the Statute of Anne and if so, to what extent. The outcome of the case was inconclusive[42] but it allowed Lord Mansfield (previously William Murray and a good friend of Pope), who acted on behalf of plaintiffs, to develop in detail his pro-author views.

Lord Mansfield may still have had those views in the back of his head as Chief Justice of King's Bench a few years later. Moreover, *Tonson* laid the ground for the next big case, *Millar v Taylor*.[43] By then, Mansfield was on the bench and, writing with the majority in a three to one decision, ruled that the author's common law copyright existed in perpetuity in both published and unpublished works. Various members of the court based their decision on Lockean, labour-based arguments[44] and/or general (im)propriety arguments. Justice Edward Willes, for instance, wrote that it 'is certainly not agreeable to natural justice, that a stranger should reap the beneficial pecuniary produce of

---

[38]   To further demonstrate the importance of British copyright history on US (state) common law copyright, one could cite s. 985 of the California Civil Code, which is directly inspired by *Pope v Curll*. It provides as follows: 'Letters and other private communications in writing belong to the person to whom they are addressed and delivered; but they cannot be published against the will of the writer, except by authority of law'. It is fairly apparent that the writer's right to prohibit is not a property right.

[39]   See Cornish and Llewelyn, *supra* note 4, 304. As also noted by Prof. Patterson, several orders of the Court of Assistants made it cleat that the stationers had to show they had the author's consent. See Patterson, *supra* 69. However, authors themselves could not copyright. With respect to published works, it was a publisher's right only until the Statute of 1709. See ibid., 5.

[40]   (1761) 1 Black W 301, 96 ER 169.

[41]   King's Bench, Common Pleas and Exchequer.

[42]   In fact, the case was dismissed for collusion between the parties. Apparently, a pact had been made to get the court to recognize the author's perpetual common law right. See Patterson, *supra*, 165–7.

[43]   (1769) 4 Burr. 2303.

[44]   See *supra* note 31.

another man's work'. Interestingly, Justice Richard Aston wrote that the 'invasion of this sort of property is as much against every man's sense of it, as it is against natural reason and moral rectitude'.[45] What Justice Aston had in mind was clearly a full property interest, the scope of which was further explicated by Lord Mansfield:

> ... it is just that an author should reap the pecuniary profits of his own ingenuity and labour.[46] It is just, that another should not use his name, without his consent. It is fit that he should judge when to publish, or whether he will ever publish.[47]

In this brief quote, we find three components of the full modern copyright, namely: the right to control economic exploitation of the work; the right to prevent its publication; and the 'moral right' not to see one's name used without consent, though not the dual nature of the latter right's justification (author *and* public). Lord Mansfield explained that an author's name 'ought not to be used, against his will. It is an injury, by a faulty, ignorant and incorrect edition, to disgrace his work and mislead the reader'.[48]

The question of common law copyright surviving the statute did not die until *Donaldson v Becket*. Thomas Becket and a group of booksellers, who had purchased the rights to *The Seasons* and other Thomson poems, obtained an injunction in Chancery against Edinburgh bookseller Alexander Donaldson, who had reprinted the poems after the expiry of statutory protection. The case[49] made its way to the peers, who ended up overturning the injunction and deciding that no common law copyright in published works had survived the Statute of Anne. But a narrow victory it was.[50] On the question whether the author's common law right survived authorized publication, the common law judges, who had been asked to provide their opinion to the peers (who, in those days, all voted, lawyers and laymen alike), voted 6 to 5 against the right. According to Professor Rose, the vote was actually 6–5 in favour of the authors but was not reported correctly.[51] The case was a turning point in copyright history:

---

45   Quoted in Rose*, supra*, 79.
46   Terms which will reappear in the early twentieth century, when the notion of 'originality' will be defined by UK courts.
47   98 Eng. Rep. 201, 252.
48   Ibid., 256. I digress for a minute to note that property-based narratives are very appealing nowadays of course, especially in the United States, because they conform to and support the classical ('liberal') discourse about priority of the individual and the sanctity of property. See Rose, *supra*, at 85. In the United States, property is also a policy 'given' because it is constitutionally protected.
49   (1774) 2 Bro. PC 129; 4 Burr. 2408.
50   See Cornish and Llewelyn, *supra*, 347–8.
51   See Rose, *supra*, 98–111.

The legal principle at stake in the Donaldson case has significant ethical implications. If copyright is a form of limited monopoly granted through statute, based on policy considerations, and not an absolute common law right, the ethical burden of proof shifts to copyright holders to show that their property interests are more important than the public good of having access to information. The ethical issue takes a metaphysical turn when we ask, as we shall in section II, just what it is that constitutes the intellectual property protected by copyright. Again, if the 'substance' of intellectual property is constituted by statutory fiat, then the limitations of the right are not analogous to limitations of natural rights.[52]

By 1770, it was clear that there was a common law right only to prevent first publication, and a statutory right that prevented reprinting of a book for 14 years – a term which would eventually be extended. In getting to this conclusion, arguments based on moral impropriety had at least as much weight in swaying Parliament and the courts as labour-based narratives. In fact, copyright in eighteenth century Britain may be characterized as moving from *propriety to property*.

Professor Brad Sherman's work has shown[53] that the subsequent evolution of copyright law in the UK during the nineteenth century[54] was that of a system open to influences of emerging international norms[55] and developments in Prussia, Saxony and France. Heuristically, this evolution is less important for the purposes of understanding the foundations of the Canadian system.

2.   The Canadian narrative

If one were to try to identify the purpose of copyright law in Canada, official government documents would provide no clear guidance. In fact, it is often believed that this quest is unnecessary and unproductive:

Copyright is in effect a right to prevent the appropriation of the expressed results of the labours of an author by other persons. That an author should have this right, at

---

52   Alfino, M. (1991), 'Intellectual Property and Copyright Ethics', http:// guweb2.gonzaga.edu/faculty/alfino/dossier/Papers/COPYRIGH.htm (accessed 15 September 2007), 3. (As Professor Alfino also noted: 'Blackstone asserted an analogy between intellectual property and real property over which one has a right of occupation. If Blackstone is right then public access to copyrighted works is not a public right but a kind of visitation right. Copyright infringement is thus not so much theft as trespassing.').

53   See Sherman, Brad (1995), 'Remembering and Forgetting: The Birth of Modern Copyright Law', *I.P.J.* **10**, 1.

54   If it ever was. Authorial advocates were fully aware of Kantian and natural rights justifications used on the Continent, as is apparent in Defoe's writings, amongst others.

55   Including both bilateral treaties and the Berne Convention of 1886 (see *infra* note 121). See Sherman, *supra*, 8–12.

least for a limited period, is generally recognized – on the ground of justice, expediency, or both.

The right is regarded by some as a 'natural right' on the ground that nothing is more certainly a man's property than the fruit of his brain. It is regarded by others as not a natural right but a right which the state should confer in order to promote and encourage the labours of authors. . . . We find it unnecessary to go on record with a conclusion of faith in either doctrine to the exclusion of the other.[56]

The absence of a clear focus was still visible in 1971, when copyright was aggregated with other intellectual property as a facet of 'innovation policy':

The laws of patents, copyrights, trademarks and registered industrial designs must therefore be seen as taking their place in a much broader group of innovation policies. In the aggregate, innovation policy must seek not only to achieve an appropriate commitment of resources to innovation and to improve the efficiency of individual policies towards this end, but also to arrive at an appropriately balanced mixture of different policies working together.[57]

. . . All four [patents, copyrights, trademarks and registered industrial designs] work in essentially the same way. The state creates an incentive for individuals and firms to do more of certain things by granting them limited rights in intangibles.[58]

Commenting on the 1971 Report, the 1985 Committee which produced 'A Charter of Rights for Creators'[59] stated:

The *Report on Intellectual and Industrial Property* was issued in January 1971. The Council was of the view that intellectual property should be included in any discussion of economic policy. The economic aspects of copyright were highlighted, with consumers' interest as an important focus of the debate. Two members of the Council, representing labour interests, did not concur completely and felt that the Report should have been more pro-creator. The economic approach also led to concerns about the balance of payments implications of copyright, concerns that recur to this date.[60]

Keyes and Brunet[61] went perhaps farther than any other in trying to provide the best narrative. In providing its own view as to the proper foundation of copyright protection, the Committee added:

---

56   Royal Commission on Patents, Copyright, Trade Marks and Industrial Designs (1957), 'Report on Copyright', Ottawa [Ilsley Commission], 9.

57   Economic Council of Canada (1971), 'Report on Intellectual and Industrial Property, Information Canada', Ottawa, January, 12.

58   Ibid., 31.

59   House of Commons, Standing Committee on Communications and Culture (1985), 'A Charter of Rights for Creators – Report of the Subcommittee on the Revision of Copyright', Ottawa: Supply and Services Canada.

60   Ibid., 2.

61   Keyes, A.A. and C. Brunet (1977), 'Copyright in Canada – Proposals for a Revision of the Law', Ottawa: Government of Canada.

In most countries it is generally accepted that creators are entitled to a degree of protection for their work, on the grounds that a creator should benefit from the fruits of his labour. If creators are guaranteed a minimum protection, they will be encouraged to create new works, thereby enriching the cultural life and fabric of the country and adding to the store of information.[62]

The report goes on to state:

The English law, from which the Canadian Act is derived, has developed copyright law as a species of property rights, as distinct from personality rights, notwithstanding the difficulties of reconciling the modern day peculiarities of authors' rights with the concept of property. . . . Copyright law in Canada reflects the theory of intellectual property which emphasizes authors' property interests.[63]

And this: 'The purpose of copyright, as expressed in the past, has been to guarantee the private property rights of creators'.[64]

In 1984, the government released another copyright report, namely a White Paper infelicitously entitled 'From Gutenberg to Telidon'.[65] It began with the following stipulation: 'Copyright in Canada is the legal recognition of the exclusive right of a creator to determine the use of a work and to share in the benefits produced by that use'.[66] The White Paper subscribed to a justification of copyright on a natural rights (property) basis and explained that, although copyright was an important incentive for creation, it was not the main force that leads to new creations. Consequently, the report suggested that a utilitarian justification for copyright was unfounded.

From the preceding quotes, it is easy to see that in Canada neither the government nor Parliament ever adopted a consistent copyright narrative, tapping instead haphazardly several possible policy justifications.[67] As Professor Scassa noted:

---

[62]   Ibid., 2.

[63]   Ibid., 4–5.

[64]   Ibid., 22.

[65]   (1984), 'From Gutenberg to Telidon: A White Paper on Copyright', Ottawa: Supply and Services Canada. To use Telidon, a technology many Canadians would not be able to identify, as the other end of a chain that began with the invention of the printing press was a stretch.

[66]   Ibid., 1.

[67]   Though it has been said that while 'copyright claims to own information on the basis of labour *per se* have not been accepted in the USA, [ ] decisions in Canada, and Australia have been more receptive to such claims'. Brian Fitzgerald, 'Theoretical Underpinning of Intellectual Property: "I am a Pragmatist But Theory is my Rhetoric"' (2003) 16 *Canadian Journal of Law and Jurisprudence* 179, 181.

The history of copyright reform in Canada ... suggests legislative ambivalence about the purpose of copyright law. At one point, proposals for copyright reform in Canada emphasized protection of the inherent right of the author to the fruits of his or her labour. More recently, courts and authors have adopted the view that copyright legislation serves to provide a limited monopoly to authors as an incentive to produce works that will benefit society.[68]

Can Canadian Courts fill the policy gap(s)?

One could argue that a policy for copyright is emerging at the Supreme Court of Canada. In the Supreme Court trilogy of *Théberge*, *CCH* and *CAIP v SOCAN*,[69] the Court has provided parts of the missing Canadian copyright narrative. This narrative is neither complete nor perfectly articulated,[70] but the importance of those cases should not be underestimated. Absent a clear (and unlikely) different direction from Parliament, the Supreme Court's dicta will provide Canada's narrative for years to come – at least to the extent that it will shape the decisions of lower courts.

First, a quick presentation of the cases. *Théberge* was an action brought by a well-known Canadian artist, Claude Théberge, who had licensed a printing press to make posters of one of his works. An art gallery (with no privity of contract with the artist) purchased the posters and used a resin-based

---

[68] Scassa, Teresa (2003–4), 'Originality and Utilitarian Works: The Uneasy Relationship between Copyright Law and Unfair Competition', *University of Ottawa Law and Technology Journal* **1**, 51, 57. Carys Craig has argued that Lockean theory (essentially the protection of one's labour in transformation of things found in nature, while leaving enough for others) underpins several judicial decisions in Canada in her comments about the purpose of copyright law in Canada:

> Scholarly writing in the area of copyright law frequently lends weight to the natural rights approach to copyright law. As is the case with judicial pronouncements, scholarly appeal to Locke's acquisition theory is often implicit, simply taking the author's right to own as the foundational assumption. Particularly interesting, however, is the relative frequency with which academic literature directly invokes Lockean labour theory as axiomatic in the copyright realm. This body of literature, whether ultimately supporting or refuting a Lockean justification for copyright, is evidence in itself of the powerful grip of his theory over the legal imagination in this area. Indeed, Locke's labour theory is so commonly invoked in examinations of copyright doctrine that one might be forgiven for believing that he explicitly defended intellectual property rights, or for that matter, that copyright legislation explicitly affirmed Lockean theory. (footnote omitted)

Craig, Carys J. (2002), 'Locke, Labour and Limiting the Author's Right: A Warning Against a Lockean Approach to Copyright Law', *Queen's Law Journal* **28**, 1, 21.

[69] *Théberge v Galerie d'Art du Petit Champlain inc.* [2002] 2 SCR 336 [Théberge]; *CCH Canadian Ltd v Law Society of Upper Canada* [2004] 1 SCR 339 [CCH]; and *Society of Composers, Authors & Music Publishers of Canada v Canadian Assn. of Internet Providers* [2004] 2 SCR 427 [SOCAN].

[70] See Craig, *supra* note 67, 18–20.

process to transfer the ink from the poster onto canvases, thus creating painting-like reproductions. The central question before the Court was whether there had been an unauthorized reproduction of the painting. The Court found in the negative by a 4–3 vote, because, according to the majority, a 'reproduction' involves an increase in the number of copies in existence, which had not happened in ink because the ink transfer process destroyed the poster copy as it created the canvas-backed reproduction. Interestingly, although the Court found that there had been no primary infringement, it proceeded to explain the role of exceptions in, and origins of, Canadian copyright law.

The second case, *CCH*, was a case brought by legal publishers against the Ontario Bar, whose 'Great Library' was providing a photocopy service to its members. Photocopies could be made on the spot or sent to members (lawyers) across the province of Ontario. Photocopies filed as evidence were of judicial decisions, law review articles and chapters from legal textbooks. The Court had to decide whether the photocopies were reproductions of (original) works and, if so, whether copyright had been infringed. In a decision arguably informed by access to justice considerations the Court found that most of the materials were original, but that the photocopies were not infringing because the Bar could invoke the fair dealing exception of research (on behalf of its patrons).

The last case in the trilogy *SOCAN*, dealt with an appeal of a decision by the Copyright Board of Canada (which, like the UK Copyright Tribunal, sets tariffs in certain instances where collective management organizations are in place) concerning use of music on the internet. The Canadian performing rights collective SOCAN was trying to get a tariff in place to collect fees from Internet Service Providers (ISPs) for music streaming. The Court found that ISPs had no liability because (as ISPs) they had no control over the content.

The first policy volley was fired in *Théberge*:

> The Copyright Act is usually presented as a balance between promoting the public interest in the encouragement and dissemination of works of the arts and intellect and obtaining a just reward for the creator (or, more accurately, to prevent someone other than the creator from appropriating whatever benefits may be generated). . . .
>
> The proper balance among these and other public policy objectives lies not only in recognizing the creator's rights but in giving due weight to their limited nature. In crassly economic terms it would be as inefficient to overcompensate artists and authors for the right of reproduction as it would be self-defeating to undercompensate them. Once an authorized copy of a work is sold to a member of the public, it is generally for the purchaser, not the author, to determine what happens to it.
>
> Excessive control by holders of copyrights and other forms of intellectual

property may unduly limit the ability of the public domain to incorporate and embellish creative innovation in the long-term interests of society as a whole, or create practical obstacles to proper utilization. This is reflected in the exceptions to copyright infringement enumerated in ss. 29 to 32.2, which seek to protect the public domain in traditional ways such as fair dealing for the purpose of criticism or review and to add new protections to reflect new technology, such as limited computer program reproduction and 'ephemeral recordings' in connection with live performances.

This case demonstrates the basic economic conflict between the holder of the intellectual property in a work and the owner of the tangible property that embodies the copyrighted expressions.[71]

While still partly inspired by Lockean labour-desert rationale, *Théberge* arguably: (a) identified the purpose of copyright ('a balance between promoting the public interest in the encouragement and dissemination of works of the arts and intellect and obtaining a just reward for the creator'); (b) adopted economic concepts[72] to evaluate the alignment of the Act's interpretation with that purpose; and (c) concluded that the chattel rights of the owner of the poster outweighed the interests of the owner of the copyright in the underlying artistic work (in this case, the artist himself).

Théberge's teachings lie at the core of copyright law. The Court tells us that users, who are also very often owners of copies of protected works, have 'rights'. Some of those rights follow from their ownership of a copy. Other rights stem from exceptions that limit the reach of the author's exclusive rights. It is the combination of both sets of rights that creates the appropriate 'balance' in copyright law, i.e., a level of protection that sufficiently protects authors and other owners of copyright, whether seen *ex ante* as an incentive to create (investment in the publication, production or dissemination of copyright works) or *ex post* as a reward for that creation and/or investment, without creating deadweight loss (or generating social costs without corresponding benefits in the form of access to new creations). The Court showed reluctance in trampling those 'rights' of users,[73] which it defined both as the owners of copies and the beneficiaries of statutory exceptions.

---

71   *Théberge*, paras 30–3.
72   And, as Jagdish Bhagwati noted: '. . . economists use cost-benefit analysis, which means . . . a utilitarian form of analysis instead of a [property] rights based approach'. See Bhagwati, Jagdish (2004), *In Defense of Globalization*, Oxford: Oxford University Press, p. 183.
73   There would be an ontological debate worth having: Is copyright a restriction on the otherwise free use of ideas (in which case a right to use is the default) or is copyright starting from a principle of protection/restriction and then one can argue that it should be inherently balanced?

In *CCH*,[74] beyond confirming the adoption of *Théberge's* 'balanced approach', the Court tackled two truly fundamental aspects of copyright law, namely the notion of originality and the scope of fair dealing. The Court examined the British and American notions of originality and ostensibly opted for a middle path that, operationally, is similar to the US standard established in *Feist*. The Court chose not to follow the 'basic' (if not simplistic) notion of UK law as portrayed in the *University of London Press* case,[75] because it concluded that a 'raw' skill and labour ('sweat of the brow') approach was unsatisfactory. Trivial and mechanical labour will not do; something more is required.

The Court stopped the wheels of infringement for similar reasons: it would be incompatible with the quest for 'balance' to limit recourse to technologies that can be used for clearly non-infringing purposes, such as a photocopy machine. In concluding that end-users have a right of fair dealing, the Court exhibited reluctance to extend copyright into the private sphere of end-users. Logically, it concluded that asking the Great Library to monitor and enforce copyright on behalf of rights-holders would tip the balance too much in favour of the right-holders themselves. In interpreting the scope of exceptions, the Supreme Court took the view that it was necessary to interpret fair dealing broadly in light of the Act's purpose.[76]

The Court's decision in *CCH* is another clear indication of the limits of copyright's reach and of an attempt to align it with its purpose, in particular when its power to exclude should yield to other rights. In deciding that end-users did not have to get permission, the Court reinforced the view that those end-users should normally not have to get a licence to access content. Copyright issues should ideally be dealt with elsewhere in the distribution chain (e.g., at the level of distributors and databases), not in the hands of end-users. That narrative is clear and, in my view, unmistakably in keeping with British copyright history: the proper sphere of economic copyright rights consists of commercially relevant uses and reuses.

In *SOCAN,* unsurprisingly, the Supreme Court found that ISPs were not

---

[74] A detailed case comment on *CCH* was previously published by this author. See Gervais, Daniel, 'Canadian Copyright Law Post-*CCH*', *I.P.J.* **18**, 131–67.

[75] *University of London Press v University Tutorial Press* [1916] 2 Ch 601. Actually, one would be foolhardy to attempt to provide a single definition of originality in UK law in light of recent decisions. For a brief discussion, see Bently and Sherman, *supra* note 23, at 80–98; and for international aspects, see Gervais, Daniel (2004), 'The Compatibility of the "Skill and Labour" Originality Standard with the Berne Convention and the TRIPs Agreement', *European International Property Review* **26**, 2, 75–80.

[76] *CCH*, para. 51.

liable to copyright owners when they act as mere conduits of content. The decision adopted a resolutely economic/utilitarian approach[77] linked to a search for the underlying purpose of copyright law. The Court's analysis led quite logically to a public good/public interest analysis. The choice of applying instrumentalist reasoning[78] was logical for the same reasons: copyright's purpose is not to 'protect' authors (or other owners of copyright), but rather to maximize the creation, production and dissemination of knowledge and access thereto. In other words, protection is not an end, in and of itself, but rather, a means to achieving that purpose, which implies that the level of protection must be properly calibrated.

The Court also pondered the importance of copyright protection (and its underlying purpose of maximizing the creation and dissemination of works) against competing general welfare objectives:

> The capacity of the internet to disseminate 'works of the arts and intellect' is one of the great innovations of the information age. Its use should be facilitated rather than discouraged, but this should not be done unfairly at the expense of those who created the works of arts and intellect in the first place.
>
> The issue of the proper balance in matters of copyright plays out against the much larger conundrum of trying to apply national laws to a fast-evolving technology that in essence respects no national boundaries.[79]

In other words, if the internet is a public good, the ISPs are its guardian, even though they are in it for profit. As such, it would be economically inefficient to impose a liability on them merely to transit content they do not control.

Carved from the same wood as *Théberge* and *CCH*, *SOCAN* set limits to the breach of copyright. It also directly confronts copyright's purposes with other, potentially different policy objectives. The Court also showed great reluctance in imposing liability on intermediaries which, while they are

---

[77]   I use the terminology somewhat loosely here. It may be useful to add that utilitarianism is consequentialist (goals-oriented): intellectual property is a good thing because 'good' (new creations and inventions) stems from it. Utilitarianism is a form of collective consequentialism, where the 'good' results are assessed at the level of the general welfare.

[78]   The concept of utilitarianism deals with the maximization of good to society. It is linked to the writings of Jeremy Bentham and John Stuart Mill. Instrumentalism assesses actions in relation to their objective. Thus, actions are tools to achieve certain goals. The instrumentalist utilitarianism view is to see law as an instrument to achieve the greatest good for society. Thus, intellectual property is useful because it encourages creativity and encourages people to share their creations with others, thus benefiting society as a whole.

[79]   *SOCAN*, paras 40–1.

professionals in their own right (in this case, ISPs; in *CCH*, the Great Library), are not professionals *of the copyright business*,[80] at least not to the extent that their roles are considered here. The subtext, I suggest, is that the 'business of copyright' should be handled by those who publish, produce and disseminate works and actually choose the content that gets disseminated (broadcasters, publishers, etc.). Another implication of the decision is that copyright, as a statutory scheme, is not 'property', and as such the property-related rhetoric of theft and piracy is suspect.

Canada thus has jurisprudential pieces of a narrative puzzle. It is not complete, but general principles can be sketched out from the Supreme Court trilogy. The Canadian copyright narrative, if it is allowed to emerge, is good news for at least one simple reason: the presence of a statement of principles will provide heuristic help in enhancing both understanding and predictability.

To take a counter-example, the United States seems to have forgotten its core narrative after 1976, especially after it let a group of lobbies write the Digital Millennium Copyright Act of 1998.[81] As a result, it is now in a policy split between, on the one hand, a simple, even simplistic property-based discourse[82] used as a rhetorical expedient to convince Congress to pass new rights to fight internet distribution and, on the other hand, a pragmatic trade regulation approach. The results are well known, as are the negative public relations and commercial results of the invasion of the private sphere of internet users.[83] ' "[P]iracy" seems to function as a rhetorical tool, implicitly advocating a normative agenda in favour of some kind of property or ownership . . . effectively using "robbery" as a trope to advocate property

---

[80]   Those would include legitimate professionals of the copyright industries (e.g. publishers, producers, broadcasters) or illegitimate ones (e.g. resellers of pirated CDs or DVDs).

[81]   Pub. L. No. 105–304, 112 Stat. 2860 (1998).

[82]   See Keith Aoki, who notes that:

'[I] laid out the theme of the disaggregation of a unitary vision of "property" in twentieth century United States law and introduced the relative countermovement in United States copyright law toward hardening and expanding intellectual property owners' rights. This movement is doubly ironic because even in the heyday of absolutist notions of "private property", copyrights were an exception: They were limited rights promulgated pursuant to public regulation, a mapping that is obscured when viewed through the occluding lens of romantic authorship.

Hale, Robert L. (1923), 'Coercion and Distribution in a Supposedly Non-Coercive State', *Political Science Quarterly* **38**, 470.

[83]   See Gervais, Daniel (2004). 'The Price of Social Norms', *Journal of International Property (US)* **12**, 1, 39.

rights for authors'.[84] While Professor Hughes has shown that recourse to this terminology is not of recent origin, it seems undeniable that it is increasingly used to feed anti-instrumentalist narratives.[85]

3.   Moving forward

3.1.   The two faces of copyright

According to the emerging Canadian narrative, copyright is perhaps best viewed as a coin. On the economic side, born from the Stationers' Monopoly and the Statute of Anne and anchored in the need to organize markets for copyright works, we find a set of rights that, though poorly expressed, were designed to prevent commercially relevant uses and reuses of protected works. For 300 years, this right was traded among copyright professionals, including authors, publishers, producers, broadcasters, etc. In the past five years, it has also been used against end-users – which is the source of much of the tension – and greatly increased attention paid to copyright law and policy[86] in the public eye.

Yet, it is simply wrong to forget that copyright policy has, and always has had, a second side, namely an author's right to prevent first publication and to be identified as the author of a work (in appropriate circumstances). That part of copyright is conveniently attributed to civil law systems and its 'moral right', but that is simply incorrect. True, moral rights include a right of attribution of authorship,[87] and civil law systems contain a right of disclosure ('divulgation') that allows authors to prevent first publication.[88] But the moral right also includes other rights, including the right to oppose mutilation, whereas the right of attribution of authorship and the

---

[84]   Hughes, *supra*, 1010.

[85]   Congress did at one time at least, seemed to agree:

'In enacting a copyright law Congress must consider . . . two questions: First, how much will the legislation stimulate the producer and so benefit the public, and, second, how much will the monopoly granted be detrimental to the public? The granting of such exclusive rights, under the proper terms and conditions, confers a benefit upon the public that outweighs the evils of the temporary monopoly.' H.R. Rep. No. 2222, 60th Cong., 2d Sess. 7 (1909).

Quoted in *Sony Corp. of America v Universal City Studios, Inc.*, 464 US 417, 430 (1984).

[86]   See Gervais, Daniel (2005), 'The Purpose of Copyright Law in Canada', *University of Ottawa Law and Technology Journal* 2, 315.

[87]   See Article 6*bis* of the Berne Convention (see *infra* note 121); and André and Henri-Jacques Lucas (2001), *Traité de la propriété littéraire et artistique*, 2nd edn, Paris: LiTec, 301–34.

[88]   See ibid.

right to oppose first publication have been part of the common law since the 1700s.[89]

Copyright, even in common law systems, has thus always had a dual nature: economic and authorial.[90] Forgetting this Janus-faced history may explain a number of significant misunderstandings. When realigning copyright to function better, for example in the internet environment, one should not lose sight of the fact that we are dealing with the 'economic' face of the right.[91]

As one commentator noted:

---

[89]   There is no room in this chapter for such a discussion, but it is also interesting to note that the emergence of the 'author' is neither culturally nor politically neutral. As Professor Coombe noted:

> Beyond the obvious – that the author emerges along with the ascendancy of the European bourgeoisie, rising literacy, the decline of aristocratic patronage, and the growing hegemony of market exchange economies – it should be noted that the author/work configuration was central to the functioning of the 'bourgeois public sphere' which (as Habermas and others have argued) was organized through the medium of print around activities of readership. Such activities presupposed an 'author' whose 'work' was the intentional 'expression' of a unified self addressing other rational selves capable of reading and evaluating such works to debate the ideas contained therein – to the ends of generating public dialogue to influence public goals. The constitutive exclusionary elitism of this model aside, it is worth stressing here that the author's control was limited to the work (in contemporary vocabulary, as an 'incentive' to disseminate it socially, so that the ideas and information it 'contained' would be available for the greater political good of public dialogue). (footnotes omitted)

Coombe, Rosemary J. (1996), 'Authorial Cartographies: Mapping Proprietary Borders in a Less-Than-Brave New World', *Standard Law Review* **48**, 1357, 1359.
This explains some of the difficulties in applying copyright concepts to different cultural contexts, such as traditional cultural expressions of indigenous peoples. See also Gervais, Daniel (2005), 'Traditional Knowledge & Intellectual Property: A TRIPS-Compatible Approach', *Michigan State Law Review* 137–66.
[90]   For lack of a better term. As James Boyle noted, referring to the 'romantic' view of authorship:

> The writer does not write [only] for money, nor is she interested in anything other than the perfection of her work. The author is presumed to have an almost transcendental insight – something which cuts beneath the mundane world of everyday appearance. This transcendental right or genius plays a very important role in establishing the author as the ruler of the text.

Boyle, James (1987), 'The Search for an Author: Shakespeare and the Framers', *American University Law Review* **37**, 625–43, 629. Peter Jaszi also commented in that connection that 'far from being a non-controversial, generalized "source" of copyright doctrine, [authorship] in fact is the specific locus of a basic contradiction between public access to and private control over imaginative creations'. Jaszi, Peter (1991), 'Metamorphoses of Authorship', *Duke Law Journal*, 457.
[91]   Obviously, the non-economic side, which I would call the authorial rights side, may have economic impacts.

[A]t its core, natural rights protect two aspects of copyright. First is the Lockean notion that authors are entitled to possess the fruits of their labours. Second, until divested by first publication in exchange for statutory benefits, authors enjoy sovereignty over their works. Unfortunately, similar to the analysis of copyright's intangible nature, the philosophical framework of natural rights provides little normative guidance towards the shape of copyright or its continued development.[92]

Copyright is a commercial right, and that is largely a good thing. It has led to the protection of works that may not have had 'aesthetic merit' but that prevented judges from delving into considerations too close to censorship for comfort. Being treated as commercial right has allowed a democratization of creativity following from the abandonment of merit.[93] It may also have made copyright more culturally neutral. But copyright is not only commercial in nature. First publication, for example, 'transcends both the economic issues and the limited risk of premature access. [The US] Congress recognized how critical the musician's first exposure could be to the success or failure of the artist. Success in the marketplace may be economic, associated with the number of copies sold, or it may be aesthetic, captured in music reviews, critical acclaim, and professional reputation within the industry. These aesthetic successes may someday translate into economics . . .'[94] One could think of academics whose pay stub is not (directly) linked to the number or quality of publications, but for whom attribution may be particularly important.

This duality is not to be confused with the 'rights-holders v user' dialogue. Some have argued that the interests of both groups coincide, while others see it as a perennial conflict. In fact, both views seem to oversimplify greatly, for at least two reasons. First, in individual cases – as in the many anecdotes used as rhetorical ammunition to show that copyright 'does not work' – there may very well be a conflict between a user and a rights-holder. Classes of users who are negotiating the price of a repertory of works, or applying to the Canadian Copyright Board or a similar body for a tariff, are also in a conflict situation. Those conflicts are inevitable in a marketplace, and one does not see why they should magically disappear given that the rights apply to intangibles. Second, there is no clear dividing line between 'users' and 'rights-holders'. Authors create using other people's ideas and work. They also use (consumptively) works of others. At bottom, everyone (and not both 'sides') should

---

92   Garon, *supra* note 3, 1306.
93   See Ginsburg, Jane (1990),'Creation and Commercial Value: Copyright Protection of Works of Information', *Columbia Law Review* **90**, 1890. (Noting, in reference to *Bleistein v Donaldson Lithographic Co.* (188 US 239 (1903)) that 'the receptivity of copyright to both creativity and commercial value' had allowed US courts to protect works that lack aesthetic merit.)
94   Ibid., 1312.

have an interest in making the copyright system achieve its objectives. User groups who claim 'it should all be free' know that their demands are patently unrealistic. The claim by certain rights-holders who want to lock up content and be paid for every use, whether they have a realistic expectation of income or not, is similarly unfounded. With this in mind, I suggest a way to move forward that is within our reach.[95]

3.2. Realigning copyright with its purpose

The internet   The economic rights' fragments contained in most national copyright laws are not particularly useful in mapping out uses of digital works, especially on the internet.[96] Copyright fragments have lost their meaning to users and rights-holders alike. In actuality, contracts and licensing arrangements for copyright works do not usually refer to the specific rights enumerated in this section or if they do, it is an afterthought.[97] Contracts typically define the uses that should be allowed, and not which fragments of rights are needed.

> Simply put, contractual licensing arrangements for some works develop into an intractable morass of ownership interests and licensing obligations. . . . works [fall] prey to intricate licensing arrangements, ownership bankruptcies, and other fissures, [one could add right reversions[98]] in the chain of copyright title . . . [T]o the extent that only some authors have the financial ability to license these building blocks [the various rights fragments], the actual and transaction costs of licensing disproportionately disadvantage those artists without funds and access to legal services.[99]

---

[95]   For smaller scale proposals, such as facilitating rights management, see Gervais, Daniel (2005), 'Use of Copyright Content on the Internet: Considerations on Excludability and Collective Licensing', in M. Geist (ed.), *In the Public Interest: The Future of Canadian Copyright Law*, Toronto: Irwin Law, 517–49.

[96]   See Einhorn, M. and L. Kurlantzick (2002), 'Traffic Jam on the Music Highway', *Journal of the Copyright Society of the USA* **8**, 417 ('Since these rights are controlled by different parties and agents, the complexity of the system leads to a gridlock of control that may hinder development.').

[97]   A contract to allow Web-casting normally refers to the function of broadcasting, independently of whether a communication to the public, one or more reproductions, or adaptations may take place. The problem is that rights ownership is still by and large, especially in the area of collective management, owned by different entities based on the rights, not the functions. While a single economic transaction should take place, several legal transactions are involved. See A. and B. Kohn (2000), *Kohn on Music Licensing (2nd ed.): 2000 Supplement,* New York: Aspen Law & Business, 398–9.

[98]   Under the national laws of several countries, rights revert to the author's heirs independently of any contractual transfer. Under s. 14(1) of the Canadian Act, reversion occurs 25 years after the author's death.

[99]   Garon, *supra*, 1317.

In the internet era, the exploitation and use of a work (often multi-media) operates in some respects as a fiction *vis-à-vis* the Copyright Act.[100] The rights 'fragments' (reproduction, public performance, communication to the public, rental, display, now making available, etc.) are a vestige of a haphazard process of rights accretion that characterizes how the Act, and many other national laws and international treaties, have evolved.[101] Part of the resulting problem is that rights are formulated in terms of the *nature of the use* (copying, performing, etc), while exceptions are formulated in terms of the *purpose* (e.g. fair use for criticism, etc.).

Internationally   At the international level, the three-step test[102] is the main norm to determine the compatibility of exceptions to copyright with international instruments including the TRIPS Agreement. It is relevant in this context because that test is not based on the *nature* of the use, but rather on the *effect* of the use. It would thus seem logical to conclude that a way to avoid applying copyright where it does not belong (and where it directly clashes with other rights) is to recast it in terms of the effects of uses of protected works. I recently suggested[103] that the best way to achieve this was to start not from the 'rights' but with the exceptions. The reason is simple. Exceptions are designed to determine where copyright should not apply in light of its underlying purpose. If one were to reverse that test, the universe that would remain would be what, in fact, copyright was meant to protect. In other words, if one agrees with the premise that fair dealing and other exceptions reflect an appropriate set of criteria to balance the rights of copyright holders and the needs and interests of users, I suggest it could serve as the basis to build the copyright of the future.[104] Because the three-step test is the accepted international standard to determine whether an exception to copyright in national legislation is TRIPS-compliant, that solution would also be in keeping with extant international norms.

What I suggest is reversing the three-step test based on the assumption that what exceptions (whether fair use in US law or the three-step test at the multilateral level) do not allow is what copyright intended to protect in the first place.[105]

---

[100]   See Einhorn, M. and L. Kurlantzick (2002), *supra* note 96, 417; and Lemley, Mark (1997), 'Dealing with Overlapping Copyrights on the Internet', *Dayton Law Review* **22**, 548, 565–6.

[101]   See WIPO (1986), *Berne Convention Centenary 1886–1986*, Geneva: WIPO.

[102]   See Gervais, Daniel (2004), 'The Reverse Three-Step Test: Towards a New Core International Copyright Norm', *Marquette Intellectual Property Law Review* **9**, 1, 13–21.

[103]   See ibid.

[104]   See Okediji, Ruth (2000), 'Toward an International Fair Use Doctrine', *Columbia Journal of Transnational Law* **39**, 75, 168–69.

[105]   See Gervais, *supra* note 102.

Such an approach is powerful because it both solves the issues related to the nature-based bundle now used in most national laws and is by definition TRIPS-compliant. If only uses not allowed by the three-step test are effectively protected (i.e. only uses allowed under the three-step test are exempted), there can be no violation of Berne or TRIPS.

How does one reverse the test? A simple way is to ask: if fair dealing is fair, then what use is unfair? I submit that 'unfair' (i.e. protected) dealing would be use that does not meet the two real steps of the Berne three-step test, that is, use that interferes with normal commercial exploitation or unreasonably (unjustifiably) prejudices the copyright holder's rights. Any use that demonstrably and substantially reduces financial benefits that the copyright owner can reasonably expect to receive under normal commercial circumstances would be 'unfair' without authorization. How one measures unfairness and interference with normal commercial exploitation in this context is fundamental. I suggest that the question should not be whether a user got actual or virtual 'value' without paying (the property rhetoric[106]) but whether the user should have obtained the content through a normal commercial transaction (the economic approach[107]).

Three observations are in order, however. First, this clearly applies only to *published* content.[108] A right to prevent first publication must remain. Second, it is not because a work is unavailable in a given form that taking is *ipso facto* fair because no normal commercial transaction is possible. Rights-holders must be given a certain degree of flexibility in how they make works available on various markets and in various formats. It also means, however, that market practices are relevant. The question to ask is whether the type of use or user is one that would normally be licensed (on a transactional or collective basis). Is the kind of material normally (only) available on a commercial basis? Finally, it is essential to view normalcy of commercial exploitation as a dynamic notion that is influenced by technological development and consumer behavior. It is clear, in my view, that the internet may have changed what 'normal commercial exploitation' means.

The second step of the Berne test, namely the unreasonable prejudice to

---

106   As Professor Alfino noted: '. . . policy arguments which proceed primarily by a retrieval of abstract thought on the metaphysical principles of property are inadequate'. *Supra* note 52.

107   See United-States – Section 110(5) of the US Copyright Act, WTO Document WT/DS160/R, 15 June 15 2000, ¶ 6.225.

108   A right of 'first publication', well rooted in UK law, exists in most national laws. In the US, fair use of unpublished material has been limited by a number of court decisions. See O'Neill, Kate (2001), 'Against Dicta: A Legal Method for Rescuing Fair Use from the Right of First Publication', *California Law Review* **89**, 369.

legitimate interests of the rights-holder, is one of *public interest* v *author's rights*. The relevant rights must be those protected under the Act. This is where the reasoning blends the two steps (without, one hopes, becoming circular). The author has a right in respect of any commercially significant use (use that would normally be the subject of a commercial transaction) and any situation not covered by this right would be one that is not subject to normal commercial exploitation *and* is justified by a valid public interest purpose.

In re-scoping the economic component of copyright rights, one should also distinguish straight commercial uses from transformative uses. A commentator[109] has suggested that copyright in its present form does not leave 'enough and as good' and is thus in conflict with the Lockean proviso against hoarding. In the same vein as the fourth factor codified in section 107 of the US Copyright Act,[110] if one were to adopt a test of commercial significance, derivative/transformative uses would be free to the extent that they did not demonstrably affect the market for the original work. There would be a logical presumption that a simple, non-transformative adaptation (change of medium), though it requires significant creative input (e.g. translation, making a film out of a novel) does have that significant impact. In addition, the authorial side of the copyright coin requires that the author of the original

---

[109] '. . . copyright principles that accord property ownership to a labourer where his labour is sufficiently separate from the "parent idea" and award ownership to the owner of the "parent idea" where the new work bears too much resemblance to the original. The person who truly has something to "add" to the cultural discourse (as opposed to merely reproducing another's prior contribution) will benefit from the same rules of acquisition as the first labourer. It is true that if the defendant's work is not substantially similar to the plaintiff's copyrighted work, there is no infringement of the copyright. However, where a defendant's work is, as a result of copying, substantially similar to the plaintiff's, prima facie infringement will be established regardless of the "labour added". The question we ask in a copyright infringement action is whether the defendant's work is substantially similar to a "substantial part" of the plaintiff's work, rather than whether the work taken from the plaintiff constitutes a substantial part of the defendant's work. . . . As noted by Judge Learned Hand, "no plagiarist can excuse the wrong by showing how much of his work he did not pirate" (in *Sheldon v Metro-Goldwyn Pictures Corp.*, 81 F.2d 49 at 56 (2d Cir, 1936)).' Craig, *supra*, at 26–8.

[110] 17 USC It reads in part as follows:

'. . . the fair use of a copyrighted work, . . . for purposes such as criticism, comment, news reporting, teaching (including multiple copies for classroom use), scholarship, or research, is not an infringement of copyright. In determining whether the use made of a work in any particular case is a fair use the factors to be considered shall include –

. . .
(4) the effect of the use upon the potential market for or value of the copyrighted work.'

work be involved. Uses such as parodies would be fair game,[111] while commercial uses (or perhaps more accurately uses on a commercially relevant scale) would be the subject of an exclusive right. There would be no need for private use[112] or fair dealing provisions thus greatly simplifying the Act. Fair uses would be those that meet the three-step test, and uses beyond that would require an authorization.

The suggested approach is not revolutionary. On the contrary, it is solidly and realistically anchored in the historical purpose of copyright. It is also in line with international norms, which this author sees as a key factor in any decision that a WTO member may make to improve its copyright system. It is not a public interest sieve for copyright infringements, but I suggest that excluding non-commercially relevant uses from the economic copyright rights would greatly reduce the harm that, according to 'public interest' advocates, the copyright system is causing.

---

[111]   This may be the most difficult issue in copyright law, namely the border between protected 'expression' and unprotected 'ideas' (see TRIPS Agreement, Article 9(2)). To what extent should copyright be a right in the form or *Gestalt* and not in the thoughts, tastes and passions that generated the 'work'? The question can be tackled from several angles. To what extent is copyright protection applicable only to the objectified work, not to the subjective fuel used to create it? What is the point of inflexion past which protection against the creation of derivatives imposes too high a social welfare cost on other creators? What is the proper level of abstraction of copyright law, or should it be formulated as the protection of the concrete and specific forms of literary and artistic expression (at a finer degree, each 'category' of protected works is itself subject to abstraction)? See B. Sherman, *supra*, 15–22. It is also harder to measure the exact input of incremental authors. As Hettinger aptly noted, 'A person who relies on human intellectual history and makes small modification to produce something of great value should no more receive what the market will bear than should the last person needed to lift a car receive full credit for lifting it'. Hettinger, Edwin (1989), 'Justifying Intellectual Property', *Philosophy and Public Affairs* **18**, 31, 38. Yet because copyright law does not distinguish between 'minor' incremental works and those that result from a major creative effort, it is up to courts to modulate the level of protection. It can also be said (using Saussurean structuralist terminology) that copyright protects the signifier, not the signified (the idea/expression dichotomy), and if one posits that ideas are more valuable than a particular expression thereof, then copyright's inherent limits are good for human progress and the public domain. This was lamented by T.H. Farrer in 1882: 'Original thought and observation, the highest form of mental labour, go unprotected, whilst literary manufacture, a very inferior product of the intellect, alone obtains protection. . . . [Copyright thus has a] tendency to encourage bad writers at the expense of good ones . . . it tends to make books bad, numerous and dear.' As quoted in Feltes, Norman N. (1991), 'International Copyright: Structuring "the Condition of Modernity" in British Publishing', *Cardozo Arts and Entertainment Law Journal* **10**, 543.

[112]   Naturally, government could decide to maintain a levy scheme, but its nature would then be clear.

3.3. The trade connection

There is progressive alignment of trade and intellectual property policy. It started in the United States in the 1980s[113] (notably through section 301 of the Trade Act[114]) and culminated in the 1994 WTO TRIPS Agreement.[115] This has at least two important consequences. First, trade law is pragmatic, something illustrated by the fuzzy notion under WTO law of 'nullification or impairment' of benefits or the doctrine of 'reasonable expectations'. Second, trade remedies are generally predicated on a showing of adverse impact on trade, and the protection of intellectual property by trade rules does not seem to mesh with its ideological defence as a 'property' right.[116] On the contrary, the linkage with trade seems to reinforce the instrumentalist/consequentialist approach to intellectual property regulation.

The United States may need to pick which legal horse it wants to cross the copyright infringement river: if it chooses trade, it must accept pragmatism and the related, three-step test-compatible need to show loss of reasonably available income streams. From that viewpoint, its recent rhetorical reliance on property may thus be at odds with a strategy that was otherwise highly successful by US copyright and patent lobbies to link intellectual property and trade.[117]

The admixture of trade rules and intellectual property norms was neither easy nor obvious. Until the establishment of the World Trade Organization and the entry into force of the TRIPS Agreement in 1995, intellectual property was an exception to free trade rules.[118] But if the mix is now accepted as a given,[119] then one must accept the consequences of that choice.

---

[113]   See Sell, Susan (2003), *Private Power, Public Law*, Cambridge: Cambridge University Press.

[114]   US Trade Act of 1974, as amended (19 USC § 2411) and the so-called 'Special 301' mechanism contained in s. 1303 of Omnibus Trade and Competitiveness Act of 1988. See http://www.osec.doc.gov/ogc/occic/301.html (accessed 6 October 2006).

[115]   WTO Agreement on Trade-Related Aspects of Intellectual Property Rights, 15 April 1994, Marrakesh Agreement Establishing the World Trade Organization, Annex 1C, Legal Instruments – Results of the Uruguay Round vol. 3, 1869 UNTS 299, 33 ILM 81 (1994).

[116]   On 5 October 2006, Reuters published a press release stating that the United States would oppose Russia's entry into the World Trade Organization until an MP3 'file-sharing' service known as allofmp3.com was shut down. See 'U.S. pushes Russia in WTO talks to close MP3 site', CNetnews, http://news.com.com/U.S.+pushes+Russia+in+WTO+talks+to+close+MP3+site/2100-1028_3-6122879.html?tag=html. alert

[117]   See Gervais, Daniel (2005), 'Intellectual Property and Development: The State of Play', *Fordham Law Review* **74,** 505–35.

[118]   See Article XX(d) of the *GATT* and Gervais, Daniel (2003), *The TRIPS Agreement: Drafting History and Interpretation*, 2nd edn, London: Sweet & Maxwell, at 5–9.

[119]   See Bhagwati, *supra* note 72.

Article 9 of the Agreement on Trade-related Aspects of Intellectual Property Rights (TRIPS) in April 1994[120] incorporates most substantive provisions of the Berne Convention into TRIPS,[121] though it also states that WTO 'Members shall not have rights or obligations under this Agreement in respect of the rights conferred under Article 6*bis* of that Convention or of the rights derived therefrom'.[122] In other words, the moral right to claim authorship (or to remain anonymous) and the right to 'object to any distortion, mutilation or other modification of, or other derogatory action in relation to [a protected] work, which would be prejudicial to [the author's] honour or reputation' is excluded from TRIPS. By excluding moral rights the TRIPS Agreement arguably split the copyright coin. If one eschews the rather simplistic view of the moral right (as implemented in common law jurisdictions) as a Continental, Kantian concept imposed on reluctant countries, and sees it rather as one which has been part of common law copyright – at least with respect to the right to claim authorship and the right to prevent first publication, which may conceptually be linked to a reputation-based right such as the right to oppose a mutilation of a creative work – then by removing the non purely economic component from its normative framework, TRIPS may have weakened the intrinsic equilibrium of copyright and, hence, the 'power to convince' that copyright has traditionally enjoyed. It may have become a pure statutory entitlement among many others, one designed to allow for limited market control.[123]

While this desire to maximize profit and control protected works may be entirely legitimate – and a fair exercise of the copyright industries' duties to their shareholders – the policy debate has become not one of fairness to authors but rather of how much money it is fair for those companies (not authors) to make. This may explain part of the resistance of various user groups and insistence that 'CDs and DVDs are too expensive' and the related, if generally intuitive, perception that copyright works are public goods.[124] As Jon Garon noted:

---

[120]   See Gervais, *supra* note 118, 12–26.
[121]   Berne Convention for the Protection of Literary and Artistic Works, 1886, 828 UNTS 221. Reference is made here to the Paris Act of 1971.
[122]   Which are generally considered to be the rights under 10(3) and 11*bis*(2) – the moral rights component only – as well as rights under Article IV(3) of the Appendix. See Gervais, *supra* note 118,125.
[123]   See Gervais, Daniel (2005), 'Towards A New Core International Copyright Norm: The Reverse Three-Step Test', *Marquette Intellectual Property Law Review* **9**, 1–37.
[124]   There is e.g. long-recognized social value in providing access to information. As Jon Garon has pointed out, however, copyright works are not true public goods (i.e. non-exclusive and non-rivalrous, such as air, sea and free-flowing water) even though some of their delivery mechanisms are (e.g. over-the-air television and, arguably, the internet). Garon, *supra*, 1333–5.

[t]he format of the digital file results in a conflation of ideas, information, and the copyrighted expression, as the 'computer file' becomes the unitary metaphor for all three attributes of the work. The file metaphor and the unlimited copying combine to transform all copyrighted works into public goods . . . To put the final nail in the copyright coffin, the anonymity and international scope of the internet has raised questions about whether legal constraints can serve any meaningful role on the internet.[125]

By staking their copyright claim in the soil of trade, natural rights-based views – and with them many of the perceived fairness – of copyright are no longer convincing. For user groups and developing countries implementing TRIPS and TRIPS Plus rules,[126] it has become a numbers game, i.e. not one where players can defend a position strictly based on the propertization of creative works.

Property confers advantages by ensuring investment and development of resources. The social costs of excludability are acceptable because 'the losses that people suffer from exclusion are small compared to the gains that they get both from their ability to privatize their labor and from their ability to enter into trade . . .'.[127] In other words, in the main propertization is a clear *Pareto* improvement, but copyright may be different. In classic property theory, for instance, possession is considered key and the law essentially reinforces the physical control that can be exerted by the owner (by fencing, etc.). No such metes and bounds exist in copyright law. This probably explains why property rights in intangibles have been the subject of many a scholarly debate. The non-rivalrous, non-excludable nature of intangibles[128] and the (perceived) public good nature[129] of at least some copyright works have already weakened the property discourse.[130,131]

---

125   Ibid., 1336. See also Gervais, Daniel (2004), 'The Price of Social Norms: Towards a Liability Regime for File-Sharing', *Journal of Intellectual Property Law* **12**, 1, 39–73.

126   See Ostergard Jr., Robert L. (2002), *The Development Dilemma: The Political Economy of Intellectual Property Rights in the International System*, New York: LFB Scholarly Publishing; and Gervais, Daniel (2005), 'Intellectual Property, Trade & Development: The State of Play', *Fordham Law Review* **75**, 505–35.

127   Epstein, *supra* note 18, 22.

128   Use is non-excludable, but profit making through distribution of a work is. See Gervais, Daniel and Elizabeth F. Judge (2005), *Intellectual Property: The Law in Canada*, Toronto: Carswell, 2–3.

129   See *supra* note 124 and accompanying text.

130   See Hettinger, Edwin (1989), 'Justifying Intellectual Property', *Philosophy and Public Affairs* **12**, 31, 35–8. See also Landes, William M. and Richard A. Posner (2003), *The Economic Structure of Intellectual Property Law*, Cambridge, Mass.: Belknap Press. A number of scholars, such as Professor Richard Epstein, have argued that the gulf between property rights in tangible and property rights in intangibles is narrower than may appear at first glance. By the same token, they recognize that the difference in the nature of the resource requires a distinctive configuration of the property rights in question, one with limited duration and free or fair use exceptions to

Ethics no longer guide us in the context of aggressive commercial exploitation, 'because of the breakdown of traditional social structure or matrix of social practices within which ethical questions have either been resolved or lack a motivation'.[132] In fact, social norms may be moving away from the industry control rhetoric and may give rise to other compensation models.[133] It is not insignificant to note that surveys show that stealing a physical object such as a CD is generally considered theft, while downloading music from peer-to-peer networks is not.[134] The tangible nature of the good matters, even though its value depends entirely on the non-tangible component (i.e. the music). The social norms do not reflect an understanding of downloading as *malum in se*, as a natural rights justification would suggest, but rather as an (annoying) *malum prohibitum*, and a prohibition that should be revisited (if not the norm itself then the way it is used and enforced). The lower level of internalization of the rule leads one to expect that a higher degree of technical control or legal enforcement will be required, i.e. exactly what can be observed in the marketplace.

The trade link and the pragmatic nature of trade rules, and their enforcement in the GATT/WTO context,[135] have forced copyright holders to find a new exposition of the principles according to which their investment should be protected, in what circumstances and to what extent. Term, scope (or rights and exceptions) and rights management are all on the Holmesian table[136] set by the incorporation of copyright in trade. 'This is the age of the finance

---

minimize negative social welfare impacts. Epstein suggests that adopting a more consequentialist analytical grid may be Ariadne's thread out of the justificatory labyrinth.

[131]   Ibid., 5–6.

[132]   Alfino, *supra* note 52, 10.

[133]   See Gervais, Daniel (2004), 'The Price of Social Norms: Towards a Liability Regime for File-Sharing', *Journal of Intellectual Property Law* **12**, 1, 39–73.

[134]   See 'On the Self-Evidence of Copyright', archive.cpsr.net/essays/2001/ CPSRCCJU7.htm (accessed 6 October 2006), 3.

[135]   See Jackson, John H. (1997), *The World Trading System: Law and Policy of International Economic Relations*, 2nd edn, Cambridge, Mass.: MIT Press.

[136]   'The assumption that people are justified in defending what they have become accustomed to is obviously an assumption heavily biased toward the status quo. There will naturally be people who want to change the way things are, but on Holmes's theory, these people are simply attempting to shift some part of the aggregate social burden from one set of shoulders to another. "Justice" and "fairness" are slogans propping up particular struggles, not eternal principles, and reform is a zero-sum game. But if we flip Holmes's theory over onto its back, so to speak, the implications are reversed. For the friends of the status quo have no greater claim to the principles of justice and fairness than its enemies do.' Menand, Louis (2002), *The Metaphysical Club,* London: Flamingo, 63–4.

minister. . . . The game of nations is now geo-monopoly.'[137] Copyright policy is not, or no longer, an exception. Whether that was for the best remains to be seen.

Conclusion

The Canadian copyright systems imported, or were at least inspired by, elements of UK law and the complex and at times obscure British history of copyright which was born out of the ashes of a censorship-tainted licensing system guaranteeing a monopoly to members of the Stationers' Company. The transition from a publisher's right to an author-centric concept happened in the years that preceded the adoption of the Statute of Anne. To a certain extent authors were instrumentalized to secure rights for publishers as assigns of authors. Common law copyright was then essentially limited to unpublished works and the right to be recognized as the author of a published work.

In the United States, for the purposes of interpreting Constitutional and other eighteenth-century law, considering contemporary legal practices that the Framers would be familiar with is undoubtedly useful to understand their context and what they would have been reacting against. In that context, British copyright history is relevant also from a US perspective. Yet US courts recognized the difficulty of referring to UK copyright principles or history because it is far from crystalline. In addition, given the US's Revolutionary history, US courts were free to supply a narrative of their own, through thinkers such as Jefferson and Madison. And, to a certain extent they did. US law weaves utilitarian/instrumentalist (essentially the 'incentive' theory) and natural rights and fairness elements. It seems, however, that in the late 1990s that narrative was shelved and that a simpler, property-centric rhetoric was

---

[137]   Thomas L. Friedman, quoted in Jackson, *supra*, at 4. At least one other well-known economist is not convinced about the merits of the linkage and even sees threats to the integrity of the trading system, 'For virtually the first time, the corporate lobbies in pharmaceutical and software had distorted and deformed an important multilateral institution, turning it away from its trade mission and rationale and transforming it into a royalty collection agency. The consequences have been momentous, Now every lobby in the rich countries wants to put its own agenda, almost always trade-unrelated, into the WTO.' Jagdish Bhagwati, *supra*, 183. One could reply that the US is progressively abandoning the multilateral approach and uses its substantial clout to get deals on a bilateral or regional basis, in many of which dispute-settlement is often mostly irrelevant because the US is both the net importer and by far the bigger player and thus much less sensitive to 'retaliation'. As it has done with a number of WTO and NAFTA decisions, the US can thus, 'realpolitikally' ignore negative rulings while insisting on enforcement of those it wins. See e.g. Owens, Richard (2003), 'TRIPS and the Fairness in Music Arbitration: The Repercussions', *European Intellectual Property Review* **25**, 2, 49–54.

preferred, even though copyright's entry into the 'property' family was a difficult adoption at best.

Now may be the time to adopt a different approach, one that is conscious of principles and objectives. Rather than appeasing the maximum number of lobbies, legislators should focus on the adoption of a Canadian narrative, using the recent Supreme Court dicta as guidance. The practice of developing detailed rules built on an absence of foundations should be jettisoned. This chapter suggests a view that reconciles the economic and authorial aspects of copyright and proposes a new copyright norm aimed at commercially significant uses.

4 Can and should misappropriation also protect databases? A comparative approach
Estelle Derclaye[1]

Introduction

Article 13 of the Database Directive[2] provides that

> [t]he Directive shall be without prejudice to provisions concerning in particular . . . unfair competition. . . .

It therefore allows Member States to protect databases by unfair competition law in addition to the *sui generis* right. In other words, database producers can protect their databases by the *sui generis* right and unfair competition simultaneously if their national laws allow it. This chapter aims at discovering whether this additional protection against unfair competition over-protects databases and if it does, remedies are suggested. It is concerned only with the database right, which protects the investment in collecting, verifying or presenting data, and not copyright, which protects the structure of the database. Over-protection exists when the same subject-matter (here investment in databases) is protected more than once by similar types of protection at the same time. I call this type of over-protection 'simultaneous over-protection'.[3] It is against the intellectual property paradigm that an effort be rewarded twice. More protection leads to rent-seeking and all the negative effects of monopolies. Over-protection must therefore be avoided. This chapter examines the protection of databases against parasitism.[4] Unfair competition acts

---

[1] Lecturer in Law, University of Nottingham.
[2] Directive 96/9/EC of the European Parliament and of the Council of 11 March 1996 on the legal protection of databases, OJ L77/20, 27.03.1996 ('the Directive').
[3] Two other types also exist. There is *a posteriori* over-protection if the intellectual property protection has expired but the database can still be protected against parasitism and there is negative over-protection when no intellectual property protection is available at all but the action for parasitism is. These are examined in the author's thesis (2008), *The Legal Protection of Databases: A Comparative Analysis*, Cheltenham, UK and Northampton, MA, USA: Edward Elgar.
[4] The terms, the 'theory of parasitism', 'tort of parasitism' and 'parasitism' will be used interchangeably. Parasitism is also commonly known as slavish imitation, slavish copying or misappropriation depending on the country. For the purposes of this

other than parasitism, such as disparagement, trade secret protection or misleading advertising, are not aimed at protecting investment but at protecting reputation, secrecy or guarding against false allegations. Thus, there is no cumulation as the subject-matters protected under the two laws are different. Unfair competition law is not harmonised in Europe. Therefore, national laws must be reviewed. Analysis of the law of a few Member States is sufficient to prove there is, at least in some, over-protection. To this aim, the laws of the United Kingdom, Ireland, France and Belgium have been chosen.

Before tackling the issue of simultaneous over-protection, a broad overview of the unfair competition legal framework in Europe is in order.

1.   Unfair competition in Europe

Unfair competition in the European Union remains largely unharmonised.[5] So far only two acts of unfair competition, namely misleading and comparative advertising, have been harmonised.[6] Despite this lack of harmonisation, each Member State must comply with articles 1–12 and 19 of the 1967 version of the Paris Convention for the Protection of Industrial Property of 1883 as required by article 2 of TRIPs.[7] Article 10bis of the Paris Convention states:

(1)   The countries of the Union are bound to assure to nationals of such countries effective protection against unfair competition.

(2)   Any act of competition contrary to honest practices in industrial or commercial matters constitutes an act of unfair competition.

(3)   The following in particular shall be prohibited:

---

chapter, the word 'parasitism' will be chosen to refer to all these concepts because it is the term most used in France and Belgium.

5   Henning-Bodewig, F. and G. Schricker (2002), 'New initiatives for the harmonisation of unfair competition law in Europe', *EIPR* 271–2.

6   Council Directive 84/450/CEE of 10 September 1984 relating to the approximation of the laws, regulations and administrative provisions of the Member States concerning misleading advertising, OJ L250/17, 19.09.1984 and Directive 97/55/EC of Parliament and Council of 6 October 1997 amending Directive 84/450/EEC concerning misleading advertising so as to include comparative advertising, OJ L290/18, 23.10.1997. See also the regulation of advertising in Council Directive 89/552/EEC of 3 October 1989 on the coordination of certain provisions laid down by Law, Regulation or Administrative Action in Member States concerning the pursuit of television broadcasting activities, OJ L298, 17.10.1989, p. 23. See also G. Schricker (1991), 'European harmonisation of unfair competition law – a futile venture', *IIC* 788; Henning-Bodewig and Schricker, above fn. 5, pp. 271–2.

7   TRIPs has no special section on unfair competition and it refers to it only in places, namely in article 39 on the protection of undisclosed information and article 22.2.b in the section on geographical indications.

1. all acts of such a nature as to create confusion by any means whatever with the establishment, the goods, or the industrial or commercial activities, of a competitor;
2. false allegations in the course of trade of such a nature as to discredit the establishment, the goods, or the industrial or commercial activities, of a competitor;
3. indications or allegations the use of which in the course of trade is liable to mislead the public as to the nature, the manufacturing process, the characteristics, the suitability for their purpose, or the quantity, of the goods.

Parasitism is not mentioned in the illustrative list of article 10bis(3).[8] It can only be prohibited under article 10bis(2). However, there is no further definition of what is an act of unfair competition beyond an act contrary to honest practices in industrial or commercial matters. Therefore, the Convention does not force Member countries to prohibit parasitism. Since there is neither international nor European harmonisation of parasitism, it is still regulated on a purely national basis.

2. Misappropriation and parasitism

2.1. The United Kingdom and Ireland

The legal concepts of unfair competition and of parasitism do not exist in the United Kingdom. Despite the obligation under article 10bis of the Paris Convention[9] and calls by many authors for a law against unfair competition,[10] the United Kingdom has continually rejected the legal concept of unfair competition as such[11] as well as a general clause establishing a tort of unfair

---

[8] J. Schmidt-Szalewski (1994), 'La distinction entre l'action en contrefaçon et l'action en concurrence déloyale dans la jurisprudence', *RTD Com.* 455, at 462.

[9] It is arguable that the United Kingdom complies with article 10bis of the Paris Convention because it is unclear whether article 10 bis(2) requires acts other than those enumerated in article 10bis (3) to be considered unfair. See Robertson, Aidan and A. Horton (1995), 'Does the UK or the EC need an unfair competition law?' *EIPR* 568, at 572.

[10] W. Cornish (1972), 'Unfair competition? A progress report', *Journal of the Society of Public Teachers of Law,* **12**, 126; G. Dworkin (1979), 'Unfair competition: is the common law developing a new tort?', *EIPR* 241; H. Brett (1979), 'Unfair competition – not merely an academic issue?', *EIPR* 295; P. Burns (1981), 'Unfair competition – a compelling need unmet', *EIPR* 311; A. Booy (1991), 'A half-way house for unfair competition in the United Kingdom – a practitioner's plea', *EIPR* 439; Robertson and Horton, above fn. 9, at 581–2.

[11] G. Schricker (1995), '25 years of protection against unfair competition' *IIC* 782, at 785; Robertson and Horton above fn. 9, at 568 (during the passing of the Trade Mark Act 1994 there was lobbying for an unfair competition law but the government resisted it).

competition.[12] As a result, there is no statute on unfair competition, neither specific nor general.[13] There is no general civil liability statutory provision as in France,[14] but courts developed a series of different unfair competition torts to which they applied different rules, namely passing off, injurious falsehood, defamation, interference with contractual relations, interference with trade by unlawful means, deceit, conspiracy, intimidation and breach of confidence.[15] English courts are conservative and are reluctant to create new causes of action,[16] especially a general unfair competition cause of action,[17] and still have not recognised a tort of misappropriation or parasitism.[18] Therefore, in the United Kingdom, misappropriation as such is not unlawful.[19] Passing off always requires a risk of confusion[20] and the other torts are not concerned with rendering copying *per se* illegal.

In conclusion, as there is no British tort of misappropriation, none of the issues addressed in this article occurs in the United Kingdom. The same is

---

[12]   W. Cornish (1974), 'Unfair competition and the consumer in England', *IIC* 73, at 74; Dworkin above fn. 10, at 242; F. Beier (1985), 'The law of unfair competition in the European Community, its development and present status', *IIC* 139, at 156; Robertson and Horton, above fn. 9, at 568.

[13]   The only exception is misleading advertising which the United Kingdom had to implement due to the relevant European Directives, see *supra*.

[14]   See below section 2.2.1.

[15]   Burns above fn. 10, p. 311; Robertson and Horton above fn. 9, p. 568.

[16]   Burns above fn. 10, p. 311; Cornish, William and David Llewelyn (2003), *Intellectual Property: Patents, Copyright, Trade Marks and Allied Rights*, 5th edn, London: Sweet & Maxwell, p. 18, nn. 1–22. Courts believe this power belongs exclusively to Parliament.

[17]   G. Dworkin (2004), 'Unfair competition: is it time for European harmonisation?', in D. Vaver and L. Bently (eds), *Intellectual Property in the New Millennium: Essays in Honour of William R. Cornish*, Cambridge: Cambridge University Press, 175, at 177.

[18]   An attempt to establish a general tort of unfair competition and misappropriation was killed off by the Privy Council in the *Cadbury Schweppes Pty Ltd v Pub Squash Pty Ltd* [1981] 1 All ER 213, commented on by G. Dworkin (1981), 'Passing off and unfair competition and opportunity missed', MLR, 564, pp. 566–7. The defendant had reaped where she had not sown but there was no misrepresentation. The court stuck to the strict conditions of passing off and the claimant lost. The Privy Council (per Lord Scarman) refused to create a tort of misappropriation because it encountered criticism in the United States and Australia. Lord Scarman also emphasised the need to preserve the freedom to compete: 'A defendant, however, does no wrong by entering a market created by another and there competing with its creator. The line may be difficult to draw; but unless it is drawn, competition will be stifled.'

[19]   J. Adams (1992), 'Unfair competition: why a need is unmet', *EIPR* 259, at 260.

[20]   Robertson and Horton, above fn. 9, at 569; Adams, above fn. 19, at 259; Beier, above fn. 12, at 156; S. Byrt (2003), 'Le *passing-off* au Royaume-Uni: des leçons a tirer?', 213 *RIPIA* 55, n. 213.

valid for Ireland, another country where parasitism is absent.[21] In other words, in those two countries, unfair competition law does not over-protect databases which are protected by the *sui generis* right.

2.2. France

This section examines the legal basis of the protection against parasitism and states under which conditions courts found copying another's creation unlawful. It does not aim at retracing in detail the history of the notion nor of the case law[22] but only to give a picture of protection against parasitism as it currently stands in France. This is sufficient to determine whether French law against parasitism over-protects databases.

2.2.1. Legal basis French unfair competition law is based on the principle of the freedom to copy. This principle dates back to the Decret d'Allarde of 2–17 March 1791[23] which provides for the principle of freedom of commerce and industry. According to this principle, undertakings are free to compete and the competitive prejudice is normally lawful. Thus, every competitor has the right to attract the customers of her competitors. The corollary of this principle is that everyone is free to sell similar or even identical products. As far as intellectual products are concerned, it means that everyone is free to copy or imitate another's creation.[24] This is not illegal *per se*. This principle is affirmed by courts and the vast majority of commentators.[25] The principle is

---

[21]   M. Davison (2003), *The Legal Protection of Databases*, Cambridge: Cambridge University Press, p. 127.

[22]   For more detail, see e.g. J. Passa (1997), *Contrefaçon et concurrence déloyale*, Publications de l'IRPI no. 15, Paris: Litec; M. Buydens, *La protection de la quasi-creation*, Larcier: Bruxelles, 1993.

[23]   Also known as Loi Le Chapelier. P. De Candé (2004), 'L'action en concurrence déloyale est-elle menacée par l'évolution du droit de la propriété intellectuelle?', *Prop. Int.*, p. 492; Passa, above fn. 22, at 13.

[24]   A. Puttemans (2000), *Droits intellectuels et concurrence déloyale*, Bruxelles: Bruylant, p. 234; Buydens above fn. 22, p. 678.

[25]   E. Golaz (1992), *L'imitation servile des produits et de leur presentation, étude comparée des droits français, allemand, belge et suisse*, Génève: Droz, p. 105; J.-J. Burst (1993), *Concurrence déloyale et parasitisme*, Paris: Dalloz, p. 1; Buydens, above fn. 22, at 655, 677, 683; M. Buydens (1993), 'La sanction de la "piraterie de produits" par le droit de la concurrence déloyale', *Journal des Tribunaux* 117, at 119, 123, fnn. 22 and 23; Passa, above fn. 22, at p. 13; M.-L. Izorche (1998), 'Les fondements de la sanction de la concurrence déloyale et du parasitime', 51(1) *RTD Com.* 17, at 19; A. Bertrand (1998), *Le droit français de la concurrence déloyale*, Paris: Cedat, pp. 16 ff.; De Candé (2004), at fn. 23 above, including the authors and decisions cited by all. *Contra*: P. Le Tourneau (2000), 'Retour sur le parasitisme', *Dalloz*, Chronique, 403, at 405 (the simple parasitic copy of another's work with an interested goal is a breach).

also called the principle of pre-emption. It means that competition is free and that limitations on competition can be set only by Parliament.[26]

The principle of the freedom to copy is subject to two exceptions. First, the legislature can grant certain intellectual property rights to certain deserving creations. In this case, copying is no longer free but is an infringement of the right holder's exclusive right. Second, courts declared certain types of copying contrary to honest practices in commercial matters on the basis of unfair competition law.

French unfair competition law (*concurrence deloyale*) is based on civil liability, i.e. on article 1382 of the Civil Code ('CC').[27] The three requirements of any civil liability action (breach (*faute*[28]), damage and causal link) must therefore be proven to establish that an act of unfair competition occurred. Several acts of unfair competition are prohibited by courts on this basis, including parasitism.

2.2.2.   The concept of parasitism and conditions of application   Parasitism occurs when a third party, without incurring any expenditure, uses the fruit of the efforts made by another by following in her wake. The copied creation must not be banal, nor be a necessary and functional form.[29] Only the copying of 'arbitrary' forms is parasitic. In other words, it is the act of copying another's creation, even if the copy is not slavish,[30] and does not create a risk

---

26   A. Kamperman Sanders (1997), *Unfair Competition Law: The Protection of Intellectual and Industrial Creativity*, Oxford: Clarendon Press, p. 11.
27   Golaz above fn. 25, at 60–1.
28   The main element of the tort is that there must be a 'faute'. This corresponds to the breach of the duty of care in the British tort of negligence. The term 'breach' will be used to designate the *faute*.
29   Buydens above fn. 22, at 707, 721; Passa above fn. 22, at 272; Schmidt-Szalewski above fn. 8, at 466–7.
30   The act of copying another's creation is also referred to as slavish or quasi-slavish copying. Slavish or quasi-slavish copies are simply identical or quasi-identical copies of another person's creation unprotected by an intellectual property right. Passa, above fn. 22, at 242. *Contra*: Strowel, A. and J.-P. Triaille (1993), 'De l'équilibre entre le droit de la concurrence et la propriété intellectuelle. A propos de la proposition de loi Godfrain sur les "créations réservées" ' 2 *DIT* 25, at 26 (slavish copies are those which create a risk of confusion). The notion of parasitism requires the avoidance of efforts and does not require that the copy be slavish or quasi-slavish, although it will generally be the case. Y. Saint-Gal (1956), 'Concurrence parasitaire ou agissements parasitaires', *RIPIA* 37. It is not the slavish character of the copy which constitutes the breach; the breach is the avoidance of efforts. Passa, above fn. 22, at 249 ff.; Izorche above fn. 25 and decisions cited. However, generally, when one slavishly or quasi-slavishly copies something, she inevitably always avoids effort. Slavish copying therefore always has as a consequence that the copying product will be cheaper since the copier

of confusion, by which someone (the parasite) benefits unduly from the creation, efforts, investment or know-how of another person without herself making any such efforts and thereby saving the costs necessary in the creation of the original product.[31] It can now be understood why courts called the tort 'parasitism'; the copier acts like a parasite, nourishing herself upon the efforts of another person without making any effort herself.[32] However, the Court of Cassation has sometimes ruled that it is not necessary for the victim of parasitism to prove she made efforts or investments.[33] The notion of parasitism encompasses parasitic competition (*concurrence parasitaire*) and parasitic acts (*actes parasitaires*). The difference between the two is that in the first case, the two parties are in competition with one another and in the second, they are not.

As parasitism is based on civil liability, to win the action, breach, damage and causal link must be proven. However, courts interpreted those requirements very loosely over the years. This has had the effect that there is no need to prove any of these three requirements to win the action.[34] The breach is the proof of parasitism. As has been seen above, in some cases it is not even necessary to prove avoidance of efforts. Proof of copying will be sufficient. As to damage, courts generally infer it from the breach itself. It generally consists in the vague notion of 'commercial turmoil'[35] or can simply be a

by definition always avoids the research and presentation costs. Parasitism and slavish copying can therefore be said to be synonyms or quasi-synonyms. Consequently, I will refer to parasitism only and this will encompass slavish and quasi-slavish copying.

[31] E.g. Puttemans above fn. 24, at 236; Golaz above fn. 25, at 228. There are two notions of parasitism, a broad one (parasitism exists if the copied creation necessitated some effort or investment) and a narrow one (parasitism exists only if the copied creation necessitated important efforts). See e.g. M. Malaurie-Vignal (1996), 'Le parasitisme des investissements et du travail d'autrui', *Dalloz* 177, at 180.

[32] Sometimes parasitism is also referred to as 'economic parasitism' to distinguish it from parasitism occurring in nature. The term 'parasitism' will be used to describe economic parasitism.

[33] Contrast Cass. com., 26.01.1999 [2000] *D.*, Jurisp. 87, cited by P. Le Tourneau (2001), 'Folles idées sur les idées' *CCE*, Chronique no. 4, 8, at 12; Cass. com., 30.01.2001, *D.*, 2001, n. 24, p. 1939, *Bull. Civ.* IV, 27; JCP G 2001, I, 340, nn. 29 comment by Viney; *D.* 2001, Jurisp. 1939, comment by Le Tourneau; *Prop. Int.* 2002, n. 3, p. 101, comment by Passa with Cass. com., 20.05.2003, case no. 01–11212, available on www.legifrance.gouv.fr cited by J. Passa (2003), 'Responsabilité civile – concurrence' *Prop. Int.* 448–9 (claimants have to establish the amount of investment necessary for a product to be copied and show to what extent litigious behaviour allows them to benefit from it).

[34] Golaz, above fn. 25, p. 64.

[35] See e.g. Cass. com., 22.02.2000 [2000] CCC, com. 81, comment of Malaurie-Vignal; Cass. com., 25.04.2001 [2001] *PIBD* 726, III, 451; *Guerlais v Tillaud Boisouvres*, Cass. com., 01.07.2003, Juris-data no. 2003–019892, cited by J. Schmidt-Szalewski,

moral prejudice.[36] It is not necessary to prove a loss of turnover or of clients,[37] unless the creator seeks damages.[38] In addition, it is possible to take legal action while the damage has not yet happened (i.e. when the parasite is just attempting to commit the act of unfair competition) to prevent it from happening.[39] As far as causation is concerned, as unfair competition acts do not always lead to a decreased turnover, courts are flexible on the certainty of the causation and often skip the requirement altogether.[40]

As can now be seen, the conditions of the action against parasitism are very lenient. Proof of copying is often sufficient to have the copying stopped. Because in practice damage and causation need not be established, the action is used more usually to stop the behaviour complained of[41] and has come to resemble a restrictive injunction or cease and desist order.

2.2.3.   The case law   How is protection against parasitism received by French courts now? The case law of the Court of Cassation is unclear. As the highest court's case law does not give guidance, the whole French case law is unsettled.

The Court of Cassation continually contradicts itself. Generally, it is clearly in favour of the tort of parasitism.[42] Thus, it is unlawful to reproduce a

---

Comment, *Propriété industrielle*, November 2003, 29; Golaz, above fn. 25, p. 64; M.-L. Izorche, 'Concurrence déloyale et parasitisme économique', in Y. Serra (2001), *La concurrence déloyale, Permanence et devenir*, Paris: Dalloz, 27, at 31–2.

[36]   Cass. 22.05.2002, case no. 99–21579, available on www.legifrance.gouv.fr, cited by J. Passa (2003), 'Responsabilité civile – concurrence', *Prop. Int.* 84, at 85.

[37]   Cass. com., 22.10.1985, *Bull. Civ.* IV, no. 245. See also J. Passa, 'Responsabilité civile – distribution' [2002] *Prop. Int.* 100.

[38]   Cass. com., 16.01.2001 [2001] CCC, com. 59, comment of Malaurie-Vignal, cited by J. Passa, above fn. 37, at 100.

[39]   See e.g. P. Le Tourneau (2001), 'Le bon vent du parasitime', *CCC*, January, 4–6, at 6.

[40]   J.-M. Mousseron (1992), 'Entreprise: parasitisme et droit', *JCP E* **6**, 14, at 24; Burst, above fn. 25, p. 182.

[41]   P. Roubier (1948), 'Théorie générale de l'action en concurrence déloyale', *Revue Trimestrielle de Droit Commercial*, 541, at 589; Golaz, above fn. 25, p. 63; Burst, above fn. 25, p. 154, 174 citing CA Douai, 21.12.1989 [1990] *PIBD* III, 316; Passa, above fn. 37, at 100 ff.

[42]   See e.g. Cass. com., 21.06.1994 [1994] *PIBD*, III, 514 cited by Passa, above fn. 25, p. 273; Cass. com., 27.06.1995 [1995] *RJDA*, p. 1129 (parasitism does not require proof of confusion) cited by Malaurie-Vignal, above fn. 31, at 181; Cass. com., 26.01.1999 [2000] *D.*, Jurisp. 87, cited by Le Tourneau, above fn. 33, at 12; Cass. com., 30.01.2001, *D.*, 2001, no. 24, p. 1939, comment of Le Tourneau; *Bull. Civ.* IV, 27; *JCP* G 2001, I, 340, n. 29, comment by Viney; *Prop. Int.* 2002, p. 101, comment by Passa (plagiarism of a catalogue); Cass. com., 27.03.2001 [2001] *CCC*, n. 123, p. 4, comment by Malaurie; *PIBD* 725, III, 408; Passa, above fn. 36, pp. 100 ff.; Cass. 15.01.2002,

creation (e.g. a catalogue, a trade mark) even if this reproduction does not entail a risk of confusion. The position of the Court recently, however, is that there is no parasitism when the copier herself also invested herself or has made some, even minor, differences to her product even if she copied to avoid effort.[43] On the other hand, in other decisions from the late 1990s to date, the Court did not accept that parasitism alone is an act of unfair competition; instead it required a risk of confusion.[44] And in two decisions of 2002, the Court held that it is not unlawful to sell products identical to those of another undertaking which are unprotected by an intellectual property right.[45] These decisions are difficult to reconcile with other decisions of the Court of the same period (2001–2003) which clearly favour the prevention of parasitism.[46] While the most recent decisions show that the Court seemingly prefers to keep the tort of parasitism alive, the current situation is unsettled as the Court has continually oscillated between the two positions over the last few years.

The vast majority of the decisions of the Courts of Appeal and of First Instance also favour of the tort of parasitism.[47] However, they remain split.

22.05.2002, 18.06.2002 and 08.10.2002, cited by J. Passa (2003), 'Responsabilité civile – concurrence', *Prop. Int.* 84, at 85; Cass. 08.07.2003, case no. 01-13293 cited by Passa, above fn. 32, at 448–9; Cass. com., 29.10.2003 [2004] *PIBD* 778, III, 47, cited by J. Passa (2004), 'Responsabilité civile – concurrence', *Prop. Int.* pp. 683 ff.; Cass. 01.07.03, case no. 01-00628, available on www.legifrance.gouv.fr.

[43]   Cass. com., 18.06.2002 [2003] *PIBD* 755, III, 22 cited by J. Passa (2003), 'Responsabilité civile – concurrence', *Prop. Int.* 84, at 85; Cass. com., 17.12.2002 [2003] *PIBD* 764, III, 278, cited by J. Passa, above fn. 32, at 448–9. Thus the Court of Cassation limits the hypotheses of parasitism to pure slavish imitations. That was not the position of the previous case law. Ibid.

[44]   Cass. com., 21.10.1997 [1998] *PIBD* 645, III, 21; Cass. com., 27.01.1998 [1998] *PIBD* 657, III, 362; Cass. com., 05.10.1999 [2000] *PIBD* 691, III, 75 cited by J. Passa (2000), 'Propos dissidents sur la sanction du parasitisme économique', *Dalloz Cah. Dr. Aff.*, Chronique, no. 25, 297, at 306; Cass. com., 16.01.2001 [2001] *Bull. Civ*, IV, no. 13; *CCC*, Comm. 43, comment by Malaurie-Vignal; *JCP* IV 1421; Cass. com., 13.02.2001 [2001] *PIBD* 723, III, 354. See also Passa, above fn. 36, pp. 100ff.

[45]   Cass. com., 18.06.2002 [2002] *PIBD* 754, III, 578, cited by Passa, above fn. 42, p. 684; *Distribution Casino France v Ratureau*, Cass. com., 09.07.2002 [2003] *CCC*, Jan. 2003, p. 11; *Prop. Int.* p. 82, comment by Passa.

[46]   Above fn. 42–3.

[47]   Golaz, above fn. 25, at 106; Passa, above fn. 22, at 267 ff.; Bertrand, above fn. 25, at 47 fn. 122 and 123; p. 48 fn. 124, and decisions cited. As far as databases are concerned, parasitism was found in two recent cases. *Edirom v Global Market Network*, T. Comm. Nanterre, 27.01.1998 [1999] *DIT*, 99/3, p. 42; [1998] *Expertises*, p. 149, comment by Ragueneau (act of posting paper database on the internet, performed before the entry into force of the Directive, is parasitic); *Tigest v Reed Exposition France et Salons Français et internationaux*, CA Paris, 12.09.2001, [2001] *Legipresse*, no. 187, Dec., pp. 215–25; [2001] *D.*, no. 35, p. 2895; [2002] *JCP*, no. 1, pp. 25–31, comment by Pollaud-Dulian; [2002] *PIBD* 740, III, 198–201; [2002] *RIDA*,

For instance, a section of the Paris Court of Appeal[48] as well as the Versailles Court of Appeal[49] firmly rejects the tort of parasitism and requires that a risk of confusion be present for an act of copying to be unlawful.

In conclusion, the situation in France is unclear. The Court of Cassation's most recent decisions condemn parasitism but in view of its other recent conflicting decisions, the status of the tort of parasitism is uncertain. Additionally, although the majority of the lower courts are in favour of preventing parasitism, they remain split. As France has a long tradition in favour of the prevention of parasitism, it is very likely that the tort is still alive.

2.3.   Belgium

As for France, this section examines the legal basis of the tort of parasitism and its conditions in Belgium. It does not aim to retrace in detail the history of the notion nor of the case law[50] but only to give a picture of protection against parasitism as it currently stands in Belgium.

2.3.1.   Legal basis   Belgian unfair competition law is also based on the principle of the freedom to copy. This principle is also based on the French Decret d'Allarde, which is still applicable in Belgium[51] and is indirectly consecrated in article 96 of the Lois sur les Pratiques du commerce et sur l'information et la protection du consommateur ('LPCC').[52] This means that everyone is free to copy or imitate another's creation.[53] This principle of the freedom to copy is firmly affirmed by Belgian courts and literature.[54]

---

no. 192, p. 433 *affirming* TGI Paris 22.06.1999 [1999] *PIBD* 686, III, 494; cited by J. Passa (2002), 'Responsabilité civile – concurrence', *Prop. Int.* 103, at 106 (acts of copying and marketing a paper database, performed before the entry into force of the Directive, are parasitic). Very few lower courts have rejected the tort of parasitism. See Passa, above fn. 22, pp. 58–9, 286, who identified only a couple of decisions.

[48]   Passa, above fn. 44, at 306; Passa, above fn. 37, at 112–13; Passa, above fn. 33, at 448–9.

[49]   Passa, above fn. 47, at 103; De Candé, above fn. 25, at 495, and decisions cited.

[50]   For more detail, see e.g. Buydens, above fn. 22; Puttemans, above fn. 24.

[51]   Strowel and Triaille, above fn. 30, p. 26.

[52]   M.B. 29.08.1991; in force 29.02.1992 (Act on commercial practices and on information and the protection of the consumer). Buydens above fn. 22, p. 678.

[53]   Puttemans above fn. 24, at 234; Buydens, above fn. 22, at 678; Buydens, above fn. 25, at 188.

[54]   See for instance, Cass. 04.11.1954, *Ing.-Cons.*, 1954.249; Prés. Trib. Com. Brussels, 03.06.1970, *JCB* 1971, III, 413, note De Gryse; Trib. Com. Courtrai 30.03.1987, *Pratiques Commerciales*, 1987.I.291; CA Antwerp, 30.05.1988, *Rev. Dr. Com. Belge*, 1988.949; CA Brussels, 24.08.1995, unreported, cited by Van Bunnen, *Journal des Tribunaux*, 1997, p. 62; Prés. Trib. Com. Namur, 22.05.1996, *Journal des*

As in France, this principle suffers two exceptions. First, the legislator grants certain intellectual property rights to certain deserving creations. In this case, copying is no longer free but an infringement of the right holder's exclusive right. Second, courts have declared certain types of copying contrary to honest practices in commercial matters on the basis of unfair competition law. Like French unfair competition law, that of Belgium was initially based on article 1382 of the Civil Code ('CC').[55] However, the civil liability action soon proved unsuitable because it is slow and expensive, damage must be proved and stopping the behaviour preventively is not possible.[56] Therefore, in 1934, specific legislation was enacted to enable the injured competitor to get a restrictive injunction or cease and desist order (*action en cessation*).[57] The difference between the two actions is that the civil liability action requires proof of damage and cannot be used to put an end to the behaviour complained of while the *action en cessation* does not require proof of actual damage and allows the claimant to put an end to the behaviour. The 1934 legislation was replaced by an act of 1971 on trade practices.[58] This act abandoned the requirement of a competitive relationship between parties to a suit and also protected consumers' interests.[59] The act of 1971 was replaced by the current LPCC, which retains the same principles as the 1971 act. The central provision of the LPCC is article 93 which provides that '[a]ny act contrary to honest practices in commercial matters by which a trader prejudices or can prejudice the professional interests of one or several traders is forbidden'. There is no further definition so the number of acts which can be considered contrary to honest practices in commercial matters is potentially infinite and is determined by courts. Finally, the *action en cessation* has not replaced the civil liability action, so it remains possible to act under traditional civil liability.[60]

2.3.2. Case law Parasitism was rarely considered unlawful until a decision of 1936.[61] In that case, the court condemned the defendant for slavish copying

---

Tribunaux*, 1997, p. 62, obs. L. Van Bunnen; CA Liège, 13.10.1998, *Rev. Dr. Com. Belge*, 1998/6, p. 410. Buydens, above fn. 25, at 119 and fn. 20 for further decisions and commentators; F. De Visscher (2003), 'L'action en concurrence déloyale comme moyen de protection en Belgique', *RIPIA*, no. 213, p. 51, at 52–3; Golaz, above fn. 25, p. 117; Passa, above fn. 44.

55 Golaz, above fn. 25, at p. 68.
56 Buydens, above fn. 22, at p. 656; Golaz, above fn. 25, at p. 68.
57 Royal Decree no. 55 of 23 December 1934.
58 Loi sur les pratiques du commerce of 14 July 1971, M.B. 30.07.1971, p. 9087.
59 E. Ulmer (1973), 'Unfair competition law in the European Economic Community', *IIC* 188; Beier, above fn. 12, at p. 154.
60 Golaz, above fn. 25, at p. 68; Buydens, above fn. 22, at pp. 656–7.
61 Buydens, above fn. 22, at p. 710.

because it allowed her to sell her product at a cheaper price.[62] Other decisions followed that trend[63] until the highest court endorsed it in 1954.[64] The first decision to mention expressly the terms 'parasitic competition' and to apply the theory dates from 1959.[65] In the 1960s and 1970s, the reference to parasitic competition grew[66] and in the 1980s, parasitism was systematically used by competitors whose creations had been copied and was widely accepted by the courts.[67] So in Belgium until recently, decisions against the tort of parasitism were rare.[68] The most recent decisions apply neither the narrow nor the broad conception of parasitism but reject the tort in its entirety, thus making one believe that the tort of parasitism has actually died. It seems to be largely admitted now that a copy can only be prohibited if it creates a risk of confusion in the mind of the public.[69] Two recent cases which follow this trend actually

---

62   See Pres. Trib. Com. Brussels, 24.07.1936, *Ing.-Cons.*, 1937, p. 18. See Buydens, above fn. 22, at p. 710; Buydens, above fn. 25, at p. 122; Passa, above fn. 22, at p. 266.

63   Trib. Com. Brussels, 03.06.1937, *Ing.-Cons.*, 1937, p. 85; Trib. Civ. Charleroi, 24.06.1939, *Ing.-Cons.*, 1939, p. 125, cited by Passa, above fn. 22, at p. 266 and Buydens, above fn. 25, at p. 122.

64   Cass. 04.11.1954, *Ing.-Cons.*, 1954, 249.

65   Trib. Com. Brussels, 14.02.1959, *Ing.-Cons.*, 1965, 258, comment by De Caluwe. See Buydens, above fn. 22, at p. 710; Buydens, above fn. 25, at p. 123; Golaz, above fn. 25, at p. 226; Y. Saint-Gal (1981), 'Concurrence et agissements parasitaires en droit français et belge', in *La concurrence parasitaire en droit comparé, Actes du Colloque de Lausanne*, Genève: Droz, 1981, 133, at 141.

66   Golaz, above fn. 25, at p. 228. See e.g. Prés. Trib. Com. Courtrai, 13.06.1974, *JCB* 1975.III.194, comment by De Caluwé; Prés. Trib. Com. Malines, 15.09.1977, *JCB* 1980.III.39, comment by De Caluwé and J. Billiet; Ghent, 20.01.1978, JCB 1978.III.573; Trib.Com. Brussels, 29.10.1979, *Ing.-Cons.*, 1980, p. 31.

67   See CA Antwerp, 30.05.1988, *Rev. Dr. Com.*, 1988, p. 949; CA Brussels, 14.03.1989, *Ing.-Cons.*, 1989, p. 115; Trib. Com. Brussels, 09.06.1989, *Rev. Dr. Com.*, 1991, p. 331; Trib. Com. Verviers, 10.10.1989, *Ing.-Cons.*, 1990, p. 178; Trib. Com. Namur, 29.11.1990, *Ing.-Cons.*, 1991, p. 172, all cited by Passa, above fn. 22, at p. 273. See also Buydens, above fn. 22, at p. 712; Buydens, above fn 25, at p. 123, citing a number of decisions, fn. 76.

68   See e.g. Prés. Trib. Com. Brussels, 17.12.1969, *Ing.-Cons.*, 1972, p. 82 (not unfair to use brochures whose form is identical to those of the claimant when this form is not original and is used by competitors), cited by Saint-Gal, above fn. 64; Prés. Com. Brussels, 07.11.1974, *JCB* 1975, 385 (the copying of commercial and technical documentation consisting of banal representations and resulting from no creative expensive effort was not judged an act of parasitic competition); Trib. Com. Brussels, 05.05.1980, *Ing.-Cons.*, 1980, p. 356.

69   Passa, above fn. 44, at pp. 304 and 306, citing Trib. Com. Namur, 22.05.1996, *Journal des Tribunaux*, 1997, p. 62; Trib. Com. Antwerp, 09.10.1997, *AJT*, 1997–8, p. 581; CA Liège, 17.02.1998, *Rev. Dr. Com. Belge*, 1998/6, p. 415, comment by Putzeys; CA Liège, 13.10.1998, *Rev. Dr. Com. Belge*, 1998/6, p. 410.

relate to parasitic acts concerning databases. They were decided before the entry into force of the Directive. In the first one,[70] the court held that Kapitol Trading, which had copied in their entirety the files (numbers, names and addresses of subscribers) of the Belgian first telecommunications operator, Belgacom, did not benefit from the name, creative work or investments of Belgacom. Hence, Belgacom did not win on parasitic competition. In the second case,[71] the defendant had copied the claimant's address file. The judge held that the file was not protected by copyright and it would be against the freedom of commerce to recognise a special protection for it. In sum, the case law prior to the Directive applied the freedom to copy strictly; the LPCC cannot grant the database producer an exclusive right which is not organised by a specific statute.[72] There have been no further cases confirming this trend.

In conclusion, the situation as regards parasitism in Belgium is uncertain. It is not clear whether the theory of parasitism survives and if so what its conditions are.[73] Whereas the recent decisions seem to show that parasitism is dead, there are no Court of Cassation decisions to confirm this.

3. Simultaneous protection

After this general overview of the status of the French and Belgian tort of parasitism, this section examines whether the protection of the *sui generis* right and parasitism for databases can be cumulated, in other words whether an infringement action can be combined with an unfair competition action for parasitism. If this is the case, the section will determine whether this simultaneous protection over-protects databases. Thereafter, the question whether the *sui generis* right holder has a choice between the infringement and unfair competition actions will be examined.

3.1. Is simultaneous protection possible?

3.1.1. France As the unfair competition and infringement actions are distinct and have a different cause and object, they can be cumulated.[74] This

---

70 *Belgacom v Kapitol Trading*, Prés. Com. Brussels., 19.07.1995, *Ann. Prat. Comm.* 1995, p. 788, comment Byl; *R.D.C.*, 1996, p. 747. See also Puttemans, above fn. 24 at p. 442; Strowel, Alain and Estelle Derclaye (2001), *Droit d'auteur et numérique: logiciels, bases de données et multimedia, droit belge, européen et comparé*, Bruxelles: Bruylant, p. 340, n. 388.

71 See Prés. Trib. Com. Courtrai, 06.09.1996, *R.D.C.*, 1997, p. 47, comment by De Vuyst and p. 442, Puttemans, above fn. 24.

72 Puttemans, above fn. 24, at p. 442.

73 The legislator also believes that the theory of parasitism is unclear. See Puttemans, above fn. 24, at p. 445, fn. 2009, citing Exposé des Motifs, Doc. Parl., Ch., 1997–8, no. 1535/1–1536/1, p. 6.

74 Passa, above fn. 22, p. 73; Golaz, above fn. 25, p. 84.

possibility to cumulate is expressly provided for in articles L. 615–19 al. 2 and L. 716–3 of the Intellectual Property Code ('IPC') which state that actions in infringement of patents or trade marks which also raise an unfair competition question are brought exclusively before the Court of First Instance (*tribunal de grande instance*).[75] As far as databases are concerned, article L. 341–1 ff. of the IPC provides a civil liability action. Article L. 341–1 paragraph 2 of the IPC states that *sui generis* protection is without prejudice to copyright or other protections on the database.

The two actions are subject to the fulfilment of their respective conditions.[76] The unfair competition action thus complements the infringement action.[77] This complementary nature means that there can be cumulation as long as the acts of unfair competition complained of are distinct from the infringement acts. Therefore, there can only be a condemnation for unfair competition if a breach distinct from infringement can be established. If there is not, the unfair competition action is rejected. Courts and commentators are anonymous on this point.[78] The existence of a distinct breach can be explained by the fact that the damages for infringement must be granted on the principle of integral reparation of the prejudice. The same act cannot serve as the basis of an unfair competition action because there would be no prejudice to repair.[79] The claimant

---

[75]   Passa, above fn. 22, p. 73.

[76]   Ibid.

[77]   Roubier, above fn. 41, at p. 555; Passa, above fn. 22. pp. 2, 73; Bertrand 1998, *op cit.* fn. 25, p. 25. However, the Court of Cassation has affirmed (Cass com., 22.09.1983 [1984] *D.*, 187) that the action in unfair competition requires a breach while the action in infringement sanctions the infringement of a privative right. The two actions have different causes and different aims; one does not complement the other. See also Golaz, above fn. 25, p. 84 (the action in unfair competition is independent of the infringement action; it is not the accessory, the complement or the consequence of the infringement action. However courts cumulate the actions as long as there are facts distinct from infringement).

[78]   See e.g. Cass. com., 23.05.1973, *Bull. Civ.* IV, no. 182; *Villeroy & Bosch*, CA Paris, 16.11.2001, Juris-data, no. 2001–170988. Roubier, above fn. 41, at p. 557; Burst, above fn. 25, at pp. 2, 146; Bertrand, above fn. 25, at pp. 153–4; Passa, above fn. 22, at p. 2; Golaz, above fn. 21, at pp. 84–5; X. Desjeux, 'La reproduction ou copie servile et l'action en concurrence déloyale dans la jurisprudence française' [1976] JCP, ed. CIJ, no. 17, at 240; P. Le Tourneau (1993), 'Le parasitisme dans tous ses états', Dalloz, 42ᵉ Cahier, Chronique, 310, at 311 citing Mousseron, Jean-Marc (1990), 'Responsabilité civile et droits intellectuels', in *Mélanges Chavanne*, Paris: Litec, 1990, 247; Izorche, above fn. 35, at p. 33; R. Clauss (1995), 'The French law of disloyal competition', *EIPR* 550, at 552–3; Schmidt-Szalewski, above fn. 8, p. 456; Malaurie-Vignal, above fn. 31, at p. 178; De Candé, above fn. 25, at p. 493. Specifically as regards the *sui generis* right, see N. Mallet-Poujol (2003), 'Protection des bases de données', ed. Juris-classeur, n. 9, fasc. 6080.

[79]   Passa, above fn. 22, at p. 73.

cannot ask for a single global reparation since the two damages are different but she must ask for the reparation of two distinct damages.[80] In spite of this rule, many judges often grant a global sum.[81]

Commentators disagree as to what constitute acts distinct from infringement. For some, parasitism is not a distinct act. Only acts without any link to the creation (or sign) infringed, such as disparagement, misleading advertising, copying secret know-how or risk of confusion, can constitute distinct acts.[82] For others, parasitism can be a distinct act.[83]

The case law fluctuated on this point and is still unsettled. In many cases involving infringement of subject-matter protected by patent, trade mark and copyright, the Court of Cassation and some courts of appeal held that (slavish) copying, because it allows the copier to save costs and market the product at a reduced price, is an act distinct from infringement.[84] The Court of Cassation confirmed this view in recent decisions.[85] On the other hand, the Paris Court of Appeal made it very clear in a number of decisions that it is not possible to condemn for both infringement and parasitism.[86]

---

[80]   TGI Paris, 06.12.1988 [1989] *RDPI*, no. 23–4, p. 72.

[81]   Passa, above fn. 22, at pp. 73 ff.

[82]   Ibid.; Bertrand, above fn. 25, at p. 154; P.-Y. Gautier (2001), *Propriété littéraire et artistique*, 4th edn., Paris: Presses Universitaires de France, p. 186, n. 114; Mallet-Poujol, above fn. 77.

[83]   X. Desjeux (1992), 'La reprise de la prestation d'autrui: l'idée commerciale et l'investissement économique (esquisse d'un projet de loi)', *Gaz. Pal.*, Doctr. 973, at 976.

[84]   E.g. Cass. com, 30.11.1966, *Bull.*, no. 460, *Bull. civ.*, III, 407; Cass. 02.01.1969 [1969] *RIPIA* 13, cited by Desjeux above fn. 77, at p. 240; Cass. com, 25.10.1977 [1978] *D.*, IR, p. 164; *Bull. Civ.* IV, 245; Malaurie-Vignal 1996, p. 178; CA Paris, 20.12.1989 [1991] *D.*, somm., p. 91, comment Colombet; CA Paris, 01.10.1992 [1993] *PIBD* 535, III, 35, cited by Schmidt-Szalewski above fn. 8, at pp. 462–3; CA Paris, 07.04.1993 [1993] *PIBD* 548, III, 462; CA Paris, 21.06.1994 [1994] *PIBD* III, 583; CA Versailles, 05.04.2001 [2002] *PIBD* 734, III, 38 cited by J. Passa (2002), 'Responsabilité civile – distribution', *Prop. Int.* 81. For more decisions, see Passa, above fn. 22, at pp. 249, 274–5; ibid., (2002), 'Responsabilité civile – distribution', *Prop. Int.* 81; Golaz, above fn. 25, p. 106 fn. 268–72; p. 241, fn. 872.

[85]   *Comité national olympique et sportif français v Groupement d'achat des centres Leclerc,* Cass. com., 11.03.2003 [2003] *CCC*, August–Sept. 2003, p. 24 (imitation of a trade mark is a fact distinct from trade mark infringement); Cass. 08.07.2003 [2003] *PIBD* 773, III, 519, cited by De Candé, above fn. 25, at p. 496.

[86]   CA Paris, 31.10.1991 [1992] *Ann. Prop. Ind.*, p. 213; CA Paris, 05.11.1992 [1993] *RDPI*, no. 47, p. 50; CA Paris, 20.09.1995 [1996] *Gaz. Pal.*, 1, somm. 166; CA Paris, 20.03.1996 [1996] *PIBD* III, 419; [1996] *RDPI*, no. 65, p. 62; CA Paris, 22.05.1996 [1996] *Gaz. Pal.*, 2 somm. 508; CA Paris, 03.07.1996 [1996] *Gaz. Pal.*, 2 somm. 504; CA Paris, 12.12.2001 [2002] *PIBD*, 740, III, 196, cited by Passa, above fn. 83.

How have courts applied these principles to databases? Courts are split on the issue of whether parasitism is an act distinct from *sui generis* right infringement.

The great majority of courts ruled that copying a protected database is not an act distinct from *sui generis* right infringement. In *France Telecom v MA Editions*,[87] MA Editions had copied France Telecom's phonebook. The court ruled that the database was protected and the extractions were illegal and condemned on the basis of infringement of the *sui generis* right. The court rejected France Telecom's argument based on enrichment without cause because the acts were illegal on the basis of the law implementing the Directive in France.

In *Groupe Miller Freeman v Tigest Communication*,[88] Tigest was held to infringe because it had extracted all the information contained in Groupe Miller Freeman's ('GMF') *sui generis* right-protected catalogue for commercial purposes. The court held therefore that there could be no additional condemnation on the basis of parasitism since the acts of copying were not distinct from the infringement acts.[89] The same conclusion was drawn by the Court of First Instance of Paris in another case involving GMF against another defendant.[90] In this case, the court rejected the action based on parasitism because the parasitic acts were a direct consequence of illegal extraction of the contents of a database and could not be distinguished from them. In a decision of March 2002,[91] the Paris Court of Appeal held the *sui generis* right infringed but rejected the action for parasitism. It held that the defendant's attempt to benefit from the investments made by the claimant was not distinct from the unlawful extraction under the *sui generis* right.

In *Cadremploi v Keljob*,[92] Keljob extracted and re-utilised daily a qualitatively substantial part of Cadremploi's database of job advertisements without the latter's authorisation and was held to infringe Cadremploi's *sui generis* right. Keljob's acts did not create a risk of confusion between Cadremploi's and Keljob's web sites because the internet user was warned that she was leaving Keljob's web site and transferred to Cadremploi's site. Since

87   T. Com. Paris, 18.06.1999, *D.*, 2000, no. 5, p. 105.

88   TGI Paris, 22.06.1999 [1999] *PIBD*, 686, III, 494.

89   Interestingly, the court qualified the same acts, but occurring before 01.01.1998, of parasitic. This clearly shows that the *sui generis* right has replaced parasitism for databases. See below, this section.

90   *Groupe Miller Freeman v Neptune Verlag*, TGI Paris, 31.01.2001, available on www.legalis.net.

91   *Construct Data Verlag v Reed Expositions France*, CA Paris, 20.03.2002 [2002] *PIBD*, 746, III, 331–4.

92   TGI Paris, 05.09.2001 [2001] *Legipresse*, no. 187, Dec., pp. 219–21, comment by Tellier-Loniewski.

customers' diversion was a consequence of the extraction, it was not an act distinct from *sui generis* right infringement and the unfair competition action was dismissed.

In *Tigest v Reed Exposition France et Salons Français et internationaux*,[93] the defendant copied the claimant's paper catalogue. This took place before and after the entry into force of the Directive. For the acts committed after the entry into force, the court condemned for infringement of the *sui generis* right and rejected parasitism as not distinct from infringement. In *Editions Neressis v France Telecom Multimedia Services*,[94] Neressis's *sui generis* right in its database of advertisements was infringed by the defendant. Neressis's argument that the extraction and commercial use of its database was an act of unfair competition as the defendant had appropriated its investments without paying was rejected as these acts were not distinct from infringement of the *sui generis* right.

So far, three courts have found that parasitism is an act distinct from *sui generis* right infringement, albeit in indirect ways. In a decision of 2003,[95] EIP's reproduction of Jataka's database, a CD-ROM containing a list of French municipalities, was held to infringe Jataka's *sui generis* right. In addition, EIP was condemned for unfair competition because it had disseminated the contents of the database and usurped Jataka's clients. But usurping clients by distributing a copy of a protected database is parasitism. In *OCP Repartition v Salvea*,[96] OCP created a database listing the names of hundreds of thousands of pharmaceutical products and their descriptions. OCP sold this database on CD-ROM and made it available on the internet on subscription. Salvea reproduced notices coming from OCP's database on its internet site. The court held that OCP's database was protected by the *sui generis* right. Salvea's copy was slavish and the court found Salvea liable for *sui generis* right infringement. The court however also found Salvea liable for acts of unfair competition, i.e. that Salvea benefited from OCP's investments. Salvea was ordered to pay under the two causes of action albeit the damage was the same under both heads (to benefit from OCP's investments by copying its database merges with *sui generis* right infringement). As a result, the claimant was compensated twice for the same damage. Finally, in *Consultant Immobilier v Aptitudes Immobilier*,[97] the court held that the defendant had

---

[93] *Tigest v Reed Exposition France et Salons Français et internationaux*, CA Paris, 12.09.2001 [2001] *Legipresse*, no. 187, Dec., pp. 215–25; [2001] *D.*, no. 35, p. 2895; [2002] JCP, no. 1, p. 25–31, comment by Pollaud-Dulian; [2002] *PIBD* 740, III, 198–201.
[94] TGI Paris, 14.11.2001, available on www.legalis.net.
[95] *Jataka v EIP*, TGI Strasbourg, 22.07.2003, available on www.legalis.net.
[96] Trib. Com. Paris, 19.03.2004, available on www.legalis.net.
[97] Trib. Com. Nanterre, 14.05.2004, available on www.legalis.net.

infringed the claimant's *sui generis* right in its clients list. Additionally, the court found the defendant liable for unfair competition because it appropriated the claimant's files which were an element of the claimant's business. Again this act merges with the infringement of the claimant's *sui generis* right.

As there has been no Court of Cassation decision on the specific issue of simultaneous protection of databases and the lower courts are split, the issue is unresolved. A majority of the few commentators who have written on the possibility of cumulating an action in unfair competition for parasitism and an action in infringement of the *sui generis* right think that, as the *sui generis* right codified parasitism in respect of databases, cumulation is not possible.[98] In the same vein, the commentators have held that enrichment without cause is now encompassed by the *sui generis* right.[99]

In conclusion, although the majority of courts do not allow the cumulation of the unfair competition action for parasitism and the action in *sui generis* right infringement, a few courts do. This creates simultaneous over-protection.

3.1.2. Belgium   The LPCC prohibits the cumulation of the action for infringement of an intellectual property right and the *action en cessation* for unfair competition.[100] The prohibition is found in article 96 LPCC, which states: 'Article 95 does not apply to infringement acts which are prohibited by the statutes on patents, trade marks, designs and models, and copyright and neighbouring rights'. Article 95 LPCC provides that: 'The president of the commercial court declares the existence and orders the cessation of an act . . . which constitutes an infringement to the provisions of this statute . . . .'

Article 96 LPCC therefore prevents the holder of an intellectual property right from acting under both actions before the president of the commercial

---

98   P. Gaudrat (1999), 'Loi de transposition de la directive 96/9 du 11 mars 1996 sur les bases de données: le champ de la protection par le droit *sui generis*' 52 (1) *RTD com.* 86, at 89; Passa, above fn. 22, at p. 294; Mallet-Poujol, above fn. 77, n. 147; Gautier, above fn. 81, n. 114 (if the database producer does not win on the basis of the *sui generis* right because there is no infringement, she should not win on the basis of the parasitism theory either because no breach is identifiable). See also J. Passa (2002), 'Responsabilité civile – concurrence', *Prop. Int.* 103, at 107. *Contra*: L. Tellier-Loniewski, Comment [2002] *Legipresse*, no. 96, III, p. 194.

99   A. Brüning, comment on *France Telecom v MA Editions*, T. com. Paris, 18.06.1999 [1999] *Expertises* 308.

100   This was already provided in the specific legislation of 1934 and was rewritten in art. 56 of the 1971 act. It actually codified a decision of 16 March 1939 of the Court of Cassation, *Pas.*, I. p. 150; *Ing.-Cons.*, p. 55. See Golaz, above fn. 25, p. 92; A. Puttemans (1998), 'La loi sur les pratiques du commerce et les droits de propriété intellectuelle', in F. Gotzen (ed.), *Marques et concurrence*, Bruxelles: Bruylant, 1998, p. 236.

court (*tribunal de commerce*).[101] Article 96 LPCC does not expressly mention the *sui generis* right. However, it can reasonably be assumed that the *sui generis* right is included in the prohibition because it is a neighbouring right. Indeed, the Civil Procedure Code has assimilated the *sui generis* right to a neighbouring right.[102] In addition to article 96 LPCC, article 12.A of the Trade Mark Act as well as article 14.5 (now 14.8) of the Designs Act provide for the same prohibition, i.e. it is not possible to act on the basis of unfair competition for acts which are only an infringement.[103] A similar prohibition does not exist in the copyright and patent acts. Despite the silence of the two acts, it has been argued that this approach can be extrapolated to other intellectual property rights.[104] Some courts seem to conform to the prohibition of cumulation,[105] but other courts still circumvent it.[106]

How does the prohibition of article 96 LPCC work in practice? Article 96 LPCC is interpreted strictly both by courts and commentators.[107] This strict interpretation leads to an exception to the rule of non-cumulation. The justification for this exception is based on the different aims of the two actions: the infringement action only protects the creator while the unfair competition action aims to protect the undertaking of the trader against unfair acts of other traders.[108] Thus, while

---

[101]   Puttemans, above fn. 24, at p. 228; Puttemans, above fn. 99, at p. 236.

[102]   Puttemans, above fn. 24, at p. 441 and fn. 1995. See art. 1481, al. 1 and 569 al. 1, 7°, of the Civil Procedure Code.

[103]   A. Delcorde (1995), 'Droits intellectuels et pratiques du commerce', in *Liber Amicorum A. de Caluwé*, Bruxelles: Bruylant, p. 111; D. Dessard (1997), 'L'action en cessation et les droits de propriété intellectuelle', in Gillardin, J. and D. Putzeys, *Les pratiques du commerce, Autour et alentour*, Bruxelles: Publications des FUSL p. 149. Art. 14.5 provides 'acts which would only constitute infringement of a design may not be subject to an action under the legislation against unfair competition'. Art. 12.A provides 'regardless of the nature of the action instituted, no one may judicially claim protection for a symbol which is considered a mark within the meaning of article 1 unless she has filed it in due form and where applicable, has had the registration renewed'.

[104]   Delcorde above fn. 103, at p. 112.

[105]   Ibid., at pp. 112–13. In 1995, in *U v Delvaux* (unreported), the *tribunal correctionnel* of Brussels avoided this double condemnation and considered the relevant criminal provision did not apply to infringement acts.

[106]   Puttemans, above fn. 24, at p. 260 who notes that before the new copyright act of 1994, courts often cumulated actions and this still occurs nowadays in the area of advertising and trade marks. Delcorde notes that, before 1995, *correctionnel* tribunals in Brussels were pursuing simultaneously on the basis of copyright or trade mark infringement and on the basis of unfair competition and the *tribunal correctionnel* of Brussels pronounced two distinct sanctions (decisions are unreported).

[107]   Dessard, above fn. 103, at p. 150; Puttemans, above fn. 24, at p. 255; Puttemans, above fn. 24, at p. 321.

[108]   Puttemans, above fn. 24, at p. 329.

it is not possible to cumulate both actions if they tend to prohibit the same act (e.g. the infringement of an intellectual property right), it is possible to act under both actions if the acts of unfair competition complained of are based on acts *distinct* from infringement acts.[109] In the 1939 Court of Cassation case where the rule is rooted, it was held that the prohibition of the cumulation of actions did not prevent the holder of a trade mark from acting in unfair competition for the dishonest acts which can *accompany* infringement.[110] Article 13, paragraph 1, indent 2 of the act implementing the Software Directive in Belgian law[111] also provides that any claim which is based at the same time on an infringement act and an unfair competition act must be introduced exclusively before the first instance court.[112] This proves that it is possible to act under both statutes. The accompanying act must be distinct from the infringement act.[113] The case law and literature have upheld this principle.[114] In conclusion, if the act is distinct from the infringement act, it is possible to introduce the *action en cessation* before the President of the commercial court.[115]

The question is therefore, as in France, what an act distinct from infringement is. Commentators disagree on this. Some think that both a risk of confusion and the narrow conception of parasitism (i.e. the systematic and characterised looting by the copier of the efforts of the copied) constitute acts contrary to honest practices, detachable from the infringement of the intellectual property right.[116] But they then add that if the risk of confusion or parasitic behaviour merges with infringement, the claimant cannot win on the basis of unfair competition.[117] Others believe that parasitism cannot succeed where there is a statute granting specific protection to the innovator.[118] As, in our view, the *sui generis* right is a codification of parasitism by a special statute, a parasitic act always merges with an act infringing the *sui generis* right. In conclusion, parasitism, be it in its broad or narrow sense, cannot be an act

---

[109]   Golaz, above fn. 25, at p. 93 referring to art. 73, para. 1, indent 2 of the Patent Act of 28 March 1983; Buydens, above fn. 22, at p. 709; Puttemans, above fn. 24, at p. 239.

[110]   Cass. 16.03.1939, Pas., I, p. 150.

[111]   Act of 30 June 1994 implementing in Belgian law European Directive of 14 May 1991 relating to the legal protection of computer programs, M.B. 27.07.1994, in force 06.08.1994.

[112]   Puttemans, above fn. 24, at p. 254.

[113]   Ibid., at p. 255; Buydens, above fn. 22, at pp. 716 ff.

[114]   Puttemans, above fn. 24, at p. 254.

[115]   Except for computer programs, see above, where it is before the Court of First Instance.

[116]   Puttemans, above fn. 24, at pp. 242, 255–7.

[117]   Ibid., at p. 255.

[118]   Delcorde, above fn. 103, at pp. 113–14.

distinct from infringement. Only the risk of confusion, disparagement, misleading advertising and other acts contrary to honest practices can constitute distinct acts.

Very few decisions if any in the field of copyright have distinguished the infringement act from the act of unfair competition. The main reason is, as we shall see below, that many infringements acts have been condemned under the unfair competition action because the claimant can, in its summons, omit the term 'infringement' and only mention unfair competition.[119]

How do these principles apply to databases? In relation to databases, Puttemans has claimed that it is clear from the *travaux préparatoires* of the act implementing the Database Directive in Belgian law that it is not possible to protect databases which fulfil the requirements of the Directive by the theory of parasitism.[120] However, it is not as clear from the *travaux préparatoires* as Puttemans would like to make us believe. The *travaux préparatoires* simply state that the creation of a new *sui generis* right was envisaged instead of harmonising unfair competition laws to protect database contents. They are silent as to whether *sui generis* right-protected databases can also be protected by parasitism. In our view, as in France, databases can only be protected additionally against unfair competition if a distinct act (e.g. misleading advertising, disparagement of the database producer) occurs. However, in view of the muddled state of the case law, courts may allow the two counts to succeed even if the act is in fact not distinct from infringement.

3.2. Does the sui generis *right holder have a choice between the infringement and unfair competition actions?*

3.2.1. France An important question is whether the holder of the *sui generis* right has a choice between infringement and unfair competition actions. Indeed, having a choice can lead to over-protection because the conditions for an unfair competition action for parasitism are less stringent than those for a *sui generis* right. Normally, the principle of pre-emption should apply and there should be no choice. If there is an infringement of the *sui generis* right, the holder must act on that basis. Let us see how the lawmaker and the courts have tackled this issue.

Article 12.2 of the Civil Procedure Code obliges the judge to re-categorise an unfair competition action into an action for infringement of an intellectual property right if an unfair competition action is alleged instead of an infringe-

---

119   Puttemans, above fn. 24, at p. 348.
120   Ibid., at p. 445, citing Exposé des Motifs, Doc. Parl. Ch., 1997–1998, no. 1535/1–1536/1, p. 6 and Rapport Van Overberghe, Doc. Parl., ch., 1997–8, no. 1535/7, p. 4.

ment action.[121] Thus, the intellectual property right holder victim of an infringement cannot choose one or the other action. She must proceed under an infringement action.

The majority of commentators believe that an unfair competition action is not or should not be a substitute for an infringement action.[122] In other words, the intellectual property right holder should not be allowed to choose between infringement and unfair competition actions. She must act on infringement. A 1978 decision of the Court of Cassation is often cited to support this argument.[123] The Court held that the aim of an unfair competition action is to ensure protection of the person who cannot avail herself of any privative right. Commentators believe that this means that *a contrario* an intellectual property right holder cannot use an unfair competition action (for parasitism in the case of databases).[124] If infringement is alleged but is not found and the claimant does not allege a distinct act of unfair competition, the unfair competition action is rejected.[125] However, a minority of commentators believe that the database producer can choose between acting on the basis of infringement of the *sui generis* right or on unfair competition because the Directive does not seem to exclude it.[126]

Despite article 12.2 of the Civil Procedure Code forbidding choice, a number of courts allowed the unfair competition action for parasitism rather than the infringement action not only when there was infringement of the *sui generis* right but also of other intellectual property rights and also when the infringement was not established.[127] The Court of Cassation recently

---

[121]   Passa, above fn. 22, at 72 (except for trade marks: the victim of a trade mark infringement can under certain conditions, act under unfair competition rather than trade mark law).

[122]   Schmidt-Szalewski, above fn. 8, at pp. 456, 458 citing Cass. com., 23.05.1973, *Bull.civ.* IV, no. 182; Clauss, above fn. 78, at pp. 552–3; Passa, above fn. 22, at p. 72; Le Tourneau, above fn. 25, at p. 403; Le Tourneau, above fn. 39, at p. 5.

[123]   Cass. com., 04.07.1978 [1979] *Ann. Prop. Ind.* 366, cited by Burst, above fn. 25, at pp. 2–3.

[124]   Burst, above fn. 25, at pp. 2–3; 146; Le Tourneau, above fn. 78, at p. 311.

[125]   Golaz, above fn. 25, at p. 87.

[126]   Lucas, André and Henri-Jacques Lucas (2001), *Traité de la propriété littéraire et artistique*, 2nd edn., Paris: Litec, 2001, p. 636, nn. 817–2.

[127]   Desjeux, above fn. 78, at p. 240. See e.g. TGI Paris, 19.03.1993 [1993] *PIBD* 548, III, 439 cited by Schmidt-Szalewski above fn. 8, p. 465 (concerned infringement of copyrighted software, the infringement action was rejected because there were not enough similarities between the two programs, but the court condemned the defendant for parasitism). In *ABC Renovation v Les Maisons Barbey Maillard*, CA Paris, 10.12.2003, RG no. 2003/17581 cited by Passa, above fn. 41, at 683 ff., the Paris Court of Appeal allowed a claim exclusively based on parasitism and held the defendant liable on this count only although the subject-matter (a catalogue of drawings) was protected by copyright.

validated this choice between the two actions. In 2001, it held that the plagiarism of a catalogue which imitates both substance and form is parasitic.[128] There can be plagiarism when there is no confusion and parasitism can subsist even if the parasitic acts do not concern elements which cost efforts and investments to the maker of the catalogue. No mention was made of the *sui generis* right.

As far as databases are concerned, it is not clear from the case law whether courts allow the option between the infringement and unfair competition actions. It is mainly in early decisions that courts do not refer to the *sui generis* right but only to parasitism. This is perhaps due to the claimants' ignorance of the new *sui generis* right or perhaps because the acts were committed before the entry into force of the Directive. In a decision of 1998, the reproduction of a database of customs tariffs was held to be parasitic.[129] No reference was made to the *sui generis* right. In *Le Serveur Administratif v Editions Législatives*,[130] Les Editions Legislatives' dictionary including 400 collective conventions was reproduced almost identically by Le Serveur Administratif. The court found the dictionary protected by copyright since its arrangement of the conventions was original. It held that in addition to infringing the copyright in the database, the defendant committed parasitic acts and created a risk of confusion in the public's mind due to similarities between claimant's and defendant's works. Surprisingly, the *sui generis* right was not discussed.[131]

In *Cadremploi v Keljob*,[132] the Court of First Instance of Paris held that Keljob's use of Cadremploi's database elements – and thereby the investments made by Cadremploi – without paying was parasitic. It thus enjoined Keljob from using Cadremploi's database of job advertisements. Although the court

---

[128] *Glock France v Becheret*, Cass. com., 30.01.2001 [2001] *D.*, no. 24, p. 1939, comment by Le Tourneau; *Bull. Civ.* IV, 27; JCP G, I, 340, no. 29, comment by Viney; [2002] *Prop. Int.*, p. 101, comment by Passa.

[129] *Encyclopédie Douanière v Conex et Agence fiscale,* T. Comm. Valenciennes, 20.01.1998 [1998] *Expertises* 196.

[130] *Le Serveur Administratif v Editions Législatives,* TGI Lyon, 28.12.1998 [1999] *RIDA*, no. 181, p. 325; [1999] *RTD Com.* 52(4), pp. 866–9, comment by Françon, *aff'd* CA Lyon, 22.06.2000 [2001] *Expertises* 74–8; [2001] *Prop. Int.* 54–5, comment Sirinelli.

[131] P. B. Hugenholtz (2001), 'The new database right: early case law from Europe', 9th Annual Conference on International Intellectual Property Law and Policy, Fordham School of Law, 1, at 7; Sirinelli, comment on *Le Serveur Administratif v Editions Legislatives,* CA Lyon, 22.06.2000 [2001] *Prop. Int.* 54–5.

[132] *Cadremploi v Keljob,* TGI Paris (ref.), 08.01.2001 [2001] *PIBD*, 721, III, 294–6; *CCE*, May 2001, p. 27.

mentioned earlier that Cadremploi was justified in invoking *sui generis* right protection, it did not rule on that basis.[133] In a decision of the Court of Appeal of Aix-en-Provence,[134] parts of the claimant's web site (sections of a statute) were copied by the defendant. Nowhere did the court refer to the web site as a database, but it could well have been classified and protected as such. The problem was surely that the part extracted and re-utilised was not substantial. The claimant based its action solely on tort and not on infringement of the *sui generis* right and the court held the defendant liable only for parasitism. Nonetheless, in a decision of 2002,[135] the *sui generis* right was not infringed because a substantial part had not been taken and the court rejected the unfair competition action since there were no distinct acts. This latter case means that it is not possible to act on parasitism when the conditions of the intellectual property right are fulfilled but the latter is not infringed. The option between the two actions is not allowed.

In conclusion, although statutory law makes clear that there can be no choice between the unfair competition action for parasitism and the action for infringement of the *sui generis* right, many courts allowed this option. This creates over-protection because the intellectual property right holder can bypass the stricter conditions of the intellectual property right by acting in unfair competition instead.

3.2.2.   Belgium   It has been argued that the *action en cessation* should not be used as a substitute for the infringement action.[136] In other words, if the claimant has an intellectual property right, she does not have a choice between the *action en cessation* and the infringement action; she must act for infringement of her intellectual property right only. This is in accordance with the principle of the primacy of intellectual property rights.[137] However, some claimants used the *action en cessation* rather than the infringement action and

---

[133]   However, in the appeal, despite Cadremploi's database being protected by the *sui generis* right, Keljob was held not to infringe and there was no parasitism. *Keljob v Cadremploi*, CA Paris, 25.05.2001 [2001] *PIBD*, 726, III, 455–7; *CCE*, July–August 2001, pp. 27–9.

[134]   *Jean-Louis H. v Net Fly – Strategies Networks,* CA Aix-en-Provence, 17.04.2002, Juris-Data no. 2002–179519; [2002] *JCP* G, IV, 3038; J. Passa (2002), 'Responsabilité civile – concurrence', *Prop. Int.* 103, at 107.

[135]   *News Invest v PR Line,* CA Versailles, 11.04.2002, *CCE*, July/August 2002, pp. 20–2, Comm. 98, comment Caron, also available on www.legalis.net; Passa, above fn. 33, at p. 107 (approving the decision because another reasoning would destroy the balance and coherence of the act implementing the Directive in France and would excessively limit freedom of commerce and the public domain).

[136]   Dessard, above fn. 103, at p. 150.

[137]   See above section 3.1.2.

succeeded in some cases.[138] In fact, Belgian procedural law allows it. If the summons is drafted to only cover infringing acts, the president of the commercial court is incompetent. But if the claimant drafts it to cover the same acts but describes them as unfair competition acts and does not use the term 'infringement', then the president of the commercial court is competent.[139]

Again, this creates over-protection because the intellectual property right holder can bypass the stricter conditions of the intellectual property right by acting in unfair competition instead.

Conclusion

In the United Kingdom and Ireland, it is not possible to protect a database protected by the *sui generis* right against parasitism. Hence, there is no issue of simultaneous over-protection. In France, while the vast majority of courts and commentators believe that parasitism is not a distinct act, a few courts nevertheless allow the cumulation of actions and repair the same damage twice. Thus, simultaneous over-protection is possible, although rare. Even if the statutory law makes clear that there can be no choice between the unfair competition action against parasitism and the infringement action, courts allow this option in many cases. This leads to over-protection because the intellectual property holder can bypass the stricter conditions of the *sui generis* right by acting in unfair competition instead. Another reason is that it renders the *sui generis* right useless; there is no need to resort to it since the unfair competition for parasitism absorbs it.

In Belgium, as in France, databases can only be protected by unfair competition if a distinct act of unfair competition occurs. However, there is disagreement on what such an act is, leaving the possibility open for courts to cumulate the two actions. In addition, and which is worse, the law seems to allow a choice between the *action en cessation* and infringement action, thereby rendering the *sui generis* right useless.

In conclusion, in the United Kingdom and Ireland, there is no simultaneous over-protection of databases, while in France and Belgium, it is possible. This also proves that there is a lack of harmonisation in Europe in this respect. To avoid over-protection of databases, the Database Directive should be amended to make clear that the *sui generis* right has absorbed parasitism as far as databases are concerned. Failure to do so leads to the recovery of extra damages in contradiction to the intellectual property paradigm. In addition, it should

---

138 For instance, in the *Tele-Atlas* case (Ghent, 16.11.1995 [1997] *A&M* 54 (*Nationaal Geographisch Instituut v Tele Atlas*), the existence of copyright in maps was held not to be important since the alleged infringing acts could *in se* constitute acts contrary to honest uses in the commercial field. Puttemans, above fn. 24, p. 332.

139 Ibid., p. 332.

also provide that there is no choice between the unfair competition for parasitism and the infringement actions. In other words, if the *sui generis* right is infringed, the claimant is obliged to introduce an infringement action. This safeguards its rights to claim under other unfair competition counts such as misleading advertising, disparagement etc. French and Belgian laws should also be amended to respect those changes.

5 Database copyright: the story of BHB

Charlotte Waelde[1]

1. Introduction

The British Horseracing Board (BHB), the governing authority for horseracing in Great Britain, has been fighting hard to protect its business model over recent years. BHB has been funded through a variety of mechanisms including by way of a levy imposed by the Horserace Betting Levy Board[2] on British bookmakers and horse races. In 2000 the Government announced that it proposed to abolish the levy by 2006[3] (a decision later reversed) After this date the horse racing industry would need to fund itself by way of commercial exploitation of its assets. One strategy would be through licensing data it collected during the course of its activities to bodies within the industry (such as betting agencies). Exploitation of this (and other) information was thus key to the longer-term survival of BHB. When negotiating with third parties on the terms and conditions for the re-use of the data, reaching agreement became problematic. BHB took to the courts and sued William Hill, the betting company, over its unlicensed re-use of BHB data.[4] BHB was no doubt confident that its investment in compiling the data would be protected as a result of the introduction in 1996 of the Database Directive,[5] the purpose of which was to promote and protect investment in databases.[6] When William Hill lost in the High Court it appealed to the Court of Appeal which, in turn, referred a number of questions to the European Court of Justice (ECJ) concerning the extent and scope of the sui generis database right introduced in the Database Directive.[7] The ECJ ruled (in this and three other cases referred at the same

---

1   Dr Charlotte Waelde, School of Law, University of Edinburgh.
2   Established by the Betting, Gaming and Lotteries Act 1963.
3   Hansard, 2 Mar 2000: Column: 373W.
4   *British Horseracing Board Limited and Others v William Hill Organisation Limited* [2001] 2 CMLR 12 Pat Ct.
5   European Parliament and Council Directive 96/9 on the Legal Protection of Databases (Database Directive) implemented in the UK in the Copyright and Rights in Databases Regulations 1997 (SI 1997/3032).
6   Database Directive Recital 12.
7   *British Horseracing Board Limited and Others v William Hill Organisation Limited* [2002] ECC 24 [2001] EWCA Civ 1268 CA.

time[8]) that while the definition of a database in the Directive was broad,[9] and apt to encompass BHB's database, the requisite investment for the subsistence of the database right in a database[10] did not extend to creation of material included in the database.[11] As, on the ECJ's analysis, the investment expended by BHB related to creation of the data and not to its obtaining (a criterion for the subsistence of the database right under the Database Directive), and verification had taken place at the point of creation[12] of the data, so BHB's database was not protected by the sui generis database right. In the aftermath of the Court of Appeal's application of the ECJ's judgement[13] BHB has, apparently, been the subject of various requests for renegotiation of its agreements with other organisations which rely on sourcing data from BHB for their own business model – each of which had been originally negotiated on the premise that the sui generis database right subsisted in the database.

But what about database copyright? When the case was first heard in the High Court[14] it was noted that BHB had claimed that it might well be entitled to copyright in the database but was content to sue just on the database right.[15] In a subsequent case where BHB found itself in court yet again, this time concerning the price of the supply of data to Attheraces,[16] BHB made several assertions (to Attheraces) that it owned copyright in the database. However, no arguments were presented to back the claims. So why did BHB decide not to pursue its claim for database copyright? That is not clear from the cases. One can only surmise that BHB (or more particularly BHB's advisors) thought that a claim to copyright might not succeed.

The purpose of this chapter is to examine database copyright within the UK and consider whether that decision was correct.

---

8   *Fixtures Marketing v OPAP* Case C-444/02 [2005] IP&T 453; [2005] ECDR 3 (OPAP); *Fixtures Marketing v Oy Veikkaus* Case C-46/02 [2005] IP&T 490 (Veikkaus); [2005] ECDR 2; *Fixtures Marketing v Svenska Spel* Case C-338/02 [2005] IP&T 520; [2005] ECDR 4 (Svenska).

9   *The British Horseracing Board Ltd and Others v William Hill Organisation Ltd* Case C-203/02 [2005] 1 CMLR 15 ECJ (BHB).

10   Database Directive.

11   *BHB* para 42.

12   Ibid.

13   *British Horseracing Board Ltd and Others v William Hill Organisation Ltd* [2005] ECDR 28 [2005] EWCA Civ 863 CA (Civ Div).

14   *British Horseracing Board Limited and Others v William Hill Organisation Limited* [2001] 2 CMLR 12 Pat Ct.

15   Ibid., para 22.

16   *Attheraces Ltd v British Horseracing Board Ltd* [2005] EWHC 3015 [2006] UKCLR 167 and *Attheraces Limited, Attheraces (UK) Limited v The British Horseracing Board Limited, BHB Enterprises Plc* [2007] EWCA Civ 38 CA (Civ Div).

2. Protecting databases by copyright – policy issues

Many compilations comprise aggregations of factual data whether these be in the form of, for example, lists of names and addresses,[17] betting odds,[18] or details of fixtures of sports matches.[19] Cases in the British courts concerning protection of these compilations bring sharply into focus underlying policy tensions in the law of copyright. There is general recognition of the proposition that copyright does not protect facts. But that broad statement tends to overlook two factors. The first is that when significant labour has been expended in collecting facts, the UK courts have sought to provide some protection for that investment. The second is that, when protected, protection may go beyond the way in which facts are presented (arranged). It is when these two factors combine to enjoin re-use of the facts as the basis for a second compilation differently arranged, that the meaning of the proposition becomes questionable.[20] A concern has clearly been to protect the investment by the original compiler, an approach closely allied to the adage that one man may not appropriate the fruits of another's labours:[21] If a second-comer were permitted to appropriate facts for her own purposes even in a different form, where is the incentive for the original compiler to create afresh? But how can that incentive be balanced against the need to ensure that protection does not override the public interest in dissemination of fact-based material?

Perhaps because of the absence of any form of tort of misappropriation when the early cases were heard in the courts[22] determination of the existence and extent of protection of factual databases by copyright has centred on an analysis of the level of originality in the compilation. Originality here may be in the labour and expense of creating and gathering the information to populate the

---

17   *Waterlow Publishers Limited v Rose and Another* [1995] FSR 207 CA; *Waterlow Directories Ltd v Reed Information Services Ltd* (1990) 20 IPR 69.

18   *Ladbroke (Football) Ltd v William Hill (Football) Ltd* [1964] 1 WLR 273; *Bookmakers' Afternoon Greyhound Services Ltd v Wilf Gilbert (Staffordshire) Ltd* [1994] FSR 723.

19   *Football League Limited v Littlewoods Pools Limited* [1959] 1 Ch 637; *Afternoon Greyhound Services Ltd v Wilf Gilbert (Staffordshire) Ltd* [1994] FSR 723.

20   E.g. Garnett, Kevin, K. Davies and G. Harbottle (2004), *Copinger & Skone James on Copyright*, 5th edn (Sweet & Maxwell: London), para 475.

21   *Ladbroke (Football) Ltd v William Hill (Football) Ltd* [1964] 1 WLR 273 p. 291. *Scott v Sandford* (1867) LR 3 Eq 723: 'no man is entitled to avail himself of the previous labour of another for the purpose of conveying to the public the same information'.

22   Gervais, D.J. (2004), 'The Compatibility of the Skill and Labour Originality Standard with the Berne Convention and the TRIPS Agreement', 26 *EIPR* 75. He suggests that because the tort of misappropriation was in its infancy at this time the courts were seeking 'other means to protect the expenditure of labour, even if this labour was devoid of any creativity' (p. 76).

compilation and/or in the presentation of the compilation (the arrangement). While arrangement of factual information might exhibit some originality (in the copyright sense) and thus be worthy of protection, more troubling has been whether copyright should also protect the industriousness and investment that lie behind the creation and gathering of the information. This latter is for two reasons. The first is as to whether originality in copyright law should take under its wing industriousness. The second is the breadth of protection accorded by copyright which seems to grant an over-broad monopoly in factual information.[23]

The Database Directive in Europe has harmonised the test for the subsistence of copyright in databases within Member States and resulted in changes in a number of jurisdictions, including the UK. The new standard applies to those compilations of data which fall under the definition of a database in the Directive.[24] The old law will remain relevant for those tables and compilations which do not meet this definition. The next part of the chapter will examine the law prior to the enactment of the Directive with a view to facilitating an understanding of what the old and new laws protect, considering the boundaries between the two, and highlighting whether there are gaps or overlaps in protection. With the exception of the directory cases, those considered below exhibit (in keeping with BHB) a sporting theme.

3.   Protecting databases by copyright – the framework (pre-1996)

There is a question as to whether the Berne Convention[25] mandates Member States to protect compilations of information where the contents are not themselves protected by literary or artistic copyright. Article 2(5) provides that

> Collections of literary or artistic works such as encyclopaedias and anthologies which, by reason of the selection and arrangement of their contents, constitute intellectual creations shall be protected *as such*, [emphasis added] without prejudice to the copyright in each of the works forming part of such collection

---

[23]   Lipton, J. (2003), 'Balance Private Rights and Public Policies: Reconceptualising Property in Databases' 18 *Berkeley Technology Law Journal* 773 notes that 'when applied to commercial databases, models based on copyright principles encourage the creation of overbroad private rights in large volumes of information' (p. 774).

[24]   Database Directive Article 1.2. 'Database shall mean a collection of independent works, data or other materials arranged in a systematic or methodical way and individually accessible by electronic or other means.'

[25]   Berne Convention for the Protection of Literary and Artistic Works 1886, Paris 1896, Berlin 1908, Berne 1914, Rome 1928, Brussels 1948, Stockholm 1967, Paris 1971, 1979.

which would seemingly exclude databases consisting of data which was itself unprotected. Ricketson and Ginsburg have argued that collections of data, while not falling within Article 2(5) may nonetheless be protectable as literary and artistic works under Article 2(1).[26] Their point is that the elements which make a collection of works an intellectual creation (the selection or arrangement) should also apply to make a collection of data an intellectual creation.[27] Whether or not that conclusion is correct[28] protection has been included in other Instruments. Both Article 10(2) TRIPs and Article 5 of the WCT require compilations of data or other material, in any form [TRIPS – whether in machine readable or other form], which by reason of the selection or arrangement of their contents constitute intellectual creations, to be protected *as such*. The UK has for many years held that copyright subsists in compilations of information.

4. Information gathering processes and originality

As will be seen when the detail of the cases is discussed below, each exhibits a different type of work pattern or process in the gathering and presentation of information for a compilation. The examples range from the very simple, where the compilation might contain a list of names and addresses of individuals or businesses perhaps arranged alphabetically by region (*the directory cases*); through those examples where existing information is used, such as that on football fixtures, to create different information for defined business needs, such as the preparation of betting odds (*the betting cases*); to the more complex scenario where information is created as part of the business itself, such as football league and greyhound racing fixtures (*the sporting cases*). In each, the compiler goes through a series of steps before finally arriving at the end product: the compilation.

In general, and despite repeated attempts by counsel during argument, British courts have at times acknowledged, but have generally not chosen to focus on, the various stages, types of information and labour expended in each part of the process of preparation of the compilation. But the skill and labour have been key to the protection of these compilations as it is the standard by which originality has been judged: it is only those compilations which attain the requisite standard which have been accorded protection. Most often the courts have considered the overall degree of skill, labour and judgement

---

[26] Ricketson, S. and J. Ginsburg (2006), *International Copyright and Neighbouring Rights: The Berne Convention and Beyond*, 2nd edn. Oxford; Oxford University Press.
[27] Ibid., para 8.89.
[28] Ibid., para 8.90.

involved[29] throughout the process to determine whether the resultant compilation is original and thus the proper subject for copyright protection. At times, where it has been clear that one part of the process (such as an alphabetical arrangement) lacks in the requisite originality level for protection, greater emphasis will be placed on the labour and expense in gathering the information together. At other times, where the labour in creating or gathering information has been meagre,[30] emphasis has been placed on the expression. The two are sometimes distinguished by terminology such as quantity or pre-expressive labour (the creation and gathering) and the quality or expressive labour (the arrangement and presentation). Whether sufficient has been expended in either or both has been a matter of degree.[31]

5. The cases: process and originality

5.1. Directory cases

One of the earliest cases to consider copyright in a simple compilation – a directory of names and addresses – was *Kelly v Morris*.[32] Mr Kelly compiled a directory, the Post-Office London Directory . Mr Morris, the second-comer, also compiled a directory, the 'Imperial Directory of London'. Mr Morris used Mr Kelly's directory, not by copying the names and addresses directly, but by giving information derived from the Post-Office London directory to his canvassers, who then checked its accuracy. So the process would have originally involved Mr Kelly deciding on the scope of his directory. He (or his canvassers) would have gathered the relevant information. This information was then arranged in the directory. There seems to have been no discussion on whether copyright subsisted in the Post Office London Directory, which appeared to be accepted. The question was rather whether Mr Morris had infringed the copyright in that Directory by using some of the information in his own information gathering processes and ultimately his directory. The court took the view that in the case of a directory, the second-comer had to do what the first had done:

> In case of a road-book, he must count the milestones for himself. In the case of a map of a newly-discovered island . . . he must go through the whole process of

---

29   Originality in the context of literary works, copyright has been said in several cases to depend upon the degree of skill, labour and judgment involved in preparing a compilation. E.g. *G. A. Cramp & Son Ltd v Frank Smythson Ltd* [1944] AC 329.

30   *Ladbroke (Football) Ltd v William Hill (Football) Ltd* [1964] 1 WLR 273 at 287.

31   *A. Cramp & Son Ltd v Frank Smythson Ltd.* [1944] AC 329.

32   (1865) 1 Eq 697.

triangulation just as if he had never seen any former map, and, generally, he is not entitled to take one word of the information previously published without independently working out the matter for himself, so as to arrive at the same result from the same common sources of information.[33]

This focus on the second-comer saving the labour and trouble in getting information set the subsequent tone for a number of other compilation cases such as *Morris v Ashbee*.[34] This dealt with a list of names and occupations of traders carrying on business in London presented in alphabetical order and in groups. Ashbee cut information from Morris's directory and gave this to the canvassers to check. So the process in compiling the information was much the same as in *Kelly v Morris*. The labour and expense of gathering the information had been expended by Morris. The information was used by Ashbee in the collation of his own directory. As the court pointed out, the plaintiff incurred the labour and expense of getting the information and then of making the compilation:

> [T]he substance of the judgment [in Kelly v Morris] is, that in a case such as this no one has a right to take the results of the labour and expense incurred by another for the purposes of a rival publication, and thereby save himself the expense and labour of working out and arriving at these results by some independent road. If this was not so, there would be practically no copyright in such a work as a directory.[35]

It also appears that the court was satisfied that the arrangement of the original directory had not been taken: nonetheless there was infringement of copyright.[36]

These early directory cases were referred to in two twentieth century directory cases, *Waterlow Publishers Limited v Rose and Another* [37] and *Waterlow Directories Ltd v Reed Information Services Ltd*.[38] Both concerned directories containing information on solicitors. As regards the decision taking, creation gathering and compilation of the information, the processes are much the same as in *Kelly* and *Morris*. In both the concern was over the re-use of the information from the first directory as a source from which to check and gather

---

33   Ibid. 'So in the present case the Defendant could not take a single line of the Plaintiff's Directory for the purpose of saving himself labour and trouble in getting his information' (pp. 701–2).

34   (1868) LR 7 Eq 34.

35   Ibid., Giffard VC at 40–1.

36   *Morris v Ashbee* (1868) LR 7 Eq 34, 'the defendants have satisfied me that the plaintiff has no grounds for complaining of their having taken the plan of his work' (p. 38).

37   [1995] FSR 207 CA.

38   (1990) 20 IPR 69.

further information in compiling a second. In both infringement was found.[39] As with *Morris v Ashbee*, in *Waterlow v Rose* it was stressed that the materials had been re-arranged in the second.

In *Waterlow v Rose* the Court said that the following points could be discerned from Morris and Kelly:

(a) the mere fact that material is checked with the data subject and verified as accurate or updated and authorised by him for insertion in the infringing directory does not mean that there is no infringement;

(b) the fact that there is no infringement of the plan of Waterlow's work or of the arrangement and layout of the information does not mean that there is no infringement of the compilation.[40]

To this might be added the more general proposition that a person may not copy entries from a directory and use that information to compile his own directory (he may not take a short cut).[41]

Reflecting on the process of compilation of these directories, it seems the courts have recognised that there are two forms of labour – that expended in collecting the information and that in writing it down. While the two have not been clearly distinguished, emphasis has been placed on the industriousness (expense) in the creation and gathering together of the information. It is when that is appropriated by another that infringement is found.

5.2.   *Betting cases*

The *betting cases* exhibit a different type of process or activity also involving the compilation of information, but in addition the use of existing information to create something different. The gambling industry makes use of existing information to calculate odds on which bets may be placed. *Ladbroke (Football) Ltd. v William Hill (Football) Ltd.*[42] (*Ladbroke*) concerned a coupon which displayed bets that could be made on weekly league matches. A question was whether the coupon was protected by copyright. As Lord Devlin explained, a bookmaker may offer odds on the outcome of the matches in a number of different ways. He may compile a list of the games to be played, and odds may be offered against the gambler picking winners from the whole list. An alternative may be to offer restricted lists of selected matches in which

---

39   *Waterlow Directories Ltd v Reed Information Services Ltd* (1990) 20 IPR 69 was an application for an interlocutory injunction – it was found that actual copying onto a word processor had taken place.

40   *Waterlow Publishers Limited v Rose and Another* [1995] FSR 207 CA, p. 222.

41   E.g *Independent Television Publications Limited v Time Out Limited and Elliott* [1984] FSR 64 Ch D 69.

42   [1964] 1 WLR 273.

there can be infinite variations such as home wins, away wins and draws. Again the gambler is invited to bet on winners and losers.[43] In both examples existing information as to the football league matches (such as the timing of the matches, the experience of the players) is used by bookmakers to calculate the odds, and in both examples the odds are agreed upon, and offered in the form of a coupon. The argument had been made by counsel that the labour involved in working out which odds to offer should be considered as distinct from the labour involved in writing those odds down: the former should be ignored, but the latter should not. Lord Evershed did acknowledge that there might be a difference:

> when all the hard work has been done in deciding upon the wagers to be offered, there still remains the further distinct task, requiring considerable skill, labour and judgment (though of a different kind) in the way in which the chosen wagers are expressed and presented to the eye of the customer.[44]

However none of the judges seemed happy to ignore the labour expended in deciding which bets should be offered (Lord Devlin called this an 'unsound point'[45]). That said, in coming to the conclusion that there was an infringement of copyright in the original coupon, it would appear that the majority were of the view that the form and presentation of the layout had been infringed. There was recognition that the defendants had put substantial skill into compiling their own documents but had ended up with

> a coupon which was a remarkably close parallel to that of the respondents . . . not only in that the appellants' coupon contained 15 out of 16 of the headings to be found in the respondents' coupon, and substantially in the same order, but also in that the lay-out and presentation of these wagers, including the appendant notes, follow substantially the precedent found in the respondents' coupon.[46]

Bookmakers' Afternoon Greyhound Services Ltd v Wilf Gilbert (Staffordshire) Ltd[47] (*Greyhound Services*), also a betting case, this time dealt with forecast dividends used in the greyhound racing industry. The forecast dividend was arrived at by way of a formula which took into account factors such as starting odds. This formula was programmed into a computer so that the dividend

---

43   Ibid., p. 289.
44   Ibid., p. 281. See also *Elanco Products Limited v Mandops (Agrochemical Specialists) Ltd* [1980] RPC 213; [1979] FSR 46.
45   *Ladbroke (Football) Ltd v William Hill (Football) Ltd* [1964] 1 WLR 273, p. 290.
46   Ibid., p. 283.
47   [1994] FSR 723.

could be produced quickly after each race had been run and then compiled into a list. So the process was the use of existing information on races, the development of a formula, and then the running of the formula in conjunction with the information to produce the dividend. On whether copyright subsisted in the dividends, the court considered these were the result of 'a repetitive job requiring a certain amount of education and thereafter a meagre amount of labour'.[48] This meagre labour was not sufficient to produce an original literary work in a single forecast. Neither did copyright subsist in a compilation of the forecast dividends produced after the day's racing as there was no skill or judgment, and only minimal labour, in writing them down twelve times. 'They amount to a mere collocation to which copyright does not attach'.[49]

So it would seem that in some betting cases where new information is produced from existing sources meagre labour such as through the application of a standard formula will be insufficient to confer originality on the result, particularly where there is minimal labour in reducing the dividends to writing. However, where that labour is more than meagre and in particular where the resultant document represents labour, skill and effort in presentation, then copyright will subsist in the result.

5.3.   *Sporting cases*

More complex are those cases where protection is sought for information that is created by the organisation as a part of the function that it carries out: in other words, the organisation determines the information. In the *sporting cases*, it is the process of deciding which matches or races should be played or run, when, where and by whom or by which dog. An early case considering this type of activity was *Football League Limited v Littlewoods Pools Limited*[50] (*Football League*). The question here was as to whether the scheme for the production of a list of games to be played by members of the league in the form of a chronological fixture list (in other words, who should play which games and when) was capable of being protected by copyright, and if so, whether copyright was infringed by reproducing parts in betting coupons. The court accepted that there was no copyright in information as such, but only in the composition or language used to express that information.[51] However, where the information was presented in a particular way, then it became a question of fact and degree as to whether the skill and labour involved in the representation was entitled to copyright. Again counsel urged the court to

---

48   Ibid., p. 736.
49   Ibid.
50   [1959] 1 Ch 637.
51   Ibid., p. 651. An analogy was made with the composition of the next MCC team to play the Ashes: the selectors could not claim the exclusive right to publish it.

distinguish the labour expended in the creation of the information from that used in the presentation and arrangement.[52] The court acknowledged that there might be different aspects of originality to be taken into account when it said that if the activity in developing the scheme leading up to the production of the dates and times of the games was an apt subject for copyright protection then that represented 'much skill, labour, time, judgment and, above all, ingenuity, and on this view, therefore, is entitled to copyright'. Ultimately, however, the court was unwilling to dissect the efforts put into the final output in the way suggested by counsel but rather concluded that copyright did subsist in the chronological list, taking into account 'the entire skill, labour, time, judgment and ingenuity of the League, their servants and agents'.[53] The court also found that a substantial part had been reproduced in the betting coupons.

Greyhound Services[54] not only concerned betting, but it also dealt with the question as to whether copyright subsisted in advance programmes for greyhound races and race cards. The advance programme was prepared by deciding on the scheduling of races, which included selecting the dogs to run and allocating dogs to traps based on past form, including where the dog would position itself in races, where it had finished in past races and whom it had beaten. The information in the advance programme was included in the race card along with details as to ownership, colour, breeding and the date of whelping. The court found that considerable skill, labour and judgment were involved in preparing both the advance programme and the race cards and that copyright subsisted in each.[55] In so doing, what was notable was the stress that the court laid upon the creation of the information: 'Considerable skill is used to select appropriate dogs for appropriate races and to provide both novel and competitive races'.[56]

What is noticeable in these *sporting cases* is that while the courts have been unwilling to distinguish clearly between the labour involved in the creation of the information and the reduction of that information to tangible form, there is much emphasis on the skill, industriousness and expense in the creation of the information by the body responsible for scheduling the event. The skill and labour expended in reducing that to writing, while present, seems less important.

By analysing the cases in this way, it would appear that the widely held view that copyright subsists not in factual information (including information

---

[52]   Ibid., p. 643.
[53]   Ibid., p. 656.
[54]   *Bookmakers' Afternoon Greyhound Services Ltd v Wilf Gilbert (Staffordshire) Ltd* [1994] FSR 723.
[55]   Ibid., p. 744.
[56]   Ibid., p. 734.

created to schedule future events) but only in the composition or language used to express that information needs to be re-thought. That the courts have accepted there is originality in the labour (industriousness) element expended in the creation and gathering of facts[57] (including pre-determined facts) and have enjoined re-use of those facts in a second compilation, even in re-arranged form, suggests that factual information is indeed protected.[58]

6.   BHB – process and originality

Having analysed the cases and considering BHB's information creation and gathering functions, BHB might have felt comfortable in betting its future on being able to assert copyright in its compilations of information on the horse racing industry and thus having the ability to license the content to third parties and the power to prevent unauthorised reproduction. However, things have changed with the introduction of the Database Directive and the enactment of a new (and higher) standard of originality for the subsistence of copyright in databases.

The purpose of the next section is to examine this new standard and consider the implications for the subsistence of copyright in compilations of information which fall under the definition of a database.

7.   Database Directive

The discussion so far has concentrated on the law in the UK prior to the enactment of the Database Directive.[59] This Directive provides for copyright

---

57   The cases have not been consistent in protecting labour expended in producing information. In *PCR Ltd v Dow Jones Telerate Ltd* [1998] FSR 170, statistical information was compiled as part of a crop forecasting service. This was presented as part of a report. However, in deciding what labour should be taken into account for the subsistence of copyright, the labour of collecting the basic data information together was not relevant.

58   One of the clearest acknowledgements is by Laddie J in *Autospin Oil Seals Ltd v Beehive Spinning* [1995] RPC 683. '[I]t is not the mere form of words or notation used which justifies copyright protection for a compilation, it is the author's skill and effort expended in gathering together the information which it contains'. And '[I]t is clear that the physical effort of writing down names and addresses to produce a street directory does not of itself justify the creation of compilation copyright in it. It is the effort and skill expended in finding out who lives at which addresses in which road which merits protection' (p. 698). The law differs in other jurisdictions. The most cited cases are Canada *Tele-Direct (Publications) Inc v American Business Information, Inc* (1997) 154 DLR (4th) 328 and *CCH Canadian Ltd. v Law Society of Upper Canada* [2004] 1 SCR 339, 2004 SCC 13. *US Feist Publications, Inc v Rural Telephone Service Co, Inc* 499 US 340 (1991); Australia *Desktop Marketing Systems Pty Ltd v Telstra Corporation Limited* [2002] FCAFC 112.

59   Ibid., n. 4.

protection for those databases which, by reason of the selection or arrangement of their contents, constitute the author's own intellectual creation.[60] The
Directive also introduced a sui generis database right which gives to the maker
of the database (the person who provides the investment necessary for such
compilation)[61] exclusive rights to prevent unauthorised extraction and re-util-
isation of a substantial part of the contents of the database[62] so long as there
has been substantial investment in obtaining, verifying or presenting the
contents of a database consisting in the deployment of financial resources,
and/or the expending of time, effort and energy.[63] A key point in relation to
this measure is that it was introduced to protect the investment in storage and
processing systems (whether electronic or paper).[64] The focus of the sui
generis right is not therefore on the data per se, but on the investment in the
system used to process the data.

Prior to discussing the existence and scope of database copyright, it is
useful to outline what the courts have said in relation to the scope of the sui
generis right and its application to BHB's database. This will enable an appreciation of the respective areas of protection by way of the sui generis right and
database copyright and also highlight where there may be gaps in protection.

As was mentioned above, in *British Horseracing Board v William Hill* [65]
BHB sought to rely on the sui generis right in its dealings with William Hill.
When the ECJ came to interpret the sui generis right, it seemed accepted that
BHB's database containing information on inter alia over one million horses,
and pre-race information on races held in the UK fell within the definition of
a database. However, the investment by BHB related to the *creation* of the
data and not to its obtaining as required by the Directive.[66] The ECJ said relevant investment in obtaining

> must . . . be understood to refer to the resources used to seek out existing indepen-
> dent materials and collect them in the database and not [emphasis added] to
> resources used for the creation as such of independent materials.[67]

So the materials to be placed in the database must already exist as independent
materials. Any investment expended in creation of materials (as was the case

---

60   Database Directive Article 3.
61   Database Directive Article 7.
62   Database Directive Article 8.
63   Database Directive Recital 40; Article 7.
64   As was emphasised by the ECJ it is to 'promote the establishment of storage
and processing systems for existing information'. *BHB*, para 31.
65   Ibid., nn. 3, 6, 8, 12.
66   *BHB*, para 38.
67   *OPAP*, para 40.

with BHB) would not count towards the subsistence of the sui generis right. In addition, the investment by BHB in the verification of the data took place at the time at which the data was created, and so once again was irrelevant for the subsistence of the sui generis right.[68]

It should be noted that BHB made the data available to users by way of digital bits, rather than in hard copy form – so there was no discussion on arrangement, at least in the copyright sense. In a related case before the ECJ at the same time, the question of relevant investment in the presentation of the contents of a database was considered. The ECJ said that this referred to:

> ... the resources used for the purpose of giving the database its function of processing information, that is to say those used for the systematic or methodical arrangement of the materials contained in those database and the organisation of their individual accessibility.[69]

It thus appears that relevant investment is that which is linked to the presentation features that are integral to the processing system as such, for instance the way in which the data are arranged within a database, and not to the presentation of any data that might be placed in the database, nor in the presentation of any data that might come out of the database (such as data presented in the form of a coupon or race card).

So in *BHB*, the ECJ distinguished between the various stages that go into the creation, verification and presentation of information in the sporting industry when in a processing system. Investment in the creation of material does not count for the sui generis right. Neither does verification (checking) of that information where it is related to its creation. Investment in the presentation of the information will only be relevant where it is directed towards the systematic or methodical arrangement of the information. When the case was applied in the Court of Appeal, counsel urged the court to 'deconstruct' the process of information gathering carried out by BHB. This the Court refused to do, holding that the ECJ had focussed on the final database[70] and what marked it out from what had come before was BHB's stamp of authority.

Nonetheless, the judgement by the ECJ suggests that account should be taken of the process of obtaining, verification and presentation necessary to make up the final database in order to determine whether relevant substantial investment has been expended in one or more of the parts. This also suggests that the British courts may be required to make similar distinctions when considering whether copyright subsists in a database.

---

68   *BHB*, para 34.
69   *OPAP*, para 43; *Svenska*, para 27; *Veikkaus*, para 37.
70   *British Horseracing Board Ltd and Others v William Hill Organisation Ltd* [2005] ECDR 28 [2005] EWCA Civ 863 CA (Civ Div), para 29.

8. Database copyright

The standard for copyright protection of a database in the Copyright Designs and Patents Act 1988 (CDPA) now provides that a literary work includes 'a table or compilation *other* [emphasis added] than a database'. Where a database satisfies the definition, then the copyright standard found within the Directive (and implemented in national law[71]) will be relevant to determining whether or not copyright subsists in a database. Those tables and compilations which fall outwith the definition of a database will be protected under the standard of copyright discussed above.[72]

A starting point in considering the scope of database copyright is Recital 15 of the Database Directive which states:

> Whereas the criteria used to determine whether a database should be protected by copyright should be defined to the fact[73] that the selection or the arrangement of the contents of the database is the author's own intellectual creation; whereas such protection should cover the structure of the database.

Echoing this is the emphasis in Recital 35 on selection, arrangement and structure. That Recital requires that exceptions should take account of the fact that copyright applies only to the selection or arrangements of the contents of a database; and that the exceptions relate to the structure of the database.

Key points to be drawn from this are

- There must be *selection* or *arrangement* of the contents;
- The selection or arrangement must be the author's own *intellectual creation*;
- Protection covers the structure of the database.[74]

8.1. *Selection or arrangement – pre-database cases*

Given that the Database is a new measure, care should perhaps be taken in relying on earlier case law dealing with compilations in deciding what might be meant by selection and arrangement. As indicated above, the courts have been reluctant to separate out the various stages underlying the preparation of

---

[71]   By way of the Copyright and Rights in Databases Regulations 1997 (SI 1997/3032).

[72]   Copyright Designs and Patents Act 1988 (CDPA), s 3(1)(a). In implementing the Directive changes were made to the CDPA. The legislation now provides that a literary work includes 'a table or compilation other than a database'.

[73]   In *Navitaire v Easyjet Airline Co and Bulletproof Technologies Inc* [2004] EWHC 1725 (Ch) the court noted that the French text is 'devront se limiter au fait que', which, the court said, is clearer (para 274).

[74]   Note the difference in wording as compared with the Berne Convention, TRIPs and WCT, where reference is made to 'as such'.

compilations. This same reluctance might mean the courts were unwilling to elaborate on what was meant by these terms. Indeed, no mention of selection is made in either of the *Waterlow directory cases*. In the *betting case* of *Ladbroke*, it was argued by counsel that selection took place at the point of deciding on which wagers should be offered[75] while the court referred to the selection of bets from the vast range of possible bets that might be offered.[76] In the *sporting case* of *Greyhound Services* there was mention of selection in the context of selecting the dogs, the racecourses and which races were to be run, while in *Football League* it was acknowledged that once the fixtures had been determined, there was no element of selection in reducing the list to paper; this was merely a mechanical effort.

On arrangement, the *directory case* of *Waterlow v Rose* made mention of the fact that the tables were arranged geographically.[77] In the *betting case* of *Football League* reference was made to arrangement in the context of arranging the matches. In the *sporting case* of *Ladbroke*, while the word arrangement was not used, there was emphasis on the way in which the wagers were expressed and presented to the eye of the customer.[78] In *Greyhound Services* there was reference to the arrangement of greyhound races as well as some acceptance that the arrangement of the information on the paper, while not original, contained an original selection of dogs.

It would appear from these cases that selection has been considered important in the context of creation of information.[79] Arrangement on the other hand seems to be more relevant in the context of presentation of the information.

---

[75]   *Ladbroke (Football) Ltd v William Hill (Football) Ltd* [1964] 1 WLR 273, p. 276.

[76]   Ibid., p. 287.

[77]   *Waterlow Publishers Limited v Rose and Another* [1995] FSR 207 CA, 'Look up Birmingham and you get a list of the firms of solicitors in Birmingham' (p. 212).

[78]   Ibid., p. 281.

[79]   *G. A. Cramp & Sons, Limited v Frank Smythson* [1944] AC 329 HL is instructive for the question of selection of a number of tables included in a diary copied from another diary. These included a calendar for the year, postal information, a selection of 'days and dates' for the year, tables of weights and measures, comparative timetables, a percentage table, and the like. Seven of these were copied by Cramp for inclusion in their diary. It was agreed that no claim to copyright was made in any of the seven tables taken individually nor in relation to the order in which the tables appeared in the diary (the arrangement). Thus the question was over the selection of the tables. In denying that the selection was protected by copyright, Lord MacMillan said: 'There is no evidence available to show how or why the particular selection was made . . .To my mind, the collection is of an obvious and commonplace character, and I fail to detect any meritorious distinctiveness in it . . . The inclusion or exclusion of one or more of the tables constituting the ordinary stock material of the diary-compiler seems to me to involve the very minimum of labour and judgment . . . If any compilation could be held

What then might amount to selection and arrangement for the purposes of database copyright? At this juncture it is necessary to consider three further elements relevant to determining the subsistence of database copyright. The first is that the originality test for database copyright is now the author's own intellectual creation. The second is to re-emphasise the distinction the ECJ made in BHB as between the creation and obtaining of data and information for the purpose of the subsistence of the sui generis database right, and consider the relevance for the subsistence of copyright. The third is that protection is said to extend to the structure of the database.

8.2. *Author's intellectual creation*

Both Recital 15 of the Directive (above) and Recital 16 refer to the author's intellectual creation:

> Whereas no criterion other than originality in the sense of the author's intellectual creation should be applied to determine the eligibility of the database for copyright protection, and in particular no aesthetic or qualitative criteria should be applied.

This standard for database copyright is one that is familiar from civilian legal systems, and is generally thought by most commentators to be higher than the traditional British test of skill labour and effort. The suggestion is that the originality must now in some way represent the personality of the author.[80]

The British courts have had little opportunity to elaborate on the test. It was mentioned in passing in the High Court in *British Horseracing Board v William Hill*[81] where Laddie J, referring to Recitals 15 and 16 of the Directive, said that

> ... for copyright to subsist, it must be shown not only that there is a relevant collection of information but that it is also original. Although there is no requirement to demonstrate aesthetic or qualitative criteria, there must be a quantitative baseline of originality before protection is acquired.[82]

The reference to 'quantitative baseline of originality' might be questioned. It may be that Laddie J was keen to stress that there must be more than minimal originality (which would be in keeping with the higher standard the test

---

to fall short of displaying the qualities requisite to attract copyright, the respondents' collection of seven tables is such a one' (p. 338).

[80]   Bently, L. and B. Sherman (2004), *Intellectual Property Law*, 2nd edn., Oxford: Oxford University Press (Bently and Sherman), p. 103.

[81]   *British Horseracing Board Ltd v William Hill Organisation Ltd* [2001] 2 CMLR 12 [2001] RPC.

[82]   Ibid., para. 28.

suggests), perhaps worried by the absence of the need to demonstrate either aesthetic or qualitative criteria. It might however be a mistake to equate the quantitative originality to which he refers with the type of 'more than meagre' labour skill and effort discussed above in the compilation cases, most notably in those which concern the creation of information. It would seem that 'intellectual creation' requires something other than industriousness in creation, most particularly as it is linked to the selection or arrangement of the materials.[83]

8.3.   Selection or arrangement (creation or obtaining) – post-Database Directive

So what then might amount to selection or arrangement? It seems that while both may be present, either may be sufficient (by reference to the use of 'or'). As discussed above, the word 'selection' has been used in case law to describe the process of choice when creating information (selection of the dogs to run; selection of the games to be played). But that is selection in the process of creation, and not selection from what exists. Even if it is accepted in these cases that the degree of originality in 'selection' is such that it meets the test of 'intellectual creation', it is in the creation of the materials. Only if intellectual creation in the process of creation and selection are merged could it be relevant for the subsistence of database copyright. Selection could exist where the information already exists: for example poems or selected recipes, although here a comprehensive collection, would suggest there is no process of selection in what should be included. If there is something more, for instance work in deciding that poems are by a particular author, then it has been suggested that might be sufficient to meet the test of selection.[84]

More difficult in the *directory cases* is where selection is made at the point at which the decision is taken as to which materials should be included (all solicitors in Birmingham); or in the *betting cases* where the selection is made at the point at which it is determined which wagers should be included on a coupon; and in the *sporting cases* it is as to the selection of horses or dogs to run in which race and when. In other words, it would appear that intellectual creation (if any) comes at the point at which decisions are made as to the type of material to be created and/or that material is created. This type of selection would seem not to meet the test of intellectual creation for the subsistence of database copyright. In other words, the industriousness (skill labour and effort) that has been protected by the UK courts as an element in originality in creation would seem irrelevant for the subsistence of database copyright. Indeed it would seem hard to elevate the type of industriousness referred to by

[83]   Bently and Sherman, para 3.2.1.
[84]   Ricketson, and Ginsburg, above n. 26, para 8.87.

Laddie J in the compilation of a directory as 'not in any conventional sense "literary" ' [85] to the level of intellectual creation. A similar argument can be made where the courts have conceded that it is effort and investment that has been protected in the *betting* and *sporting cases*.

Arrangement is perhaps easier to conceptualise. Materials may be arranged in many ways. From the simplest of *directory cases* where information is arranged alphabetically, to the more complex *sporting cases* where information is arranged in race card or coupon. The question is whether these types of arrangement are apt to stretch to the level of the author's own intellectual creation or whether something more is needed. An alphabetical list is unlikely to qualify; nor an arrangement which is standard in the industry. It may be that some central idea or theme will be required which determines the arrangement of the collection and which, in turn, distinguishes it from other arrangements.[86]

One question does arise over arrangement when the information is in the form of an electronic database. As discussed above, 'presentation' for the purposes of the sui generis right refers to the systematic or methodical arrangement of the materials in the database, their organisation and individual accessibility. Beyond this, it must be questioned whether data in an electronic database could meet a higher standard of intellectual creation to be protected by database copyright. Certainly, when data are printed out (such as in the form of a coupon or race card) then the selection of materials from the database, or the scheme that has been devised for their arrangement on paper, might meet the test of intellectual creation. It seems that the presentation of materials within an electronic database is better suited to be protected by way of the sui generis database right than by copyright.

8.4. *Selection, arrangement and structure*

One final element to consider is the linking of author's intellectual creation, selection and arrangement to the structure of the database. As indicated above, Recital 15 states that protection extends to the structure of a database. What is

---

[85] *Autospin Oil Seals Ltd v Beehive Spinning* [1995] RPC 683, p. 697.

[86] Some guidance could be taken from those cases in which copyright in collective works has been considered. For example, in Austria a number of cases (dealing with copyright in collective works rather than database copyright) exhibit a similar requirement for the collection and sorting or arranging or co-ordinating of material according to a central idea – one that must distinguish the collection from other collections. *R v Re Quotation of News Pictures* [2002] ECC 20 OGH (A). An ordering or arrangement according to external features is not sufficient – what is necessary is a collection and sifting of the parts according to a specific controlling concept *Re Copyright in Editors' Names* [1996] ECC 44 OGH (A).

meant by structure? The word seems to suggest that it might be linked with 'arrangement'. Where the contents of a database are arranged in a particular way, that results from the way the materials are structured. If protection extends to the structure, that would prevent a second-comer from reproducing that structure in a second compilation but not from re-arranging the material. Recital 38 would appear to suggest that structure is indeed linked to arrangement when it states that

> the increasing use of digital recording technology exposes the database maker to the risk that the contents of his database may be copied and rearranged electronically, without his authorisation, to produce a database of identical content which, however, does not infringe any copyright in the arrangement of his database.

This would seem to imply that rearrangement of the contents of a database would not amount to an infringement of database copyright. So in those cases discussed above where it is accepted that there was no reproduction of the arrangement of the materials, there would be no infringement of copyright. Where there has been substantial investment in the obtaining, verification and/or presentation of the materials and a substantial part is extracted and/or re-utilised, the sui generis right would be infringed and that would protect against re-arrangement. Such an outcome would seem to be in keeping with the intention that database copyright does not extend to the contents of the database.[87]

However, the text of the Database Directive itself is not so clear. Article 5.3 provides that in respect of the expression of a database which is protected by copyright, the author of a database shall have the exclusive right to carry out or to authorise inter alia translation, adaptation, arrangement and any other alteration. What in this context is meant by 'arrangement' in particular when linked to 'any other alteration'? In the directory cases discussed above, if database copyright subsisted, would that prevent the use of the facts in the first directory by the compiler of the second, albeit re-arranged? While the focus may not be on whether the second-comer has 'used' the information from the first, it might question whether the arrangement has been altered. The result in substance may be little different from the *directory, betting* and *sporting cases* discussed above. In other words, where the information is used it might infringe even if presented in re-arranged form. If however one regards the intellectual creation in the *selection* as key, then only where that subsists, should it be possible to enjoin the re-arrangement of the contents. Take the example of intellectual creation residing in working out whether selected poems are by a particular author which are then arranged alphabetically. Here

---

87   Database Directive Article 3.

database copyright would reside in the selection poems and not their arrangement. As the arrangement is not protected, then reproducing that should not infringe. However, reproducing a substantial part of the selection, however arranged, would infringe the intellectual creation in the selection, and could thus be enjoined. Such a conclusion might suggest that the scope of database copyright is broader when tied to selection rather than to arrangement. This, in turn, might require careful consideration as to what qualifies as selection.

Turning back to the *directory, betting* and *sporting cases*. As has been argued, the intellectual creation (if any) resides in the creation of the materials and not in their selection (in the database copyright sense). When made available in hard copy form, the materials might be arranged in such a way as to meet the test of intellectual creation in arrangement (for example *Ladbroke*). Which would mean that for directories, betting information and information on football fixtures and greyhound races made available in digital form, database copyright does not subsist.

There have been few cases which have considered the scope of database copyright within Member States, and fewer still which have arisen after the ECJ handed down judgment in *BHB* and the related cases. One case where the German Federal Supreme court had the opportunity to do so was *Re a Musical Hits Database*.[88] The court considered the meaning of selection or arrangement, author's intellectual creation and structure. The case concerned the use of a repertoire of musical hits made available by the claimants (a marketing company) in the form of weekly charts. The defendant publishers made available a CD Rom of musical hits in Germany, which they arranged alphabetically and chronologically. Some of the information on this CD Rom came from the claimants' repertoire. The court held that the claimants' compilation did not satisfy the test of database copyright. The compilation was arranged by way of rankings, titles and artists together with information on the position of the music in the charts. This did not 'display any structure necessitating personal intellectual creation'. In other words, the arrangement flowed from the purpose of a list of musical hits.[89]

Here it would seem that the court linked structure to arrangement and to intellectual creation. It still does leave open the question as to whether, if database copyright did subsist in the claimants' compilation by virtue of the selection of the materials, the defendants would have been enjoined from re-using the contents in re-arranged form, or even relying on the contents of the compilation in order to gather their own original content.

---

88   [2006] ECC 31 BGH (Ger).
89   German Copyright Act (UrhG) § 97(1) in conjunction with § 4.

9. Conclusion

So it would seem that UK law has changed with regard to the protection of data-bases by way of copyright.[90] For those collections falling under the definition of a database, the historical industriousness in the creation, selection and gathering of information – or indeed any intellectual endeavour that goes into deciding which materials should be created or gathered – should not be accorded copyright protection. The arrangement criterion may only be satisfied where it does not automatically follow on from the nature of the material selected (or created) or is not commonplace or, to borrow a phrase from the Austrian courts, where the material has been arranged according to a controlling concept.[91]

British courts may need to focus more clearly on the various steps involved in the creation, selection and arrangement of contents of databases, determine when selection and arrangement amounts to intellectual creation, and consider the extent to which the scope is linked to the structure of a database. Taking such steps would facilitate proper consideration of the boundaries between the sui generis right and database copyright. The sui generis right can protect genuine investment in obtaining verification and presentation of the contents of a database, while database copyright can protect genuine intellectual creation in the selection or arrangement. Fears as to over-broad protection granted to fact-based compilations by copyright can be assuaged.

So was BHB right in not pursuing a copyright claim? The answer to that would appear to be yes. For BHB, any intellectual creation was in the creation of materials, and not in the selection of existing materials. At issue was the licensing of data (and not its availability in printed form). In addition, and as has been argued above, it seems hard to accept that database copyright would subsist in the arrangement of information in an electronic database.

So what of BHB and other sporting organisations, directory makers and the betting industry? Indeed what are the implications for other sectors deeply engaged in the creation and licensing of information, such as geospatial data providers and the scientific community?[92] Where data is created it would appear that there is little protection under intellectual property (IP) law. In other words, there is a gap.

This in turn begs the question as to whether this is a problem and, if so, for whom. For those who supported protecting industriousness by copyright on the

---

90   There is recognition in the Database Directive that the standard will change for some countries; see for example Recital 60.

91   *Re Copyright in Editors' Names* [1996] ECC 44 OGH (A).

92   Hey, A.J.G. and A.E. Trefethen (2003), 'The Data Deluge: An e-Science Perspective', in Berman, F., G.C. Fox and A.J.G. Hey (eds),. *Grid Computing – Making the Global Infrastructure a Reality,* Chichester: Wiley and Sons, chapter 36, pp. 809–24.

grounds that it gave the necessary incentive to the author, it would be problematic.[93] Not only is industriousness unlikely to be protected by database copyright but in addition, when linked to creation of the materials, it will be unprotected by the sui generis right. But that assumes that protection really does provide an incentive. In the database sector that is questionable. One of the reasons given for the introduction of the Database Directive was to give the necessary incentive by way of the sui generis right and thus boost production. It has been noted that the numbers of databases in Europe did indeed rise in the aftermath of the introduction of the Database Directive[94] – but fell back soon thereafter – and that was when it was thought that the scope of the sui generis right was broad (i.e. before the rulings of the ECJ). Indeed, in a review of the workings of the Database Directive the European Commission has acknowledged quite candidly that the measure has not boosted production of databases as had been anticipated.[95]

Will the absence of protection for 'created' databases increase dissemination? Simply because there is no IP protection for the contents of databases does not mean that the industry will make the contents freely available and to a greater extent than they were made freely available when it was thought protection subsisted.[96] IP protection is not essential for the commercial exploitation of the contents of electronic databases. Database makers frequently use combinations of contract and digital rights management when licensing data to third parties – which they are perfectly entitled to do. Competition will affect the behaviour of the smaller players in competitive markets and put pressure on both licensing terms and prices. Competition law may regulate terms and conditions offered to third parties where the provider is in a dominant position.[97] Beyond that, and in the absence of a legislative

---

[93]   Denicola, R.C. (1981), 'Copyright in Collections of Facts: A Theory for the Protection of Non-fiction Literary Works', 81 *Columbia Law Review* 516 '. . . effort of authorship can be effectively encouraged and rewarded only by linking the existence and extent of protection to the total labor of production. To focus on the superficial form of the final product to the exclusion of the effort expended in collecting the data presented in the work is to ignore the central contribution of the compiler' (p. 530).

[94]   Hugenholtz P.B., S.M. Maurer and H.J. Onsrud H.J. (2001), 'Europe's Database Experiment', *Science*, **294**, pp. 789–90.

[95]   DG Internal Market and Services Working Paper, 'First evaluation of Directive 96/9/EC on the legal protection of databases', Brussels, 12 December 2005.

[96]   It would be most interesting to know how the commercial framework for making the contents of databases available may have changed in the aftermath of the ECJ's rulings (if at all).

[97]   *Attheraces Ltd v British Horseracing Board Ltd* [2005] EWHC 3015 [2006] UKCLR 167 and *Attheraces Limited, Attheraces (UK) Limited v The British Horseracing Board Limited, BHB Enterprises Plc* [2007] EWCA Civ 38 CA (Civ Div). See also OPSI report on its investigation of a complaint (SO 42/8/4): 'Intelligent Addressing and Ordnance Survey'.

framework, there appears little to control the behaviour of database providers. In other words, without the legislative framework which includes public interest goals including, inter alia, the advancement of education and science[98] database makers are relatively free to behave as they please.

Should then the framework for the protection of databases be re-thought?[99] If BHB and other industries of that ilk feel that the absence of both database copyright and the sui generis right is detrimental to their long-term future, then they may well press for a re-appraisal of the system. Taking into account the lessons learnt from the Database experiment,[100] this could provide the perfect opportunity for re-thinking the balance between private rights and the public interest.

---

[98]   The Database Directive contains a number of exceptions or limitations on both database copyright and the sui generis right. For example, where database copyright subsists, then Member States can limit the right where the use is for the sole purpose of illustration for teaching or for scientific research. Database Directive Article 6.2(b).

[99]   If copyright laws do not derive their authority from human creativity, but instead seek merely to compensate investment, then the scope of protection should be rethought and perhaps reduced. Ginsburg, J. (2003), 'The Concept of Authorship in Comparative Copyright Law', 52 *De Paul L Rev*, 1063, p. 1064.

[100]   Ibid., fn. 94.

6 'Une chose publique'? The author's domain and the public domain in early British, French and US copyright law

Jane Ginsburg[1]

Introduction

The public domain is all the rage.[2] It is invoked to breach copyright's encroaching enclosure of the cultural commons of the mind. The heralds of our 'remix culture'[3] deploy the public domain to smash that icon of the entertainment–industrial complex, the Romantic Author. But even before the Author became Romantic, he still served as a shill for concentrated industry, then the printing-bookselling complex.[4] Authors' moral claims of laborious

[1]   Morton L. Janklow Professor of Literary and Artistic Property Law, Columbia University School of Law. This is a shorter version of an article published in *Cambridge Law Journal* 65, 636 (2006), which in turn was based on the Inaugural Emmanuel College International Intellectual Property Lecture, delivered at Emmanuel College, University of Cambridge, 11 May 2006. Many thanks for research assistance to Matthew Batters, Columbia Law School class of 2006, without whom this project could not have been completed, and to Caleb Edwards, Columbia Law School class of 2008 and Christina Jodidio, University of Paris II class of 2007. Thanks also to Clarisa Long, Henry Monaghan, Thomas Nachbar, William R. Cornish, Lionel Bently, and especially Anne Barron.

[2]   The volume of academic writing on the public domain has vastly increased since the signal articles of David Lange, 'Recognizing the Public Domain', and of Jessica Litman, 'The Public Domain'. See, e.g., Bernt Hugenholtz and Lucie Guibault, *The Future of the Public Domain* (collection of essays on the public domain from multiple contributors, including Pamela Samuelson and Julie Cohen); Tyler T. Ochoa, 'Origins and Meanings of the Public Domain'; James Boyle, 'The Second Enclosure Movement and the Construction of the Public Domain'; Mark Rose, 'Nine-Tenths of the Law: The English Copyright Debates and the Rhetoric of the Public Domain'; Pamela Samuelson, 'Mapping the Digital Public Domain: Threats and Opportunities'; Yochai Benkler, 'Free as the Air to Common Use: First Amendment Constraints on Enclosure of the Public Domain'; Lawrence Lessig, *The Future of Ideas: The Fate of the Commons in a Connected World*. For a more skeptical view of 'commons' discourse, see Anupam Chander and Madhavi Sunder, 'The Romance of the Public Domain'.

[3]   See, e.g., Lawrence Lessig, *Free Culture: How Big Media Uses Technology and the Law to Lock Down Culture and Control Creativity*.

[4]   See, e.g., Mark Rose, 'The Author as Proprietor: Donaldson v Becket and the Genealogy of Modern Authorship' ('it might be said that the London booksellers

entitlement merely masked the power grab of the printers. If we speak of a grab, we imply that copyright was seized from somewhere. So whence, in that account, was copyright wrested? From the public domain.

It is not my purpose here to take issue with the expanding normative role for the public domain. I do not for a moment dispute that the public domain is today and should remain copyright's constraining counterpart. In its composition, my idea of the public domain may differ from some of yours, but we probably agree that there is and should be an ever-growing corpus of material over which no author or successor in title may exercise a private right. What provokes this essay, by contrast, are what I perceive to be anachronistic assertions of the 'immemorial' quality of today's aggressive concept of the public domain.[5] Some of these arguments look to me like the Roche-Bobois 'provincial' line of furniture: modern pieces with nicks and wormholes introduced to impart antique appeal. The normative claims for the public domain should persuade on their own, without the added patina of ancient precept. I therefore propose to examine what were the respective domains of author and public at copyright's inception, in eighteenth to nineteenth-century Britain, France and America. I acknowledge immediately that the search uncovers more ambiguity than certainty, more matters for further inquiry than tidy findings. I hope I will leave you with many questions, and that some of you will rise to the bait of seeking fuller answers.

1.   Britain

We might start the inquiry into the respective domains of author and public with the observation that the term 'public domain' did not exist in early copyright law.[6] This does not necessarily mean that the broader concepts that the 'public domain' today embraces did not exist in some form in the eighteenth

---

invented the modern author, constructing him as a weapon in their struggle with the booksellers of the provinces').

[5]   See, e.g., Ochoa, note 2 above, p. 222; Ronan Deazley, *Re-Thinking Copyright*; L. Ray Patterson, 'Free Speech, Copyright, and Fair Use', p. 25 (the stationer's copyright 'purported to preempt' the public domain while the Statute of Anne 'created, or at least reestablished' the public domain); James Boyle, note 2 above, pp. 37–40 (arguing that a second enclosure movement is eating away at intellectual property that was previously in the public domain), Negativeland, 'The Public Domain: Two Relationships to a Cultural Public Domain', p. 251 (the 'ancient, universal view of art's potential subject matter' encompassed everything, and has slowly been encroached by the development of capitalism); See also, Lawrence Lessig, 'Dunwody Distinguished Lecture in Law: The Creative Commons', p. 764 (the public domain is a resource 'that creators throughout history have drawn upon freely').

[6]   See, e.g., Mark Rose, note 2 above, p. 84 ('In the early period, [there was] no positive term in which to speak affirmatively about the public domain').

century, but simply that no single handy locution captured them. Eighteenth-century jurists employed terms like '*publici juris*',[7] or, in France, '*propriété publique*',[8] but they may not have meant it in the way some modern expositors use 'public domain', to mean the non-proprietary primordial soup from which we all sup, and freely digesting, bring forth further expression for the common delectation.

To ascertain the meaning of these terms at copyright's inception, we might ask: In the beginning, in Britain, France and the US, was a published work a public thing? I start with publication because the printing press gave rise to the conditions to which copyright and its predecessor privileges responded: the mass, and potentially uncontrolled, reproduction of copies of works, and the eventual rise of a population capable of reading them. For almost as soon as there were printing presses there also came printing privileges.[9] Ruling authorities perceived two problems that privileges might resolve. Publishing would further the Renaissance revival of the classical authors as well as enhance the communication of contemporary Latin and vernacular literature and scholarship. Along with making desirable works more available, however, uncontrolled publishing could also disseminate undesirable ideas. Second, uncontrolled publishing could discourage the financial undertaking required to print books: second-comers could undercut the profits of the first. Limiting the number of printers would serve both the crown by controlling the ideas, and the publisher by controlling competition.

With the printing privileges in place, the new copying technology was unlikely to have given rise to expectations of public entitlement to make and distribute copies. On the contrary, a 1677 King's Bench decision stated: 'printing was a new invention, and therefore every man could not by the common law have the liberty of printing law books' (*Company of Stationers v Seymour*).[10] Thus a published work would not have been a 'public thing'.

But in England the printing privileges lapsed. The licensing act expired in 1695, and no statutory regime of exclusive rights replaced it until 1710, with the Statute of Anne.[11] We might therefore consider whether this period

---

7   See, e.g, speech of Lord Camden in *Donaldson v Beckett*, p. 999.
8   See, e.g., report of Le Chapelier, *Archives parlementaires (Assemblée nationale)*, p. 210, discussed below, section 3.
9   The first printing privileges were granted by the city-state of Venice in the second half of the fifteenth century. On the history of printing privileges see generally, Bruce Bugbee, *The Genesis of American Patent and Copyright Law*, pp. 12–56; Frank Prager, 'A History of Intellectual Property from 1545 to 1789'.
10   See also John Feather, *Publishing, Piracy and Politics*, p. 46.
11   An Act for the Encouragement of Learning by Vesting the Copies of Printed Books in the Authors or Purchasers of such Copies, 8 Anne c. 19 (1710).

fostered an expectation of public entitlement to published works which would have supplied the framework for interpreting the subsequent Statute of Anne. That is, should the Statute of Anne be seen as derogating from a prior public domain default, or does the statute fit within a proprietary landscape which persisted despite the expiration of the printing privileges?

Two factors make it unlikely that during this fifteen-year period a concept of the public domain as the first principle would have taken root. First, while the Stationers' Company no longer enjoyed a royal monopoly, it still maintained a significant economic and technological advantage. The guild largely controlled the means of publishing, and it controlled its membership.[12] So long as the guild could discipline its members into respecting each others' exclusivity, the conditions for propagating a public domain would not arise.

Second, the lapsing of the Licensing Act may have terminated the vesting of exclusive rights in booksellers. But that did not necessarily mean that the concept of exclusive rights to copy and disseminate works of authorship died along with the printers' monopoly. Rather, another claimant to those rights appeared – the author, along with a philosophical and legal theory to connect the author to the rights. Although John Locke urged the expiry of the Licensing Act, largely because he objected to the Stationers' 'Monopoly of all the Clasick Authers and scholars',[13] he also collaborated on the text of a new licensing bill, which did not pass, but which would have vested both initial printing and reprinting rights in the author. Locke's draft appears to accept the premise of authorial proprietary rights: the text provides that the prohibition on printing was 'to secure the Author's property in his copy'.[14] This proposal is the precursor to the Statute of Anne, the world's first enactment to place the exclusive right initially in the hands of authors, rather than of printer-booksellers.

By the late seventeenth century, authors' claims may, therefore, have been recognized as a matter of natural justice. But does natural justice translate into enforceable rights? Before authors were vested with statutory rights, could

---

[12]   For self-regulation within the printing and bookselling trades during the period between the licensing act and the Statute of Anne, see generally Isabella Alexander, '*The Metaphysics of the Law*', para. [2.3]; Feather, see note 10 above, pp. 65–6; Cyprian Blagden, *The Stationers' Company: A History*, pp. 175–7.

[13]   John Locke, *Memorandum against the Renewal of the Licensing Act*. Self-interest may have played some role in Locke's objections: a bookseller's previously granted printing privilege in Aesop's Fables blocked Locke's endeavor to publish his own edition. See Lewis Hyde, 'Frames from the Framers: How America's Revolutionaries Imagined Intellectual Property', p. 11.

[14]   See Appendix to E.S. De Beer, *The Correspondence of John Locke*, p. 795. See generally, Laura Moscati, 'Un "Memorandum" di John Locke tra *Censorship* et *Copyright*'.

they advance a common law claim to exclusive rights in their works? I have found no cases preceding the Statute of Anne in which an author alleged a trespass of his property rights in a published, or unpublished, work. That authors might enjoy enforceable *incorporeal* property rights in their works may well have been a new concept.[15] The term 'literary *property*' appears to have been coined around 1707, when it was invoked in a petition from members of the guild to the House of Commons as part of the Stationers' ongoing attempt to restore the expired Licensing Act.[16] Less than three years later, in an earlier draft of the Statute of Anne, the preamble vaunts the rights of 'authors . . . in whom ye undoubted Property of such Books and Writing as the product of their learning and labour remains . . .'.[17] If the concept of authorial property had not by 1710 received judicial imprimatur, the proposition that authors' intellectual labor justified a right perhaps cognizable at common law seems at least to have gained currency.

If authors' rights did not detract from a pre-existing public domain, we might nonetheless posit that the Statute of Anne created both copyright and the concomitant public domain. For if the statute delineated the author's domain (and, derivatively, the bookseller's, too), then everything the statute left out might be deemed *publici juris*. But that is taking a highly positivist view of the Statute of Anne. The effect of an interpretation that makes the statute the sole source of authors' rights is to create (or to perpetuate) a vast zone of non-property encircling the statute. Copyright becomes a little coral reef of private right jutting up from the ocean of the public domain. In fact, the respective domains of author and public appear to have been much less clearly marked. If we stick with aquatic landscapes, we might say that the realm of copyright was a shoreline of uncertain contours. If the Statute of Anne separated the waters from the lands, it did not clearly tell us which was which.

I propose four ways to ascertain whether authors' rights were confined to the terms of the statute. Two address the existence of copyright, the others its scope. If the Statute of Anne furnished the sole basis for literary property, then the following propositions should be true:

1. Subject matter not included within the statute was not protected;
2. Protection for covered subject matter depended on compliance with statutory formalities;

---

[15] For the evolution of the concept of incorporeal property rights in works of authorship, see generally Brad Sherman and Lionel Bently, *The Making of Modern Intellectual Property Law*, pp. 19–35. For the parallel, albeit later, evolution in France, see Laurent Pfister, 'La propriété littéraire est-elle une propriété?'.

[16] See Feather, note 10 above, p. 56.

[17] Ibid.

3. Rights not included within the statute were not protected;
4. The duration of rights was limited to the statutory term.

As we will see, only the last of these proved ultimately to be correct, and it was hotly debated, even deplored, at the time by significant expositors of the common law.[18] More importantly, resolution of the duration issue did not fully contain the author's domain. English judges continued both to grant extra-statutory protections, and to interpret hospitably claims that pushed the limits of statutory scope.

Let's begin with *Subject Matter*. The Statute of Anne covered 'any book' (8 Anne c. 19 s. 1), a term the text did not define. A later enactment, the 1735 Hogarth's Act,[19] provided for exclusive rights in prints and engravings. One might infer from the passage of a law specifically directed at certain works of art that 'book' was limited to literary works, in book form. Moreover, if the statute was creating new proprietary rights subtracted from the public domain, one might anticipate that the statutory grant would be narrowly construed. Most of the early cases did concern literary works in book form, but not all. Some addressed unpublished letters[20] and manuscripts,[21] an unpublished play,[22] published roadmaps[23] and, finally, musical compositions,[24] including music sold as single sheets.[25] In the cases of maps and musical compositions, a generous reading of 'book' could bring them within the statute, but such a technique of statutory interpretation implied a property-friendly premise inconsistent with a view of copyright as derogating from a public domain default and therefore compelling narrow construction. Indeed, to fit musical compositions within 'any book', Lord Mansfield in his 1777 decision in *Bach v Longman* elevated the statute's preamble, which referred to 'books and other writings' (2 Cowp. at 624, 98 Eng. Rep. at 1274) into operative language.

Similarly, beginning in 1741, with Alexander Pope's suit against Edmund Curl for unauthorized publication of letters written by Pope and sent to recipients from whom Curl apparently obtained them,[26] the English courts

---

[18]   In the US, *Donaldson* was also criticized by the legal academy, see James Kent, *Commentaries on American Law*, pp. 314–15.

[19]   An Act for the Encouragement of the Arts of designing, engraving and etching historical and other Prints, by vesting the Properties thereof in the Inventors and Engravers, during the Time therein mentioned, 8 Geo. II c. 13 (1735).

[20]   See, e.g., *Pope v Curl*.

[21]   See, e.g., *Duke of Queensberry v Shebbeare*; *Southey v Sherwood*.

[22]   *Macklin v Richardson*.

[23]   *Carnan v Bowles*; *Cary v Faden*; *Cary v Longman and Rees*.

[24]   *Bach v Longman*.

[25]   *Clementi v Golding*.

[26]   *Pope v Curl*.

routinely enjoined the unauthorized publication of letters and manuscripts.[27]
A manuscript might both be considered a 'book' (or an incipient one), and be
assimilated to a chattel under its author's physical dominion. But letters were
both less book-like, thus less clear candidates for statutory coverage; and,
having been sent to their intended recipients, had left the physical control of
their authors. A traditional trespass claim thus would have been rather attenu-
ated. But Lord Hardwicke surmounted the chattel problem with vaulting ease.
Yes, the recipient had the 'property of the paper', he ruled, but the author's
dispatch of the physical medium did not transfer the property in the words.
The right of first publication thus was distinct from the ownership of the letter
or the manuscript.

This brings us to our second inquiry, regarding *Formalities*. Was the first
publication right a statutory property right or a common law property right?
The overall focus of the statute was directed towards the regulation of the
printed, published copies – and the guild that purveyed them. Indeed, the
printer/bookseller centrism of the Statute of Anne has led many scholars to
conclude that the author, having lent rhetorical flair to the preamble and moral
appeal to the preceding lobbying,[28] was nearly irrelevant to the actual regime
the Statute established.[29] Part of that regime included the conditioning of the
statute's remedies on compliance with formalities. These requirements,
notably registration of the work with the Stationers' Company upon publication, were per se irrelevant to unpublished works.[30] The role of formalities in
a copyright system can tell us a lot about the premises underlying protection.
If copyright is conditioned on compliance with formalities, then the right may
be viewed in purely positivistic terms. No registration, no right, full stop.

The statute imposed the registration requirement out of fear that 'persons
[might] through ignorance offend against' the author's or proprietor's exclusive rights.[31] That might imply that, absent registration of the work, the
public was entitled to assume that the work was free to be printed or
reprinted. In other words, the default position, away from which the author or
proprietor must educate the public through proper registration, would be free

---

27   Ibid.; *Duke of Queensberry v Shebbeare*; *Southey v Sherwood*; *Perceval v
Phipps*, Ves. & Beam, p. 24, Eng. Rep., p. 277; *Thompson v Stanhope*, Ambler R., p.
740, Eng. Rep., p. 477; *Gee v Pritchard and Anderson,* Eng. Rep., p. 679.
28   See, e.g., Mark Rose, *Authors and Owners.*
29   See, e.g., Lyman Ray Patterson, *Copyright in Historical Perspective*, p. 147
(suggesting that giving the right to authors was merely a convenient means to attack
the Stationers' monopoly); Feather, see note 10 above, p. 51.
30   See 8 Anne c. 19 s. 2. Moreover the term of protection ran from first publication, see s. 1.
31   Ibid., s. 2.

appropriability. This in turn would suggest a skeptical and skimping view of the proprietary right.

The caselaw, however, indicates a different view. The courts concluded that formalities conditioned only the special statutory remedies; common law remedies remained available when the author or proprietor had not registered the work with the Stationers' Company.[32] Thus, the statutory claim sat atop an established common law structure of rights, enhancing, but not defining, the available relief.

Let us turn to the third proposition, that the statute articulates the full and sole *scope of the right*. The Statute of Anne vested authors and proprietors with the rights to print, reprint and sell. In modern copyright parlance, these are the rights to reproduce and distribute the work.[33] If these are the only legally cognizable rights, we would expect courts to reject any claims to protect a work against unauthorized public performance, or against unauthorized adaptation. Once again, the caselaw serves up an ambiguous response.

We will first consider the scope of the rights to print and reprint. If these were limited to dissemination of copies of the work in the same form and contents as originally published, then partial copying, or revision of the prior work, would not have been held to infringe. The courts did devise a doctrine of 'fair abridgement', permitting second-comers to update, correct, summarize, or partially copy copyrighted works. The basis of the fair abridgement rule, however, seems to me more consistent with a labor-based property concept than with a narrow application of statutory text. In the 1740 decision in *Gyles v Wilcox*, concerning the alleged copying of a law book, Lord Hardwicke considered whether 'all abridgements' should 'be brought within the meaning of this act of parliament'. Books that 'are colourably shortened only' were 'undoubtedly within the meaning of the act of parliament, and are

---

[32]   See, e.g., *Blackwell v Harper*; *Beckford v Hood*.

Later interpretations of Hogarth's Act, however, required the engraver to have placed the date of first publication upon all distributed copies. See, *Thompson v Symonds*, Term. R., p. 45, Eng. Rep., p. 26 (Lord Kenyon CJ: 'The date is of importance, that the public may know the period of the monopoly'); *Harrison v Hogg*, Ves. Jun. p. 327, Eng. Rep., p. 656; *Newton v Cowie* (esp. per Best CJ: 'It is impossible to suppose the legislative intended that the public should not have the protection afforded them by the first act against fraudulent continuance of the monopoly beyond the term prescribed by that act'). In *Brooks v Cock*, [1835] Ad. & El. pp. 140–41, Eng. Rep., p. 366 Lord Denman CJ rejected the analogy with *Beckford v Hood*, 'It is the proprietor's own fault if he suffers a hardship. It is easy for him to comply with a regulation which is very simple and useful, and which makes the date part of the description of the plate to be protected'.

[33]   See, e.g., 17 USC § 106(1)(3); Copyright, Designs and Patents Act, 1988 c. 48 § 16(a)(b) (Eng.).

a mere evasion of the statute', he declared. But a 'fair abridgement' falls outside the act because a 'real and fair abridgement . . . may with great propriety be called a new book, because . . . the invention, learning, and judgment of the author is shewn in them' (Atk. p. 143, Eng. Rep. p. 490). In other words, because he has expended mental labor, a fair abridger is an author, too. The labor rationale that justifies the first author's property also confines it. The colorable shortener (or, to use Justice Story's later US characterization of the same lowlife figure, the facile user of the scissors[34]) is not an author because he has contributed nothing of his own to the prior work. In the case of a fair abridgement, by contrast, we encounter not an absence of property rights, but two contending property rights, both arising out of 'invention, learning, and judgment'.

The other right we will explore is the public performance right. The Statute of Anne did not cover this, which is understandable in light of parliament's focus on the printing trade. But if a play were performed without authorization, what recourse would its author or proprietor have? The few performance right cases decided before parliament enacted a performance right in 1833[35] are inconclusive, with relief both granted and denied.[36] The most interesting for our purposes is *Murray v Elliston*, an 1822 decision of the King's Bench concerning an unauthorized performance of a tragedy by Lord Byron. The defendant, stressing that the statute did not extend to performance rights, asserted that no remedy could exist outside the statute. But the defendant also advanced an additional rationale for dismissing the action. Expounding on 'the nature of copyright', defendant's counsel urged:

> If [a] book be not in all reasonable strictness such as may be called the author's own book, as if it be a bona fide abridgement, *Gyles v Wilcox* shews that the author has no remedy. Now, in the present case, a theatrical exhibition falls within the principle above laid down. Persons go thither, not to read the work, or to hear it read, but to see the combined effect of poetry, scenery, and acting. Now of these three things, two are not produced by the author of the work, and the combined effect is just as much a new production, and even more so than the printed abridgement of a work. (B. & Ald., p. 660, Eng. Rep., p. 1332)

The court's laconic dismissal of the action offers a clue to which of the two arguments the judges may have found most persuasive: 'an action cannot be maintained . . . for publicly acting and representing the said tragedy, *abridged*

---

34   See *Folsom v Marsh*, F. Cas., p. 345. On *Folsom v Marsh*, see generally, R. Anthony Reese, 'The Story of Folsom v Marsh', p. 259.

35   An Act to amend the Laws relating to Dramatic Literary Property, 3 Will. IV c. 15 (1833).

36   See, *Coleman v Wathen*; *Morris v Kelly*; *Morris v Harris*, p. 285.

in the manner aforesaid . . .' (B. & Ald., p. 661, Eng. Rep., p. 1332) (emphasis supplied). I suggest we have here not an absence of statutory rights, but an excess of conflicting common law claims.

We turn now to the last of our four propositions, addressing the *duration of copyright*. Here, the statute definitively trumped any pre-existing or concurrent common law rights. I do not propose to re-tell the oft-told tale of *Donaldson v Beckett*,[37] but simply to observe that because the Peers did not address the five questions put to the judges, and most of them gave no reasons at all for their votes, we do not know which if any of the following propositions *Donaldson v Beckett* stands for: that there was no common law copyright; that any common law copyright expired upon publication; that the Statute of Anne pre-empted common law copyright entirely; that the Statute of Anne pre-empted common law copyright to the extent it overlapped with statutory copyright, but left untouched those areas not specifically addressed by the statute. [38]

The controversy over common law copyright that culminated in *Donaldson* is also known as the 'battle of the booksellers',[39] but some of its most heated rhetoric concerned authors. These included the lofty pronouncements of Lord Mansfield and Blackstone,[40] as well as interested parties' broadsheets, extolling authors' labor-based claims to literary property.[41] The other side tended to excoriate booksellers' greed, and to emphasize the public interest in the spread of ideas.[42] Lord Camden's speech in *Donaldson*, if carefully

---

[37]   For prior re-tellings, see, e.g., Ronan Deazley, *On the Origin of the Right to Copy*, pp. 191–210; Mark Rose, 'Author as Proprietor' note 4 above; Feather, note 10 above, pp. 89–95; Howard B. Abrams, 'The Historic Foundation of American Copyright Law'; Augustine Birrell, *Seven Lectures on the Law and History of Copyright in Books*, pp. 99–138.

[38]   4 Burr. at 2408, 98 Eng. Rep. at 357–8, 2 Bro. at 144–5, 1 Eng. Rep., pp. 846–47, 17 Parl. Hist. Eng., pp. 970–1.

[39]   See Birrell, note 37 above, p. 99.

[40]   See, 'Speeches or Arguments of the Judges of the Court of King's Bench', p. 94 (Lord Mansfield's opinion in *Millar v Taylor*, pronouncing what is 'just' for authors); Sir David Rae, Lord Eskgrove, 'Information For Mess. John Hinton, and Attorney; Against Mess. Alexander Donaldson, and Others', p. 44 (citing book 2, chapter 26, § 8 of Blackstone's Commentaries).

[41]   Francis Hargrove, 'An Argument in Defence of Literary Property', p. 21; Anon., 'Information for John MacKenzie of Delvine', pp. 10–11; James Ralph, 'The Case of the Authors by Profession or Trade', p. 2; William Enfield, LL.D., 'Observations on Literary Property', pp. 19–20.

[42]   J. MacLaurin, 'Considerations on the Nature and Origin of Literary Property', p. 34 ('The perpetuating the Monopoly of Books, must inevitably enhance their Prices beyond all Bounds, the infallible Consequence of which is to retard, and indeed stop altogether the Progress of Learning'); Anon., 'A Memorial for the Booksellers of

excerpted, would take pride of place on anyone's Top Ten list of public domain advocacy. For example:

> If there be anything in the world common to all mankind, science and learning are in their nature *publici juris*, and they ought to be as free and general as air or water. . . . Why did we enter into society at all, but to enlighten one another's minds, and improve our faculties, for the common welfare of the species? Those great men, those favoured mortals, those sublime spirits, who share that ray of divinity which we call genius . . . must not . . . hoard up for themselves the common stock. (Parl. Hist. Eng., p. 999)

But read a little further, and we discover a less seductive vision. Lord Camden goes on to lament filthy lucre's defilement of the pristine calling of authorship:

> Glory is the reward of science, and those who deserve it, scorn all meaner views: I speak not of the scribblers for bread, who teaze the press with their wretched productions; fourteen years is too long a privilege for their perishable trash. It was not for gain that Bacon, Newton, Milton, Locke, instructed and delighted the world; it would be unworthy of such men to traffic with a dirty bookseller for so much a sheet of letter press. (Ibid. p. 1000)[43]

Given the rise of the professional author in the eighteenth-century, this snarling feature of Lord Camden's oration was retrograde even in its day.[44] As Catherine Macaulay then wryly observed, the need to pay the 'sordid butchers and bakers . . . are evils which the sublime flights of poetic fancy do not

---

Edinburgh and Glasgow', p. 12; Thomas Hayter, 'An Essay on the Liberty of the Press, Chiefly as it Respects Personal Slander', pp. 38–9. See also 'A Letter from a Gentleman in Edinburgh, to his Friend in London; Concerning Literary Property', p. 15 (charging that self-interest underlay Blackstone's espousal of the booksellers' position).

[43] Lord Camden's rhetoric evokes that of Boileau, almost a century earlier, deploring those who 'disgusted with glory and famished for gain/indenture their muse to a bookseller/and convert a divine art into a mercenary trade'. See Boileau, 'Chant IV', *Art poétique* (1688–96), reprinted in Guillame Picot (ed) (1984):

> Je sais qu'un noble esprit peut sans honte et sans crime
> Tirer de son travail un tribut légitime
> Mais je ne puis souffrir ces auteurs renommés
> Qui, dégoûtés de gloire et d'argent affamés,
> Mettent leur Apollon au gages d'un libraire
> En font d'un art divin un métier mercenaire.

[44] On 'the development of authorship as a business' in the eighteenth century, see, e.g., Victor Bonham-Carter, *Authors by Profession*, pp. 11–32; Brean S. Hammond, *Professional Imaginative Writing in England*; A.S. Collins, *Authorship in the Days of Johnson*.

always soar above'.[45] Camden's stance, and the outcome in the case, also evoked the ire of legal commentators of the time. Gilles Jacob's 1797 *Law Dictionary* attributes to Cambridge law don Edward Christian the confrontational assertion that because *Donaldson* 'was contrary to the opinion of Lord Mansfield, of the learned Commentator [(Blackstone)], and of several other judges ... every person may still be permitted to indulge his own opinion upon the propriety of it, without incurring the imputation of arrogance'.[46] And such indulgences abounded, as a host of early nineteenth century commentators seemed committed to diminishing *Donaldson*'s impact, as Deazley demonstrated in his book *Re-Thinking Copyright*.

2.   France

Let us leave the cabal of British commentators and travel across the Channel to consider how the French envisioned the respective domains of author and of public. French copyright today is generally considered, at least by 'les anglo-saxons' – by which the French curiously mean anglo-americans – to be fundamentally authorial property-oriented.[47] Even the public domain, in the strict sense of copyright-expired works, is not absolutely property-free: authors' moral rights are perpetual, and can be invoked to protect the integrity of works whose authors have been dead well past the statutory post-mortem period.[48] The risk of rampaging moral rights-bearing remote heirs is not theoretical, as the publishers of a purported sequel to *Les Misérables* learned recently to their dismay.[49]

But it was not always thus. Of the three copyright systems here reviewed, France's was at first the closest to acknowledging a public domain default, emphasizing the public's property as the backdrop to private rights. Like

---

[45]   Catherine Macaulay, *A Modest Plea for the Property of Copyright*, p. 15.

[46]   Giles Jacob, *The Law Dictionary*, 'Literary Property', 1st page, col. 2 of entry.

[47]   By many French, too: a basic course in literary history and theory declares, 'the French conception is personalist and favors the interest of the author over that of society, all the while permitting the free public circulation of ideas' – Antoine Compagnon, Course, 'What is an Author', lesson 9, Intellectual Property, course given at the University of Paris IV-Sorbonne, division of French and comparative literature, www.fabula.org/compagnon/auteur9.php

[48]   See Code de la propriété intellectuelle, art. L-121-1, cl. 2.

[49]   See *Pierre Hugo v Editions Plon*, note Pollaud-Dulian (Victor Hugo during his lifetime rejected all requests to create sequels to *Les Misérables*; the publisher who presents new novels as the continuation of *Les Misérables* therefore violates Hugo's perpetual moral rights; court awards damages to Hugo heir and to literary authors' society, but reversed: 04-15.543 Decision no. 125 of January 2007 Court of Cassation. First civil chamber, holding that the Court of Appeals' reasoning failed to establish how Victor Hugo's moral rights had been violated).

England, France had a longstanding regime of printing privileges. These, however, ended not with the whimper of the lapsing of the Licensing Act, but with the bang of the night of August 4, 1789, and the general abolition of all privileges.[50] Whatever the lingering *de facto* power of the *corporation des libraries de Paris*, *de jure* and politically the message was clear: henceforth, the press is free, not only of censorship, but also of proprietary claims.

The first French copyright enactment did not restore private rights in printed works; instead it created a dramatists' public performance right. This was not the principal motivation for the Law of January 13, 1791. Rather, the dramatists' first objective was to destroy the exclusivity the *Comédie Française* had sought to maintain over the works of Corneille, Racine and Molière. The dramatists situated their second demand, for control over their works, within the rhetoric of the public domain. According to Le Chapelier's report, the dramatists' petition 'does not hesitate to admit that after the five-year period [following the author's death], the authors' works are a public property' (*Archives parlementaires*, *Assemblée nationale*, January 13, 1791, p. 210).

Turning, after much execration of the *Comédiens*, to the dramatists' property right, Le Chapelier opened with a ringing affirmation of the principle of authorial property:

> The most sacred, the most legitimate, the most indisputable, and if I may say so, the most personal of all properties is the work which is the fruit of a writer's thoughts.

This excerpt also makes the top ten list for selective quotation, because property-enthusiasts tend to leave Le Chapelier at this rhetorical high point, before he lets the other shoe drop.[51] He continues:

> But it is a property of a different kind from all the other properties. [Once the author has disclosed the work to the public] the writer has affiliated the public with his property, or rather has fully transmitted his property to the public. However, because it is extremely just that men who cultivate the domain of ideas be able to draw some fruits of their labors, it is necessary that, during their whole lives and some years after their deaths, no one may, without their consent, dispose of the product of their genius. But also, after the appointed period, the public's property begins, and everyone should be able to print and publish the works that have contributed to enlighten the human spirit. (*Archives parlementaires*, *Assemblée nationale*, January 13, 1791, pp. 212–13)

---

[50]   Or more accurately, a couple of bangs, because, despite the abolition of privileges, the Paris Book Guild was not definitively suppressed until the decree of March 17, 1791, see Carla Hesse, *Publishing and Cultural Politics*, pp. 47–56.

[51]   See, e.g., Frédéric Rideau, *Une convergence oubliée*, p. 263 n. 751 (pointing out that quotations from Le Chapelier are 'frequently truncated'). For an attempt to trace the origins of the truncation, see Jane C. Ginsburg, 'A Tale of Two Copyrights: Literary Property in Revolutionary France and America', pp. 131, 144 n. 50.

Article 2 of the proposed law declares that the works of authors who have been dead for five years 'are a public property' (ibid., p. 214). There is no ambiguity about the end point of the author's domain. Moreover, Le Chapelier's concept of the public domain appears more extensive than expiration of term. The public's property interest is incipient as soon as the author discloses his work. Authors' labors justify their temporary property rights, but the public's more fundamental claims form an ever-present background.

France did not enact a reproduction right until 2 years later (Law of July 19–24, 1793), though laws were proposed in the interim, one of which strongly emphasized authors' proprietary rights, melding a variety of justifications, including France's debt to the writings of authors that shaped 'the opinion that smashed all forms of despotism in France'.[52] This proposal included special statutory remedies more rugged than the Statute of Anne's damasking of infringing copies. An infringer would be exposed in the public square for three hours, chained to a placard labeled 'thief infringer'[53] – an idea for today's record companies' pursuit of illegal file sharers?

The 1793 Report of Lakanal accompanying the law installing a reproduction right begins defensively, deeming property in the 'productions of genius' the 'least contestable, the one whose increase cannot harm republican equality, nor offend liberty'. The rhetoric grows warmer, extolling 'such a great revolution as ours' for making clear the simple justice of recognizing that property right. Lakanal later rebuts Le Chapelier's characterization of a published work as a 'propriété publique': it makes no sense, he contends, for the author's right to disappear at the very moment at which he exercises it. In contrast to Lord Camden's elevation of the author who writes only for glory, Lakanal contemptuously dismisses that notion, querying, 'By what stroke of fate must it be that the man of genius, who devotes his waking hours to the instruction of his fellow citizens, might look forward only to a sterile glory, and might not claim the legitimate tribute of such noble work?' (*Archives parlementaires*, July 19, 1793, p. 186).

Revolutionary rhetoric deliberately paired the author's domain with the advancement of revolutionary ideals. Authors deserve exclusive rights not only because they bring forth the products of 'genius', but particularly because that genius bears a strongly republican stamp. Nonetheless, the concept of 'propriété publique' was also a revolutionary rallying cry. It instituted what has been called 'a "public domain" of democratic access to a common cultural inheritance'.[54]

---

52   Report of François Hell, *Archives parlementaires*, September 28, 1791, p. 533, quoted in Rideau, see note 51 above, p. 261.
53   See Rideau, note 51 above, p. 262 n 744.
54   Carla Hesse, 'Enlightenment Epistemology', p. 129.

The 'propriété publique' concept lingers in the text of the laws, particularly regarding the *role of formalities*. The 1792 law amending the public performance right conditioned the vesting of the right on compliance with a notice-giving obligation (Decree of 1792, arts 4–6), although that was later withdrawn. The 1793 law conferring reproduction rights imposed a requirement of deposit of copies with the national library (Law of July 19–24, 1793, art. 6). It is difficult to discern from the sparse caselaw addressing formalities whether French courts perceived them as conditions precedent to acquiring rights, or as means of perfecting pre-existing rights necessary to initiate an infringement action,[55] or yet as a condition subsequent whose non- fulfillment would divest the author of the copyright he initially enjoyed.[56] That the question was raised at all nonetheless indicates that the courts were uncertain of the boundary between the author's domain and the public's.

By contrast, two of our other tools for separating the author's domain from the public's – *subject matter* and *scope of rights* – delineate a capacious authorial exclusivity, because the 1793 Act grandly covered 'écrits en tout genre' (writings of all kinds) (Law of July 19–24, 1793, art. 1); and the combination of the 1791 and 1793 acts was interpreted to cover the waterfront of rights, which may explain why France did not supplant these texts with a more fully developed code until 1957.

As for our fourth yardstick, *duration*, we have seen that the term, while potentially much longer than the Statute of Anne's, was unambiguously terminal. Because the positive law was clear, the advocates of perpetual copyright pressed their case before the legislature. The period lasting until the law of 1866, setting the term of copyright at life plus 50 years, saw increasingly acrimonious

---

[55]   See Rideau, note 51 above p. 270.

[56]   See Judgment of October 23, 1806, 1.299; Judgment of November 26, 1828, 2.159. Both of these held that deposit of copies, rather than simply meeting a procedural requirement, gave rise to the copyright. In Judgment of March 1, 1834, 1.65, the Cour de Cassation states that the 1793 law 'guarantees literary property, upon condition of deposit of two copies with the Bibliothèque nationale' and refers to the 'loss of that property right through failure of deposit' ibid. at 75. As a result of this decision, the question whether deposit under the 1793 law created, perfected, or merely served to prove the copyright became moot: the court held that subsequent enactments (in 1810, 1814, and 1828) had substituted a different deposit requirement for that set forth in art. 6 of the 1793 law. See also Judgment of January 20, 1818, p. 5, considering compliance with formalities as giving rise to exclusive rights. The court states the plaintiffs 'published the work in 1816 and fulfilled all the formalities prescribed for acquiring the exclusive right to sell' ibid., pp. 12–13. Plaintiff's advocate made the same assumption when he contended that a French national first publishing abroad could nonetheless obtain copyright protection in France by completing the formalities to which the privilege is subject. Ibid., p. 8.

debates over the nature of copyright.[57] Perpetualists argued that authors' rights were property, and property rights must, by their nature, endure forever.[58] Their antagonists, whom I'll dub public domainists, emphasized that the rights contended for were by their nature incorporeal and therefore incapable of ownership.[59] A copyright thus could only be a contract between the author and society, in which the author received a limited term of exclusivity in recompense for his contributions to society. Joseph Prudhon, of notorious hostility to property in general, thundered against one of the draft perpetual copyright bills:

> By enacting such a law, the legislature will have done far worse than paying the author an exorbitant price, it will have abandoned the principle of the *chose publique*, of the intellectual domain, and at great harm to the community. . . . Let us not disinherit humanity of its domain . . . Intellectual property does not merely encroach on the public domain; it cheats the public of its share in the production of all ideas and all expressions.[60]

Déjà vu all over again? Some of this nineteenth-century French anti-copyright rhetoric sounds a lot like today's cyber-libertarian 'copyleft' avant la lettre.[61] But notwithstanding Prudhon and others of like mind, France in 1866 adopted a law which, albeit not perpetual, installed one of the longest copyright terms in the world.

3.   The United States
We come, at last, to the United States. The pre-Constitutional State copyright statutes revealed multiple motivations, mixing Statute of Annesque encouragements of learned men to write useful books with strong affirmations of

---

57   For a collection of the reports accompanying the various bills and rehearsing the arguments, see Fernand Worms, *Etude de la propriété littéraire*.

58   See, e.g, Edouard Laboulaye, *La propriété littéraire au XVIIIème siècle*, pp. 18–19 (literary property is the same as other real property, and the author's right in it is a 'droit perpétuel dans son principe'); J.-B. Jobard, *Organon de la propriété intellectuelle*, pp. 54–5, 269.

59   See, e.g., Augustin-Charles Renouard, *Traité des droits des auteurs*, p. 203 ('Le droit au privilège est le prix du travail; c'est une rémunération dont la loi garantit la jouissance exclusive comme prix d'échange et dette de reconnaissance par lesquels la société paie l'utilité et le plaisir qu'elle retire de l'ouvrage. Il dérive de la qualité d'auteur'); Edouard Calmels, *De la propriété et de la contrefaçon des œuvres de l'intelligence*, pp. 33–4; Paul Clément, *Etude sur le droit des auteurs*, pp. 72–9 (doctoral dissertation with extensive demonstration of how post-publication rights cannot fit *usus, fructus, abusus* characteristics of civil law property).

60   Joseph Prudhon, 'Les Majorats Littéraires', pp. 140, 152–3.

61   Laurent Pfister, 'La propriété littéraire est-elle une propriété?', pp. 117–19.

authors' labor-based natural property rights.[62] The Constitutional copyright clause also melds public domain and authorial property rationales. It empowers Congress 'to promote the Progress of Science and Useful Arts by securing for limited Times to Authors and Inventors the exclusive Right to their respective Writings and discoveries' (US Const., art. I, § 8 cl. 8). The goal of the property right is to enhance public knowledge, but the rights – though limited in time – are 'secure[d]', not 'granted', by Congress. In 1787, when the clause was drafted, selection of the term 'secured' may have meant that the Framers understood copyright to have been a natural right pre-existing at common law.[63] At least, James Madison in *Federalist 43* prompted that conclusion, for, in justifying the power granted to Congress to provide for copyright and patents, he asserted that 'The copyright of authors has been solemnly adjudged, in Great Britain to be a right of common law' (*The Federalist Papers, No. 43*, p. 279).

If the starting point for federal copyright seemed to assume the author's pre-existing property rights,[64] the first statutes, enacted in 1790 for maps, charts and books (1790 Act, §§ 3 and 4), and in 1802 for prints and engravings (1802 Act, § 1), point in a different direction. The statutes were heavily inspired by (not to say largely plagiarized from) the Statute of Anne and Hogarth's Act. But the *formalities* imposed were more burdensome than their English counterparts.[65] More importantly, where the English statutes and their judicial interpretations confined formalities to specific statutory remedies,[66]

---

[62]   The statutes are collected in Thorvald Solberg (ed.), *Copyright Enactments of the United States: 1783–1906*, pp. 1–21. See also, Francine Crawford, 'Pre-Constitutional Copyright Statutes'. See particularly the statutes of Massachusetts and Connecticut. But see Alfred C. Yen, 'Restoring the Natural Law: Copyright as Labor and Possession', pp. 530–1 (early decisions indicate that courts perceived these statutes to express primarily economic motivations).

[63]   For a review of various meanings to ascribe to 'securing', see, e.g., Edward C. Walterscheid, 'Inherent or Created Rights: Early Views on the Intellectual Property Clause', pp. 92–8 (inter alia, the Preamble to the US Constitution states that one of the purposes of the Constitution is to 'secure the blessings of liberty to ourselves and our posterity'; the Constitution didn't grant liberty – the War of Independence did that – but it was designed to protect and reinforce it). See also Edward C. Walterscheid, *The Nature of the Intellectual Property Clause*, pp. 210–12.

[64]   But cf. Hyde, see note 13 above, pp. 18–27 (contending that the Framers conceived of copyright within the British land-ownership metaphors, but added a civic republican gloss which prompted them to think of intellectual (and of real) property as conferred for use for the public good).

[65]   The 1790 Act required deposit of the work with the clerk of the federal district court upon publication of the work (§ 3), and deposit of three copies with the Secretary of State within six months of publication (§ 4). The 1802 Act further required a notice of copyright in at least one newspaper within one month of publication (§ 1).

[66]   See discussion above.

the US statutes conditioned the existence and enforceability of the right on compliance with the notice, registration and deposit formalities. Indeed, one early decision excluded a 'daily price quote' from the realm of copyrightable subject matter on the ground that the ephemeral nature of the work ill-adapted it to comply with the requisite notice and deposit formalities (*Clayton v Stone*).[67]

With respect to *rights protected*, the general US approach was highly positivistic. Congress, not the courts, established and expanded the scope of copyright. *Stowe v Thomas* (23 F. Cas. 201 (CCED Pa. 1853)) is a notable example. Harriet Beecher Stowe complained of the unauthorized German translation of *Uncle Tom's Cabin*. But the statute then afforded rights only to print, publish and vend. The court characterized statutory copyright as a derogation from the public domain. It ruled that once Stowe's work was published, it 'bec[a]me as much public property as [the creations] of Homer or Cervantes' (ibid., p. 208). Only those rights specified by the statute survived the dedication to the public that publication effected.

The legal positivism characterizing *Stowe* and similar decisions received fullest expression in *Wheaton v Peters*, which is sometimes called the US counterpart to *Donaldson*, because the Supreme Court there rejected common law copyright in published works.[68] The dispute, however, concerned compliance

---

[67]   Republican fears of monopolies may have motivated the institution and judicial requirement of strict observance of statutory formalities. See, e.g., L. Ray Patterson and Craig Joyce, 'Copyright in 1791', p. 941. On intellectual property and early American monopoly-phobia, see, e.g., Hyde, note 13 above, pp. 13–29; Paul J. Heald and Suzanna Sherry, 'Implied Limits on the Legislative Power', p. 1169; Yochai Benkler, 'Constitutional Bounds of Database Protection', p. 570 (the founders understood copyright as a monopoly to be 'carefully circumscribed'). But see Tom Nachbar, 'Constructing Copyright's Mythology', p. 45 (modern scholars' attribution of anti-monopoly animus to the framing of early US copyright laws is overstated); Edward C. Walterscheid, 'To Promote the Progress of Science and Useful Arts', pp. 55–6 (noting the few voices raised against giving Congress the power to grant monopolies, but concluding that 'Just as in the Constitutional Convention itself, the issue of the limited monopolies authorized by the Intellectual Property Clause seems never to have been a point of contention in the state ratifying conventions. Although it was generally received with favor by those who thought about it, with Jefferson being the notable exception, the reality is that among the much more momentous issues addressed with respect to the new Constitution, very few actually gave much thought to it'); Paul M. Schwartz and William Michael Treanor, 'Eldred and Lochner', pp. 2364, 2384–5 (originalist arguments do not withstand careful examination, which reveals a spectrum of attitudes including support for monopolies among the Federalists and – in a limited manner – from the future Republicans).

[68]   See, e.g., Patterson and Joyce, note 67 above, p. 928 n. 45; Howard B. Abrams, see note 37 above, p. 1178.

with formalities, not expiration of the statutory term.[69] Henry Wheaton had been the reporter of the decisions of the Supreme Court. His successor Richard Peters not only published new volumes covering new decisions of the Court, but also reissued Wheaton's reports. Wheaton's claim encountered the objection that he had no federal statutory rights because he had failed to comply with the multiple formalities imposed by the 1790 and 1802 statutes. Although insisting he had acquitted himself of those obligations, Wheaton also rejoined that if his statutory copyright claim failed, he nonetheless enjoyed enforceable common law rights. A three to two majority of the court followed Peters' argument that, whatever the state of affairs in England, in the US, copyright was purely statutory. The court determined that there was no federal common law (33 US, p. 658), and, as to the States, Pennsylvania, where Wheaton's reports had first been published, had had no common law of copyright in published works. The State copyright statutes of the pre-Constitutional period having been supplanted by the federal statute, it was solely to the 1790 and 1802 enactments that Wheaton must look for his post-publication rights. Congress having created the right, compliance with every jot and title of statutory formalities was essential to its vesting and enforceability.

Wheaton had tried to support his claim of common law rights by stressing that the Constitutional copyright clause and the 1790 Act 'secured' the exclusive rights of authors, rather than 'vesting' them, as had the Statute of Anne. If the Constitution gave Congress the power to 'secure' authors' rights, the argument went, that must imply that the rights pre-existed the Constitution. The majority made short work of this contention. It observed that the constitutional clause employs 'securing' with respect to both the writings of authors and the discoveries of inventors. Yet it is clear that patents were not protected at common law. The word cannot, the majority insisted, at once mean pre-existing rights for copyright and newly created rights for patents. If the word is to have the same meaning for both, then it can only mean a new grant (ibid., p. 661). The drafting history of the patent-copyright clause suggests that this reading was not in fact inevitable,[70] but the syntactical nuances of variant

---

[69]   There seems not to have been much if any agitation in the US in favor of perpetual post-publication copyright, perhaps because the US, in contrast to England, did not have a printer-booksellers' monopoly. See Nachbar, note 67 above, p. 45 (US publishers in fact were hostile to long copyright terms). Curtis' 1847 treatise on copyright, the first of its kind in the US, does not take issue with the limited duration of US copyright. On the contrary, he deems it desirable for both practical reasons (the dissipation of the right across successive generations of heirs), and policy considerations (quid pro quo). See George Ticknor Curtis, *A Treatise on the Law of Copyright*, pp. 23–5.

[70]   See Bugbee, see note 9 above, p. 126 (Madison's record of the proposals before the Convention set out a list drawn up by Madison including the following: 'To secure to literary authors their copyrights for a limited time' and 'To encourage by

1787 texts would not have mattered: In 1834, any argument built on 'securing' was doomed to fail, for reasons extraneous to competing conceptions of the author's and the public's domains.

The reasons go back to 1798, when the New York legislature granted Robert Livingston 'the sole right and advantage of making and employing the steam boat'.[71] Livingston teamed up with Robert Fulton and in April 1808, having obtained numerous extensions of the monopoly, they launched a 20-ton steamboat capable of going up river on the Hudson at the stately speed of four miles an hour. Whereupon the New York legislature granted them another five years' exclusivity, with the possibility of further grants to a total of 30 years. When Thomas Gibbons' challenge to the steamboat monopoly reached the US Supreme Court (*Gibbons v Ogden*), the monopolists' counsel advanced the same argument that had succeeded in the New York state courts. In broad outline, the argument went as follows. The Constitution provides for Congress's power to 'secure' the exclusive rights of authors and inventors. The term 'securing' implies pre-existing rights. Copyright is such a right, as it has been recognized as a right at common law. Madison in *Federalist 43* adverted to this and further urged that inventions for the same labor-rewarding reasons ought also to come within Congress's power to regulate through a patent system. Thus, even though historically there was no common law patent, nonetheless the logic supporting common law copyright ought to apply to patents as well. In other words, there should be residual authority to recognize patents at common law. But, because there was no federal common law, the relevant source of law securing the monopolies would be the common law of the several States.[72]

The steamboat monopolists thus built from the foundation of 'securing' an elaborate construct whose practical effect would have eviscerated federal power. New York's steamboat monopolies were creating precisely the kinds of barriers to interstate trade that had hobbled the new nation under the

---

premiums & provisions, the advancement of useful knowledge and discoveries'; and a list by Charles Pinckney including 'To grant patents for useful inventions' and 'To secure to Authors exclusive rights, for a . . . certain time'). For a detailed exploration of the drafting history of the patent-copyright clause, see Dotan Oliar, 'The Immediate Origins of the Intellectual Property Clause'.

[71]   The facts of the steamboat controversy are taken from *Livingston v van Ingen*. See also, Albert J. Beveridge, *The Life of John Marshall*, pp. 397–460.

[72]   See, e.g., in *Gibbons*, 1824 LEXIS US, pp. ***61–6; ***177–82 (petitioner); *Livingston v van Ingen*, Emmet for Petitioners ('Congress have not power to confer a boon or reward. Its power is merely to secure a right for a limited time. . . . The state grants and creates an estate, and rewards the inventor. The patent merely secures the property to the inventor for a certain time. It proceeds as to authors, on the common law notion; as to inventors, on natural rights').

Articles of Confederation – and that had occasioned the adoption of the federal constitution in the first place.[73] *Gibbons v Ogden* is today celebrated as one of the cornerstones of the federal Commerce power.[74] In grounding the decision for *Gibbons* on that power, Justice Marshall's opinion sidestepped the roiling patent power controversy. The relevance of *Gibbons v Ogden* to our exploration of the respective domains of author and public in early US copyright, I suggest, is to have taken 'securing' out of contention as a basis for non-statutory authors' rights pre-existing and concurrent with the federal statute. 'Securing' had become a by-word for States' rights, for national sub-units' exercise of an economic regulatory power which could undermine the larger nation state.

I do not wish to leave you with the impression that, after *Wheaton*, there was no common law copyright in the US, and that, accordingly, the author's domain was strictly limited to the narrow realm of the federal statutes. The public domain began with publication. An unpublished work, as a chattel, remained the object of State common law rights, and this was still true until 1978.[75] Over time, moreover, US courts elaborated a parallel universe of common law rights in works which, albeit technically 'unpublished' because they had not been distributed in copies to the general public, had nonetheless encountered significant, indeed sometimes massive public exposure, particularly through public performance.[76] The rather strained notion of publication was motivated in large part by courts' awareness that, were the work to be deemed 'published', and had the author not complied with all applicable federal statutory formalities, the work would go into the public domain, and all protection, state or federal, would be lost.[77] Thus, even in a system as positivist

---

[73]   See, e.g., Federalist 22 (Hamilton) (defect of system under Articles of Confederation is absence of national power to regulate commerce, and consequent 'interfering and unneighborly regulations of some States, contrary to the true spirit of the Union').

[74]   See e.g., IV Beveridge, note 71 above, p. 447 ('It is not immoderate to say that no other judicial pronouncement in history was . . . so interwoven with the economic and social evolution of a nation and a people. After almost a century, Marshall's Nationalist theory of commerce is more potent than ever . . .').

[75]   The 1976 copyright act abolished the publication threshold for entitlement to federal copyright, which now 'subsists' as of the creation and fixation of the work, see 17 USC § 102(a).

[76]   See, e.g., *Estate of Martin Luther King v CBS*, ('I Have a Dream' speech technically 'unpublished' despite delivery before live audience of thousands, and television and radio broadcast to millions); see generally, William S. Strauss, Study No. 29, 'Protection of Unpublished Works'.

[77]   See, e.g., *Estate of Hemingway v Random House*, p. 349 ('the courts are reluctant to find that an author has 'published' so as to lose his common-law copyright').

Courts' efforts to avoid forfeitures may also explain the somewhat tortured US caselaw relating to sound recordings; see Study No. 29, note 76 above, pp. 202–4. In

as US copyright, judges found occasion to recognize authors' extra-statutory rights, or, if you prefer, to compromise the public domain.

Conclusion

In *Conclusion*, it is so well established today that copyright cannot, and should not, last forever,[78] that it may be difficult to understand the appeal of perpetual common law copyright in published works. But in both Britain and especially France, demands for perpetual copyright persisted into the nineteenth century. The expression 'fall into the public domain', which appears to have originated in mid-nineteenth-century France to denote the end of the copyright term, evokes the devastation of a fall from grace. Indeed, the nineteenth-century poet Alfred de Vigny amplified the sense of desolation: he evoked the expiration of copyright as 'tomber dans le gouffre du domaine public' – to fall into the sink hole of the public domain.[79]

Gallic hyperbole notwithstanding, I think perpetuity was the punchline of a syllogism whose first proposition may have been the most important for authors' rights advocates: an author's intellectual labor gives rise to property rights; property rights are perpetual; therefore the author's right must be perpetual, too. To question the perpetuity of the right may be to unravel the syllogism, and thus to undermine its premise. If copyright is not perpetual, then it cannot be property. If it is not property, then authors' efforts are denigrated; authors become uniquely disadvantaged among those who labor.[80]

---

this instance, two different forfeitures loom, first of the recorded musical composition, and second of the recorded performance. Under the 1909 Act regime, if sale of phonograms constituted 'publication', and the recorded composition had not previously been published with notice or registered, then the sale of the recording would cast the composition into the public domain. With regard to the recorded performance, sound recordings were not included within federal copyright subject matter until 1972 (Pub. L. No. 92–140, 85 Stat. 391 (1971)), as amended by Pub. L. No. 93–573, 88 Stat. 1873 (1974) (federal protection for sound recordings fixed and published with notice on and after February 15, 1972). As a result, were pre-1972 recordings deemed 'published', they would have immediately gone into the public domain. Hence the judicial rulings that the sale and distribution of phonograms did not 'publish' the performances, which, accordingly, remained subject to common law copyright. See *Capitol Records v Naxos of America*; *Capitol Records v Mercury Records Corp.*

[78]   But see UK CDPA 1988 c. 48 § 301 (potentially perpetual royalty right in J.M. Barrie's *Peter Pan*), discussed in Catherine Seville, 'Peter Pan's Rights: "To Die Will be an Awfully Big Adventure" ', pp. 3–7.

[79]   Alfred de Vigny, 'De mademoiselle Sédaine et de la propriété littéraire, Lettre à messieurs les Députés', pp. 107, 112–13.

[80]   Cf. E. Laboulaye, *Etudes sur la propriété littéraire en France et en Angleterre*, p. xii (criticizing the 1793 French copyright law for making authors' rights 'of all property rights the most humble and the least protected').

This, to echo Lord Mansfield's celebrated litany in *Millar v Taylor*, is not 'just' (4 Burr., pp. 2398–9; 98 Eng. Rep., pp. 252–3). Finally, there may have been more than felt justice animating the calls for an endless author's domain; then, as now, copyright advocates have had literary affinities, unfulfilled artistic yearnings reluctantly redirected toward juridical rather than creative endeavors. Blackstone himself was one of these closeted copyright lawyers.[81] Yielding to his Arcadian urges, in 1744 he penned the wistful 'Lawyer's Farewell to his Muse', which, in conclusion, I shall unfairly – but mercifully – abridge:

> Adieu, celestial Nymph, adieu:
> Shakespear no more thy sylvan son,
> Nor all the art of Addison,
> Pope's heav'n-strung lyre, nor Waller's ease,
> Nor Milton's mighty self must please:
> Instead of these, a formal band
> In furs and coifs around me stand;
> With sounds uncouth and accents dry
> That grate the soul of harmony,
> Each pedant sage unlocks his store
> Of mystic, dark, discordant lore;
> And points with tott'ring hand the ways
> That lead me to the thorny maze.
> There, in a winding, close retreat,
> Is Justice doom'd to fix her seat,
> There, fenc'd by bulwarks of the Law,
> She keeps the wond'ring world in awe,
>
> Then welcome business, welcome strife,
> Welcome the cares, the thorns of life,
> The visage wan, the pore-blind sight,
> The toil by day, the lamp at night,
> The tedious forms, the solemn prate,
> The pert dispute, the dull debate,
> The drowsy bench, the babling Hall,
> For thee, fair Justice, welcome all!

Bibliography

Abrams, Howard B. (1983), 'The Historic Foundation of American Copyright Law: Exploding the Myth of Common Law Copyright', *Wayne Law Review*, **29**, 1119–91.

Alexander, Isabella (2005), 'The Metaphysics of the Law': Drawing the Boundaries of Copyright Law 1710–1911', unpublished thesis, University of Cambridge.

---

[81]   Joseph Story also joins the coifed company of *poètes manqués*; in 1800, perhaps in youthful indiscretion (he was 21), he published an 83-page poem, 'The Power of Solitude'. His son seems to have deemed the effort worthy of obscurity, for he did not include it among Story's posthumously published miscellaneous papers; see William Wetmore Story (ed.), *The Miscellaneous Writings of Joseph Story*.

Anonymous (1747), 'A Memorial for the Booksellers of Edinburgh and Glasgow, Relating to the Process against them by some of the London Booksellers; which Depended before the Court of Session, and is now under Appeal', reprinted in (1974), *The Literary Property Debate: Seven Tracts, 1747–1773*, New York: Garland Press.

Anonymous (1769), 'A Letter from a Gentleman in Edinburgh, to his Friend in London; Concerning Literary Property', reprinted in (1974), *Freedom of the Press and the Literary Property Debate: Six Tracts, 1755–1770*, New York: Garland Press.

Anonymous (1771*)*, 'Information for John MacKenzie of Delvine, Writer to the Signet, and Others, Trustees Appointed by Mrs. Anne Smith, Widow of Mr. Thomas Ruddiman, Late Keeper of the Advocates Library, Pursuers, against John Robertson, Printer in Edinburgh, Defender', reprinted in (1974), *The Literary Property Debate: Seven Tracts, 1747–1773*, New York: Garland Press.

Anonymous (1771), 'Speeches or Arguments of the Judges of the Court of King's Bench', reprinted in (1974), *The Literary Property Debate: Seven Tracts, 1747–1773*, New York: Garland Press.

Benkler, Yochai (1999), 'Free as the Air to Common Use: First Amendment Constraints on Enclosure of the Public Domain', *New York University Law Review*, **74**, 354–446.

Benkler, Yochai (2000), 'Constitutional Bounds of Database Protection: The Role of Judicial Review in the Creation and Definition of Private Rights in Information', *Berkeley Technical Law Journal*, **15**, 535–603.

Beveridge, Albert J. (1919), *The Life of John Marshall*, Boston: Houghton Mifflin.

Birrell, Augustine (1899), *Seven Lectures on the Law and History of Copyright in Books*, London: Cassell.

Blackstone, William (1744), 'The Lawyer's Farewell to His Muse', in *A Collection of Poems in Six Volumes by Several Hands* (1763), London: R&J Dodsley.

Blagden, Cyprian (1960), *The Stationers' Company: A History 1403–1959*, London: George Allen & Unwin.

Boileau Despréaux, Nicolas, 'Chant IV', reprinted in Guillame Picot (ed.) (1984), *L'art poétique/Boileau; suivi de Horace, Epitre aux Pisons; avec une notice sur les traités d'art poétique depuis l'Antiquité, une biographie chronologique de Boileau, une étude géneérale de son œuvre, une analyse méthodique de son 'Art poétique', des notes des questions par Guillaume Picot*, Paris: Bordas.

Bonham-Carter, Victor (1978), *Authors by Profession*, London: Society of Authors.

Boyle, James (2003), 'The Second Enclosure Movement and the Construction of the Public Domain', *Law and Contemporary Problems*, **66**, 33–74.

Bugbee, Bruce (1967), *The Genesis of American Patent and Copyright Law*, Washington: Public Affairs Press.

Calmels, Edouard (1856), *De la propriété et de la contrefaçon des œuvres de l'intelligence*, Paris: Cosse.

Chander, Anupam and Madhavi Sunder (2004), 'The Romance of the Public Domain', *California Law Review*, **92**, 1331–73.

Clément, Paul (1867), *Etude sur le droit des auteurs*, Grenoble: Maisonville et fils.

Collins, A.S. (1927), *Authorship in the Days of Johnson*, London: R. Holden.

Compagnon, Antoine, 'What is an Author, lesson 9, Intellectual Property', www.fabula.org/compagnon/auteur9.php, accessed 24 August 2006 (course given at the University of Paris IV-Sorbonne, division of French and comparative literature).

Crawford, Francine (1975), 'Pre-Constitutional Copyright Statutes', *Bulletin of the Copyright Society*, **23**, 11–37.

Curtis, George Ticknor (1847), *A Treatise on the Law of Copyright*, Boston: C.C. Little and J. Brown.

Deazley, Ronan (1994), *On the Origin of the Right to Copy: Charting the Movement of Copyright Law in Eighteenth-Century Britain (1695–1775)*, Oxford: Hart Publishing.

Deazley, Ronan (2006), *Re-Thinking Copyright: History, Theory, Language*, Cheltenham and Northampton, MA: Edward Elgar.

De Beer, ES (ed.) (1979), *The Correspondence of John Locke*, Oxford: Clarendon Press.

De Vigny, Alfred (1841), 'De mademoiselle Sédaine et de la propriété littéraire: Lettre à messieurs les Députés' reprinted in Jan Baetens (ed.) (2001), *Le Combat du droit d'auteur: Anthologie historique*, Paris: Les Impressions Nouvelles.

Enfield, William (1774), *Observations on Literary Property*, reprinted in (1974), *The Literary Property Debate: Eight Tracts, 1774–1775*, New York: Garland Press.

Feather, John (1994), *Publishing, Piracy and Politics: An Historical Study of Copyright in Britain*, New York: Mansell.

Ginsburg, Jane C. (1994), 'A Tale of Two Copyrights: Literary Property in Revolutionary France and America', in Brad Sherman and Alain Strowel (eds), *Of Authors and Origins: Essays on Copyright Law*, Oxford and New York: Clarendon and Oxford University Press.

Guibault, Lucie (2006), *The Future of the Public Domain*, The Hague: Wolters Kluwer Law and Business.

Hamilton, Alexander, *Federalist Paper No. 22*, reprinted in Edward Earl Mead (ed.) (1941), *The Federalist*, New York: The Modern Library.

Hammond, Brean S. (1997), *Professional Imaginative Writing in England, 1670–1740: 'Hackney for Bread'*, Oxford and New York: Oxford University Press.

Hargrove, Francis (1774), 'An Argument in Defence of Literary Property', London, printed for the author.

Hayter, Thomas (1755), 'An Essay on the Liberty of the Press, Chiefly as it Respects Personal Slander', reprinted in (1974), *Freedom of the Press and the Literary Property Debate: Six Tracts, 1755–1770*, New York: Garland Press.

Heald, Paul J. and Suzanna Sherry (2000), 'Implied Limits on the Legislative Power: The Intellectual Property Clause as an Absolute Constraint on Congress', *University of Illinois Law Review*, 1119–97.

Hesse, Carla (1990), 'Enlightenment Epistemology and the Laws of Authorship', *Representations*, **30,** 109–37.

Hesse, Carla (1991), *Publishing and Cultural Politics in Revolutionary Paris 1789–1810*, Berkeley, CA: University of California Press.

Hyde, Lewis (2005), 'Frames from the Framers: How America's Revolutionaries Imagined Intellectual Property', Berkman Center for Internet and Society, Research Paper No. 2005–08, 1–34.

Jacob, Giles (1797), *The Law Dictionary*, London: Andrew Strahan.

Jobard, J.-B. (1851), *Organon de la propriété intellectuelle*, Paris: Mathias.

Kent, James (1826), *Commentaries on American Law*, Part V, lecture XXXVI, New York: O. Halsted.

Laboulaye, E. (1858), *Etudes sur la propriété littéraire en France et en Angleterre*, Paris: Durand.

Laboulaye, Edouard (1859), *La propriété littéraire au XVIIIème siècle*, Paris: Hachette.

Lange, David (1981), 'Recognizing the Public Domain', *Law and Contemporary Problems*, **44,** 147–78.

Lessig, Lawrence (2003), 'Dunwody Distinguished Lecture in Law: The Creative Commons', *Florida Law Review*, **55,** 763–77.

Lessig, Lawrence (2004), *Free Culture: How Big Media Uses Technology and the Law to Lock Down Culture and Control Creativity*, New York: Penguin Press.

Lessig, Lawrence (2001), *The Future of Ideas: The Fate of the Commons in a Connected World*, New York: Random House.

Litman, Jessica (1990), 'The Public Domain', *Emory Law Journal*, **39,** 965–1023.

Locke, John (1694), *Memorandum against the Renewal of the Licensing Act*, reprinted in E.S. de Beer (ed.) (1979), *The Correspondence of John Locke*, Oxford: Clarendon Press.

Macaulay, Catherine (1774), *A Modest Plea for the Property of Copyright*, Bath: R. Cruttwell.

MacLaurin, J. (1767), 'Considerations on the Nature and Origin of Literary Property', reprinted in (1974), *Freedom of the Press and the Literary Property Debate: Six Tracts, 1755–1770*, New York: Garland Press.

Madison, James, *Federalist Paper No. 43*, reprinted in Edward Earl Mead (ed.) (1941), *The Federalist*, New York: The Modern Library.

Moscati, Laura (2003), 'Un "Memorandum" di John Locke tra *Censorship* et *Copyright*', *Rivista di storia del diritto italiano*, **LXXVI,** 69–89.

Nachbar, Tom (2002), 'Constructing Copyright's Mythology', *Green Bag 2d.*, **6**, 37–46.

Negativeland (2003), 'The Public Domain: Two Relationships to a Cultural Public Domain', *Law and Contemporary Problems*, **66**, 239–62.

Ochoa, Tyler T. (2002), 'Origins and Meanings of the Public Domain', *University of Dayton Law Review*, **28**, 215–67.

Oliar, Dotan (2006), 'The Immediate Origins of the Intellectual Property Clause' (on file with the author).

Patterson, Lyman Ray (1968), *Copyright in Historical Perspective*, Nashville, TN: Vanderbilt University Press.

Patterson, L. Ray (1987), 'Free Speech, Copyright, and Fair Use', *Vanderbilt Law Review*, **40**, 1–66.

Patterson, L. Ray, and Craig Joyce (2003), 'Copyright in 1791: An Essay Concerning the Founders' View of the Copyright Power Granted to Congress in Article 1, Section 8 Clause 8 of the Constitution', *Emory Law Journal*, **52**, 909–52.

Pfister, Laurent (2005), 'La propriété littéraire est-elle une propriété? Controverses sur la nature du droit d'auteur au XIXe siècle', *Revue Internationale de droit de l'auteur*, **205**, 117–209.

Prager, Frank (1944), 'A History of Intellectual Property from 1545 to 1789', *Journal of the Patents and Trademark Office Society*, **26**, 711–60.

Prudhon, Joseph (1862), 'Les Majorats Littéraires: Examen d'un projet de loi ayant pur but de créer, au profit des auteurs, inventeurs et artistes, un monopole perpétuel', in Jan Baetens (ed.) (2001), *Le Combat du droit d'auteur*, Paris: Les Impressions Nouvelles.

Rae, David (1773), *Information for Mess. John Hinton, and Attorney; Against Mess. Alexander Donaldson, and Others*, reprinted in (1975), *The Literary Property Debate: Six Tracts: 1764–1774*, New York: Garland Press.

Ralph, James (1758), 'The Case of the Authors by Profession or Trade, Stated with Regard to Booksellers, the Stage, and the Public', reprinted in (1974), *Freedom of the Press and the Literary Property Debate: Six Tracts, 1755–1770*, New York: Garland Press.

Reese, R. Anthony (2005), 'The Story of Folsom v Marsh: Distinguishing Between Infringing and Legitimate Uses', in Jane C. Ginsburg and Rochelle Cooper Dreyfuss (eds.), *Intellectual Property Stories*, New York: Foundation Press.

Renouard, Augustin-Charles (1838), *Traité des droits des auteurs*, Paris: J. Renouard et cie.

Rideau, Frédéric (2004), *La Formation du droit de la propriété littéraire en France et en Grand-Bretagne: Une convergence oubliée*, Aix-en-Provence: Presses universitaires d'Aix-Marseille-PUAM.

Rose, Mark (1993), *Authors and Owners: The Invention of Copyright*, Cambridge, MA: Harvard University Press.

Rose, Mark (1994), 'The Author as Proprietor: Donaldson v Becket and the Genealogy of Modern Authorship', in Brad Sherman and Alain Strowel (eds), *Of Authors and Origins: Essays on Copyright Law*, Oxford and New York: Clarendon Press and Oxford University Press.

Rose, Mark (2003), 'Nine-Tenths of the Law: The English Copyright Debates and the Rhetoric of the Public Domain', *Law and Contemporary Problems*, **66**, 75–87.

Samuelson, Pamela (2003), 'Mapping the Digital Public Domain: Threats and Opportunities', *Law and Contemporary Problems*, **66**, 147–71.

Schwartz, Paul M. and William Michael Treanor (2003), 'Eldred and Lochner: Copyright Term Extension and Intellectual Property as Constitutional Property', *Yale Law Journal*, **112**, 2331–414.

Seville, Catherine (2003), 'Peter Pan's Rights: "To Die Will be an Awfully Big Adventure"', *Journal of the Copyright Society*, **51**, 1–77.

Sherman, Brad and Lionel Bently (1999), *The Making of Modern Intellectual Property Law: The British Experience, 1760–1911*, Cambridge and New York: Cambridge University Press.

Solberg, Thorvald (ed.) (1963), *Copyright Enactments of the United States: 1783–1906*, Copyright Office Bulletin No. 3, 2nd edn, rev., Washington: Copyright Office, Library of Congress.

Story, William Wetmore (ed.) (1852), *The Miscellaneous Writings of Joseph Story: Associate Justice of the Supreme Court of the United States and Dane Professor of Law at Harvard University*, Boston: C.C. Little and J. Brown.

Strauss, William S. (1963), Study No. 29, 'Protection of Unpublished Works', in (1963), *Studies on Copyright, Arthur Fisher Memorial Edition*, South Hackensack, NJ: F.B. Rothman.

Walterscheid, Edward C. (1994), 'To Promote the Progress of Science and Useful Arts: The Background and Origin of the Intellectual Property Clause of the United States Constitution', *Journal of Intellectual Property Law*, **2**, 1–56.

Walterscheid, Edward C. (1995), 'Inherent or Created Rights: Early Views on the Intellectual Property Clause', *Hamline Law Review*, **19**, 81–105.

Walterscheid, Edward C. (2002), *The Nature of the Intellectual Property Clause: A Study in Historical Perspective*, Buffalo, NY: W.S. Hein.

Worms, Fernand (1878), *Etude de la propriété littéraire*, 2 vols, Paris: A. Lemerre.

Yen, Alfred C. (1990), 'Restoring the Natural Law: Copyright as Labor and Possession', *Ohio State Law Journal*, **51**, 517–59.

Statutory Law

1790 Act, §§ 3 and 4.

1802 Act, § 1.

17 USC § 102(a).

17 USC § 106(1)(3); Copyright, Designs and Patents Act, 1988 c. 48 § 16(a)(b) (Eng.).

An Act for the Encouragement of Learning by Vesting the Copies of Printed Books in the Authors or Purchasers of such Copies, 8 Anne c. 19 (1710).

An Act for the Encouragement of the Arts of designing, engraving and etching historical and other Prints, by vesting the Properties thereof in the Inventors and Engravers, during the Time therein mentioned, 8 Geo. II c. 13 (1735).

An Act to amend the Laws relating to Dramatic Literary Property, 3 Will. IV c.15 (1833).

Code de la propriété intellectuelle, art. L-121-1, cl. 2.

Decree of 1792, arts 4–6, *Bulletin annoté des lois, décrets et ordonnances*, p. 273 (1834).

Law of July 19–24, 1793.

Pub. L. No. 92–140, 85 Stat. 391 (1971).

Pub. L. No. 93–573, 88 Stat. 1873 (1974).

UK CDPA 1988 c. 48 § 301.

US Const., art. I, § 8 cl. 8.

Cases and Reports

Bach v Longman, [1777] 2 Cowp. 263, 98 Eng. Rep. 1274.

Beckford v Hood, [1798] KB 7 TR 620, 101 Eng. Rep. 1164.

Blackwell v Harper, [1740] Ch 2 Atk 93, 26 Eng. Rep. 458.

Brooks v Cock, [1835] 3 Ad. & El. 138, 140–1, 111 Eng. Rep. 365.

Capitol Records v Mercury Records Corp., 221 F2d 657 (2d Cir. 1955).

Capitol Records v Naxos of America, 4 NY3d 540 (2005).

Carnan v Bowles, [1786] 2 Bro CC 80, 28 Eng. Rep. 45, 29 Eng. Rep. 1168, 1 Cox 283.

Cary v Faden, [1799] 5 Ves 24, 31 Eng. Rep. 453.

Cary v Longman and Rees, [1801] 1 East 358, 102 Eng. Rep. 138.

Clayton v Stone, 5 F. Cas. 999 (CC SDNY 1829).

Clementi v Golding, [1809] 2 Camp. 25, 170 Eng. Rep. 1069.

Clementi v Goulding, [1809] 11 East 244, 103 Eng. Rep. 998.

Coleman v Wathen [1793] KB, 5 TR 245, 101 Eng. Rep. 137.

Company of Stationers v Seymour [1677], 1 Mod 256.

Donaldson v Beckett, 4 Burr. 2408, 98 Eng. Rep. 257, 2 Bro. 129, 1 Eng. Rep. pp. 837, 17 Parl. Hist. Eng. p. 953.

Duke of Queensberry v Shebbeare, [1758] 2 Eden 329, 28 Eng. Rep. 924.

Estate of Martin Luther King v CBS, 194 F.3d 1211 (11th Cir. 1999).

Estate of Hemingway v Random House, 23 NY2d 341, 349 (1968).

Folsom v Marsh, 9 F. Cas. 342 (CC D.Mass. 1841).

Gee v Pritchard and Anderson, [1818] 2 Swan 402, 36 Eng. Rep. 670.

Gibbons v Ogden, 22 US 1 (1824).

Gyles v Wilcox, [1740] Ch 2 Atk. 141, 26 Eng. Rep. 489.

Harrison v Hogg, [1827] 2 Ves. Jun. 323, 30 Eng. Rep. 654 (1794).

Judgment of January 20, 1818, Cass. crim., 52 J. Pal. 5.

Judgment of March 1, 1834, Cass. crim., [1834] Dev. & Car. 1.65.

Judgment of November 26, 1828, Cour royale, Paris, [1828] 9 Dev. & Car. 2.159.

Judgment of October 23, 1806, Cass. crim., [1808] 2 Recueil Général des Lois et des Arrêts, [Dev. & Car.] 1.299.

Livingston v van Ingen, 9 Johns 507 (NY Sup. 1812).

Macklin v Richardson, [1770] Amb 694, 27 Eng. Rep. 451.

Millar v Taylor, 4 Burr. pp. 2303; 98 Eng. Rep. 201.

Morris v Harris, Unreported (Ch 1814), cited in Richard Godson (1823), *Practical Treatise on the Law of Patents for Inventions and of Copyright*, London: Saunders and Benning.

Morris v Kelly, [1820] Ch 1 Jac. & W. 481, 37 Eng. Rep. 451.

Murray v Elliston, [1822] KB 5 B. & Ald. 657, 106 Eng. Rep. 1331.

Newton v Cowie, 4 Bing. 234, 130 Eng. Rep. 759.

Opinion of Judge Hopkinson, Appendix II to *Wheaton v Peters*, 1834 US LEXIS 619 p. ***51.

Perceval v Phipps, [1813] 2 Ves. & Beam. 19, 24, 35 Eng. Rep. 225.

Pierre Hugo v Editions Plon, Paris Court of Appeals, decision of March 31, 2004, 202 RIDA (October 2004). Reversed: 04-15.543 Decision 125 of 30 January 2007, Cour de Cassation – First civil chamber, http://www.courdecassation.fr/jurisprudence_publications_documentation_2/actualite_jurisprudence_21/premiere_chambre_civile_568/arrets_569/br_arret_9850.html.

Pope v Curl, [1741] 2 Atk. 342, 26 Eng. Rep. 608.

Report of François Hell, *Archives parlementaires*, September 28, 1791.

Report of Lakanal, *Archives parlementaires*, July 19, 1793 p. 186.

Report of Le Chapelier, *Archives parlementaires (Assemblée nationale)* January 13, 1791.

Southey v Sherwood, [1817] 2 Mer. 435, 173 Eng. Rep. 1006.

Stowe v Thomas, 23 F. Cas. 201 (CCED Pa. 1853).

Thompson v Stanhope, [1774] Ambler R. 737, 740, 27 Eng. Rep. 476.

Thompson v Symonds, [1792] 5 Term. R. 41, 45, 101 Eng. Rep. 23.

Wheaton v Peters, 33 US 591 (1834).

7 Draw me a public domain

Valérie-Laure Benabou[1] and Séverine Dusollier[2]

'Draw me a sheep!'

. . .

'This is only his box. The sheep you asked for is inside.'
(Antoine de Saint Exupéry, *The Little Prince*)

Introduction

Like the sheep of the Little Prince, the public domain is presumed to be existing but is actually very hard to draw precisely. It is mostly viewed as a mere
box into which the objects once protected by intellectual property, or never
liable to its protection, are deemed to be 'falling'. But no one knows what
happens next, after the fall: what becomes of the sheep once it is inside the box?

So far, 'European Intellectual Property' (if one can consider there is a
common body of intellectual property in Europe, whether in legislation or in
legal scholarship), has had little impact on issues related to the public domain.[3]
The question has never been evoked as such during the harmonisation of the
field; case-law is lacking; doctrine is only just emerging.[4] In contrast, in the
United States, the public domain has been a favourite theme for scholarly
research and writing in recent years: many have denounced the 'enclosure of
public domain'[5] or have pleaded for its defence against undue appropriation.[6]

---

[1]   Professor at the University of Versailles – Saint-Quentin-en-Yvelines, France.

[2]   Professor at the University of Namur, Belgium.

[3]   The hypothesis of a positive status for the public domain that is developed in
the present contribution will be specifically limited to its impact on copyright rules for
mere material reasons even though the proposal sets out to analyse its relationship also
with other intellectual property rights.

[4]   See, for instance, B. Hugenholtz and L. Guibault (eds), *The Public Domain of
Information*, The Hague: Kluwer Law International, 2006 (including many contributions from US scholars); S. Choisy, *Le domaine public en droit d'auteur*, Paris: Litec,
2002.

[5]   As it was first phrased by one of the seminal scholarship works about the
shrinking public domain, see J. Boyle, 'The Second Enclosure Movement and the
Construction of the Public Domain', 66 *Law and Contemporary Problems* 33 (2003).

[6]   D. Lange, 'Recognizing the Public Domain', 44 *Law and Contemporary
Problems* 147 (1981); J. Litman, 'The Public Domain', *39 Emory Law Journal* 965
(1990); J. Boyle, 'A Politics of Intellectual Property: Environmentalism for the Net?',

Central to most of these writings is the importance that the public domain has in a democratic society where cultural diversity and freedoms to create, to innovate and to take part in the cultural environment are considered as fundamental objectives. Current reflections about the public domain recall that a strong and vivid public domain is a pivotal element of the common heritage of humanity and that, consequently, it should be made available to all and be preserved from undue privatisation and encroachment.

Such thinking relies on the idea, too often forgotten, that the public domain was the beginning of intellectual property, and of copyright. For copyright is forged from pieces of land taken from the public domain. Public domain, the absence of any restrictions on the products of the mind and of creation, or freedom to copy, is the rule while intellectual property rights are the exception. Yet, the territory of intellectual property has constantly grown and expanded over the realm of the public domain to such an extent the public domain increasingly looks like the exception.[7] The extension of the duration of copyright, the creation of new objects of rights and the broad interpretation of the criteria for protection were milestones in that expansion. The intellectual commons, as some have started to dub the contents of the public domain, are increasingly at risk of being commodified, of falling into the private domain of intellectual property rights.

Current scholarship on the public domain, despite its wishful thinking about the need to preserve the public domain, does not endeavour to draw it precisely, nor the box that should be containing it.

The objective of the present contribution is to try to sketch the first lines of a proper regime for the public domain, to build the rules through which it could resist encroachment by private property. We will not specifically address this phenomenon of constant extension of the principles of intellectual property: this point has already been made obvious by various publications.

---

47 *Duke Law Journal* 87 *(1997)*; Y. Benkler, 'Free as the Air to Common Use: First Amendment Constraints on Enclosure of the Public Domain', 74 *New York University Law Review* 354 *(1999)*; R. Coombe, 'Fear, Hope, and Longing for the Future of Authorship and a Revitalized Public Domain in Global Regimes of Intellectual Property', 52 *DePaul Law Review* 1171 (2002–3), p. 1173; R. Merges, 'A New Dynamism in the Public Domain', 71 *University of Chicago Law Review* 183 (2004); N. Ochoa, 'Origins and Meanings of the Public Domain', 28 *Dayton Law Review* 215 (2002); as well as all the contributions at the Public Domain conference, held in Duke University in 2002 and published in 66 *Law and Contemporary Problems* (2003); E. Samuels, 'The Public Domain in Copyright Law', 15 *Journal of the Copyright Society* 137 (1993); K. Aoki, 'Authors, Inventors and Trademarks Owners: Private Intellectual Property and the Public Domain', 16 *Columbia – VLA Journal of Law and the Arts* 1 (1993).
   7   Honoré de Balzac, *La peau de chagrin.*

Neither will we analyse the 'composition' of the public domain, save for delineating the elements which a new regime of public domain should encompass.

The difficulty is that, in most countries, the public domain receives no positive definition, either in its contents, or in its regime. The growth of intellectual property rights has led to the paradoxical situation where the principle has become an obscure notion and the exception to the rule of reference.

The starting point of this chapter is the impression that current depictions of the public domain tend to blur the real nature thereof and weaken attempts to preserve it. If many efforts to design the boundaries of public domain seem to have been unsuccessful, at least to draw a single image of 'the' public domain, this may be due to the erroneous idea that there are things which, by their very nature, cannot be owned. This romantic view of the public domain, as an open field[8] where everyone can go, is appropriate neither to describe the reality of the actual trend of privatisation of the commons, nor to struggle against it. There is no 'natural state' of the public domain; its composition is fundamentally a matter of political choice. Only an attribution of a specific regime to things which would otherwise be subjected to privatisation on economic grounds can turn the situation round. This political position is certainly a function of the economic and cultural interests of each State and therefore highly variable in time and space.

The imprecision of the public domain may be the cornerstone of its vulnerability, as is the metaphor used to depict it: as if by its very name, the public domain were a fortress immunised from any commodification and privatisation. We will demonstrate in the first section of this chapter that the conception of the public domain is fallacious in the sense that the actual regime of the public domain is one that operates to facilitate its ongoing encroachment. A first and necessary step in the construction of a solid regime for the public domain would thus be to deconstruct the way we conceive and make it operate in copyright laws.

Based on this deconstruction, we will, in Section 2, adopt a new definition for the public domain by trying to focus on the function of a desirable public domain and to figure out what 'belonging' to the public domain actually means, once an element is considered to be part of it. To achieve this goal, we will suggest that the public domain has not only to be looked at through the lens of intellectual property, as a receptacle of a formerly protected work or as a dead zone of protection, but should be considered on its own, as a positive notion which needs to be defined and protected. On these grounds, a specific regime for the public domain could be set up.

An adequate regime for preserving the public domain and the free availability of its elements should answer the following questions: How can this

---

8   'Les idées sont de libre parcours', as Desbois used to say.

freedom be maintained and the shrinking of the public domain be stopped? Has the public domain to be made legally 'immune' from appropriation, and if so, how? How should the 'non-appropriation' rule be sustained by a legal regime protecting the public domain? How should the effective accessibility of the public domain be guaranteed?

1.   The vacuity of the public domain regime

1.1.   The current definition of the public domain
At the beginning of the copyright era, the ineluctable fall of works into the public domain, once a (short) period of time had lapsed, was considered as being a key counterpart of the property grant, as being one side of the trade-off embedded in copyright. The limitation of intellectual property in time was indeed to constitute a public domain where contents could be used freely by members of the public. It aimed at achieving a balance between proprietary protection and public availability, thus creating two separate domains, constituted by the passing of time. The erection of private property was only a limited intrusion into the public domain that should remain the norm. J. Ginsburg has shown that this predominance of the public domain was present in the early regimes of both literary and artistic property both in France and in the United States.[9] In 1774, in *Donaldson v Beckett*,[10] one of the seminal cases in copyright in the UK, the House of Lords voted in favour of the principle that copyright should be limited in time, insisting on the public interest in preserving the public domain as the rule. The need to protect the public domain, as constructed through the rule of limited-time protection, was strong enough to deny any attempt at extended commodification.

Despite this strong emphasis on the public domain, no rule appeared in the early copyright laws to make this public domain effective, save for the limited duration of the right.

First the public domain was not inscribed as such in the copyright regime. Even today, the terms 'public domain' rarely appear in the provisions of the law and no specific rules are attached to the public domain or to its elements. Due to a lack of legal definition, the contents of the public domain are diversely determined. The public domain in copyright is generally defined as the realm of elements that are not or no longer protected, whether because they are not liable to protection by copyright (as with ideas, or works that are not

---

    9   J. Ginsburg, 'A Tale of two Copyrights: Literary Property in Revolutionary France and America', in B. Sherman and A. Strowel (eds), *Authors and Origins – Essays on Copyright Law*, Oxford: Clarendon Press, 1995, p. 145.
    10   1 Eng. Rep. 837 (HL 1774).

original) or because the protection of copyright has expired (works whose author has died more than 70 years ago). Some even restrict that definition to the latter category, to works that were protected but, due to the lapse of time and expiration of the term of copyright protection, have 'fallen' into the public domain.[11] Nevertheless, many agree that the public domain comprises all intellectual assets that are not protected by copyright, thereby opting for a definition that is the inverse of the scope of copyright protection.

On the other hand, the terminology used, that of the 'public domain', is a powerful one that still seems to convey the early conception of a realm of elements protected by and isolated from private property. The public domain is a very abstract idea shaped in a very concrete territorial metaphor. The 'domain' evokes a particular place, clearly bordered, almost tangible. In most writings on the public domain, the metaphor is almost taken literally: the public domain is that territory where no intellectual property rights apply, a domain where anybody is free to enter and to help herself. As to the attribute of 'public', it sounds as if, by nature, the elements concerned were a public property, collectively enjoyed, as if the publicity of the domain was, in itself, sufficient to ensure public access by anybody thereto. The terminology employed is one of the main causes of the somewhat naïve rhetoric that has evolved around the notion of the public domain.

1.2.   The limits of such definition and its defensiveness against commodification

This metaphor, in which all discourse on the public domain is rooted, is limited and fallacious on several counts.

First, opposing the public domain to the private domain of copyright gives only a partial view of what is not touched upon by the monopoly granted by copyright and of the freedoms enjoyed by the public. Such a traditional view of the public domain does not include copyright exceptions or any use of a protected work that is free. Only elements that are not protected by copyright, whatever the circumstances of their use, are deemed to belong to the public domain. This limitation of the public domain to unprotected elements portrays the public domain as a place separated from intellectual property rights. The private domain of intellectual property, characterised by exclusive rights, monopolies, and authorisation/prohibition schemes, appears to be fenced off from the public domain, as if both domains were contiguous, though separate, as if the domain of commoditised and privatised assets faces the domain of freely available resources, with no connection or relation between them. On one side, there would be the perimeter of intellectual property protections,

---

[11]   Choisy, *op. cit.*

where copyright's exclusive rights would be the sole area for commodification process and action, whereas, on the other and opposite side, the public domain, where unprotected elements or the commons would lie, would be the only place where artistic creation could take place without infringing the right held by an author. As a consequence, critics of the expansion of copyright are easily brushed aside by the proponents of a strong copyright regime using the following argument: commodification by nature occurs in the field of copyright, leaving the public domain as such untouched.

Another consequence of a reverse-copyright definition of the public domain is equally worrisome. The touchstone of the definition being the lack of copyright protection, it does not enable the public domain to be viewed as a collection of elements to which a rule of inappropriability would apply. The negativity of the definition does not help to give status to the public domain, but only reinforces its perception as an empty territory where no protection applies, either through an intellectual property right, or by a rule of positive protection against private reservation. One can say that the public domain is a commons, in the sense of the *Code Civil*, where commons are defined as 'goods that are owned by nobody and whose use is common to all'. Having said that, that does not ensure that anybody could easily access and enjoy any element of the public domain, nor that such an element would be buttressed against any reservation, by contract or by a technological measure. Yet, the terminology of the public domain seems to indicate the public nature of the resources contained therein. The use of the word 'domain' itself points to a separate and enclosed place and its qualification as 'public' tends to label the public domain as naturally and inherently immune from private reservation, which would contradict the negative definition of the term. The ensuing binary rhetoric of 'the intellectual property v the public domain', clothed with the metaphor and terminology of the public domain, hides the real epistemology of the public domain where private and public are much more intertwined.

Indeed, as it is conceived in copyright law, the public domain does not at all create a separate site not liable to any privatisation, although the terminology of the public domain inclines to signify it. Only a few elements of the so-called public domain are completely safe from falling into the realm of intellectual property.[12] Contrary to what the public/private logic suggests, the

---

[12]   See the elements that are explicitly excluded from the ambit of copyright protection, for instance official texts of a legislative, administrative and legal nature (save for the Crown's Copyright in the UK), as enabled by article 2(4) of the Berne Convention. News of the day can equally be deemed to be a legal exclusion from copyright protection, or to be an application of the idea/dichotomy expression. Yet, even in this case, commodification is not rendered impossible through for example database *sui generis* protection.

public domain often serves private property[13] and this interdependent relationship is rooted in the history and economics of intellectual property.[14] Actually, commodification is equally at work when granting exclusive rights on some intellectual creations *and* when leaving other intellectual productions in what is called the public domain. This can be better explained by considering some different elements of what is called the public domain.

For example, the idea/expression dichotomy works as a first exclusionary principle. Only the expression is protected by the copyright; the idea is said to be free for everybody to use. The notion of 'ideas' as unprotected in copyright also covers facts, principles, methods, news of the day, mere information or concepts, as noted by article 9(2) of the TRIPS Agreement and by the article 2(8) of the Berne Convention. As a second step, copyright law only welcomes within its ambit works that are considered original, even though that notion is rather loosely defined. It is rare that the law defines the notion of originality, save for the definition ('the author's own intellectual creation') that has been applied, in the European Union, to software, databases and photographs.

Rather than delineating a public domain as a field free from reservation, the joint operation of the two rules (idea/expression dichotomy and criteria of originality) works by leaving ideas, not already expressed in an original form, in a fallow land where they are only waiting for human authorship to save them from an 'un-property' destiny.

Besides, originality as a criterion for propelling a creation into copyright protection conveys a predominant idea in intellectual property, i.e. the principle that any creation due to human agency should be entitled to private protection. The threshold imposed by originality is indeed very low as it suffices that the work bears, depending on the country of protection, either the imprint of the personality of the author or some skill and labour. The trigger for protection is thus highly subjective while being very minimal given the construction of originality as any intellectual involvement, any stamp of personality imposed upon nature.[15]

The preceding observations are in line with the traditional Lockean justification of property right, according to which the labour of a human being grants him property in the product of his labour, any resource being free for every man to appropriate through his labour. Rooting the justification for copyright in the theory of Locke, as the early laws on copyright did, shapes the public domain

---

13   A. Chander and M. Sunder, 'The Romance of the Public Domain', 22 *California Law Review* (2004), p. 1352.
14   C. Rose, 'Romans, Roads, and Romantic Creators: Traditions of Public Property in the Information Age', 66 *Law and Contemporary Problems* 89 (2003), at 96.
15   B. Edelman, 'The Law's Eye: Nature and Copyright', in B. Sherman and A. Strowel, *Of Authors and Origins*, Oxford: Clarendon Press, 1995, p. 83.

as a 'private-property-to-be'. It is then all the more difficult to describe the public domain as containing, *per se*, the elements enabling to limit the commodification by intellectual property. No positive regime of the public domain can be obtained from the elements defining the ambit of copyright.

The very structure of copyright law sustains this ambiguity and explains, for example, the difficulty of granting a right over traditional knowledge and/or defending it from undue appropriation. Traditional knowledge and folklore (except where traditional knowledge is subject to customary laws granting other forms of ownership and rights) have some difficulty in enjoying copyright (and patent) protection, since they are generally not new but ancient, not individual but collective, not vested with authorship but largely mixed with nature and tradition. Public domain has always been the repository of traditional knowledge and folklore in classical views of intellectual property, which facilitates its exploitation and appropriation by industrial entities.[16] It shows that the (now global) regime of intellectual property denies exclusivity to other forms of intellectual production, knowledge or cultural expression, and uses the empty concept of public domain as a lever to consolidate the private rights of others.[17]

Another example can be found in the duration of copyright. A key part of the public domain encompasses works which used to be protected but have fallen into the public domain after the lapse of copyright duration. Whereas the passage of time was considered in the early enactment of copyright laws as a public interest rule ascertaining the rapid constitution of a public domain, the term of copyright has been constantly and regularly lengthened without any due consideration of the ensuing status of the public domain.[18] Many reasons have been advanced to justify this repeated extension,[19] but strikingly, the

---

[16]   T. Cottier and M. Panizzon, 'Legal Perspectives on Traditional Knowledge: The Case for Intellectual Property Protection', in K. Maskus and J. Reichman (eds), *International Public Goods and the Transfer of Technology under a Globalized Intellectual Property Regime*, Cambridge: Cambridge University Press, 2005, p. 570; R. Coombe, 'Protecting Cultural Industries to Promote Cultural Diversity: Dilemmas for International Policymaking Posed by the Recognition of Traditional Knowledge', in Maskus and Reichman, *op. cit.,* pp. 602–4; A. Chander and M. Sunder, op. cit., at p. 1331; Carlos M. Correa, *Traditional Knowledge and Intellectual Property – Issues and Options Surrounding the Protection of Traditional Knowledge*, Geneva: Quaker United Nations Office, 2001.

[17]   Chander and Sunder, *op. cit.*, at p. 1355.

[18]   The EU Directive on copyright duration, adopted in 1993, extended the term of the right to 70 years after the death of the author without much consideration of its effect on the public domain. To keep pace with the European extension, the United States has similarly lengthened the duration of copyright by the Copyright Extension Act of 1998 (known also as the Sony Bono Act).

[19]   Some are related to the protection of the creators and their heirs and their participation in the benefits of exploiting the works, but most of the time, the demand

adverse effect on the limitation of the public domain has rarely been evoked and weighed in the balance. When the US Copyright Term Extension Act was challenged before the Supreme Court on the basis of its unconstitutionality, the latter upheld the law with only a meagre reference to the effects of extended duration on the public domain.[20] Instead of adhering to a view of the term of protection that would have drawn a clear line between protected works and the public domain as in *Donaldson v Beckett*, the Supreme Court admitted that the duration of copyright could be regularly extended as long as the Congress could proffer a rational basis for that extension.[21] That implies that the public domain, once constituted by the rule of the term of protection, is not immutable, that it does not take its definitive form once for all. The passing of time does not hence form a solid buttress against attempts at an extended commodification.

Another example of the vacuity of public domain status relates to the exclusion of works from copyright protection on the grounds of public policy concern, for example the exclusion of official texts where the general interest of making sources of law available to citizens is more important than the copyright of their authors. It would be logical that such elements are in the public domain and should resist appropriation. However, the seemingly positive nature of that public domain is thwarted by the possible reservation, through a database right, of a collection of such official texts. Here the human intervention sufficient to remove data and information from the public domain should only be a financial or time investment devoted to obtaining and verification of the contents of the database, as it results from the criteria chosen by the Database Directive.[22]

Public domain emptiness can also be illustrated by the movement of open access in software or in other fields of creation for there is actually no scope for a rightholder to relinquish a work into the public domain by a voluntary

---

for extended protection comes from industry, hence from the market, which would like to enjoy an unlimited monopoly over some works.

[20] 537 US 186 (2003).

[21] Economic needs are considered to be a particularly strong motive for extending protection. Delivering the opinion of the court, Justice Ginsburg notes that the task of defining the scope of the limited copyright monopoly assigned to Congress aims to give the public appropriate access to the works, hence to constitute an effective public domain of literary and artistic works. However, in the notion of appropriate access to copyrighted works, Justice Ginsburg insists upon the need for an appropriate protection of the work and of the copyright holders, namely referring to statements made by members of Congress that equate the duration to the 'necessary life of copyright', i.e. the term during which works will be commercially exploited (see Opinion of the Court, footnote 14).

[22] Database Directive 96/9, 11 March 1996, OJ L77/20, 27 March 1996.

act. Unlike other intellectual property rights such as patent or trademark,[23] the lack of exploitation of copyright has no consequences for the duration of protection. In the 'droit d'auteur' model, ownership is triggered by the mere act of creation. One cannot refuse the 'title' once it has been granted, the 'authorship' being consubstantial with the phenomenon of creation. There are no registration formalities, fees, costs, conflict with public policy which could possibly deter the author from being protected by a monopoly. Had he wanted not to be protected as such, the creator has no way of escaping from the legal pattern. In most of legislations, it is not clear whether the rightholder can renounce the full exercise of its exclusive rights. Even if one admits this relinquishment, the work now abandoned to the public domain is not protected by this new status against any attempt at appropriation.

The open access licences are in someways an expression of a voluntary or 'agreed' public domain.[24] Though the decision over making the work available still belongs to the author, the latter cannot reverse his choice once he has disclosed the work for an open use. Instead of enduring the loss of control after the term of copyright protection, the author decides to 'relinquish' the legal exclusivity he has received from the law, to offer common access to and/or use of his work. One can see in such licences nothing but an exotic form of assignment of copyright, or in the style of the expression 'copyleft' – a reverse notion of copyright. But because of the *de facto* irrevocability of consent in most licences, it is also possible to consider this phenomenon as a variant of the public domain, the start of which being triggered by the rightholder's will.[25]

However, in order to protect the work or its derivations from being commodified, the open access schemes rely on licences based on proprietary copyright and impose free access to the work and to its modifications. Such recourse to property rights and contractual tricks is a weak answer to the lack of positive status of public domain elements, since it does not confer the legal certainty that the public domain status would do and, by using the very tool that they are trying to fight, constitutes an ambiguous response to copyright expansion.[26]

To conclude on that point, the depiction of the public domain as an open territory, free for others to take, devoid of any idea of property or undue privatisation, as a global commons, beneficial to the informational, cultural or technological needs of the world, is to some extent a naïve perspective. There is as

---

[23]   For revocation of a trademark see e.g., article L714–5 French Intellectual Property Code.

[24]   On the existence of an agreed upon public domain, see M. Clément-Fontaine, 'Les oeuvres libres', thesis, Montpellier, December 2006, not published, p. 420ff.

[25]   Clément-Fontaine, *op. cit.*, p. 494.

[26]   S. Dusollier, ' The Master's Tools v the Master's House: Creative Commons v Copyright', 29 *Columbia Journal of Law & Arts* 271 (2006).

much of a commoditised view of intellectual production in the notion of the public domain as in the notion of the private domain of intellectual property. The evolution of the intellectual property regime shows that the public domain is not so much an open territory from which some limited lands are grabbed to form islands of exclusivity as a way of allocating rights of access to intellectual resources, whether in the form of exclusive property or in the form of non-exclusive liberties. A negative definition of the public domain considered as a default theory and not as an area reserved to collective use is thus not very helpful to preserve the public domain from an extension of the scope or duration of copyright or other property rights.

2. A positive regime for the public domain

Most copyright laws are intrinsically unsuitable for preventing the elements of the public domain from being commodified either by those who are being granted an intellectual property monopoly or by the mere owners of the unique source of the element in a position to refuse access to others (owner of the material who can thus apply technical protection measures). The results are therefore the possibility that some may confiscate the common and shared use of the intellectual production, subject to a new or ongoing protection.

Regarding the lack of answers given by copyright legislation, in an attempt to suggest some of the principles that could contribute to building the foundations of a positive public domain, one must explore the possible solutions not only within the intellectual property system but also and, maybe to a greater extent, outside it.

This positive regime for the public domain should first determine the definition and contents of the public domain to be so protected (Section 2.1), the objective of protection pursued by such a regime (Section 2.2) before going into the detail of what such a regime might look like (Section 2.3).

2.1. A new definition: what public domain?

We have already said that the current definition of the public domain focusing on a lack of copyright protection was rather limited. The public domain is generally defined as encompassing elements that are not or no longer protected by copyright, hereby opting for a structural notion of the public domain.

Conversely, one can relate to the definition to the very function pursued by the notion of the public domain in the copyright regime. In our view, the public domain is the principle to which the private right of copyright derogates. Any limitation of copyright, whether in its existence or its exercise, should then be a return to the principle of the public domain.

From that perspective, one can say that the freedom to copy entailed by the public domain occurs at different places within the copyright regime, not only outside its scope of protection but also within the rules of protection itself, namely in the gaps between the exclusive rights and the exceptions. Besides, if the ultimate objective of the public domain is to foster the availability of works, it does not matter that this availability is achieved through a rule of no protection or through a limitation of the exercise of the right.

This has been aptly described by J. Cohen[27] who proposes to switch, for strategic reasons, to another definition of the public domain that would no longer be centred around the lack of protection but would include all freely available resources for intellectual production, such as fair use or other copyright limitations and exceptions. J. Cohen suggests that the commons should be seen as a set of cultural and creative practices that would form a better basis on which to build a strong theory and protective regime of the public domain and argues for a new metaphor, that of the 'cultural landscape'.[28] If the function of the public domain is to enable productive practices, whether cultural, creative, or purely cognitive or consumptive, and to exempt them from the exercise of an exclusive proprietary right, it should include not only elements in which such rights are non-existent, but also resources or practices that are left untouched by the exercise of those rights.

The fact that the work is still somewhat protected and that its access might be open only to those who fulfil the conditions of the exception is of no importance. Many functions can indeed be assigned to the public domain: public access to culture, to information, sharing of the elements of common heritage, a source of inspiration for creators and the core element of the freedom to create. But most of these functions are intertwined: the creator has certainly been a reader before beginning to write, a mere part of the audience before composing a symphony. . . . The journalist using a piece of information in a newspaper article is both acting as an author – freedom to create – and as a messenger of content – freedom of expression, access to culture, etc.

From a sociological point of view, the commons or the public domain should be a field where the public can enter without stepping on the intellectual rights of anyone. Economically speaking, it should cover the assets or uses of such assets for which no transaction can take place. The public domain could thus greatly benefit from a definition that would include in its realm copyright exceptions and limitations. It would also come close to the definition of the public domain put forward by UNESCO as 'the realm of all works or objects of related rights, which can be exploited by everybody without any authorisation, *for instance*[29] because protection is not granted under national or international law, or because of the expiration of the term of protection'.

---

[27]   J. Cohen, 'Copyright, Commodification, and Culture: Locating the Public Domain', in Hugenholtz and Guibault, *op. cit.*

[28]   Ibid., p. 38.

[29]   Emphasis added.

Even though the two examples given refer to unprotected elements, the core definition, by emphasising exploitation without a need for authorisation could well encompass copyright exceptions or any other circumstances where a copyrighted work can be freely used.

Therefore, the public domain might comprise the following elements:

- elements not protected by copyright (ideas or non-original works);
- works whose term of protection has expired;
- works excluded from protection (official texts, the question of Crown in the UK should also be addressed);
- exceptions to the exclusive rights;
- freedom of use not covered by the exclusive rights (e.g. the right to intellectually enjoy and access the work that is not covered by any exclusive rights held by the author).

2.2. *The key objectives of a new regime of the public domain: what for?*

The first function of the public domain would be to enable and guarantee a free and equal use of some intellectual resources, whether the resource is *per se* not 'copyrighted' or its use open in some circumstances. If such a 'broad' approach of the public domain is to be favoured, the regime should guarantee both freedom and equality of access.[30] In order to achieve this goal, one might prohibit any kind of monopoly of the element 'included' within the public domain.

Repelling any monopoly over public domain resources can be accomplished through a compulsory rule rejecting 'exclusivity'.[31] In this way conflict with a subjective right, such as copyright on derivative work, trademark, or physical ownership, could be avoided. When the element is still protected by copyright but its use free under some circumstances, it is not so much exclusivity that should be forfeited as the possibility of excluding others from the use. For instance, as far as copyright exceptions are concerned, the rightholder still enjoys exclusivity over her work but has to admit a rivalry in the use covered by the exception.

Introducing shades into the public domain depiction and regime might also help to achieve its objectives. So far the public domain has been described as a mere entity, a kind of melting pot in which each element loses its individuality to become part of a whole. But one might imagine that positive protection of the public domain would have different layers depending on the functions allotted to it. Thinking of the public domain not as a horizontal

---

[30]   M.-A. Chardeaux, *Les choses communes*, Paris: LGDJ, 2006, no. 211. The author suggests considering the *droit moral* as a public policy regime corresponding to the second paragraph of article 714 of the Civil Code.

[31]   Like the '68 French motto, 'il est interdit d'interdire'.

notion but as a pyramidal one may refine the definition of a positive status: it may encompass various hypotheses for which the answers would differ, yet still remain within the public domain system.

Depending on the values that the public domain is supposed to be representing, the rules governing its mechanism may vary significantly. Is it really aimed at allowing public access for everyone to all its constituents? Or, on the contrary, is the public domain consistent with the idea of a selection of tolerated uses, of beneficiaries and/or of conditions of access? If the principle of such a choice is agreed upon, who will be entitled to decide it: the State, the rightholder or the public itself? All these questions make one wonder whether the public domain should be drawn as a monolithic framework or composed of concentric circles.

At least three concentric circles could compose the public domain.

Its 'hard kernel' would be constituted, as it is today, by productions of the human mind that still resist copyright – if not patent – i.e., ideas. For ideas, unlike works, are not *per se* subject to protection.

Obviously, even when such ideas take the form of original expressions and leave the public domain, the object of protection is a new one, i.e. an original work, keeping untouched the idea now contained or reworked in the work itself. In that sense the idea never really leaves the public domain field and can be used again by anyone anytime, as long as it remains abstract. Because of their ubiquity, ideas remain resistant to copyright protection focused on form and not on content.

It is nevertheless paradoxical that the exclusion-of-ideas principle, usually considered as being the milestone of the public domain is not even supported by a clear statement according to which ideas are never to be protected by copyright. This principle lies, *inter alia*, in the Software Directive but is not mentioned as such in the Berne Convention though article 2, paragraph 8 excludes 'news' (and not ideas) from its range of protection. Conversely, article 2 of the WIPO Copyright Treaty of 1996 explicitly excludes ideas, procedures, methods of operation or mathematical concepts from scope of copyright protection.

A second layer would be composed of other elements for which a public policy concern requires free access thereto and/or which should be immune from any exclusivity. The production of the mind could there be protected by copyright as to its criteria but its public utility is stressed. It encompasses non-original works, works in which copyright has expired, and works excluded from the scope of protection, such as official texts.

Whatever choice the legislation makes as to the extent, scope, and strength of the public domain, its hard kernel and its second circle may at least guarantee concurrent uses of the elements included. Such a level of competition presupposes the setting up of a system formally repelling exclusivity and easing common access.

One should nevertheless bear in mind a shortcoming of what is quite a radical vision of the public domain: the possible lack of incentives to innovate. For example, withholding from future creators any possible protection of their derivative work would go far beyond what is necessary to meet public domain requirements. The expression of the 'exclusion' rule might therefore take such a proportionality test into account.

Another layer of public domain could encompass elements at the periphery, receiving a lesser level of positive protection consisting of preserving the rivalry of uses or a rule of 'unexcludability'. There would lie the exceptions or the possibility of getting access to protected works in order to be able to read or view them. In comparison with the actual copyright regime, where such rivalry results for instance from recognition of an exception, but is not in itself protected, a positive regime for the public domain should ensure effective enjoyment and preservation of such free and rival use.

The regime should seek to exclude the possibility of constituting over public domain resources a reservation in contradiction to public domain status but would also vary along with its purposes. Depending on the type of elements concerned, this rule might be achieved by a prohibition of any exclusivity or by a mere prohibition on excluding others from the use. For instance, the absence of exclusivity means that some intangible elements should be formally excluded from any private system, in a similar way to the protection of the commons in environmental or public international laws.[32] Meanwhile, in the second circle, one might find items of the so-called public domain over which there continues to be a certain measure of control exercised by the rightholder. The obligation of maintaining the rivalry of use would not contradict a possible control by the State or an agency, either to protect the integrity of the work or to collect fees on its exploitation thereof in order to sustain the protection of the public domain status thereof.

2.3. *The positive protection of the public domain: how?*

This pyramidal view of the public domain where positive protection of its elements varies from a prohibition on regaining exclusivity to the obligation to sustain rival uses would require both the adoption of new rules in intellectual property laws and the setting up of the material conditions to effectively enable access to and enjoyment of public domain resources.

To ascertain public domain efficiency one might enforce these minimum principles through at least two ranges of rules: the first category would consist

---

[32]   See for instance protection as a commons of the Antarctica, the seas, or the recent declaration of UNESCO about the human genome considered as the common heritage of mankind.

of impediments to monopoly; the second would enumerate the positive obligations required to achieve the goals allotted to the public domain.

2.3.1.   The impediments to a regained monopoly over the public domain   As a first, and key rule in securing the nucleus of the public domain against undue privatisation, a specific law – dedicated to its regime – must assert that some elements – ideas, news, and discoveries – are not subject to any kind of property whatsoever, and free for all.

The 'no' rules may for example consist of a clear prohibition on cumulating different layers of intellectual property rights over the same object.[33] Once copyright has been granted on a specific creation, one might consider that no trademark can be registered on this very creation after the term of copyright protection even by the author himself, if this trademark would prevent the free use of the sign as such. Though very carefully, the Directive on Designs and Models has already introduced a rule distributing the protections between designs and copyright. Previous disclosure of a work destroys its novelty, which renders impossible an extension of the duration of protection by an adjunct of design and model monopoly after the term of copyright. Such a system might also prevail between copyright and patent, as far as novelty is concerned.

It should be expressly mentioned in copyright laws that no monopoly or reservation can be regained on works that have fallen into the public domain, be it by the effect of the exercise of another copyright, by the deposit of a trademark or any other intellectual or material property right, or by a technological measure. This prohibition on cumulating other ways of reservation over what is not protected by copyright would be limited to the verification that the exercise of the right or of the factual control unduly impedes access to or enjoyment of the public domain element. For instance, a trademark might well cover a design no longer protected by copyright in the limits of the speciality of the trademark protection, but it should not grant a protection that exactly substitutes for the former protection of copyright and prohibits the use of the resource in all circumstances. Mickey Mouse, once it falls into the public domain (if ever!), or any other cartoon character, can serve as a trademark for specific products but its protection as a trademark cannot result in transforming users of Mickey for uses other than branding products covered by the trademark, and especially authors of derivative works, into infringers. Technological measures can encapsulate public domain elements but this factual control cannot deprive users from getting access to all copies of such elements, or from reproducing or communicating technically protected elements.

---

[33]   See part II of the ALAI Congress, New York, 13–17 June 2001 Adjuncts and Alternatives to Copyright, ALAI, 2002.

This prohibition on reconstituting a monopoly over public domain assets is already applied by some case law, in copyright and more broadly in intellectual property. For example, a French tribunal has limited the exercise of the copyright of two authors of a contemporary work of art included in a public and historic place of Lyon, on the ground that entitling them to prohibit the reproduction of their work on postcards would impede the free reproduction of the historical palaces surrounding it.[34] The key argument of the decision was that the public domain status of such buildings constrains and limits the exercise of the copyright held by the authors of a derivative work to the extent required by the necessity of preserving free access to and reproduction of this public domain. The decision was confirmed on appeal but on different grounds, as if this reasoning on the public domain was too dangerous to handle.[35]

The European Court of Justice has also declined to protect some three-dimensional trademarks where the result would be to prevent free access to and use of the element in question, not protected by a patent.[36] In its conclusion in the *Linde* case, the General Advocate relied on the fact that 'the public interest should not have to tolerate even a slight risk that trade mark rights unduly encroach on the field of other exclusive rights which are limited in time, whilst there are in fact other effective ways in which manufacturers may indicate the origin of a product'.[37]

A last example of this prohibition on regaining a lost monopoly is given by the French controversy over the scope of 'material property' and its extension to the image of a 'thing', that is to say to the intellectual elements embedded in material objects. For some time recognised as an attribute of property right, the exclusive right to control the image, and thus the reproduction, of a material property has finally been rejected by the Court of Cassation.[38] The claim of the owner of the material was actually an important threat to the principle of common access that underlies the intellectual public domain. One way to construe the Cassation decision is to admit that the Court has recognised that the status of the public domain prevails over any attempts to invoke a new monopoly in intellectual work.[39] One commentator has referred to article 4 of

---

34   TGI Lyon (1ère ch.), 4 April 2001, *RIDA*, October 2001, note Choisy.
35   Lyon, 1ère ch., 20 March 2003, *CCE*, September 2003, p. 23, note Caron.
36   CJCE, *Linde AG, Winward Industries Inc. and Radio Uhren AG*, 8 April 2003, C-53/01 to C-55/01.
37   Opinion of Advocate General Ruiz-Jarabo Colomer delivered on 24 October 2002, at p. 29.
38   On the whole debate, see B. Gleize, 'La protection de l'image des biens', thesis, Montpellier, 2004; Cass. fr. (ass. plén.), 7 May 2004, *D.*, 2004, Jurisprudence, p. 1545, note J.-M. Bruguiere and E. Dreyer.
39   V.-L. Benabou, 'La propriété schizophrène, propriété du bien et propriété de

the Duration Directive (which grants a limited right to the first publisher of a public domain work)[40] to prove that physical ownership was not a sufficient foundation for exclusivity over the intellectual content of a work. Only the publisher, as such and not as a mere passive owner of the manuscript, is, by a special text, being granted this exclusivity. The goal of this provision, i.e. wide disclosure of a work so far not revealed, was supposed to apply a specific rule that can either be read as the creation of a neighbouring right for the first publisher or as one within the regime of the public domain, as an exception to the common use.

Equally the status of the works relinquished by their authors into the public domain should be explicitly ascertained. We have seen earlier that, absent a positive protection of the public domain against re-appropriation, authors who wish to decline the protection of copyright increasingly resort to copyleft strategies that embed a contamination clause, strategies that are often legally fragile and disputable.[41]

A public domain regime – inside or outside copyright law – should give authors the legal means to abandon their rights in a way that would guarantee and formalise the new status given to the work, so that no new monopoly could make this intention void.

A last idea (last from our viewpoint at least) would be to make all elements of the public domain immune to undue reservation by technological measures or contracts. Technological measures and contracts can be part of a business model that distributes and gives access to public domain materials, such as a commercial service deserving protection on its own, but the actual operation of such a model should never be allowed to prohibit free reproduction of such material when authorised by the status of the public domain, whether the resource is no longer protected or the use is justified by an exception or by the mere consultation of the work.

In this respect, the European rules governing the combination between exceptions and technical protection measures should be reconsidered. Not only are they illogical but they are also highly difficult to enforce. In the French Intellectual Property Code, for example, exceptions are written in such a way that once the author has disclosed his work, he can no longer prohibit

---

l'image du bien en le renouveau du droit de propriété', *Droit et Patrimoine*, March 2001, no. 91; 'La guerre des droits n'aura pas lieu', *Auteurs et Médias*, April–June 2005, pp. 103–9.

40   M. Cornu, 'Droit sur l'image photographique d'un immeuble – Prérogatives du propriétaire de l'immeuble', *RIDA* October 1999, pp. 149–81. Also see this author on the public domain in general, particularly, 'La mise hors commerce des biens culturels comme mode de protection', *Legicom*, no. 36, 2/2006, p. 75.

41   On this point, see S. Dusollier, 'Sharing Access to Intellectual Property through Private Ordering', 74 *Chicago-Kent Law Review*, 101 (2007).

certain detailed and limited uses. Nevertheless, according to the Infosoc Directive, if the work is 'recovered' by a technical protection measure, the rightholder (who?) can ignore some (but not all!) of the exceptions. Yet, the French law implementing the directive, while creating a very sophisticated system of conciliation between exceptions and technical protection, has forgotten to wipe out the genuine wording, keeping therefore 'the prohibition of prohibition'. The result is that the provider of the technological protection measure may bar certain uses which cannot be banned by the author even though the technological measure is supposed to be protected only if it covers a protected work! The Belgian system, by clearly saying that some exceptions are compulsory, is strengthening the public domain.

Making exceptions mandatory, as it is the case in Belgium, would be part of our positive regime of the public domain, as well as the obligation imposed on technological measures operators to enable the free exercise of *all* copyright exceptions. Apart from this impediment rule, a general obligation on those having recourse to contractual or technical methods should be added to enable the reproduction and communication of the intellectual works or content once they are not protected by copyright, since protection of the service they provide should not extend to intellectual content, covered as it is by a public domain status. But this kind of positive obligation already belongs to the second category of rules ascertaining the effectiveness of the public domain.

2.3.2.   A positive obligation towards the availability of the public domain It does not suffice to inscribe in the law the legal rules applying to the public domain; actual access thereto should also be promoted.

Equally, as already mentioned, one must look carefully at such exclusion rules as their result may be a loss of incentive to innovate or to invest. Yet the risk is low and can easily be avoided, at least from a theoretical point of view, by considering public domain not as a no-ownership but as a common-ownership area (*res communis*). To make possible this common use, the regime of the public domain should first guarantee public access to the assets concerned. Such access should at least enable material access to the element (i.e. access to a copy thereto), as well as intellectual or cognitive access (i.e. the possibility to enjoy the element, thus to read, view or use) for free.

Dependent on this effective access is an obligation to preserve and conserve the public domain. If we look at the system used for sharing natural resources such as Antarctica, the high seas, or other commons, it is obvious that there exists a loose obligation to preserve the resource. However, mere conservation might not be sufficient to make the intellectual public domain alive; because the existence of the public domain is only justified in this field by public diffusion of the content, there is also a need to display or disseminate the resource to a certain extent.

That preservation/exploitation obligation could rest upon the State, in its mission to protect the cultural heritage, but also upon the community of users of public domain elements.

There is, to our knowledge, no such thing in the current European legislation on copyright as a system organising or maintaining public access to a work. During the author's life, the moral right to divulge – when recognised – even seems totally in contradiction to an obligation to preserve.

Yet, moral right is not *per se* inconsistent with the rationale of the public domain. For example, in France, the *droit moral* continues after the end of exploitation rights. Even if the work can theoretically be employed by anyone, the user may not violate the right of the author over his name or quality nor distort the genuine expression of the work. Entrance into the public domain does not allow totally free use of the item, which remains somewhat protected. Yet, such control is not necessarily incompatible with the logic of free and equal use.[42] It is not an authorisation to use which is granted by the rightholder and anybody has access to the production of the mind without paying royalties. The *droit moral* shall remain only to make sure that the genuine intention of the artist is not betrayed and, along the way, it assumes the function of conservation of the work (right of integrity and of paternity). Although it is not in general considered as such, the *droit moral* may contribute to protecting the work against undue privatisation by applying to everyone but the genuine author the same conditions for the use of the work. The obligation to respect the integrity of the work and the paternity of the author can be considered as an expression of the obligation of preservation. To keep an environmental metaphor, the rightholder, his heirs or any agency entitled to do so will look after the work to prevent its possible 'pollution' and disappearance as such. In this perspective, perpetuity and prohibition of assignment of the *droit moral* contribute to achieving long-lasting and faithful access to the elements of the public domain.[43]

Other models can be used to achieve a common access and/or common use: the French 'depot legal' and the European texts on access to public information or cultural items.[44] While the French system is limited in its aims of conservation

---

[42]   See, in this sense, Cour de Cassation no. 04-15.543, 30 January 2007 in the *Les misérables* case. The supreme court has overruled the Court of Appeal decision and has considered that, if the right of paternity and integrity of the work subject to adaptation are respected, freedom of creation prohibits interdiction by the author or his heirs of a sequel to the work under the terms of the exploitation monopoly they are beneficiaries of.

[43]   See Chardeaux, *op. cit.,* no. 211.

[44]   Directive 2003/98, 17 November 2003, on the re-use of public sector information; Recommendation of the Commission, 24 August 2006, on digitalisation and access to the cultural element and digital conservation.

and making certain sites available only for researchers,[45] the Directive has a wider scope. According to article 3, it considers that 'Member States shall ensure that, where the re-use of documents held by public sector bodies is allowed, these documents shall be re-usable for commercial or non-commercial purposes . . . Where possible, documents shall be made available through electronic means.'

The conditions of access might even suggest an underlying condition of interoperability, as for example article 5, paragraph 1 of Directive 2003/98, suggests:

> Public sector bodies shall make their documents available in any pre-existing format or language, through electronic means where possible and appropriate. This shall not imply an obligation for public sector bodies to create or adapt documents in order to comply with the request, nor shall it imply an obligation to provide extracts from documents where this would involve disproportionate effort, going beyond a simple operation.

The constant need for access to the public domain will not only require its elements to be locked in a secure box but also for them to be offered in an open standard.

To ascertain access, not only must the material conditions be preserved but also identification of works belonging to the public domain and the diffusion of this information must be kept up to date. In this perspective, the recommendation on digitisation and online accessibility of cultural material and digital preservation of 24 August 2006, article 6[46] considers it necessary to create mechanisms in order to facilitate the exploitation of orphan works or of works which are no longer published, to make a list of known orphan works and of works in the public domain.[47]

---

[45] Though recently expanded to the electronic depot legal by the law of 1 August 2006.

[46] Commission Recommendation of 24 August 2006 on the digitisation and online accessibility of cultural material and digital preservation, 2006/585/CE, OJEU, 31.08.2006, no. L236/28.

[47] Article 6: Improve conditions for digitisation of, and online accessibility to cultural material by:

(a) creating mechanisms to facilitate the use of orphan works, following consultation of interested parties,

(b) establishing or promoting mechanisms, on a voluntary basis, to facilitate the use of works that are out of print or out of distribution, following consultation of interested parties,

(c) promoting the availability of lists of known orphan works and works in the public domain,

(d) identifying barriers in their legislation to the online accessibility and subsequent use of cultural material that is in the public domain and taking steps to remove them.

Finally, as regards use, the Directive 2003/98 recalls a non-discrimination principle as to which, 'any applicable conditions for the re-use of documents shall be non-discriminatory for comparable categories of re-use'.

Ensuring public access to public domain elements would in some cases require encroachment upon the property rights of whoever owns the sole material copy of the work, now unprotected by copyright. In that case, the law should confer on the State or one of its agencies the right to get access to that material copy to make the reproductions necessary for the preservation and access obligations resulting from its public domain status. Such a right would be the equivalent, for the public domain, of the right granted, in some countries, to authors, to get access to the material embodiment of their work to the extent required by the necessity to exploit their copyright.

2.3.3.   A public domain with remuneration?   It may be difficult to achieve the goals allotted to the public domain if no one wants to sustain the positive obligations mentioned above, as some of these may require money, time and/or technical skills.

It is not clear whether common and equal access is actually better achieved through free access or by the payment of a lump sum by everyone or through a cross-compensation system in which the commercial users would support the upkeep of the public domain for others. The answer may also depend on the question of who will have to sustain this cost: the State, specific users, or the public.

The d*omaine public payant* doctrine has always considered that the entrance of an item within the public domain after a certain period of time would not mean that the use of the work would necessarily become 'free of charge' for all.[48] Such a system might be kept in mind, for instance, when copies of the public domain are made available through technological measures of protection.

Consideration should also be given to the situation where public access to an asset is rendered impossible, not because of an intellectual property right but since there is no incentive to publish. In this case, the status of the public domain could be a deterrent. Hence, one might consider the possible entrance

---

[48]   The doctrine in favour of this theory is pleading for an ongoing royalty on the commercial exploitation of any work, notwithstanding the expiration of the duration of the monopoly. See A. Dietz, 'Le droit de la communauté des auteurs: un concept moderne de domaine public payant', *Bulletin du droit d'auteur*, January 1990, pp. 14–26.

Essentially, access to the work would be unconditional but its exploitation could only be made in counterpart of a fee paid to a community of living authors so as to stimulate creation and cultural development.

into a temporary 'ownership area' but with charge. For the rightholder, exclusivity would only be granted to the extent that 'he' would open up public access to the asset, which would otherwise be impossible to achieve under a common and free access regime.

A glimpse of such a system has already been implemented in the article 4[49] of the 'Term' Directive[50] for the protection of previously unpublished works. This provision, though granting extra-exclusivity even after the work falls within the public domain, makes the public interest prevail over the interest of the owner of the manuscript by granting a monopoly to the publisher, that is to say, to the one who will disseminate the very substance of the work by disclosing it publicly. Faced with a choice between gratuitousness and public access, the Directive has preferred the second course.

Though reconstitution of any exclusivity might be banned in principle, in conceiving a positive status for the public domain, one might not completely exclude the possibility of introducing a special and temporary right – the nature of which might vary according to the circumstances – granted to the person who will actually disclose the assets, in order to ensure the effectiveness of public access.

Conclusion

Ignoring the need for a regime of the public domain is not neutral, but has an impact on public acceptance and the legitimacy of intellectual property and might endanger it in the long run.

This overview of the possible protection of the 'public domain' through positive rules of delimitation, access and preservation outlines that the notion cannot be adequately articulated by a single regime and/or a single rule. In a positive vision of the public domain, the public domain should henceforth be considered as contingent, not because of the existence of the monopoly, but for the reason that it is evolving in accordance with a combination of values. Among these values are freedom, equality and solidarity as to the costs of this new openness. If we adopt a pyramidal vision of the public domain, the nucleus would be the result of a high dose of these principles to the extent they

---

[49] Article 4: 'any person who, after the expiry of copyright protection, for the first time lawfully publishes or lawfully communicates to the public a previously unpublished work, shall benefit from a protection equivalent to the economic rights of the author. The term of protection of such rights shall be 25 years from the time when the work was first lawfully published or lawfully communicated to the public.'

[50] Former Council Directive 93/98/EEC (OJ L290, 24.11.1993, p. 9) codified by a Directive 2006/116/EC of the European Parliament and of the Council of 12 December 2006 on the term of protection of copyright and certain related rights (codified version).

are consistent with each other. For example, the traditional image of the public domain (here the top of the pyramid) presupposes free access for all: no authorisation, no condition, no payment, no discrimination, the widest community of users possible, eternal length.

Yet, public domain should also encompass other uses, even if they are more restricted. Renouncement of one's monopoly claim for the public benefit, as long as the consent of the rightholder is clear and irreversible, might also contribute to an original expression of the public domain. Access to the intellectual content is then in general free, not subject to authorisation but use might be conditional. The same statement can be made for 'exceptions' to the rights: they allow equal access not to all, but to anyone who fulfils the conditions enumerated. Access and/or use might not be gratuitous even if, most of the time, the onus of the payment is divided throughout a public still distinct from the actual audience or directly supported by the State.

Common access, non-exclusive licence, non-discrimination for re-use, evolving formats of conservation of the item, a list of orphan works, the possible revival of works that are not exploited any more . . . New texts should contain suggestions of practical principles which would give full effect to the public domain. Yet, discussion about effective access to and preservation of the public domain should still get under way at the European level. Isn't it time for the Little Prince to open the box?

8   Could multimedia works be protected as a form of audiovisual works?

Irini Stamatoudi[1]

1. Introduction

During the last few years multimedia products have experienced exponential growth on the international market.[2] This growth has in turn produced a need for their immediate protection. Although it is clear that multimedia products are considered to be works for the purposes of copyright,[3] and therefore are protected as such, it is not immediately clear under which specific category of copyright works, if any, they come.[4] This is important, especially for those countries, such as the UK, where classification of a work is necessary in order for the work to attract copyright protection.

The experience of copyright lawyers and others to date shows that there is, arguably at least, a strong presumption that data including or mainly composed of sound and images, which are projected onto a screen, fall within

---

[1]   Dr, Director of the Greek National Copyright Organisation.

[2]   The multimedia market has seen an exponential growth in terms of turnover in the first half of the 1990s. Various estimates are available and whilst all of them show huge growth on average, the figures for 1995 and 1996 ($12.5 to 17 billion) were between 5 and 10 times higher than those for 1989 or 1992 ($1.2 to 3.2 billion). For further details see Vercken, G. (1996), *Practical Guide to Copyright for Multimedia Producers*, European Commission, DGXIII, pp. 16 seq. Other sources indicated that the growth in turnover was expected to continue and that by 1997 it could reach the figure of $23.9 billion, excluding video games. See Interactive Multimedia Association (Annapolis, USA), as referred to by Radcliffe, M. (1995), 'Legal issues in new media technologies', *The Computer Lawyer*, 12 (12), 2.

[3]   Sirinelli, P. (1994), *Report on Multimedia and New Technologies*, France: Ministère de la Culture et de la Francophonie. Sirinelli, P. (1994), *Le Régime Juridique et la Gestion des oeuvres multimédias*, Paris: CERDI (Centre d'études et de recherche en droit de l'informatique de l'Université Paris Sud. Institute of Intellectual Property), Sirinelli, P. (1994), *A Proposal of the New Rule on Intellectual Property for Multimedia*, Japan. Strowel, A. and E. Derclaye (2001), *Droit d'Auteur et Numérique: Logiciels, Bases de Données, Multimédia*, Brussels: Bruylant. Pollaud-Dulian, F. (2005), *Le Droit d'Auteur*, Paris: Economica, pp. 270 seq.

[4]   For an extensive discussion regarding the copyright protection of multimedia works, see Stamatoudi, I. (2002), *Copyright and Multimedia Works: A Comparative Analysis, Cambridge: Cambridge University Press*.

the category of audiovisual works. Unless multimedia works are projected onto a screen, their contents cannot be read, accessed or manipulated by users. Thus, if we are to judge multimedia works according to their appearance or looks alone, we could argue that the one category of protection which seems most capable of accommodating multimedia products is that of audiovisual works. That aside, US and European courts, when dealing with the first cases concerning primitive forms of multimedia works, i.e. video games, came to the conclusion that these works were audiovisual works.

This chapter will examine whether this initial presumption corresponds to the actual characteristics and needs of multimedia works when the issue is considered in detail. It will also consider whether the inclusion of elements of image and sound in a multimedia work is enough to place it under the legal umbrella of audiovisual works or related categories such as cinematographic works, films or motion pictures.[5] Because of the physical constraints of this chapter, in terms of time and space, I will limit the discussion to whether multimedia works qualify as films under the UK Copyright, Designs and Patents Act 1988 (CDPA 1988). To this end I will only examine the actual characteristics of films (as these are put forward by the law, the case-law and the literature) and not the suitability of the provisions in the regime of protection for films. The latter issue forms a separate discussion that falls outside the scope of this chapter.

2.   Definition of multimedia products

The term 'multimedia products' has been used increasingly in the last few years with different meanings. However, a common characteristic in all those meanings is the fact that they all involve a combination of more than one distinct expression, e.g. sound, image, text, etc. Yet, this is not enough to establish the appearance of a new type of work or form of communication. The combination of more than one expression is something well-known both in our present as well as in our past copyright experience. Newspapers and magazines combine text and images. Films combine sound and images, databases can combine any form of expression. Yet, no one refers to these works as multimedia works. That alone makes us think that multimedia works must be something else, although not necessarily something entirely different.

Arguably, what makes multimedia works a different species of works are

---

5   Art. 95 of the German Copyright Act refers to 'moving pictures' as a notion which adds to the notion of cinematographic works. The former seem to include any sequence of images or images and sounds which are not cinematographic works, in the sense that there is no performance involved.

two essential additional elements. The mere inclusion of different kinds of expressions does not allow a work to qualify as a multimedia work. On top of that these expressions have to be *integrated*. They have to be combined with each other to such an extent that any distinction or any attempt at distinguishing between the various expressions and elements initially included in the work is either impossible or makes no sense. If that is not the case then we only have a juxtaposition of materials which perhaps adds nothing or at least does not add a lot to the fact that these materials are different in nature. In such a case the separate protection of the various materials alone would equal the protection of the work as a whole and would confer on it an adequate degree of protection under copyright. If these materials were somehow originally arranged, the work would immediately qualify for protection either as a compilation or as a database.[6] In this case one could refer to compilations or databases and multimedia works interchangeably and no questions relating to the nature of the work could arise at all.

In addition, multimedia works are *interactive*. They allow their users to interact with the information they carry, not simply by giving simple instructions to the machine or by choosing a limited number of available pathways, but also by manipulating and interfering with the materials contained in them and to such an extent that they can morph and blur them. The outcome of such activity should not immediately or necessarily be recognisable as one of the elements initially included in the work. That should not mean of course that the user should himself necessarily engage in the activities of morphing and blurring but at least the potential for such manipulation should be there. In other words a substantial degree of interactivity should exist.

Other characteristics are that multimedia works are necessarily digital works since they cannot operate without the aid of a software tool. On top of that the amount of expressions and elements usually contained in a copyright work is large so as to allow a substantial degree of involvement and manipulation on the part of the user. Yet, these characteristics are more or less implied by the former ones (integration and interactivity), which define more characteristically the nature of a multimedia work.

Therefore multimedia works should for the purposes of this chapter be defined as follows:

> *works which combine on a single medium more than one distinct kind of expression in an integrated digital format, and which allow their users, with the aid of a software tool, to manipulate the contents of the work with a substantial degree of interactivity.*

---

[6] If it did not come under other categories of copyright works, e.g. films.

Primitive forms of multimedia products may contain all the aforementioned elements but to a lesser extent. For example the various elements contained in the work may not be integrated to an inseparable and indistinguishable degree. Alternatively authors may interact with the work but not to a substantial degree. They may only make simple choices amongst the limited number of options provided by the producer of the work, which in their turn can only give rise to a predefined sequence of images (e.g. certain types of video games) or which can affect only the selection or arrangement of the various elements contained in the work rather than the content and substance of those elements (e.g. an electronic encyclopaedia such as Microsoft Encarta). However, these works (which can be referred to as the first generation of multimedia products) would fall foul of the definition of multimedia works as it is set out in this chapter. This is essentially so because these works share characteristics with conventional and existing types of copyright works (e.g. films or databases) rather than introducing a new type of work. Therefore they can be protected adequately by existing copyright legislation and they raise no points of concern. This chapter sets out to examine whether sophisticated forms of multimedia work (which can be referred to as the second generation of multimedia products) fit in easily with the definition of films under the CDPA 1988.

3.   Multimedia works as audiovisual works

3.1.   Multimedia works as de jure *audiovisual works*

3.1.1. Complex works   Audiovisual works are, like multimedia products, 'complex' works, which in most cases combine *de facto* more than one type of work, i.e. image and sound. The latter is however not a necessary element of their nature. The complexity of audiovisual works, wherever this complexity exists, is not a vital and essential component of their definition. The national copyright laws of the various states do not expressly refer to it. On the contrary, the existence of more than two different types of works is an essential element in the definition of multimedia products. In addition to that it is not only the case that different kinds of works are combined to form a multimedia product, but that the number of the combined works is well above that found in any traditional film or audiovisual work, even in those cases where the latter works combine both sound and image. Thus, the difference in quantity unavoidably becomes a difference in quality as well (a limited number of works compared to a vast number of works). In addition, in the case of films the constituent works have been combined so as to form an amalgamation of sound and image where these two co-exist and are independent at the same time. In the case of multimedia products the works contributed are assimilated, and nothing of their independence is retained.[7]

One could argue that national laws on audiovisual works have been worded and construed in such a way as to read that creations bringing together data of any nature, other than image or where images are not prevalent, and also data which, though prevalent, do not form a sequence of animated or moving images, are excluded from the scope of protection of audiovisual works.[8]

On the basis of the above observation the following should be pointed out. By definition certain data do not fall within the category of moving images. This is the case where the law of a country requires pre-existing moving images to be recorded as a film, and the data recorded do not meet the requirement. Another case is where certain data, though not moving images by nature, can still be recorded in such a way as to form a moving image. The question here is whether it suffices for the law of a country that the motion of images derives from the recording of the data and not from the nature of the data itself as moving images. In the CDPA 1988, there is no requirement for the data to actually be a moving image, even before they are recorded.[9] Yet, in the Copyright Act 1956, which the CDPA 1988 replaced, it was implied that the image had to be moving in nature before it was recorded.[10] If this were still the case the scope of audiovisual works would be substantially restricted, and it would *de facto* present severe difficulties to any attempt to fit multimedia works into the category of audiovisual works. Data which are not a moving image and which cannot form a moving image even if one tries to record them as such are any kind of still images, e.g. photographs, artistic works, diagrams, text or other.

In contrast to audiovisual works, multimedia products combine various types of works. This feature is a key element of their nature. Multimedia works

---

7   Koumantos, G. (1996), 'Les aspects de droit internationale privé en matière d'infrastructure mondiale d'information', *koinodikion*, 2.B, pp. 241 seq., at p. 243.

8   Groupe Audiovisuel et Multimédia de l'Edition (1994), *Questions juridiques relatives aux oeuvres multimédia* (Livre Blanc), Paris; see also Deprez, P. and V. Fauchoux (1997), *Lois, contrats et usages du multimédia*, Dixit, at p. 48.

9   According to section 5B CDPA 1988, a film is 'a recording on any medium from which a moving image may by any means be produced'.

10   See Turner, M. (1995), 'Do the old legal categories fit the new multimedia products? A multimedia CD-ROM as a film', *EIPR* (3), pp. 107 seq., at p. 108. The wording of the Copyright Act 1956 was that cinematographic works were 'any sequence of visual images recorded on material of any description (whether translucent or not) so as to be capable, by the use of that material (a) of being shown as a moving picture, or (b) of being recorded on other material (whether translucent or not), by the use of which it can be shown'.

are by definition complex creations,[11] composed of contributions of different types of works.[12] These contributions consist of works that are not restricted to a mode of adaptation and transformation in order to fit into the format of an audiovisual work, as is the case with audiovisual works and films. The wide and diverse range of individual creative contributions that a film incorporates consists not only of the labour of adapting the story and setting the scene of the film. Items such as script, acting, directing, filming, sound recording, responsibility for make-up, clothing, lighting, music, properties and so on are also included in this.[13] These contributions do not necessarily consist of works, in the sense of intellectual property law. In other words they are not works which fall within one of the categories of intellectual property and are protected as such. They consist of technicalities, which do not possess any originality or creative character in the traditional sense. Indicative of this point is the fact that, although many people contribute to the production of a film or an audiovisual work, it is only to a few that the law grants the status of authors. It grants author status to those who have contributed actual works to the production of the film (e.g. the director, the author of the script or adaptation, etc.). Thus, the complexity of audiovisual works, when compared with that of multimedia works, is qualitatively different. It is only the combination of image and sound in an audiovisual work which is comparable with a multimedia work. But, even here, it is apparent that legislation on audiovisual works has been designed to accommodate works combining only image and sound, whilst text or other data are either of secondary importance or are left out entirely.[14]

Even in those cases where something more than images is included in an audiovisual work, the number of works incorporated is always limited. Perhaps because of the technology available at the time of the drafting of the various national laws, films were never thought capable of including more than two kinds of works, i.e. image and sound, together with some minimal amount of text (e.g. opening and closing titles). They were probably not thought capable of incorporating more than one kind of image, sound, or text. Even when such a three-element combination was made, no one would refer to vast numbers of works or amounts of data. The mere inclusion of works,

---

[11]   Gautier, P. (1994), 'Les oeuvres multimédias en droit français', *RIDA*, pp. 93 seq.

[12]   B Edelman, '*L'oeuvre multimédia, une essaie de qualification*' [1995] 15 *Recueil Dalloz Sirey* 15, pp. 109 seq., at p. 110.

[13]   See Laddie, H., P. Prescott and M. Vitoria (1995), *The Modern Law of Copyright and Designs*, 2nd edn, London: Butterworths, at p. 365.

[14]   I.e. in cases where text is included in the film, in most cases it includes only the opening and closing titles.

other than the aforementioned, or the inclusion of data, for example numbers, where image was not a prevailing element (or which could not be presented as data), automatically made any lawyer exclude them from the definition of audiovisual works. The additional layer of content as such came within the definition of literary works or other categories of works, hence the difference between the contents of an audiovisual work and a multimedia product.

3.1.2. 'Image' as a prevalent element   One of the essential characteristics of audiovisual works that is contained in every single national definition is the presence of images. As we explained earlier, there is no express exclusion of other elements from the definition of audiovisual works. On the contrary, sound is also referred to as being potentially included. However, the prevailing element is always the image.[15] The requirement of the image as the dominant element in an audiovisual work also pre-defines the purpose of an audiovisual work. Audiovisual works are meant to be shown, either in public or privately. They are not meant to be read, as would be the case with literary works.

'Image' is a notion that is somehow larger than the notion of a 'picture'. The term 'picture' was found in the Copyright Act 1956, which was replaced by the CDPA 1988. It seems more difficult for the term 'picture' to include images that are not derived from pictures as such, but from computer-generated devices which can transform data into image, as would be the case for example with a computer-programmed automatic puppet show[16] or a figure

---

[15]   Indeed A. Lucas argues that even though the law does not specifically stipulate that an audiovisual work should consist exclusively of sequences of moving images, one would no doubt be stretching the meaning of the words unduly if one regarded a work that includes only a limited number of sequences of moving images as audiovisual works. In most cases the components of a multimedia work will be of a diverse nature and the work will miss the coherence that goes with a normal audiovisual work. Nevertheless putting such a work into the inappropriate straitjacket of the category of audiovisual works does not seem suitable. Lucas, A. (1996), 'Multimédia et droit d'auteur', in AFTEL, *Le Droit du Multimédia: De la Télématique à Internet*, Les Editions du Téléphone, pp. 113 seq., at pp. 145–6. See also Lucas, A. (1996) 'Les oeuvres multimédias en droit belge et en droit français', in Doutrelepont, C., P. Van Binst and L. Wilkin (eds), *Libertés, droits et réseaux dans la sociétés de l'information*, Brussels: Bruylant, 55, at 67; Bitan, H. (1996), 'Les rapports de force entre la technologie du multimédia et le droit' (1996), *Gazette du Palais* (26.1.1996), 12; Pasgrimaud, H. (1995), 'La qualification juridique de la création multimédia: termes et arrire-pensées dans vrai-faux débat', *Gazette du Palais* (11.10.1995); and Edelman, B. (1995), 'L'oeuvre multimédia, une essaie de qualification', *Recueil Dalloz Sirey*, 15, pp. 109 seq.

[16]   See Laddie et al., *The Modern Law of Copyright and Designs*, at p. 377.

generated by a computer by putting bits and pieces of the image of well-known artists together and programming their moves. Thus, images do not have to stay unchanged from the traditional format in which they are found in conventional films. Apart from two-dimensional images, three-dimensional images, holograms and virtual reality shows are also covered. Images can also be produced by digitised pre-existing information and computer-generated displays, such as the 'attract' mode of an arcade game (video game in which a moving picture is generated by computer).[17] The fact that the new technologies make these images far more diverse and complicated than the ones found in conventional films, as well as the fact that these kinds of pictures are not usually found in films as we traditionally know them, should not affect the notion of the image as this notion is enshrined in the national definitions of audiovisual works.[18]

It follows logically from the above that the medium from which an image is produced or generated, and the support, linear or non-linear, on which it is reproduced and communicated, should not affect the notion of the image. For that very reason no special support or medium is required by the law. Images can either be produced by filming, putting drawings ('cells') together (as in cartoons), or they can be computer-generated (as with the special effects in films such as *The Day After*, *Independence Day* and *Jurassic Park*).

In the light of the above, any multimedia product in which (moving) images form the main element should qualify as an audiovisual work. However, in multimedia products, though they are expressed in an audiovisual way[19] and though they look like an audiovisual work, images are rarely the most important element.[20] This is especially so in cases where a multimedia work is an adaptation to an electronic format of an encyclopaedia or other work which was primarily fixed, or could be fixed, on paper. In such a case one might wonder whether the transfer of a work from a paper support to a CD-ROM is a new mode of exploitation, where separate contracts, transfer of rights by the author and additional remuneration is required, or whether it is another use covered by the rights conferred by the initial contract. If it is the

---

[17]　Ibid.

[18]　See the thoughts of Turner, M. (1995), 'Do the old legal categories fit the new multimedia products? A multimedia CD-ROM as a film', *EIPR*, 3, pp. 107 seq., at p. 108.

[19]　See Linant de Bellefonds, M. (1995), Note under CA Paris, 16 May 1994, *JCP*, t. II, p. 22375.

[20]　The need to know which is the prevalent element in a work (or contents of a work) is not only dictated by the definition of the separate kinds of works themselves, but is also the essential/accessory test run by the courts in many countries in order to find the nature (essence) of a work. See Edelman, 'L'oeuvre multimédia', at p. 114, and note 44.

latter no separate transfer of rights and supplementary remuneration are required.[21] The view, which seems to be closer to the reality and needs of authors, is that digitisation is indeed a separate mode of exploitation usually known as electronic rights. This is also implied by the fact that 'electronic rights' of authors are not automatically transferred to publishers and producers unless they are precisely defined in the licensing contract. If they are not, any legal presumption works against their transfer and in favour of the authors.[22] An example of a multimedia product is an encyclopaedia which is put on CD-ROM. Although the encyclopaedia is shown on the screen, the user simply reads it. Images are accessory, whilst text is the main element. Its transfer from paper onto CD-ROM should not alter the nature of the work, even if adaptations to match the new mode of exploitation are made, e.g. interactive retrieval and browsing of information. Of course, separate licensing of rights is required as well as additional remuneration. In the Anglo-Saxon tradition this area is predominantly left to the contractual relationship between the parties. Very few, if any, statutory provisions regulate these issues.

However, does the existence of text, or of text as a prevailing element, exclude these works from the notion of audiovisual works altogether? The attempt of various lawyers to include teletext and Minitel within the ambit of audiovisual works has only shown that in certain cases this should not be so. According to them, text shown on a screen performs the same task as an image. In this sense teletext is an audiovisual work.[23] Yet, this would confuse, if not discredit, the boundaries between audiovisual and literary works, and would unjustifiably place too much emphasis on the medium of communication, culminating in the medium defining the nature of the work, rather than the work itself. In addition, the qualification of works as audiovisual would no longer be possible, since in practice such a solution would lead to all kinds of works being placed indistinguishably in one copyright

---

[21] See ibid., at p. 115.

[22] Most continental systems seem to have a theory in *dubio pro autore* which means that the terms of any licence or assignment have to be interpreted restrictively and that in case of doubt the author is assumed only to have assigned the absolute minimum of rights that are necessary for the specific exploitation that was envisaged in the contract. This theory is also known in Germany as the Zweckübertragungstheorie. (On its applicability in a multimedia context see Kreile, J. and D. Westphal (1996), 'Multimedia und das Filmbearbeitungsrecht', *GRUR*, pp. 254 seq., at p. 254.) However, in Britain there is no such theory. On the contrary, it is fair to say that the presumption works the other way round. See Vercken, *Practical Guide to Copyright for Multimedia Producers*, at p. 114.

[23] See Berenboom, A. (1995), *Le nouveau droit d'auteur et les droits voisins*, Brussels: Larcier, at p. 193.

basket. If copyright is to be redefined this is definitely not the most appropriate way to go about it.[24]

3.1.3. 'Sequence of moving images' and interactivity

A *DE MINIMIS* RULE   The inclusion of images as such does not suffice for a work to qualify as an audiovisual work. Most national laws require, expressly or impliedly, the existence of 'moving images'.[25] Yet, what each national law refers to or implies by 'moving images' is not immediately obvious. The notion of 'moving image' can be construed either narrowly or broadly. In either case a *de minimis* rule should be applied. A moving image is not just a changing image.[26] Nevertheless, despite the variety of definitions, there is at least a common link

---

[24]   Even if in the future the various categories of copyright works are abolished, the regime of protection will have to be adapted to cover all needs. This is clearly not the case now.

[25]   The requirement of a 'moving image' is found in national copyright acts in relation to films (i.e. UK), motion pictures (i.e. US) and cinematographic works (i.e. France and Germany), and not in the definition of audiovisual works as such (it exists in the preparatory works of the Belgian Commission of the Chambers of Justice in relation to audiovisual works, Report De Clerck, LDA, at p. 181). (In fact, the lack of this requirement in the definition of audiovisual works seems to be the distinctive line between audiovisual works and films.) Yet, since most countries provide only a single definition (e.g. only for films or only for audiovisual works), they mean or use the aforementioned definitions interchangeably or by analogy (see e.g. the Greek Copyright Act which refers to films before their fixation as audiovisual works and after their first fixation as films). The fact that this analogy is very common in reality derives also from the Berne Convention, which assimilates all works using the process of cinematography or something analogous to it. Since, as we explained in the first section of this chapter, the category of audiovisual works is held to be the broader category which contains the rest, and since the most common sort of audiovisual works are cinematographic films, we will use the term audiovisual works and films interchangeably for the purposes of this chapter. Moreover, we hold that the notion of moving images, wherever it is not expressly mentioned (as it is e.g. in the British, US and French Copyright Acts in relation to films and cinematographic works), is implied by the strong relationship of audiovisual works to the rest of the aforementioned categories. We also hold that the European definition of films, as this is enshrined in the Rental and Renting Rights Directive (Council Directive (92/100/EEC) on rental right and lending right and on certain rights related to copyright in the field of intellectual property, [1992] OJ L346/61), and which refers to films as designating cinematographic, or audiovisual works or moving images, does not imply any essential or actual difference between the three. It only tries to encompass these cases where national laws might want to or do differentiate in relation to the scientific definitions they use for the aforementioned categories of works. However, this does not admit or legitimise such differentiations.

[26]   Turner, M. (1995), 'Do the old legal categories fit the new multimedia products? A multimedia CD-ROM as a film', *European Intellectual Property Review*, 3, pp. 107 seq., at p. 108.

with the notion of motion. Is motion a recording of apparently identical images, which have, however, been recorded at different moments, or do the images themselves have to communicate or create the impression of some kind of movement? If the second option is adopted then even when images are filmed with a traditional filming technique, if the average person cannot see with the naked eye that movement exists, the moving images, though moving in reality, are not held to be 'moving' for the purposes of the law. However, such a solution would disregard the essential criterion that is contained in the Berne Convention, namely the use of cinematography or a technique analogous to cinematography. If the first option is adopted then we could argue that the recording process is sufficient to qualify a work as an audiovisual work. It may not communicate movement in all instances but at least the potential for movement is there. A straightforward example is that of a plant, which grows extremely slowly. Even if a single picture is taken every hour over a period of three months, once projected as a film at a speed of 24 pictures *per se*cond little or no movement may be visible. Nevertheless this is an audiovisual work due to the technique used and scientifically speaking there is constant movement even if this is not readily perceived. An even more extreme example is found in a shot of a desert landscape, which is used to create a certain atmosphere. A one minute shot may continue to offer the viewer exactly the same view of the landscape. Nevertheless due to the use of the cinematographic technique and its potential for movement this is also an audiovisual work.[27]

Fixed frames or still images alone are excluded altogether.[28] A sequence of fixed frames sewn together (sequence of *images inanimés*) should also be excluded.[29] Berenboom alleges that the latter should not be the case as long as

---

[27]   As will be seen later the particular technique that is used to reproduce images is not of primary importance. What is, however, of importance is the content of the product and the fact that a certain type of recording has been made. For example, the shooting of pixels onto a television screen does not define the type of work. A photograph can be reproduced in that way on a screen, and so can a text. What counts here is the process of recording, as well as the content of the recording.

[28]   A series of archive photographs should not fall within the category of audiovisual works, Strowel, A. and J.-P. Traille (1997), *Le droit d'auteur, du logiciel au multimédia* (*Copyright. From Software to Multimedia*), Brussels: Bruylant, at p. 360.

[29]   See also Edelman, 'L'oeuvre multimédia', at p. 114. See *contra* Strowel and Traille, *Le droit d'auteur,* in relation to a series of slides which, according to their view, qualify as an audiovisual work, at p. 360. We hold the opposite view, similar with the one shared by Corbet, J. (1997), *Auteursrecht,* Brussels: Story–Scientia, at p. 38 and the Belgian Association of Copyright, oral process of 2 April 1992 on audiovisual works. Nimmer, D. (1995), (*Nimmer on Copyright,* New York: Matthew Bender) holds that although a show of slides qualifies as an audiovisual work, under the US Copyright Act, it does not qualify as a film because it fails to confer the impression of movement to the viewer, vol. 1, §2.09 [C].

these fixed frames have undergone a montage which allows them to unfold in such a way as to create the impression of motion.[30] In his view a succession of fixed frames should qualify as an audiovisual work, and he refers as an example to the film of Chris Marker, *La jetée*. His view comes very close to confusing the boundaries between artistic works and audiovisual works. If the notion of moving images is so broadly construed and approached, then there is nothing essentially different between the viewing of an artistic work and the viewing of a series of moving images on a screen. In this case the unfolding (the technical French term is '*déroulement*') of these images can no longer be distinguished from a trip round an exhibition or even from turning the pages of a book if these images or pictures are found in a conventional book.[31] In this sense a multimedia work containing fixed frames, which can be retrieved and browsed through according to the needs and commands of the user, and which do not impart an impression of motion or a continuous impression of motion occupying the greater part of their contents, cannot qualify as an audiovisual work. They come closer to literary works, databases or artistic works.

TWO WAYS OF CONSTRUING THE NOTION OF 'MOVING IMAGES'   If the *de minimis* rule rules out fixed frames altogether, the French view is broader. According to this view, the images have to be related and linked to each other in such a way that they can unfold, subject to a scenario for example.[32] By 'related to' and 'linked to each other' one does not mean that the images have to be relevant only to each other, or just follow one another in a logical sequence. They have to be sewn together in such a way that even if they are not 'moving images' right from the start, e.g. filmed as moving images or computer generated as such, they can at least impart the impression of motion to the viewer when they are communicated.[33] Thus, it is submitted that it is the sequence of images that should be recorded and not just the visual images.[34] The sequence of images when combined with the other ingredients of a film should be capable of producing a moving picture in a 'fluent movement'. Yet, the degree of that fluency is a question of fact, subject to the judgment and discretion of the

---

[30]   Berenboom, *Le nouveau droit d'auteur et les droits voisins*, at p. 193.
[31]   Especially in the case of an encyclopaedia; see also Edelman, 'L'oeuvre multimédia'.
[32]   Group Audiovisuel et Multimédia de l'Edition (1994), *Questions juridiques relatives aux oeuvres multimédia*, Paris: Livre Blanc, at p. 20.
[33]   This is also the American view. See § 101 US Copyright Act, under the entry 'moving pictures'. From a British perspective it could be argued that s. 5B(1) CDPA 1988 is wide enough in scope to include this possibility.
[34]   Laddie et al., *The Modern Law of Copyright and Designs*, at 385–6.

judge. It is alleged, though, that this 'fluent movement' can even derive from pictures taken in a rapid sequence (e.g. by still cameras in motor races capturing almost every second of action), if the gaps between them are small enough.[35] In this case

> the resulting spool might satisfy the definition of 'cinematograph film' even though the photographer was using neither a cine camera as commonly understood nor had any intention of making a moving picture[36].[37]

If the notion of 'moving images' is construed narrowly, one could argue that what the law is really looking for are actual moving images and in certain cases, perhaps, images that are moving before they are recorded as films. Under UK law this is particularly so after the replacement of the definition of films in the Copyright Act 1956 by that of the CDPA 1988. Under the former one could perhaps have assumed that the moving image had to exist before it was recorded,[38] but the CDPA 1988 no longer requires the pre-existence of the 'moving image'. An actual moving image can be an image taken by a cine camera, generated by a computer so as to be in motion. Yet, this narrow legal approach would leave out of the scope of the law the individual drawings (cells) included in cartoon films, which worldwide are held to qualify as films.[39] It is true however that these are held to qualify as films after they are collected, put in sequence and recorded on any medium (not only on pellicule) in such a way that motion can arise.[40]

If the first view is adopted it may be easier to fit multimedia works into the category of audiovisual works and films. These are clearly not images that already move before they are recorded but one could assume that most multimedia works introduce some kind of impression of movement. This becomes clear when one looks at an even more radical approach

---

[35] Even if the gaps are not small enough, in the way they have been described in the text, a reasonably fluent picture might still be produced if the subject was moving slowly enough, e.g. the filming of a germinating seed with a slow cine camera which is then speeded up for display. Ibid., at p. 386.

[36] Ibid., at pp. 385–6.

[37] Under German copyright law a 'sequence of moving images' is interpreted as a series of images and sounds that creates the impression of moving images. See Schricker, G. (1987), *Urheberrecht, Kommentar*, München: Verlag C.H. Beck, at p. 1002; 2nd edn, 1999, at 1371; and Nordemann, W., K. Vinck and P. Hertin (1994), *Urheberrecht*, Stuttgart: Kohlhammer, 1994, at p. 523.

[38] Turner, 'Do the old legal categories fit the new multimedia products?', at p. 108.

[39] See Koumantos, G. (2002), *Pnevmatiki idioktissia*, 8th edn, Athens: Ant. N. Sakkoula, at p. 132.

[40] Laddie et al., *The Modern Law of Copyright and Designs*, at p. 378.

which requires an audiovisual work to be just a series of related images which are intrinsically intended to be shown by the use of machines.[41] Most multimedia works could indeed be said to contain a series of related images and the issue of movement is more or less side-stepped. It is submitted though that whichever approach is adopted, multimedia works do not fit well with the category of audiovisual works and that each link remains artificial.[42]

'SEQUENCE OF MOVING IMAGES' AND INTERACTIVITY　At this stage we should examine which element the requirement of 'sequence' adds[43] to that of 'moving images'. It is clear that 'moving images' might be present in a work without necessarily forming a sequence or else a unity. Fragments of films, cartoons, documentaries, frames in motion, such as described earlier in relation to motor races or sprinting, these alone do not allow a work to qualify as an audiovisual work or a film. A characteristic example of such a case is a collection of fragments of films shown in the 1980s and 1990s. This encyclopaedia of films does not present a unity in the sense that the notion of a film requires.[44] Rather it comes within the ambit of a database, as this is defined in the EU Database Directive.[45] The moving pictures included in a film have to be coherent and united in serving one particular project, plot, scenario or otherwise. Simple audiovisual 'touches', or 'spreads' of fragments of moving

---

[41]　See e.g. §101 US Copyright Act 1986. A similar approach is adopted under Spanish and Dutch copyright law. See also Esteve, A. (1998), 'Das Multimediawerk in der spanischen Gesetzgebung', *GRUR Int.*, pp. 1 seq.

[42]　Desurmont, T. (1997), 'L'exercise des droits en ce qui concerne les "productions multimédias" ', in *WIPO International Forum on the Exercise and Management of Copyright and Neighbouring Rights in the Face of the Challenges of Digital Technology*, Spain: Sevilla, pp. 169 seq., at p. 176.

[43]　The CDPA 1988 does not contain this element *expressis verbis*. We analyse later in the text whether it nevertheless forms part of the concept that is contained in the Act.

[44]　According to Cornish a digital encyclopaedia which does not produce moving images does not fit within the definition of films, Cornish, W. (1999), *Intellectual Property Law*, 4th edn, London: Sweet & Maxwell, pp. 532–3.

[45]　There is, of course, a part of the literature that would consider such a collection of works as being an audiovisual work. Yet, if this kind of collection qualifies as an audiovisual work, it cannot qualify as a database at the same time, because, as Laddie has pointed out (and it seems logical), different categories of works are intended to accommodate different (and mutually excluding) kinds of works. In addition to that, in those national laws where the notions of databases have been placed under the wider umbrella of literary works, there is one more argument against the parallel protection of a work as an audiovisual work and as a literary work. These two categories of works are not only logically exclusive, but also expressly mutually exclusive from a legal point of view.

images are not covered.[46] According to Edelman,[47] if we have a collection of fragments of audiovisual works, without these works co-existing in a legal sequence or coherence (*sans queue ni tête*), it is not an audiovisual work we are dealing with but a collection of citations. The regime of protection for audiovisual works should not apply. In this case the resemblance comes closer to literary works, databases or the reading of a book than to the performance/showing of a film.

What is not clear at this point is whether the sequence of moving images which is required should be uninterrupted or not. In some national laws, interactivity in relation to conventional films was an unknown concept. Films were traditionally designed and produced subject to a linear form, inextricably linked with and dependent on the unfolding of images that were sewn together, so as to produce the effect of continuous motion. In other words, the viewer who was seeing the film was a passive receiver, whose task was no more than to watch the 'story' from the beginning to the end. The notion of interactivity, which is embedded in multimedia works, is by definition contradictory to any uninterrupted linear unfolding of a sequence of images, favouring a dialogue between the user and the system and the interference by the former with the latter according to his needs and choices.[48]

Nevertheless, this conclusion or observation is not watertight. There is also a part of the literature which contends that interactivity is not a notion completely alien to the area of audiovisual works and films. Films in their first expression did not possess any interactivity at all. But later, slow or quick motion commands became available, as well as freeze frame, scanning, time shifting[49] and other options. The choose-your-own-end films, which appeared on the market at the time, offered a better example of a primitive form of interactivity. The viewer does not only have a passive role (i.e. viewing the film

---

[46]   According to Turner, 'Do the old legal categories fit the new multimedia products?', at p. 108, the requirement of 'moving images' in the British definition of films 'obviously covers some of the displays that may be produced on screen by a multimedia product'. Yet, he finds it doubtful whether it covers animation, the different levels of compression below full motion video, screen scrolling and all other movements that are generated on screen.

[47]   'An audiovisual work can only be protected if it exists as a work. This means that it needs to have a certain degree of coherence in the sense that the sequences of images need to form a certain unit', Edelman, 'L'oeuvre multimédia, une essaie de qualification', at p. 114.

[48]   Deprez, P. and V. Fauchoux (1997), refer to interactivity as 'la négation du déroulement linéaire, au profit d'accès commandés par l'utilisateur', *Lois, contrats et usages du multimédia*, Paris: Dixit, at p. 48.

[49]   Recording of a film so that it can be viewed at a later more convenient time by the viewer.

only in the way it is presented). He intervenes and pre-determines the end of the film by selecting from the choices available. Yet, the aforementioned commands which were available to viewers of films were not commands inherent in the notion of films. They were essentially commands made available by machines, such as video cassette players, which could manipulate the image to a certain extent. (Films are not structured to serve such purposes. They are not structured in fragments so that their contents can be accessed independently.) These commands are referred to by Choe[50] as the first sperm of interactivity, or manual interactivity, and should be distinguished from the film itself, which presents no interactive options whatsoever. In addition manual interactivity was not only a primitive form of the actual interactivity that modern multimedia products present, but it was so basic and limited that it is qualitatively different from the one possessed by multimedia products today. It did not allow for any substantial dialogue between the viewer and the film, only for the exercise of certain primitive commands. These commands in no way turned the passive viewer into an active user and manipulator. Although they presented certain options, impinging on the development (stopping and starting) of the picture, in no way did they offer the ability to manipulate and reconstruct the image itself.

In the case of choose-your-own-end films, the viewer is not afforded any substantial degree of action. He is not allowed to 'enter' the image itself and transform it. What he is allowed to do though is to interfere with the sequence of images presented to him. This has little to do with interactivity, since changing the sequence of images is only one of the interactive possibilities, and a very basic one at that. The case of choose-your-own-end films can be compared with that of video games. Video games, which allow for the intervention of the player and thus allow for a degree of interactivity, were found in many jurisdictions to qualify as audiovisual works.[51] Specifically, in

---

50   Choe, J. (1994), 'Interactive multimedia: a new technology tests the limits of copyright law', *Rutgers Law Review*, 46, pp. 929 seq., at p. 935.
51   Cass. Ass. Plen., 7 March 1986, [1986] D. 405, concl. Cabannes, note B. Edelman; *Atari c Valadon*, TGI Paris, 8 December 1982, Expertises 1983 no. 48, p. 31(*France*). *Atari games Corp. v Oman*, 888 F.2d 878 (DC Cir. 1989) and 979 F.2d 242 (DC Cir. 1992); 964 F.2d 965 (9th Cir. 1992), 115 S. Ct. 85 (1994); *Computer Associates International, Inc. v Altai*, Inc., 982 F.2d 693, 703 (2nd Cir. 1992); *Stern Electronics, Inc., v Kaufman*, 669 F.2d 852, 855–6 (2d Cir. 1982); *Williams Electronics, Inc., v Artic International*, Inc., 685 F.2d 870, 874 (3rd Cir. 1982); *Midway Mfg. Co. v Strohon*, 564 F. Supp. 741, 746 (ND Ill., 1983; *Midway Mfg Co. v Artic International Inc.*, 704 F.2d 1009, 1011 (7th Cir. 1983) (*USA*). *Pac Man decision*, as referred to in [1984] EIPR, at D-226 (*Japan*). *Nintendo c Horelec*, Court of First Instance, Brussels, 12 December 1995, [1996] IRDI 89 (*Belgium*). *Amiga club decision*, Oberlandesgericht Köln, 18.10.91, [1992] GRUR 312 (*Germany*).

Midway Mfg. Co. v Artic International, Inc., the American Court held that even if the sequence of images varies after any new use of the game by the player, the notion of 'a series of related images', as this is referred to in §101 of the US Copyright Act, is still not affected. The work still possesses a certain unity, which is enough to allow the work to qualify as an audiovisual work.

The element of interactivity which video games possess is more advanced than the one possessed by the choose-your-own-end films. But it is more limited in degree. It allows for no more than a variation in the presentation of the sequence of the set of images which are included in these works. The user restricts his options in choosing option A, B or C. In fact A, B or C follow automatically after a first choice of action is made by the user/player. Nevertheless, this kind of interactivity has not reached those levels which are usually possessed by multimedia works, where the user has an even more active and creative role.[52] One such example is a palette where colours and designs are offered to the user with which he can reconstruct or create from scratch. Another is where various possibilities are offered for musical composition by adding melodies, changing keys or missing out instruments in an orchestra, and so on. This kind of result is often reached through the use of techniques such as morphing and blurring. In these cases the intervention of the user exceeds the level of options and reaches the level of reconstruction or new unpredicted creation.[53] In this context, it is difficult to understand how any sequence of moving images can be maintained.[54]

There is a serious argument that with regard to the definition of moving images, for example, UK law has been construed widely enough to encompass any notion of interactivity, especially in view of the lack of any precise prerequisite of 'sequence of moving images'. However, this argument looks weak in view of the practical reality as presented above. It seems that these moving pictures should exist in a sequence, or at least in some sort of coherent unit. Even if that requirement is not mentioned expressly in the law, it must purposively be derived from it, especially if it is referred to in relation to the notion of a film which represents a certain form in our minds. This, of course, does not mean that this form is not subject to evolution. Yet, we all know that the

---

[52] The Green Paper also requires a minimum degree of interactivity, Green Paper on Copyright and Related Rights in the Information Society, COM (95) 382 final, at 19.

[53] Always in the context of the choices offered, which can however be great enough to render the outcome unpredictable.

[54] Yet, it always remains open to discussion whether video games are a separate category of works, or whether they are multimedia products. In the latter case they can still be considered to require separate protection from that afforded to other multimedia products.

excessive stretching of certain notions and categories, as well as the departure from the historical interpretation of a certain provision, creates problems and presents gaps in the laws of the states. Most laws have been designed to accommodate certain forms of works and rarely others which could not have been foreseen at the time. In this case interactivity and especially 'reconstructive' creative interactivity cannot easily co-exist with this idea of unified moving pictures.[55] Nevertheless we should not ignore the tendencies derived from the example of video games, especially if these are held to be a kind of multimedia work. In the judgments referring to them it was not perhaps the actual nature of video games that gave rise to these decisions as much as their expression, appearance and need for protection.[56] This must have seemed appealing and must have come as a relief to the national judges who found themselves facing a gap in the law.

CONCLUDING REMARKS   It is submitted that, despite all the apparent similarities, the concept of moving images creates serious problems concerning the classification of multimedia products as films or audiovisual works. The apparent similarities are over-emphasised by the common use of the technique of projecting images onto a television screen in the form of pixels and by the fact that in both cases some form of movement or activity seems to be involved. As section 5B CDPA 1988 makes clear, the particular technique used to reproduce the moving images is not important. The essential element is found in the substance of the work, in the images that are projected onto the screen. It is submitted that these images are different, rather than similar in nature.

Let us return to section 5B CDPA 1988 for films. The essence of a film is that moving images are reproduced. The moving nature of the images is the crucial element. Sound can be an interesting addition, but it is not even necessary, let alone required. The essential element of moving images involves in some way the concept of a pre-defined sequence of images. The sequence of

---

[55]   Schack argues that the advanced form of interactivity that is found in modern multimedia works means that a multimedia work can no longer be considered to be similar to a film. Schack, H. (1997), *Urheber- und Urhebbervertagsrecht*, Tübingen: Mohr Siebeck, at p. 101. *Contra* Desurmont, 'L'exercise des droits en ce qui concerne les "productions multimédias",' at p. 176.

[56]   See in this respect Bertrand, A. (1991), *Le droit d'auteur et les droits voisins*, Paris: Masson, at p. 509. Ibid., 1983,'La protection des jeux video', *Expertises*, no. 56, at p. 230; and Edelman, 'L'oeuvre multimédia', at p. 110, where he alleges that a 'multimedia work is characterised on the one hand, by the intervention of a computer program that allows for interactivity and on the other hand by an audiovisual expression'. This audiovisual expression seems to have prevailed in the judgments of the judges before whom the video games cases came.

images creates the movement and it has been defined in advance by the makers of the film. The user gives one command and is then presented with a sequence of many images. This sequence may be the whole film or a rather limited section of it. In the latter case the viewer is invited to introduce a new command to release a new sequence of images. The content of the latter sequence may be influenced by the specific command given by the viewer. A limited and primitive form of interactivity is possible, but that interactivity leads only to the release of pre-defined sequences of moving images.

Multimedia presents a different picture. A variety of images are projected onto a television or computer screen. Still images, such as photographs and text are combined with moving images.[57] The images as such, and especially the moving images, are not the essence of a multimedia product. Not only are non-moving images involved, the sound element is also of equal importance to the final product. The essential aspect of a multimedia product is found in the combination and in the integration of the various expressions. That integration leads to an advanced form of interactivity which allows the user to create his or her own version of the work while using it. The user picks and chooses from a wide variety of elements, expressed in different media, to make for example a personalised tour of the ancient Greek cultural heritage, as it is found in the various museums in Greece. Often the use of the multimedia product will involve a certain form of movement and at the very least, movement from one screen to another will create an impression of movement. However that movement is often not based on recorded 'moving' images that are reproduced from the recording, but on the interaction of the user with the various materials that are made available for interaction. Looked at in this way the similarity is rather with a set of (un-)related photographs that can always be stitched together and shown at a rate of 24 photographs *per second* to create an impression of movement. We are trying to define the nature of a product that allows for interactivity. In this context we must return in our example to the individual photographs. They remain photographs in nature. Any subsequent use cannot change that, even if such use can lead to the creation of an additional work. It is therefore submitted that a multimedia product should not be classified as a film simply because its use would allow the user to create a sequence of moving images that could qualify as a film. The essence of the multimedia work lies in the element of interactivity. It does not have to be a recording that is made in a particular technical way the first time round for moving images to necessarily result from its normal intended use. It could rather be seen as a set

---

[57]   According to Cameron, D. (1996), multimedia works are not films since they essentially contain text rather than images. 'Approaches to the problems of multimedia', *EIPR*, 3, pp. 115 seq., at p. 116.

of elements and data, a database in its non-legal sense, that is combined with software that allows for a sophisticated form of interactivity.

3.1.4.   Fixation/recording   Fixation or recording, as provided for in the national laws on audiovisual works and films, would not be a hurdle for multimedia products to qualify as audiovisual works. Under section 5B of the CDPA 1988, the notion of films has been drafted very widely in relation to the medium in which a work can be fixed. Almost any recording falls within this definition. Some examples are films carried on celluloid, filmstock, print, negative, magnetic tape, videotape films, recordings on laser discs, CD-ROMs, DVDs and in computer memories. Thus, copyright in relation to films is not tied to any particular technology.[58] In the light of this, although multimedia products are always put in a digitised format, whilst films are communicated or transmitted in an analogue format, this differentiation is one made *de facto* and not derived from the wording or the spirit of the law and thus does not affect the law. Whether digitisation is included within the definition of films or not in relation to their recording, is not a contested issue. According to the record of the discussions at the time of the introduction of this law, it was stated in the House of Lords[59] that the definition of films was intended to include recording on magnetic tape, but that since it was impossible to foresee what new technologies for recording and presenting moving pictures might arise in the future, the object of the definition was to avoid tying the definition to any particular sort of fixation.[60] No specific method of recording is required. Thus, according to Turner,

> digitisation is clearly a reproductive process analogous to older processes such as Braille and Morse code in reducing creative work into a binary form.[61]

In relation to the medium required, he mentions that

> neither the medium from which the moving image is produced, nor the means of producing the image are of relevance [to a film] and can therefore clearly include a CD or other formats of multimedia products just as much as it does celluloid or video tape.[62]

In addition, one can contend that the medium in which a work has been recorded (either originally or derivatively) should also not affect the nature of

---

[58]   Laddie et al., *The Modern Law of Copyright and Designs*, at p. 377.
[59]   Hansard, 16 February 1956, cols 1085–6.
[60]   Laddie et al., *The Modern Law of Copyright and Designs*, at pp. 374 and 383.
[61]   Turner, 'Do the old legal categories fit the new multimedia products?', at p. 108.
[62]   Ibid.

the work, if, of course, the work has been fixed or transferred into the new medium without any substantial modifications, adaptations or alterations.[63]

Thus, if multimedia products were to qualify as audiovisual works, the fact that they are in a digitised format, capable of being manipulated by the user with the aid of a computer, and the fact that they are communicated to third parties through both material and non-material media, does not contradict the notion of fixed audiovisual works as found in the CDPA or other national Copyright Acts, and consequently does not create any definitional problems.[64]

4. Summing up

Multimedia products are not *de jure* audiovisual works.[65,66] First, moving images are rarely the prevailing element in a multimedia work. Multimedia works combine different types of works, and it is usually either text or still images that are their major element. Moreover, their purpose is not to be shown in public, and consequently watched by viewers. They are meant to be communicated to private individuals and are not intended to be viewed by a larger public. This is so since the general task of a multimedia work is to allow a dialogue between the system and the user. This dialogue, of course, presupposes the element of interactivity, which as such is a negation of any continuous sequence of images, linked together and constituting a unity. Fragments of sequences of moving images alone do not allow a work to qualify as a film or an audiovisual work. This becomes more apparent if one looks into the terminology used in the area of multimedia and that used in audiovisual works. A multimedia work is supposed to be read, watched and heard, and also to be used at the same time, while a film is simply to be watched. The person receiving the information in the first case is a user, with an active role, and even on occasion a creative one, whilst in the second he or she is a passive viewer. The

---

[63] Gautier, P. (1994), 'Les oeuvres multimédias en droit français', *RIDA*, pp. 93 seq.; and Edelman, 'L'oeuvre multimédia', at p. 114 and at p. 110, where he contends that the concept of the 'document', or that of the 'support' should not be decisive in the characterisation of a work.

[64] See also Cornish, *Intellectual Property Law*, at pp. 531 seq.

[65] See also the doubts expressed by Kreile and Westphal, 'Multimedia und das Filmbearbeitungsrecht', at p. 255.

[66] Edelman, 'L'oeuvre multimédia', at p. 114; and Turner, 'Do the old legal categories fit the new multimedia products?' at p. 109, who contends that perhaps multimedia products will be squeezed into the films definition on a case-by-case basis. This approach also receives support from Wittweiler, B. (1995), 'Produktion von Multimedia und Urheberrecht aus schweizerischer Sicht', *Ufita*, 128, pp. 5 seq., at p. 9; and see also Koch, F. (1995) 'Software – Urheberrechtsschutz für Multimedia – Anwendungen', *GRUR*, pp. 459 seq., at p. 463. With regard to difficult cases, there is always the risk that these cases might make bad multimedia law.

notion of interactivity is altogether absent in audiovisual works or films, whilst it is a vital component in multimedia. All the above, of course, do not preclude the case where a film can be designed and fixed as a multimedia work. If that occurs, of course, all the components of a film are present and the work should qualify as an audiovisual work. The existence or not of the interactivity element should then be assessed on its own merits. If the work has been designed in order to produce moving images, then this lets it stand out from the normal multimedia case in which the essence is not moving images, but interactivity.

Some French judgments dealing with multimedia products seem to be moving in the same direction.[67] In fact an encyclopaedia on CD-ROM was found not to qualify as an audiovisual works on two grounds. First, because it did not present a linear unfolding of sequences of images since the user could intervene and modify the order of sequences by means of interactivity. And second, because it did not contain a succession of moving images but only fixed sequences which could contain moving images. These two characteristics made the work lie outside the scope of audiovisual works under Article L 112–2 of the French Copyright Act. It was also mentioned that when this particular provision was drafted there was no way that multimedia works were the sort of work which could potentially be included in this definition. This could only be done by analogy. A similar case was decided by the Court of Appeal of Versailles.[68] An interactive video game on CD-ROM was found not to come under the scope of audiovisual works by reason of the fact that it was interactive as well as because the 'audiovisual part' of the work was an accessory to the software part of the work in which it was included. In both these decisions it is obvious that interactivity was found to be an essential part of a multimedia work which does not sit well with the notion of an audiovisual work (as perceived under French law) since it contradicts the existence of a linear sequence of moving images or at least a sequence of images.

[67]   TGI Paris (3e ch.), 8 September 1998, *RIDA*, July 1999, no. 181, p. 318 (*Casaril c Arborescence France*), confirmed by Paris (4e ch.), 28 April 2000, *RIDA*, January 2001, no. 187, p. 315 (*Havas Interactive c Casaril*).

[68]   Versailles (13e ch.), 18 November 1999, *RIDA*, July 2000, no. 185, p. 407; D., 2000, no. 20, somm. Comm., p. 205 (*Vincent c Software International, Schmid et Tramis*). There are a few more interesting French cases: TGI Paris, 28 January 2003, Com, -com, -élec., April 2003, no. 35, p. 17. TGI Nanterre, 26 November 1997, Expertises, April 1999, p. 117.

9 Adequate protection of folklore – a work in progress

Silke von Lewinski[1]

1. Introduction

Adequate protection of expressions of folklore has been claimed, discussed and tested for a much longer time than protection of other aspects of indigenous heritage, such as traditional knowledge or traditional names, signs and insignia. Yet, it seems that the ideal solution has not yet been found. In the past few years, however, considerable progress has been made in respect of the concrete drafting of tailor-made provisions, not least as a result of enhanced knowledge of the particularities of indigenous heritage. This chapter will focus on two documents which may be considered to represent the most advanced state of the art in the field to date, namely the Draft Substantive Provisions elaborated by the WIPO Secretariat on the basis of its earlier documents and comments by governmental, intergovernmental and non-governmental experts,[2] and the Regional Framework for the Protection of Traditional Knowledge and Expressions of Culture adopted by the Secretariat of the Pacific Community as a model law for the Pacific Island countries that wish to enact legislation in this field.[3] Before analysing the different model provisions, a résumé of the previous attempts to achieve protection of folklore and the possibilities of protecting folklore by existing intellectual property or similar rights will be presented.

2. Previous attempts to achieve protection of folklore at the international and national levels

2.1. The Berne Convention

It is not astonishing that the earliest attempts to achieve protection for folklore were made in the context of international copyright law, namely of the Berne

---

[1]   Dr., Head of Department, Max Planck Institute for Intellectual Property, Competition and Tax Law, Munich; Adjunct Professor, Franklin Pierce Law Center, Concord, NH, USA.
[2]   WIPO Doc WIPO/GRTKF/IC/9/4, Annex, pp. 11 ff. Reprinted from WIPO Doc GRTKF/IC/8/4.
[3]   ISBN 982-203-933-6; Model Law of 2002.

Convention for the Protection of Literary and Artistic Works. After all, expressions of folklore occur in the literary and artistic domain and appear, from the outside, like copyright works. It is also not astonishing that folklore was discussed for the first time at the 1967 Stockholm Revision Conference of the Berne Convention, which was the first revision conference taking place after most former colonies had become independent states and had started to represent their own interests as developing countries. Although folklore exists also in industrialised countries such as Australia, New Zealand, Canada and the USA, where indigenous peoples continue to live in their ancestral ways, folklore is of particular importance for developing countries where it is likely to be economically more important, at least in international relations, than the creation and export of contemporary works. In addition, the integration of a new subject matter into an existing international treaty would have saved the enormous effort of motivating a sufficient number of countries to join in order to adopt a completely new treaty.

Despite the obvious advantage of including folklore in the Berne Convention – an approach strongly supported by many (in particular developing country) delegations — this approach was not successful in the long term. The doubts about its appropriateness had already emerged during the discussions at the Stockholm Conference. In particular, delegations were sufficiently aware of the fact that folklore was different from authors' works in different aspects.[4] Therefore, they did not adopt the proposal by the Indian delegation to include 'works of folklore' in the non-exclusive list of literary and artistic works of article 2(1) of the Berne Convention.[5] Instead, the proposal of a working group was adopted as the new article 15(4) of the Berne Convention. It did not mention the word 'folklore' by intention, due to the difficulties in defining it. One may deduct only from the Report of Main Committee I that this new provision was supposed to apply mainly to folklore.[6] This solution was found against the background that folklore is usually not published and that one can usually identify only a particular geographical area from which a certain expression of folklore stems rather than any individual author or group of authors. Accordingly, article 15(4) of the Berne Convention was adopted as follows:

> (4)(a)   In the case of unpublished works where the identity of the author is unknown, but where there is every ground to presume that he is a national of a country of the Union, it shall be a matter for legislation in that country

---

4   On these differences see hereunder pp. 12–13.
5   Records of the Intellectual Property Conference at Stockholm (1967), vol II, Geneva 1971, p. 1152, paras 126, 127.
6   Records, op. cit., p. 1173, para 252 and p. 918, para 1509.2.

to designate the competent authority which shall represent the author and shall be entitled to protect and enforce his rights in the countries of the Union.

(b) Countries of the Union which make such designation under the terms of this provision shall notify the Director-General by means of a written declaration giving full information concerning the authority thus designated. The Director-General shall at once communicate this Declaration to all other countries of the Union.

Accordingly, this solution was based on the assumption that expressions of folklore would in principle be copyright works created by individual authors or groups of authors who would, however, be unknown, so that a competent authority would have to represent the author. This provision was an attempt to cover the phenomenon of community-based folklore by existing rules dealing with individual authorship. The fact that India alone has made the necessary designation of a competent authority under article 15(4) of the Berne Convention[7] may indicate that this approach to protect folklore was not the appropriate one.

2.2. *Model laws*

Further steps were taken thereafter in order to provide for protection of folklore. First, adoption of model laws at the international level was chosen rather than the elaboration of a treaty. In particular, the Committee of Governmental Experts of UNESCO and WIPO adopted in 1976 the Tunis Model Law with a view to assisting developing countries in drafting their own copyright laws in general.[8] Again, the issue was dealt with in the larger framework of copyright protection and also represented only a minor part of the entire model law. Although the provisions took into account a number of particularities of folklore, for example by not requiring the fixation thereof and providing for a specific definition of folklore as well as for an unlimited duration of its protection,[9] they were not completely adapted to the specific features of folklore, in particular to its collective nature.

Only two years later, a Committee of Governmental Experts was convened by WIPO and UNESCO at the request of the WIPO Governing Bodies in 1978 in order to discuss the protection of folklore. Its work resulted in the adoption of the Model Provisions for National Laws on the Protection of Expressions of Folklore against Illicit Exploitation and Other Prejudicial Actions in

---

[7] Nordmann (2001), pp. 25 ff.

[8] Tunis Model Law on copyright with a commentary drafted by the Secretary of UNESO and the International Bureau of WIPO, Copyright 1976, pp. 165 ff.

[9] See in particular § 1(3) in connection with §§ 6, 18(iv), 5bis and 6(2) of the Tunis Model Law, op cit.

1982.[10] Unlike the Tunis Model Law, this model law was based on a sui-generis system dealing exclusively with the protection of folklore. The protection was still similar to copyright protection in many ways. The defined subject matter of protection, namely expressions of folklore, was made subject to acts that had to be authorised by a competent authority or community, supplemented by exceptions to such rights of authorisation. The source of any identifiable expression of folklore had to be indicated. In addition, the Model Provisions covered the issues of enforcement and protection of foreign folklore as well as its relationship with other forms of protection.

Upon the basis of these Model Provisions, the Group of Experts on the international protection of expressions of folklore by intellectual property, convened by WIPO and UNESCO in December 1984, discussed a draft treaty in order to meet the needs of an international legal framework for the protection of folklore. This was based on national treatment.[11] Yet, a number of problems were perceived for which no immediate solutions were found. For example, the identification of expressions of folklore to be protected in other member countries was considered difficult. Nor was a solution seen for expressions of folklore extending beyond national borders. Also, the scope of international obligations under the Draft Treaty was considered vague. The Group of Experts eventually considered adoption of an international treaty in the field as premature and recommended that experience of the protection of folklore at national level should first be gained.[12] International ambitions faded after this discouraging result.

2.3.   Recent attempts and the WIPO Intergovernmental Committee

Only twelve years later, the topic was revived first in the context of the preparation of WIPO for the Diplomatic Conference 1996 where new treaties on the protection of copyright, on the protection of performances and phonograms as well as on the sui-generis protection of databases were put on the agenda. Developing countries might have felt that these treaties would mainly benefit industrialised countries and tried to establish a link between the planned database treaty and a possible international treaty for the protection of folklore

---

[10]   Copyright 1982, pp. 278 ff. On the Model Provisions see for example Kuruk (1999), p. 815 and Ficsor (1999), pp. 7–12.

[11]   See the Draft Treaty for the Protection of Expressions of Folklore against illicit Exploitation and other Traditional Actions (1984), reprinted in Copyright Bulletin of UNESCO 1985, para 9.19 no 2, pp. 34 ff and Copyright 1985, pp. 47 ff (with comments).

[12]   Report on the Meeting of the Group of Experts on the International Protection of Expressions of Folklore by Intellectual Property convened by WIPO and UNESCO, Copyright 1985, pp. 40 et seq, in particular para 14.

from which they might derive some benefit. In reaction to this claim, the Committee of Experts which prepared the 1996 WIPO treaties recommended in February 1996 to the Governing Bodies of WIPO that WIPO should organise an international forum for the exploration of issues concerning the preservation and protection of expressions of folklore, the intellectual property aspects thereof and the harmonisation of different regional interests.[13] Such a forum was indeed later organised in Phuket, Thailand, in April 1997, together with UNESCO.[14] It adopted a very ambitious action plan to be submitted to the competent organs of UNESCO and WIPO: In addition to regional consultations, a committee of experts was to be established in cooperation with UNESCO in order to 'complete the drafting of a new international agreement on the sui-generis protection of folklore . . . in view of the possible convocation of a Diplomatic Conference, preferably in the second half of 1998'.[15]

As developments have shown, this plan was not realistic. Nevertheless, the topic had a certain leverage in the context of the then emerging, new issues of the possible protection of biological resources and associated traditional knowledge. The WIPO and the United Nations Environment Program (UNEP) began work in these areas with a joint study in 1998 concerning the role of intellectual property rights in the sharing of benefits arising from the use of such resources and knowledge. Further steps and claims by Member States of WIPO in these two areas then became the driving force for the establishment of the new Intergovernmental Committee on Intellectual Property and Genetic Resources, Traditional Knowledge and Folklore in 2001 at WIPO. Also, from 1998 on, WIPO carried out fact-finding missions in the fields of genetic resources, traditional knowledge and folklore, resulting in the final report of 2001.[16] From 2001 until summer 2007, the Intergovernmental Committee has met eleven times and achieved considerable progress in particular as regards the availability and compilation of information on existing protection and continuing challenges. Many studies on different aspects were carried out, questionnaires have served to gain up to date information on existing suigeneris protection and its enforcement and, not least due to the knowledge gained, awareness of the issues and the level of detail in discussions has risen considerably. The discussions in the Intergovernmental Committee have also

---

[13] Report on the Meeting, WIPO Doc BCP/CE/VI/16-INR/CE/V/14, para 269.

[14] UNESCO publication no CLT/CIC/98/1 and WIPO publication no 758/E.

[15] UNESCO/WIPO, World Forum on the Protection of Folklore/Geneva 1998, p. 235.

[16] WIPO Report on Fact-Finding Missions of Intellectual Property and Traditional Knowledge (1998–9), Intellectual Property Needs and Expectations of Traditional Knowledge Holders, Geneva, April 2001, WIPO Publication no 768. See also Wendland (2002a) pp. 488 ff.

shown that it is necessary and worthwhile to have a closer look than before at the particular features of folklore and indigenous heritage in general. Whatever the final outcome of the Committee's work – soft law, such as non-binding recommendations, a model law for national legislation or even a treaty – the advancement of awareness and knowledge alone, as acquired in particular through the process within the Intergovernmental Committee, is definitely progress as compared to earlier work in the field.

3. Existing protection of folklore by intellectual property and sui-generis rights

3.1. *Copyright and neighbouring rights*
The fact that copyright in most cases does not protect expressions of folklore as such is largely agreed on by scholars as well as in political discussion. It is therefore not necessary to elaborate in detail on the reasons for the general incapacity of copyright to cover expressions of folklore as such. These reasons include individual authorship under copyright versus the communal character of folklore, the limited duration of copyright and, in this context, the originality level, as well as, in certain countries, the fixation requirement versus the continuous and oral nature of folklore.[17] Yet, it has to be acknowledged that folklore has been considered as being protected by copyright in specific cases, in particular where folklore has been expressed by a living author and where the required originality level is extremely low, such as in Australia.[18]

It must be stressed that only the protection of folklore as such is at stake. In contrast, individual works created on the basis of folklore can be protected. Where, for example, contemporary aboriginal artists create individual works which fulfil the general requirements of copyright, then these individual works are protected under the general rules. These rules also include the limited duration of protection after the author's death and the limited scope of protection: Only creative additions by the author are protected, rather than the elements of pre-existing folklore, such as symbols, stories, techniques and styles, which have been integrated into the contemporary painting. Accordingly, and in compliance with the general rules, copyright protection will extend only to original elements. Consequently, the closer the new work's reference to or integration of the expressions of folklore, the more restricted will be the scope of protection.

---

17   For an extensive discussion of these obstacles for protection see in particular Lucas-Schloetter (2004), pp. 291–8.
18   *Bulun Bulun and Another v R&T Textiles Pty Ltd and Another* (1998) 41 IPR 513, 520.

Copyright and neighbouring rights protection may apply also to works or achievements that are made in the context of expressions of folklore. A number of examples may be given. In particular, different kinds of recordings of folklore may result in protection for the recordings rather than for the folklore itself. A photographer who fixes folklore will receive copyright in the photographic work or a neighbouring right in a non-copyrightable photograph; the producer of a recording of folklore music or the producer of a film fixing folklore dances can be protected as a phonogram producer or a film producer respectively in relation to the phonogram or film (as opposed to the folklore as such). Also, researchers who collect expressions of folklore and arrange them in a certain order may be protected for such collections (i.e. not the folklore itself) if the general copyright conditions for collections are fulfilled. Performers of folklore may be protected in respect of their performances (not the folklore as such) and even have to be so under recent international law, namely article 2(a) of the WIPO Performances and Phonograms Treaty 1996. In most of these cases, indigenous communities would not in fact benefit from such protection, since they usually do not make fixations or collections of their own folklore. However, performers of folklore will often stem from indigenous communities and therefore benefit from protection in their performances, so that in this case the communities may be protected indirectly in respect of the folklore performed.

3.2.   Other intellectual property rights

Apart from copyright and neighbouring rights law, design law is also not satisfactory as a means of protection. It applies only to two- or three-dimensional objects with artistic qualities made for industrial application. Its requirements of novelty, originality, formalities and industrial application will often not be fulfilled; in addition, even if they were fulfilled in an individual case, its short duration of between five and 25 years would not correspond to the nature of folklore as living heritage. Trademarks and geographical indications may be a viable way of indirectly protecting folklore, where expressions of folklore are marketed. These intellectual property rights may serve the authenticity needs of indigenous peoples by clearly designating the origin of the expressions of folklore and decreasing the market for 'copycat' products. Accordingly, while the right-holders cannot prevent others from using the expressions of folklore, they can prohibit them from using the trademark or geographical indication in the context of these expressions, to the advantage of the authentic expression of folklore in the market. To this extent, trademarks and geographical indications can be useful to indigenous communities. In addition, registration by associations (rather than individual right-owners only) is possible, in particular in the case of collective and certification marks. Also, their term of protection lasts as long as the mark is used. Yet, the disadvantages of protection by trademarks and geographical indications include the need to register the mark or to gain governmental recognition as a regional association benefiting from a geographical indication, the costs of trademark registration and maintenance and the knowledge needed about these procedures, such as the best marketing strategies and connected efforts.[19]

To some extent, the law of unfair competition may also provide protection for folklore, in particular in the form of trade secret protection,[20] which is a case of unfair competition in civil law jurisdictions and a case of 'breach of confidence' under the common law concept. It only applies where the expression of folklore is secret and confidential, namely known only to those who are authorised by indigenous customary law to know it, and where a confidentiality obligation exists. In these cases, protection is granted against the utilisation of folklore without authorisation. Another case of unfair competition is the protection of the commercial reputation acquired by an indigenous community, for example in the field of indigenous art. In such a case, others may be prevented from behaving in a way which would affect the reputation of the community. As may be seen, the relevant instances are quite specific and limited to situations involving commercial transactions.[21] Contracts may be helpful only where an outsider is forced to conclude a contract in order to get access to the folklore, such as in the case of secret folklore. Also existing laws outside intellectual property, such as norms on the protection of cultural heritage or human rights, will usually not serve as a basis for concrete protection.

3.3   Sui-generis laws

Not least on the basis of the WIPO Model Provisions 1982, many countries have introduced sui-generis protection systems.[22] Although such laws, like the Model Provisions, have taken into account the particular features of folklore to some considerable extent, it seems that they have not been applied or enforced in many countries.[23] The fact that sui-generis protection in many countries seems to exist only on paper rather than also in reality may be due to a number of factors, such as the following: In many developing countries, much more basic and urgent problems have to be tackled, such as the supply of clean water, the fight against AIDS, the supply of sufficient food, medicine etc. Another factor may be the often low appreciation of folklore in developing

---

[19]   For more details on the advantages and disadvantages of trademark protection, see Kur (2004), pp. 86–9 and regarding geographical indications, Lucas-Schloetter (2004), pp. 311f.

[20]   Art 39 TRIPS Agreement.

[21]   For more details see Lucas-Schloetter (2004), pp. 312–15.

[22]   See in detail ibid., pp. 286–91.

[23]   Wendland (2002b), p. 115.

countries in so far as they continue to strive to copy western models rather than following their own traditions, for example where western business suits are used instead of traditional dress. Also, depending on the country, indigenous communities may often not have the power to fight for the enforcement of such protection, in particular where tensions prevail between indigenous communities and non-indigenous governments.

3.4.   Customary law

Finally, one of the existing legal means of protecting expressions of folklore has been largely neglected for a long time: customary laws and protocols of indigenous communities. Their main deficiency is that, in principle, they do not apply to outsiders or otherwise outside the communities, so that the most important cases of misappropriation of folklore cannot be pursued on this basis.[24] Yet, in search of protection models on a national, regional or international basis, it is worthwhile exploring customary laws and protocols in respect of expressions of folklore. Very little is yet known and, where expressions of folklore are covered by customary rules, such rules may be quite diverse in the different communities. Therefore, only those examples which have been made known, especially in the framework of Australian court decisions such as *Bulun Bulun*,[25] or those known from anthropological research can be given here. WIPO's work certainly goes in the right direction where it tries to encourage research in the field of customary law and gives some indications of relevant aspects.[26] A look at customary law is worthwhile not least because it may reflect the different world views of indigenous communities and thereby clearly show the basic differences between an indigenous and western approach in dealing with expressions of folklore.

Although no generalisation is possible, certain characteristics of indigenous world views can be described as being frequent. In particular, indigenous peoples usually have a holistic view of the world in which every element, such as the land, animals, plants, humans, their ancestors and spirits, is interrelated and has to be respected equally. The high importance of the land and the natural environment is another common feature. Relationships with all elements of the world including the members of a community are also of major importance and are best expressed through mutual respect. Expressions of folklore usually have a much deeper meaning and function than music, art,

---

[24]   On the application of customary laws and protocols in situations involving outside elements through tribal courts and federal courts in the USA, see Cooter and Fikentscher (1998), pp. 559 ff.

[25]   *Bulun Bulun*, op. cit., at 513.

[26]   http://www.wipo.int/tk/en/consultations/customary_law/guidelines.pdf, accessed 15 September 2006.

dance, etc in western societies: Rather than only serving as entertainment, they often present the link of an individual member of the community with the other members, the land, the ancestors and the entire surrounding world. Making a design, dancing a ceremonial dance or singing a folklore song often serves to re-establish these links, to reconnect and bring into harmony the individuals with their surrounding world. Such activities reaffirm self-identification and thereby strengthen the identity of an entire community and the position of its individual members within the community, and may even be essential for its survival as a distinct community. The context of self-determination also becomes evident here. Expressions of folklore may even contain concrete information which may be useful for the life or even survival of an indigenous community, such as information on the topography of the surrounding land, on the places of waterholes in a desert, and so on.

Indigenous communities are usually characterised by their collective focus as opposed to individualistic, western-style societies. Therefore, western notions of 'property' or 'intellectual property' do not exist in a comparable way in such communities. One should rather speak of community or tribal ownership or, even better, custodianship for the benefit of the community. Often, customary laws determine concrete persons, families, clans or other groups within the community as being exclusively permitted to reproduce or otherwise use expressions of folklore and in what context they may do so. Such rules often do not apply in the same way to all existing expressions of folklore but vary according to the specific expression of folklore. Also, some expressions may be secret and under the exclusive custodianship of one person or a group of persons, while others may be known to the entire community.

Such exclusive 'rights' of use usually bring about a corresponding responsibility to exercise custodianship in accordance with customary law. Receiving knowledge about a particular expression of folklore and the way of using it properly may be seen as a gift which requires the receiving person to give something back to the community, in particular by fulfilling his responsibilities in respect of such an expression of folklore. If anyone uses expressions of folklore in a way not permitted by customary law or otherwise goes against customary rules in general, sanctions usually aim at re-establishing the relationship which was broken by the improper behaviour. Therefore, instead of confining infringers in prisons or asking for monetary damages, infringers may be asked to perform a dangerous hunting action or other acts which would benefit the community, or otherwise show that he or she values the customary laws and agrees to be bound thereby.

Another characteristic feature of customary law is its dynamic and oral nature. In the same way as expressions of folklore and other aspects of indigenous heritage evolve constantly as they are being practised and transmitted from generation to generation orally rather than being fixed in static form, so too the customary law is usually not laid down but known and further developed by particular persons or groups within the community. It is evident that the nature of this customary law would not meet the requirements of western civilisation for legal certainty.

4. The most recent Draft Provisions of WIPO and of the Model Law 2002 of the Pacific Community

4.1. Overview

The preceding analysis has shown that indigenous world views, in particular in respect of indigenous heritage, including expressions of folklore, are fundamentally different from western thinking and, in particular, from concepts such as intellectual property rights. So far, the protection models contained in particular in the Tunis Model Law and the 1982 Model Provisions were based on the model of copyright protection, subject to certain modifications, and on similar sui-generis provisions respectively. It seems obvious that, in reality, it would hardly be possible to make customary laws applicable beyond the affected communities and difficult to have them respected in the framework of rules on applicable law even within one country. Yet, it seems not only appropriate but also necessary for better protection of expressions of folklore beyond indigenous communities to take account of customary laws as much as possible. Certain attempts to do so have already been made by Australian courts, in particular where a fiduciary relationship was recognised obiter dicta on the basis of customary law, leading to fiduciary obligations of an indigenous artist towards the community not to exploit the work in a way contrary to customary law and, in case of an infringement, to take appropriate action to restrain and remedy the infringement.[27] Yet, there is no guarantee that courts, even under the common law system, would take account of the customary law of indigenous communities in the future. Therefore, another, more promising approach is to integrate certain elements of customary law into legislative norms – whether they are national, regional or international norms. This approach has been taken in particular in the most recent Draft Provisions of WIPO and in the Model Law of the Pacific Community. The following subsection will present and analyse in particular the WIPO Draft Provisions.

The individual articles of the WIPO Draft Provisions (hereinafter 'Draft Provisions') concern similar matters as would be covered by norms on copyright or other intellectual property protection: The subject matter of protection, beneficiaries, acts of misappropriation (scope of protection), management of rights, exceptions and limitations, term of protection, formalities, sanctions/remedies

---

[27] *Bulun Bulun*, op. cit., at 531.

and exercise of rights, transitional measures, relationship with intellectual property protection and other forms of protection, preservation and promotion, and international and regional protection. Although this structure may look similar, at first sight, to traditional intellectual property rights norms, the draft articles show a number of remarkable deviations, as shown below.

4.2.   Subject matter of protection

The subject matter of protection is designated in article 1 Draft Provisions as ' "traditional cultural expressions" or "expressions of folklore" '. This alternative use of both notions reflects the underlying controversy about the proper designation of the subject matter of protection: 'Folklore' is considered by some as having a negative connotation, stemming from colonial times when folklore was considered as 'primitive'. When WIPO therefore chose to use the term 'traditional cultural expressions', others stated to the contrary their preference for 'expressions of folklore', which they considered as a generally established term without any negative connotation.

These terms are then defined as 'any forms . . . in which traditional culture and knowledge are expressed, appear or are manifested . . .'. The definition explicitly covers tangible and intangible forms and then gives a list of examples of such forms of expression and combinations thereof, including verbal expressions from stories to words, signs, names and symbols, musical expressions and expressions by action such as dances and other performances – which can all be, but need not be, fixed in material form – as well as tangible expressions such as paintings (including body painting), terracotta, textiles, musical instruments and architectural forms. All these different forms of expression must fulfil the following three conditions in order to be protected subject matter: First, they must be products of creative intellectual activity. It is worth noting that such activity may include both individual and communal creativity. The definition therefore also covers expressions actually realised by individuals but, as may be seen from the following two conditions, only if the expressions represent the identity of the community and belong to the community. The fact that an individual may have produced an expression of folklore does not however mean that the individual person would also be the beneficiary of the protection. Eventually, creation by the individual under the additional conditions (2) and (3) is regarded as the product of a communal creative process, so that the community will control the use of the expression and be the beneficiary of any protection.

Secondly, the forms of expression must be characteristic of a community's cultural and social identity and cultural heritage. Indeed, these characteristics reflect the very reason for the need to protect expressions of folklore, namely the fact that folklore, as practised, constantly re-establishes the links of community members among each other and with the surrounding world and thereby assists in reaffirming the identity of the community. 'Characteristic' for such identity and cultural heritage of the community should be understood in particular as what is the authentic expression of the community.

Thirdly, it is necessary that these forms of expression are maintained, used or developed by the community or by those individuals in the community with the right or responsibility to do so in accordance with customary law and practices. This condition reflects the common feature of folklore as living heritage as well as the reason for the need to protect folklore: folklore is important for a community as long as it is not only characteristic of it but also as it is being 'lived', namely practised, even through further development. Where folklore is no longer living and no longer serves the self-identification and linkage of the community to its ancestors, other members of the community and all elements surrounding them, it is no longer of importance for the community and therefore not in need of protection.

4.3. *Beneficiaries of protection*

While the beneficiary of copyright protection is the author who creates a work, and the beneficiary of performers' protection is the performer who performs a work, the beneficiary of expressions of folklore has been proposed to be the communities rather than any individual who may have been at the start of an expression of folklore. Communities are recognised as beneficiaries only if the custody, care and safeguarding of the folklore are entrusted to them in accordance with their own customary law and practices and if they maintain, use or develop the folklore as being characteristic of their cultural and social identity and cultural heritage.[28] These conditions are again consistent with the purpose of protection, which is inherently linked to the fundamental role of expressions of folklore for the identity of a community. Accordingly, the communal character of expressions of folklore as opposed to individual authorship has been taken into account in this provision.

The Model Law for the Pacific Community seems to be even more precise: The beneficiaries under article 6 of the Model Law are the 'traditional owners of traditional knowledge or expressions of culture' who are defined, in article 4 of the same Model Law, as

(a) the group, clan or community of people; or
(b) the individual who is recognised by a group, clan or community of people as the individual;
in whom the custody or protection of the traditional knowledge or expression of culture are entrusted in accordance with the customary law and practices of that group, clan or community.

---

[28] Art 2 of the Draft Provisions.

This definition even takes account of the inner structure of communities where individuals are recognised by the group, clan or community as being the custodians of a particular expression under customary law. This technique of referring to the relevant customary law in order to determine the beneficiary of protection seems to be a good approach: It would not be helpful to the communities if any abstract person who is not necessarily the custodian of the folklore were designated as the beneficiary of protection, nor would it be possible to fix any such person or groups of persons within a community, such as a shaman, as always being responsible for all kinds of expressions of folklore. Indeed, such custody rules may be quite complicated, vary from community to community and may even evolve over time. The best way of taking into account such customary law is the legal technique of reference which leaves a certain flexibility and honours the dynamic nature of customary law. Admittedly, the need to find out which community has custody of a particular expression of folklore and which person inside such a community is the custodian on behalf of the community according to the respective customary law may be a deterrent for outsiders who wish to use expressions of folklore, particularly if these persons are used to legal certainty. Such practical concerns would have to be addressed by different mechanisms such as, in particular, the establishment of a central authority which could either establish a contact with the relevant community or even act on behalf of the community.[29]

In article 2 of the Draft Provisions, WIPO uses the term 'indigenous peoples and traditional and other cultural communities' in order to be as comprehensive as possible and, in particular, to include also cases where folklore is regarded as belonging to all the people of a particular country, as claimed in particular by Egypt and Morocco.[30] In such cases, the term 'cultural communities' could include all nationals of an entire country. Article 2 of the Draft Provisions also takes into account cases where more than one community is custodian of a particular expression of folklore; in this case, all in whom the custody is entrusted according to customary law and practices would be beneficiaries. The question of allocation of rights or distribution of benefits among them would be addressed by rules on the management of rights and on formalities.[31]

Since the question of who is the beneficiary of protection also determines the allocation of rights and potential benefits from their exercise, it is not astonishing that a potential conflict of interests between governmental delegations

---

[29]   This aspect of management of rights is taken into account separately, namely in art 4 of the Draft Provisions and in part 4 of the Model Law for the Pacific Community, see below at p. 223.

[30]   WIPO doc GRTKF/IC/7/15 prov, paras 69 and 85.

[31]   Arts 4 and 7 of the Draft Provisions, see comments hereunder.

and representatives of indigenous groups is reflected in the discussions of the Intergovernmental Committee, in particular as regards the determination of beneficiaries. While indigenous groups have claimed that they were strictly opposed to any role for governmental agencies in this respect, and even in the managing of any rights, governmental delegates, in particular of African countries, have claimed that the role of the state in the preservation and protection of folklore should be taken into account in the context of beneficiaries of protection.[32]

4.4. Contents and scope of protection

The contents and scope of protection have been designated in the Draft Provisions as 'acts of misappropriation'.[33] Different scopes of protection have been proposed in respect of different kinds of folklore: The broadest scope of protection would be provided for expressions of folklore of particular cultural or spiritual value to a community, on the condition that they are registered or notified. Less strong protection is provided for other folklore that is not registered or notified, and very specific protection is provided for secret folklore. The broadest scope of protection for registered or notified expressions of a particular cultural or spiritual value or significance for the community is provided in the form of necessary, 'free, prior and informed consent' (PIC), which in part corresponds to a classical exclusive right in the field of intellectual property (IP); however, PIC does not allow for the possibility to grant licences and sell rights and thereby reduces the danger of commodification. Since users would have to obtain such prior consent and since it may be difficult for them to find out from whom and for which expressions of folklore such consent is necessary, the condition that these expressions be registered or notified as further specified[34] facilitates the task of the users. If communities decide that certain expressions of folklore are so important that this highest form of protection should be claimed for them, and if they fulfil these formalities, they shall enjoy not only economic rights comparable to classical exclusive rights in the field of copyright,[35] but also rights which are comparable to the moral rights of paternity and integrity in the field of copyright as well as a form of defensive protection by which the acquisition or exercise of IP-rights

---

32 WIPO doc WIPO/GRTKF/IC/7/15 prov, para 85 (Morocco).
33 Art 3 of the Draft Provisions.
34 Art 7 of the Draft Provisions.
35 Art 3(a)(i) first indent of the Draft Provisions mentions the rights of 'reproduction, publication, adaptation, broadcasting, public performance, communication to the public, distribution, rental, making available to the public and fixation (including by still photography) of the traditional cultural expressions/expressions of folklore or derivatives thereof'.

over the folklore or adaptations thereof can be prevented. All these rights are provided in respect of folklore other than words, signs, names and symbols. In respect of the latter, any use, acquisition or exercise of IP-rights over them or their derivatives 'which disparages, offends or falsely suggests a connection with the community concerned, or brings the community in contempt or disrepute' can be prevented; this latter protection certainly goes beyond what is comparable to copyright protection.

Lower protection for non-registered or notified expressions of folklore has been described as adequate and effective legal and practicable measures to ensure what might be called the paternity right (identification of a community as the source of any work derived from folklore), the right of integrity, protection against false attribution in the broadest sense in respect of folklore belonging to a particular community and a statutory right of remuneration or benefit sharing (instead of an exclusive right or PIC), but only where the exploitation is for a gainful intent, and on terms determined by a managing agency in consultation with the relevant community.[36] The role of the agency may again facilitate the user's task of finding out the person to address for negotiation and payment of remuneration.

Finally, in respect of secret folklore, adequate and effective measures shall ensure that unauthorised disclosure, subsequent use, acquisition and exercise of IP-rights over them can be prevented.

While existing sui-generis laws had already chosen either for protection by exclusive rights or simple rights of equitable remuneration, as well as rights comparable to moral rights in order to take account of non-economic interests, the differentiation of several levels of protection which can be influenced by communities through the decision to register or not to register seems to be new. Such a system might be too close to western thinking and not truly adapted to the needs of indigenous communities, in particular as regards the (admittedly optional) registration or notification which is in contradiction to the dynamic, oral nature of indigenous heritage, and as concerns the reference to civil or criminal sanctions.[37]

In contrast, the Model Law of the Pacific Community establishes a list of acts subject to PIC, and specifies that PIC is required only for non-customary uses, whether or not commercial, and clarifying that the traditional owners themselves are entitled to use expressions of folklore in the exercise of their traditional cultural rights without the need for PIC. 'Customary use' is defined as the use of expressions of culture in accordance with customary laws and

---

[36]   Art 3(b) of the Draft Provisions.
[37]   See for example the protection of non-registered folklore in its integrity and against false attribution in art 3(b) of the Draft Provisions.

practices of the traditional owners.[38] In addition to these economic rights, traditional owners are also granted moral rights in the form of the right of attribution of ownership in relation to the expression of culture, the right against false attribution and the right of integrity or to object to any derogatory treatment.[39] Such simple protection might be better adapted to the needs of indigenous communities. The interests of potential users can still be taken into account through the intervention of a central authority, even without the need to register or notify the folklore.[40]

4.5. Management of rights

As with the 1982 Model Provisions, article 4 of the Draft Provisions provides for certain tasks to be allocated to an agency in respect of the management of rights. Where PIC in respect of registered expressions of folklore is provided, the agency may act at the request and on behalf of the relevant community in order to grant authorisations, and collect any benefits for the use of folklore. Where a statutory right of remuneration is provided, it may monitor uses and establish remuneration, where requested. It is important to note that the Draft Provisions offer the alternative possibility that authorisation for use is granted by the community directly where it so wishes. Where authorisation is granted by the agency, article 4 of the Draft Provisions provides that this should be done in 'appropriate consultation with the relevant community, in accordance with their traditional decision-making and governance processes'. Also, where benefits are collected by the agency, they 'should be provided directly by it to the community concerned'. Also in the context of the remuneration right, the agency should only act where so requested by the community and consult with it concerning the establishment of the remuneration.

This provision has been quite controversial. On the one hand, it may be useful to involve such an agency in the management of rights for a number of reasons: Some communities may need assistance in properly negotiating contracts and monitoring the uses made of their expressions of folklore, due to language or communication problems in western languages, a lack of experience, a weak bargaining position etc. An agency may be advantageous to users also, since it may help them to find the relevant beneficiaries and to obtain easier access to the relevant holders of expressions of folklore. On the other hand, allusions have been made to the potential threat that benefits would not,

---

[38]   Art 4 of the Model Law 2002.
[39]   Art 13 of the Model Law 2002.
[40]   On the procedure of managing the rights under the Model Law 2002 see below and part 4 of the Model Law 2002.

or not fully, reach the relevant communities, at least if state agencies were involved. A number of representatives of indigenous peoples have stressed this point and opposed any mention of an agency at all.[41] In any case, it seems appropriate to require not only consultation with the communities before authorisation is granted or remuneration is established through the agency, but to require the agency also to follow the wishes expressed by the community after consultation.

While the WIPO Draft Provisions are deliberately kept rather flexible and limited to certain principles, articles 14–25 as well as 36–7 of the Model Law 2002 of the Pacific Community describe in detail the conditions to be fulfilled and the procedure of application for obtaining the authorisation of the traditional owners of expressions of folklore. They lay down, for example, the specifications to be made by the prospective user regarding the intended uses, the tasks of the authority towards the user and the traditional owners, including measures to search for the respective traditional owners, to help clarify disputes about ownership by referring the matter to be resolved according to customary law or other means as agreed by the parties, its role in the conclusion of a user agreement, etc. In any case, the provisions give priority to the decisions of the traditional owners. For example, the authority has an obligation to give a copy of the application by the user to those persons who it is satisfied are the traditional owners and, in addition, has to publish a copy of the application in a national newspaper or even broadcast details of the application, so that any further potential traditional owners have the opportunity to approach the authority within a deadline of 28 days. Where a dispute about ownership arises, it is again very important that the provisions refer back to customary law or other means chosen by the parties for the resolution of the dispute. Only if, after further procedural steps have been taken, no traditional owner can be identified or no agreement on ownership has been reached within a certain period of time, may the authority determine, after consultation with the Minister, that it is the traditional owner for the purposes of the Act, in which case the benefits arising under such an agreement must be used for traditional cultural development purposes.[42]

Regarding the conclusion of agreements with users, it is important to note that the Model Law 2002 leaves full control over the contents of the agreement and over the conclusion thereof to the communities. In particular, it is the traditional owners themselves who must decide whether to reject or accept the application and enter into negotiations. The authority only has the role of

---

[41]   See for example the Saami Council, WIPO doc GRTKF/IC/9/.

[42]   Art 19 of the Model Law 2002; regarding the procedure of application and search for the traditional owners see arts 15–18 Model Law 2002.

advising the traditional owner and acting as a kind of agent towards the applicant, for example by transmitting the decisions of the traditional owners to the applicant.[43] In respect of the contents of a user agreement, the Model Law 2002 contains a list of items which should be included in such agreements, such as sharing of financial or other benefits, compensation for use, duration of the use to be allowed, disclosure requirements, education and training requirements for the applicant, choice of law in relation to disputes, respect for moral rights etc.[44] Such provision is certainly useful because it reminds the traditional owners of the most important issues to be tackled in such an agreement.

In the process of negotiation, the authority again plays mainly an auxiliary role. For example, it is the traditional owners who, after drafting an agreement, must refer the proposal to the authority for its comments. Where the authority has the impression that the traditional owners do not have sufficient information to make a full and informed decision or that the proposed agreement does not adequately protect their folklore, the authority may assist the traditional owners by requesting the applicant and the traditional owners to meet with it in order to discuss the proposed agreement. Again, the final decision on acceptance, rejection or modification of any comments made by the authority on the agreement will rest with the traditional owners.[45] In a case where the traditional owners reject the proposed agreement, it is again the authority which will advise the applicant of that decision. This role as an agent may in many cases strengthen the bargaining position of the traditional owners, just as the described forms of assistance can do. Yet, the Model Law 2002 also leaves open the possibility for a user to apply directly to the traditional owners for their prior and informed consent. In this case, the authority still has to be informed by the prospective user about the proposed agreement, upon which the authority will comment and advise about other prospective traditional owners. The fact that no user agreement can be concluded without such information being delivered by the prospective user to the authority shows that the Model Law intends to protect the traditional owners from being trapped in possibly disadvantageous contracts. This system of management of rights under the Model Law 2002 seems to be very well considered and balanced.

4.6. Exceptions and limitations
The idea of providing for exceptions and limitations regarding the protection of expressions of folklore has been taken over from classical intellectual property

---

43 Art 20 of the Model Law 2002.
44 Art 22 of the Model Law 2002 includes even more specific items.
45 Art 21 of the Model Law 2002.

rights both in the WIPO Draft Provisions and in the Model Law 2002 of the Pacific Community. Both include a number of classical copyright exceptions such as for purposes of teaching, learning, research, criticism or review, reporting news or current events, judicial or legal proceedings, incidental uses, subject to indication of the source of the folklore. In addition, under the WIPO Proposal, these uses must be compatible with fair practice and not be offensive to the community.[46] While it may be questioned whether such classical exceptions would be appropriate in respect of expressions of folklore, the following specific limitations are certainly most ingenious from an indigenous peoples' point of view: Protection must in no way hinder the normal, customary uses, transmission, exchange and development of folklore by members of the relevant communities and is limited to uses outside the traditional or customary context.[47]

4.7.   The duration of protection

The duration of protection has been one major stumbling block for the application of copyright which expires, where the legal fiction of anonymous authorship is applied, 50 years after the work has been lawfully made available to the public or, where no publication has taken place, there is no obligation to protect the anonymous work, where it is reasonable to presume that its author has been dead for 50 years (article 7(3) of the Berne Convention). The need to protect expressions of folklore is rooted in its importance as living cultural heritage or, in other words, as an essential element of the daily life of indigenous peoples. Accordingly, it seems only logical that, once protection is granted, it continues to exist as long as such cultural heritage is living through the practice of folklore in the communities. Therefore, it is only consistent that WIPO has proposed to link the duration of protection to the continuous fulfilment of the criteria for protection under article 1 of the Draft Provisions which refer, in particular, to the maintenance, use and development of expressions of folklore by the communities.[48] For secret folklore, protection as secret folklore of course continues to exist only as long as the folklore remains secret.[49] Upon the suggestion of participants at the Intergovernmental Committee to provide for different terms of protection in relation to different forms of expressions of folklore, WIPO has also proposed that those expressions of folklore which have been registered (in order to obtain the highest form of

---

[46]   Art 5(a)(iii) WIPO Draft Provisions and art 7(4) of the Model Law 2002.

[47]   Art 5(a)(i), (ii) of the WIPO Draft Provisions and, similarly, art 7(3) and, at the end, (2) of the Model Law 2002.

[48]   For the other conditions see above pp. 218–19; art 6 of the Draft Provisions lays down the rules on duration.

[49]   Art 6(ii) of the Draft Provisions.

protection through PIC) remain protected as long as they remain registered. Yet, this condition should be interpreted so that such folklore could, after deletion from the register, at least continue to be protected simply through the proposed remuneration right.[50]

Similarly, and more simply, the Model Law 2002 of the Pacific Community only states that 'traditional cultural rights continue in force in perpetuity'.[51] The indefinite term of protection has been opposed by some who have argued that copyright and other intellectual property rights would also be limited in time for the benefit of the general public.[52] Yet, this argument is not convincing because the determination of the duration of protection should always follow the purpose of protection. While, for example, the limited duration of patents is due to the objective of giving an incentive to research in order to obtain progress in science, or where copyright intends to reward the author and secure an income for the two following generations, the purpose of protecting folklore is completely different, namely to secure the control of indigenous peoples over their living heritage in order to allow them to continue their lives in the ancestral ways. In addition, there is even one intellectual property right which is linked to the ongoing use of the object of protection, because its protection is needed as long as it is being used, namely trademark protection.

4.8. Formalities

In respect of formalities, the WIPO Draft Provisions propose that, in principle, the recognition of protection of folklore should not be subject to any formality but that registration or notification should be necessary in order to obtain the highest level of protection, namely protection through PIC.[53] Registration or notification in this case is intended to serve legal certainty and transparency in favour of researchers and other users. Yet, a number of set-backs are brought about by any such procedure, in particular the fact that folklore is dynamic and transmitted from generation to generation only orally; its fixation would go against the nature of folklore by freezing it in a static manifestation. The problem that fixations of folklore may be protected by copyright or neighbouring rights mostly in favour of researchers or others outside the communities[54] has been addressed by a provision suggesting that such intellectual property rights

---

[50]   For the different levels of protection, see the proposed art 3 and comments here above, pp. 221–3.

[51]   Art 9 of the Model Law 2002.

[52]   See for example the comments by the EC and Member States, WIPO Doc GRTKF/IC/9/4, p. 30 n 49.

[53]   Art 7(a), (b) of the WIPO Draft Provisions; for the highest level of protection see art 3(a) of the Draft Provisions and comments here above, pp. 221–2.

[54]   See above, p. 213.

should be vested in or assigned to the relevant community.[55] It is however not entirely clear whether such provision would be in compliance with existing copyright and neighbouring rights law, including in particular international law. Legal certainty, transparency and even the clarification of ownership in case of disputes on traditional ownership in specific cases could possibly be better resolved under the Model Law 2002 of the Pacific Community which does not require registration.[56]

4.9.   Sanctions, remedies and exercise of rights

Article 8 of the WIPO Draft Provisions on sanctions, remedies and exercise of rights is rather broad and recommends accessible, appropriate and adequate enforcement and dispute resolution mechanisms, including in particular criminal and civil remedies. Again, the Model Law 2002 of the Pacific Community is much more detailed and includes, besides traditional civil remedies, an order that the defendant make a public apology for the contravention and any orders that the court considers appropriate in the circumstances.[57] It explicitly refers to mediation, alternative dispute resolution procedures and customary law and practices regarding possible ways of resolving disputes.[58] One might even think of further customary law sanctions where appropriate.[59]

4.10   Transitional measures

Closely linked to the question of the duration of protection is the question of transitional measures, once a specific protection regime is adopted. For the same reasons as set out in the context of duration,[60] it is only logical to make any such new legal norms applicable to all existing expressions of folklore which fulfil the criteria of protection, while a certain flexibility is useful in respect of uses of folklore which had begun before the coming into force of the legal norms. Such a consistent approach has been chosen by article 9 of the WIPO Draft Provisions and, similarly, articles 3 and 35 of the Model Law 2002. At the same time, it corresponds to frequently followed models in the field of copyright and neighbouring rights law.[61]

---

[55]   Art 7(b)(i) of the WIPO Draft Provisions.

[56]   For the procedure under the Model Law 2002, see here above, pp. 224–5.

[57]   Art 31(1)(d) and (h) of the Model Law 2002.

[58]   Art 33 of the Model Law 2002; its art 34 in addition leaves unaffected any other rights of action or remedies provided under any other acts or laws.

[59]   The detailed provisions on enforcement are contained in arts 26–34 of the Model Law 2002.

[60]   See above, comments on art 6 of the WIPO Draft Provisions.

[61]   See, for example, art 18 of the Berne Convention, integrated also in art 9(1) of the TRIPS Agreement, art 14(6) of the TRIPS Agreement in respect of neighbouring rights, and in the WCT and WPPT.

Against this broad approach, it has been argued that folklore so far has been in the 'public domain' and therefore could not be carved out from it. This argument is not convincing because it only corresponds to the western intellectual property system so far established but conflicts with the customary law under which folklore has always been protected. In addition, even in the classical intellectual property system, there have been many instances where subject matter was not protected before; for example, where a country adhered to any international treaty and, upon accession, had to protect also pre-existing subject matter, or where a new form of intellectual property protection was created and, from then on, covered existing objects which beforehand had never been protected by intellectual property, such as the sui-generis protection of databases under EC law.[62]

4.11.   Relation to intellectual property and certain measures

Finally, Article 10 of the WIPO Draft Provisions clarifies that the specific protection of folklore envisaged does not replace and is complementary to any existing protection applicable to folklore under intellectual property laws and legal and non-legal measures for the protection and preservation of folklore. Accordingly, where an existing intellectual property right applies in an individual case,[63] the specific folklore protection may apply cumulatively. This is nothing new: Even in the field of classical intellectual property rights, such overlaps are known. Such an overlap of protection is justified on the grounds that both the purposes of protection and the conditions thereof differ in the case of each intellectual property or specific folklore right. Accordingly, these systems of protection remain consistent in themselves.

4.12.   International and regional protection

As regards the most important protection beyond national borders, namely international and regional protection, article 39 of the Model Law 2002 opens up the possibility of concluding reciprocal agreements stating that the same protection as provided under the national law is provided also to expressions of folklore originating in the other country. Article 11 of the WIPO Draft Provisions recommends that beneficiaries should be the nationals or habitual residents of individual countries and that foreign beneficiaries should enjoy the same rights as the nationals of the country of protection, as well as rights and benefits specifically granted by international provisions. In other words, the suggestion follows the well-established principles of

---

[62]   On this issue of public domain see also von Lewinski (2004), pp. 391–3.

[63]   On the limited possibilities of applying intellectual property rights to folklore see above, pp. 212–14.

national treatment and minimum protection known in the classical field of intellectual property.

5. Outlook

The issue of international protection is however the most controversial, as reflected in the current discussions of the Intergovernmental Committee of WIPO. Industrialised countries are more or less strongly opposed even to discussing any options for international protection, while developing countries, in accordance with the current mandate of the Intergovernmental Committee, are strong *demandeurs* thereof. Given this difficult situation, it would probably be wiser first to work on the development of regional agreements, which should preferably be based on models such as the Model Law 2002 for the Pacific Community. It is true that there is not yet abundant evidence for the fact that such systems of protection may properly function. It is even somewhat disturbing to learn that the individual Pacific islands still seem to be somewhat reluctant to implement the Model Law 2002 into local law. Although customary law has been taken into account to quite some extent, it seems that the Model Law is still too far away from rules with which local communities could feel comfortable. To promote knowledge and possibilities for implementation, the Secretariat of the Pacific Community has issued very detailed guidelines for national legislation based on the Model Law in 2006. In general, it will be necessary to refine any models according to local or regional particularities.

Apart from the need to show that systems of protecting folklore may indeed work, it is still deplorable that industrialised countries show so little readiness to even talk about the possibility of a binding treaty in the future. Given that developing countries have proved very cooperative in the past regarding classical intellectual property treaties from which they themselves often do not gain as much as they lose, it would have been appropriate if industrialised countries would now reveal the same sense of cooperation – all the more since it is very likely that any treaty, if ever concluded, would have relatively small economic 'losses' from the point of view of the industrialised countries but great profits in terms of good will. The need to regain good will from developing countries has already become evident: For around three years, developing countries have strongly shown their muscles in different international fora on other issues and have already slowed down, if not paralysed, most discussions in different international organisations. In particular, in the field of intellectual property, for example, discussions in respect of the planned treaties on patent law and on the protection of broadcasting organisations have been affected by objections and hesitations from developing countries. Yet, looking at the essence of the claims to protect indigenous heritage, including folklore, leads us back to a very basic concept: What is really needed in this area, in particular on the side of those representing western civilisations, is a sincere readiness to listen to the other side, to try to understand and accept the existence of different world views, concepts of property and so on, a readiness to be less egocentric and less focussed on own benefit only – in short: mutual respect. It seems it could be so simple.

Bibliography

Cooter, R. and W. Fikentscher (1998), 'Indian Common Law: The Role of Custom in American Indian Tribal Courts', *American Journal of Comparative Law*, **46**(3), 287 and 509.

Ficsor, M. (1999), 'Indigenous Peoples and Local Communities: Exploration of Issues Related to Intellectual Property Protection of Expressions of Traditional Culture (Expressions of Folklore)', ATRIP Paper GVA/99/27, pp. 1–20.

Kur, A. (2004), 'Trademarks, Public Certification Systems and Geographical Indications', in Silke von Lewinski (ed.), *Indigenous Heritage and Intellectual Property*, The Hague, Netherlands: Kluwer, pp. 86–90.

Kuruk, P. (1999), 'Protecting Folklore under Modern Intellectual Property Regimes: A Reappraisal of the Tensions between the Individual and Communal Rights in Africa and the United States', *American University Law Review*, **4**, 769–848.

Lucas-Schloetter, A. (2004), 'Folklore', in Silke von Lewinski (ed.), *Indigenous Heritage and Intellectual Property*, The Hague, Netherlands: Kluwer, pp. 259–377.

Nordmann, M. (2001), *Rechtsschutz von Folkloreformen*, Baden-Baden, Germany: Nomos.

von Lewinski, S. (2004), 'Final Considerations', in Silke von Lewinski (ed.), *Indigenous Heritage and Intellectual Property*, The Hague, Netherlands: Kluwer, pp. 379–96.

Wendland, W. (2002a), 'Intellectual Property Law, Traditional Knowledge and Folklore: WIPO's Exploratory Program', *International Review on Industrial Property and Copyright*, **33**(4), 485–504 and 606–21.

Wendland, W. (2002b), 'Intellectual Property and the Protection of Cultural Expressions: The Work of the World Intellectual Property Organization (WIPO)', in W. Grosheide and J. Brinkhof (eds), *Cultural Expressions and Indigenous Knowledge*, Antwerp, The Netherlands: Intersentia, pp. 101–38.

10 Regulating competition by way of copyright limitations and exceptions

Thomas Dreier[1]

1. Copyright, conflicts of interest and limitations and exceptions

Current copyright debate is dominated by the clash of interests between those advocating an extension of, or an increase in legal exclusive protection on the one hand, and those advocating, quite to the contrary, that the exclusivity of copyright should be reduced on the other hand. In particular, producers of works fight for an extension of copyright, whereas users, often 'spoiled' by recent opportunities of free access to copyrighted materials, oppose any attempt to limit the scope of existing copyright limitations and exceptions if not to abolish them altogether. In the digital and networked environment, copyright constraints are felt by end-users because, in the analogue world, the end-user was out of the copyright picture, owing to the fact that the acts he undertook with regard to copyrighted material – reading a book or viewing a performance – were copyright free.

The sharpening tone of this clash is generally attributed to the advent of digital and networking technologies. Copying without loss of quality and at almost no marginal cost plus almost unlimited possibilities of dissemination and communication, in particular in person-to-person filesharing networks, all cause a nightmare to rightholders. In contrast, the reaction of rightholders, which consisted in convincing the international community and the European legislature to strengthen existing protection by broadening the reproduction rights to cover even transient acts, to introduce a new right of making available to the public and, most of all, to grant legal anti-circumvention protection to technical protection measures and protection against the alteration or removal of rights management information, all caused the user community to complain that their fundamental rights of freedom of access to information and freedom of expression are being violated.[2]

---

[1]   Professor of Law; Dr. iur.; M.C.J. (NYU); Director, Institute for Information Law, University of Karlsruhe, and Honorary Professor, University of Freiburg, Germany.

[2]   For an early account see e.g. Dreier, *Copyright Law and Digital Exploitation of Works – The Current Copyright Landscape in the Age of the Internet and Multimedia*, 1997.

Where exactly individual authors stand in this clash of interests, however, is not so clear. On the one hand, if authors are interested in copyright at all, they want to have strong protection as well. That is particularly of importance for those authors who derive their main income from their creative activity, either directly as employed creators or indirectly by receiving royalties out of the proceeds of the exploitation of their copyrighted works. On the other hand, authors are generally interested in wide dissemination of their works, and this might be in conflict with the publisher's pricing policy (indeed, the relationship between authors and publishers has for long been described as a symbiosis, a term which in biology designates a way of living together which is beneficial for both parties, even if, or because, each of the partners benefits in a different way from the other). Also, as creators, authors want to use preexisting material in a creative way, getting inspired by it and transforming it into new creations.

1.1.   Exceptions and limitations: the focus on the private copying exception
Since the main clash of interests is between rightholders and end-users, the current debate by and large focuses on copyright limitations and exceptions which benefit individual end-users.

In particular, the debate focuses on the appropriate scope, if any, of the private copy exception in the digital environment. Against are the rightholders, who want to have this exception either abolished altogether in the digital field, or at least for it to be limited in scope; in favour are end-users, who generally want to see the private copy exception also applying in the digital area.

Whereas international copyright law, by way of the so-called three-step test (according to which any limitation contained in national copyright law must be limited to certain specific cases, not conflict with the normal exploitation of the work and not unreasonably prejudice the rightholders' legitimate interests[3]), itself strives to set certain limits in this respect, the EU Directive 2001/29/EC on copyright in the information society[4] in fact undertook a harmonizing effort. However, owing to the fact that not even the private copying regime in the analogue world had been harmonized in the EU, it hardly came as a surprise that the harmonizing effect of the Directive as regards digital copying remained minimal. However, it was already an achievement to legislate, at the European level, that rightholders should at least 'receive fair compensation' for private copying (something which is, however, not specific

---

[3]   Art. 9(2) of the Berne Convention, art. 13 TRIPS, art. 10 WCT, art. 16(2) WPPT and art. 5(5) of EU Directive 2001/29/EC.
[4]   OJ L167 of 22 June 2001, p. 10.

to digital private copying, since the same condition also applies to analogue private copying[5]). Moreover, in its list of the 21 copyright limitations and exceptions enumerated in art. 5(1)(3), the EC Directive 2001/29/EC on copyright in the information society has both opened up and limited the possibilities for additional copyright exceptions and limitations which indirectly benefit the end-user without addressing him as such. Such limitations include, but are not limited to, the making and sending of copies by libraries to persons who can invoke, for themselves, the private use exception, or the exception for personal research; the making available of protected works by libraries to its customers via dedicated terminals, or the making available either of parts of works or whole newspaper and journal articles to limited user groups within schools and universities.

Of course, there are several good reasons for focussing on the end-user. First, apart from the use of copyrighted material in analogue form, which only involves copyright-free listening, viewing and reading, the use of copyrighted material in digital form brings with it acts of reproduction by the end-user, which according to a traditional interpretation of copyright law are covered by the general reproduction right. Second, with digital copying technology and almost endless storage capacity, the end-user now also has at his disposal the technical means to make additional copies of copyrighted material at almost no cost and without loss of quality, thus completing a historical development which started with the dissemination of early reprography machines and, later on, magnetic tape recorders and VCRs. It follows that the end-user, who used to be a person not subject to copyright law, has become a new player and an important figure in the copyright arena. Because of this, end-users are henceforth directly affected by the scope and exercise of exclusive rights. Moreover, the use of technical protection measures – employed by rightholders who wish to protect their content against piracy and unauthorized taking and use as well as in order to control access and use-possibilities of different kinds and prices – also affects the freedom of the end-user to deal with the data-sets that represent someone else's copyrighted material. Indeed, the social, legal and policy issues raised are by no means trivial.

1.2.   Exceptions and limitations: the public interest and other functions
But there is more to be said about exceptions and limitations than that they regulate what the end-user of copyrighted material may do with regard to copyrighted material. Indeed, there have already been several attempts to

---

5   Art. 5(2)(a) and (b) of EU Directive 2001/29/EC. – For discussion, see, e.g., Bechtold, in: Dreier and Hugenholtz (eds.), *Concise European Copyright Law*, 2006, Information Society Dir., art. 5 note 3(b).

structure existing copyright limitations and exceptions according to each individual limitation's or exception's individual purpose.

First, it is generally said that exceptions and limitations are all in the public interest, in that they facilitate access to, and use of, copyrighted material under certain narrowly defined circumstances and conditions. The problem, however, with such a general approach is that any definition of what is the 'public' interest meets with considerable difficulties. It is difficult to define a truly 'public' interest as distinct from the interests of the individual participants in the production, dissemination and consumption of copyrighted material. Is the 'public' interest the sum total of all private interests involved, or is it some 'higher' interest, other than, and different from, each of the individual interests? Of course, in spite of this uncertainty in defining a 'public' interest, it appears that there is some legal interest propagated by the copyright exceptions and limitations, which would not be internalized by granting exclusive rights alone, and which is thus integrated in the copyright system by way of providing exceptions and limitations.

Second, although it appears that in each country, exceptions and limitations have historically grown under different conditions, power relationships, political circumstances and national mentalities, these otherwise not internalized interests and hence the exceptions and limitations which propagate them, may be somewhat summarily classified in at least three groups.[6] Without going into too much detail, these three groups are limitations and exceptions which are (1) serving very strong, overriding public interests, such as freedom of information (e.g. limitations and exceptions for news reporting or reporting of administrative, parliamentary or judicial proceedings) and freedom of expression (such as citation rights or the right to use protected works for the purpose of caricature, parody or pastiche); (2) serving other public interests which the national legislature considers strong enough in order to justify a deviation from the principle of exclusive right (e.g. limitations and exceptions concerning the use of works during religious celebrations or official celebrations, or reproductions of broadcasts made by social institutions pursuing non-commercial purposes, such as hospitals or prisons, etc.); and, finally, (3) correcting market failure (which is at least part of the rationale for e.g. the private copying exception,[7] but also for limitations and exceptions such as the one allowing the free use of works of architecture or sculpture, designed to be located permanently in public places, etc.).

---

[6]   See, in particular, Guibault, *Copyright Limitations and Contracts – An Analysis of the Contractual Overridability of Limitations on Copyright*, 2002.

[7]   For an early analysis see, in particular, Gordon, 'Fair Use as Market Failure: A Structural and Economic Analysis of the Betamax Case and its Predecessors', 82 *Columbia Law Review* 1600 (1982).

Third, it might be added that several other exceptions and limitations can be explained by the fact that although the use acts in question are covered by broadly formulated exclusive rights, they are only of little or no independent economic value (such as e.g. the exception for temporary acts of reproduction in networks and in the course of lawful use;[8] ephemeral recordings made by broadcasting stations for their own broadcasts,[9] etc.). Similarly, some exceptions and limitations ensure that the existence of exclusive rights which are merely 'ancillary' to the main activity of use do not result in subjecting this activity to the consent of the rightholder, if the copyright law contains an exception or limitation with regard to that main activity (one such example is the general possibility, under art. 5(4) of Directive 2001/29/EC on copyright in the information society, to extend the exceptions and limitations granted regarding reproduction rights to the right of distribution 'to the extent justified by the purpose of the authorized act of reproduction'; also, it should be noted that the European Court of Justice (ECJ) has limited the reproduction right with regard to advertising goods with regard to which the distribution right had been exhausted[10]).

1.3.   Exceptions and limitations: the aspect of regulating competition
However, this is still not all that can be said about the function of exceptions and limitations.

Already, copyright as such is not limited to regulating the relationship between authors/rightholders and end-users, but it likewise regulates the relationship between authors and publishers, and competition between those who offer copyrighted material on the market. Such competition may be horizontal on the primary level amongst authors, or on a secondary level amongst producers who produce directly competing products which contain copyrighted material (to the extent to which copyright law grants additional rights to the result of the activities of the producers, as is notably the case with phonogram and film producers, with broadcasters, and, most recently in Europe, makers of databases,[11] it threatens competition on the secondary level

---

8   Art. 5(1) of EU-Directive 2001/29/EC.
9   Art. 5(2)(e) of EU-Directive 2001/29/EC.
10   ECJ, case C-337/95 – *Parfums Christian Dior/Evora*, ECR I-6013 (1997).
11   Directive 96/9/EC of the European Parliament and of the Council of 11 March 1996 on the legal protection of databases, OJ L77 of 27 March 1996, p. 20, providing both for copyright protection (arts 3 et seq.) in the selection or arrangement of the contents and sui-generis protection (arts 7 et seq.) for investment in obtaining, verification or presentation of the contents of a database. For the scope of the sui-generis right see ECJ, case C-203/02 – *British Horseracing Board*, ECR 2004, I-10415; cases C-338/02, C-444/02 and C-46/02 – *Fixtures Marketing*, ECR I- 10497, I-10549 and I-10365 (2004).

of product dissemination as well as competition on the primary level). Moreover, competition may also exist in a vertical way between those who produce copyrighted material at the source or 'upstream', and others, who offer their services 'downstream', on the basis of other upstream authors'/rightholders' copyrighted material.[12] Here, competition arises not because of the comparable characteristics of the two products in question, but because the upstream author/producer wants to control commercially marketed transformations, adaptations and aggregations of pre-existing copyrighted works by downstream authors/producers. As far as the exclusive rights of copyright are concerned, this downstream competition is generally regulated by the protection requirement of originality (which includes the legislative decision not to grant copyright protection to the mere contents of otherwise protected works), by the limited term of protection, by the regulation of the adaptation right and the exception of free use as well as by the doctrine of partial taking.

It is worth noting that like copyright in general, some of the exceptions and limitations also regulate competition. Like use acts that are not covered by exclusive rights at all, exceptions and limitations which retract certain uses from the requirement of consent to be given by the original author/rightholder also open up these particular uses for competition amongst third parties who all benefit from the exception or limitation alike. This is at least the case where exceptions and limitations, rather than directly benefiting the end-user, indirectly benefit him by privileging an intermediate user who performs the copyright-relevant act (e.g. reproductions made by publishers under the exception for handicapped people, or school books produced under privileges granted to publishers of school books with the aim of benefiting school children).

This aspect, i.e. that copyright exceptions and limitations also regulate competition, generally tends to be overlooked if exceptions and limitations are merely discussed in their function of benefiting the end-user, or by referring to such vague notions as 'overriding public interests'. Of course, competition may certainly be one such public interest which eventually can override exclusive rights, as is demonstrated by cases like *Magill*,[13] But a discussion based on the general notion of overriding public interests does not focus on the aspect of competition, and hence does not grasp the impact which copyright exceptions and limitations have on competition amongst those market

---

[12]   For general discussion of barriers to entry for follow-on innovation in patent law see Reichman, 'Of Green Tulips and Legal Kudzu – Repackaging Rights in Subpatentable Innovation,' 53 *Vanderbilt Law Review* 1743 (2000).

[13]   ECJ, joined cases C-241/91 and 242/91 of 6 April 1995, *Radio Telefis Eireann (RTE) and Independent Television Publications Ltd (ITP)/Commission*, ECR I-743 (1995).

participants who base their products and services on pre-existing copyrighted material and provide value-added products and services. Moreover, there are a number of cases that have been decided at the national level concerning exceptions and limitations that regulate competition in the sense just described, cases which can not fully be understood if they are analysed only from the point of view of indirectly benefiting the end-user. However, the aspect of downstream competition is of particular importance in the information society, since information products and services are to a large extent based on pre-existing copyrighted material that is owned by someone else.

Therefore, it is the purpose of this chapter to examine a little further the issue of regulating downstream competition by way of exceptions and limitations – in particular with regard to value-added information products and services. To this effect, after a brief description of information value-added services and the need for competition in the field of value-added services (Section 2), the legal framework of international and European copyright law will briefly be examined where exceptions and limitations serve the purpose of vertical downstream competition (Section 3). As an example, German case law in both analogue and digital information value-added services is presented (Section 4), before some conclusions are drawn (Section 5).

In sum, it is submitted for discussion that competition amongst those intermediate commercial users with regard to uses of copyrighted works that are permitted by many exceptions, is more than just a reflex response to the intended benefit that shall accrue to the end-user. Rather, it is argued that in the information society, there is a fundamental need for competition in downstream value-added information services on the basis of upstream information. A broad legal right to exclude publicly available information from being included in value-added services or being listed by search engines operated by third parties risks leading to a compartmentalization of the internet into guarded zones and most likely to an undue restriction of competition, and thus would most likely interfere with the free flow of information and the public benefits associated with the networked architecture of the internet. Regulating downstream competition with regard to value-added information products and services is therefore a vital concern in the information and knowledge society, and part of that regulation is achieved by copyright exceptions and limitations.

2.   Competition in the field of value-added services

The reason for the relative inattention given by copyright scholarship to this aspect of copyright exceptions and limitations regulating vertical, or downstream, competition may be that in the analogue world, such vertical or downstream competition was largely confined to the distribution of one and the same material object embodying copyrighted material at different levels of commerce. In other words, the scenarios to be looked at here were limited to cases such as translations and adaptations, as well as to special cases of news reporting, such as reproduction and public communication of speeches held in the public domain, of newspaper articles or of copyrighted works which are visible from public streets and places or on the occasion of newsworthy events.

However, vertical downstream competition is particularly acute when it comes to information and information services. Information economics and the information society are to a large extent characterized by vertical downstream competition, at least to a much larger extent than traditional copyright industries in the analogue world. This has to do with the fact that in contrast to traditional copyrighted works – a novel, a musical composition, a painting – which often used to be incorporated in a single material object or product and which were marketed as such, today's copyrighted works are to a much larger extent used as the basis for new works and new services which consist in selecting and providing access to existing works and the information they contain. In other words: in much the same way as information in general, copyrighted information also serves as the basis for the creation of additional information. To be clear, what is meant by copyrighted information is, of course, not mere information which due to its lack of originality cannot claim copyright protection as such (and which therefore can be freely used), but rather the informative content of copyrighted works, which is often so 'dense' as to itself benefit from copyright protection. Information is not only reproduced, but it is indexed, referred to and cited, it is selected, repackaged, recombined and it is, last but not least, enhanced on its way from the source to different commercial and private downstream users.

In one way or another, all of these activities tend to add value to the information in its initial form. This gives rise to the question whether adding such value should be subject to the consent of the rightholder upstream at the source, or whether adding this value should be opened up to competition by third parties downstream.

2.1. *Information value-added services*

Before this question can be answered, an – albeit brief – characterization of information value-added products and services seems to be called for, in the way it is used for the purposes of this chapter. In general, an information value-added product or service offers, on the basis of pre-existing copyrighted material, a service or a product which adds value to the original information product. Such services or products may consist in searching for, and referencing, other information or simply in opening access to existing information products, as well as in selecting, aggregating and regrouping pre-existing information. Such information value-added products or services satisfy a different or more specific information need than that satisfied by the production and dissemination of the initial products and the provision of the initial services. The existence of such different needs is a strong indicator of the existence of markets for those value-added products and services which are different from the markets for the original works in question.

In the analogue world, the simplest examples of such services are library catalogues, indexes, anthologies and encyclopaedias. Another still largely analogue example, although one already closer to the issue to be discussed here, are document copy and delivery services. In the digital environment, search engines that come up with hyperlinks which point to the particular sources the user of the search engine has looked for have to be identified as information value-added services. Searching, retrieval and saving also make up so-called personal online video-recorders (online PVRs), which provide information about broadcasting programs, receive signals, enable access to a central recording device and provide individual storage of the broadcasts recorded upon commission by a private customer. Also, services that recombine existing information products in order to create a new product or service have to be mentioned, such as services which recombine information stored in different databases or press-clipping services. A press-clipping is certainly more than a single newspaper, but it is also less than the number of newspapers from which articles are being extracted, because it would take a prohibitive amount of time for a single user to search through all the newspapers for articles they are interested in. Hence, there is value added as well.

In all likelihood, this list is not complete, since information technology allows for a growing number of business models which focus on activities as intermediaries in searching, receiving, storing, reproducing, processing and delivering information of all sorts, some of which is contained in copyright works or subject matter protected by neighbouring or related rights. Also, we might see in the future services which automatically retrieve, process and alter pre-existing information. However, such value-added services will still take some time to be offered in view of the fact that current information technology is not yet able to perform semantic searches and transformations.

2.2. *The need for competition in the field of value-added services*

Before the legal framework for the treatment of information value-added services is examined in Section 3 below, the question has to be answered why markets for information value-added services should be opened up to competition by downstream third parties, rather than being monopolized by, or under the exclusive control of, the upstream original producer or author.

Here, the preliminary question is why there is a need for information value-added information. This question is a simple one. It is easy to see that value-added information services are very useful to the user. But even on a more fundamental level, it can be observed that in an information society which is characterized by an information overflow, we will, in view of our limited capacity for attention, depend to an increasing extent on navigators and information-agents that help to retrieve, store, combine and impart the information available according to our individual information needs. Information overload is the problem, much more than having available and accessible too little information. In addition, it makes perfect sense to use the potential of information and communications technology (ICT) in order to improve our information engineering and management. In doing so, we will hopefully reach, or even create, a better world.

However, it is another matter to compellingly demonstrate that it is not sufficient to have these services offered by the holders of copyright in the primary materials, but that there should be room for competition by third parties. The question therefore borders the general question why competition is better than no competition, or, more precisely, under what circumstances competition is better than sole exploitation by the holder of an exclusive right. But although this question is as old as it is general, certain characteristics of information markets point in the direction of opening up markets for information value-added services to competition by third parties, at least to some extent. First of all, the market for the initial, upstream product is different from the markets for downstream value-added information products and services. Second, although it may well be that derivative products, different product versions and eventually even value-added services may follow 'naturally' from the inherent economic mechanisms of information economics,[14] it is not to be overlooked that value-added information products and services usually draw from multiple sources and that, therefore, they cannot be offered by any single holder of rights in the original material alone. Indeed, if upstream rightholders got together in order to offer downstream products and services, this would invariably lead to a narrowing of downstream competition. In cases where the downstream information product or service draws from all upstream sources, there would then be no competition at all. Third, as information products, the upstream products will often be sole source products, i.e. the information contained therein can only be obtained from this particular one source (e.g. weather data recorded only by one satellite), or the source is the only meaningful source because of its particular characteristics (e.g. the article of a particular newspaper on a certain news item, rather than the article of another newspaper on the same news item). In those cases, the substitutability of the information to be included in any downstream product or service is limited, if not non-existent.[15] Finally, even in

---

[14] For a comprehensive overview see Shapiro and Varian, *Information Rules*, 1998.

[15] Of course, it should be noted that the notion of 'sole' source does not describe an absolute property of the information provided by the source. Rather, in view of the fact that the value of certain information depends both on prior knowledge and on the information needs of the recipient of the information (the receiving end of the

cases where the downstream product or service could be offered by the holder of the rights in one or several upstream products, developing and implementing the downstream service or product is costly and certainly time-consuming so that absent the competitive pressure of third parties entering the market, there might be some unnecessary delay before consumers are offered these downstream value-added information products and services. In some cases, a deliberate time delay may even be called for from the business point of view of the holder of the copyright in the upstream works, because the delay helps him to maximize the revenues generated by exploiting the upstream material without satisfying any downstream demand. At any rate, under an exclusive rights scheme, competition in downstream information value-added markets requires that the holders of the rights in the upstream material grant licences to third parties on a non-exclusive and non-discriminatory basis. However, in general this does not happen where existing exclusive rights that are not otherwise limited by copyright exceptions or limitations allow for exclusive licensing or blocking downstream markets altogether.

3.   The framework of international and European law

3.1.   *Regulating competition within copyright*
As far as the legal reaction to these issues is concerned, the focus so far has by and large been on the control of the all too broad scope of the exclusive rights granted by copyright to be corrected by the external means of competition law. This is not the place to discuss what is, and what ought to be, the proper relationship between copyright granting a legal monopoly on the one hand, and competition law on the other. Suffice it to recall that although acting on the basis of copyright is not completely shielded from control by competition law, competition law only comes in late, operates an a posteriori control and is a heavy instrument based on a rather cumbersome enforcement mechanism. Indeed, there is something to be said in favour of balancing propriety and non-proprietary competition aspects directly within copyright.[16] Apart from the misuse of dominant market positions, which

---

communicative act which takes place between sender and receiver), the singularity of the information contained in a particular source, and hence its substitutability by other information provided by other sources is of a relative nature. Hence, in order for 'sole source' information to be a workable notion, it must refer to information needs that are typical of certain classes of information recipients.

[16]   For further detail, see e.g. Dreier, 'Balancing Proprietary and Public Domain Interests: Inside or Outside of Proprietary Rights?', in Dreyfuss, Zimmerman and First, *Expanding the Boundaries of Intellectual Property – Innovation Policy for the Knowledge Society*, 2001, pp. 295 et seq.

undoubtedly is the core domain of competition law, copyright, although having to work on an a priori judgment of typical factual situations, can handle questions of competition at a much greater level of detail. After all, doesn't copyright, by granting exclusive rights to some market participants and not to others, already regulate competition, both on a horizontal and on a vertical level? So why shouldn't it likewise do so by crafting appropriately fine-tuned exceptions and limitations?

3.2. The existing framework of copyright exceptions and limitations

However, it appears that the rules on exceptions and limitations that are contained in both international and European copyright law, do not – at least not primarily – address the issue of downstream competition. In particular, neither international nor EU copyright law expressly mentions value-added information products and services, nor are value-added information products and services expressly granted special treatment.

At the European level, Directive 2001/29/EU starts from the assumption that 'providing for a high level of protection of intellectual property, will foster substantial investment in creativity and innovation, including network infrastructure, and lead in turn to growth and increased competitiveness of European industry, both in the area of content provision and information technology and more generally across a wide range of industrial and cultural sectors'.[17] As the citation demonstrates, the focus is on the 'competitiveness' of European industry, rather than on 'competition' amongst individual firms. Exceptions and limitations shall, according to the EU Directive, provide for '[a] fair balance of rights and interests between the different categories of rightholders, as well as between the different categories of rightholders and users of protected subject-matter must be safeguarded'.[18] Again, no reference is made to regulating downstream competition. In addition, exceptions or limitations are only – and rather vaguely – referred to with regard to 'the public interest for the purpose of education and teaching'[19] and several other similar public interests.[20] For the rest, the main focus of the EU legislature is on achieving harmonization for the benefit of the 'smooth functioning of the internal market'. It follows that the public

---

[17] Directive 2001/29/EC, Recital 4.
[18] Directive 2001/29/EC, Recital 31.
[19] Directive 2001/29/EC, Recital 14.
[20] Recital 34 of Directive 2001/29/EC, lists 'exceptions or limitations for cases such as educational and scientific purposes, for the benefit of public institutions such as libraries and archives, for purposes of news reporting, for quotations, for use by people with disabilities, for public security uses and for uses in administrative and judicial proceedings'.

interest of providing for competition in general, and for downstream competition in the area of providing value-added information products and services, can only be factored into the exceptions listed in art. 5(2) and (3) of the EU Directive 2001/29/EC by way of statutory interpretation, to the extent that this is possible under the existing wording and as far as this is in conformity with the purpose of an individual exception or limitation. It is, of course, a different matter, in what ways European copyright should take care of the interests of competition, under an ideal copyright regime in the future. However, this question has to be reserved for further studies. The present chapter only intends to bring to light the fact that exceptions and limitations are likewise regulating competition, in particular in downstream markets of information value-added products and services, as well as what the existing legislative framework looks like.

Interpreting existing copyright exceptions and limitations have to obey the limits set by the so-called three-step test,[21] which has made its way from an international limitation placed upon the exceptions to the reproduction right under art. 9(2) of the Berne Convention to the general rule as contained in art. 13 TRIPS, and following arts 10 WCT/16 WPPT and art. 5(5) of the EU Directive 2001/29/EC on copyright in the information society. According to the second and third steps, exceptions and limitations may, even if they are restricted to certain special cases, not be applied in a way which conflicts with the normal exploitation of the protected work, nor may they do so in a way which prejudices the legitimate interests of the rightholder. Again, as a limitation on limitations, this test only focuses on the interests of the rightholder, but this time, in doing so and in not focussing on the purposes of the exceptions, it does not outlaw the taking into consideration of the aspect of competition when Member States are either crafting new, or interpreting already existing, exceptions and limitations contained in national law. In other words, from the perspective of the three-step test, regulating competition by way of exceptions or limitations is perfectly all right, as long as this does not conflict with normal exploitation and does not otherwise unduly prejudice the legitimate interests of rightholders.

How much of downstream competition can then be incorporated into permissible copyright exceptions and limitations, in particular in the digital and networked context? In this respect, EU Directive 2001/29/EC, in its Recitals, gives a hint by pointing out that since the provision of exceptions or limitations by Member States should, in particular, 'duly reflect the

---

[21]   See Recital 44, EU-Directive 2001/29/EC. For a comprehensive analysis of the three-step test see, in particular, Senftleben, *Copyright, Limitations & the Three-Step Test – An Analysis of the Three-Step Test in International and EC Copyright Law*, 2004.

increased economic impact that such exceptions or limitations may have in the context of the new electronic environment, the scope of certain exceptions or limitations may have to be even more limited when it comes to certain new uses of copyright works and other subject-matter'.[22] Of course, this again is only one side of the coin. The other side is that in order to achieve an optimum of overall efficiency, a legal system likewise has to give due leeway for an appropriate use of existing and future information and communication technologies and provide for competition, in order to avoid monopoly rents which ultimately lead to the under-consumption of intellectual property goods. In normative terms, of course, it all hinges upon the proper interpretation of what has to be regarded as 'normal' exploitation and 'unreasonable prejudice'.

It is not the purpose of the present chapter to discuss these issues in general. Rather, they shall be briefly discussed – as an illustrative case study – in the light of recent German case law on downstream competition in information value-added products and services.

4. A case study: German case law

Although a thorough comparative law analysis seems to be called for in order to analyse the issues raised in a more detailed way, the discussion shall be limited here to German cases. The choice of German cases – while certainly being influenced by the author's nationality and hence familiarity with the German system – is mainly due to the fact that over the last few years, the Federal German Supreme Court (Bundesgerichtshof, BGH) has already produced a whole series of cases concerning value-added information services.[23] However, analysis of these German decisions may prove to be useful even outside Germany, because the arguments raised will most likely be the same, or at least similar, in other jurisdictions as well.

---

22 Recital 44, EU Directive 2001/29/EC.
23 Other decisions of lower courts are not discussed here. It should be mentioned, however, that recently, litigation has started regarding the permissibility, under copyright, of personal online video recorders; see Court of Appeals of Cologne, 9 September 2005, GRUR-RR 2006, 5; Regional Court of Braunschweig, 8 June 2006, K&R 2006, 362; Regional Court of Munich, 19 May 2005, ZUM 2006, 583. Up until now, the courts have concluded that in these cases, the reproductions were made by the person offering the service and not by the end-user as privileged under the private use exception contained in § 53 of the German Copyright Act. Under German law, from this it follows that such a service is only permissible if offered cost-free. However, so far, the courts could not agree whether or not the recording of the broadcasts for download by the end-users was an act of making the broadcasts publicly available.

4.1.   The cases

In 1997, it all started with a case where a bank had offered its customers a service which consisted of mailing copies of articles which the bank had researched in its own archive according to a search formulated by the client.[24] In 1998, the service of digitizing analogue archives for the in-house use of the service's customers had to be decided,[25] followed in 1999 by a case concerning the service of mailing articles upon request by a public library, which had made its catalogues available online.[26] Likewise, the question of whether electronic press-clipping services are covered by the exception which allows for analogue press-clipping services against the payment of a fee to the collecting societies, was before the German Federal Supreme Court in 2002.[27] And in 2003 the legitimacy of unauthorized hyperlinking to online articles had to be decided.[28]

To sum up the Court's holdings: the services the Court did not allow third parties to perform without the consent of the holders of the rights in the original copyrighted material were, on the one hand, digital archiving services by third parties (even if the digitized archives were only intended for in-house use by the employees of the respective clients) as well as the mailing of analogue copies upon the basis of a prior search by a third party. On the other hand, the Federal Supreme Court did allow both the mailing of copies by public libraries (even where the catalogues had been made available online) and electronic press-clipping services. Although it should be added that in these cases, equitable remuneration has to be paid by the third party offering the service in order to compensate for the economic loss resulting from the service to the rightholders' exploitation interests; in the case of press-clippings this duty to pay a reasonable remuneration was already provided for under German copyright law, whereas in the case of the mailing of copies by public libraries, the remuneration right was 'invented' by the Court by way of analogy with already existing duties to pay remuneration under existing non-voluntary licensing schemes. Moreover, it has to be noted that in the case of electronic press-clippings, the Court limited the scope of the statutory exception to scans which the subscriber to the press-clipping service could systematically search, in order to ensure that the use-intensity of the copies legally made under the copyright limitation did not exceed what the historical legislature had intended to exempt from exclusive copyright control. Finally, hyperlinking has been

---

[24]   BGH, 16 January 1997, GRUR 1997, 459 – *CB-Infobank I*; BGH, 16 January 1997, GRUR 1997, 464 – *CB-Infobank II*.
[25]   BGH, 10 December 1998, GRUR 1999, 324 – *Elektronische Pressearchive*.
[26]   BGH, 25 February 1999, GRUR 1999, 707 – *Kopienversanddienst*.
[27]   BGH, 11 July 2002, GRUR 2002, 963 – *Elektronischer Pressespiegel*.
[28]   BGH, 17 July 2003, GRUR 2003, 958 – *Paperboy*.

regarded by the German Federal Supreme Court as violating neither the reproduction right nor the making-available right, nor any right that might be enjoyed by the database that was searched by the service and to which the link goes.

4.2. Analysing the issues

But it is not the outcome as such that is of importance. Indeed, discussing the decisions in detail against the background of existing German copyright law would amount to an analysis of national law which is not called for here. Rather, what is of interest here are the arguments which the Court used in order to arrive at the results just mentioned. As divergent as the outcomes of the cases may, at first sight, appear, the argumentation of the Federal Supreme Court shows a high degree of consistency.

As a preliminary remark, it should be noted that none of these cases touched upon the issue of derivative works, i.e. to what extent the respective value-added information services had to be considered as adaptations or as free uses of pre-existing copyrighted material. Rather, all activities touched upon the reproduction right – and some of them in addition on the new making-available right – and hence were concerned with the question whether or not value-added activities are covered by statutory exceptions and limitations to these exclusive rights, notably by the private copying exception[29] and, in the case of electronic press-clipping services, by the statutory press-clipping exception.[30] The main issue faced by the Court was to find, by way of statutory interpretation, to what extent these exceptions, which had initially been drafted in view of, and as a response to, traditional analogue reproduction techniques, could and should also apply to digital reproduction techniques, especially in view of the dissemination possibilities offered by networked communication infrastructure.

In answering this question the Court started with the traditional assumption, according to which the exclusive right is regarded as the rule and the limitation as the exception, so that in case of doubt, any exception should be narrowly construed. However, in the press-clipping decision, the Court had somewhat given up this approach and taken the view that the task should be one of maintaining in the digital world the balance struck by the historical legislature in the analogue environment between the interests of the rightholder on the one hand, and the interests of the persons privileged by the respective exception, on the other. In a way this later holding seems to distance itself somewhat from the initial statement contained in the first of the decisions discussed, according to which the extent of the statutory limitation

---

[29] § 53 of the German Copyright Act.
[30] § 49 of the German Copyright Act.

should be judged in the light of the technical circumstances of the time in which the limitation was enacted. The Court then arrived at some further conclusions.

First, the Court noted that the private use exception is not limited to acts undertaken by private persons themselves. Rather, third parties also benefit from the privilege granted by the private use exception to their customers with regard to acts undertaken for, and on behalf of, these customers, unless the law expressly states otherwise.[31] Hence, third parties are free to offer, without the permission of the respective rightholders, all acts which the persons privileged under the private use exception are allowed to perform themselves.

Second, the Court limited these acts undertaken by third parties to the technical act of making copies. On the one hand, in the opinion of the Court, this does not preclude that the making of copies is accompanied and facilitated by an additional service such as providing the originals for copies to be made, an online catalogue and an automated ordering process. Hence, referring to the overriding significance for the general public of having open access to relevant information, the Federal Supreme Court held that such a copy and delivery service by public libraries is still covered by the private use exception benefiting the individual users of that service, although remuneration would have to be paid in order to compensate the rightholders for the heightened use made of, or use-possibilities created with regard to, their analogue works. On the other hand, the Court concluded that to offer an additional research service is going beyond the limits of the statutory private use exception and therefore infringes upon authors' exclusive reproduction rights. The Court argued that the combination of making copies with a prior research service would exceed the limits of the private use exception as initially intended by the legislature.

Third, the Court looked to the overall effect which an authorization-free activity of private copying might have on the exploitation of the original copyrighted subject matter. The Court concluded that the digitization of analogue archives in order to make these archives electronically available in-house to the employees of the entity which had commissioned the digitization, infringes the exclusive right of the rightholders. The decisive argument was that the

---

[31]   Indeed, prior even to the implementation of EU Directive 2001/29/EC on copyright in the information society, the copying of copyrighted material on image and sound-carriers was only allowed to be made by third parties if no remuneration was paid. It should be noted that in the course of implementing EU Directive 2001/29/EC, the German legislature imposed the same limitation on digital private copies made by third parties. Henceforth, the making of *digital* private copies by third parties is only permitted if no remuneration is paid (see § 53(1) of the German Copyright Act as amended by Law of 10 September 2003, BGBl. I S.1774).

digital archive opens up a much higher use intensity – and it also allows the employees to build up their own archives – than the one privileged by the historical legislature in an analogue environment. Indeed, the historical legislature seems to have crafted the archiving exception only for rather limited purposes, for example to secure the stock of works or to allow space-saving storage on microfiche. Similarly, in the case of electronic press-clipping services, the perceived danger of a much higher intensity of use of material in digital form led the Court to limit the exception for digital press-clipping services to services which only use picture files that cannot automatically be searched after downloading. In sum, the heightened electronic use possibility did not make the Court conclude that electronic press-clipping services should be prohibited altogether. Rather, the Court allowed electronic press-clipping services under the existing press-clipping exception, but at the same time controlled the effects of that freedom by way of limiting the technology to be used in order to benefit from this particular exception. The solution thus retained may be seen as a compromise between a too far-reaching exclusive right on the one hand, and the danger of infringement of the normal exploitation of the original copyrighted works by the original rightholder, on the other. Of course, the decision thus artificially limits the possibilities of using existing information and communication technology which would allow for a much better and user-friendly service.

Fourth, another issue of interest in this regard is to what extent illegal acts of copying and making available by users of the value-added service in question should be taken into account when it comes to assessing the effect which digital value-added services might have on the exploitation of the original copyrighted material. With regard to this issue, a certain shift in the argumentation of the Court can be observed. In the case concerning the digitization of analogue archives, the Court seems to hold the customer – and via the customer the person offering the digitization service – accountable for further legal and illegal use-acts of users further down the line. In contrast, the electronic press-clipping case contains an obiter dictum according to which at least unlawful use acts by subsequent users of the value-added digital service cannot be taken into account when it comes to determining the exact scope of the existing statutory copyright exception.

Fifth, in the case involving hyperlinking to sources which are publicly available on the internet, the Court – after concluding that there was a violation neither of the making-available right, nor of the reproduction right, nor of the sui-generis database right, and after finding that deep-linking likewise did not constitute an act of unfair competition – explicitly recognized the value added by the activity of opening up a variety of information sources on a common platform. This was a much more clear-cut statement than the general statement, often repeated, that the public interest to have uncomplicated access to existing information has to be 'balanced with' the proprietary interest of the rightholders. The Court thus finally made it clear that some room has to be left for information value-added services to be offered by third parties.

Another question is to what extent an interpretation which deviates from the principle of literal and narrow interpretation of existing copyright exceptions, and which carefully opens the existing exceptions up to the new digital environment, can be upheld under the now all-encompassing three-step test. In reaching its conclusions, the German Federal Supreme Court has indeed at various instances made explicit reference to international copyright law's three-step test. Whereas in the first of the decisions discussed here, art. 9(2) of the Berne Convention was only briefly mentioned by the Court, in the later case concerning the mailing of copies by public libraries, the Court gave the discussion of the three-step test a somewhat broader room. Finding that the private use-exception with regard to the mailing of individual copies upon request constitutes a 'special case', the Court concluded that the legitimate interests of rightholders could, and ought to, be remedied by the payment of a remuneration. This decision thus guarantees that the public has easy access to relevant information while at the same time safeguarding the monetary interests of the rightsholders. This claim for remuneration had not been foreseen by the legislature at the time of enacting the private copying exception, but in view of the three-step test the Court felt both empowered and under an obligation to create it by way of judge-made law. It should be noted, however, that somewhat oddly the Court left aside the question of a potential conflict between the library's activity of mailing analogue copies upon request and normal exploitation, i.e. with the second step of the three-step test. Similarly, only a mere hint of the statutory claim for remuneration is to be found in the decision regarding electronic press-clippings. However, the second step was discussed by the Court with regard to the hyperlinking service within the framework of the legality of repeated and unsubstantial taking under the provision of the German Copyright Act which implemented art. 7(5) of EU Directive 96/9/EC on the legal protection of databases. Of course, here the case was rather clear-cut, since the Court could point to the fact that mere links, even if accompanied by small citations of the articles linked, did not substitute for consumption of the articles linked, but rather incited the user of the value-added linking service to consult the original. Moreover, the repeated and systematic linking to the databases in question did not conflict with their normal exploitation either.[32]

---

[32]   This result now receives additional support from the recent ECJ decisions regarding the scope of the sui-generis database right (see note 10).

In sum, it can be held that the German Federal Supreme Court did not explicitly discuss the issues at bar under the perspective of competition. In the press-clipping service case, the issue of proper participation of the authors of the individual articles played a major role, which, in the opinion of the Court, is obviously better secured by a claim of remuneration administered by a collecting society than by participation of the authors in the proceeds generated by the producers of the respective journals. However, at least in the *Paperboy* decision, the Court for the first time explicitly recognized the value added by the activity of opening up a variety of information sources on a common platform. At least under the present circumstances, such a service presupposes that the activity of the service in question is open to third parties and, hence, to downstream competition.

5. Some conclusions

In the evolving information society too much information is the problem rather than too little. In view of the huge amount of information available, there is a growing need for products and mostly services that search and compile information according to individual users' individual information needs. Or, to put it in more general terms, in the information society, there is a need for downstream value-added information services on the basis of upstream information, no matter whether or not the upstream information is protected by copyright. In the years to come, these value-added information services will be subject to legal discussion and, of course, intense fights over market share. A broad legal right to exclude publicly available information from being included in value-added services or being listed by search engines operated by third parties would invariably lead to a compartmentalization of the internet into guarded zones as well as to an undue restriction of competition, and thus interfere with the free flow of information and the public benefits associated with the networked architecture of the internet. The preceding 'case study' of case law handed down by the German Federal Supreme Court illustrates quite well both the issues raised with regard to the permissibility of value-added information services based on someone else's copyright by third parties and the legal constraints of the international and European legislative copyright framework. However, several lessons can be learned.

One lesson is that a formalistic approach which postulates that the exclusive right has to be considered as the rule and the limitation as the exception, and that consequently, in case of doubt, exceptions should be narrowly construed, does not necessarily lead to appropriate results. Neither does, of course, the opposite approach which starts from the assumption that an absence of exclusive rights is the general rule and exclusive rights are the exception, and that consequently, in case of doubt, limitations to exclusive right will have to be broadly construed. Both approaches tend to favour only one group of market participants. Rather, the starting point should be to recognize that with regard to value-added information services, there are two different groups of players, i.e. the upstream initial rightholders, and the downstream third party providers of value-added services.

Rather than sticking to a formalistic approach, the decisive criteria should be to secure a proper freedom for healthy competition with regard to value-added information services, both at the upstream and the downstream level, while at the same time not disregarding the legitimate interests of copyright holders. Enabling competition at the downstream level, however, means admitting that parties are legally in a position to offer downstream value-added information services without necessarily and in all cases having to license the upstream information. To begin with, this implies that the application of technologies is not limited to technologies as they existed at the time the limitation was enacted. In particular, it should not be made a principle that limitations are per se limited to analogue exploitation activities. Rather, one should look at the purpose which a particular exception is supposed to achieve. If, for example, the interest of the general public in a free flow of relevant information can only, or best, be achieved by way of competition with regard to downstream value-added information services, then the interpretation of statutory exceptions or limitations should take this aspect properly into account as well. Of course, in doing so, factual and economic changes resulting from digital and networking technology have to be taken into account. This means not only focusing on heightened use possibilities, but also considering that in the digital environment the position of the person offering the value-added service is somewhat different from the position of the traditional producer of copyrighted works. While, on the one hand, end-users become ever more involved in undertaking copyright-relevant acts, on the other hand the number of intermediaries is likewise increasing in the new value-chains of producing, transmitting and making accessible copyrighted information. As the German cases have demonstrated, in many cases now the producer of value-added information services just helps end-users to benefit from the private copying exception.

Of course, this leads to the rather thorny issue of deciding under what circumstances a downstream market can be left to exclusive exploitation by the holder of copyright in the upstream market (e.g. because otherwise the economic basis for the production of the copyrighted work upstream would be jeopardized, or because there is no need to open up the downstream market for competition due to the fact that there is already sufficient substitutability, and hence competition, in the downstream market), and under what circumstances the downstream market should be opened up to competition by third parties by way of an exception or limitation (because of lack of substitutability and, hence, of competition in the downstream market). The answer to this issue needs further examination, which cannot be done here.[33]

Moreover, irrespective of whether existing exceptions or limitations are interpreted by the courts, or whether new exceptions or limitations are introduced into national law by legislative amendments, the limits of what is currently possible are prescribed by the three-step test. If one accepts the proposition that exceptions and limitations also serve the purpose of enabling competition – a proposition which the present chapter intends to demonstrate – then the interpretation of the three-step test can, and indeed should, take into consideration the effects which a broader or narrower interpretation has on competition in the downstream market, in particular for value-added information services. In other words, if it is accepted that the three-step test works both as a limitative and as an enabling clause, then the second step ('normal exploitation') can no longer be interpreted as comprising any and all future downstream exploitation possibilities of copyrighted material in value-added information services. Because if it does, there will be no room whatsoever for competition with regard to downstream value-added services (apart from the fact that there will then be no room for the third step, the 'unreasonable prejudice'). From this point of view, it appears understandable, if not logical, that the German Federal Supreme Court was looking for a solution by way of compensating the higher use intensity opened up by digital and networked technology, rather than of preventing it by way of extending the exclusive right. Also, this might explain the relatively little attention the German Federal Supreme Court has so far paid to the second step ('normal exploitation'). In this respect, a comparison can also be made to art. 7(5) of the EU Database Directive 96/9/EC, which – much more sensibly – does not exactly duplicate the three-step test, but rather has the second and third steps as alternatives ('acts which conflict with a normal exploitation of that database *or* which unreasonably prejudice the legitimate interests of the maker of the database', emphasis added). Thus, adequate remuneration may not only eliminate any prejudice caused to the maker of the database by insubstantial taking (third step), but likewise may compensate for a conflict with the normal exploitation of the database (second step).

Finally, it can only be pointed out here that accentuating the aspect of copyright as regulating competition leads to similar considerations regarding, in the context of value-added information services, the notion of what is not protected as mere 'information'; how far exclusive copyright protects against

---

[33]   An attempt to cast this distinction in statutory language is currently being undertaken by the Wittem Project for a Uniform European Copyright Code, work undertaken by an informal study group of European copyright scholars.

the making of transformative and value-adding derivative works; and what constitutes an unreasonable prejudice to the legitimate interests of the maker of a database protected by a sui-generis right against repeated and systematic extraction and/or re-utilization of insubstantial parts of the contents of the database.

In sum, the arguments put forward in this chapter may serve to strike a new balance between the interests of rightholders, providers of value-added information services and, ultimately, end-users. Such a balance takes into account the competition-regulating effect of exceptions and limitations.

11 Competition in the field of collective management: preferring 'creative competition' to allocative efficiency in European copyright law

Josef Drexl[1]

1. Introduction

The European Union is in search of a concept for collecting societies. It has been questioned whether the traditional system, based on national monopolies, is still adequately responsive to the evolving reality and needs of cross-border digital exploitation of music in particular. Yet, in the offline sector, individual collecting societies remain unable to monitor the use of licences and enforce rights against infringements abroad. Therefore, and for the time being, the internal market for copyrighted works cannot function without the cross-border cooperation of collecting societies based on bilateral reciprocal representation agreements. In the field of digital exploitation, however, the traditional system needs to be reconsidered.

How does the European legislature react to the impact of digitalisation on collective rights management? In recent years, Community institutions have adopted positions that are not necessarily consistent. The need for a European system of collecting societies that serves the interests of authors and performing artists in particular and takes into account the cultural and social dimension of collecting societies was recognised by a resolution of the European Parliament at the beginning of 2004.[2] The Commission, too, became active in

[1] Director, Max Planck Institute for Intellectual Property, Competition and Tax Law; Honorary Professor of Law, University of Munich.

[2] European Parliament Resolution of 15 January 2004 on a Community framework for collective management societies in the field of copyright and neighbouring rights (2002/2274(INI)), [2004] OJ EC No. C 92, p. E/425; http://www.aepo.org/usr/docs%20coll%20man%20of%20rights/resolution%20Echerer%2015%20January%202004.pdf#search=%22European%20Parliament%20resolution%20on%20a%20Community%20framework%20for%20collective%20management%20societies%20in%20the%20field%20of%20copyright%20and%20neighbouring%20rights%22. Even better known is the so-called Echerer Report, named after the rapporteur Raina A. Mercedes Echerer, which preceded and proposed the later resolution; see http://www.europarl.europa.eu/omk/sipade3?L=EN&OBJID=31582&LEVEL=2&MODE=SIP&NAV=X&LSTDOC=N.

2004, publishing a Communication on collective administration of rights.[3] This Communication promised an integrated approach, not limiting a future Community framework to specific forms of exploitation (e.g. in digital form), specific categories of works or single aspects of the regulation of collecting societies. Yet, in 2005, the Commission suddenly took a different path by adopting the so-called Recommendation on the management of online rights in musical works.[4] The Recommendation has to be seen in the context of the Commission's endeavours to fight the so-called Santiago and Barcelona Agreement,[5] a model for reciprocal representation agreements for the collective administration of online rights in musical works, which was

---

[3]   Communication of 16 April 2004 from the Commission to the Council, the European Parliament and the European Economic and Social Committee – The Management of Copyright and Related Rights in the Internal Market, COM(2004) 261 final = http://europa.eu.int/eur-lex/en/com/cnc/2004/com2004_0261en01.pdf; see also Tuma, Pavel (2006), 'Pitfalls and Challenges of the EC Directive on the Collective Management of Copyright and Related Rights', *European Intellectual Property Review (EIPR)*, **28**, 220 (with a review of a possible directive that could be adopted in line with the Communication).

[4]   Commission Recommendation of 18 October 2005 on collective cross-border management of copyright and related rights for legitimate online music services, [2005] OJ EC No. L 276, p. 54; Corrigenda, [2005] OJ EC No. L 284, p. 10. Adoption of this Recommendation was preceded by a Commission Staff Working Document of 7 July 2005 – Study on a Community initiative on the cross-border collective management of copyright, http://ec.europa.eu/internal_market/copyright/docs/management/study-collectivemgmt_en.pdf, which opened a new, though very short, public consultation that finally proved to have little effect on the Commission position; on this document see Schmidt, Manuela Maria (2005), 'Die kollektive Verwertung der Online-Musikrechte im Europäischen Binnenmarkt', *Zeitschrift für Urheber- und Medienrecht (ZUM)*, **2005**, 783; Tuma, above n. 3, at 227 et seq. The later Commission Staff Working Document of 11 October 2005 – Impact assessment reforming cross-border collective management of copyright and related rights for legitimate online music services, SEC(2005) 1254 = http://ec.europa.eu/internal_market/copyright/docs/management/sec_2005_1254_en.pdf, which accompanies and explains the policy of the Recommendation, is in line with the working paper of July 2005. As to the Commission's policy, see also Lüder, Tilman (2006), 'Working Toward the Next Generation of Copyright Licenses', presented at the 14th Fordham Conference on International Intellectual Property Law and Policy, 20–1 April 2006, http://ec.europa.eu/internal_market/copyright/docs/docs/lueder_fordham_2006.pdf; Majer, Ludwig (2006), 'Handlungsoptionen der EU-Politik im Bereich der Verwertungs-gesellschaften', in Karl Riesenhuber (ed.), *Wahrnehmungsrecht in Polen, Deutschland und Europa*, Berlin: De Gruyter, 147.

[5]   The two agreements are reprinted in Spada, Paolo (ed.) (2006), *Gestione collettiva dell'offerta e della domanda di prodotti culturali*, Milan: Guiffrè, at 253 (Santiago) and 261 (Barcelona); see also Capobianco, Antonio (2004), 'Licensing of Music Rights: Media Convergence, Technological Developments and EC Competition Law', *European Intellectual Property Review (EIPR)*, **26**, 113, at 119.

deemed by the Commission to be in conflict with EC competition rules. The Santiago Agreement, though allowing multi-territorial and multi-repertoire licensing (the so-called one-stop shop), attracted the Commission's criticism for centralising the power to grant such licences in the hands of the domestic society of the country of the licensee's business establishment. This 'economic residence clause' excluded competition between domestic societies as licensors, whereas the IFPI/Simulcasting Agreement, the model for reciprocal representation agreements regarding the licensing of the related rights of phonogram producers in the field of simulcasting and webcasting, allowed such competition to a limited extent and, therefore, was exempted from the cartel prohibition by the Commission in 2002.[6] With regard to the Santiago Agreement, the collecting societies escaped further action by the Commission by simply not extending the agreement's application beyond the end of 2004. This caused a highly inappropriate situation not only for users, who suddenly lost the advantage of the one-stop shop, but also for right-holders, who now had to fear that users would simply refrain from acquiring the licences and infringe the rights.[7] According to then applicable traditional reciprocal representation agreements, users had to 'shop around'

---

[6]   Decision of 8 October 2002, COMP/C2/38.014 – *IFPI/Simulcasting*, [2003] OJ EC No. L 107, p. 58. According to the IFPI/Simulcasting Agreement, the global royalty to be paid for the multi-territorial and multi-repertoire licence is predetermined by the aggregate of the tariffs fixed by the individual societies and calculated according to the volume of the public reached in the different countries. Hence, price competition is mostly limited to the part of the global royalty that is meant to cover the administration costs of the society granting the licence. The European Commission nevertheless accepted this form of calculation. In its exemption decision, the Commission (above at para. 110) argued that an individual society would refuse to authorise their counterparts in other countries to grant multi-territorial licences with regard to its repertoire if the other societies were allowed to 'dump' the level of royalties the authorising society deemed appropriate with regard to the use in its own country. However, the Commission (above paras 99–107) only granted the exemption after the IFPI/Simulcasting Agreement had been changed to the effect that the society granting the licence would always distinguish, in setting up its tariffs, between the 'copyright royalty' and the 'administration fee'. The Commission thereby tried to introduce more transparency into the licensing practice in favour of users. Nevertheless, the Commission's approach was very much criticised in legal writing; see Mestmäcker, Ernst-Joachim (2005), 'Agreements of Reciprocal Representation of Collecting Societies in the Internal Market – The Related Rights of Phonogram Producers as a Test Case (Simulcasting)', *Revue internationale de droit d'auteur (RIDA)*, **203**, 62, at 113–21.
[7]   In the same sense Lincoff, Bennett M. (2001), 'A Plan for the Future of Music Rights Organizations in the Digital Age', in Rochelle C. Dreyfuss, Diane L. Zimmermann and Harry First (eds), *Expanding the Boundaries of Intellectual Property*, Oxford: Oxford University Press, 167, at 174 et seq.

anew and request territorially limited online rights from all national collecting societies.[8]

Instead of recommending that collecting societies adopt the IFPI/ Simulcasting model for reciprocal representation agreements, the Recommendation of 2005 opts for a totally new system which expects collecting societies to directly grant cross-border licences for works belonging to their respective repertoires. This new approach has the obvious advantage of not relying on reciprocal representation agreements; collecting societies are supposed to compete for right-holders and to license their rights directly to users. Still, this system departs from the one-stop-shop principle. The Recommendation's approach causes search costs at least for online users who may have problems finding out which society holds the rights to the music they want to use on the internet.

The Recommendation only relates to online rights in the musical sector. Still, it is obvious that the system cannot differ for online rights in audiovisual works. The Recommendation may even affect the administration of offline rights. Collecting societies increasingly depend on income from the online market. If some collecting societies lose out in the competition for online rights, these societies may well have problems effectively administering offline rights in their respective territories. In addition, national legislatures, which are also addressees of the Recommendation,[9] will not distinguish in the domestic law on collective administration between what lies within the scope of application of the Recommendation and what lies outside of it. Finally, the Recommendation sets the trend of the new EC copyright policy and has to be expected to be relied upon by the Commission when crafting any future legal instrument in the field of collective administration of copyrights. To sum up: Whereas the Recommendation seems to constitute a mere sector-specific and non-binding instrument, it may well remodel the landscape of collecting societies in the EU at large.

The following analysis concentrates on only one, albeit a very important, aspect of the new policy, namely the Recommendation's specific competition-

---

    [8]   As to the traditional form of licensing, see Lincoff, above n. 7, at 172–4. The need to collect national licences stems from the territoriality principle of copyright and the conclusion drawn from this principle that the making available of copyrighted subject-matter on the internet would potentially infringe domestic copyright law worldwide. This view relies on the so-called Bogsch theory, initially developed for satellite broadcasting. It explains that states may apply their copyright law to acts of transmission committed outside their territory provided that these acts target their public. For a more thorough analysis, see Drexl, Josef (2006), 'Internationales Immaterialgüterrecht', in *Münchener Kommentar BGB*, 4th edn, Munich: C.H. Beck, p. 812, at nn. 157–73.

    [9]   See Nos 16 and 19 of the Recommendation.

policy approach.[10] According to the Commission, an ideal system of collective administration in the EC has to rely on competition between collecting societies for right-holders. In the following, it will be shown that the Commission only argues in terms of a static competition-policy model, focusing on output, price and quality in the sense of allocative efficiency, without taking into account the purpose of copyright law to promote creativity and, what is very important in the European context, cultural diversity. The analysis therefore argues for a policy based on the dynamics of creativity. Such a policy should avoid market foreclosure effects in favour of internationally well established titles and singers and to the disadvantage of new developments in music and of national music. Whereas the Recommendation does not differentiate between different categories of right-holders and thereby favours the copyright industry, which is predominantly interested in producing for existing tastes and markets, the following analysis recommends a system of collective management that is based on a principle of non-discriminatory market access for all kinds of music.

2.   Why markets for copyright need collective administration

Right at the outset, the question needs to be answered whether and when markets are in need of collective administration.

The need for collective administration cannot be analysed without identifying the economic rationale for having a copyright law in the first place. Copyright law is meant to solve a market failure. The subject-matter of copyright protection meets the two requirements for a public good,[11] namely of being non-exclusive and unrivalrous. In a world without legal protection, one who invests in the production of such a public good, but cannot control its use, would necessarily produce an external benefit for others. Conversely, recognition of a property right internalises such externalities[12] and, thereby, creates the necessary incentives for the provision of such goods by private market participants. Copyright law is therefore considered to be based on a trade-off

---

[10]   Other critical aspects concern, for instance, the conformity of the Recommendation with the principle of territoriality of copyright; see Rabe, Hans-Jürgen (2006), 'Grenzen gemeinschaftsweiter Linzenzierung durch das Territorialitätsprinzip des Internationalen Urheberrechts', in Karl Riesenhuber (ed.), *Wahrnehmungsrecht in Polen, Deutschland und Europa*, Berlin: De Gruyter, p. 174. See also Tuma, above n. 3, at 228, who is critical of the fact that direct multi-territorial licensing would clash with the existence of 25 different copyright systems.

[11]   See, for instance, Landes, William M. and Richard A. Posner (1989), 'An Economic Analysis of Copyright Law', *Journal of Legal Studies*, **18**, 325, at 326.

[12]   See Demsetz, Harold (1967), 'Toward a Theory of Property Rights', *American Economic Review*, **57 II**, 347, at 349.

between the costs of limiting access to a work and the benefits provided by the incentives to create copyrightable works.[13]

However, in the copyright world, granting the copyright does not suffice to enable the author to administer the economic rights effectively.[14] This is especially true in situations in which users request access to works of a large number of different authors and with regard to uses that are difficult for the individual author to control. Accordingly, there are basically two reasons why copyright markets require and create collective administration: First, collective administration saves transaction costs for right-holders and users.[15] Collecting societies assemble large portfolios of works and grant blanket licences for the whole repertoire to users who are interested in having easy access to works of different right-holders. Secondly, whereas the individual right-holder is not able to monitor licences given to a large number of users and to enforce her rights against infringements, collecting societies can build up effective control systems that serve the interests of all the right-holders they represent. This second argument is also important in explaining the existence of the system of reciprocal representation agreements between national collecting societies. Each society runs a control system only for its national territory, whereas financing a similar control system abroad as well would create prohibitive costs. Therefore, reciprocal representation agreements traditionally oblige and authorise each collecting society to license and control the rights of right-holders affiliated to the other society with regard to exploitation in the respective national territory. This two-pronged economic rationale has also been approved by the European Court of Justice. The ECJ held that, in principle, reciprocal representation agreements only restrain competition in the sense of Art. 81(1) EC if licences granted between the societies are 'non-exclusive' in the sense that such agreements do not exclude direct access to the repertoire of the societies by users established abroad.[16]

---

13   Landes and Posner, above n. 11, at 326.
14   In general, on the rationale of having collective administration, see Christian Handke, Paul Stepan and Ruth Towse (2007), 'Development of the Economics of Copyright', in Josef Drexl (ed.), *Research Handbook on Intellectual Property and Competition Law*, Cheltenham, UK and Northampton, MA, USA: Edward Elgar, at para. 8 (forthcoming); Kretschmer, Martin (2002), 'The Failure of Property Rules in Collective Administration: Rethinking Copyright Societies as Regulatory Instruments', *European Intellectual Property Review (EIPR)*, **24**, 126, at 127 et seq.
15   See, for instance, Snow, Arthur and Richard Watt (2005), 'Risk Sharing and the Distribution of Copyright Collective Income', in Lisa N. Takeyama, Wendy J. Gordon and Ruth Towse (eds), *Developments in the Economics of Copyright*, Cheltenham, UK and Northampton, MA, USA: Edward Elgar, p. 23.
16   See Case 395/87 *Tournier* [1989] ECR 2521, para. 20; Case 110/88 *Lucazeau v. SACEM* [1989] ECR 2811, para. 14.

In the online world, however, this economic rationale for collective administration may well be questioned.[17] As to the first argument on saving transaction costs, the internet considerably facilitates direct transactions between the right-holder and users. Large internet music platforms may replace the functions of collecting societies.[18] In the so-called *Daft Punk* case, decided in 2002, the Commission accordingly held that, because of the ability of authors to enter into direct contact with potential users over the internet, collecting societies abuse their market-dominant power in the sense of Art. 82 EC if they force authors to license their rights to a collecting society.[19] As to the second argument, it is of course true that online exploitation also requires a system of monitoring and enforcement. However, whether a local control system is still required for the enforcement of online rights is less clear. Adoption of the IFPI/Simulcasting Agreement, which explicitly gives a right to users to request a multi-state licence from a collecting society abroad, confirms that at least some collecting societies think that cross-border licences can be monitored.[20] In the light of these differences, it may well be possible to replace

---

[17]   From recent writing, see, in particular, Katz, Ariel (2006), 'The Potential Demise of Another Natural Monopoly: Digital Right Management and the Future of Collective Licensing', *Journal of Competition Law and Economics*, **2**, 245, in which he analyses how new technologies affect the general justification of collective administration. See also Ricolfi, Marco (2006), 'Figure e tecniche di gestione collettiva del diritto d'autore e dei diritti connessi', in Paolo Spada (ed.), *Gestione collettiva dell'offerta e della domanda di prodotti culturali*, Milan: Giuffrè, p. 6.

[18]   See also Katz, above n. 17, at 247 et seq., describing the example of the Canadian Rights Clearing House (RCH) as a tool for licensing copyrights online.

[19]   Decision of 12 August 2002, Case COMP/C2/37.219 *Banghalter & Homem Christo gegen SACEM*, http://europa.eu.int/comm/competition/antitrust/cases/decisions/37219/fr.pdf (only available in French). According to its rules, the French SACEM denied membership to the two composers, Banghalter and Homem Christo, working for the punk group Daft Punk. SACEM's rules required that certain rights would have to be administered by a collecting society, not necessarily SACEM. The composers wanted to exclude certain rights from the contract with SACEM. Whereas some of these rights were administered by the British Performing Rights Society (PRS), the composers intended to administer the remaining rights individually.

[20]   Accordingly, the Commission, in its decision of 8 October 2002 exempting the IFPI/Simulcasting Agreement from Art. 81(1) EC, has held that online monitoring is actually possible; see Case COMP/C2/38.014 *IFPI/Simulcasting* [2003] OJ EC 2003 No. L 107, p. 38, para. 17. Other collecting societies doubt this and indicate that a user, in the case of simulcasting, is also in need of a licence for terrestrial broadcasting. Since the latter can only be granted by the local collecting society, it is further argued that the IFPI/Simulcasting Agreement has not really changed the practice of licensing. However, after extension of the application of the IFPI/Simulcasting Agreement to mere webcasting, hence, without simultaneous terrestrial broadcasting, this counter-argument seems no longer convincing.

collective administration by individual administration completely, at least to the extent that important right-holders, such as large music publishers, can run their own internet platforms for licensing online rights and monitor their rights themselves.[21] To sum up: The different technological environment does not only question the need for the application of traditional reciprocal representation agreements to online rights. Collective administration also has to compete with the individual administration of online rights by large institutional right-holders, such as the music publishing companies in particular.

It has to be kept in mind that the initial question of whether markets are in need of collective administration is only meant to identify the purely economic function of collecting societies. This does not exclude a non-economic rationale, based on objectives of social and cultural policy in particular.[22] A good example is given by Community law itself. Article 4 of the Rental and Lending Right Directive[23] provides for an unwaivable remuneration right of the author in a situation where the exclusive rental right has been transferred. According to Art. 4(3) of the Directive, this remuneration right can only be transferred to a collecting society. Thereby, EC law protects authors against the buy-out of the rental right by the copyright industry.[24]

---

[21]   Cf. Katz, above n. 17, at 252, who reviews new technologies for monitoring the use of rights online and points out that such technologies could of course also be used for individual administration.

[22]   Similarly, some authors highlight that the functions of collecting societies cannot be reduced to a means of solving market failure; see, e.g., Ricolfi, above n. 17, at 8.

[23]   Council Directive 92/100/EC of 19 November 1992 on rental right and lending right and on certain rights related to copyright in the field of intellectual property, [1992] OJ EC No. L 346, p. 61.

[24]   Towse, Ruth (2006), 'Copyright and Artists: A View from Cultural Economics', *Journal of Economic Surveys*, **20**, 567, at 573, sees this legislation as a reaction to a 'perceived market failure for equity rather than efficiency reasons'. In implementing the Directive, the German legislature, for instance, availed itself of the option left by Art. 4(4) of the Directive and made collective administration of the remuneration right mandatory; see § 27(3) German Copyright Act. However, this does not mean that authors are better protected in Germany than in other countries. Authors are equally protected in the EU against a buy-out by the prohibition to transfer the remuneration right to anybody other than a collecting society. To make collective administration mandatory in addition only excludes the ability of the author to administer the mandatory right individually. Consequently, the mandatory character of collective administration, at least in this case, serves the interest of store operators who know that payment to the collecting society covers all the works they offer for rental. This conclusion is in line with the arguments of the German legislature, who wanted to bundle all remuneration rights together. In addition, however, the legislature intended to guarantee financing for social funds for authors run by the collecting societies; see Loewenheim, Ulrich (2006), in Gerhard Schricker (ed.), *Urheberrecht, Kommentar*, Munich: C.H. Beck, § 27 n. 20.

The non-market-oriented rationale of protecting individual authors against the buy-out of their rights by the copyright industry has to be kept in mind when it comes to competition between collective and individual administration. If large companies of the copyright industry prevailed in this systemic competition, and collective administration of online rights consequently disappeared, such a development would most harm the creative authors and performing artists.

3. Collecting societies and monopoly power

Collecting societies in EU Member States usually hold monopolies in their respective national markets. Some states even provide for a legal monopoly. Austria, for instance, has quite recently adopted a new law on collective administration,[25] which explicitly states that only one society will receive the necessary authorisation to administer a specific right.[26] In contrast, other countries do not legally guarantee a monopoly; still, their legislatures may react to the development of natural monopolies with specific regulation. The German law, with its Act on collective administration of copyright,[27] is a good example of this second approach.[28] Obviously, both approaches are at odds with the Commission's assumption that competition between collecting societies can work.

In the following, two questions need to be distinguished: (1) Should the law depart from the principle of competition and provide for a legal monopoly? (2) Will markets for collective administration always end in a natural monopoly?

As to the first question, copyright lawyers on the continent sometimes

---

[25] Bundesgesetz über Verwertungsgesellschaften (Federal Act on collecting societies), Bundesgesetzblatt für die Republik Österreich I No. 9, of 13 January 2006, p. 1. The new law entered into force on 1 July 2005; see also Handig, Christian (2006), 'Das neue österreichische Verwertungsgesellschaftsgesetz (VerwGesG 2006)', *Gewerblicher Rechtsschutz und Urheberrecht Internationaler Teil (GRUR Int.)*, **2006**, 365.

[26] § 3(2), 1st sentence, of the Act on collecting societies. The provision reads as follows: 'Für die Wahrnehmung eines bestimmten Rechts darf jeweils nur einer einzigen Verwertungsgesellschaft eine Betriebsgenehmigung erteilt werden.' The previous act of 1936 did not include such a provision. Nevertheless, the legislature of 1936 had made it clear in the legislative documents that collecting societies should enjoy a monopoly in their respective area of activity; see Handig (2006), above n. 25, p. 167.

[27] Gesetz über die Wahrnehmung von Urheberrechten (Urheberrechts-wahrnehmungsgesetz) of 9 September 1965.

[28] For quite a recent overview of the law on collective societies in EU Member States, see Florenson, Paul (2003), 'Management of Authors' Rights and Neighboring Rights in Europe', *Revue internationale de droit d'auteur (RIDA)*, **196**, 3.

warn that introduction of competition in the market for collective administration would reduce the income of right-holders.[29] However, copyright law, from a market-oriented perspective, so far has the sole objective of solving a public-goods problem, and of enabling right-holders to market their rights. It does not pursue monopoly rents for authors.[30] Accordingly, the ECJ is willing to apply Art. 82 EC, the Community provision on the control of abuse of market dominance, with a view to controlling the level of royalties fixed by collecting societies.[31]

Still, providing for a legal monopoly may make sense as a reaction to an unavoidable natural monopoly. Markets may not necessarily select the best, i.e., most efficient collecting society, whereas regulation of the legal monopoly can stipulate criteria for selecting the best society and provide for a specific procedure to be taken when potential competitors wish to replace the incumbent. Such regulation can actually be found in the new Austrian law. A society that has been granted the 'single' authorisation for the administration of a given right cannot expect to hold this authorisation forever. Later application by a new entrant obliges the competent authority to invite existing societies to apply for the same authorisation.[32]

These arguments in favour of regulating collecting societies, however, depend on the validity of the natural monopoly assumption. In economic writing, this assumption finds broad support.[33] Still, in recent years, it has increasingly been questioned.

Already in 1992, Besen, Kerby and Salop argued that the entry of a new society into the market would be possible to the extent that the incumbent society did not apply a policy of open membership on a non-discriminatory

---

[29]   See, for instance, von Lewinski, Silke (2005), 'Gedanken zur kollektiven Rechtewahrnehmung', in Ansgar Ohly, Theo Bodewig, Thomas Dreier, Peter Götting, Maximilian Haedicke and Michael Lehmann (eds), *Perspektiven des Geistigen Eigentums und Wettbewerbsrechts: Festschrift für Gerhard Schricker*, Munich: C.H. Beck, p. 401, at 405 et seq.

[30]   See also Drexl, Josef (2006), 'Auf dem Weg zu einer neuen europäischen Marktordnung der kollektiven Wahrnehmung von Online-Rechten der Musik? Kritische Würdigung der Kommissionsempfehlung vom 18. Oktober 2005', in Karl Riesenhuber (ed.), *Wahrnehmungsrecht in Deutschland, Polen und Europa*, Berlin: De Gruyter, p. 193, at 226.

[31]   See Case 395/87 *Tournier* [1989] ECR 2521, paras 34–46.

[32]   § 3(3), 2nd sentence, of the Act on collecting societies. Whether new entrants have a decent chance of contesting the authorisation granted to other collecting societies is open to question. According to § 3(2), 2nd sentence, in the absence of evidence to the contrary, there is a presumption that existing collecting societies better fulfil their duties and obligations under the law as the main criterion for selection.

[33]   See, for instance, Handke et al., above n. 14, at 8.

basis.[34] The argument seems convincing: Without regulation, collecting societies would refuse to manage rights that increased their administrative costs by more than they contributed to its income. In such a situation, there is room for new societies to enter the market.[35]

In a recent article, Ariel Katz reviewed all the potential benefits of a monopoly in the field of collective management of copyrights.[36] As a general conclusion, Katz admits that collecting societies, by granting blanket licences for their respective repertoires, achieve economies of scale and scope, but still he is critical about the assumption that such benefits can only be achieved by a monopoly.[37] By economies of scale, Katz refers to the benefit of allocating fixed administrative costs among a larger number of managed rights.[38] By economies of scope, Katz describes the advantage to the users and licensees of having access to a larger repertoire.[39] Still, Katz identifies reasons for the emergence of a natural monopoly.[40] For instance, he mentions the costs of enforcement. The co-existence of several collecting societies in a market would thus increase such costs for the simple reason that, in infringement proceedings, an individual society would be required to prove that the rights that had been used illegally actually belong to its repertoire.[41] As to the said economies of scope, Katz accepts the 'one-stop shop' argument about saving search and negotiating costs but, nevertheless, he questions whether these benefits are really worth the cost of opting against a market that comprises

---

[34]　Besen, Stanley M., Sheila N. Kerby and Steven C. Salop (1992), 'An Economic Analysis of Copyright Collective', *Virginia Law Review*, **78**, 383, at 397–405.

[35]　Besen et al., above n. 34, at 401 et seq., illustrate their argument by alluding to the successful creation of BMI in 1940 by broadcasters in the US who wanted to break ASCAP's monopoly.

[36]　Katz, Ariel (2005), 'The Potential Demise of Another Natural Monopoly: Rethinking the Collective Administration of Performing Rights', *Journal of Competition Law and Economics*, **1**, 541.

[37]　Katz, above n. 36, at 590.

[38]　Ibid., at 554.

[39]　Ibid., at 581.

[40]　Ibid., at 591.

[41]　Ibid., at 556 et seq. and 559. A good example of justifying the argument is provided by German case-law. German courts have established the so-called 'GEMA Vermutung', a presumption based on the monopoly position of the German GEMA, according to which, in an infringement litigation, the user has the burden of proof as to the fact that works used by him are not managed by GEMA; see, in more detail, Riesenhuber, Karl and Alexander von Vogel (2005), 'Die Rechtsbeziehungen der GEMA zu den Nutzern', in Reinhold Kreile, Jürgen Becker and Karl Riesenhuber (eds), *Recht und Praxis der GEMA*, Berlin: De Gruyter, p. 633, at nn. 5–11. This presumption also relates to the repertoire of foreign collecting societies that are administered by GEMA in the framework of reciprocal representation agreements.

several collecting societies.[42] Most interestingly, Katz argues that these cost-saving benefits of the monopoly are overstated given the high concentration of the music industry, with the major publishing companies controlling 80% of the market and each of them holding large portfolios of rights.[43] Although Katz, in principle, accepts the argument according to which blanket licences granted by monopolistic societies reduce the risk of infringement on works users publicly perform, he still argues that an alternative competition-oriented solution could be found, for instance by insurance companies offering coverage for the risk of infringement.[44] Apart from those potential benefits, Katz also asks whether monopolies held by collecting societies are contestable.[45] Here, he admits that new entrants would only be successful if they could offer a repertoire that is large enough to offer a reasonable substitute.[46] Obviously, Katz does not question the natural monopoly assumption as such. He rather argues in favour of a solution according to which regulation would have to replace the natural monopoly by a more competition-oriented form of collective administration.

The two economics articles, by Besen et al. on the one hand and Katz on the other hand, provide interesting insights into the working of the markets in collective management of copyrights. Still, they both seem to pursue allocative efficiency as the goal of regulation and therefore do not take into account the essential copyright goal of promoting creativity.

Besen et al. very much aim at identifying the conditions of a copyright system that offers the optimal volume of copyrighted works at the lowest prices. They therefore criticise a regulatory system that requires collecting societies to accept all right-holders as members, since such a system would lead to the production of a larger than efficient volume of works.[47] Whereas Besen et al. evaluate collective administration of copyrights only in terms of quantity and price for existing markets (allocative efficiency), copyright is, above all, meant to promote creativity in the sense of dynamic competition. In contrast to the model of allocative efficiency, modern competition policy should focus more on the dynamic aspect of competition than on pure price competition. The European Commission has best explained this concept of dynamic competition as a goal of its policy in the Guidelines on Transfer of Technology, where Intellectual Property (IP) law and competition law are described as two complementary elements of a coherent regulatory framework

---

[42]   Katz, above n. 36, at 571.
[43]   Ibid., at 575 et seq.
[44]   Ibid., at 576 et seq.
[45]   Ibid., at 578–82.
[46]   Ibid., at 580.
[47]   See Besen et al., above n. 34, at 397.

that triggers sustainable competition for innovation.[48] Of course, these Guidelines only refer to technology, including software, and not to copyright in general. Still, there is no reason why the same philosophy should not apply to copyright as a whole. The question, therefore, would be how to conceive a market for collective management that best enhances creativity.

The approach applied by Katz is open to similar criticism. His analysis is very much inspired by the concern that the natural monopoly assumption 'seriously distorts the pricing system for music' by not taking into account available competition-oriented options.[49] Katz thereby overlooks the fact that price competition may matter less than dynamic, creativity-enhancing competition. Nevertheless, Katz himself, somehow unwillingly, gives hints as to how such dynamic competition might be implemented best. Very convincingly, he alludes to the 'superstar phenomenon'.[50] Katz does so in order to describe a specific benefit of the blanket licence. Users of music, like radio stations, do not know in advance which songs are going to be most successful and which are not. The blanket licence guarantees that users will have access to superstar music at the right time. Yet, Katz does not ask the 'preliminary' question of how a collecting society, or an intermediary, like a large music publishing company, can know what kind of music will be liked most by the public. This question, however, seems essential if one allows collecting societies to refuse to manage the rights for individual works as a condition for making competition possible. The reason why Katz does not ask this question seems quite obvious. In his model of allocative efficiency, he only tries to guarantee access to already existing works. Pre-selection of works by collecting societies and music publishing companies may however exclude very creative works that would be accepted by the public. This is a strong argument in favour of a system of collecting administration based on a principle of open and non-discriminatory access for all works. Whereas according to Besen et al. such a system would promote the emergence of a natural monopoly, it would allow maximum access for all works to the market in which ultimately the consumer will decide on who becomes the 'superstar' for a certain time. Non-discriminatory access by works to the market should however not only be preferred for mainstream music. This principle would in particular promote market access for highly innovative forms of music and music with a strongly minority character, whereas, motivated by maximising income, competing collecting societies would predominantly pre-select in the light of the existing

---

[48]   Para. 7 of the Commission Notice – Guidelines on the application of Article 81 of the Treaty to technology transfer agreements, [2004] OJ EC No. C 101, p. 2.

[49]   Katz, above n. 36, at 591.

[50]   Ibid., at 574.

average taste of the public.[51] Hence, imposing an obligation on collecting societies to accept all right-holders on a non-discriminatory basis is not only mandated by pre-existing market dominance but also by the need to establish 'creative' competition between works. As shown by Besen et al., such a system, however, would directly lead to a natural monopoly.

It may be added that Besen et al. focus their analysis on the possibility of entry into the market as a condition of competition. Market entry of additional societies, however, does not automatically lead to more competition. This is actually demonstrated by the US example of the co-existence of ASCAP and BMI, to which the authors nevertheless allude.[52] It seems that most users of public performance rights acquire licences from both societies.[53] This may indicate that the repertoires of both societies are not substitutes, but rather complementary in the sense that certain users cannot operate with the blanket licence granted by one of the societies only. Instead of competing for users, ASCAP and BMI seem to hold a collective market-dominant position vis-à-vis users. With regard to right-holders, however, ASCAP and BMI may well compete.

4.   Competition in favour of right-holders or consumers?

In its policy underlying the Recommendation on the management of online rights, the Commission is convinced that competition among collecting societies can work and, therefore, relies on a model of 'competition for right-holders' (the so-called right-holders option).

What are the basic features of this right-holders option? The right-holder, according to this model, is expected to choose his or her collecting society.[54] To achieve this, the Recommendation explicitly states a right of right-holders to choose freely the 'collective rights manager' and to define freely the scope of the rights entrusted to that manager:[55]

---

51   See also Josef Drexl (2007), 'Le droit de la gestion du droit d'auteur en Allemagne après l'adoption de la recommandation européenne sur la gestion collective en ligne dans le domaine musicale', *Propriétés intellectuelle* 2007, 33 (forthcoming), with more extensive arguments on the negative effects of the Commission's model for competition between collecting societies on cultural diversity.

52   Beson et al., above n. 34, at 401 et seq.

53   See Einhorn, Michael (2001), 'Intellectual Property and Antitrust: Music Performing Rights in Broadcasting', *Columbia-VLA Journal of Law and the Arts*, **24**, 349, at 362.

54   See No. 3 of the Recommendation, as well as para. 9 of the recitals to the Recommendation.

55   No. 3 of the Recommendation. Thereby, the Recommendation takes a principle as its starting point that is no longer a problem; see Tuma, above n. 3, at 228, who argues that the problem is the lack of the one-stop shop rather than deficiencies regarding the freedom of right-holders to choose the collecting society.

Right-holders should have the right to entrust the management of any of the online rights necessary to operate legitimate online music services, on a territorial scope of their choice, to a collective rights manager of their choice, irrespective of the Member State of residence or the nationality of either the collective rights manager or the right-holder.

The collecting society is then supposed to license these rights directly to the users. Since such a licence can only refer to the society's own repertoire, the Commission model has the obvious disadvantage of departing from the one-stop shop.[56] Apparently, the Commission does not deem this to be a decisive problem. On the contrary, the Commission expects collecting societies to specialise in specific categories of music. According to the Commission, such specialised repertoires would much better target the needs of commercial users, like webradio stations, that likewise concentrate their programs on specific types of music.[57]

Since the Recommendation has no binding effect, the Commission prefers a gradual migration from the current system with reciprocal representation agreements to the right-holders option. The Commission recommends that right-holders 'should have a right to withdraw any of the online rights and transfer the multi-territorial management of those rights to another collective rights manager'.[58] Once such a transfer has taken place, 'all collective rights managers concerned', hence, including the one to which the rights have been transferred, 'should ensure that those online rights are withdrawn from any existing reciprocal representation agreement concluded amongst them'.[59] The collecting societies are not legally obliged to behave as the Commission recommends. If, however, the collecting societies do not behave as recommended, the Commission may well return to its warning[60] and try to implement the right-holders option by a binding legal instrument.[61]

---

[56]   See also above n. 1.
[57]   See Commission Staff Working Document of 7 July 2005, above n. 4, at 3.3 and 4.1.
[58]   No. 5(c) of the Recommendation.
[59]   No. 5(d) of the Recommendation.
[60]   See the speech given by the Commissioner for the Internal Market, Charlie McCreevy, given at the 'UK Presidency Conference on Copyright and the Creative Economy' on 7 October 2005, http://europa.eu/rapid/pressReleasesAction.do?reference=SPEECH/05/588&format=HTML&aged=0&language=EN&guiLanguage=en.
[61]   Such an instrument, as part of the internal market legislation, would however have to be passed by the Council and the European Parliament. In the light of the European Parliament's Resolution of 2004 (above n. 2) and the effects on existing principles of collective administration in the Member States, it is quite doubtful whether the two institutions would support such a Community instrument.

The Commission thinks that competition for the right-holders would optimise the service provided by the collecting societies as 'collective rights managers'.[62] This kind of competition relates to both the quality and the price of the service. The Commission argues that competition will pressure the collecting societies to develop licensing schemes that best serve the interests of the right-holders. Without relying on reciprocal representation agreements, the licensing activity of the collective rights managers is under the direct control of the right-holders. In addition, the Commission expects that the royalties finally paid to the right-holders will be higher without the reciprocal representation agreements.[63] The risk that collecting societies will discriminate between the rights of their own members and the rights they license under reciprocal representation agreements would no longer exist.[64] The involvement of only one collecting society in the licensing of online rights would reduce the costs of administration considerably. And, since 'collective rights managers' would compete with each other, they would be forced to keep their own costs low.

Yet, the advantages expected for right-holders from competition will only be forthcoming if such competition is workable in the first place. The foregoing analysis on collective administration of copyrights as a natural monopoly[65] sheds doubt on the validity of the Commission's assumptions.

The Commission overlooks the fact that competitive markets are based on the principle of 'freedom of contract', but not on a general 'right of free choice' for customers. The latter concept would actually argue in favour of a duty to contract on the part of the collective rights managers. As Besen et al.[66] explained, such a duty to contract, which amounts to a policy of open access to an individual society on a non-discriminatory basis, cannot be combined with a system in which collecting societies compete. An enforceable right of

---

[62]   It is interesting to see that the Recommendation prefers the term of 'collective rights manager' to the more common term of 'collecting society'; see No. 1(e) of the Recommendation. Similarly, the French version prefers the term 'gestionnaire collective de droit' to the generally used term of 'société de gestion collective'. In contrast, the German version sticks to the traditional term 'Verwertungsgesellschaft'.

[63]   See the Impact Assessment, above n. 4, at 4.11; see also Schmidt, above n. 4, at 785.

[64]   Such potential discrimination was a fundamental concern of the Commission's policy. The Commission even produced statistical data according to which collecting societies transferred much less income to their partner societies in the framework of reciprocal representation agreements than one would expect in the light of the share of the foreign repertoire in the domestic market; see Commission Staff Working Document of 7 July 2005, above n. 4, at 1.4.2 (p. 25).

[65]   Above at s. 3.

[66]   Above at n. 33.

all right-holders to choose their collective rights managers freely would promote the emergence of a natural monopoly. In contrast, if one sticks to the principle of freedom of contract, less popular music may have difficulty finding a collective rights manager who thinks such music worth administering. To sum up: The Commission promises both competition and free choice for right-holders. However, economically speaking, it is not possible to achieve both objectives at the same time. Whereas the first option risks leading to a European monopoly, but guarantees access of all rights to the system of collective administration, the second option safeguards the chance of having more than one society competing for right-holders, but excludes less popular music from access to the system of collective administration.

Whereas the above-cited principle of free choice suggests the opposite, the Recommendation and the accompanying Commission documents make it very clear that it is the second option that the Commission wants to implement. A duty to contract would need to be explicitly stipulated by law. The Recommendation neither explicitly provides for a duty to contract, nor could it do so for lack of any binding effect.[67]

Hence, it is the principle of freedom of contract that governs the right-holders option. In fact, the Commission itself indirectly admits that the collective rights managers are at liberty to reject the administration of individual rights by arguing that collective rights managers will and should specialise in certain categories of music.[68] Such specialisation obviously requires that the collective rights managers are able to select music according to their preference. Obviously, mainstream popular music, which mostly uses the English language and is popular across national borders within the European Union, will benefit most from this kind of competition. In contrast, music based on less widely used languages will most likely be administered by the dominant collecting society in the country where the specific language is spoken. The Hungarian society will manage rights in Hungarian music; the Greek society will administer rights in Greek music. Music only liked by minorities may have problems finding an interested collecting society. And finally, there is no guarantee that, in particular, 'innovative' music that may even pave new ground for popular music will find a collective rights manager at all, given the specialisation the Commission advocates. To sum up: Competition will work for some but not all right-holders.

This analysis leads us to another, maybe even more important fallacy of the Commission model. It is certainly true that, from an economic perspective,

---

[67]   A duty to contract with right-holders can however be found in national law, such as the German one; see § 6 Urheberwahrnehmungsgesetz (Act on Collective Administration). However, this duty only relates to the administration of rights relating to German territory, which actually defines the scope of application of the German Act.

[68]   See Commission Staff Working Document of 7 July 2005, above n. 4, p. 36.

right-holders can be conceived as recipients of a service consisting in the collective management of their rights. However, the right-holders simultaneously provide an input into the market for music. The Commission seems to completely exclude this second dimension of collective administration from its analysis, although economic theory should instruct the Commission that the preferences of the end-users of music will be decisive for what will actually be offered in the market. Hence, a more convincing competition policy would be expected to develop a workable model for collective administration from the perspective of consumers. This is not to say that the model should serve the interests of consumers only. On the contrary! Only if consumers are best provided with the music they like can the system be expected to produce maximum income for right-holders. Collective rights managers can only transfer to right-holders what was earlier paid to them by users. This simple economic wisdom was actually disregarded by the Commission, which, in describing its model for competition, focused almost exclusively on competition through better services. To select a competent collecting society, how much individual societies can pay their right-holders will be more important.

Conceptualising a competition law analysis from the perspective of consumers necessarily brings us back to a very essential argument made by Katz, namely that commercial users never know who the 'superstar' is going to be.[69] In other words, tastes and trends in music are highly unpredictable. This not only explains the economic advantage of having a blanket licence system in collective administration. It also provides strong support for the one-stop-shop principle. Commercial users will necessarily have problems judging the popularity of the individual repertoire of several collective rights managers in advance. Moving away from the one-stop-shop principle would not only create search costs, because commercial users would have to find out which society manages the rights for the music they want to use. Commercial users would also feel economic pressure to switch continuously between repertoires. An analysis based on the preferences of consumers consequently demonstrates that, even in the case of popular (mainstream) music liked in the whole of the EU, for which several collecting societies may compete for right-holders, commercial users would be best advised to acquire licences from all collecting societies that manage rights for a given category of music. This will be true in particular for mainstream popular music, characterised by many releases and fast-changing preferences of the public.

The interest of commercial users in having easy access to all repertoires regarding one category of music coincides with the interest of right-holders in maximising their own income.

---

[69]   See above at n. 50.

In order to bring the most money into the system of collective administration, it is essential to enable commercial users to offer a most attractive programme to the public. Having the superstar is one factor, diversity is another. Nothing is more boring to the public than a radio channel with a very narrow selection of titles. The more attractive a programme is, the more income this programme will attract, be it from the consumer directly or from advertising. A competition policy in favour of right-holders, therefore, should enable the one-stop shop, which guarantees easiest access to all repertoires and avoids considerable search costs.

5. Preferring 'creative competition' to 'allocative efficiency'

Collective administration according to the model of the IFPI/Simulcasting Agreement, with the one-stop-shop principle and the freedom of the commercial users to choose a collecting society freely,[70] has its own price. It has to rely on reciprocal representation agreements, which necessarily create additional costs of administration and may incite individual societies to discriminate against right-holders of other societies when it comes to the distribution of royalties.

The following analysis will demonstrate that the IFPI/Simulcasting model is nevertheless the option to be preferred. In contrast to the Commission's right-holders, the IFPI/Simulcasting Agreement goes beyond a simple concept of allocative efficiency and promotes a concept of creative competition.

As indicated in the introduction,[71] the term of 'allocative efficiency' refers to a static competition policy that predominantly focuses on price and output. Economic theory, however, tells us that dynamic competition for better products and innovation may promote wealth and consumer interests much more than does the mere optimal allocation of existing resources through the price mechanism of markets.[72] The concept of 'dynamic competition' was mostly

---

[70] In contrast to the 'right-holders option' preferred by the Commission, the IFPI/Simulcasting model may also be called a 'commercial users option'. On this terminology, see Drexl, above n. 30, at 197.

[71] Above at s. 1.

[72] These ideas on dynamic competition were first developed by Schumpeter, Joseph R. (1942; new edition 1976), *Capitalism, Socialism, and Democracy*, New York, NY: Harper & Brothers, pp. 81–6, who created the now oft-cited concept of 'creative destruction'. According to this concept, monopolies are not so bad after all, since they will always be overturned after a while by competitors offering more innovative products. Modern economists sometimes question the validity of the neoclassical static model of perfect competition altogether as unrealistic, and refer to dynamic competition as the only convincing model; see, e.g., Blaug, Mark (2001), 'Is Competition Such a Good Thing? Static Efficiency versus Dynamic Efficiency', *Review of Industrial Organization*, **19**, 37, at 44 et seq.

developed in the light of the patent paradigm. Copyright, however, at least as far as rights administered by collecting societies are concerned, is not technology-related and does not aim at promoting innovation, but creativity. This is why we will use here the term 'creative competition' instead of 'dynamic competition'.

In none of its documents does the Commission distinguish between the two concepts of competition. The arguments put forward in favour of the right-holders option, namely the objective of improving the quality of the services provided by collective rights managers and of keeping administration costs low, underline the Commission's emphasis on allocative efficiency.[73] The effect of the Recommendation on creativity is hardly taken into account. With a rather superficial argument, the Commission can only argue that transfer of higher royalties to right-holders may increase investment in creativity.[74]

In the Commission model, both commercial users and collecting societies have to identify the music they want to offer to the public at the time of acquiring the respective rights. Since the Commission conceives the collecting societies as regular market participants – so-called collective-rights managers – their decision on which rights they accept for collective management and which rights they reject has to be based on a business rationale. Accordingly, they face the difficult task of deciding what kind of music will be successful in a given market. Specialisation in regard to a specific category of music would not suffice. 'Collective rights managers' would still have to distinguish attractive from non-attractive music within a given category. Therefore, collective rights managers will tend to make a decision on the basis of the existing tastes of the public. Actually, such an approach would be in line with the concept of allocative efficiency. Businesses should satisfy the needs of consumers. Whereas existing tastes may be identified, it is almost impossible to know what consumers might like in the future. Collective rights managers that accept music that deviates from the existing average taste take economic risks. Therefore, collecting societies that now bring their business strategies in line with the Recommendation have a strong incentive to concentrate on popular music that is liked throughout the EU.

Obviously, the phenomenon of specialisation as a specific feature of the Commission model plays a major role in assessing the impact of the Commission model on creative competition.[75] Specialisation of collecting societies splits up a comprehensive market for all music into separate markets

---

[73]　See also above at s. 1.

[74]　See, however, the argument made above at 4, according to which departure from the one-stop shop may well reduce the level of royalties paid by users to the collecting society in comparison to the model of the IFPI/Simulcasting Agreement.

[75]　See already above at section 4.

relevant for different categories of music. These separate markets will have their own specific structures. For mainstream popular music liked across national borders, several collecting societies may well try to compete and acquire an attractive repertoire for cross-border licensing. To the extent that competition for right-holders is sustainable, and does not end up as a natural monopoly, the Commission model would actually generate large income, which, under the pressure of competition, would be passed to the right-holders. The situation would be very different for music based on less spoken languages, for which there is a real danger that only one society, namely the relevant domestic society, will exercise market dominance, also to the disadvantage of right-holders. Instead of protecting the interest of right-holders vis-à-vis such a monopoly, the Commission only relies on an unjustified principle of free choice for the right-holder. The situation may well be worst for most creative and 'innovative' music that still has to prove its market viability, but will not find a collective rights manager at all. Hence, the Recommendation favours mainstream popular music most, whose market value can be judged best, and tends to create market-access barriers for more 'national' and innovative music.

In contrast, a competition-oriented system that promotes cultural diversity and creativity would have to guarantee non-discriminatory market access to all categories of rights and then leave it to consumers to decide which music they like most. Such a system would actually require a duty to contract for the individual collecting societies with regard to all right-holders, enabling the right-holders to choose the competent collecting society. The model of the IFPI/Simulcasting Agreement meets these requirements. Of course, it largely excludes competition between the societies with regard to both price and the licensed repertoire.[76] This exclusion of competition between collecting societies, however, is the price to be paid for establishing a level playing field for creative competition between all works. Such a system requires that all music, including innovative music that has yet to find its market, can actually reach the public without discrimination.

6. 'Creative competition' in the digital environment in particular
In a preceding part of the analysis,[77] it was asked whether economic arguments on the need for collective management are also pertinent when it comes to digital exploitation of rights. It was stated that the two economic advantages of collective management, namely saving transaction costs and spreading the

---

[76] As to the calculation of the global royalty for the multi-territorial and multi-repertoire licence, see above n. 6.
[77] Above at section 2.

costs of building up a control system amongst all right-holders is less stringent in the area of digital exploitation. This is why collective administration competes with individual administration in the digital environment.[78] Here, the question remains how systemic competition between collective and individual administration impacts on 'creative competition'.

Individual online exploitation is not equally accessible for all right-holders. Commercial users of online rights do not want to use single rights, but music titles. Such titles, however, involve a number of different rights, namely the copyright of the composer and the song writer, the neighbouring rights of the performing artists and the phonogram producers. Therefore, individual exploitation over the internet can only work if the relevant rights are licensed in a bundle. This is why original right-holders, authors and performing artists, will only be able to license directly to users in exceptional circumstances. In most cases, the producer or the music publishers are the 'natural' organisers of bundled administration. They can and do 'collect' all the rights necessary for licensing 'titles'. In addition, the music publishing companies are able to build up important repertoires of titles, similar in size to the repertoires of large collecting societies. Therefore, one wonders why the large music publishers, the so-called major companies, together holding 80% of the European music market, would have to use the system of collective management in the first place, since they could license their repertoires across borders just as the Commission now recommends for the collecting societies.

For original right-holders, authors and performing artists, the Recommendation, which stipulates a right of free choice for all right-holders, cannot keep the promise made to authors and performing artists as original right-holders. In the real world of the market economy, commercial users will require collective rights managers to offer repertoires that include all the rights needed for the use of individual titles. Since the collecting societies will only be able to get such bundles of rights for attractive music titles from the copyright industry, they are forced to cooperate with the music publishing companies. This analysis is confirmed by a development shortly after the adoption of the Recommendation. Music publishing companies and major European collecting societies became active simultaneously.[79] They started to cooperate in building up platforms from which online rights could be

---

[78] Whereas this competition between collective and individual competition plays an important role in the Commission's Communication of 2004 on collecting societies above n. 3, it does not seem to play any role for the Commission's policy leading to the Recommendation of 2005; for a more detailed critique, see also Drexl, above n. 30, at 216–20.

[79] On the first experience of the Recommendation, see Lüder, above n. 4, at 17–19.

licensed.[80] Whereas the Commission initially expected competition between individual collecting societies, competition seems to be evolving among a limited number of such platforms that pool the repertoires of the cooperating partners. The Head of the Commission's Copyright Unit, Tilman Lüder, obviously takes this development as evidence of the Recommendation's success.[81]

However, this development proves that the Commission's policy best serves the interests of large institutional right-holders, the music publishing companies in particular. Only these right-holders can use their market power to rearrange the system of licensing online rights in Europe. The Recommendation does not lead to better services by collecting societies in favour of authors and performing artists, as a superficial reading of the Commission documents may however suggest. It rather blurs the distinction between the three groups of persons, namely the right-holders, the music publishing companies and the collecting societies, as well as between individual and collective administration. Music publishing companies fulfil the Recommendation's definition of a right-holder as 'any natural or legal person that holds online rights'.[82] To the extent that they have now started cooperating with collecting societies in operating platforms for online rights, the actual business conduct of collecting societies and music publishing companies can no longer be distinguished. In addition, both 'collective rights managers' – in the sense of the Recommendation[83] – and the music publishing companies manage rights that are derived from other right-holders. A distinction may only be made insofar as music publishers have fully been assigned the rights and manage them for themselves, whereas the collective rights managers act on behalf of right-holders. This latter and decisive feature of the definition of collective rights managers does not help the original right-holders. Since

---

[80]   This policy holds true especially for EMI Music Publishing, who, at the beginning of 2006, entered into a contract with the British collecting society MCPS-PRS Alliance and the German GEMA with a view to establishing such a platform for the licensing of EMI's Anglo-American repertoire.

[81]   See Lüder, above n. 4, at 17–19.

[82]   No. 1(g) of the Recommendation avoids any distinction between authors and performing artists as original right-holders on the one hand and the copyright industry that acquires rights from the authors and performing artists on the other. The Recommendation only refers to the interests of original right-holders, namely to 'artists, including writers and musicians' in para. 3 of the recitals, where the Commission cites the European Parliament's Resolution. And even here the Recommendation, as throughout its whole text, avoids the legal terms of 'authors' and 'performing artists'.

[83]   According to No. 1(e) of the Recommendation, collective rights managers provide services regarding the management of copyright and related rights in the sense of lit. (a) to several right-holders.

music publishers are considered right-holders themselves, the Recommendation wilfully makes the collecting societies more dependent on the music publishing companies.[84]

The Recommendation does not only promote the very interests of the music publishing companies.[85] It also negatively affects 'creative competition'. The music publishing companies are not creative themselves. Rather, they have a strong interest in the best marketing of their respective repertoire. Their market strategy, therefore, aims to cater for the average taste of the public and to keep that taste stable for the longest time possible. 'Dynamic' developments in music, namely 'innovative' trends and music with a more distinct national character, go against this strategy. It is no wonder that the first two initiatives for the establishment of platforms for cross-border licensing touched the Anglo-American repertoire of EMI on the one hand[86] and the Anglo-Hispanic repertoire, including Latin American music, of the British collecting society MCPS-PRS Alliance and Spain's SGAE on the other hand.[87] Obviously, the Commission's model only promotes popular entertainment music, often with a non-European cultural background, to the disadvantage of innovative trends and cultural diversity in Europe.

7. 'Creative competition' and Europe's competitiveness in international markets

Despite the truly global character of digital exploitation of works of music on the internet, the Commission opted for a model that is geographically limited to the territory of the EU. In the light of the objective of promoting 'creative competition', the additional question needs to be asked whether this model is

---

[84]   Most strikingly No. 13(a) of the Recommendation stipulates a principle of non-discrimination with regard to categories of right-holders and all elements of the management service. This principle reacts to the situation in some EU Member States where the collecting societies only accept authors and performing artists as members. For the Commission's critique on such a practice, see Commission Staff Working Document of 7 July 2005, above n. 4, at 1.1.4.3 (pp. 13 et seq.). In contrast, Kretschmer, Martin (2003), 'Copyright Societies Do Not Administer Individual Property Rights: The Incoherence of Institutional Traditions in Germany and the UK', in Ruth Towse (ed.), *Copyright in the Creative Industries*, Cheltenham, UK and Northampton, MA, USA: Edward Elgar, p. 140, very much criticises joint membership of music publishers and authors or performing artists in collecting societies, since the publisher may dominate the societies.

[85]   This is confirmed by the Head of the Commission's Copyright Unit Tilman Lüder, who welcomes the development that some collecting societies have now offered publishers more seats on their board, in line with the 'economic weight principle' of the Recommendation; see Lüder, above n. 4, at 18.

[86]   EMI cooperates with the British collecting society and the German GEMA.

[87]   See Lüder, above n. 4, p. 18.

internationally compatible and whether it actually promotes competitiveness in the European economy.

The Commission is extremely silent on this topic. Only in its impact assessment, accompanying the adoption of the Recommendation, does the Commission briefly mention that its model may convince right-holders from outside the EU to entrust their online rights to collective rights managers within the EU.[88]

For a closer analysis, it is necessary to distinguish between the two fundamental aspects of collective administration, namely the licensing of rights and the enforcement of such rights against infringing acts. From the perspective of European competitiveness, the most important objective does not consist in convincing as many right-holders of the world to authorise European collecting societies with cross-border licensing, but to guarantee that commercial users from outside the EU respect the rights of right-holders based in the EU and actually pay for the respective licences. Whereas the IFPI/Simulcasting Agreement enables easy access to the multi-territorial licence for commercial users, who can get this licence from the domestic collecting society, the Commission model requires users from outside the EU to request the licence from the competent European collecting society. Even if the competent collecting society runs an electronic platform in English that can be accessed without problems from everywhere in the world, the Commission's approach increases the transaction costs and the risk that users outside the EU in particular will not request a 'European' licence. Especially with respect to less well-known music of European origin, the search costs of finding out which collecting society actually administers the rights may convince foreign users either not to use that music or simply to infringe the copyright.

As to enforcement, problems are even greater. Whereas reciprocal representation agreements would at least oblige the local collecting society to act against alleged infringers, collective rights managers have to enforce the rights administered by them within the judicial system of the country where the potential infringer is situated.[89] Although the Recommendation clearly states

---

[88]   Impact assessment, above n. 4, at 4.8. (p. 29).

[89]   Here, the problem may well arise that domestic law does not accept the standing of collecting societies from abroad. German law, for instance, only recognises the standing of collecting societies that hold an authorisation for managing rights with regard to German territory; see § 1(3) German Act on Collective Administration (Urheberrechtswahrnehmungsgesetz). Foreign collecting societies that want to license rights with regard to Germany can get such authorisation. However, if they do not respect the duties under German law, the authorisation may be withdrawn; see § 4(1) No. 2 German Act on Collective Administration. For a more detailed analysis of the application of German law to cross-border licensing, see Drexl, above n. 51.

that enforcement of the copyright and related rights forms part of the service collective rights managers provide, the Commission does not give any consideration to the difficulties a duty to enforce the online rights in any other country of the world would entail.[90]

To sum up: The Commission model may well reduce the likelihood that the online rights of EU right-holders will be respected globally. In contrast, the Recommendation favours mainstream popular, mostly Anglo-American music to the disadvantage of music with a European background. In contrast to the IFPI/Simulcasting Agreement, the Commission model tends to reduce the flow of royalties from non-EU users to EU right-holders and simultaneously enhances the flow of royalties in the opposite direction. The approach of the Commission weakens the international competitiveness of works based on European creativity by making it more difficult to enter a functioning international system of collective administration on a non-discriminatory basis.

8.   Conclusion

With the adoption of the Recommendation on the management of online rights for musical works, the European Commission took the first steps toward the regulation of collecting societies in the European Union. With a view to promoting a workable cross-border system of licensing for online rights, the Commission has opted for a new system of 'direct licensing' without relying on reciprocal representation agreements.

In formulating its new policy, the Commission develops a competition-oriented concept of collective rights managers competing for right-holders. The Recommendation promises to confer upon right-holders a right to choose freely between collective rights managers and to define independently the online rights to be entrusted to such managers. However, in reality, the Recommendation tends to trigger a process of specialisation by the collecting societies in different categories of music, which will lead to separate markets relevant to different categories. Each market will develop its own specific structure and define the actual ability of right-holders to access the new system. Competition for right-holders, as imagined by the Commission, will only have a chance with regard to some categories of musical works, most importantly mainstream popular music, which enjoys high consumer demand across Europe. In contrast, music using a language spoken only in one or very few countries will continue to be managed solely by the respective national society. New types of music, whose market potential is still unknown, and

---

90   In contrast, see Tuma, above n. 3, at 226, who warns that disrupting the system of reciprocal representation agreements by imposing direct licensing could seriously affect the ability to enforce the rights even in other EU Member States.

music only liked by a minority of the public may have difficulty finding a 'specialised' collective rights manager at all; this music therefore runs the risk of being excluded from the new system altogether.

Hence, the Commission model discriminates between different kinds of music. It promotes the interest of music publishing companies holding large repertoires in mainstream popular music. Initial experience shows that these companies are now beginning to cooperate with collecting societies to build up digital platforms for cross-border licensing of their rights.

The foregoing analysis questions the Commission's policy in the light of the overall objective of copyright law to promote creativity. Whereas the Commission is very much enamoured of the idea of promoting 'innovative' business models for cross-border licensing of online rights,[91] it misses the point of giving due consideration to the creativity-enhancing rationale of copyright law itself. The 'innovative' new form of licensing advocated by the Commission is actually based on a purely static competition policy – in the sense of allocative efficiency – that focuses exclusively on output and price. The Commission prefers a copyright policy that serves the average taste of consumers across Europe and tries to maximise the income of the undertakings in control of the rights in such mainstream music. The Recommendation achieves this goal by forcing the collecting societies into cooperation with the music publishing companies and by creating entry barriers to less widely popular music. Collecting societies thereby risk losing their innocence and their capacity to act as credible defenders of the interests of creative authors and performing artists vis-à-vis the copyright industry. In contrast to the Commission's policy, the foregoing analysis argues in favour of a system based on 'creative competition'. The fundamental objective of such a policy would consist of enabling all kinds of music equal access to the online market. Instead of establishing a level playing field for competition between collecting societies to the benefit of music publishers, the Commission should work for a level playing field for competition between works. Only the latter approach will enhance creativity in Europe, with its large multi-cultural background, and promote cultural diversity and the competitiveness of European music in international markets.

It has to be admitted that this concept of 'creative competition' has to face considerable lack of competition between collecting societies and has to rely on cooperation between collecting societies on the basis of reciprocal representation agreements. However, the model advocated today by the Commission is less competition-oriented than it seems. Even with regard to mainstream popular music, operators of co-existing platforms for licensing

---

[91] See, in particular, recent statements by Lüder, above n. 4, at 10–12.

online rights can exercise market dominance vis-à-vis commercial users, like webradio stations, who need to get licences from all platforms in order to offer an attractive programme to their audience. Most importantly, however, the Commission policy weakens the position of creative authors and performing artists. Today's problems in the field of cross-border digital exploitation of rights highlight the need for European principles regarding the functions and duties of collecting societies vis-à-vis the users on the one hand and the creative authors and performing artists as their most important members on the other. The Commission Recommendation clearly fails to live up to this challenge by promoting the business interests of those undertakings that are least in need of enhanced market power.

12 Individual and collective management of copyright in a digital environment
Marco Ricolfi[1]

Introduction

What does the future hold for the collective administration of copyright and related rights in a digital environment? Certainly, at the moment the legal and organisational landscape in this area is rapidly changing, particularly in the European Union and in the Member States.[2] At times, it even appears that in the long run collective rights management and collective rights management organisations (CRMOs) might end up being altogether displaced from the digital environment. Indeed, according to some observers, the alternative to CRMOs consists of technology-based tools, usually described as digital rights management (DRM). As DRM enables rightholders to individually monitor and meter the use of copyright protected works, resort to it would ultimately make CRMOs redundant. According to a different school of thought, however, the future alternative to collective management is to be found in the opposite direction, or, more specifically, in the setting up of levy-based neo-regulatory devices, such as a mechanism sometimes described as a 'governmentally administered reward system' which, in the long run, would phase out copyright in the entertainment sector.

Thus CRMOs, which since the second half of the nineteenth century have made a remarkable contribution to the advancement of culture and to the progress of the media industries in our societies and until the present day have managed to remain powerful organisations, are currently subject to a strong wind of change.

To understand why this is so, and to explore the possible outcomes, some background may be in order.

---

[1]   Professor of Law, Faculty of Law, University of Turin, Italy.
[2]   See Commission Recommendation of 18 October 2005 on collective cross-border management of copyright and related rights for legitimate online music services, in OJ L 276 of 21 October 2005, 54 ff. as amended in OJ L 284 of 27 October 2005, 10 ff.

History of a comet

It is well known that the management of copyrighted works may either be individual or collective. Historically, the latter form of management follows the former. The time interval between the two was however short. While copyright was introduced in England in 1709 and on the European continent its protection was exalted as the most sacred of rights in 1793, at the height of the French Revolution, it did not take long before creators became aware that it was impossible for them to enforce their new rights individually.

The story has it that the composer Paul Bourget realised that it was impossible for him to be simultaneously present in all the cafés of Paris, let alone of the rest of France, to assiduously monitor that his music was not being exploited without his authorisation. No doubt Bourget was not the only creator to come to this conclusion. But the reason we still single him out for recollection is that his initiative started a movement which eventually led to the creation of the first CRMO in France and therefrom in the rest of the world.[3] In due course CRMOs were monitoring not only cafés, but also theatres, as well as concert halls, dance schools and all the other establishments where works are performed, to make sure that the copyrights of their members were not being infringed.[4] From that point on and for well over the next hundred

---

[3]   For accounts of this episode see M. Kretschmer (2002), 'The Failure of Property Rules in Collective Administration: Rethinking Copyright Societies as Regulatory Instruments', *European Intellectual Property Review (EIPR)*, **24,** 126 ff. at 127; M.F. Makeen, *Copyright in a Global Information Society: The Scope of Copyright Protection Under International, US, UK and French Law*, Deventer: Kluwer Law, 2000, 15.

[4]   On the birth in 1850 of the French CRMO SACEM (Société des Auteurs, Compositeurs et Editeurs de Musique) see, also for additional references, W. Fikentscher (1995), 'Urhebervertragsrecht und Kartellrecht', in F.K. Beier, H.P. Goetting, M. Lehmann and R. Moufang (eds), *Urhebervertragsrecht*, in *Festgabe für Gerhard Schricker zum 60. Geburtstag*, München: C.H. Beck'sche Verlagsbuchhandlung, 149 ff. at 182; F. Melichar (2003), 'Das Recht der Verwertungsgesellschaften', in U. Loewenheim (ed.), *Handbuch des Urheberrechts*, München: C.H. Beck, 674 ff., 677–79. For the USA, where ASCAP (American Society of Composers, Authors and Publishers) was set up in 1913 and BMI (Broadcast Music, Inc.) followed in 1939, see Julie E. Cohen, Lydia Pallas Loren, Ruth Gana Okediji and Maureen O'Rourke (2002), *Copyright in a Global Information Economy*, New York and Gaithersburg: Aspen Law & Business, 440 ff. and R.P. Merges (1996), 'Contracting into Liability Rules: Intellectual Property Rights and Collective Rights Organisations', *California Law Review*, **84**, 1293 ff., at 1329 ff. A wide comparative overview is to be found in Makeen, *Copyright in a Global Information Society*, supra at note 2, 18 ff. For a law and economics perspective see A. Katz (2006), *The Potential Demise of another Natural Monopoly: New Technologies and the Future of Collective Administration of Copyrights*, *Journal of Competition Law and Economics*, **2**(2), 245–84, and previously S.M. Besen, S.N. Kirby and S. Salop (1992), 'An Economic

years, CRMOs proved extremely successful in carrying out their original mission.[5]

During all that period of time and until the digital revolution finally set in, the respective roles of individual and collective management of copyrighted works remained pretty clear. What is worth remarking on in this specific connection is that the continued growth of collective management was never at the expense of individual management, as it would have been if we were dealing with the case of a zero sum game.

Indeed, in our systems individual and collective management were always in the kind of reciprocal relationship we can observe between the head and the tail of a comet. First, creators enter into individual contracts, e.g. with publishers, record companies, entertainment businesses and movie producers, which then engage in what is sometimes called the *primary* exploitation of the work. Once the work has been launched and turns out to be successful on the initial market, it may have one or more additional runs of life in what are correspondingly described as forms of *secondary* exploitation. Indeed, music, plays or movies may eventually be broadcast over radio and television, or, if the work is performed in theatres, the performance itself may also be broadcast. Normally it is at this later stage that collective management and CRMOs come into the picture; and as a rule the intensity of the secondary exploitation depends on the extent of the success of the primary one, very much as the tail of a comet follows its head, according to our simile.

Let us now look for a moment at the head of the comet. In the analogue world, the public did not usually obtain access to the work directly from the creator.[6] In particular, books and records needed to be printed; and for this purpose some kind of 'factory' was required, to manufacture what in effect were fixed, stable, material or – as the expression now goes – 'hard' copies of

---

Analysis of Copyright Collectives', *Virginia Law Review*, **78**, 383 ff. For additional references see J.A.L. Sterling (2003), *World Copyright Law,* London: Sweet & Maxwell, 499 ff.

5   While in the last few decades mainstream scholarship has focused on collective management as an efficient economic mechanism to minimise transaction costs, more recent scholars have underlined that the reasons for success of CRMOs, particularly in continental Europe, are also strongly correlated to political and cultural factors, such as the rise of the nation states and the role played by governments in fostering this aim by intervention in cultural institutions and how these factors weakened considerably in the second part of the last century: for a persuasive account see D. Sarti (2006), 'Gestione collettiva e modelli associativi', in P. Spada (ed.), *Gestione collettiva dell'offerta e della domanda di prodotti culturali*, Milano: Giuffrè, 30 ff., at 45 ff.

6   Except in a very limited number of very special cases, such as the bohemian painter personally seeking out patrons to sell his paintings or the wandering gipsy carrying around his violin.

the work. In turn these hard copies needed to be stored, transported, distributed, before reaching the shelves where the public would finally find them. It was difficult for creators to engage in all these steps; and that is why, as a rule, they preferred to resort to businesses to set up the characteristic trilateral relationship between creator, business and the public, which is typical of primary exploitation of copyrighted works.[7]

In this regard, it can certainly be said that this was a quite long-winded way of establishing contact between the work and the public. But then, if we turn our attention to the area we earlier described as the tail of the comet, to secondary exploitation of works, it is easy to see that there the route for accessing the market was significantly longer. Here, additional classes of businesses, such as radio or television stations, had to appear, before the work could be brought to such new markets; and these businesses in turn had to deal with CRMOs, which in the meantime had signed up both the creators and their assignees.

From analogue to digital: three novel features

The emergence of digital technology and of the internet has posed formidable challenges both to collective management and to the continued viability of CRMOs. So much has been said about the intersection of digital technology, the net and copyright in the last two decades, that I shall certainly refrain from engaging in a recapitulation of the state of the art in this vast domain.[8] In this connection I shall refer to just three expressions, which in my opinion capture well the three novel features of the digital age which have the greatest impact on the role of CRMOs.

The first two are adverbs: *anywhere, any time.*

Anywhere. While radio and TV could reach only a limited slice of the earth, which usually had some loose correspondence with geopolitical borders, the net is everywhere and nowhere in particular. To have access, on demand or otherwise, it does not matter where the receiving end or the transmitting end may happen to be located.

Any time. In the past, the architecture of networks was point-to-mass: from one transmitting end to innumerable receiving ends, intended for simultaneous

---

[7]   See in this connection W.R. Cornish (1996), *Intellectual Property: Patents, Copyright, Trade Marks and Allied Rights*, London: Sweet & Maxwell, 401.

[8]   See among others P. Torremans and I. Stamatoudi (eds) (2000), *Copyright in the New Digital Environment: The Need to Redesign Copyright*, London: Sweet & Maxwell; L. Lessig (1999), *Code and Other Laws of Cyberspace*, New York: Basic Books, 122 ff.; P. Spada (1998), 'La proprietà intellettuale nelle reti telematiche', *Riv. dir. civ.*, I, 635 ff.; B. Hugenholz (ed.) (1996), *The Future of Copyright in A Digital Environment,* The Hague: Kluwer Law International.

reception by each and all members of the audience at the same time. This is the way radio started to function in the early tens of the last century and television in the forties. Today, the architecture is essentially point-to-point. Yes, we also have terrestrial digital radio and television, simulcasting and webcasting, which are – or may be – point-to-mass. But we also have digital audio and video transmission and distribution, which are point-to-point and thus interactive. In the latter settings, it is the end-user who decides at which time she will access the relevant digital content. Which, correspondingly, is accessible on demand, any time.

The last expression is an adjective: *perfect*. Digital copies, as contrasted to analogue, are perfect. Any digital copy is as good as the original. Yes, of course digital copies also tend to be infinite and costless, but what is more important for present purposes: they are perfect.

The impact of the three novel features on collective and individual management of copyright

But then, in which way do these novel features impact on CRMOs and on the reciprocal roles of collective and individual management? Let us go back to each of our three proxies for the internet.

Anywhere

CRMOs are territorial; they feel on shaky ground when markets integrate. Whatever can they conceivably still be doing when the net, which is everywhere and in no particular place, creates the greatest of all possible markets for copyrighted goods, i.e. a world market accessible in every remotest corner of the globe with all the goodies available through it around the clock?

To have access, on demand or otherwise, it does not matter where either the receiving end or the transmitting end – or, more to the point: the provider, the server – happen to be located. So which CRMO has authority over which provider?[9] What are we going to look at? The provider's registered office? The top level domain of its site? The principal place of business? The place where the servers are located? The place where its users are located? Let us visualise legitimate providers, such as webcasters, subscription services, music and media stores. Why should they not strive to get established where

---

    9   A clear presentation of the issue and of the available alternatives is in B.M. Linkoff (2001), 'A Plan for the Future of Music Performance Rights Organizations in the Digital Age', in R. Cooper Dreyfuss, D. Leenher-Zimmermann and H. First (eds.), *Expanding the Boundaries of Intellectual Property: Innovation Policy for the Knowledge Society*, Oxford: Oxford University Press, 167 ff. and, for the necessary updates, A. Capobianco (2004), 'Licensing of Music Rights: Media Convergence, Technological Developments and EC Competition Law', *EIPR*, **26**, 113 ff., 118 ff.

the lowest-cost CRMO is located? But then, if they do so, how can they lawfully webcast and stream and sell music into countries where a different CRMO has jurisdiction?

This is the easy part, though, because the real challenges to the old order arise in connection with the other two proxies for the internet.

Any time

Copyright law is used to adapting to technological change. As a new way of exploiting works becomes technologically feasible, copyright evolves to provide rightholders with additional prerogatives. This was the case when radio and television initially emerged; and once again when consumer electronics enabled users to make cheap analogue copies, particularly of music and of text.

We have just seen that, as a result of the internet, the architecture has become point-to-point rather than point-to-mass. Works are available online; they reside all the time on the servers of the provider and access to them is activated at the receiving end, on demand from the user.

This new mode of exploitation immediately raises a number of issues.

Traditionally, rightholders used to have an exclusive right over point-to-mass communication, which in the Berne Convention[10] and in EU secondary legislation is designated as communication to the public, in the USA as public performance.[11] What then was the legal status of the online mode? This question arose as the online mode, while sharing with traditional communication to the public the fact that the work is communicated to a dispersed public,

---

[10]   Arts. 11(1)(ii), 11-*bis*, 11-*ter*(1), 14(1)(ii) and 14-*bis*(1) of the Berne Convention for the Protection of Literary and Artistic Works, 9 September 1886 as last revised in Paris, 24 July 1971 (hereinafter Berne Convention).

[11]   It should however be noted that terminological complications may arise in this connection, as (i) in various legal systems, the exclusive right which in EU parlance is described as communication to the public (see Art. 3 of Directive 2001/29/EC of the European Parliament and the Council of 22 May 2001 on the harmonisation of certain aspects of copyright and related rights in the information society, in *OJ* L 167 of 22 June 2001, 10 ff., hereinafter EUCD) and in the USA as public performance (see 17 USC § 106(4)), is elsewhere categorised under a different designation, such as *représentation* (in France), broad- and cable casting (in the UK), *Vorführungs- und Senderecht* (in Germany; see §§ 15(2)(1), 19(4), 15(2)(3) and 20 UrhG); (ii) in some of these legal systems, such as the UK, the notion of communication to the public constitutes the broader category to which both public performance (there understood as taking place before an audience in attendance) and broad- and cable casting belong; and finally, (iii) in the French legal system the term *représentation* covers both the broader category which in the UK would be designated as communication to the public and its two individual components. Henceforth, to simplify matters, we shall use the EU terminology, unless otherwise specifically noted.

members of which are located in different places, has also the additional specialised feature whereby by definition such communication is not simultaneous, as each individual member decides for herself the timing of her access.[12] At first, the question was whether this new, interactive feature was covered by the pre-existing exclusivity over public communication. The reply came in the form of two new copyright treaties,[13] intended to complement the Berne Convention[14] by adding the interactive, or 'making available', feature to the old exclusivity over public communication.[15]

Not surprisingly this solution in turn opened up a number of new issues, including the question whether CRMOs retained their prerogatives also over this new stick in the bundle of exclusive rights conferred upon rightholders by the different legal systems.

Perfect
This would have been a difficult issue to sort out by itself.[16] An additional complication arose, however, as a result of the third proxy for the internet mentioned earlier, whereby digital copies are perfect.

---

[12]   On the further complication, whereby digital online transmission may involve digital distribution of copies, see the next paragraph

[13]   World Intellectual Property Organization (WIPO): Copyright Treaty, 20 December 1996, (1997) ILM **36**, 65 ff. (hereinafter WCT); World Intellectual Property Organization: Performances and Phonograms Treaty, 20 December 1996, (1997) ILM **36**, 76 ff. (hereinafter WPPT).

[14]   As a Special Agreement under Art. 20 of the Berne Convention itself.

[15]   Art. 8 of WCT reads: 'Without prejudice to the provisions of Articles 11(1)(ii), 11 *bis*(1) (i) and (ii), 11*ter*(1) (ii), 14 (1)(ii) and 14*bis*(1) of the Berne Convention, authors of literary and artistic works shall enjoy the exclusive right of authorising any communication to the public of their works, by wire or wireless means, including the making available to the public of their works in such a way that members of the public may access these works from a place and at a time individually chosen by them'. See also the corresponding wording in Art. 14 WPPT.

[16]   As CRMOs derive their rights from their members, a reply to any question concerning CRMOs' prerogatives depends on the determination of the preliminary issue as to whether the interactive feature is vested in the creators or belongs to their assignees, such as music publishers. In the different legal systems the outcome is in turn bound to be influenced by the separate issue of whether, under the relevant national legislation, the rule providing exclusivity over the interactive feature is considered to confer a new right or to clarify the original legislative grant. To the extent that the first reply prevails, legal systems are also bound to differ significantly on the question of whether future rights may be contractually assigned in advance, where the solution tends to be in the affirmative in common law systems but in the negative in continental European civil law systems (on the basis of the mandatory provisions discussed by P. Florenson (2003), 'Management of Authors' Rights and Neighbouring Rights in Europe', *Revue Internationale de droit de l'auteur*, 2 ff., 10 ff.).

In this connection we should engage in a brief detour and consider that, particularly in the field of music, on top of the copyright concerning music as such, there had all along been a second layer of protection concerning the sounds fixed in the recording of a given performance. In the USA this additional protection had taken the form of a separate copyright in sound recordings, in Europe it took the shape of a neighbouring right, granted to the so-called producers of phonograms. In the analogue world, however, this second layer had never been protected under a full property right. Indeed, in the USA the copyright in sound recordings, while covering reproduction and distribution of the sound recording, did not extend to their 'public performance'. In the EU the corresponding right gave rise to a limited claim to compensation in connection with the communication to the public of protected subject matter.

It is easy to see why this approach made a lot of sense in a situation where record companies retained full exclusivity over the manufacture and sale of records and thus had complete control over the primary exploitation of the work. If the work eventually made it over the air, in the form of radio or television broadcasts, then this occurrence was seen as a clear case of secondary exploitation. In this connection, record companies either staked no claim, as happened in the USA,[17] where they rested content in the fact that the added popularity gained by broadcast music would in turn increase the sales of records; or they staked claims limited to monetary compensation, as happened in Europe.

It is also easy to see why all this had to change, as soon as digital technology made available over the net audio files – or musical 'tracks' – which are (nearly) perfect substitutes for the original material, physical and stable copies, i.e. records first and then CDs. In this new context, it was arguable that digital transmission was still a case of secondary exploitation, as it disseminates the work through a network exactly as happens with radio or television broadcasts. The analogy may sound defensible to the extent that we attach importance to structure: in either case the work passes through a network before reaching a dispersed audience. From a functional viewpoint, however, the analogy does not hold at all. Tracks are as good as records and CDs, in a world where PCs, i-pods, and other hand-held devices are equivalent to CD players and have completely displaced record players and tape recorders. Moreover, as soon as they are downloaded, it is very difficult to deny that tracks are the functional equivalent of records and CDs; and that correspondingly an act of primary exploitation, specifically in the form of the distribution of copies, has occurred.

Now, coming back to the heart of the matter, the very perfection of digital

---

[17]   See 17 USC § 106(6).

copies is the reason why, while the debate was still going on concerning the issue of whether the interactive feature of copyright in creative works still belonged to CRMOs, the holders of copyrights in sound recordings in the USA and their European siblings, the holders of the neighbouring right in phonograms, were able to quickly and successfully bargain for a full property right on the same interactive feature as far as their sound recordings or phonograms rights were concerned.[18] Failure to do so, they argued, would mean that perfect digital copies would totally destroy their bricks-and-mortar franchise. This legislative coup was quite a success; and it was obtained, it should be noted, in an area where traditional CRMOs, which derive copyrights from creators of the work and their assigns, have no say.

An interim assessment

What then is the impact of these developments on the role of CRMOs and on the reciprocal roles of collective and individual management?

At first glance, we have reason to say that business is quite clearly taking the offensive. Indeed, as far as copyright in works is concerned, business is trying to wrest away from CRMOs the interactive feature of the exclusive right to public communication of copyrighted works, in spite of the fact that in the past this latter and more general right traditionally used to belong to collective administration and CRMOs. I do not know that this effort has been totally successful yet. Certainly, in the USA rightholders – which in the field of music tend to be music publishers – have a concurrent power to license what is there referred to as public performance[19] and this concurrent power extends to the interactive feature. In Europe the situation is more nuanced. Here CRMOs are keen to insist that their exclusivity extends to the interactive feature of what is here designated as the right of public communication. This may well be so, at least in principle.[20] Except that, as we shall presently see, the smaller CRMOs are clearly losing ground in this specific regard.[21]

In any event the overall balance of power has in the meantime clearly shifted. Indeed, as far as the second layer of protection is concerned, be it

---

[18] For the US see the Digital Performance Rights in Sound Recordings Act of 1995 (Pub. L. No. 104-39, 109 Stat. 336 (1995)) as amended in 1998; for Europe see Art. 3(2) EUCD. For additional detail see Cohen et al. (2002), *Copyright in a Global Information Economy*, supra at note 4, 444 ff. and V. Espinel (1999), 'The U.S. Recording Industry and Copyright Law: An Overview, Recent Developments and the Impact of Digital Technology', *EIPR*, **21,** 53 ff., at 57 ff. (noting that the American notion of interactivity is in this connection broader than the one adopted in Europe).

[19] As a result of several antitrust consent decrees: see Katz, *The Potential Demise of another Natural Monopoly*, supra at note 4, 46 and 72.

[20] And see the discussion supra at note 16.

[21] See infra, text accompanying notes 33–4.

conceptualised as the American copyright in sound recordings or as its European counterpart, the neighbouring right in phonograms, businesses were quick to secure a fully monopolistic right over its interactive feature.[22] They thereby acquired a strong foothold in digital transmission and distribution of works over the networks, based on a legal position over which, as we have just seen, traditional CRMOs have no say. Which does make sense in many ways.[23] Indeed, as we noted, digital files are a perfect substitute for the stable, physical and material copies which used to constitute primary exploitation. Moreover they seem to constitute a section of this market which is finally growing after a number of disappointing years, and – even more to the point – promise to stem the losses arising from what record companies regard as widespread 'piracy'. It can therefore be readily understood that businesses wish to have a free hand in this respect.[24] It is quite likely that, from their perspective, the job will be completed only when CRMOs are excluded altogether from the interactive feature of copyright in music; but in the meantime securing exclusivity over the interactive feature relating to phonograms goes quite a long way towards control of this business sector.

What is possibly less obvious but even more striking is that creators seem at long last also to have a chance of gaining some control over the exploitation of their works. In this connection, technological and legal evolution appears to impact more on individual management than on collective administration. It would seem that even in the area of primary exploitation individual management, understood as the setting up of a relationship between creator and business, no longer has the same compelling rationale it used to have in the past. Digital copies are (nearly) perfect; and can be duplicated at no cost at the

---

[22]   Music in digital form is (nearly) perfect and may therefore be perceived as a competitive threat even if the real-time transmission (streaming) does not entail any reproduction and is not interactive. Also in this specific regard USA holders of copyright in sound recordings have obtained a position of exclusivity (as confirmed by the decision *Bonneville International Corp. v Peters* 153 F. Supp. 2d 763 (ED Pa. 2001), whereby only terrestrial over-the-air transmissions, as opposed to digital webcasting, may be exempted), which is much stronger than the claim to compensation available in this connection to European phonogram producers.

[23]   It should however be noted that creating multiple layers of monopoly over the same item on behalf of different categories of rightholders (here: a copyright in the work and a separate full monopoly on the sound recording/phonogram) may entail the risks described by M.A. Heller (1998), 'The Tragedy of the Anticommons: Property in the Transition from Marx to Markets', *Harvard Law Review*, **111**, 111 ff. In this specific case the risk is greatly mitigated by the fact that the same entities (here: music publishers) may be at the same time assignees of the former right and associated with the holders of the latter (here: record companies).

[24]   Subject, of course, to the limits deriving from overlapping multiple layers of monopoly: see supra at note 23.

receiving end. Therefore, in a number of situations neither the 'factory' nor the physical distribution chain is indispensable any more.[25] It appears therefore that creators can more and more often access markets without engaging in the trilateral relationship which used to characterise dealings in copyright. As a result, the long route from creators to the public may at some point become much shorter. Today creators set up their own sites and make books and music directly accessible to the public therefrom, either independently or in cooperation with businesses.[26] Currently, social networking and user-generated content are all the rage.[27]

From this perspective, the notion of individual management acquires a new dimension. Indeed, it designates the setting up of a direct relationship between creators and the public, rather than between creators and business. Here business appears to be on the defensive, as much as they appeared on the offensive in their relationship to CRMOs.

The European reply in the field of collective management of cross-border offerings of music for online services

The starting point
In recent times the European Union has tried to take up the challenges which the new digital environment poses in the specific area of online music services. This is a sector which appears to have the potential for a very high growth rate, as is shown both by the success of i-tunes and by the efforts of competitors, such as MS and Tesco, to imitate it.

However, in Europe the setting up of a provider of online music services has to face difficulties which would hardly be conceivable in the USA. Since the service has an inherently cross-border character, for the reasons we earlier explored, and in the EU the interactive feature of the right of communication to the public is still believed to belong to CRMOs, currently a provider of online music services is required to go around, hat in hand, to all 27 of the EU CRMOs to get from each of them clearance for the service.

---

[25]   Both developments were anticipated a number of years ago: see E. Volokh (1995), 'Cheap Speech and What it Will Do', *Yale Law Journal*, **104**, 1805 and I. De Sola Pool (1983), *Technologies of Freedom*, Cambridge and London: The Belknap Press of Harvard University Press, 249–51.

[26]   The cooperative variety appears very frequent, though, and has been resorted to from the very beginnings of the phenomenon, when Stephen King set up a site to allow readers to download his latest short story, 'Riding the Bullet', at $2.50 per download, in association with his publisher, Scribner: for a full account see J. Epstein (2000), 'The Rattle of Pebbles', *The New York Review of Books*, 27 April 2000, 55 ff., at 57–8.

[27]   Pew/Internet Home Broadband Adoption 2006, 28 May 2006.

This characterisation may sound quite surprising and particularly so if one remembers that European CRMOs for a long time engaged in reciprocal representation agreements, such as the so-called Santiago Agreement for the licensing of the right of communication to the public. These agreements provide for both multirepertory licences (whereby a CRMO gets authority in its own country also for the repertoires of the sister CRMOs) and multiterritory licences (whereby a CRMO may give clearance not only for its own country but also for the territories of sister CRMOs). Why then could not a business desiring to enter the business of providing online music in Europe just seek out an appropriate CRMO and get all the required clearances through it?

The fact is that reciprocal representation agreements have in the meantime run into serious antitrust troubles. Indeed, the emergence of the internet had raised for European CRMOs the difficult question I discussed earlier: which CRMO has authority over which provider? Apparently European CRMOs sought a way out of this difficult dilemma by agreeing to apportion among themselves the candidate providers on the basis of the territory where the latter had their main offices ('economic residency clause').[28] The EU Commission objected that this arrangement sounded rather like a territorial market-sharing agreement.[29] Therefore European CRMOs thought it advisable to cancel all reciprocal representation agreements as of 31 December 2004.

This is why from 2005 onwards a business intending to set up a European provider of online music services is, as I indicated earlier, required to go around, hat in hand, to all 27 EU CRMOs to get clearance for the service from each of them.

The three options
Against this background we may also understand why the EU Commission decided with uncharacteristic speed to do something about this unfortunate situation. On the 18 of October 2005 it issued a Recommendation,[30] on the

---

[28] See the Notice issued by the EU Commission on notification of the cooperation agreements (Case COMP/C2/38.126 – BUMA, GEMA, PRS and SACEM), in OJ C 17 May 2001, 145, 2 ff.

[29] EU Commission Notice in Cases COMP/C2/39152 – BUMA and COMP/C2/39151 SABAM (Santiago Agreement – COMP/C2/38126), in OJ 17 August 2005 C 200, 11 f.

[30] See Commission Recommendation of 18 October 2005 on collective cross-border management of copyright and related rights for legitimate online music services, supra at note 2. For thorough – and critical – comments see Stellungnahme des Max-Plank-Instituts für Geistiges Eigentum, Wettbewerbs- und Steuerrecht zuhanden des Bundesministerium der Justiz betreffend die Empfehlung der Europäischen Kommission über die Lizenzierung der Musik für das Internet vom 18.Oktober 2005 ('005/737/EG) (2006), *GRUR Int.*, 222 ff. and Josef Drexel (2006), 'Auf dem Weg zu

basis of extensive findings and policy discussions published just a few months earlier.[31]

In the Commission's view, currently we have three options to deal with the present situation of online music services.

The first, which consists of doing nothing at all about it, is described by the Commission as clearly unacceptable and therefore should be rather described as a non-option.

The second option is based on the idea of going back to reciprocal representation agreements among CRMOs after deleting the economic residency clause. This approach can therefore be described as 'Santiago without residency'; and, since it would give providers the possibility to shop around to seek out the European CRMO giving clearance for their cross-border offer of online music at the best combination of price and service, it could also be quite accurately described as the providers' option.

There is also a third option; and this is the one which the Recommendation favours finally. Underlying this third option is the idea that CRMOs should compete against each other for the custom of creators and rightholders, rather than for that of online music providers. In this perspective, CRMOs should compete over demand for their inputs, copyrighted works, rather than in the offer of their outputs, clearances thereof. Thus adoption of the third option means that both creators and rightholders, whatever their nationality or residency, should be able to freely select the CRMO of their choice; that they should be able to make different choices in connection with the different categories of rights, thereby in a way

---

einer Neuen europäischen Marktordung der kollektiven Wahrnehmung von Online-Rechten der Musik? – Kritische Würdigung der Kommissionempfehlung vom 18.Oktober 2005', in Karl Riesehuber (ed.), *Wahrnehmungsrecht in Polen, Deutschland und Europa*, Berlin: De Gruyter, 193 ff.

31   See Commission of the European Communities, Commission Staff Working Document, Study on a Community Initiative on the Cross-Border Collective Management of Copyright, Brussels, 7 July 2005 and Commission Staff Working Document, Impact Assessment Reforming Cross-Border Collective Management of Copyright and Related Rights for Legitimate Online Music Services, Brussels 11 October 2005, SEC(2005) 1254. To a certain extent the Commission's work built on the positions expressed by the Resolution of the European Parliament on a Community framework for collecting societies for authors' rights 2002/2274 (INI) adopted by the Plenary Session of the European Parliament on 15 January 2004, which in turn was based on the Report by the Committee on Legal Affairs and Internal Market, Rapporteur Raina A. Mercedes Escherer, dated 11 December 2003. V. EP 1999–2004, Session Document Final A5-0478/2003 11 December 2003. In this connection see A. Dietz (2004), 'European Parliament versus Commission: How to Deal with Collecting Societies', *IIC* **35**, 809 ff. (exploring the tensions between the respective positions of the two institutions).

'unbundling' them; except that where the grant to the CRMO of their choice has a Community-wide dimension.[32]

A tentative assessment

What do we make of a proposal based on the third option? It is clear that here a number of technical problems still need to be worked out.

First, the old, Santiago-type reciprocal agreements were, as indicated, the basis for multirepertory and multiterritory licensing, because each CRMO managed in its own territory the works of rightholders who were also members of a sister CRMO. Now a licence from a CRMO to a provider under the third option would be monorepertory-multiterritory. This is quite a different notion: each CRMO would directly manage the rights of its own members even in states of other CRMOs. This might have significant repercussions on infringement actions. Indeed, it seems to me that the old presumption, whereby each CRMO is deemed to have authority for all the works which may happen to be used in its own state,[33] may now be called to question, as any rightholder may be represented either by the local CRMO or by any other CRMO which happens to be operating Community-wide for one of its members. Thus enforcement may henceforth presuppose specific evidence of which works have actually been used by the defendant and of the affiliation of each of their creators to the plaintiff CRMO. As a result costs are bound to escalate.

Second, I am not sure at all that a CRMO located in a given Member State really has the know-how to license works also for all the other 26 member States, if one considers how vast to date are the divergences in applicable laws in crucial areas such as initial ownership of works, conflict of laws or mandatory provisions.

But this is the technical side; perhaps it can be sorted out more or less effectively.

My impression is that the real difficulties with the third option lie elsewhere. Indeed it is quite reasonably feared that, under these arrangements, the bigger players and in particular music publishers will take their business to a

---

[32]   See items 3 and 5(a) and (b) of the Recommendation, supra at note 2. For a critical discussion of the underlying model see Drexel, 'Auf dem Weg zu einer Neuen europäischen Marktordnung der kollektiven Wahrnehmung von Online-Rechten der Musik?', supra at note 30, 204 ff.
[33]   Which is quite popular in continental European countries: for Germany see reference to the so called 'Gema Vermutung' and its limits. F. Melichar, 'Das Recht der Verwertungsgesellschaften', supra at note 3, 730 ff. and for Italy the decision of the Court of Appeals of Florence of 17 October 2002, *Video Firenze s.r.l. v SIAE*, *IDA* 2004, 81 ff., based on the assumption that all works used in the Italian territory are managed by SIAE, unless otherwise shown by the defendant.

few large European CRMOs, such as GEMA in Germany and MCPS-PRS Alliance in the UK. It is predictable that this development will lead to an oligopolistic market structure;[34] and that this will in the long term translate into an advantage for commercially successful, English language music, to the detriment of minor music communities, which will have to fall back on the services of smaller, shrinking national CRMOs.[35]

There is an even more remarkable aspect of the action undertaken by the EU Commission. The initiative has chosen to deal with a very limited part of the challenges we have identified earlier. Indeed, the case could be made that the European proposal deals only with one of the three novel features we discussed, i.e. with the 'anywhere' aspect; and chooses to ignore the other two ('any time'; 'perfect'). This limitation is clearly intentional; and can be highlighted by contrasting the approach recommended by the Commission with the two much more ambitious alternatives to collective administration in a digital environment currently advanced from other quarters. As we shall presently see.

Digital rights management: a neo-proprietary and market-based alternative to collective management

A radical technological option to cut off CRMOs
The beauty of DRM, according to its usually enthusiastic supporters, consists in the combination of conditional access and control of use plus its self-enforcing feature. *Access:* this is the digital lock feature, whereby access is made conditional on compliance with what Larry Lessig would call code,[36] i.e. conditions such as prior payment, regional area restrictions and the like. *Use:* after the green light has been given to access, certain uses are allowed, others are (technologically) restricted or disabled, e.g. by dictating (i) whether

---

[34]   This argument is articulated on the basis of the concept of network externalities by the Stellungnahme des Max-Plank-Instituts, supra at note 30, 223. In this connection see also P. Tuma (2006), 'Pitfalls and Challenges of the EC Directive on the Collective Management of Copyright and Related Rights', *EIPR*, **28**, 220 ff., 228 f.

[35]   It should be noted, however, that this fear has been countered by the argument advanced by the Working Documents of 7 July 2005, supra at note 31, 35 f. and of 11 October 2005, supra at note 31, 24 and 30, whereby even smaller CRMOs may play important roles, by concentrating on specialised markets and contributing to the success of niche categories of works. This is indeed a possibility; but only empirical evidence may prove or disprove this argument. In the meantime, it has been reported (by Andrew Edgecliffe-Johnson (2006), 'Shake-up for Online Music Rights', *Financial Times*, 23 January) that EMI's publishing arm is giving the collective management of its catalogues to GEMA and MCPS-PRS Alliance for the entire EU.

[36]   Lessig, *Code and Other Laws of Cyberspace*, supra at note 8.

the file can be copied onto a hard disk and, if so, how many times; (ii) whether it may be transferred to portable devices or not; or (iii) whether it may be burnt on a CD or not. *Self-enforcing features*: if the initial and continuing conditions are not met, DRM supplies the functional equivalent to a court injunction: the delinquent user (or machine) is just cut off.

Against this background, the proposal is often made that all the monitoring and metering in which allegedly old, cumbersome and outdated CRMOs are still engaged be replaced – or rather 're-internalized' – by resort to the flawless monitoring and metering technology offered by DRMs.

The argument comes in several components.

First, it is argued that the idea that CRMOs are a remedy for market failure has now become obsolete. Direct transactions between copyright holders and users may indeed have been impossible in the past, when both supply and demand were highly fragmented. In that specific context CRMOs may for a long time have offered sufficient economies of scale and scope to support the claim of being natural monopolies.[37] However, this claim is belied now as a consequence of a number of developments. Successful creators are few and hold a majority of the works which are in strong demand.[38] Also professional users typically come in limited numbers. As a result, while there may still be a need for intermediaries, in fields like music these may well be found among music publishers rather than in CRMOs.[39] Even businesses investing in the creation and dissemination of works have in the meantime proved to be extremely successful intermediaries. This is what the practice of 'source licensing' proves, whereby, to offer a single but significant example, movie producers in the US acquire all incidental copyrights from the creators of the different components packaged within a single movie, and make them available downstream to theatres, broadcasting stations, and to the distributors of videocassettes, CDs and DVDs and, in the future – if I may add – to broadband distribution. So, the avenues to carry works from creators to users through 'less restrictive alternatives'[40] than old CRMOs are opening up.

Second, DRM may be visualised as a device for replacing collective management through individual management. What is meant here is no longer the old individual management we came across in the analogue world, the initial relationship between creators and business, which would enable the latter to eventually bring the work to the market. Here individual management rather refers to the setting up of a direct contractual relationship between the

---

[37]   Katz, *The Potential Demise of another Natural Monopoly*, supra at note 4, at 15 ff. and 39 ff.
[38]   Ibid., at 37.
[39]   Ibid., at 40.
[40]   Ibid., at 28.

rightholders on the one side and the end-users of works on the other. Under this approach DRM enables rightholders to grant access (usually in the form of a 'licence') to copyright protected works on pre-set terms, such as a given price for any category of end-user and for each mode of use (or package of modes of use).

The mechanism based on DRM seamlessly internalises all the different steps through which CRMO-based enforcement normally unfolds and thereby enables rightholders, even while distributing digital copies over a network, to dispense with the services of CRMOs. Indeed, it is the technology itself which carries out the whole job of monitoring and metering, by checking so to say from within the licensed digital copy that the work is not put to uses additional to those contractually provided for and technologically enabled. In the event agreed-upon restrictions are overstepped, no resort to the courts is needed, as was necessary in the analogue past when CRMOs were in charge. The beauty of DRM is that, if this happens, the digital copy is automatically disabled without the need for a judge to grant an injunction. Thus DRM has within it a self-enforcing feature which makes files it protects functionally equivalent to traditional physical property, except that it has the advantage over old analogue material copies of also being protected by the equivalent of a standing injunctive order.[41]

Thus DRM-protected files, while clearly differing from material copies of works, such as books or CDs, because the former are intangible while the latter are tangible, share with them a common feature: they both constitute a discrete portion of reality. Therefore rightholders may exchange the DRM-protected file, in a direct transaction between the rightholder on the one side and final user on the other, in what for all purposes amounts to a market. Thereby rightholders may obtain whatever price the market will bear for that specific good, instead of remaining content with a monetary claim to a share of the pool of the net proceeds which a CRMO may have collected for a given class of uses of a given class of works. In a nutshell, via DRMs rightholders recover full protection under a property rule in lieu of the CRMO-administered liability rule which in the past used to prevail in connection with works disseminated through networks.[42]

---

[41]   In this context the law becomes ancillary, but not irrelevant. Its role is no longer to enforce copyright, but to mete out harsh punishment to those who engage in the circumvention of technical protection measures or contribute to it.

[42]   It may be interesting to note that this development would represent a total reversal of the sequence which was brilliantly analysed, for the time period between 1850 and 1990, by Merges (1996), 'Contracting into Liability Rules: Intellectual Property Rights and Collective Rights Organisations', supra at note 4.

A tentative assessment

What do we make of this approach?

Again, there may be a number of technical difficulties in it. I will just mention a couple of them. As a lawyer, rather than a technologist, I am always under the impression that technology-based solutions are extremely vulnerable. We are told all the time that any technical protection measure ends up being hacked; and maybe this is indeed the case also with DRM.

From a law and economics perspective, I am inclined to think that at this stage our legal systems have been creating so many categories of rightholders[43] and given out so many overlapping layers of full property rights, in combinations which moreover may even vary dramatically from one legal system to another, that it seems quite unlikely to me that all these categories will come together and agree on terms and conditions of exploitation[44] and that these may additionally happen to be valid and enforceable in each and all of the jurisdictions in which DRM-protected works are to be made available.

The case has however been made that the really big question raised by DRM is a different one that has to do with the very constitutional basis of the grant of copyright. The objection here is that copyright protection is granted on the basis of a constitutionally mandated balancing act between the prerogatives of holders on the one hand and claims to access by the public, on the other. From this perspective, first sale doctrine, or exhaustion of rights in European parlance, is specifically intended to make sure that once a copy of a copyrighted work is marketed, then the work becomes accessible to the public at large. Also fair uses and other exceptions and limitations to copyright monopoly have a similar constitutional dimension. This area of freedom would be severely curtailed, it is quite plausibly argued, if permissible uses were to be unilaterally determined by rightholders on the basis of technology and technology-based contracts, rather than by the choices of the relevant legal systems.[45]

---

[43]   From holders of copyright in the work, holders of copyright over the sound recording, performers and so on, as far as music is concerned; but in movies all this gets much more complicated.

[44]   For a classic analysis whereby negotiations over property rights are liable to break down when several parties are involved and these may indefinitely hold out see G. Calabresi and A.D. Melamed (1972), 'Property Rules, Liability Rules and Inalienability: One View of the Cathedral', *Harvard Law Review*, **85**, 1089 ff., 1127.

It should be noted however that A. Katz, *The Potential Demise of another Natural Monopoly*, supra at note 4, 24 ff. makes a case for the emergence in the circumstances referred to in the text of incentives to the creation of 'marketable cleared parcels of rights' on the basis of an agreement among all the rightholders involved.

[45]   For a forceful statement of this position see P. Spada (2002), 'Copia privata ed opere sotto chiave', *Riv. dir. ind.* I, 591 ss.; the comment by C. Geiger (2004), 'The Private Copy, a Freedom Endangered in the Digital Environment?' to Tribunal de

I quite sympathise with this view.

Nevertheless, it also seems to me that DRM-based approaches do have a certain allure, at least to those who believe that the cure of market failures may be found in market-based mechanisms. As I earlier indicated, at least in some sectors, such as music and books, it makes sense that digital text and audio files are considered as functional equivalents of books, records and CDs. And, if this is the case, then it would seem to me that it may also make some sense that rightholders are permitted to resort to technological devices which extend to digital files the same property rights-based and strongly market-oriented regime which by and large has so far proved successful with tangible copies of works.

Killing them softly? A radical public-law minded regulatory option

Of course, one can doubt the very idea that it is for the market to cure market failures and also embrace the idea that DRMs are constitutionally objectionable. If we start off from these assumptions, we may prefer to go radically the other way. Why then not decide to face the challenges raised by the internet by replacing the market mechanism of copyright with a totally different regulatory device, intended to compensate the different contributions which go into the creation and distribution of works and be done once and for all with the legacy of the past, the old, boring and cumbersome machinery we have inherited? If we decide to go this way, copyright and along with it CRMOs, would gradually and more or less graciously be phased out, to become at some point a memory of an ancient past.

The case for a 'governmentally administered reward system'

This is indeed roughly what the proposed 'alternative compensation system', also designated as a 'governmentally administered reward system' and proposed by leading American liberal scholars[46] sets out to do.

What are the details? This plan would apply to the digital exploitation of all copyrightable works which their holders chose to register under a new system, to be administered by the American Copyright Office. Compensation would

---

grande instance de Paris, 30 April 2004, *Perquin et UFC Que Choisir v SA Films Alain Sarde, Sté Universal Pictures Video Fr. et al., IIC* **36,** 148 ff.; L. Lessig (2002), *The Future of Ideas: The Fate of Commons in a Connected World,* New York: Vintage Books, Random House, and J. Cohen (1999), 'WIPO Copyright Treaty Implementation in the U.S.: Will Fair Use Survive?' *EIPR,* **21,** 236 ff.

[46]   W. Fisher (2004), *Promises to Keep: Technology, Law and the Future of Entertainment,* Stanford, CA: Stanford University Press, ch. 6. The outline for a broadly similar proposal is to be found in Spada, 'La proprietà intellettuale nelle reti telematiche', quoted supra at note 8.

derive from a mix of taxes, levied on recording equipment, on CD burners, on personal video recorders (PVRs), including set top boxes and the typically American device represented by TiVo, MP3-players and ISP-mediated access to the net. The tax rates applicable on these items would increase at the same pace as the proportion of works fed into the system increases to the total. How would allocation and distribution of this income to the benefit of contributors to the creation and distribution of works take place? The monies would be administered by a special department of the American Copyright Office, on the basis of a number of techniques which are not all that different from the ones currently used by traditional CRMOs, i.e. surveys to establish audience shares, reporting by some users (such as non-interactive webcasters). The corresponding mechanisms might well be fine-tuned through digital technology to combine automated reporting with privacy and to make sure that the system could not be tampered with to artificially inflate data.

Would this system be voluntary? Not really. In the proposal, there is no obligation to register.[47] But failure to do so would imply forfeiture of compensation rights under the new system. Accordingly old copyright would gradually be phased out as earlier copyright-protected works went into the public domain; and the old property right would finally be replaced by what in fact is a Reichman-style compensatory liability rule.[48]

What do we make of this approach? It seems to me that in this case too there is a number of technical difficulties, which it may be possible to fix in some way; but the whole idea seems to raise larger questions which again I am afraid it is not so easy to shrug off.

Issues of compliance with the Berne Convention and TRIPs
The first thing to consider is that Berne Convention provisions, as frankly acknowledged by the proponent of the system, 'would seem to forbid the curtailment of copyright law necessitated by the proposed regime'.[49] Indeed the case may be made that Berne Convention requires that the rights it provides for are protected under a property rule rather than a liability

---

[47]   Fisher, *Promises to Keep. Technology, Law and the Future of Entertainment,* supra at note 46, ch. 6, at 4.

[48]   See J.H. Reichman and T. Lewis (2005), 'Using Liability Rules to Stimulate Local Innovation in Developing Countries: Application to Traditional Knowledge', in K.E. Maskus and J.H. Reichman (eds), *International Public Goods and Transfer of Technology under a Globalized Intellectual Property Regime,* Cambridge: Cambridge University Press, 337 ff. and earlier J.H. Reichman (2000), 'Of Green Tulips and Legal Kudzu: Repackaging Rights in Subpatentable Innovation', *Vanderbilt Law Review,* **53,** 1743 ff.

[49]   Fisher, 'Promises to Keep: Technology, Law and the Future of Entertainment', supra at note 46, ch. 6, at 44.

rule.[50] While the Berne Convention leaves some leeway under Arts 9(2), 11-*bis*(2) and 13 and similarly Art. 13 TRIPs provides for 'limitations and exceptions' to full copyright protection, it may still be disputed that these provisions would cover the reward system envisaged.

To begin with we may wonder whether what we earlier referred to as the interactive feature of the right of public communication may be subject to the special regime enabled by Art. 11-*bis*(2) of the Berne Convention. One may indeed point out that the 'rights mentioned in the previous paragraph' to which § 2 of Art. 11-*bis* refers are just point-to-mass broadcasts or, in plain English, radio and television broadcasts; and on this basis make the case that therefore no flexibility is provided for point-to-point performances and for the interactive feature which is characteristic of them. Were this the case, we should then conclude that the plan cannot encompass this mode which lies at the heart of the internet revolution and therefore it is dead before being born.

I do not believe this is the case, however. First, Art. 8 WCT was adopted 'without prejudice to the provisions of . . . Art. 11-*bis*(1)' of the Berne Convention; and this language is compatible with the idea that the provisions of Art. 11-*bis*(1) deal not only with point-to-mass but also with point-to-point communication to the public, because otherwise, the initial proviso would appear – pun unintended – pointless. Second, WCT is accompanied by Agreed Statements; and the Agreed Statement to Art. 8 WCT reads: 'It is further understood that nothing in Art. 8 precludes a Contracting Party from applying Art. 11-*bis*(2)'.[51] Which, I submit, means that the interactive feature to which Art. 8 WCT refers is also subject to the possibility of introducing the special regimes enabled by Art. 11-*bis*(2).

This is far from being the end of the story, however. Any exception to or limitation on copyright protection, including the one provided for by Art. 11-*bis*(2) of the Berne Convention, still has to comply with the strict test of permissibility currently laid down in Art. 13 TRIPs: 'Members shall confine limitations and exceptions to exclusive rights to certain special cases which do not conflict with a normal exploitation of the work and do not unreasonably prejudice the legitimate interests of the right holder'.[52]

Moreover the plan envisages not only diffusion but also distribution of works through digital networks. Now, distribution through downloads in turn

---

[50]   I developed this argument at some length in M. Ricolfi (2006), 'Is There an Antitrust Antidote against IP Overprotection within TRIPs?' *Marquette Intellectual Property Law Review*, **10**, 305 ff., 349 f.

[51]   See also the Agreed Statement to Art. 10 WCT.

[52]   For an introduction to the issues which arise in coordinating international provisions on exceptions and limitations to copyright see T. Heide (1999), 'The Berne Three-Step Test and the Proposed Copyright Directive', *EIPR*, **21**, 105 ff.

entails reproduction. And this means that the requirements set in this specific connection both by Art. 9(2) and by Art. 13 TRIPs have also to be met simultaneously. Which is not an easy proposition.[53]

Conclusively, it seems to me that we have a genuine issue of consistency of the proposed plan with current international obligations. Not that I make too much of this difficulty. Certainly it is not a minor one. As dutifully noted by the proponent of the plan, Prof. Fisher, the Berne Convention nowadays enjoys the dubious privilege of being 'incorporated by reference' into the TRIPs Agreement. As TRIPs is in turn part of the 'whole package' concept of the 1994 WTO/GATT Agreement, there is no way to opt out of it. The only way is 'to obtain a modification of the Berne Convention' with the consent of all its members *and*, if I may so add for the sake of completeness, with the consent of all TRIPs/WTO signatory countries. This is as unlikely as it gets. The hurdles are more or less infinite. For instance: anybody advising developing countries would insist that any such amendment be made conditional on simultaneously meeting *their* demands, including, just to mention the inescapable, cancelling subsidies and protection for Northern agriculture and textiles.

Nevertheless the proposal is worth discussing on its merits. It is a clear invitation to think outside the box. To implement it, treaties have to be amended? So what? Let us amend them; and if this entails a shake-up of other issues, as it may well be in a situation where issue linkage prevails, this may even be for the better.[54]

So, what should we think about the merits of the plan, then?

---

[53]   In this connection, G.B. Dinwoodie and R. Cooper Dreyfuss (2004), 'International Intellectual Property Law and the Public Domain of Science', *Journal of International Economic Law*, **7**, 431 ff, 439 f., make the case that the notion of 'normalcy' under the different fair use provisions in TRIPs should be given a normative, rather than empirical, meaning. This reading is at least in part supported by two WTO Panel decisions (Panel Report 17 March 2000, Canada – Patent Protection of Pharmaceutical Products, WTO/WT/DS114/R, at 7.69 and Panel Report 15 March 2005, European Communities – Protection of Trademarks and Geographical Indications for Agricultural Products and Foodstuffs, WT/DS174/R, at 7.633). However, I am afraid that if we stick to the idea that digital text, audio and video files are the functional equivalents of analogue books, records and movies, as we probably should do, considering both are primary exploitations (the head rather than the tail of the comet), then it gets difficult to deny that the idea of normalcy implies that the exploitation of such files through digital networks should be reserved to rightholders.

[54]   As indeed would be the case if, per chance, this led to demands for the cutting of agriculture subsidies, as I was more or less bizarrely suggesting earlier in the text.

A cyberspace-induced revival of national insulationism?
Well, I am quite dubious. To begin with, there is a feature in it which does not ring convincing at all to me. We have seen what makes cyberspace different: that perfect copies are made available any time anywhere. Cyberspace is global. You cannot any longer segregate geographical areas along the borders set up by the ancient sovereigns. A decade ago this feature had led Johnson and Post to insist on a declaration of the independence of the cyberspace from the nether world of bricks-and-mortar reality.[55] Now what is this latest of proposals about? A separate American regime for music and entertainment in the cyberspace. It sounds like turning Johnson and Post upside down by a sort of declaration of digital independence of the US from the rest of the world. One is reminded of an old catch-phrase of the past: Socialism in one country. Except that now we know how that other story ended.

And then, has it not been said that it is easier to empty an ocean with a sieve than to establish borders within the internet? On the providers' side, what about American webcasters, ISPs, music and media stores and subscription services setting up shop, or rather a shingle, in some remote jurisdiction, to avoid paying their dues under the US tax-and-royalty regime? On the demand side, as Chinese people have long become technology-savvy enough to access the internet through foreign jurisdictions to avoid censorship, would not American consumers do the same to save a few hundred bucks a year in taxation?[56] Even physical, hard goods, such as blank disks, are being shipped by the ton through the internet, exactly as Canadian medicines were shipped across the border through internet mail orders.

In the end, going back to insulationism – or is it insularity? – does not seem to me actually the most persuasive of replies to the challenges of global cyberspace.

A tentative assessment

Let us for a moment assume that all the legal and technical difficulties I have just raised may be taken care of. Still there would remain a possibly fatal flaw which we have to consider. We should not forget, it may be argued, that the plan deals with downloads of audio and video files and thus it deals with the primary exploitation of works, or, at least, about a functional equivalent to it, rather than about secondary exploitation. Once again: we are dealing with the

---

[55]   D.R. Johnson-D. Post (1996), 'Law and Borders: The Rise of Law in Cyberspace', *Stanford Law Review*, **48**, 1367 ff.
[56]   Once again, the emergence of what are called 'geolocation services', which are said to be capable of pinpointing where a broadband internet user is located (see Andrew Baxter (2006), 'World Cup to Tackle Broadband Bar', *Financial Times*, 3 May) might take care of this difficulty.

head, rather than the tail of the comet. In this connection our societies have so far been setting up a legal framework on the basis of the assumption that creators are induced to create and businesses to take the risk of investing along the long route which leads from the creation of a work to its initial dissemination on the market only when their rights are protected under a full property rule. The rationale for the choice of this type of entitlement is that full property protection ultimately enables rightholders to charge whatever price the market will bear.

The 'neo-regulatory' plan I have been describing subverts these long-held assumptions. In the plan, the final 'price', the compensation, would be set by the ancient regulators, sovereign states. Moreover such compensation would be set in exchange for the whole package of all registered works, rather than for each individual work separately considered. Therefore, it will become impossible for rightholders to engage in the educated guess of anticipating demand for a given work in each segment of the relevant market and of setting the price accordingly. Indeed, they will find that they cannot conceivably fathom in advance what share of the pool will finally be allocated to each of them, when the complex computational machinery has crunched out the final calculations. This is bound to create a difficult situation for making decisions about investment and risk taking, which require ex ante predictions of income rather than unpredictable, ex post windfalls. In a way this means that by accepting a mechanism such as the one advocated by the plan, we may be forced to adopt for the head of the comet a business model which may function only for the tail. It may therefore well be argued that the whole logic of the incentive mechanism which has been characteristic of copyright protection will dangerously come to an end without a proper replacement.

This objection is totally respectable, if certainly not novel in its ultimate foundations. Indeed, it just reiterates the time-honoured, but far from undisputed, idea that markets are superior to regulation. This is the Coase of 1960 against Pigou all over again. Which may make sense, possibly; even though no specific reason is present in this particular context to favour the former over the latter.

The European Union's position on collective management revisited: homage to hesitancy?

We are now in a position to clearly see in which way the European position is to a large extent partial and incomplete. While it deals with the issues to which the word 'anywhere' alludes, it fails to engage with the headings 'any time' and 'perfect'.

In fact, the position of the EU Commission tends to remain hazy and vague about the much wider issues which both the neo-proprietary and neo-regulatory approaches discuss. For sure we can surmise that regulatory options are not the most favoured choice for European institutions. They were briefly considered in connection with compulsory licensing of components inputs for multimedia works about a decade ago;[57] but the Commission hastily withdrew.[58]

The EU Commission is equally cautious in connection with DRMs. It seems to consider them as an exogenous factor, or, in other words, pure technology, which has to be tamed and domesticated to make it compatible with normative design.[59] In doing so, it fails to take into account that DRMs are the centerpiece of the neo-proprietary approach and anathema under the neo-regulatory one. As to the contentious issue of whether the interactive feature of the right of communication to the public belongs to CRMOs or to rightholders individually, which is indeed crucial to decide who has the upper hand in the three-way battle for the control of dissemination of digital copies of works over the net, the Commission often appears characteristically uncertain even about the law as it is in the present legal context.[60]

These hesitations are quite understandable. As we earlier indicated, the two alternative approaches we just discussed ultimately go to the root of the old dilemma between markets and regulation. Probably it is not for European institutions, which do not have sufficient democratic legitimacy, to engage in such sweeping choices; and particularly so when we are talking about sectors which impact on culture and national identities, where the role of the national sovereigns, the member States of the EU, remains very large under current and proposed European arrangements.[61]

Maybe there are additional reasons why we could argue that the hesitation of European institutions to take sides in the broader dilemma makes sense today. The alternative between markets and regulation originates from the nineteenth century and dominated the so-called short century which has just come to an end. We do not know for sure whether this same dilemma is going to remain crucial also for the next century. Possibly we even have special

---

57 European Commission, Green Paper 'Copyright and Related Rights in the Information Society' of July 1995, Brussels, 72.

58 Green Paper, supra at note 57, 75. This is not to say that European institutions a priori discard resort to regulatory devices; rather that they prefer to do so in an ad hoc fashion. Indeed, even a component of the so-called third option for the management of the cross-border offer of music services has a strong regulatory element, in the part in which it suggests that the rightholders should grant CRMOs Community-wide licensing powers.

59 Working Documents of 7 July 2005, supra at note 31, 39 and of 11 October 2005, supra at note 31, 10.

60 See the apparently contradictory statements made in this connection in the Working Documents of 7 July 2005, supra at note 31, 18, 19 and 25.

61 Arts 151 EU Treaty; III–81 of the Draft European Constitution.

reasons to doubt it, particularly in the sector of culture and media, where, it is sometimes argued, the future alternative will be a quite different one, and will concern the choice between freedom and control. If this is so, then it may turn out that it is more than appropriate for European institutions to avoid engaging in old dilemmas; and particularly so if at the same time they try to be true to their unique quasi-federalist mission by leading the way in the exploration of future landscapes.

From the long route from creators to the public to the short route: a glimpse into the future

A change of scenario

Indeed, putting together the pieces we have been collecting so far, it appears that the stage scenario is rapidly changing precisely in the area of collective and individual management of copyrighted works. More specifically, it is time we finally became aware that in our post-post-industrial age, creators and the public take one step forward, businesses and CRMOs take two steps backwards. Correspondingly, the long route which used to lead the work from its creator to the public by passing through different categories of businesses and CRMOs is gradually being replaced by a short route, which puts in direct contact creators and the public[62] and takes the shape of the new form of individual management which is characteristic of the digital environment.

In the previous pages I briefly sketched the reasons for this evolution. The time has now come to have a second look at them. In the past direct access to the market by creators was confined to a very limited number of very special cases. Otherwise, it could be taken for granted that business was needed to bring works from creators to markets. The kind of business which appeared indispensable had features which in the last two centuries came to be familiar to us. First it had to make substantial outlays to figure out whether there was a market for the work; then again it had to invest and take large risks for the mass production of material copies of works and for their distribution; and this on a scale which increased in step with the extension of the markets. Hollywood and the record labels are appropriate cases in point.

In the digital environment all this changes dramatically.

On the production side, we have already noted that perfect digital copies make 'factories' of physical, material copies of works redundant, at least in principle. It may be argued that this is true only for additional copies, the ones which can be costlessly multiplied after what we could call the initial embodiment, the prototype or the 'master', has first been created; and to this it may

---

62   See also supra, text accompanying notes 25–27.

be added that for the latter the required investment is still huge. This objection has indeed been raised a number of times;[63] but it becomes less and less defensible as time passes. The role of software and of digital technology in the creation and fixation of music is increasing all the time; and their cost is decreasing in parallel. What is specially remarkable is that this same development is now reaching the movie industry. Until recently this sector of the entertainment business appeared to be the last bulwark in which capital-intensive business could be considered really indispensable. But this is becoming less and less true as each day passes.[64] Jean Cocteau predicted that the tools required for the creation of a movie would at some point in time become as cheap as paper and pencil; and digital technology is proving his vision right.

On the distribution side a similar – possibly less visible, but certainly more striking – process is taking place. This is so because, as I have already mentioned, digital goods to be distributed through the net are light rather than heavy, and use up a limited amount of storage space. But even more so because the technological endowment held by the public at the receiving end has in the meantime changed profoundly. Even in the past the end-user had to make an investment in technology of sorts, by purchasing a radio or a TV set, a record player or a tape recorder. The novel feature is that since the beginning of the digital age the scale of a minimum unit of the technological endowment at the receiving end – e.g. the memory of a PC – is largely in excess of the average needs of the consumer;[65] and as a rule each unit is interoperable with all the others. A similar analysis can be reiterated in connection with file-sharing. Whatever legal assessment we may make of this practice, its ultimate technological ramifications cannot be doubted. Here we have enormous excess capacity residing with the public at large at the receiving end; and this excess capacity can be mobilised to create distributive networks of extraordinary scale, scope and effectiveness.[66]

These technological determinants enable creators to make works directly

---

63   See P. Auteri (2006), 'Diritti d'autore, nuove tecnologie e Digital Rights Management', in M.L. Montagnani and M. Borghi (eds), *Proprietà digitale: diritti d'autore, nuove tecnologie e Digital Rights Management*, Milano: EGEA.
64   For a few striking examples see 'Filmmakers, Musicians, Artists Do it Themselves', in *USA Today*, 1 April 2005.
65   As noted by Y. Benkler (2004), 'Sharing Nicely: On Shareable Goods and the Emergence of Sharing as a Modality of Economic Production', *Yale Law Journal*, **114**, 272 ff., 277.
66   As indeed aptly described by the decision of the US Supreme Court of 27 June 2005, *Metro-Goldwin-Mayer Studios Inc. et al. v Grockster, Ltd. et al.*, 125 S. Ct. 2764 (2005). On the potential for distribution offered by open spectrum access see Lessig, *The Future of Ideas*, supra at note 45, 78 ff., 218 ss., 240.

available to the public. In turn, an increasingly large number of members of the public are themselves grabbing the opportunity offered by the technology available at the receiving end to transform themselves into producers and distributors of works. Thus the short route not only goes from creators to the public but may turn part of the public into creators.

To make a long story short: both the production and distribution functions migrate from business to the public and there they can rely on excess resources available at each consumption unit. These, if individually of small scale, may be multiplied by very large numbers to provide almost infinite manufacturing and distribution capacity in a way that dwarfs past industry investment and makes them to a large extent redundant. The stage scenario is indeed changing. Social sharing enters; business exits.

The missing box

If this is so, then maybe the closing question would be whether the two opposite approaches we discussed so far, which favour respectively neo-proprietary and neo-regulatory projects for the digital environment, have got their agenda for the next few decades right. This I strongly doubt; and specifically because both approaches confine themselves to considering issues typical of the long route and ignore the specifics of the emerging short route and of the relationship between the latter and the former.

To elaborate a bit on the point, let us consider again for a minute the two alternatives. The former bets on markets, on the decentralised price mechanism and on business firms. The second lays its hopes on the most traditional of remedies to market failure, regulation; but, in advocating sovereign intervention to correct externalities created by markets, it takes for granted firms and prices. There is reason to believe that these two visions leave out of the picture phenomena which are essential under the current scenario.

The missing portion may be visualised by considering a simple matrix concerning economic choices. This matrix may be designed as follows:[67]

CHOICES	Market	Non market
decentralised	price	X
centralised	firm	regulation

---

[67]   This matrix is taken from the extraordinarily important work of Benkler, 'Sharing Nicely', supra at note 65, 276. The rest of this section is also based on Benkler's work.

It has been noted[68] that usually we concentrate on the three boxes which have labels (price, firm,[69] and regulation). As a rule, it does not occur to us that choices may also take place in accordance with the way indicated in the box marked X, that is in a way which is at the same time decentralised and non-market.

The are two interesting things in this little chart.

The first is that production and distribution of works in accordance with the so-called short route would appear to be taking place in ways which are at the same time decentralised and non-market and thus conform to the box designated X. Decentralised and non-market choices are based on social exchange and therefore on mechanisms based on reciprocity and cooperation, rather than on price. This can be seen quite clearly at work in the fields of open source software and Creative Commons licensed works; and the relevance of this production and distribution mode seems confirmed by the growing amount of user-generated content available online. This is why the short route, with which we have been dealing so many times by now, is taking off: it is sustained by social sharing.

Of course traditional economic analysis has always doubted the long-term sustainability of social sharing and asked which incentives form its basis. The initial reply was that latent creativity will always be unleashed, as soon as the obstacles created by monopolistic control are removed. While this kind of reply was at best incomplete, we have in the meantime come to realise[70] that social sharing has its own specific production and distribution functions; and that the structure of incentives for the production and distribution of the goods and services provided through social sharing, while different from that on which the market mechanism is based, may be no less viable than that provided by markets and, more to the point, is increasingly sustained by the structural determinants of current technology.

The other interesting thing in the chart is that the neo-proprietary and neo-regulatory approaches cover the price and regulation boxes but totally ignore box X.

This seems a very serious limitation to me. First, because in box X we find works which are made available through the short route. Second, because the

---

68   By Benkler, 'Sharing Nicely', supra at note 65, 276.
69   For all purposes, the term 'firm' used henceforth should be considered equivalent to the expression 'business'; except that in this section we prefer to resort to the former, rather than to the latter which we employed up till now, because here we are discussing contributions which use the former expression and this same expression is more appropriate in the context of formal economic analysis.
70   Particularly through the work of Benkler, 'Sharing Nicely', supra at note 65, 296–343.

short route is becoming so significant, as it is based on social sharing and, in turn, the technological conditions for the emergence of social sharing seem to be on the rise. This is why both neo-proprietary and neo-regulatory approaches are proposing an agenda which is increasingly incomplete.

An agenda for the future

If this is so, then we can see why the institutional design cannot be confined to rules concerning the long route, on which all the approaches we have examined so far have concentrated. The institutional design must also incorporate rules concerning the short route, which is based on social rather than market exchange. And it must also fashion rules concerning the peaceful coexistence of the two sectors, the one which is offering works by the long route and the one offering them by the short one.

This is a primary necessity; and it seems to me that it is here to stay. Indeed, there are very strong reasons to believe that large business firms, organised along strong top-down hierarchical command structures and having access to capital markets, still have a fundamental role to play for many years to come; but also that an increasingly important role will be played by the new actors and the new business models. And if this is so, then the two breeds of actors are bound to step up their reciprocal interactions. After all, even programmers of open source software may offer it on the market for a price;[71] creators who license their works under a non-commercial Creative Commons licence are keen to capitalise on the online success of their music to earn nice fees when performing live.[72] Even Mr Murdoch seems to have been quite bent on acquiring MySpace.

In this new context, policy makers should give adequate consideration to the fact that even the distinction between primary and secondary exploitation, which once was fundamental, loses its meaning. A work may initially become successful by being promoted for free, by making it available through the short route, e.g. over a site. As a next step, the creators may earn nice performing fees before some audience, cashing in on the popularity they have previously acquired. At this stage their music may so to say enter the long route, possibly to be recorded on a CD, which may eventually be disseminated, point-to-mass or point-to-point. It may be argued that in such situations it does not make

---

[71]   It is often noted, in this connection that the adjective 'free' is used as in the expression free speech, not free lunch and indicates that source code is made available under no restriction, not that programmers do not get paid.

[72]   This is one of the express aims of the Brazilian project 'Canto Livre': see R. Lemos, 'Brazil's "Canto Livre" Project: the Emergence of Society's Creativity', http://static.world-information.org/infopaper/wi_ipcityedition.pdf, accessed 16 November 2005.

sense any longer to speak of primary and secondary exploitation, of the head and of the tail of a comet, because the very sequence of acts of exploitation no longer needs to start from a 'factory'. Maybe the comet has been replaced by a Milky Way Galaxy. And policy makers should take this into account.

Of course, we do not know much about the future. So much is changing all the time and so quickly, that it is impossible to make predictions. Nevertheless we can anticipate with some confidence that in the future production and distribution of works will originate from two different sectors, the one based on property and markets, the other on social sharing; and that the rate of interaction between the two sectors will be very high but will take shapes which are much more unpredictable than the ones the old comet analogy would suggest.

This is why any agenda for the management of works in a digital environment should meet at least three requirements. First, the agenda should incorporate rules which are appropriate not only for the long route but also for the short route. Second, it should make the two sets of rules interoperable, i.e. such that the continued existence and specific contribution of the two sectors is maximised. Third, obstacles inherited by the past which unduly inhibit the emergence of the short route should be gradually phased out in ways which should minimise the disruption of the workings of the old route.

This is quite a tall order; but, luckily, it is a task which is left for some other occasion and maybe for a younger generation of scholars.

Still, a somewhat longer comment may be in place here, to sketch out a few normative implications of the developments discussed in the text. In the long run, to the extent that works generated by social exchange reach a critical mass and flourish, the criticism concerning DRMs we earlier discussed may gradually lose ground. Indeed, would there still be a constitutional problem in the event DRMs disable the further distribution and fair uses, say, of the British Encyclopedia, at the moment in which Wikipedia becomes a viable or even superior alternative to it? At some point, we may also wish to consider whether governmentally administered reward systems, which indeed face the objection that they may provide insufficient incentives for the high investment-high risk production and distribution of works which is characteristic of market-based mechanisms, as indicated *supra* in the text, may turn out to be an appropriate starting point to support sharing-based creation and distribution of works.

There are also more urgent normative issues raised by the emergence of the sector of sharing and by its coexistence with the market-based sector. While in connection with the latter there is an ongoing discussion as to whether what we designated as the interactive feature of the right of communication to the public belongs to CRMOs or to businesses (see *supra* at note 16 and accompanying text), in connection with works created and distributed on the basis of social exchange the main question is the extent to which creators themselves retain the freedom to engage in the same interactive feature. Indeed a number of CRMOs claim that, as the interactive feature belongs to them, creators are not allowed to make works available for free on the net. This is quite an understandable position, as the making available of a work for free might destroy the possibility of licensing it for a fee, which is CRMOs' job. Nevertheless, to the extent we believe that the emergence of works based on sharing is to be encouraged, we should begin to ask whether in this specific connection it is appropriate to make sure we have in place rules which either (i) give creators the chance to be members of a CRMO only for some works, instead of all, thereby retaining the possibility of individually managing the rest, e.g. by making them available for free over their sites or dedicated, cooperative portals; or (ii) provide for 'dual licensing', whereby creators retain freedom over the licensing of their works for non-commercial uses while CRMOs take care of commercial uses of the same; or, even (iii) do away with the continental European exclusivity feature, embracing the American idea whereby collective management of works does not prevent creators from engaging in individual management or even concurrently relying on additional intermediaries. The coexistence of the two sectors is also bound to raise questions which have to do with the establishment of a level playing field between the two models. In this connection, it should be asked whether, to the extent creators in the sharing sector give up some of their copyrights (as happens in connection with free software or Creative Commons licences), users of 'free' works should be entitled to obtain a discount over the blanket licence rate or tariff otherwise applicable to them, such a discount being in principle based on the proportion of 'free' works they use compared with the total. Similarly, as CRMOs are entrusted with the task of collecting levies or fees in connection with statutory licences or extended collective management schemes, and collect them on the basis of parameters, such as blank tapes, digital memory or hours of programming, which bear no relation with the kind of work which is being exploited, it may be asked whether creators of works who are not members of CRMO, as it is often the case for creators engaged in sharing, should also receive a pro-rata portion of the proceeds.

13 Copyright law and scientific research
Reto Hilty[1]

Introduction

Copyright is increasingly failing to fulfil its function with respect to the creation of scientific work. The researcher is obliged to transfer his copyright to commercial exploiters if the scientific content he has created is to be disseminated in any way. However, this dissemination is increasingly being effected in electronic form exclusively, leading to serious problems for scientists with respect to third-party research results – particularly where technical protection measures are used. This is because such protection measures frequently concern vital information on which further research depends. Thanks to this dependency, a number of exploiters have succeeded in imposing prohibitive conditions on access and use, a constellation of facts that is given short thrift in modern copyright law. Specifically, the EU Directive on Copyright in the Information Society is designed one-sidedly to protect the entertainment industry, and the European legislature is thus thwarting the efforts to make Europe the leading centre for research. The present chapter shows where the individual problems are and what corrections are urgently necessary in European law.

1. The problem

Only a few years ago, it would have been presumptuous to describe copyright and scientists as being in a relationship of tension. The scientific research results are protected by copyright in terms of the manner in which they are presented – i.e. their 'form'.[2] In contrast, copyright is not intended to cover

---

[1]   Director, Max Planck Institute for Intellectual Property, Competition and Tax Law, Munich; Professor at the Universities of Zurich and Munich.

[2]   Thus Art. 9 Abs. 2 TRIPS explicitly: 'Copyright protection shall extend to expressions and not to ideas, procedures, methods of operation or mathematical concepts as such' and, with practically identical wording, Art. 2 WCT. See also Section 102 (b) of the US Copyright Act: 'In no case does copyright protection for an original work of authorship extend to any idea . . .'. Copyright, Designs and Patents Act of 1988 (CDPA 1988) lacks such a clear statement. This principle can best be found in Section 21 (5) CDPA 1988: 'No inference shall be drawn from this section [adaption of the work] as to what does or does not amount to copying a work'. See also Laddie, H., P. Prescott and M. Vitoria (2000), *The Modern Law of Copyright and Designs*, London,

'content' as such, and as a result freedom of opinion can fundamentally not be affected – at least that is the general approach.[3]

UK *et al.*: Butterworths, at paras 3.77 *et seq.* and especially at para 3.80: 'The task of the courts is not to apply an "ideas/expression dichotomy" doctrine but the provisions of the Act, which mention no such rule. What the Act does do is stipulate that what is protected is an original work, and that the right may be infringed by taking any "substantial part" of it'.

[3] Cf. for recent expressions of this approach, for instance Jeroham, H.C. (2004), 'Urheberrecht und Freiheit der Meinungsäußerung, Rechtsmissbrauch und Standardschikane', *GRUR Int.*, **53** (2), 96 *et seq.* In fact, the discussion has been more differentiated for some considerable time in more recent theory. Cf. as an example Loewenheim, Ulrich (2003), 'Schutzgegenstand', in Ulrich Loewenheim (ed.), *Handbuch des Urheberrechts*, Munich, Germany: Beck, para. 7 note 8 *et seq.*; Macciacchini, Sandro (2000), *Urheberrecht und Meinungsfreiheit*, Zurich, Switzerland: Stämpfli, pp. 21 *et seq.* On the original approach, found above all in the USA, of copyright being understood as an instrument of free expression, see *Harper & Row, Publishers, Inc. v Nation Enters.* 471 US 539, 558 (1985); on the relationship of tension see also Yen, A.C. (1989), 'A First Amendment Perspective on the Idea/Expression Dichotomy and Copyright in a Work's Total Concept and Feel', *Emory Law Journal*, **38** (2), 393, 398–407; for criticism, see above all Litman, J. (1990), 'The Public Domain', *Emory Law Journal*, **39** (4), 965, 977; for an in-depth study, see in particular Geiger, C. (2005), 'Droit d'auteur et droit du public à l'information', *Recueil Dalloz*, (38), 2683 *et seq.* In Great Britain, it was above all in the 18th century that case law addressed this issue, generally treating it under common law property, such as in the cases of *Millar v Taylor* (1769) 4 Burr. 2301, and *Donaldson v Beckett* (1774) 4 Burr. 2407. See also Bently, Lionel and Brad Sherman (2004), *Intellectual Property Law*, Oxford, UK: Oxford University Press, p. 172 note 51. Generally, it is apparent that the debate in Great Britain is being conducted less in the context of the freedom of opinion (logically, since this is not guaranteed in a constitution). Concerning Art. 10 of the Human Rights Act 1998 and Art. 10 ECHR (freedom of expression) cf. the case of *Ashdown v Telegraph Group Ltd.* [2001] EWCA Civ. 1142, cited by Garnett, Kevin, Jonathan Rayner James and Gillian Davies (eds) (2005), *Copinger and Skone James on Copyright*, London, UK: Sweet & Maxwell, paras 3-260, note 55 and 22–83 *et seq.*, as the leading case for copyright taking second place to freedom of opinion. The priority of public interest is expressed in Section 171 (3) CDPA 1988. Cf. *ibid.*, at paras 22–82. On the public interest and the copyright limitations in the UK see Davies, Gillian (2002), *Copyright and the Public Interest*, London, UK: Sweet & Maxwell, paras 4-024 *et seq.* As further examples from case law, Davies also cites *Newspaper Licensing Agency Ltd. v Marks and Spencer plc* [2001] RPC 76 (CA), and the related House of Lords decision [2001] ECDR 28. On the *Ashdown* case see *ibid.*, at para. 4-035. See also Garnett, Kevin and Gillian Davies (eds) (2001), *Copinger and Skone James on Copyright. First Supplement to the Fourteenth Edition*, London, UK: Sweet & Maxwell, paras 9-05B *et seq.* Only Bently and Sherman go into somewhat more detail in this direction, *supra* 2, at p. 174, with references to case law: 'The exclusion of "ideas" from the scope of protection is an important judicial technique that is used to reconcile the divergent interests of Copyright owners against the interests of users, creators, and the public more generally. These interests include, but

In fact, in principle this is an absolute necessity, at least if we include considerations of a constitutional nature.[4] However, technical developments have rapidly shown that this notional two-fold division as reflected in positive rights could in reality mutate into a dangerous phantom.

By adopting the Directive on Copyright in the Information Society,[5] the European legislature attempted to provide a response to the huge developments in the field of information technology. We would not be far wrong to suggest that the legislation was strongly influenced[6] by (representatives of) commercial interests in the entertainment industry.[7] In all the sensitive

---

are by no means confined to: the public interest in ensuring that new works can be made dealing with the same topic, or subject matter; the public interest in ensuring that Copyright protection does not undermine the free use of functional ideas (other than those protected by designs); . . .; the public interest in free expression; . . .'. As a review on the 'idea/expression dichotomy' in Great Britain see also Bently and Sherman, *supra* 2, at p. 173, with the oft-cited comments by Lord Hoffmann: *Designers Guild v Russell Williams*, [2002] 1 WLR 2416 *et seq.*; Strokes, S. (2005), 'The Development of UK Software Copyright Law', *CTLR*, **11** (4), 129 *et seq.*; Garnett *et al.*, *supra*, para. 2-06.

   4   Art. 10 of the European Convention of Human Rights states, on the right to the freedom of expression: 'This right shall include the freedom . . . to receive and impart information . . . without interference by public authority'. Although this right does not establish claims against private persons, an 'interference by public authority' would include a state arranging a protective right in such a way that the freedom to receive ideas is restricted. The same idea is contained in Art. 27 of the United Nations Declaration of Human Rights of 1948, para. 1 of which – i.e. before para. 2 in which the right to the protection of the moral and material interests resulting from scientific production is laid down – states: 'Everyone has the right . . . to share in scientific advancement and its benefits'. For the basics on this entire issue see Geiger, *supra* note 3.

   5   Directive 2001/29/EC of the European Parliament and of the Council of 22 May 2001 on the Harmonisation of Certain Aspects of Copyright and Related Rights in the Information Society (OJ L 167 dated 22 June 2001, pp. 10 *et seq.*).

   6   The Royal Society (2003), 'Keeping Science Open: The Effects of Intellectual Property Policy on the Conduct of Science', www.royalsoc.ac.uk/ displaypagedoc.asp?id=11403, note 2.7: 'The recent copyright and database legislation in Europe is in a large part a response to the rapid developments in electronic storage and transmission of information. The legislation has been driven by commercial interests unrelated to science and is likely to have significant – and detrimental – effects on science' (Last access to all websites referred to in this chapter on 14 September 2006).

   7   Pressure from the entertainment industry in the USA led to an amendment of the international treaties (WIPO Copyright Treaty – WCT, WIPO Performances and Phonograms Treaty – WPPT) and the adoption of the Digital Millennium Copyright Act (DMCA) in 1998. This development is to be understood as a reaction to the new (digital) technologies that have increased the possibilities for private use of culture industry products and thus constitute a threat to the relevant markets. At European level, the Directive on Copyright in the Information Society was adopted three years

problem constellations, the national legislatures are impeded by the apparently immovable factor of the requirements laid down by the European legislature.[8]

A group that has been very directly affected by the current developments in copyright is that of scientists. They have suddenly become aware that copyright is not only capable of providing them with protection for their achievements, but also that under certain circumstances it can become an obstacle, specifically if research is carried out using modern information technologies. The background is that the balance of interests that has always been inherent in copyright is at risk of being undermined by technical developments. This sophisticated system of exceptions that has in the past given copyright a differentiated aspect and works in Great Britain through what are known as the 'fair dealing[9] provisions' is, as has been described and regretted on many an occasion,[10] exposed to severe interference if technical protection mechanisms are superimposed on copyright protection. The problem is not simply that certain acts – of themselves permitted on the basis of the exception provisions – are prevented by actual measures.[11] Rather, the Achilles' heel is to be found in the

---

later, and contains the DMCA's main prohibitions on the circumvention of technical protection measures (TPMs). For details, see Hilty, R.M. (2005/6), 'Five Lessons about Copyright in the Information Society', *Journal of the Copyright Society*, **53** (1–2), 110–13.

[8]   For criticism see Hilty, R.M. (2005), 'La transposition de la directive sur le droit d'auteur et les droits voisins dans la société de l'information. Analyse critique et prospective', *Propriétés Intellectuelles*, (15), 140.

[9]   As an example of many see Cornish, William R. and David Llewelyn (2003), *Intellectual Property*, London, UK: Sweet & Maxwell, paras 11–36 *et seq.*; on 'recent case law on fair dealing' see Davies, *supra* note 3, at paras 4-031 *et seq.*

[10]   Cf. as an example Hugenholtz, P.B. (2003), 'Copyright, Contract and Technology – What Will Remain of the Public Domain?', *Cahiers du CRID*, (18), 85; Vinje, T. (1996), 'Brave New World of Technical Protection Systems: Will there still be room for Copyright?', *EIPR*, **18** (8), 436 *et seq.*; Koelman, K.J. (2000), 'A Hard Nut to Crack: the Protection of Technological Measures', *EIPR*, **22** (6), 279; Buydens, M. and S. Dusollier (2001), 'Les exceptions au droit d'auteur dans l'environment numérique: evolutions dangereuses', *CCE*, (10), 15; Foged, T. (2002), 'US v EU Anticircumvention Legislation: Preserving the Public's Privilege in the Digital Age', *EIPR*, **24** (11), 525–42; Bechthold, Rainer (2004), 'Das Urheberrecht und die Informationsgesellschaft', in Hilty, R.M. and A. Peukert (eds), *Interessenausgleich im Urheberrecht*, Baden-Baden, Germany: Nomos, pp. 67, 72; Geiger, C. (2004), 'Der urheberrechtliche Interessenausgleich in der Informationsgesellschaft – Zur Rechtsnatur der Beschränkungen des Urheberrechts', *GRUR Int.*, **53** (10), 819 *et seq.*; Hilty, R.M. (2005), 'L'avenir du droit d'auteur dans le dilemme numérique', *Revue Lamy du Droit de l'Immateriel*, (1), 49 *et seq.*; Dusollier, S. (2005), *Droit d'auteur et protection des oeuvres dans l'univers numérique*, Brussels, Belgium: Larcier, pp. 160 *et seq.*

[11]   An example is the situation where the protection expires after the end of the protected period but the technical protection continues to prevent free accessibility. See

independent legal protection that international copyright law now demands for such technical protection measures (TMPs).[12] The consequence of this two-stage legal protection is first of all that the previous differentiation in the form of the system of exceptions at the first level – the pure copyright protection – is lost at the second level, since TPMs cannot distinguish between privileged and forbidden uses as intended by the legislature. In other words, a statutory exception effectively 'fails' where TPMs are used.[13] In addition, it is sufficient to use technical measures to protect non-protected elements together with specific protected works or parts of works, since a single protected element is sufficient to permit the legal protection of the TPM, with the consequence that the law also secures the inviolability of the access to the unprotected elements.[14] Finally, the legal protection of such TPMs means that even the users who from the technical point of view are able to solve the problem themselves (by overcoming the TPMs so as to create the privileged access intended by the law) are a priori prevented from doing so since otherwise they would be exposed to the risk of a conflict with copyright – in which

---

for instance Branstetter, C. (2003), 'Anti-Circumvention: Has Technology's Child Turned against its Mother?', *Vanderbilt J. Transnational L.*, **36** (5), 961, 978 (2003); Strowel, A. and S. Dusollier (2001), 'La protection légale des systèmes techniques: analyse de la directive 2001/29 sur le droit d'auteur dans une perspective comparative', *Propriétés Intellectuelles*, (1), 18; Koelman, K.J. (2002), 'The Protection of Technological Measures vs. the Copyright Limitations', *Copyright World*, (122), 18.

[12] Art. 11 WCT/Art. 18 WPPT. This is implemented in the USA in the form of the Digital Millennium Copyright Act (DMCA), in Europe in the Directive on Copyright in the Information Society, Art 6, *supra* note 5. On the US approach see for instance Lessig, Lawrence (2004), *Free Culture*, New York, US: Penguin Press, pp. 156–60; for a comparison of laws, Foged, *supra* note 10, or Koelman, *supra* note 10, at pp. 272–80; Dusollier, *supra* note 10, passim.

[13] Accurately, Lessig, *supra* note 12, at p. 148: 'It is code, rather than law, that rules'; critically even at an early date, Samuelson, Pamela (1995), 'Copyright, Digital Data, and Fair Use', in Mackaay, E., D. Poulin, P. Trudel and G. Basque (eds)., *The Electronic Superhighway*, The Hague, Netherlands: Kluwer, p. 12; Vinje, *supra* note 10, at 436 *et seq.*; Hoeren, Thomas (2001), 'Access Right as a Postmodern Symbol of Copyright Deconstruction?', in Ginsburg, J. and J. Besek (eds), *Proceedings of the ALAI Congress June 13–17, 2001*, New York, US: Columbia University, p. 356; Geiger, Christophe (2005), 'Hindert das Urheberrecht den freien Zugang zu Wissen? Für einen angemessenen Interessensausgleich im Urheberrecht', in Fisaum (ed), *Geistiges Eigentum von Hirsch bis Heute 28*, Ankara, Turkey: Ankara Üniversitesi Basimevi, p. 28; Strowel, A. (2001), 'La protection des measures techniques: une couche en trop?', *A&M*, (1), 93.

[14] Cf. Peukert, Alexander (2002), 'Digital Rights Management und Urheberrecht', *UFITA*, (3), 709 and in particular note 45; *idem* (2003), 'Technische Schutzmaßnahmen §§ 95a bis d UrhG', in Ulrich Loewenheim (ed.), *supra* note 3, para. 34 note 6, with reference to the limit of abuse of the law.

the legal protection of TPMs is integrated – despite the privilege basically intended by the legislature.[15]

Against this background, the scientist's problem is obvious: technical progress – above all in its effect on online use – may initially have given him the unimagined possibility of accessing content that was previously inaccessible or only accessible with considerable difficulty. At the same time, however, this technology can now be used to impose unreasonable conditions on his access to the content he needs.[16] The scientist may be expected to accept economically unreasonable conditions for the new forms of use as long as the traditional information channels – i.e. ultimately the book or the printed journal – continue to be available without restriction. In the worst case, the scientist simply does not use the most recent information technologies, but at least he does not suffer a disadvantage as against the previously known research possibilities. However, if business models prevail in which information is provided entirely by means of databases accessible online – a development that is currently clearly observable in the field of scientific periodicals – the problem of access becomes a question of the scientist's survival.[17]

It is here that the problem to be discussed in the present chapter starts. The concept of copyright may have been intended so as not to protect information as such, but only its specific form of expression. However, from a practical point of view, the well-known and oft-cited dichotomy between 'form' and 'content' is no longer of any use when TPMs are used. Admittedly, the legal protection of such TPMs initially requires the existence of copyright protection – and to this extent 'only' the protection of form.[18] However, in practical terms, the use of TPMs necessarily means that anyone using this technology also has control over the contents; it is obvious that technical restrictions cannot be limited to the form of expression. In other words, anyone who holds the rights to a TPM – the copyright holder (usually, however, not the original

---

[15]   In the light of Art. 6 para. 4 subpara. 4 of the Directive on Copyright in the Information Society. See section 3.1.

[16]   On the relevant development see below sections 2.1. and 2.2.

[17]   Cf. for more depth, for instance, Samuelson, P. (2001), 'Anticircumvention Rules: Threat to Science', www.sciencemag.org/cgi/content/full/293/5537/2028?ijkey=sJ5V2ve/PTGkU&keytype=ref&siteid=sci. See also Lessig, *supra* note 12, at p. 147.

[18]   The necessity for copyright (or related right) protection of technically protected content initially follows implicitly in international law from the reference to the consent of the 'authors' (Art. 11 WCT) or of the 'performers or producers of phonograms' (Art. 18 WPPT). In European law, the base is even more clearly – and more accurately – the 'rightholder of any copyright or any right related to copyright as provided for by law' (Art. 6 para 3 of the Directive); conversely it can be concluded that in the absence of the existence of such rights there is no legal protection for the TPMs.

rightholder, i.e. the artistic creator himself) – in the final analysis has full control over the information.[19]

However, it is doubtful whether the implications of this de facto extension of protection resulting from the legal protection of TPMs are in fact understood in the current discussion on copyright. The focus is on far more popular topics whose implications are less radical, and it is rarely that the question is addressed of 'whether' participation in cultural life is at all possible, the concentration instead being on the 'how' of this participation.[20]

In the field of science, on the other hand, it is precisely this precondition – the availability of content in a suitable form – that appears increasingly under threat. The background is firstly the actual changes in the business models of a number of academic publishers, as will be examined in further detail below. Secondly – and above all – the main problem is based on a ruling in European law according to which exceptions can be made unenforceable a priori in the online sector that forms the basis for the new business models. This problem area will also be examined in further detail below.

2.   The Actual Changes and their Effects

2.1.   *Technical Development*

Basically, technical developments prevailed in the publishing sector with considerable delay. Unlike the producers of phonograms and video recordings, who were first exposed to a cold wind in the 1960s when (still analogue)

---

19   See Samuelson, P. (2003), 'Mapping the Digital Public Domain: Threats and Opportunities', *Law and Contemporary Problems*, **66** (1–2), 147, examining the relation between anti-circumvention law and public domain and concluding that the DMCA will significantly threaten the public domain and reasonable uses of digital information; Benkler, Y. (1999), 'Free as the Air to Common Use: First Amendment Constraints on Enclosure of the Public Domain', *New York University Law Review*, **74** (2), 354. See also Branstetter, *supra* note 11, at p. 978: 'If a work cannot be copyrighted or its copyright protection has expired, its owner can merely use a digital rights management tool such as encryption to protect the work, and anyone wishing to access the work would be without a practical means to do so, other than by requesting permission from the owner'; Foged, *supra* note 10, p. 526: 'Technological measures may cause material to be protected that would not have been protected by copyright laws'.

20   As an example we refer to the discussion in Germany on the lawfulness of the private copy when copy prevention is installed. This example is often used for a global discussion of whether the existing exceptions are 'strong in enforcement' – i.e. whether they enjoy priority over the legal protection of TPMs. What is easily overlooked is that there are two questions, whether one is entitled to make a private CD or a DVD for whatever reasons, and whether access to the information proper – the building blocks of science as well as of research and development of all kinds – is impeded. The distinction is also made by Geiger, C. (2005), 'Right to Copy v. Three-step Test', *CRi*, (1), 9.

electromagnetic storage media and recording devices became available at affordable prices, publishers were 'only' faced with the invention of the photocopier in the course of the 1940s.[21] However, the effort of copying individual pages and having to handle loose sheets of paper never led to a genuine substitute product that would have persuaded large parts of the population not to buy a handy bound book or to do without the convenience of regularly receiving the current issue of a journal.[22] This fact is also the reason why publishers – unlike the producers of phonograms and video recordings and the broadcasting organisations[23] – have as yet not acquired their own legal protection in terms of a related right in the international context.[24] However, even though they were in individual cases in fact affected by the possibility of photocopying – above all in the fields of journals – the possibility of the collective exercise of rights created an acceptable compensation for the lost profit. In Great Britain this was implemented in 1988 through the inclusion of a corresponding provision in the Copyright, Designs and Patents Act (CDPA). This lays down that collecting societies such as the Copyright Licensing Agency can claim licence fees for specific publishers payable for acts of reproduction by scientific organisations going beyond the exception for fair dealing.[25]

---

[21]   The first patent for xerography dates from 1942; the first marketable appliance, the Xerox 'model A', was launched on the market in 1949.

[22]   Trotter, Hardy (1996), 'Property (and Copyright) in Cyberspace', *University of Chicago Legal Forum*, 217, 224–5.

[23]   The basis is primarily the Rome Convention (International Convention dated 26 October 1961 on the Protection of Performers, Producers of Phonograms and Broadcasting Organisations).

[24]   On the comparable entitlement of his achievement to protection see Dietz, A. (1990), 'Ist die Einführung eines Leistungsschutzrechts (eines verwandten Schutzrechts) für Verleger zu empfehlen?', *ZUM*, **34** (2), 55 *et seq.* taking account of British law; Hilty, R.M. (1991), 'Gedanken zum Schutze der nachbarrechtlichen Leistung – einst, heute und morgen', *UFITA*, **116**, 41 *et seq.*; *idem* (2005), 'Vergütungssystem und Schrankenregelungen – Neue Herausforderungen an den Gesetzgeber', *GRUR*, **54** (10), 826. See also Reinbothe, J. (2004), 'Das Urheberrecht im Wandel der Zeiten', *ZEuS*, **7** (3), 373. On the special case of educational media see von Bernuth, W. (2005), 'Leistungsschutz für Verleger von Bildungsmedien', *GRUR*, **54** (3), 196 *et seq.*; on the background in Germany, see also Thoms, F. (1983), 'Zur Vergütungspflicht für reprographische Vervielfältigungen im Regierungsentwurf zur Urheberrechtsnovelle', *GRUR*, **32** (10), 543, or Sieger, F. (1989), 'Gegen ein eigenständiges originäres Verlegerrecht', *ZUM*, **33** (4), 175; on the present prospects of the Börsenverein, see Sprang, C. (2003), 'Statement des Börsenvereins des Deutschen Buchhandels', *ZUM*, **47** (special issue), 1036; for criticism, see Schack, Haimo (2005), *Urheber- und Urhebervertragsrecht*, Tübingen, Germany: Mohr Siebeck, note 1007 *et seq.*

[25]   The Royal Society, *supra* note 6, note 4.5: 'The CDPA brought in licensing schemes in response to the widespread use of photocopiers and consequent loss of revenues to publishers. Under the terms of an agreed general licence, educational and

This 'grace period' slowly came to an end as digitisation appeared on the scene and also reached the publishing sector. The technical convergence typical of digital storage made it suddenly irrelevant whether a carrier medium such as a compact disc contained music, images or text. Consequently, such a medium could be used to store the contents of a book electronically, hugely increasing the vulnerability of its producer. For now, as already previously with music recordings, anyone could create a qualitatively equivalent copy from a technical point of view (known as a clone) by merely copying it to an empty data carrier instead of acquiring the original. Nevertheless the introduction of this new technology did not yet create a stir; as compared with the traditional book market, off-line media did not in the publishing sector play a major role in terms of numbers. Presumably, the potential purchaser regarded the advantages over the book as being too small, particularly since the prices – astonishing in the light of the elimination of printing costs – hardly differed from those for books, while a CD as such becomes just as quickly out of date as a book.

Thanks to the online media, the entire information available worldwide is today linked – at least theoretically; information that is needed can be made available on the screen that the scientist views as he writes his own article. This new opportunity was rapidly taken up by numerous publishers, who set up databases, linked related content and were thus capable of marketing new products, doing precisely what the market was now demanding – one might think. Nevertheless, particularly amongst scientists there is no cause for rejoicing. Why this is the case becomes clear if we regard developments from a different point of view:

In truth, the development by no means began only when the internet started its hectic triumphal march. Even in the traditional book-printing sector, much had happened in the previous decades, although the book essentially still looked like it did 100 years ago. The decisive step was taken when expensive hot metal type was replaced by desktop publishing, i.e. ultimately the use of computers. Everything became much easier, with an extremely positive effect for publishers, who could gradually send entire armies of typesetters home as authors slowly learned to write their texts themselves on their own computers – at no cost to the publishers. Authors long ago became accustomed to having to take on responsibility for the more complex formatting; if they do not, the price they pay for publishing their texts increases. Of course, conversely, they also realised what they were capable of doing – a realisation that was to prove a boomerang for the publishers.

---

commercial research establishments pay licence fees to collecting societies such as the Copyright Licensing Agency, which act on behalf of certain publishers for copying outside fair dealing'; on collective licensing under the CDPA see generally Laddie *et al.*, *supra* note 3, at pp. 946 *et seq.*

2.2.   *Implications for the market*

However, it was astonishing that the prices for books and magazines never really fell; on the contrary, studies in the USA show that prices for periodicals have increased by a factor of almost 5 since 1985.[26] The development in Great Britain was similar, although less marked. According to a study, not only has the number of journals published each year substantially increased over the last 10 years (from 4,000 in 1993–4 to 6,500 in 2001); the average price of a journal has also increased by 58% over the same period.[27] This has been of no concern to most scientists, but not because scientists are by nature particularly appreciative of the value of the print media. On the contrary – and this is the decisive point – scientists mainly do not themselves buy the works that they need for their libraries, and instead the funds are provided by the public sector (in any event in the field of public research).[28] Consequently, the individual scientist does not protest at the current price development. In contrast, however, scientific organisations are sounding the alarm, understandably in the light of the fact that over the last few years three contradictory developments have taken place, as will be set out in brief below: (a) cuts in state funds, (b) newly identified opportunities for the exchange of information and (c) excessive profit demands by a number of publishing companies.

(a) It is more than sufficiently known that the economy of many countries is stagnating, leading to painful losses of tax revenue, and that the funds in the state coffers for financing traditional public expenditure are becoming increasingly limited. A number of countries are reacting more intelligently,[29] others

---

[26]   Cf. Albee, Barbara and Brenda Dingley (2002) 'U.S. Periodical Prices – 2002', www.ala.org/ALCTSTemplate.cfm?Section=alctssectionscont&template=/Content Management/ContentDisplay.cfm&ContentID=40416.

[27]   Report of the UK House of Commons, Science and Technology Committee (2004) 'Scientific Publications: Free for All?', www.publications.parliament.uk/pa/cm200304/cmselect/cmsctech/399/399.pdf, p. 29.

[28]   This fact incidentally had consequences in copyright law, with for instance the making of copies by – publicly financed – libraries in Germany enjoying a certain privilege. The basis for this was the *Kopienversanddienst* decision of the Federal Supreme Court NJW 1999, 1953 *et seq. – Kopienversanddienst.*

[29]   This can be said of Germany in that the previously 'Red-Green' federal government concluded a 'Pact for research and development' together with the federal provinces that provided for annual growth of 3% for major research institutions (www.bmbf.de/de/3215.php). This approach is to be continued by the present government within the framework of the 'large coalition' (www.cdu.de/doc/pdf/05_11_11_Koalitionsvertrag.pdf, note 4.1). The policy in Great Britain provides for an increase in research and development expenditure from 1.9% of national income to 2.5% by 2014, according to the Department for Education and Skills (2004) 'Science and innovation investment framework', http://news.bbc.co.uk/nol/shared/bsp/hi/pdfs/science_innovation_120704.pdf, p. 7.

less so – many have perceptibly or even dramatically reduced the funds for publicly financed research a few years ago. On the other hand, the research institutions financed in this way retain little scope. They are neither able to reduce the rent costs for laboratories and offices, nor can they simply terminate the (public) employment relationships or give notice of the collective wage agreements. All that can be reduced are procurement costs – and what must be procured for scientists is information. It goes without saying that it cannot be a question of procuring less information – this would be the end of research (and in particular of fundamental research); instead the aim is to acquire the individual 'information unit' more cheaply within the framework of what is known as the 'purchase of information'.[30]

(b) Alongside this development, new technologies indeed gave reason for hope that information would become cheaper – the keyword being the internet. Potentially, every item of information was available via the internet – often free of charge – and the question arose of why it should still be paid for. At first sight the situation appears indeed grotesque. The public sector pays to enable research. The results of this research are, however, not freely accessible to other researchers. Instead, every research institution must acquire the research results of every other – again with public funds.[31] And it should be understood that this is not because the scientific organisations are paying each other for research results, but because the researchers have handed their results to a third party – the publisher – who sells them (mostly on his own account) to other researchers. This detour was understandable as long as an expensive factor created an added value as against the pure information: the printed book or the journal. If, however, there is no longer any need to produce a tangible

---

[30]   According to the Report of the UK House of Commons, *supra* note 27, at pp. 23 and 50–1. See also Committee on Issues in the Transborder Flow of Scientific Data, U.S. National Committee for CODATA, Commission on Physical Sciences, Mathematics, and Applications and National Research Council (1997), *Bits of Power: Issues in Global Access to Scientific Data*, Washington, DC., US: National Academy Press, p. 115.

[31]   In the USA, the 108th Senate promptly responded to this problem with the bill of a 'Public Access to Science Act' (http://thomas.loc.gov/cgi-bin/query/z?c108:H.R.2613:). According to this, copyright was to be excluded 'for any work produced pursuant to scientific research substantially funded by the federal government'. However, this was not implemented. The demand that the results of publicly financed research should be made more accessible to the public was also raised here in Germany. See for instance Hilty, R.M. (2005), 'Urheberrecht und Wissenschaft', in Sieber, U. and T. Hoeren (eds), 'Urheberrecht für Bildung und Wissenschaft', *Beiträge zur Hoschulpolitik*, (2), 189 *et seq.*, and Hansen, G. (2005), 'Zugang zu wissenschaftlicher Information – alternative urheberrechtliche Ansätze', *GRUR Int.*, **54** (5), 379 *et seq.*, with further references, each with a proposal for rewording Section 38 of the Copyright Act with a binding time limit to the grant of exclusive user rights.

product, and if instead only electronic data is created and even formatted by the researcher, where is the added value for which the researcher should pay? Why should researchers who could ultimately supply each other with electronic information pay? Examined closely, this logic is without doubt too simple; but its core hits a sore point. However, it would hardly have had any effect if the third development had not occurred as well.

(c) A number of publishers began to invest in online databases at an early stage. They realised that electronic online media would at least in part replace the print media, in the field of short-lived periodicals rather than with books. A convincing example of the accuracy of the publishers' assessment of the situation is shown in the American case-law system. The advantages that users derive from regularly updated backward-compatible databases as compared with the almost unmanageable volume of printed case-law collections are innumerable. They have led to the rapid success of the suppliers of Westlaw or Lexis-Nexis.[32] An army of lawyers was willing to pay even high user fees for such services, since time is money and the time saved (alongside the increase in accuracy) was unbeatable. Naturally, a similar acceptance of this business model in the academic sector is not quite so self-evident as one might think. In this field, the time factor does not have the same importance as in business. Of more importance is the hope of finding information somewhere in the world that would otherwise be concealed. For this completeness, the researcher (or the individual research organisation) is likewise willing to pay a certain price. The question here, where there is no direct financial return through the use of online databases, is simply: what is the correct price?

Concerning the pricing of the products in question, it can be noted that the detour via the publisher has had a huge inflationary effect.[33] This detour is without doubt reasonable if a relevant added value is provided at an understandable price. Of course this added value has nothing to do with the content as such, since this is generally received by the publisher free of charge or for a comparatively marginal cost. Nor do most cases concern what is known as peer reviewing, which may indeed be organised by the publishers but ultimately, if it is genuinely to be of an academic standard, is likewise to be provided by the scientists themselves – again as a rule free of charge for the publishers. In the field of e-publishing, where the entire printing and distribution costs can be cut, genuine added value is probably only provided by the

---

[32]   LexisNexis began the Lexis Service, the first commercial full-text law information service, as far back as 1973; the companion Nexis-News and Business Information Service was founded in 1979. For details of the history, see www.lexis-nexis.com/about.

[33]   See Hilty, R.M. (2006), 'Das Urheberrecht und der Wissenschaftler', *GRUR Int.*, **55** (3), 183 *et seq.*

publisher within the framework of electronic data management, the maintenance of the entire information infrastructure and above all through the processing of electronic data or the like. Thus the answer to the question of the reasonable and hence justifiable price results automatically: if the total value of such services provided by the publisher appears very small while the price for online supply is very high, the scientific organisation is logically increasingly motivated to take matters into its own hands.

Irrespective of one's view of the actual prospects of success of the open access movement in terms of research institutions,[34] it remains the case for the moment that scientific works – irrespective of the source of their financing and form of exploitation – also enjoy copyright protection. Hence, we must also accept the fact that this protection often has an effect to the detriment of precisely those persons for whom it was actually created. Under these premises, the open access system – if the cost question just discussed is ignored for the moment – does not appear fundamentally unreasonable. For there is one objective that it could in fact achieve: the heated discussions reveal the true state of interests, a revelation that does not exactly flatter the publishers who refuse to behave cooperatively, and should at least shake them into action.

2.3. Two approaches to a solution

There can be no blaming the critical copyright lawyer for asking whether he should be satisfied with this uncertain prospect. Would it not be an act of caution to put to the test the existing legislation that obviously permits the present injustice and ask what could have been different? This leads to essentially two possibilities.

The first step is to examine the major publishing companies with their

---

[34]   For details see Hilty, *ibid.*, 183–5; *idem, supra* note 7, at 125–30, concerning the question of the principle whether a substantial investment of public money to provide public research on the basis of an open access doctrine does not already lead to an alternative economic approach, i.e. an alternative incentive model: we might consider the resulting intangible good as a public good and challenge the intervention of the legislator by granting exclusive rights. See also Arrow, K.J. (1962), 'Economic Welfare and the Allocation of Resources for Invention', in Richard R. Nelson (ed.), *The Rate and Direction of Inventive Activity: Economic and Social Factors*, Princeton, US: Princeton University Press and National Bureau of Economic Research, pp. 609, 623–5; Cooter, R. and Thomas Ulen (2004), *Law and Economics*, Boston, US *et al.*: Pearson Addison Wesley, pp. 120–2; Elkin-Koren, Niva and Eli M. Salzburger (1999), *Law, Economics and Cyberspace*, Cheltenham, UK and Northampton, MA, USA: Edward Elgar, pp. 50–5; Schäfer, Hans Bernd and Claus Ott (2004), *The Economic Analysis of Civil Law*, Cheltenham, UK and Northampton, MA, USA: Edward Elgar, pp. 456–7. On developments in Great Britain see The Royal Society, *supra* note 6, pp. 17–22 and especially note 4.10.

considerable portfolios of periodical titles from a competition law point of view. In this connection, a central role is probably played by the fact that the academic market is not just any old market but one that is subject to its own mode of operation. In particular, the possibility of publishing in a relevant high-ranking periodical plays a decisive role for specific research institutions – in particular scientific institutions. This fact possibly means that these periodicals are not substitutable for each other even if a number of publications from different publishers exist side by side, and this in two ways. Firstly, the scientist who is anxious about his reputation cannot waive publication in certain specialist journals. Secondly, anyone who needs specific content cannot simply switch to a different periodical with different content if he is looking for specific research results. In this light, there is the suspicion that the academic market should perhaps be located in the field of 'essential facilities', a classification that would have an effect if an exploiter, thanks to his market-dominant position, was able to impose unreasonable conditions on publication on the one hand or on access on the other hand.[35]

Such an approach under competition law may in extreme cases indeed have a prospect of success; however, we should not forget that the route via an antitrust-law investigation is long and stony.[36] In particular, it may be possible to make an 'example', but the battle would in principle (with the exception of certain deterrent effects of leading decisions) have to be taken up again in every case of abuse, without it being possible to address the roots of the problem in legal terms.

The second approach is accordingly directed to the source of the problems.

---

[35] Cf. also Helberger, N. (2005), *Controlling Access to Content*, New York, US *et al.*: Kluwer, pp. 166–70, 283, 284. She describes the decision of the Conseil de la Concurrence in *Apple Computer* of 9 November 2004 (Case No. 04-D-54) as the first case in Europe in which a European antitrust authority was required to decide whether an electronic content management system was to be classified as an essential facility; ultimately, however, the notion was rejected by the Court. On the grounds of the decision, see paras 96–103 and Helberger, *ibid.*, p. 167. In this context, see also the discussion of the similar decision in *Microsoft Europe* before the European Commission of 24 March 2004 (Case COMP/C-3/37.792) in Helberger, *ibid.*, pp. 168, 169, 182.

[36] It is indicative that in the European context the decisions in the field of copyright must be qualified as untypical in terms of the subject matter of protection: *Radio Telefis Eireann v Commission of the European Communities* (C-241/91P) (Magill Case) [1995] 4 CMLR 718 (ECJ); *IMS Health GmbH & Co OHG v NDC Health GmbH & Co KG* (C-418/01) [2004] 4 CMLR 28 (ECJ), while 'normal' constellations of the exploitation of the copyright exclusive status are apparently not capable of being corrected by means of antitrust law. In general on antitrust law as an external limit to copyright, see Heinemann, Andreas (2004), 'Interne und externe Begrenzungen des Immaterialgüterschutzes am Beispiel des IMS Health-Falls', in Hilty, R.M. and A. Peukert (eds), *supra* note 10, pp. 207 *et seq.*

In fact, it appears attractive from a copyright point of view to reduce the powers that result from the protective right itself a priori to such an extent that the legal position it creates can no longer be used to detrimental effect. In this connection, it must be noted that under the present system not only does the individual rightholder have hardly any negotiating power to refuse to grant copyright to the publisher if he wishes to publish in recognised media; nor is it realistic to believe that the scientific organisation for which he works might have such an option. At first sight, one might think that these organisations could, by means for instance of employment contracts, oblige scientists to grant the rights not to the publishers but to the organisations themselves, in order to avoid abuse being made of copyright;[37] however, in fact such an arrangement could become a boomerang for the organisation concerned. For, if they were to restrict scientists excessively, they would have to reckon with the possibility that they would no longer be able to recruit really good and independent researchers. To this must be added the fact that by no means all scientists are integrated within the corresponding organisations by employment contracts.

If account is taken of these problems, it would appear most effective to apply the lever to the derivative rightholder, i.e. the publisher. For in truth, neither the individual author nor the organisation for which he works is capable of abusing the rights to which he is entitled as author. This temptation lies on the contrary with the exploiter, who appears as such on the market and who, thanks to the sum of all the rights granted, in fact also acquires a corresponding potential for misuse. Consequently, it is necessary to examine where the neuralgic points of copyright are to be found that permit the undesirable use of this potential.

In order to be able to show that reducing the legal position that is conveyed by copyright is not only the most effective means against the normative force of reality (in the form of the effect of TPMs) but also best does justice to the existing (tri-polar) state of interests, it is necessary to examine in further detail the interests of the parties involved. As will become apparent, this approach can, under certain circumstances, result in a (financial) improvement of the position of the author, accompanied by increased accessibility of information to the benefit to the general public.

---

[37]   A similar demand can be found in Pflüger, T. and D. Ertmann (2004), 'E-Publishing und Open Access – Konsequenzen für das Urheberrecht im Hochschulbereich', *ZUM*, **48** (6), 436 *et seq*. Rightly critical, see Hansen, *supra* note 30, 379 *et seq*. (specifically in the light of the freedom of science guaranteed by Art. 5(3) of the German Constitution) and 381 (intervention in the freedom of publication pursuant to Section 42 of the Employee Inventions Act).

3.   Copyright considerations

3.1.   Problems of access to information

In the most recent legislation, the provision of Art. 6(4) of the Directive on Copyright in the Information Society can be regarded as symbolic of the problem just described and its disregard. Subparagraphs 1 and 2 admittedly lay down that account must be taken of the problem of TPMs just discussed,[38] if necessary by member states adopting suitable measures to ensure the enforceability of selected exceptions pursuant to Art. 5 of the Directive.[39] However, subparagraph 4 of Art. 6(4) waives this provision precisely for the most sensitive field of information communication, online use: according to this, the regulation that certain exceptions must be given priority over TPMs does not apply if the subject matter of protection is 'made available to the public on agreed contractual terms in such a way that members of the public may access them from a place and at a time individually chosen by them'.[40]

Admittedly, one might discuss the precise implications of this rule;[41] however, viewed realistically, the chances of those who according to the general rules are granted privileges in the form of exceptions being able to enforce these in connection with online material would appear poor. For instance, the researcher who obtains information from a scientific online database will be unable to make use of the relevant exception under national law. The consequences of this undermining are particularly fatal for the scientist. The privileged access to subject-specific information – the scientist's 'raw material' – is for him the sine qua non if he is to be able to pursue research, hence to further develop existing knowledge.[42]

In fact, account has always been taken of the principle of the accessibility

---

38   *Supra* section 1.

39   On the exhaustive nature of these exceptions see Recital 32 of the Directive on Copyright in the Information Society; on the relationship between exceptions and TPMs see Recitals 51 *et seq.*

40   See also Recitals 11 and 53 of the Directive, where the grounds are stated as being that the protection of technical measures should ensure 'a safe environment for the provision of interactive services'.

41   For further information see in particular Linnenborn, Oliver (2004), 'Die Richtlinie 2001/29/EG im Rückblick: Quellen zu Artikel 6 Absatz 4 über interaktive Abrufdienste', in Hilty, R.M. and A. Peukert (eds), *supra* note 10, pp. 103 *et seq.*, who sets out the historical sources of Art. 6(4) subpara. 4 of the Directive in their context.

42   See Hansen, G. (2006), 'Urheberrecht für Wissenschaftler – Risiken und Chancen der Urheberrechtsreform für das wissenschaftliche Publizieren', in M. Stempfhuber (ed.), *Tagungsband der IuK-Jahrestagung 2005*, 9 *et seq.*

of copyright works, the notion described at the beginning showing that copyright protection only covers the form of expression and not the contents. However, this separation of content and form degenerates into a purely intellectual fiction if TPMs are brought into play. For, if access to the work is protected by technical means, it is only of theoretical interest that the legal protection of the TPM is in fact 'only' related to the copyright protection of the form; it simultaneously also protects access to the content, in other words what actually constitutes the knowledge.

Such scope has hitherto never been granted to copyright – a restriction that the Directive wipes out at a stroke with the said Art. 6(4) subparagraph 4. In the light of this regulation, the discussion about exceptions in general – and those for science in particular – simply becomes obsolete as soon as information is only made available online.[43] If the term 'information society' in the said Directive is not merely intended to refer to gradually ageing information technologies, the European legislature will find it difficult to avoid having to return to the issue.[44] The following makes use of two examples to show what will also be necessary.

3.2. Information broking

The information society is characterised not only by the possibility of access to existing information but also by being able to handle the totality of available information intelligently. The present technical preconditions for the storage and networking of gigantic data quantities are far from sufficient for this purpose. What is necessary instead is a selective scanning of the unstructured mass of data in order to be able to find any usable information whatsoever.

---

[43] Similarly Ganley, P. (2004), 'Digital Copyright and New Creative Dynamics', *IJL&IT*, **12** (3), 282 *et seq.*, who regards the entire provision of Art. 6(4) of the Directive as being superfluous in the light of subpara. 4: 'Since these restrictions will naturally delimit the scope of any accompanying end-user licence agreement, individuals, when assenting to an agreement to obtain access to works made available over the internet, may inadvertently be signing away the protection of article 6.4 itself. Here we've reached the core problem with the provision. Aside from its truncated scope and uncertain oversight, the most troubling aspect is its potential redundancy. Rightholders retain absolute discretion in DRM design at the point of access through which they may themselves circumvent later safeguards. The result is an empty shell with users instead relying on the benevolence of rightholders to perform perfectly legal actions.'

[44] Similarly critical, in particular Koelman, K.J. (2004), 'Copyright Law and Economics in the EU Copyright Directive: Is the Droit d'Auteur Passé?', *IIC*, **35** (6), 626, and The Royal Society, *supra* note 6, note 6.5: 'Recent copyright legislation has more closely met the needs of the entertainment industry than those of science, and difficulties now face the science community which has relied heavily on the "fair dealing" provisions of the copyright legislation to access information'.

Even when the search machines are incomparably better than they are today,[45] this will still require a huge effort because even with relatively precisely worded search terms, weighting and value judgements will continue to be unavoidable if a distinction is to be made between the productive and the useless. Thus until further notice there will still be a need for thinking persons, although in a society where labour is divided it will not necessarily be the person searching himself who is best able to find what he really needs. Instead, it will probably make sense for many members of the information society to make use of specialised third parties whose specific skills and knowledge will decisively increase efficiency as against the searcher's own abilities. Or, put differently, there will be an increasing number of experts, namely information brokers,[46] who will be able to generate their income from creating a cost advantage as a result of the time they save as compared with the client's own search.

It is of course at this point that the copyright question arises. Even if the information broker only sits at a monitor and analyses the hits, his activity will infringe current copyright law[47] if the activity is not limited to simply displaying links[48] and if instead, for instance – in order to relieve the client of the

---

[45]   On Google's attempt to digitise entire libraries, see www.google.com/ intl/en/press/pressrel/print_library.html; on the copyright relevance of this enterprise, see Hansen, G. (2005), 'The Future of the Research Information Chain – The role of Publishers and Learned Societies – Budapest, 17.–18. März 2005, Tagungsbericht', *GRUR Int.*, **54** (7), 580; *idem* (2005) 'Angst vor digitaler Landnahme', http://archiv.tagesspiegel.de/archiv/30.03.2005/1727330.asp; Pierrat, E. and P. Allaeys (2003), 'Google print ou le leurre de la bibliothèque universelle au mépris du droit d'auteur', *Propriétés Intellectuelles*, (17), 386. On similar business models, see also Müller-Lietzkow, J. (2004), 'Open Science – Paradigmawechsel in der Wissenschaftskommunikation', *MW*, **1** (4), 201.

[46]   See Hilty, R.M. (1996), 'Die Rechtsbeziehungen rund um den Information Highway', in Hilty, R.M. (ed.), *Information Highway: Beiträge zu rechtlichen und tatsächlichen Fragen*, Berne, Switzerland and Munich, Germany: Stämpfli and Beck, pp. 442 and 481 *et seq.*

[47]   In general on the problem that – generally and hence also in connection with internet use – the copy triggers copyright protection, see Lessig, *supra* note 12, at pp. 139–45. In fact, uses that have hitherto been regarded as normal use, i.e. free under copyright law (such as reading itself), will become an interference in copyright. See Dusollier, S. (2000), 'Incidences et réalités d'un droit de contrôler l'accès en droit européen', *Cahiers du CRID*, (18), 32; Geiger, *supra* note 3, at note 242; Litman, J. (1994), 'The Exclusive Right to Read', *Cardozo Arts and Entertainment Law Journal*, **13**, 29 *et seq.*

[48]   On the limits of the lawfulness of (in particular deep) links, see Wiebe, A. (2002), in Ernst, S., I. Vassilaki and A. Wiebe (eds), *Hyperlinks*, Cologne, Germany: O. Schmidt, note 11 *et seq.* and especially note 52 *et seq.*; Hilty, Reto M. (2002), 'Zur Zulässigkeit des Link', in Weber, R.H., R.M. Hilty and R. auf der Maur (eds), *Geschäftsplattform Internet III*, Zurich, Switzerland: Schulthess, pp. 123 *et seq.*

work he would otherwise have to provide – he reproduces the hits (electroni-cally). For, the (already narrow[49]) privileges of certain users of the work by no means extend in digital use to the possibility of contracting a specialised – and usually paid – third party to handle the corresponding activity.[50] There may be disagreement as to where precisely the limits between the permitted and the no-longer permitted must be drawn. Nevertheless, even this debate appears obsolete in the light of the access problem described above, since the issue here concerns online uses, for which Art. 6(4) sentence 4 of the Directive allows TPMs to undermine all limitations. It remains a mystery how the European legislature, against this background, can argue that the aim is to 'foster the development of the information society in Europe'[51] or that the Directive in question complies with 'the fundamental principles of law . . . including . . . freedom of expression and the public interest'.[52] Even the simple identification of the development of the information society with the function of the internal market[53] shows how selectively Parliament and the Council viewed the consequences of this Directive. In any event, the possibility of promoting the information society in a manner involving a division of labour – i.e. through the use of specialised information brokers – as is usual in the modern world of business, has been scuppered by the European legislature.

Admittedly, despite all the criticism of this legislation, it must not be forgotten that suitable protection mechanisms are in many cases unavoidable if the commodity 'information' is to be made at all usable for online media. For, in general – and in any event outside the very specific field of science, where, as has been shown, alternative incentive systems would be conceiv-able[54] – considerable investments are necessary, and as a rule made by private undertakings. If such investments are to be made, there is a need for reason-able legal certainty that there are appropriate opportunities to cover the costs

---

49   In German law, in addition to the private or academic use pursuant to Section 53(1) and (3) of the Copyright Act, there is also the extremely complex interaction in Section 53(2), sentences 1–3, which fails to do justice to the needs of the modern infor-mation society and its use of the usual digital technologies.

50   Cf. for Germany Section 53(1) sentence 2 of the Copyright Act, where this narrow limit is based on corresponding provisions of the Directive on Copyright in the Information Society (in particular on Art. 5(2)(a) and (b). See also Recital 38 of the Directive on Copyright in the Information Society. Cf. Section 29 of the British CDPA as a 'fair dealing provision' for the field of research. In particular, Section 29(3) of the CDPA 1988 lays down that infringement by a third party must satisfy the requirements of Sections 37–44 of the Act.

51   Recital 2 of the Directive on Copyright of the Information Society.

52   Recital 3, *ibid.*

53   Recitals 6 and 7 *ibid.*, similarly Recital 38.

54   See above note 32.

and make a profit.[55] Conversely, the legitimate protection of commercial interests – and it is only these that can be at issue in the question of incentives for the commercialisation of copyright protected works – must necessarily end at the point where the return on the investment is in fact guaranteed; if it goes beyond this point, the free competition that is desirable will be impeded by monopoly-like legal positions. Whether and to what extent the investor is exposed to a genuine risk – and as a result needs legal protection – can hardly be given a standardised answer; in particular, it would be wrong to want to automatically apply the protection mechanisms that may in fact be needed by the exploiters in the entertainment industry to the exploiters of actual information.

Seen in this light, it is extremely doubtful whether copyright prohibitions that are intended to prevent the type of services provided by an information broker are at all desirable. If such activities satisfy an existing need, it would seem irresponsible from an economic point of view not to find a legislative approach that would actually permit them – irrespective of the consent of the rightholder concerned – since after all it is precisely such new markets that ultimately can and should create jobs.[56] Should, on the other hand, there be no demand for such services, they will disappear just as quickly as they appeared – an entirely normal process in a well-functioning market economy. If there is a demand, its satisfaction can reasonably only be prevented by a protective right if the – commercial – interests of the rightholder are unfairly prejudiced. However, it is precisely this that can be avoided by the mechanism that has been part of copyright for some time in connection with statutory licences, the payment of reasonable remuneration to the rightholder.[57]

At this point it should be noted that this discussion is not redundant a priori on the grounds of the actual effect of TPMs: their use is determined by the copyright protection granted to form – if there is no right to prohibit,[58] access

---

[55]   Recital 10 of the Directive on Copyright in the Information Society.

[56]   This is also the argument used in the Directive on Copyright in the Information Society, Recital 4, although on the grounds that this objective was to be achieved by a harmonisation of legal protection and a higher level of protection.

[57]   On the recourse to statutory licences in order to regulate access to information, see Geiger, C. (2006), 'Copyright and Free Access to Information, For a Fair Balance of Interests in a Globalized World', *EIPR*, **28** (7), at 366–80; Hilty, R.M. (2005), 'Verbotsrecht vs. Vergütungsanspruch: Suche nach den Konsequenzen der tripolaren Interessenlage im Urheberrecht', in Ohly, A., Th. Bodewig, Th. Dreier, H.-P. Götting, M. Haedicke and M. Lehmann (eds), *Perspektiven des geistigen Eigentums und des Wettbewerbsrechts – Festschrift für Gerhard Schricker zum 70. Geburtstag*, Munich, Germany: Beck, pp. 325 *et seq.*

[58]   On the conformity of such a legislative provision with European law, see Geiger, C. (2004), 'Die Vereinbarkeit einer Privilegierung von kommerziellen Pressespiegeln mit europarechtlichen Vorgaben', *KUR*, **6** (3), 70.

to information cannot definitively be prevented. Alongside the legal aspect, account must also be taken of factual matters: even against the background of the spread of TPMs, this approach by no means ends up as an anachronism, since these measures have still not received their baptism of fire. They will only be able to prevail across the board if they are accepted by consumers as a business model. But even then, marketing models without technical protection will continue to remain significant for a longer period – one need only recall the still long protected period of more recent (and still technically unprotected) products.[59]

In the legal solution by means of statutory licences, we should not be blinded by the discussion of the concept of reasonableness. For the rightholder it is always more beneficial if he can determine the price himself. However, if there is an obvious risk that a prohibitive price rather than a 'reasonable' price can be charged for the corresponding individual licence, the potential for misuse can hardly justify the use of an unrestricted right to prohibit in order to erode the public interest in the professional procurement of information.

3.3.   Added-value services

Entirely comparable approaches can be justified where a relevant added value is created with respect to services by third parties aimed at refining the collection of existing data. In particular, this data is possibly not yet in a form that meet the needs of potential users, in that the data could be linked, for instance, or processed from a technical point of view. Such professional and hence commercial refinements could practically be a preliminary stage for producing new information (e.g. new research results) based on existing information, while the absence of such services could lead to a reduction of efficiency to the detriment of the public interest.

Of course, examples of such added-value services need not be sought only in the information society of the future. On the contrary, the need on the part of large sectors of the economy, administration and specifically also science, for information about existing newspaper and magazine articles has long been known. Corresponding media monitors established themselves decades ago to meet this demand. However, even today they are still operating on the margins of legality or, thanks to existing law, are obliged to make use of

---

[59]   On the coexistence of individual and collective remuneration systems that this sometimes requires, see Peukert, A. (2003), 'Neue Techniken und ihre Auswirkung auf die Erhebung und Verteilung gesetzlicher Vergütungsansprüche', *ZUM*, **47** (special issue), 1050, 1051–3; *idem* (2004), 'DRM: Ende der kollektiven Vergütung?', *sic!*, (10), 749 *et seq*. This approach is also adopted by the draft of a Second Act to Regulate Copyright in the Information Society of 26 March 2006. See http://www.bmj.bund.de/media/archive/1174.pdf, pp. 38–40.

archaic methods (buying the necessary number of print media, cutting out and gluing the articles in question and mailing them to customers).[60] Admittedly there have long been more modern techniques available, but their use is prevented not only by copyright in general. Art. 6(4) subparagraph 4 of the Directive on Copyright in the Information Society forbids any (enforceable) exception in the case of online information.

Once again it must be pointed out that it can naturally not be a question of being able to offer such services based on copyright-protected works without restrictions. Instead, consent must be linked to a reasonable remuneration, as is probably completely undisputed by those who would like to offer such services. Precisely in the field of media monitors, the possibility of using modern technologies would lead to a significant increase in efficiency and reliability – thus benefits that are worth money and in which the rightholder could indeed participate. On the other hand, the system of a 'merely' reasonable remuneration means that there cannot a priori be a prohibition.[61] In fact, a right to prohibit with respect to added-value services would as a rule open the gate to abuse for competition law reasons, as can easily be seen in the market for media monitors in Germany.[62] The need for protection in a primary market cannot automatically be assumed for a downstream market; on the contrary, such markets should typically be regarded separately. While there may be a justification in the primary market for a monopoly in the light of the necessary possibilities for covering costs, this permits no conclusions whatsoever as to the corresponding possibilities in a downstream market.[63] Instead, it is necessary to determine separately whether the creation of added value is necessary to achieve a possible covering of costs that is sufficient overall. It may in the individual case appear appropriate to eliminate free competition there, too.

3.4. Assessment from the point of view of the interests concerned

As an interim conclusion, it can be said that the statutory licence represents a tried and tested solution for the problems of access to information. It is not

---

[60]   Cf. on this and the corresponding consequences for the German newspaper market, Hilty, *supra* note 8, pp. 141 *et seq.*; *idem* (2005), 'Vergütungssystem und Schrankenregelungen – Neue Herausforderungen an den Gesetzgeber', *GRUR*, **54** (10), 822 *et seq.*

[61]   On the conformity of such a legislative provision with European law, see Geiger, *supra* note 58, at p. 70.

[62]   In Germany, where there is an unrestricted right to prohibit the use of modern technologies by independent media monitors, the newspaper publishers themselves (cf www.pressemonitor.de) exploit around 600 titles; in Switzerland – with the corresponding exception rules and an independent media observer (www.argus.ch) – the figure is around 2,500 titles. For further details see Hilty, *supra* note 60, 823.

[63]   In this context see also Lessig, *supra* note 12, at p. 122.

only the interests of the potential users but also the interests of the authors of the works themselves that argue for such an approach. In order to give it specific form, it is necessary to recall the state of interests and the way that they are taken into account in the various legal systems.

First of all, we must examine the various statutory approaches to encouragement of the creation of intellectual works in the various legal systems. In English law, which can be regarded as a product of a range of different factors,[64] there are essentially three different justifications for the existence of copyright[65] – the natural law approach, the reward theory and the incentive theory. Irrespective of the individual arguments raised for or against the various approaches, it remains the case that in legal reality all three approaches are cited alongside each other – depending on the speaker's perspective.[66]

Two leading cases that reflect historical developments[67] are *Millar v Taylor*[68] and *Donaldson v Beckett*.[69] The former takes as its point of reference the person of the author from a natural law point of view, thereby justifying the author's common law right that results from fitness and natural justice.[70] In contrast, the second decision is based on an economic point of view and rejects the protection of ideas as property.[71] The basis for this was the risk of the author's perpetual monopoly being exercised not by the author but by the publishers.[72] It was the latter approach that was to prevail.

---

[64]   See Bently and Sherman, *supra* note 3, at p. 36. See also Cornish and Llewelyn, *supra* note 8, at para. 10-01, who speak of a 'mixed system'.

[65]   According to Bently and Sherman, *supra* note 3, at pp. 32–7.

[66]   *Ibid.*, at p. 37.

[67]   According to Burkitt, D. (2001), 'Copyrighting Culture – The History and Cultural Specificity of the Western Model of Copyright', *IPQ*, **5** (2), 151 *et seq.*, who provides an extensive comparative insight into the historical development of copyright and the underlying ideas, *ibid.*, 146–86.

[68]   *Millar v Taylor* (1769) 4 Burr. 2301.

[69]   *Donaldson v Beckett* (1774) 4 Burr. 2407.

[70]   Burkitt, *supra* note 67, at 152 citing the decision: '"I confess, I do not know, nor can I comprehend any property more emphatically a man's own, nay, more incapable of being mistaken, than his literary works," wrote Aston J. Clearly, Aston was referring to the embellishment of the author's personality in his work: a literary composition belonged to the individual author because it constituted an embodiment of that individual. The basis of literary property was not just the sweat of the author's brow, but the imprint of his personality.'

[71]   As can already be derived from what has been said so far, this notion has, irrespective of its age and the specific discussion, by no means lost significance, but appears more topical than ever in the light of the present overall problem.

[72]   Burkitt, *supra* note 67, at 152: 'Lord Camden, who opened the debate, insisted, that ideas could not properly be regarded as property, and argued forcefully against the author's common law right on the basis that it amounted to a perpetual monopoly exercised not by authors but by the booksellers who purchased their copyrights.'

In the further development of the law, copyright was uncoupled from natural law considerations, ultimately resulting in the present concept of English copyright in the 1988 Copyright, Designs and Patents Act. The legal concept of authorship (Sections 9–11 CDPA 1988) of a work is the decisive attribute that determines the legal protection of a property right (Section 1(1) CDPA 1988).[73] In most cases, the author holds the copyright in a work that he has created (Section 9(1) CDPA 1988). No major distinction is made between the creator of the work and the investor – the trend is even towards preferring the latter.[74]

Originally, the protection of moral rights was not a part of the English legal system – the creators of works were instead required to protect themselves against any infringements by means of contracts.[75] Without these precautions, they could only make use of general law (law of confidence, defamation, passing off, injurious falsehood and general economic torts).[76] Following the enforcement of rights proceedings in 1956 and 1977, which adopted a rather reserved approach to moral rights, it was only in the course of the implementation of the obligations under the Berne Convention in the 1988 Copyright Act that four different moral rights were recognised (Sections 77–89 CDPA 1988).[77] This move encountered not only support but also not insignificant criticism.[78] For some, the half-hearted implementation of Art. 6 of the Berne Convention did not go far enough, and it was even found that the future standard of protection was worse than in the USA.[79] The arguments on the other

---

[73]   For details see Bently and Sherman, *supra* note 3, at pp. 36, 114 *et seq.*; Phillips, Jeremy and Alison Firth (2001), *Introduction to Intellectual Property Law*, London, UK: Butterworths, para. 11.1 *et seq.*; Cornish and Llewelyn, *supra* note 9, at para. 10-01.

[74]   According to Cornish and Llewelyn, *supra* note 9, at para. 10-01.

[75]   On the US situation, where this is still a common legal practice, see Hilty, *supra* note 7, at 131.

[76]   See Cornish and Lllewelyn, *supra* note 9, at para. 11-66. Examples would be: *Humphreys v Thompson* [1905–10] Mac. CC 148; *Lee v Gibbings* (1892) 67 LT 263; *Frisby v BBC* [1967] Ch. 932.

[77]   Two of them in direct compliance with international obligations. Cf. Cornish and Lllewelyn, *supra* note 9, at paras 11-64, 87; on the implementation generally, Cornish, W. R. (1989), 'Moral Rights under the 1988 Act', *EIPR*, **11** (12), 449 *et seq.*

[78]   Bently and Sherman, *supra* note 3, at pp. 232 *et seq.*, with further references.

[79]   Ginsburg, J. (1990), 'Moral Rights in a Common Law System', *Ent. LR*, **1** (4), 121, 129: 'One may draw this lesson from the CDPA: in countries lacking a moral rights tradition, where legislators and copyright industries remain hostile to the premises of moral rights, enactment of a general statute may not effect substantial improvements, and may well do those rights more harm than good. I doubt that the UK legislators were more persuaded than are US legislators of the benefits of a general system of moral rights. Were we in the US now to enact an overall moral rights bill, it might well reveal the same kinds of shortcomings. Moreover, it may be harder to repair the damage done by a half-hearted statute, than to continue to work slowly towards real guarantees.'

side are essentially based on the utilitarian concept of common law copyright that it is difficult to combine with the elements from continental Europe.[80]

Despite the differences in the dogmatic approaches as compared with the European system[81] – whose natural law approach focuses on the author[82] – the question still arises whether in reality the two are in fact so different.

Moreover, is the grant of new economic rights merely intended to act as a means to the end of bolstering the economic power wielded by the copyright industry, while the interests of the real creators of works have scarcely been taken into account? In considering this question, one should particularly note that the latest rights to be introduced – above all the legal protection of techno-logical measures – obviously do not improve the creator's position. Such reme-dies further maintain the interests of the exploiter of the rights who, for instance, wishes to avoid losses from private copying. Regardless of these facts, the European Directive on Copyright in the Information Society proclaims in one consideration: 'A rigorous, effective system for the protection of copyright and related rights is one of the main ways of ensuring that European cultural creativity and production receive the necessary resources and of safeguarding the independence and dignity of artistic creators and performers'.[83] However, these new rights are nothing other than tools in the hands of the industry.

Therefore we should accept that there are three conflicting interests[84] that

---

[80]   Bently and Sherman, *supra* note 3, at p. 233, with further references.

[81]   On the relationship between the two systems, see generally Bently and Sherman, *supra* note 3, at pp. 29–30; Strowel, Alain (1993), *Copyright et Droit d'Auteur: Convergences et Divergences*, Brussels, Belgium: Bruylant, pp. 130 *et seq.*; in the context of the influence of European law-making, Bently and Sherman, *supra* note 3, at p. 44, and at p. 115 with reference to the concept of 'authorship'.

[82]   The author-centred aspect of copyright law is still animated today in the theory of the *droit d'auteur* approach, even if in practice it is of no more than marginal impor-tance in comparison with those commercial aspects of copyright which shaped copy-right from the very beginning. See Loewenheim, Ulrich (2003), 'Gegenstand, Zweck und Bedeutung des Urheberrechts', in U. Loewenheim (ed.), *supra* note 3, at para. 1 note 4-7; Schack, *supra* note 24, at paras 2 *et seq.*; for a critical view, Hilty, R.M. (2003), 'Urheberrecht in der Informationsgesellschaft: Wer will was von wem woraus? – Ein Auftakt zum "zweiten Korb"', *ZUM*, **47** (special issue), 983–1006. On the differences between the *droit d'auteur* and the copyright system see Strowel, *supra* note 81, passim; for a historical view see Ginsburg, J. (1990), 'A Tale of two Copyrights: Literary Property in Revolutionary France and America', *Tulane Law Review*, **64** (5), 991.

[83]   Recital 11 of the Directive on Copyright and Related Rights in the Information Society.

[84]   At first sight, this realisation appears profanatory, but is still hardly consid-ered in the discussion concerning the effects of exceptions on the author's interests. Nevertheless, the question of the lawfulness of statutory licences is being posed. In the USA, a whole range of proposals are currently being discussed that suggest that non-commercial file-sharing in peer-to-peer networks should be permitted using statutory

we have to distinguish.[85] The borderline between conflicting interests runs not so much between creators and consumers as greatly emphasised by the traditional perception of copyright. The very discrepancy, however, arises from the fact that the exploiting copyright industry wants to optimise its profits by all possible means at its disposal, while the end consumer wants to pay as little as possible to have access to and use of the copyright-protected works.[86]

---

licences combined with an obligation to pay a fee. See, with in part substantial differences in the details, for instance Lunney, G.S. (2001), 'The Death of Copyright: Digital Technology, Private Copying, and the Digital Millennium Copyright Act', *Virginia Law Review*, **87**, 813, 910–18; Shih Ray Ku, R. (2002), 'The Creative Destruction of Copyright: Napster and the New Economics of Digital Technology', *University of Chicago Law Review*, **69** (1), 263, 311–15; *idem* (2003), 'Consumers and Creative Destruction: Fair Use beyond Market Failure', *Berkeley Technology Law Journal*, **18** (2), 539, 566 note 160; Jacover, A. (2002), 'I Want My MP3! Creating a Practical and Legal Scheme to Combat Copyright Infringement on Peer-to-Peer Internet Applications', *Georgetown Law Journal*, **90** (6), 2207, 2250–4; Netanel, N.W. (2003), 'Impose a Noncommercial Use Levy to Allow Free Peer-to-Peer File Sharing', *Harvard Journal of Law and Technology*, **17** (1), 1, 4, 35–59; Fisher, Terry (2004), *Promises to Keep: Technology, Law, and the Future of Entertainment*, Stanford, US: Stanford University Press, pp. 199 *et seq.*; Lessig, *supra* note 12, at pp. 298, 301; Litman, J. (2003) 'Sharing and Stealing', http://ssrn.com/abstract=472141, pp. 33–42. On the compatibility of such proposals with the three-step test, see Peukert, Alexander (2005), 'International Copyright Law and Proposals for Non-Voluntary Licenses Regarding P2P File Sharing', in Grosheide, F.W. and J.J. Brinkhof (eds), *Intellectual Property Law 2004. Articles on Crossing Borders between Traditional and Actual*, Antwerp, Belgium *et al.*: Intersentia, pp. 439 *et seq.* In German literature, the importance of a statutory entitlement to a fee in the digital world is emphasised by Wittgenstein, Phillip (2000), *Die digitale Agenda der WIPO-Verträge*, Berne, Switzerland: Stämpfli, p. 162; Wandtke, A. (2000), 'Copyright und virtueller Markt in der Informationsgesellschaft – oder das Verschwinden des Urhebers im Nebel der Postmoderne', *GRUR*, **49** (1), 7; Freiwald, Sven (2004), *Die private Vervielfältigung im digitalen Kontext am Beispiel des Filesharing*, Baden-Baden, Germany: Nomos, pp. 187–9. Reference is made here to this discussion. The focus should, of course, be on the usual failure to distinguish between the effects felt by the artistic creators on the one hand and those felt by the exploiters on the other hand. But see, for instance, Peukert, A. (2004), 'Besprechung: Gounalakis, Georgios: Elektronische Kopien für Unterricht und Forschung (§ 52a UrhG) im Lichte der Verfassung', *UFITA*, (2), 566 *et seq.*, and Geiger, *supra* note 58, at 366–80.

    85   Cf. on the interests involved, Hilty, *supra* note 82, 985 *et seq.*; Cornish and Llewelyn, *supra* note 9, at paras 9-42 *et seq.*; and, in detail, Geiger, *supra* note 3, at notes 19–97.

    86   An interesting account of the relationship between competing interests within copyright law is provided by Ginsburg, J. (2002), 'How Copyright Got a Bad Name for Itself', *Columbia Journal of Law and the Arts*, **26** (1), 61–2: 'I have a theory about how copyright got a bad name for itself, and I can summarize it in one word: Greed. Corporate greed and consumer greed. Copyright owners, generally perceived to be large, impersonal and unlovable corporations . . . have eyed enhanced prospects for

As a result, if there are essentially three different positions that must all be taken into account in terms of their significance, and if the author's interests are occasionally identical with those of another party involved, there must, consequently, be important reasons if the conflicting interests of a third party are not pushed to the side. Such an interaction between different interests appears to be the case for those exceptions that entitle a third party to use a work while at the same time ensuring a payment to the author that he would otherwise not receive.[87]

Alongside this clarification of the situation of the various interests, we must necessarily also finally abandon an illusion, namely that the continuous expansion of rights to prohibit can provide the author with what we want to give him namely ' ensuring . . . cultural creativity'.[88] The assertion of a right to prohibit does not automatically provide the author with remuneration, but a claim to remuneration can do so, under certain circumstances – namely if the remuneration is necessarily subject to collective collection and if the author is necessarily entitled to a share.

Seen realistically, such statutory licences, of course, only make sense under certain factual conditions. They are primarily justified where a use escapes the power of disposal of a (derivative) beneficiary, where the claim to remuneration established instead of a right to prohibit is subject to an obligation to exploit – for it is here that the author necessarily participates in the remuneration – which in turn presupposes that the use takes place in a sector where the market for individual licences fails because of the mass of demand (or possibly also of rightholders).

At first sight, the argument for market failure could be countered by the possibility, already discussed, of the use of technical protection and control mechanisms, but this view fails to convince for two reasons. Firstly – at least to date – the artistic creator is rarely the one who is actually able (or even willing) to use these mechanisms, which are instead used by the exploiter; accordingly, the artistic creator is still dependent on the contractual relationship with the exploiter. Secondly, market failure cannot be interpreted merely as a

---

global earnings in an increasingly international copyright market. Accordingly, they have urged and obtained ever more protective legislation that extends the term of copyright and interferes with the development and dissemination of consumer-friendly copying technologies . . . Greed, of course, runs both ways. Consumers, for their part, have exhibited an increasing rapacity in acquiring and "sharing" unauthorized copies of music, and more recently, motion pictures.'

[87]   A conflict with the general interest tends to occur less in the relationship with the author than in the relationship with the exploiter. See also Geiger, *supra* note 3, at note 44 *et seq.*; Hilty, *supra* note 82, at 986 f. and 989 *et seq.* as also 999 *et seq.*

[88]   Recital 11 of the Directive on Copyright and Related Rights in the Information Society.

purely commercial problem; on the contrary, such failure can also be found in the non-existence of sufficient journalistic competition, while the insufficient pluralism of opinion is also testimony to a system that does not function properly.[89] Irrespective of these arguments, the problem of TPMs would not arise if the enforcement of the exceptions prevailed over them.[90]

3.5.   *International law and the three-step test*

It goes without saying that such demands made of the legislature cannot ignore the question whether exceptions to protect the needs of the information society are at all compatible with current international law – in particular the 'three-step test' contained in Art. 10 of the WCT and (with restrictions) in Art. 9(2) of the Berne Convention (and similarly in Art. 16(2) of the WPPT for the holders of related rights). In this context, in the light of European law, the question arises whether the prevailing view is correct, namely that the list of exceptions is to be regarded as exhaustive;[91] if so, the 'three-step test' likewise reproduced in Art. 5(5) of the Directive no doubt ultimately only has declaratory significance.[92] However, there is no need to go into further depth in this discussion here, since the considerations made here in any event require a revision of European law, and because corresponding new exceptions would be in conflict with the current Directive.

---

[89]   As an example, we can cite press monitoring services, a market that, in the light of the number of titles to be taken into account, can contribute significantly to a variety of opinion given that hardly any enterprise is capable of maintaining an overview over all these titles. While there are no exceptions that apply to this market in Germany (the case cited in note 3 only concerns in-company press reviews), Switzerland – with a system that is not incompatible with European law – permits such exceptions (Art. 19(1) c in conjunction with Art. 2 of the Copyright Act) with an obligation to exploit (Art. 20(4) Copyright Act.) In the absence of corresponding exceptions, Presse-Monitor Deutschland GmbH and Co. KG (PMG), a merger of around 175 newspaper and magazine publishers, is basically able to control the market on the basis of its unlimited exclusive rights (acquired derivatively) while the Swiss Argus der Presse AG is an independent company that can take account of all publishing products thanks to the statutory exceptions. The consequence is obvious. While PMG deals with a total of around 600 titles without a third party being able to penetrate the market, Argus, subject to competitive conditions, monitors 2,500 titles with a fraction of the market.

[90]   See above section 3.1.

[91]   In any event according to Recital 32 of the Directive on Copyright in the Information Society.

[92]   Recital 44 is restricted to the obligation to apply this test '. . . when applying the exceptions and limitations'. For a discussion of the scope of the three-step test, see in particular Senftleben, Martin (2004), *Copyright, Limitations and the Three-step Test*, The Hague, Netherlands et al.: Kluwer; specifically on the application in the English legal system, *ibid.*, at pp. 67 *et seq.* and 165–6, where he sets out the similarity to the 'fair dealing' system; for further references, see Hilty, *supra* note 57, at 343 *et seq.*

In fact, the signatory states to the most recent international copyright agreement, the WCT,[93] were fully aware of the need 'to introduce new international rules and clarify the interpretation of certain existing rules in order to provide adequate solutions to the questions raised by new economic, social, cultural and technical developments' in order to 'maintain a balance between the rights of authors and the larger public interest, particularly education, research and access to information'.[94] And it is because of this, and not only because of the objective reasons set out above, that the EU Directive cannot seriously be regarded as the cleverest of all solutions, particularly since the virtually 'violent' intervention in the balance of interests in favour of the exploiter contained in Art. 6(4) subparagraph 4 of the Directive was by no means a requirement of Art. 11 of the WCT – quite the contrary: the international regulation covers, without making any differentiation, only 'acts . . . which are not authorised by the authors concerned or permitted by law' – hence for which no statutory exception has been provided.

With the discussion on the admissibility of corresponding exceptions being conducted against this background, an indeed encouraging picture results if account is taken of the fact that the interests described above[95] of (creative) authors and – derivatively entitled – exploiters need by no means be identical. In the following, attention is therefore addressed to the – in part merely assumed – limits to the three-step test.

The Preamble of the WCT – going beyond TRIPS (which repeats the Berne Convention plus a number of extensions) – indeed recognises that there is a 'need to maintain a balance between the rights of authors and the larger public interest, particularly education, research and access to information'. At the same time, Art. 10 of the Treaty extends the three-step test intended in Art. 9(2) of the Berne Convention[96] only for acts of reproduction, to all limitations of or exceptions to copyright protection,[97] thereby complying with Art. 13 of TRIPS.[98]

---

93 WIPO Copyright Treaty of 20 December 1996.
94 According to the Preamble to the WCT.
95 See above section 3.4.
96 Revised Berne Convention dated 9 September 1886 in the Paris version dated 24 July 1971.
97 With the agreed declaration on Art. 10 of the WCT, para. 2, laying down that the scope of application of the exceptions and limitations permitted under the Berne Convention are neither reduced nor extended by Art. 10(2) of the WCT.
98 TRIPS Agreement dated 15 April 1994. The same applies to performing artists and producers of phonograms pursuant to Art. 16 of the WPPT (WIPO Performances and Phonograms Treaty dated 20 December 1996), which, however, will not be examined separately here. On this first inclusion, see for instance Bornkamm, Joachim (2002), 'Der Dreistufentest als urheberrechtliche Schrankenbestimmung', in Ahrens, H.J., J. Bornkamm and W. Gloy (eds), *Festschrift für Willi Erdmann*, Cologne, Germany: Heymanns, p. 41.

According to these international law requirements, a statutory licence (a) must be related to certain special cases, (b) must not be in conflict with the normal exploitation of the work and (c) must not prejudice the legitimate interests of the author.[99] The general opinion is that this imposes a corresponding limit on the scope of national (and European) legislation.[100]

(a)   First step: certain special cases   However, not even the meaning of the first step is beyond doubt. Admittedly, it is probably clear that the term 'certain' prevents a global introduction of statutory licences; in terms of rights, however, any individual constellation would be permissible. In contrast, theory applies both a qualitative and a quantitative approach to the term 'special case'; 'qualitatively' applies to the question whether the exception need at all serve the public interest.[101]

---

[99]   In general on this topic, see for instance Ficsor, Mihály (2002), *The Law of Copyright and the Internet – The WIPO Treaties, their Interpretation and Implementation*, Oxford, UK: Oxford University Press, pp. 284 *et seq.* (RBÜ) and 515 *et seq.* (WCT); *idem* (2002), 'How Much of What ? The Three-Step Test and its Application in Two Recent WTO Dispute Settlement Cases', *RIDA*, (192), 111 *et seq.* (RBÜ, TRIPS, WCT/WPPT); Gervais, Daniel (1998), *The TRIPS Agreement: Drafting History and Analysis*, London, UK: Sweet & Maxwell, pp. 89 *et seq.* (TRIPS); Reinbothe, Jörg (2000), 'Beschränkungen und Ausnahmen von den Rechten im WIPO-Urheberrechtsvertrag', in Tades, H. *et al.* (eds), *Festschrift Robert Dittrich*, Vienna, Austria: Manz, pp. 255 *et seq.* (WCT/WPPT); Reinbothe, Jörg and Silke von Lewinski (2002), *The WIPO Treaties 1996 – The WIPO Copyright Treaty and the WIPO Performances and Phonograms Treaty – Commentary and Legal Analysis*, London, UK: Butterworths, pp. 127 *et seq.* (WCT/WPPT); Ricketson, S. (1999), 'The Boundaries of Copyright: Its Proper Limitations and Exceptions: International Conventions and Treaties', *IPQ*, (1), 69 ff. (RBÜ), 80 ff. (TRIPS) und 86 ff. (WCT); Lucas, A. (2001), 'Le "triple test" de l'article 13 de l'Accord ADPIC à la lumières du rapport du Groupe spécial de l'OMC "Etats-Unis – Article 110 5) de la Loi sur le droit d'auteur"', in Peter Ganea, Christopher Heath and Gerhard Schricker, *Urheberrecht Gestern – Heute – Morgen – Festschrift für Adolf Dietz*, München, Germany: Beck, p. 423 (TRIPS). See also the following references.

[100]   For details of the order of priority see as an example of many, Katzenberger, Paul (1999), 'Vor §§ 120ff. UrhG', in Gerhard Schricker (ed.), *Urheberrecht. Kommentar*, Munich, Germany: Beck, note 118. See also Bornkamm, *supra* note 98, at pp. 40 *et seq.*; Dreier, Thomas (2004), 'Vor §§ 44a ff. UrhG', in Thomas Dreier and Gernot Schulze (eds), *Urheberrechtsgesetz. Kommentar*, Munich, Germany: Beck, note 21; Duggal, Raoul (2001), *TRIPS-Übereinkommen und internationales Urheberrecht*, Cologne, Germany: Heymanns, p. 103; Katzenberger, P. (1995), 'TRIPS und das Urheberrecht', *GRUR Int.*, **44** (6), 459; von Lewinski, S. (1997), 'Die WIPO-Verträge zum Urheberrecht und zu verwandten Schutzrechten vom Dezember 1996', *CR*, (7), 441.

[101]   See, each with further references, on the one hand WTO Panel (2000), 'WTO-Dokument WT/DS160/R', http://docsonline.wto.org/gen_search.asp?searchmode=simple, paras 6.108 *et seq.*, 6.105 and 6.111; on the other hand Reinbothe and

It is, of course, hardly likely that new statutory licences would fail at this first step.[102] Firstly, the scope of a statutory licence can be determined specifically depending on the preconditions of this first step. Secondly, all that is at issue here is a number of constellations in which – in the light of a qualitative approach (which in any event tends to convince in that the quantitative considerations placed to the fore by the WTO Panel[103] are taken into account in the other two steps) – not only the public interest, but in contrast even the interests of artistic creators, can be satisfied.

Against the background of the balancing of interests already discussed,[104] it would therefore not appear incompatible with the first step of the three-step test to restrict the free exercise of a user right by the exploiter – subject to the other steps – in such (special) cases in which the artistic creator receives a payment thanks to the lawfulness of a use and the associated collective assertion of rights.

(b)   Second step: no conflict with the normal exploitation of the work   The meaning of the second step is also disputed.[105] One opinion regards a statutory licence as being in conflict with the normal exploitation of the work if the

---

Lewinski, *supra* note 99, at p. 124; Senftleben, *supra* note 92, at pp. 133 *et seq.* and especially at pp. 138 *et seq.*; *idem* (2003), 'Digitales Kopieren im Spiegel des Dreistufentests: genügt die deutsche Regelung zur Privatkopie den Vorgaben des internationalen Rechts?', *CR*, (12), 916; Berger, C. (2004), 'Elektronische Pressespiegel und Informationsrichtlinie – Zur Vereinbarkeit einer Anpassung des § 49 UrhG an die Pressespiegel-Entscheidung des BGH mit Europäischem Urheberrecht', *CR*, (5), 364 *et seq.*

[102]   Generally still rejecting statutory licences, for instance Desbois, Henri, André Françon and André Kerever (1976), *Les conventions internationales du droit d'auteur et des droits voisins*, Paris, France: Dalloz, p. 207; with a detailed discussion, Senftleben, *supra* note 92, at p. 129. See also Frotz, Gerhard (1986), 'Zum Vervielfältigungsrecht des Urhebers und zu den konventionskonformen nationalen Beschränkungen – Ein Beitrag zur Fortentwicklung des Urheberrechts', in Robert Dittrich (ed.), Festschrift 50 Jahre Urheberrechtsgesetz, Vienna, Austria: Manz, p. 128.

[103]   The WTO Panel, *supra* note 100, para. 6.133, held that the exception in US copyright law for the public communication of works in business premises (Section 110(5)(B) of the US Copyright Act) failed the first step of the three-step test, since a 'substantial majority of eating and drinking establishments and close to half of retail establishments' would profit from the exception. Specifically against this quantitative approach, see Senftleben, *supra* note 92, at pp. 140–4. See also *idem* (2004), 'Die Bedeutung der Schranken des Urheberrechts in der Informationsgesellschaft und ihre Begrenzung durch den Dreistufentest', in Hilty and Peukert (eds), *supra* note 10, p. 178.

[104]   See above section 3.4.

[105]   See the overview in Senftleben, *supra* note 92, at pp. 168 *et seq.*; *idem*, *supra* note 101, at 916 *et seq.*, with further references.

rights it covers enter into competition[106] with the manner in which the rightholder could normally exploit the intangible property commercially in such a way that the rightholder is denied significant tangible economic benefits, although there are various gradations with respect to the impairment that is no longer permitted.[107] The other opinion argues that an exception is only in conflict with the normal exploitation of a work if copyright in fact covers such use.[108] In a further interpretation, it is even argued that there is only a conflict with normal exploitation if the exception denies the rightholder an actual or potential source of revenue that typically has considerable importance within the overall exploitation of the work in question.[109]

At this point, there are two elements that must not be left out of account. Firstly, the indeed important view – since upheld by the WTO Panel – that the denial of 'significant, tangible economic benefits' is not permissible, needs to make it clear that these benefits must be legitimate in the sense that it is not just any possible amount of proceeds from an exploitation based on a problematic monopoly from a competition law point of view that equally merits protection. In particular, it can be observed that the constellations of interest here as a rule concern second exploitations – for it is here, in the light of the impossibility of monitoring acts of use, that the route via the collective assertion of rights is to the fore – and it can rightly be argued that these possibilities of profit based on a type of 'leverage' are no longer part of 'normal' exploitation. It is a fact that second exploitations are often based on technical factors (created subsequently) such as possibilities for reproduction or distribution, to which the rightholder himself has not contributed. His interest in bringing such additional exploitations under his own control in the same way as the first exploitation is therefore hardly to be given any greater weight than that of the general public in profiting as much as possible from given technologies. The latter is all the more true in that the third step can in the specific case be used for this balancing of interests, and consequently the conceivable exceptions in which the legitimate interests of the rightholder extend to the second exploitation (e.g. because it is only there that the relevant value creation is possible) are still to be identified.

---

[106]   According to Senftleben it is here that there is a similarity to the 'fair dealing' system. Cf. Senftleben, *supra* note 92, at p. 70.

[107]   See WTO Panel, *supra* note 101, para 6.183; also, no doubt, Berger, *supra* note 101, at 365; tending to be even narrower, Bornkamm, *supra* note 98, at pp. 34 and 46.

[108]   Ricketson, Sam (2003), 'WIPO-Dokument SCCR/9/7', www.wipo.int/meetings/en/archive.jsp, p. 22; *idem* (1999), 'The Boundaries of Copyright: Its Proper Limitations and Exceptions: International Conventions and Treaties', *IPQ*, (1), pp. 70 and 92.

[109]   Senftleben, *supra* note 92, at pp. 180 *et seq.*; *idem, supra* note 101, at 918.

As a second element, there is the fact that the unilateral focus on the interests of the exploiter – based on the incorrect assumption that his interests are identical to those of the artistic creator – threatens to invert the meaning of the three-step test. If it is the case that the unrestricted assertion of the right to prohibit by the exploiter deprives the artistic creator of the proceeds from a possible second exploitation – while the introduction of a statutory licence with an obligation to exploit would at least allow him to participate pro rata in the proceeds – the second step of the three-step test practically requires the introduction of such statutory licences.

(c)   Third step: no unreasonable prejudice to the author's legitimate interests
These thoughts on the second step continue more intensively in the third step. The comprehensive balancing of interests now required is an even stronger argument for distinguishing between different rights and interests.

The demand for the protection of property is omnipresent in copyright. The legislature must balance different legally protected positions by taking account, in the guarantee of property, not only of the social element (in the present case no doubt in the sense of the 'public interest') that is recognised in the field of copyright, but also of the position of the freedom of opinion.[110]

This usual distinction is, of course, not sufficient. Instead, there is good cause at this point, contrary to the usual approach, for returning to the special feature of the tripolarity[111] of the interests to be taken into account in copyright. This tripolarity is characterised by the fact that the interests of the artistic creator do not necessarily correspond with those of an exploiter, that, however, at least in a monistic approach (i.e. in the absence of the transferability of copyright), both can ultimately rely on the protection of property. If the property guarantee of the artistic creator is taken seriously, the interests of the exploiter cannot be given comparatively greater weight. There is the additional factor that a conflict with the public interest tends to occur less in the relationship with the artistic creator than in the relationship with the exploiter.[112] For, what is threatening to discredit copyright in the current public perception – namely that undesirable monopoly structures (with corresponding pricing) can develop on the basis of protective rights within a framework of exploitation chains – usually takes place, as already described,[113] within the sphere of the exploiter.

A final argument in favour of the lawfulness of statutory licences – subject to remuneration – is that the prejudice to the legal position is systematically

---

[110]   See generally Davies, *supra* note 3, at paras 4-024 and 4-035.
[111]   See above section 3.4.
[112]   See also Geiger, *supra* note 3, at note 44 *et seq.*; Hilty, *supra* note 82, at 986 *et seq.*, 989 *et seq.* and 999 *et seq.*
[113]   See above section 3.3. and 3.4.

associated with compensation paid to the affected party. Admittedly, it cannot be assumed that this compensation is equivalent to the unrestricted right if copyright (without statutory licence) could be used as a lever to demand excessive prices where the statutory licences 'only' demand 'reasonable payment'. However, it is difficult to justify why this should be unlawful if the balancing of all the legally protected positions shows that (a) it is in the public interest to prevent the risk, potentially inherent in copyright law, of leverage effects that are undesirable from the point of view of social and competition policy and (b) it is precisely the statutory licence that ensures that the artistic creator benefits financially from a second exploitation.

The third step of the three-step test imposes further considerations. Firstly, it directs attention to the claim to payment – binding in the present constellation of statutory licences – as an important argument for the view that a statutory licence does not gratuitously prejudice legitimate interests.[114] Secondly, it explicitly identifies the party whose interests ought to be taken into account, a fact that, against the background that the interests of artistic creators and exploiters need not be identical, is not without significance.

The English, the French and the German versions of Art. 10 of the WCT take as their starting point for the third step the 'author', by which at least in origin is meant the artistic creator according to the wording of the Berne Convention – which distinguishes between the 'author' and any 'successor in title or other holder of exclusive user rights' (even if the protection granted according to Art. 2(6) can ultimately also be exercised by the latter). Where in contrast Art. 13 of TRIPS (like Art. 5(5) of the Directive on Copyright in the Information Society) speaks of the 'rightholder' (*Rechtsinhaber*, *détenteur/titulaire du droit*), this may be regarded as a reference to copyright countries which, like Great Britain,[115] know the approach of the 'work made

---

[114]   No doubt also Senftleben, *supra* note 92, at p. 130 and in greater depth at pp. 237 *et seq.*; Dreier, *supra* note 100, at note 21. See, already referring to the Berne Convention, Kerever, A. (1976), 'The International Copyright Conventions and Reprography', *Copyright*, **12** (7–8), 191; Masouyé, Claude (1978), *Guide de la Convention de Berne*, Geneva, Switzerland: WIPO, p. 63; Ricketson, Sam (1987), *The Berne Convention for Protection of Literary and Artistic Works*, London, UK: Kluwer, p. 484; more hesitantly, Reinbothe and Lewinski, *supra* note 99, at p. 127; Bornkamm, *supra* note 98, at pp. 47 *et seq.* See also decision of the Federal Supreme Court, *GRUR* 1999, 707, 712. The lawfulness of this approach is of course still occasionally disputed: Niemann, F. (2003), 'Pressespiegel de lege ferenda – Eine europa-, konventions- und verfassungsrechtliche Betrachtung nach BGH, Urteil von 11.7.2002 – I ZR 255/00 – Elektronischer Pressespiegel', *CR*, (2), 121; Ricketson, *supra* note 99, at p. 70.

[115]   Section 11 (2) CDPA 1988: 'Where a literary, dramatic, musical or artistic work is made by an employee in the course of his employment, his employer is the first owner of any copyright in the work subject to any agreement to the contrary'.

for hire'. It can, however, hardly be used to lead to the conclusion, at least for *droit d'auteur* countries, that after the right has being granted to an exploiter the author simply loses his (financial) protection. Even if this might appear worth considering where proprietary rights are transferable without restriction, and even if one argues in favour of complete freedom of contract – for if a legal position is abandoned, claims can no longer be asserted from a previous right based on general principles – this reduction would, at least from a German perspective, conflict with the notion of protection that is inherent in the monistic approach.[116]

If we conclude from this that the third step at least also takes account of the artistic creator's interests, it is difficult to avoid the following observations on the relationship between the artistic creator and the exploiter: statutory licences subject to remuneration of the kind discussed here are actually the first step towards enforcing the interests of the artistic creator within the framework of the collective assertion of rights, while the exploiter's interest in higher proceeds from exploitation (resulting from individual contracts) can hardly be regarded as 'legitimate' any longer if they (a) deprive the artistic creators of a remuneration of their own in the absence of a statutory licence and (b) no longer appear to be a 'reasonable' burden on the general public as is required within the framework of fee-based statutory licences.

We should, however, also recall at this point that from a factual point of view the aim cannot be to subject all possible exploitation constellations to a statutory licence. The discussion here is conducted only on the assumption that individual licensing will lead to a failure of the – not necessary merely economic – market.[117] This would have a negative effect on the general public by for instance denying access (in reasonable form) to necessary information; however, as we have seen, it would ultimately also be to the detriment of the artistic creator, who would be deprived of possible revenue.

3.6. Interim conclusion

Under all aspects, the focus regularly returns to the problem that the usual approach of an opposition between 'the author' (irrespective of the question of who actually exercises the rights) and the general public amounts to an inadmissible reduction of the real situation. This provides cause to question certain traditional dogmas in copyright – even if they have been reflected in the field of international law in abbreviated form. For, if, as is correct, we assume a (potential) tripolar split in the interests, there is a need for a more differentiated

---

[116]   It is precisely in the light of German law that the many attempts to achieve a reasonable remuneration would be reduced to farce if the artistic creator were now to be left out of the three-step test.

[117]   See above section 3.4.

approach both in the light of the fundamental rights and in the light of the three-step test required by international law.

If in this connection we remember that the notion of the protection of the artistic creator is at the heart of all copyright considerations, it is difficult to avoid regarding the institution of the statutory licence – in suitable constellations – as an appropriate means of ensuring that he receives a reasonable income. That this also means that the general public or the beneficiaries of the statutory licence themselves are able to achieve consideration of their own interests can be regarded rather as a (more or less desirable) side effect than an objective.[118] This side effect is, of course, what is primarily perceived in the legal policy discussion, since it results in a potential conflict of interests between exploiters and consumers. Even if some attention is paid to this fact, the origin of copyright protection should nevertheless not be forgotten.

Admittedly, there might still be considerable need for a discussion and clarification particularly with respect to the scope of the new exceptions to the benefit of the information society in general and science in particular, there still being in part very diffuse notions with respect to the interests involved, notions that are apparently determined by markets other than the information market. Regarded unemotionally, the consideration set out in the introduction nevertheless no doubt shows the right approach: from the very start, copyright never pursued the aim of subjecting content to an exclusive legal position. On the contrary, it is precisely this content – and in particular the sensitive product 'information' – whose free availability has always been regarded with particular prudence.[119] However, even the problem cases discussed here, in which new exception regulations are regarded as necessary, only concern content and not the form of expression that allegedly is the sole subject matter of protection. Accordingly, the interest of (derivative) rightholders in comprehensive rights of prohibition as expressed in Art. 6(4) subparagraph 4 of the Directive on Copyright in the Information Society cannot be granted protection, since it would go beyond what copyright is intended to protect.

---

[118]   In this direction, but probably going even further, for instance Peukert, Alexander (2004), 'Der Schutzbereich des Urheberrechts und das Werk als öffentliches Gut', in Hilty and Peukert (eds), *supra* note 10, pp. 11, 44 *et seq.*: 'Urheberschutz als Nutzerschutz'.

[119]   Of interest is the reference in Geiger, Christophe (2004), 'Die Schranken des Urheberrechts im Lichte der Grundrechte', in Hilty and Peukert (eds), *supra* note 10, pp. 144 *et seq.*, that it was for this reason that the 18th century philosophers championed the cause of the recognition of intellectual property in order precisely to encourage the dissemination of the ideas of the Enlightenment, thereby ensuring access to information for the population.

4. Conclusions

If the interests of the information society, which the EU wishes to encourage and develop,[120] are interpreted in the true sense of the word – i.e. as a 'knowledge society' and hence also a knowledge-focused society – and if we refuse to be blinded by the very different problems of the culture and entertainment industry (as is almost exclusively the focus in public perception), it becomes apparent that a discussion about the appropriate form of national copyright has become shadow play. The Directive on Copyright on the Information Society is focused on European law in a way that largely deprives the national legislature of the necessary scope. In truth, however, the name of this Directive proves to be highly misleading, since it is not designed to meet the needs of an information society that is worthy of the name but entirely those of the culture industry. Admittedly, the changes faced by this trade as a result of modern technology might justify a certain degree of understanding; however, when its lobbying efforts go so far that the European legislature overlooks the most fundamental national economic interests, the diagnosis is extremely worrying. There is an urgent need for a rapid adjustment, while for the moment there is no need to conduct fundamental discussions about the future structure of a modern and balanced copyright – although this will be unavoidable in the long term. Instead, it would be sufficient to concentrate on three core sectors in which the Directive on Copyright in the Information Society must be adjusted:

(1) Art 6(4) subparagraph 4 of the Directive – which globally abolishes the enforcement of exceptions against TPMs in the case of on-demand online services – must be deleted. It is a fact that this 'anticipatory obedience' on the part of the Europeans is not only not required by any international legal provision; nor is it in any way in the interests of the European economy – not even in the entertainment sector, in which the European Union appears to be highly dependent on imports.[121] There may admittedly be a need for specific protection in selective areas; however, these do not justify general solutions. Instead, such needs should be investigated very precisely in advance, and there is a need for an objective analysis and decision on whether the alleged risk to individual legal positions actually justifies the annulment of certain – but by no means all – exceptions in the fields in question. The relevant field of information – at least scientific information – should not be called into question. No private interest ultimately aimed at the achievement of profit can outweigh the

---

[120]   Recital 2 of the Directive on Copyright in the Information Society.
[121]   On the market shares in the film sector see for instance; Hilty, R.M. (2003), 'Eldred v. Ashcroft: Die Schutzfrist im Urheberrecht – eine Diskussion, die auch Europäer interessieren sollte', *GRUR Int.*, **52** (3), 202 *et seq.*

significance of this sensitive commodity and its vital importance for the general public.

(2) Specific exceptions are vital for actual scientific or knowledge-relevant information in the sense that access to this information must be and must remain guaranteed under reasonable conditions, whatever the business model used. There may be a need for deeper discussion on the form of the details of such exceptions. In particular, one must not underestimate the fact that sufficient protective instruments must exist to the benefit of the commercial exploiters of such information so that the risks of investments being usurped by third parties (particularly for instance in the field of complex online media) can be mitigated. One might even consider the introduction of a separate legal protection in terms of a related right for publishers.

In fact, a justification of copyright that is based more on 'natural law' and on purely economic 'incentive' theories places the artistic creator at the centre of considerations. While, in contrast, the protection of the exploiter – as investor – may appear just as legitimate, since he needs an incentive to make investments in the exploitation of copyright works, attempts have been made since the 1960s – above all within the framework of the Rome Convention[122] – to take account of this idea by providing the investor with a separate (copyright) related right. This instrument – which if correctly interpreted would focus on competition and hence be less susceptible to abuse[123] – basically involves much more potential than its academic penetration so far suggests. In fact, it is generally ignored since it is much more interesting for the exploiter (as derivative beneficiary) to use the much broader copyright with its longer protected period.[124] In other

---

[122]   International Convention on the Protection of Performing Artists, the Producers of Phonograms and Broadcasting Enterprises dated 26 October 1961.

[123]   On these approaches, see Hilty, R.M. (1993), 'Zum urheberrechtlichen Leistungsschutz im schweizerischen Recht am Beispiel des Tonträgerproduzenten – Versuch einer dogmatischen Begründung', *GRUR Int.*, **42** (11), 818 *et seq.*; *idem* (1994), 'Die Leistungsschutzrechte im schweizerischen Urheberrechtsgesetz', *UFITA*, **124**, 127 *et seq.*; also Weber, R. (1996), 'Schutz von Datenbanken – ein neues Immaterialgüterrecht?', *UFITA*, **132**, 5 *et seq.*; *idem* (2003), 'Dritte Spur zwischen absoluten und relativen Rechten?', in Heinrich Honsell, Wolfgang Portmann, Roger Zäch and Dieter Zobl (eds), *Festschrift für Heinz Rey: Aktuelle Aspekte des Schuld- und Sachenrechts*, Zurich, Switzerland: Schulthess, pp. 583 *et seq.*

[124]   This strategy is both unjustified and old. The London book publishers attempted as long ago as 1774 to influence the development of the law, which was wavering between natural law and a utilitarian approach, to influence it in favour of the former by spreading a romantic and misty-eyed image of the author, in order ultimately to assert his rights for themselves. Cf. Burkitt, *supra* note 67, at 153 and 185; similarly Ganley, *supra* note 43, at 306 *et seq.*: 'For centuries authorship has proven to be a convenient rhetorical device to allow publishers to colour their claims for stronger copyright protection'.

words, if copyright is increasingly returned to its origins, the protection of the artistic creator, deciding 'against' the exploiter in the event of a conflict of interests between him and the artistic creator does not necessarily mean that the exploiter is without protection. On the contrary, he will be required to mobilise the collection of protective instruments originally intended for his benefit and that constitute the answer to his investment – even if the development of the law is admittedly still in progress here, as is shown by the (ultimately system-contrary[125]) lack of a related right for the publisher.

This protective right to be introduced should, however, not be provided alongside the present (derivative) protection resulting from copyright, but instead as its replacement, in order to prevent information as such becoming a monopoly right. In other words the protection of the exploiters must aim at allowing them to act under comparable competitive conditions amongst each other, and consequently be in the form of actual competitor protection; however, under no circumstances should it go so far that it in any way prevents the intended use of what is at issue, i.e. (scientific) information of itself. In the light of the ever inherent risk of access to information being made difficult or impossible because of excessive needs for protection, account will also have to be taken of the fact that adjustment instruments going beyond copyright will have to be applied. If current antitrust law proves to be too cumbersome in many cases, the introduction of specific misuse constellations could be conceivable, the aim of which would have to be to provide access to specific unlawfully retained information in very rapid and inexpensive proceedings.

(3) Finally, copyright must take account of the real conditions in the information society, and it must not impede the advantages of a society based on the division of labour, as specifically results from specialisation. Against this background, there is no avoiding the introduction of exceptions to the benefit of third parties who at least indirectly (although they may be acting directly in their own profit-making interests) offer services in the interests of the general public, such as information brokers or the providers of added-value services. It goes without saying that such use of copyright works must be paid for appropriately;[126] this – but only this, given the state of the general public's

---

125   Cf. on the background, Hilty, R.M. (1991), 'Gedanken zum Schutze der nachbarrechtlichen Leistung – einst, heute und morgen', *UFITA*, **116**, 24, 40 *et seq.*

126   Although the division of the income obtained between the original and the derivative rightholders is a different topic that the EU would have good reasons for addressing; for details see Hilty, *supra* note 60, 826 *et seq.*, with further references. However, this is not part of the immediate context of the Directive on Copyright in the Information Society, but rather belongs in the context of the – inappropriate – Commission Recommendation 2005/737/EC concerning the licensing of music for

interest – is also required by the three-step test under international law. To exclude such services a priori, as the Directive on Copyright in the Information Society does, is in conflict with the economic interests of Europe and ultimately proves to be a slap in the face for the oft-cited information society.

---

the internet dated 18 October 2005 (OJ L 276 dated 21 October 2005, 54 *et seq.*) and generally the exploitation right in Europe. See Peukert, A. and A. Kur (2006), 'Stellungnahme des Max-Plank-Instituts für Geistiges Eigentum, Wettbewerbs- und Steuerrecht zur Umsetzung der Richtlinie 2004/48/EG zur Durchsetzung der Rechte des geistigen Eigentums in deutsches Recht', *GRUR Int.*, **55** (4), 292 *et seq.*

14 Copyright and freedom of expression in Sweden – private law in a constitutional context

Jan Rosén[1]

1. Introduction

Copyright and freedom of expression, freedom of speech in American law, are two legal phenomena with quite a lot in common, but they also carry a built-in dichotomy. Looking at Swedish law, their common/mutual features are indicated by the fact that copyright or, rather, authors' rights, had its legal breakthrough within the framework of constitutionally protected freedom of expression already in the basic Freedom of the Press Act, forming a part of the Government Form of 1809.[2] Both copyright and freedom of expression, can also be seen as a common designation of respect for the creative man's need to express himself, for the individual results of human creativity and the basic right to express it publicly. The personality rights side of authors' rights, moral rights or *droit moral*, also stresses, just like freedom of speech, a respect for an individual way of exposing thoughts in a literary or artistic form. It is true to some extent, as some would have it, that copyright is the engine of free expression.

The conflict is just as overt, as one person's right to express himself must, per definition, be limited by another person's copyright in the very form which is used for a public speech. If someone in his public address wants to expose someone else's expression there is inevitably a conflict between his right to express himself and the rights in what is expressed or, rather, the forms of what is expressed. There is nothing weird in this. Freedom of expression, while constitutionally stronger in Sweden than possibly in any other country in the world, is on closer inspection subject to a long line of limitations, which are not of a copyright nature, like those following from rules on secrecy, norms about defamation and other forms of illicit expression

---

[1]   LLD, Professor of Private Law, Law Faculty, Stockholm University.

[2]   See G.W.F. Karnell, 'Sweden', § 1, in M.B. Nimmer & P.E.Geller (eds.), *International Copyright Law and Practise*, Vol. 2, 1996. Cf. G. Petri, *Upphovsrätten och dess intressenter, Svenska Föreningen för Upphovsrätt 50 år*, Stockholm, 2004, p. 33 et seq.

or other acts of making public what should remain unpublished. Thus, copyright as a limitation on freedom of expression cannot be denied as a matter of principle.

It is certainly of interest to study more closely how this conflict, merely hinted at so far, between authors' rights and freedom of expression has been legally resolved in Sweden and to test, if valid at all, how constitutionally protected freedom of expression, i.e. as a form of fundamental law, may in fact break into the realm of private law, thus within the framework of exclusive use rights. However, some would rather describe this as an *internal* copyright issue, while others argue for the benefit of an *external* solution. As for the former, it may be claimed that the antagonism, if there is one, could be solved within copyright as a result of copyright's separation between idea and form, internationally known as the idea/expression dichotomy, following on from copyright's denial of protection for figures, facts, items of information or ideas in a general sense, thus offering protection merely for the way in which something has been expressed, thus in an original literary or artistic expression. If so, it is claimed, there isn't really a conflict between someone's right to express ideas and thoughts publicly and someone else's exclusive rights in the content of a work in its individualised form.

It is also often assumed that the 'conflict' is softened considerably by all those limitations to the exclusive rights of an author spelt out directly in the Swedish Copyright Act, in a way usually to be found in any national legislation on copyright that is comparable to the Swedish or Nordic Copyright Acts. Rules on quotations from protected works, on free display of news items, on the use of materials from public debates or for educational purposes, or to make available to the public official documents or to accomplish other forms of important informative activities with protected works, are ordinary and common examples of such limitations found in most copyright acts. Generally speaking, in Europe such limitations tend to be explicit, exhaustive and narrowly interpreted by the courts, whereas economic rights are generally drafted in flexible and open terms.

But it is also claimed that the conflict should be submitted to an external solution, basically flowing from the fact that two legal entities are opposing each other, whereby the general legal hierarchy should rank copyright and freedom of expression on different levels of precedence. The result of this would follow from how freedom of expression has been fostered constitutionally, which may vary from one country to the other. In this context it may also be examined whether the courts have found their way by using one model or the other, if and when the question has been brought to the judge's table. Also in this respect the Swedish situation will be considered somewhat below.

2. The international scene – copyright as a basic human right or as a commodity?

As has already been noted, national constitutional solutions for copyright, as well as freedom of expression, vary considerably even among countries normally fully comparable as far as legal phenomena are concerned. As an example this is true also among the Nordic countries, in spite of their long history of joint efforts to harmonise legislation. However, something strikingly characteristic of the 20th century, international treaties were drafted with a focus on basic human freedoms and rights, among which authors' rights are expressly mentioned, for instance, in the same context as freedom of expression and the annexed freedom of information.[3] Hereby, it is hardly a conflict between independent figures, but rather a question of interaction between them and an exposure of the idea that respect for freedom of expression cannot be upheld without respect for anybody's literary or artistic creativity, thus as a basic human right.

A most prominent example of the aforesaid is Article 27 of the United Nations Declaration on Human Rights of 10 December, 1948 (UNDHR).[4] It is focussed *inter alia* on the rights of anybody to *share* in the creativity of others – a kind of right to be informed and to enjoy artistic results – which is connected directly to any individual person's *rights* in the results of his or her literary and artistic creations.

Article 27 UNDHR reads:

> Everyone has the right freely to participate in the cultural life of the community, to enjoy the arts and to share in scientific advancement and its benefits.

This position is immediately followed by a statement concerning authors' rights in Article 27 (2):

> Everyone has the right to the protection of the moral and material interests resulting from any scientific, literary or artistic production of which he is the author.

It is of some interest that the Scandinavian countries, among others, in the wake of positions taken by the USA and United Kingdom, initially opposed the adoption of Article 27 (2), formulated as quoted above, namely as concerns the rights of authors and inventors in the works and considering the potential strength of the first paragraph of Article 27. How could the declaration endorse the rights of everyone to enjoy the arts and to share in scientific

---

3   See A. Kerever, 'Authors' Rights are Human Rights', *Copyright Bulletin*, 32/1999, p. 18 et seq.
4   See http://www.un.org/Overview/rights.html.

advancements of others, i.e. the results of individual human creativity, at the same time as it promotes the protection for intellectual property?[5] Obviously, Article 27 (1) concerns freedom of information to the same extent as it concerns freedom of expression. At the time when the UNDHR was drafted it was characteristic of the North American point of view, probably also valid for the Scandinavian approach, to oppose consumer interest to the benefit of purely authoritarian interests.[6] Eventually, attitudes have probably changed in favour of more mercantile and utilitarian interests, primarily within the framework of the activities of the World Trade Organization, further observed below. Still, the breakthrough of copyright, and to some extent also of other forms of intellectual property, as a basic form of human right in the UNDHR was eventually endorsed by United Nations' so-called Covenant on Economic, Social and Cultural Rights of 16 December 1966, explicitly mentioning intellectual property rights.[7]

Article 15(1)(c) of the Covenant reads:

> The States Parties to the present Covenant recognize the right of everyone … to benefit from the protection of the moral and material interests resulting from any scientific, literary or artistic production of which he is the author.

Here, copyright is not directly expressed as a human right, but rather as a natural limitation on freedom of expression. However, it is generally contended that the fundamental basis for copyright may be construed both from the so-called 'property clause' of Article 1 of the First Protocol to the European Convention on Human Rights (ECHR) and from the 'privacy clause' of Article 8 ECHR.[8]

Some have conceived Article 27 (1) as a basis for the freedom of everyone to be constructive – a true freedom of creativity – which is not exactly the same as freedom of expression or information. The former phenomenon isn't primarily a political right or a freedom to express an opinion, as freedom of expression naturally is, although freedom of creativity may be seen as a

---

[5]   See F. Dessemontet, *Copyright and Human Rights, Intellectual Property and Information Law, Essays in Honour of Herman Cohen Jehoram*, The Hague, London, Boston, 1998, p. 113 et seq.

[6]   Cf. P. Goldstein, *Copyright's Highway: From Gutenberg to the Celestial Jukebox*, New York, 1994, p. 168 et seq.

[7]   See http://www.unhchr.ch/html/menu3/b/a_cescr.htm. The Covenant's entry into force occurred on 3 January 1976.

[8]   See P.B. Hugenholtz, 'Copyright and Freedom of Expression in Europe', in Rochelle Cooper Dreyfuss, Harry First and Diane Leheer Zimmerman (eds), *Innovation Policy in an Information Age*, Oxford, 2000; cf. Kerever, op. cit., note 3 supra, at p. 18 et seq.

condition of unfettered use of the freedom of expression. On the level of exclusive rights, freedom of creativity connects rather to the question of how private law should be shaped in order to handle a creative person's need to borrow creative elements from the factual results of another author. This is a very specific question, shaped by its own logic and framing. When authors' rights are confronted with freedom of expression and information, it is more natural to evaluate the well-tested idea–expression dichotomy, whereby the answer follows from whether a use merely concerns facts, figures and material ideas of a work, or if the use relates to the form of the work, its original expression.

It may be noticed here that copyright has actually not much to say about those cases when someone's protected work is affected by a later creation emanating from another author. Probably it is fair to say that copyright, construed as it normally is in all comparable countries, is not very concerned with some kind of priority order in such 'lending' cases. The simple reason seems to be that an author's natural creative incentive is generally assumed to enhance originality, what makes it unnecessary to specify and regulate in detail the needs of later authors to copy (parts of) works already created by others. However, some would probably assume that all forms of the creative process are built on the steps of an endless stairway, where a form of dependency is always relevant between something just created and an earlier created object of a literary or artistic nature. But this type of problem is typically solved by exercising the notion of an author's literary or artistic work, in particular the rudimentary rules on adaptations, either in free connection with another work or as dependent on it, setting aside that a number of legal limitations typically offers nuances to the picture, such as the right to quote, to report on news and to use material for research and study.

The status of copyright as a basic human right and its linkage in this respect to freedom of expression is somewhat more precisely demonstrated in the European Convention on Human Rights, signed in Rome, 4 November 1950, ECHR, which was incorporated extensively in Swedish law.[9] Under the heading of 'Freedom of Expression' Article 10 ECHR reads as follows:[10]

(1)   Everyone has the right to freedom of expression. This right shall include freedom to hold opinions and to receive and impart information and ideas without interference by public authority and regardless of frontiers. This article shall not prevent States from requiring the licensing of broadcasting, television or cinema enterprises.

---

[9]   Lag (1994:1219) om den europeiska konventionen angående skydd för de mänskliga rättigheterna och de grundläggande friheterna.

[10]   There is a fairly new official translation into Swedish, valid as SFS 1998:712, based on this text in English.

(2)   The exercise of these freedoms, since it carries with it duties and responsibilities, may be subject to such formalities, conditions, restrictions or penalties as are prescribed by law and are necessary in a democratic society, in the interest of national security or public safety, for the prevention of disorder or crime, for the protection of health and morals, for the protection of the reputation or *rights of others*, for preventing the disclosure of information received in confidence, or for maintaining the authority and impartiality of the judiciary. (Emphasis added)

Obviously, the ECHR does not expressly define copyright as a human right, as Article 10 expresses it rather as a natural limitation to freedom of expression. Neither the European Court nor the EC Commission has knowingly ever tested the status of authors' rights in this sense. Still, it has repeatedly been claimed that the fundamental basis for the recognition of copyright would be construed both from the so-called 'property clause' of Article 1 of the First Protocol to the ECHR, from 20 March 1952, and from the 'privacy clause', protection of private life or family life, of Article 8 ECHR.[11] Probably, it is quite generally assumed that copyright is a basic human right also according to the ECHR.

The internationally valid picture of copyright has been somewhat blurred, though, due to mercantile and utilitarian trends in recent years affecting intellectual property *in corpore* on the world stage of trade relations. Ever since the World Trade Organization (WTO) became interested in matters concerning intellectual property (IP) law, its TRIPS Agreement from 1996 has been the basis for actions primarily in the Third World against commercialisation of pirate goods. But the TRIPS Agreement also shows IP rights as market commodities and as an instrument for exchanging techniques and know-how.[12] The EU as well as its member states are parties to the TRIPS Agreement, and so are many more countries.[13] The TRIPS Agreement tries in this respect to turn authors' rights into a tasty dish for members of governments as well as consumers, alas by having it equated to trade marks and patents.

The trade-oriented or utilitarian stamp on the solutions chosen in the TRIPS Agreement breaks through in Article 7, the 'Objectives' clause, a 'should'

---

[11]   Cf. again Hugenholtz, op. cit., note 8 supra.

[12]   See generally on the WTO and the application of the TRIPS Agreement, T. Seth, *WTO och den internationella handelsordningen*, Stockholm, 2004. Cf. J. Rosén, 'North–South, Open Source och Creative Commons – en vägande kritik mot immaterialrätten?' *NIR*, 1/2006, p. 2 et seq.

[13]   On TRIPS and a copyright-oriented approach, see T. Dreier and B.P. Hugenholtz, *Concise European Copyright Law*, The Hague: Kluwer, 2006, p. 195 et seq.

rather than a 'shall' provision, tellingly having no corresponding norm in the Berne Convention or the Paris Convention. Producers and users of technological knowledge are equal balancing weights indicating the positioning of rights and obligations.[14] In this context copyright is not placed among other human rights, but considered as a commodity, the protection of which shall be balanced against varying users' interests.[15] In short, this need for 'balance' is obviously not driven by a humanitarian perspective, for example emanating from respect for free speech, but by intellectual property rights to serving as useful commodities in a dynamic market.

Article 7 of the TRIPS Agreement reads:

> The protection and enforcement of intellectual property rights should contribute to the promotion of technological innovation and to the transfer and dissemination of technology, to the mutual advantage of producers and users of technological knowledge and in a manner conducive to social and economic welfare, and to a balance of rights and obligations.

It is quite symptomatic that one side of authors' rights, moral right, has been cut off from the agenda of developing countries, as they, if bound by the TRIPS Agreement, have the freedom not to pay any attention to moral rights issues according to Article 9 (1) TRIPS. This is somewhat paradoxical, as it may be assumed that developing countries probably have the greatest interest in recognising copyright as a human right. In particular, as copyright may form the supportive basis for claims related to the protection of folklore and other moral or human rights-oriented assets, freedom of expression ought not to be forgotten.

3. The constitutional basis for copyright

3.1. Calibrating the differences between the European and North American scenes

While questions on freedom of expression have often, but certainly not as a rule, been recognised in national constitutional law, the same can rarely be

---

[14]   Cf. J. Rosén, 'Upphovsrätten i med- och motvind', *NIR*, 6/2005, p. 570 et seq., for further references.

[15]   Cf. the preamble to WIPO's World Copyright Treaty (WCT), recognising 'the need to maintain a balance between the rights of authors and the larger public interest, particularly education, research and access to information, as reflected in the Berne Convention, . . .'. It is to be observed that the Preamble speaks of *rights* of authors and the larger public *interests* (emphasis added), not viewing rights and interests as of equal significance. See M. Ficsor, *The Law of Copyright and the Internet. The 1996 WIPO Treaties, their Interpretation and Implementation*, Oxford, 2002, p. 414 et seq.; cf. J. Reinbothe and S. von Lewinski, *The WIPO Treaties 1996*, Brussels and Munich, 2002, p. 21.

said of copyright. The most prominent, or well-known, example of such recognition is found in the USA, where the constitutional basis for copyright is quite clear, thus having an impact on its relation to freedom of speech. In the USA copyright is recognised in a phrase, stamped by utilitarian philosophy, expressed directly in the Constitution, the so-called Copyright Clause, stressing the role of copyright: '. . . to promote science and the useful arts . . .'.[16] It is beyond discussion that this clause offers copyright a quite precise constitutional status, hereby adding to copyright a certain dignity rarely to be found elsewhere from a global perspective. At least not if comparison is made with legal standards in Europe, where a direct constitutional parallel is rarely found.

But the American construction primarily opens the way for direct utilitarian public demands, as just indicated, thus limiting the scope of those exclusive rights offered to authors. This is a reason for the generous dimension of limitations on copyright within the framework of American 'fair use', thus designed with considerable latitude.

In Europe authors' rights have often been seen as something of a 'natural right', built on a mixture of proprietary and individual rights elements, in some rare instances protected also by constitutional law protecting such phenomena in particular. This may of course offer copyright a stronger position than recognised by more purely proprietary private law norms, even if the constitutional element is formally lacking. It is quite typical for the European situation to describe exclusive copyright uses fairly broadly, while legal exemptions are narrowly defined and restrictively interpreted in practice.[17]

In Germany copyright is considered to have an unusually strong constitutional position, as compared with common European circumstances. But in Germany too copyright is supported constitutionally only by interpretation – or rather it is underpinned by an implied constitutional recognition by some articles of the Federal Constitution – with however quite profound results, *inter alia* as concerns moral rights as they are kept inseparable from other functions of copyright, and thus protected via Articles 1 (1) and 2 (1) of the Federal Constitution, while rights in exclusive uses are protected by Article 14 (1), i.e. within the provisions for property rights and freedom of 'art' and 'science'.[18] Further, Article 14 (2) of the Federal Constitution shows that property rights shall serve a social function, which offers a constitutional basis for a judicious restriction of copyright for the benefit of public interest. In fact,

---

[16]   US Constitution Art. I, § 8, cl. 8.

[17]   See ALAI, *Cambridge Study Days, The Boundaries of Copyright*, Cambridge, 1998.

[18]   See F. Leinemann, *Die Sozialbindung des Geistigen Eigentums*, Baden-Baden: Nomos, 1998; F. Fechner, *Geistiges Eigentum und Verfassung*, Mohr Siebeck, 1999.

the German Federal Constitutional Court, Bundesverfassungsgericht, has more than once not only recognised constitutional support for copyright but also stated that Article 14 motivates certain limits upon copyright and has, though so far without a direct reference to freedom of expression, found that the German Constitution presupposes a balancing of authors' rights against those of the public interest.[19] In this sense the German Federal Constitution may be said to offer a basis also for a balancing of the public interest in freedom of expression and those of exclusive private law copyright.[20] In a few cases German courts have found interests of a freedom of expression nature to be strong enough to motivate statutory limitations to copyright to be used quite elastically or actually set aside.[21] In particular a few decisions of the German Supreme Court offer some guidance.[22]

In other European states encounters between copyright and freedom of expression have been much more discreet. The situation in United Kingdom is probably characteristic of the overall picture.[23] Quite recently, in the year 2000, the ECHR was incorporated into the statutory law of the UK, which triggered debates on the relation between copyright and freedom of expression and also statements in a few well-observed cases.[24] What appears typical of the UK situation, as in most other countries throughout Europe, is that the

---

[19]   See Judgments of the Bundesverfassungsgericht of 7 July 1971, Kirchen- und Schulgebrauch, *GRUR* 1972, p. 481, and of 25 October 1978, Kirchenmusik, GRUR 1980, p. 44.

[20]   See G. Schricker (ed.), *Urheberrecht Kommentar*, 2nd edition, Munich, 1999, esp. § 97 no. 19–25.

[21]   Cf. the survey on court decisions offered by Hugenholtz, op. cit., note 8 supra, p. 9 et seq.

[22]   Cf. the German Federal Supreme Court, judgment of 7 March 1985, [1987] GRUR 34, *Lili Marlene*. The Court accepted in principle that 'under exceptional circumstances, because of an unusually urgent information need, limits to copyright exceeding statutory limitations may be taken into consideration'. See also the judgment of the German Federal Supreme Court of 16 January 1997, [1997] GRUR 464, *CB-Infobank*. The Court found that the public interest in accessing information did not justify departing from the rule that statutory limitations on copyright, being narrowly construed, should be narrowly interpreted.

[23]   See M.D. Birnhack, 'Acknowledging the Conflict between Copyright Law and Freedom of Expression under the Human Rights Act', *Entertainment Law Review*, (2), 2003, p. 24. Available at SSRN: http://ssrn.com/abstract=368961 or DOI: 10.2139/ssrn.368961

[24]   See the Court of Appeal [2001] EMLR 44 (CA), *Ashdown v Telegraph Group Ltd*. Tellingly, the British Appeal Court admitted (cf. note 25 infra), that in some circumstances the *form* of expression is no less important than the *information* it conveys – sometimes the user of a work doesn't have 'alternative avenues' which they could have used to express the unprotected idea in their own manner without using the copyright owner's expression.

courts seem reluctant to apply constitutional law, or even Article 10 ECHR, in borderline copyright cases, instead testing aspects of freedom of expression through an interpretation of statutory limitations afforded by the copyright legislation itself.[25]

3.2. Constitutional positioning in Sweden

It is quite striking that no other country within the EU seems to be able to demonstrate more profound constitutional support for copyright or, rather, authors' rights, than Sweden, namely via the Government Form of 1974 (GF), which replaced that of 1809, where copyright's relation to freedom of expression is actually clarified by reference to a number of norms found in the Fundamental Freedom of the Press Act (FPA) of 1949 and the Fundamental Law on Freedom of Expression (FEA) of 1992, the latter being drafted for the protection of modern electronic media, broadcasting included. Alas, in 1976 a provision on copyright was included in the comprehensive second chapter of the GF, comprising a long list of rights and freedoms, completed in 1976, 1979 and 1994. The 1976 amendment very overtly defined authors' rights as constitutionally protected, although, as initially mentioned above, such rights had been included in a constitutional context long before that.[26]

The very basis of this order is Article 2:19 GF, as formulated in 1976, laconically indicating that '. . . authors, artists and photographers shall own the rights to their works according to norms stated in statutory law'. From this follows that there must be such legislation. As these norms, whether of a private or a public law nature, must appear in the form of statutes, there is no mandate for the Government to issue decrees or ordinances in this field of law, apart from ordinary executive decrees to already existing laws according to Article 8:13 paragraph 1 GF.[27] Obviously, this kind of order directly affects

---

[25]   See *Ashdown v Telegraph Group Ltd.* [2001] Ch. 685, and [2001] EMLR 44 (CA). In the latter case (at para. 45) the court concluded that '. . . rare circumstances can arise where the right of freedom of expression will come into conflict with the protection afforded by the Copyright Act, notwithstanding the express exceptions to be found in the Act. In these circumstances, we consider that the court is bound, insofar as it is able, to apply the Act in a manner that accommodates the right of freedom of expression. This will make it necessary for the court to look closely at the facts of individual cases (as indeed it must whenever a "fair dealing" defence is raised). We do not foresee this leading to a flood of litigation.' Cf. Birnhack, note 23 supra.

[26]   Cf. J. de Meij, 'Copyright and Freedom of Expression in the Swedish Constitution: An Example for the Netherlands?' In *Intellectual Property and Information Law: Essays in Honour of Herman Cohen Jehoram*, J. Kabel and G. Mom (eds), The Hague, London, Boston, 1998, p. 323 et seq.

[27]   Cf. SOU 1975:75 s 207 f , and prop. 1975/76:209 s 262 ff.

the courts' view on the possibility of letting copyright yield to e.g. freedom of expression interests, not already indicated among the express limitations found in the Copyright Act, as will be demonstrated below.

The rationale behind the fact that Swedish copyright law, at least with the focus on authors, artists and photographers, has been offered this profound constitutional support, is, as indicated in the preparatory works, its considered purpose to promote 'the free formation of opinion'. This specification as well as a limitation on freedom of expression is of considerable importance also as a legal source of copyright in Swedish Law, as we shall soon see.

Another limitation should also be observed, although already hinted at. The word 'copyright' ('upphovsrätt') is not used in the GF, which speaks of the rights of *authors*, *artists* and *photographers*. Included are not just authors and creative artists, in a fairly broad sense, but also performing artists, such as musicians, singers and actors. But outside this group falls e.g. designers, at least in their capacity as designers of applied art or 'useful' forms, just like inventors and any other owners of neighbouring rights, except for those performing artists just mentioned, like sound or film producers or broadcasters.[28] Probably producers of databases are also excluded, to the extent their protection is merely of a sui generis kind (not built on authoritarian original creation), according to Article 49 of the Swedish Copyright Act, although this is debatable, the crucial question being whether the creation of the database is of importance for the 'free formation of opinion'.

4. The fine line between copyright and freedom of expression in Swedish fundamental law

As an initial observation of some significance we may note that freedom of expression is regulated twofold in Swedish fundamental law. Firstly, it appears among other basic freedoms and rights of a general nature, placed as it is in the GF as the premium form of those freedoms and rights appearing in Article 1 paragraph 1, Chapter 2 of the GF, where it is framed by the following definition: 'Freedom to offer enlightenment and to express thoughts, opinions and feelings orally, by text or picture or otherwise'. In paragraph 2 of the same article of the GF this basic right is immediately followed by a norm demonstrating the freedom of information – the freedom 'to gather and to receive information and otherwise to be notified of the expression of others'. Secondly, freedom of expression appears, as was already indicated above, in the fundamental Freedom of the Press Act (FPA), as well as in the fundamental Freedom of Expression Act (FEA), the latter built on the

---

[28]   See G. Petrén and H. Ragnemalm, *Sveriges grundlagar och tillhörande författ-ningar med förklaringar*, 12th edition, Stockholm, 1980, p. 86 et seq.

former.[29] Here, freedom of expression steps forward as defined by certain forms of expression or media techniques, such as formulated in print techniques etc.

However, in the preparatory works to the FPA the possibility of having a special regulation in ordinary statutory law on the contents of printed matters was anticipated, which was considered to be effectuated on the basis of nothing more than a teleological or purpose-oriented interpretation of the FPA, accordingly without express support by the statute itself. As for such an interpretation of the purpose of the FPA, we may observe that several laws have been enacted in Sweden with reference to that anticipation in the preparatory works; prominent examples are the Marketing Practices Act (1995:450) and the Act on Names and Pictures in Advertising (1978:800). From this it follows that certain limitations on fundamental freedom of expression may, and do, occur in ordinary statutory law based solely on the interpretation of the purposes of fundamental law. The fundamental law simply does not regulate all forms of proceedings whereby a printed work is being used. The decisive elements are the meaning and purpose of freedom of expression.[30] The given definition in the GF, quoted above, hereby emerges as extremely important, particularly as it demonstrates a limitation on the scope of this specific basic freedom, namely to 'offer enlightenment and to express thoughts, opinions and feelings', thus of importance to 'the free formation of opinion'.

Therefore, naturally of specific interest in this context, it may rightly be claimed that a purpose-oriented interpretation should lead to the conclusion that anybody's use of the copyright works of other authors typically falls outside the material field of application of the FPA. Particularly as far as exclusive rights are concerned – the 'internal' copyright regulation, the idea and form dichotomy, may thus be said to cut into the constitutional or fundamental laws. But this may probably also demonstrate that exclusive copyright uses are not really to be seen as a hindrance to freedom of expression as defined by fundamental law, namely as long as means are available for the public to *convey enlightenment and thoughts* on topics of importance to freedom of expression, irrespective of the exclusiveness of copyright.[31]

This 'limitation' on freedom of expression, as this construction must be

---

[29]   The consonance of the FPA and the FEA in this respect follows obviously from the fact that the FEA came into being in the early 1990s, hereby closely modelled on the older FPA. For practical reasons this also motivates us to focus solely on the FPA in this presentation.

[30]   Cf. the preparatory report to the FPA, SOU 1947:60 s 120.

[31]   Cf. also the so-called Rättighetsskyddsutredningens (The Protection of Rights Committee) report in SOU 1978:34, Förstärkt skydd för fri- och rättigheter (Enforced protection of freedoms and rights), p. 181.

conceived, is in fact quite obvious as far as copyright is concerned, as nobody may use someone else's original work, without due permission, in order to exercise his fundamental freedom of expression. Still, as if this relation between copyright and freedom of expression was not quite distinct, there is also an express rule contouring the landscape.

Aside from the purpose-oriented interpretation of the FPA, there is also a specific *delegation rule*, an express exception in the FPA (and the FEA) to the benefit of copyright. It is found in Article 8, Chapter 1 of the FPA, which offers specific legislative measures in many fields of law.[32] It reads:

> Provisions concerning the copyright of an author of a literary or artistic work, or the producer of a photographic picture, provisions concerning rights neighbouring such copyright, and provisions prohibiting the reproduction of literary or artistic works in such a way as to infringe cultural interests, shall be laid down by law. (SFS 1988:1448)

This article, just like its parallel in the fundamental law on electronic media, clearly indicates that copyright, although basically seen as a strong support for freedom of expression in any medium, may also be a limitation on expressions in the press or electronic media. This article shall thus be seen in the context of freedom of expression and freedom of information, and that those basic rights, however prominently placed in the Government Form, may in fact be limited, as expressly follows from Article 12, Chapter 2 of the GF. According to this article expressional and informational freedoms may be limited not only by a number of distinctly phrased purposes, but also to the benefit of certain *very important purposes*, among which are primarily meant authors' rights.[33] These exceptions from the field of application of the FPA and the FLE also indicate the opinion of the lawmaker that copyright cannot be properly regulated without express support from fundamental law.

These delegation rules are thus expressed via quite a complex mass of main rules and exceptions. As for the delegation rule in the FPA, it is clear that the exception to the benefit of copyright may cover anything formally falling within its provisions, meaning that the Copyright Act and all those rights offered by it shall be fully applicable without any hindrance from the FPA.

---

[32] Delegation rules of that kind have also been applied by the enactment of legislation on the marketing of alcohol and tobacco, Article 1:9, paras 1 and 2 FPA, advertising dangerous for health and environment, Art. 1:9, para. 3, and for intelligence on creditworthiness, Art. 1:9, para. 4. Of late, child pornography has come to fall totally outside of the FPA through an amendment to Art. 1:10 FPA, thus distinctly not being part of the protection offered by basic freedom of expression.

[33] Cf. Ragnemalm and Petrén, op. cit., note 28 supra, p. 77.

Against this backdrop and the somewhat more narrow focus on copyright offered by Article 2:19 GF, what falls within that structure, i.e. what is of importance to *the formation of opinion*, shall be applied in a way not conflicting with basic principles of freedom of expression. Further, this falls in line with the idea that those limitations actually admitted according to Article 2:12 GF must never be broadly drawn so as to be a threat to the free formation of opinion, which is expressly stated in Article 2:12, paragraph 2 of the GF.

5. Practical applications

What was just said above is quite profoundly demonstrated in Swedish court practise. However, the Supreme Court has probably never tried a crystal-clear conflict between copyright and freedom of expression. But this court has many times touched upon the question and stated that it is for the lawmaker, not for the courts, to define limitations on copyright, accordingly as a given result of the impact of Article 2:19 GF.[34] As a matter of principle the point of departure for the courts is that they don't have a mandate to limit statutory copyright law to the benefit of an intrinsically important counter-interest. This question is, however, stamped in a certain way when aspects based on fundamental freedom of expression, closely linked to the strongly supported assumed necessity of the free formation of opinion, occasionally conflict with authors' rights, likewise supported by fundamental law.

The Supreme Court of Sweden stated in a well-observed case that the penalty for criminal offences of copyright in some very rare cases might be limited, thus to the benefit of an opposing freedom of expression interest but, as a matter of principle, such a step should generally be taken by the lawmaker.[35] However, the court also stated, occasionally certain situations might occur when freedom of expression interests were so profound and strong that the court simply would have to take the responsibility for a verdict of *acquittal* in a trial on an acknowledged violation of copyright. Hereby the Supreme Court referred to cases of extremity embraced by those emergency situations indicated in Article 24:4 of the Penal Code (1962:700), thus leading to acquittal or, rather, non-punishment. In the case here referred to, the Supreme Court did not find reason to use this tool, although it concerned a well-known daily paper's publication of the content of a letter sent from a potential managing director to the tax-financed Gothenburg City Theatre, on how management would be conducted if he was appointed, thus being of considerable general interest. The author's copyright in the letter should have

---

[34]   See under section 3 supra.

[35]   See NJA 1985, p. 893, *The Manifesto; Supreme Court of Sweden*, 20 December 1985, also in *GRUR Int.*, 1986, p. 739.

been fully respected, as the newspaper would have needed the author's consent to the publication, which it had not.

In another case the Supreme Court of Sweden found that the Parliament had clearly decided on the nature of the relationship between copyright and freedom of expression.[36] The Court referred *inter alia* to a statement by the Law Committee, since 1971 a permanent Parliamentary committee, indicating that the law in force must be considered to balance appropriately the different interests of the authors, on the one hand, and the free formation of opinion on the other. Further, the Supreme Court forwarded the ECHR and its power to guarantee anybody the right to freedom of expression, which may, however, be subject to such limitations or sanctions as defined by the law and necessary in a democratic society with respect to the rights of others. It also made clear the position of Swedish copyright law as being construed basically by inalienable moral rights and other rights of a personal nature.[37] However, statutory law support could be found for freedom of expression precedence over copyright, resulting in the possibility then of accepting relief from punishment for factual violation of copyright, accordingly in line with the somewhat older *Manifesto* judgment.

The Supreme Court accordingly gives quite a direct message; but for atypical situations, on occasions the lawmaker was not likely to have foreseen, probably purely emergency situations in reality, a court may have a mandate to limit copyright as given in statutory law. This basically lies in the legal construction of copyright, as has also been stressed by the Supreme Court several times in different judgments.[38] Not even such an important

---

[36]   See NJA 1998, p. 834, Mein Kampf.

[37]   For such very specific reasons copyright cannot be subject to *seizure* as long as it remains with the author or with any other person who has acquired the copyright by virtue of division of property between spouses, inheritance or will, Art. 42 of the Copyright Act. Neither can the hard kernel of moral rights be waived with a binding effect, Art. 3, para. 3 CA. There is, however, a single and specific exception to moral rights, as the owner of a building or a useful article is entitled to alter the property without the consent of the author, Article 26 (c) CA.

[38]   See NJA 1993 p. 263, *Architectural drawing* (NIR 1993 p. 263). The Supreme Court stated *inter alia* 'Given the construction of the law of copyright – authors' exclusive rights of disposition over their work constitute, it may be said, a complete and all-embracing right from which certain specific exceptions specified in legislation have been made, aimed at benefiting social interest – it is clear that the room for the courts to interpret restrictions to authors' rights, other than those stipulated therein, is extremely limited. Such restrictions appear to be practically impossible in other cases except when the situation that has arisen is atypical and barely anticipated by the legislation, and also where compelling social interest can be invoked, the regulation of more predictable cases of conflict between the author's individual interests and opposing interest must be reserved for the legislator.' (My translation). Cf. NJA 1985, p. 893,

phenomenon as the freedom of informational speech of a political nature is considered to motivate an exception from copyright protection.[39]

Quite recently the Supreme Court of Sweden has tried a related matter with a certain defiance for freedom of expression, namely whether parody, travesty or satire with reference to or actual use of someone else's literary or artistic work may cause a violation of the author's moral rights to the work used.[40] This case concerned potential uses for radio broadcasts of textual elements from the renowned children's book author Gunilla Bergström's stories about her literary figure Alfons Åberg. Those textual elements, cut from well-known sound recordings from an actor's reading of Alfons' stories, had been combined in the radio broadcast with excerpts from the soundtrack of a Danish adult film called *The Pusher*. The character of Alfons, a seriously thoughtful and charmingly observant child, hereby came to be involved in an encounter with a drug dealer, claiming Alfons had himself delivered bad quality stuff. It all ended in a fist-fight between them. Author Gunilla Bergström was not amused, sensing disrespect for her thirty years of writing very serious although entertaining Alfons stories, published in many books, and that the association with the *Pusher* movie had drawn her impeccable Alfons into something undignified and far from his character.

The radio producer added freedom of expression interests to his argumentation, claiming that the programme broadcast was a parody or travesty of Alfons as a literary character. His main objection to Gunilla Bergström's action was, however, that the programme launched a new original work, independent of the no doubt underlying texts from the Alfons books, thus not a violation of the moral rights of Gunilla Bergström.

The Supreme Court came to test the case only on the basis of copyright and the majority of the judges (three out of five) found that a 'travesty' had been

---

The Manifesto, and, very distinctly, NJA 1986 p. 702, *Public Performance in TV shops*; The Supreme Court stated: '. . . authors' rights of disposition over their work constitute . . . a complete and all-embracing right from which certain specific exceptions specified in legislation have been made, aimed at benefiting social interest. Given this construction of the law, the room for the courts to interpret restrictions to the authors' rights, other than those stipulated in the legislation, is extremely limited. It appears to be practically impossible to establish such restrictions for the purpose of benefiting interests other than those of society at large, for example, purely commercial interest.' (My translation).

[39]   Cf. again NJA 1985, p. 893, *The Manifesto*. Also in another judgment, NJA 1975 s 679, *The Flag of Sweden*, the Supreme Court stressed that political freedom of expression must under no circumstances purport 'that the protection of authors not involved in the political dispute in question would be diminished'.

[40]   See The Supreme Court of Sweden, judgment of 2005.12.23, T 4739-04, *Gunilla Bergström v Sveriges Radio AB*; NJA 2005, p. 905, Alfons.

accomplished in the broadcast programme and that it did amount to a new original work independent of those underlying works to which it no doubt referred.[41] However, the court underlined that, even if the travesty was considered to be an independent work, it might still be that it associated the presentation of another original work in such a demeaning or negative form or context as to be prejudicial to the author's literary or artistic reputation or to his individuality, i.e. a direct violation of moral rights according to Article 3 paragraph 2 of the Swedish Copyright Act. But this had not happened in this case, the majority of judges concluded. This statement of the Supreme Court demonstrates, though, that even if a travesty amounts to an original work, independent of what it refers to, it may violate someone else's moral rights.

Symptomatically, the Supreme Court hereby solved the Alfons case with an 'internal' test of copyright elements and didn't even touch upon freedom of expression aspects in its judgment.[42] Accordingly, the moral rights side of copyright was not tested, which no doubt connects firmly to basic human rights as reflected in Article 10 ECHR as well as Swedish norms on freedom of expression, whether it could at all be set aside by someone else's right to express himself, e.g. in the form of parody or travesty. In this case it was not necessary to make such a test, of course, as the court simply found the travesty acceptable for mere copyright reasons. But if the travesty on the Alfons books, whether original or not was irrelevant, had been considered to be a per se violation of Gunilla Bergström's moral rights, it still seems very unlikely that the court would have found the travesty acceptable or non-punishable with reference to freedom of expression.

6. Concluding remarks

It is of course beyond discussion that copyright in Swedish Law emerges as a very special private law phenomenon, protected by fundamental law, relating to freedom of expression but certainly not merely an element in the latter. Irrespective of the fact that both fundamental rights emanate from a common basis, it is clear that copyright is motivated also by proprietary principles, an author's rightful claim to have a decisive influence on uses of his work in the market. As for co-existence with freedom of expression or, for that matter, the

---

[41] The minority, two of five judges, found that there had indeed been a use of Gunilla Bergström's original works (the travesty was thus not in itself an original work) and, accordingly, a test whether the moral rights vested in those works were violated could and should be accomplished. However, in doing so the minority found that the act of connecting the works to the film's soundtrack was not prejudicial to Gunilla Bergström's literary reputation or to her individuality.

[42] Cf. J. Rosén, 'Alfons Åbergs integritet eller författarens? Kan parodi, travesti eller satir innefatta intrång i upphovsrätt?' *Juridisk Tidskrift*, no. 3 (2005/2006), p. 713.

potential conflict between the two, the point of departure principally lies in the assumption that only on those rare occasions when the application of copyright rules crushes very fundamental qualities of freedom of expression – when private law emerges as a solid hindrance to the free formation of opinion – may the use of the delegation rules of the FPA and the FEA lead to a balancing of interests, whereby copyright may appear overly rigid and thus motivate a setting aside of it or, rather, a restrictive interpretation of the norms of the Copyright Act. As yet, there is not one single example of that in Sweden.

So far, the courts have chosen, not very surprisingly, to try copyright cases within the framework of that legal figure, testing its own 'internal' build-up, its own built-in balancing of informational interests and, generally, freedom of expression. On those rare occasions when a conflict between copyright and freedom of expression and information is observable – without it being factually tested by a court capable of offering a decision that may form a precedent – the courts have chosen to reason on the possibility of non-punishment for violation of copyright, i.e. not a setting aside of basic copyright values, even in those atypical situations when the question is at all relevant. This attitude seems to offer quite congruent factual results from courts throughout Europe, to seek a solution to the conflict between copyright and freedom of expression within the former's internal construction. A tendency of this kind seems to flourish also among countries that do not offer copyright as strong a constitutional dimension as Sweden does.

15 On-line teaching and copyright: any hopes for an EU harmonized playground?

Raquel Xalabarder[1]

Introduction

Education never fails to be mentioned – and, often, mentioned first – as a public interest that justifies an exception to copyright. Educational purposes were already present in the first version of the Berne Convention of 1886[2] and have remained there (although in revised language) ever since. The WIPO Copyright Treaty of 1996[3] expressly referred to education in its Preamble, when 'Recognizing the need to maintain a balance between the rights of authors and the larger public interest, particularly *education, research and access to information*, as reflected in the Berne Convention' (emphasis added). And more recently, the EU Directive on Copyright in the Information Society[4] stressed its goal 'to promote learning and culture by protecting works and other subject-matter while permitting exceptions or limitations in the public interest *for the purpose of education and teaching*' (Recital 14, emphasis added).

Despite being widely accepted as a fundamental right to be balanced against authors' exclusive rights, domestic laws fail to grant uniform and comprehensive treatment to education as a copyright exception or limitation.[5]

---

[1]   Dra. Universitat Oberta de Catalunya. This chapter is based on a presentation delivered at the 2006 ATRIP Congress in Parma (4–6 September 2006), www.atrip.org, as well as a result from a research project on 'Copyright and Digital Distance Education' funded by the Universitat Oberta de Catalunya (2002–3), www.uoc.edu/in3/dt/esp/20418.html, accessed 13 November 2006.

[2]   *See* Berne Convention for the Protection of Literary and Artistic Works, of 9 September 1886, as revised in Paris on 24 July 1971 and amended in 1979 (hereinafter, Berne Convention or BC).

[3]   *See* WIPO Copyright Treaty of 20 December 1996 (hereinafter, WCT). A parallel clause can be found in the Preamble of the WIPO Performances and Phonograms Treaty of 20 December 1996 (hereinafter, WPPT).

[4]   *See* Directive 2001/29/EC of the European Parliament and of the Council of 22 May 2001, on the harmonization of certain aspects of copyright and related rights in the information society, 2001 OJ L167/10 (22.06.2001) (hereinafter, EUCD).

[5]   Usually, a distinction is made between 'limitation' to refer to non-voluntary (compulsory) licences, and 'exception' to refer to free uses. We will not make such a distinction here, and will use the term exception without distinguishing between free or remunerated uses.

As we will see, the extent and conditions of the exceptions provided for educational purposes vary, sometimes widely, among domestic laws. The lack of normative consensus is far more acute when we consider digital formats and on-line teaching.

Due to the principle of territoriality of copyright laws and the unsolved question of applicable law (especially acute when students that will be receiving the teaching materials are located in different territories), differences in national laws may become a serious impediment to the development of on-line education within a lawful framework.[6]

In face-to-face teaching, the use of works is 'self-contained' – within the walls of a physical classroom – and does not have a major economic significance. Furthermore, many teaching uses could be excused by the doctrine *de minimis non curat lex* (a small non-authorized use does not constitute an actionable infringement). For this reason, the fact that some teaching uses that took place within the walls of a classroom might not be covered by a teaching exception never worried legislators or authors.

In a digital world, this no longer holds true. Recent modifications of the exclusive rights of reproduction and making available to the public make it virtually impossible to use a work in a digital context without stepping onto the author's exclusive rights. *There is no room for* de minimis *uses in a digital environment.* If traditional copyright dealt with the exclusive control of commercial and public *exploitation* of works, digital copyright deals with controlling any *use* (any *experience:* read, listen, view, etc.) of works. The boundaries used to be intrinsic to the definition of the exclusive exploitation rights granted to authors, exceptions being – as they should be – exceptional; now, the *boundaries of copyright* can only be found in the exceptions, which – rather than exceptional – have become fundamental.[7] Yet, reinforcement of the author's exclusive rights has not been balanced by an equal reinforcement of the applicable exceptions. A clear example may be found in the disappointing Art. 6(4) EUCD.

---

[6]   In fact, failing a harmonized and certain playground for exempted teaching uses, an on-line university has two options: either face a myriad of eventual infringements in different countries (under different applicable laws) or start a 'mission impossible' search for worldwide licences. In order to mitigate the consequences of the principle of territoriality of Art. 5(2) BC, only one national law should be retained (to decide whether the teaching use is exempted or not): that of the 'degree-granting' country, regardless of where its headquarters, servers or students are located. See Xalabarder, Raquel (2003), 'Copyright and Digital Distance Education: The Use of Pre-existing Works in Distance Education through the Internet', *Columbia – VLA Journal of Law & the Arts*, **26**, pp. 101–78.

[7]   Art. 5(1) EUCD is a clear example of how important exceptions become in defining 'all-encompassing' exclusive rights.

On the other hand, as more and more works become available in digital format and are contracted on-line, *DRMs and contractual terms* may drastically reduce the scope of works that can be used freely – and I don't necessarily mean 'for free' – for teaching purposes by virtue of Art. 6(4)4 EUCD. Such a restriction on the scope of works available for teaching purposes may be to the detriment of two other fundamental rights: education and culture.

The 1948 UN Universal Declaration of Human Rights[8] acknowledges as *fundamental rights* not only the author's right,[9] but also education[10] and access to culture.[11] In fact, we should not forget that while every human being has a fundamental right to education and to participate in cultural life, only authors – those who create – have authors' rights. This should not be read so as to diminish the importance of the author's right as a fundamental human right, but it should always be kept in mind in order to find the right balance between these fundamental rights in our copyright laws.

The difficulties in clearing teaching uses[12] derive mostly from *legal uncertainty,* which benefits nobody: it brings extra-cautious educational institutions to seek unnecessary licences and empowers copyright owners to unreasonably deny[13] licenses for on-line uses or simply to set unreasonable prices and conditions, thus limiting the freedom and quality of education. Additional difficulties exist in locating the owner and obtaining timely responses, and collecting societies are not much help because they have not always been given digital rights in the works they manage.

One may argue that no exceptions would be necessary if a solid *licensing*

---

[8]   *See* Universal Declaration of Human Rights, General Assembly of the United Nations, Resolution 217 A (III) of 10 December 1948 (hereinafter, UNUDHR), www.un.org/Overview/rights.html, accessed 13 November 2006.

[9]   *See* Art. 27.2 UNUDHR: 'Everyone has the right to the protection of the moral and material interests resulting from any scientific, literary or artistic production of which he is the author'.

[10]   *See* Art. 26.1 UNUDHR: 'Everyone has the right to education'.

[11]   *See* Art. 27.1 UNUDHR: 'Everyone has the right freely to participate in the cultural life of the community, to enjoy the arts and to share in scientific advancement and its benefits'.

[12]   For a study on this topic, *see* the Harvard University Berkman Center (2006), 'The Digital Learning Challenge: Obstacles to Educational Uses of Copyrighted Material in the Digital Age', cyber.law.harvard.edu/media/files/copyrightandeducation.html, accessed 13 November 2006; *See* also Crews, Kenneth D. and Ramos, Jacque (2004), 'Comparative Analysis of International Copyright: Law Applicable to University Scholarship', www.surf.nl/copyright, accessed 13 November 2006.

[13]   Let's not forget that exclusivity grants the power to authorize and to prohibit.

system was available, and that efforts should be devoted to building such a system rather than relying on the 'old-fashioned' legal technique of exceptions. However, this reasoning forgets that exclusive rights granted to authors are not unlimited and that education and culture deserve to act as a limit on these exclusive rights, also in a digital context. The legislator should see to it that proper exceptions exist for that purpose; then, licensing will evolve within a reasonable and legally certain environment.

All that said, the purpose of this chapter is to examine the *status quo* and implications of the *teaching exceptions in the European context*, at both the community and domestic level. In addition to the specific teaching purposes exceptions, the exceptions for *quotations* are also important for on-line teaching, especially in those countries where no specific exception is provided for teaching purposes, or where the teaching exception does not cover digital uses.[14]

Before we start, it is worth mentioning that in recent years the US[15] and Australia[16] have passed specific legislation to address the use of pre-existing works for on-line teaching; and that Canada is currently considering this topic

---

[14]   Similarly, library exceptions and – to some extent – private use exceptions may also have an impact on teaching uses (at both ends: when the teacher obtains the work and prepares for instruction and when the student uses the material). Unfortunately, they go far beyond the scope of this study.

[15]   In the US, the TEACH Act of 2 November 2002 which amended the Copyright Act of 1976 (*see* www.copyright.gov/title17/, accessed 13 November 2006) was adopted to transport the instructional exceptions already existing under sec. 110 (that covered both face-to-face teaching uses and distance-teaching uses by means of radio and TV broadcasting) into a digital environment. If there is one criticism to be made of the TEACH Act it is its narrow scope, which may be somehow excused by its non-remunerated character, but which makes it clearly insufficient to cover the needs of on-line teaching. However, when examining the US scenario for teaching uses, two other facts remain fundamental: the general *fair use* defence of sec. 107 USCA and a voluntary – but widely accepted – remunerated licensing system that allows for the compilation of material for teaching purposes, even in digital format (*see*, for instance, the Copyright Clearance Center, among others).

[16]   In Australia, the Copyright Amendment (Digital Agenda) Act 2000, No. 110 (*see* www.austlii.edu.au/au/legis/cth/consol_act/caaa2000294/, accessed 13 November 2006) provides for a statutory collective licensing regime for the digital reproduction and communication to the public of all kinds of works (from digital sources, only) for educational uses (in broad terms: from use as part of instruction to the making of e-packs and e-reserves), by all kinds of educational institutions (primary or secondary institutions, universities and assimilated institutions). It is all managed by just one collective society; the remuneration fee is agreed by the parties (or, by default, set by the Copyright Tribunal) according to several parameters, such as the nature of the institution, the kind of work, the number of students, and so on. This statutory collective licence does not preclude the possibility that authors and institutions negotiate individual licences.

under an amendment to its Copyright Act.[17] We will not examine them, but will make some comparative comments where applicable.

So, let's start on common ground for all: the Berne Convention.

1.   Art. 10(2) Berne Convention: educational purposes

The teaching exception in the Berne Convention may be traced back to its very origins. Art. 8 of the Berne Act of 1886 reserved 'the liberty of extracting portions from literary or artistic works for use in publications destined for educational or scientific purposes' to national legislation. The Brussels Act of 1948 changed the matter reserved for national law under Art. 10(2) as 'the right to include excerpts from literary or artistic works in educational or scientific publications'. At the 1976 Stockholm Revision, the proposal of a minor amendment (which only affected the English text) to replace 'excerpts' with 'borrowings',[18] opened an important debate[19] that resulted in the current Art. 10(2):[20]

> It shall be a matter for legislation in the countries of the Union, and for special agreements existing or to be concluded between them, to permit the utilization, to the extent justified by the purpose, of literary or artistic works by way of illustration in publications, broadcasts or sound or visual recordings for teaching, provided such utilization is compatible with fair practice.

---

[17]   Under a broader Copyright Act reform (Bill C-60, An Act to Amend the Copyright Act, introduced in the House of Commons on 20 June 2005; *see* www.parl.gc.ca/, accessed 13 November 2006), Canada is currently examining a two-layer system for on-line teaching uses: a broad non-remunerated exception for digital teaching uses, and an *ex-lege* extension of collective reprographic licences (subscribed by educational institutions) to include digital uses. It is expected that this will stir up voluntary collective licensing and, at the same time, 'ensure that the exercise of new digital rights for creators will not hamper access to works for educational or other socially important purposes'.

[18]   It was thought to correspond better to the French text 'emprunts'. *See* WIPO (1971), 'Preparatory Document S/1', *Records of the Intellectual Property Conference of Stockholm, June 11–July 14 1967* (hereinafter, Stockholm Records), p. 48.

[19]   *See* WIPO (1976), *Reports on the Work of the Five Main Committees of the Intellectual Property Conference of Stockholm 1967*, WIPO Publication 309(E), # 93–94.

[20]   The final text proposed by the Working Group (document S/185) to amend Art.10(2) read: 'It shall be a matter for legislation in the countries of the Union, and for special agreements existing or to be concluded between them, to permit the utilization, to the extent justified by the purpose, of literary or artistic works by way of illustration in publications [broadcasts or recordings] for teaching, provided such utilization is compatible with fair practice'. *See* Stockholm Records, *op. cit. supra*, note 18, Document S/185, p. 708.

Art. 10(2) BC provides for an open and flexible exception for teaching purposes which, instead of any specific quantitative (how much can be used and how many copies) or qualitative (which kind of works) restrictions on exempted uses, is only limited on two grounds: '*the extent justified by the purpose*' and '*fair practice*', and ultimately – after the TRIPs Agreement and WCT – interpreted in accordance with the three-step test. Therefore, it applies to all kinds of works, both literary and artistic, that may be used in full or in part, provided that these conditions are met.

From its introduction in 1886, it was always agreed that, as long as the course led to an 'official' degree, this exception comprised both elementary and university teaching, in both private or public institutions, as well as distance teaching.[21]

There is no reason to conclude that on-line teaching (or any other means of distance learning, such as *pod-casting*) should be left out.[22] On the one hand, because the word 'utilization' is neutral enough to cover not only reproduction but also communication to the public (and the making available to the public[23]). And on the other, because although 'by way of illustration in publications, broadcasts or sound or visual recordings for teaching' could be read as an exhaustive list that leaves out on-line teaching, the BC Revisions[24] show that, far from constituting an exhaustive list, this language results from a specific wish to accommodate new technology.[25]

Furthermore, having accepted that digital technologies are covered under the exception, reference to *publications* favours the acceptance of teaching compilations (anthologies),[26] 'to the extent justified by the purpose' and

---

[21]   *See* Ricketson, Sam (1987), *The Berne Convention for the Protection of Literary and Artistic Works: 1886–1986*, London, Kluwer, § 9.25 and § 9.27 n. 3; *See* Ricketson, Sam and Ginsburg, Jane C. (2006), *The Berne Convention for the Protection of Literary and Artistic Works: 1886–1986*, Oxford, UK and New York, US, Oxford University Press, § 13.45.

[22]   *See* Ricketson and Ginsburg, *op. cit. supra*, § 13.44 and § 13.45.

[23]   *See* Art. 8 WCT.

[24]   From 'publications destined for educational or scientific purposes' (as in the Berne Act), to 'educational or scientific publications' (as in the Brussels Act), and to 'publications intended for teaching or having a scientific character or in chrestomathies' (as proposed in the Stockholm Program), until the current text approved at Stockholm (which added recordings and broadcasts).

[25]   The reason behind such wording was to enable educators 'to take full advantage of the new means of dissemination provided by modern technology . . . and there is no reason today to argue that it should not extend to digital fixations of works'. *See* Ricketson and Ginsburg, *op. cit. supra* § 13.45.

[26]   *See* Ricketson, *op. cit. supra*, § 9.27 n. 7: 'In many instances these [teaching anthologies] will, by their very nature, fall within the scope of publications made for teaching purposes under article 10(2)'.

'provided such utilization is compatible with fair practice,' and as usual, this will only be determined *in casu*.[27]

Which leads us to the crucial feature of this exception (and, in fact, the one that has found its way into national laws): 'by way of illustration . . . for teaching'. What does this mean? Is it different from (narrower than) the 'educational purposes' previously stated in Art. 8 of the Berne Act and Art. 10(2) of the Brussels Act? The answer is, no. The Stockholm Conference documents show that the introduction of the current wording responds exclusively to a concern about the amount of a work used (and the accuracy of the English version that ignited the revision), rather than to any modification or reduction in the concept of 'educational purposes', itself. The new language 'by way of illustration' was never intended to further restrict the scope of the educational purposes.

In short, it is an open, flexible and technology-neutral exception that obliges us to consider the kind and the amount[28] of work used, the quantity of copies made[29] and the specific implications of the technology,[30] in order to

---

27   In their last work, Prof. Ricketson and Prof. Ginsburg show some reserve:

> . . . while it is always possible that some [anthologies] may fall within the scope of Art.10(2), it is more likely that they will not. . . . it will be a distortion of language to describe an anthology of poetry (with the complete texts of the poems) or a 'course pack' consisting of chapters taken from various books about the subject to be covered in the course, as being used 'by way of illustration . . . for teaching'. Such usages are well-developed forms of exploitation in many countries subject to voluntary licensing arrangements or even compulsory licensing schemes that meet the requirements of art.9(2).

See Ricketson and Ginsburg, *op. cit. supra*, § 13.45, p. 794. Leaving aside the fact that the existence of well-developed licensing schemes in some countries is not enough to support (let alone, justify) an interpretation against the express wording of Art. 10(2) – after all, domestic laws are not obliged to provide for such an exception – it should be noticed that the two specific examples chosen by the authors are not exemplificative or exhaustive of all teaching anthologies possible.

28   *See* Ricketson, *op. cit. supra*, § 9.27 n. 2 p. 496: 'The words "by way of illustration" impose some limitation, but would not exclude the use of the whole of a work in appropriate circumstances'. *See* also Ricketson and Ginsburg, *op. cit. supra*, § 13.45, p. 791.

29   *See* Ricketson, *op. cit. supra*, § 9.27 n. 8; *See* also Ricketson and Ginsburg, *op. cit. supra*, § 13.45, p. 794:

> Just as no limitation is imposed in respect of the public which is reached by a broadcast intended for teaching purposes, so there can be no limitation on the number of copies that can be made for the same purpose. The only further qualification applied here is that the making of multiple copies must be compatible with 'fair practice'. Obviously, if this competes with the author's normal exploitation of his work and unreasonably prejudices his legitimate interests, article 10(2) should not apply.

30   According to the Agreed Statement concerning Art. 10 WCT, Member States may 'appropriately extend into the digital environment limitations and exceptions in

find *in casu* the right balance between the public interest (education) and that of the author.

All that said, we should not forget that Art. 10(2) BC is not a mandatory exception and simply sets the limits within which an exception for teaching purposes may be carried out by national laws.[31] No matter how broad and flexible the BC exception is, the exempted use of works for teaching purposes remains a matter for national law.

2.   Art. 5(3)(a) EU Copyright Directive

Among the list of non-mandatory exceptions gathered under Art. 5 EUCD, Art .5(3)(a) allows Member States to exempt any

> use for the sole purpose of illustration for teaching or scientific research, as long as the source, including the author's name, is indicated, unless this turns out to be impossible and to the extent justified by the non-commercial purpose to be achieved.

2.1.   What rights are covered under the exception?

Following the BC example, the teaching exception in the EUCD is technologically neutral and clearly intended to cover both face-to-face as well as distance education, including by digital means. Recital 42 of the EUCD expressly includes 'distance learning' under the teaching exception, and the Explanatory Memorandum accompanying the initial proposal of Directive further confirms its application to 'the new electronic environment'.[32]

Accordingly, the exception covers both rights of reproduction and communication to the public (including the right of making available to the public) and domestic laws may extend it to distribution (according to Art. 5(4)

---

their national laws which have been considered acceptable under the Berne Convention. . . . [and] devise new exceptions and limitations that are appropriate in the digital networked environment'. Digital teaching uses pose far greater risks to the author's interest than face-to-face teaching; therefore, the exception may be subject to different conditions depending on the technology used.

   [31]   *See* Ricketson, *op. cit. supra,* § 9.27 n. 1; *See* Ricketson and Ginsburg, *op. cit. supra,* § 13.45, p. 791.

   [32]   *See* Explanatory Memorandum accompanying the Commission's proposal for a Directive of 10 December 1997 (COM(97)628 final), OJ C108/6 (07.04.1998):

> It does not only cover traditional forms of using protected material, such as through print or broadcasted media, but might also serve to exempt certain uses in the context of on-demand delivery of works and other protected matter. Member States will have to take due account of the significant economic impact such an exception may have when being applied to the new electronic environment. This implies that the scope of application may have to be even more limited than with respect to the 'traditional environment' when it comes to certain uses of works and other subject matter.

EUCD). Let's see how these apply to the specific acts involved in on-line teaching.

The act of uploading the work on a server, in order to make it available to the public (students), entails both a reproduction and a communication to the public (also restricted-access recipients) and may be covered by the exception.

Temporary reproductions that enable the digital transmission and reception of the work may be covered by the mandatory temporary copies exception of Art. 5(1) EUCD. The same may hold true for RAM copies that enable the work to be displayed on the computer screen,[33] or they could be deemed part of the act of communication to the public and, consequently, follow its exemption; communication and making available to the public occur regardless of actual reception or access, but it makes no legal sense to dissociate such reception or access from the act of communication or making available, when they do take place.[34]

Permanent downloads (in any format: print-outs or digital storage) of the transmitted work made by recipients (students) will not be covered by the temporary copies exception.[35] They might be covered by the private use exception of Art. 5(2)(b), but if we draw an analogy from face-to-face teaching, the private copying exception would never exempt the reproduction of a work in multiple copies to be distributed among students for classroom use.[36] In fact, some domestic laws expressly exclude copies intended for collective use from their private copying exceptions. Finally, the EUCD being silent on this issue, nothing prevents Member States from exempting permanent student copies also as part of the teaching exception itself.[37]

In short, Art. 5(3)(a) covers any acts of reproduction and communication to

---

[33]   If, according to Recital 33 EUCD, caching and browsing qualify as temporary reproductions under Art. 5(1) EUCD, so should the reception of the transmitted work on the recipient's computer; after all, they both involve RAM copies and have the same effect: display or performance on the recipient's computer hardware.

[34]   Instead, others defend their exemption as private copies; *see* Hugenholtz, P. Bernt (1996), 'Adapting Copyright to the Information Superhighway', in Hugenholtz, P. Bernt (ed.), *The Future of Copyright in a Digital Environment,* Information Law Series no. 4, The Hague, Kluwer, 88, pp. 101–2: 'The act of screen display and related acts of temporary storage may not be restricted by copyright, in so far as these acts are necessary for private viewing, and do not qualify as communication to the public'.

[35]   *See* Art. 5(1) EUCD; downloads (copies) made by students do not qualify as 'temporary' and will most likely have some 'independent economic significance'.

[36]   *See* Ginsburg, Jane C. (1992), 'Reproduction of Protected Works for University Research or Teaching', *Journal of the Copyright Society of the USA,* **39** (181), p. 189.

[37]   In fact, some domestic teaching exceptions expressly allow as many copies as students in a class, thus proving that student copies do qualify as part of the teaching use.

the public that are necessary to carry out such teaching use: upload, transmission and reception, as well as student downloads; in addition to any technical copies which are necessary to carry that out being exempted under the temporary copies exception of Art. 5(1) EUCD.

However, Art. 5(3)(a) remains silent on two fundamental issues for on-line teaching: transformation and digitization. Since the exclusive right of transformation (derivative works) has not been harmonized in EU law, and is not affected by the EUCD, Member States are free to include translations and/or any other transformation of works within their national teaching exceptions.[38] Similarly, the EUCD silence leaves it to domestic laws and national courts to decide whether the making of a digital copy of a work that is not available in such a format is allowed or not. As long as digitization amounts to a reproduction only and since the exception is technologically neutral (not limited to specific means of exploitation),[39] there seems to be no reason not to exempt digitization of a work under the teaching exception.

2.2. What works can be used under the exception?
Art. 5(3)(a) EUCD follows the Art. 10(2) BC pattern which, instead of specific provisions as to the extent and nature of the works used,[40] prefers to rely on open-ended clauses. As a result, all kind of works[41] may be exempted for teaching uses, whether in full or in part,[42] as long as such use is 'for teaching', 'to the extent justified by the non-commercial purpose to be achieved' and in compliance with the three-step test.

2.3. Who is eligible to benefit from the exception?
The EUCD does not focus on the category (school, university, etc.) or nature (public or private, for-profit or non-profit, etc) of the educational establishment, but on the 'non-commercial' purpose of the specific educational activity.

---

[38]   Such an option is especially important for minority language countries.

[39]   It may be worth pointing out here that, unlike the Canadian and Australian laws which only permit digital uses from digital sources, the US TEACH Act expressly allows digitization of works used under the teaching exception; *See* § 110(2) US Copyright Act.

[40]   Needless to say, works under the exception must have been previously lawfully disclosed; otherwise, it would amount – according to most EU domestic laws – to an infringement of the moral right of divulgation.

[41]   For instance, works primarily intended for education, either in analogue or digital format, may in principle be covered, but the subsequent requirements may exclude them from the exception.

[42]   *See* EUCD Commission's Proposal, *op. cit. supra*, COM(97)628 final: 'only the part of the use which is justified by its non-commercial purpose may be exempted from the exclusive right'.

Determining eligibility on the basis of the nature of the institution[43] would have been easier, but also unfair. Education (either private or public, for-profit or non-profit) is the fundamental right that justifies this exception; it is only reasonable and fair that no distinction is made on that account.

So, what is a 'non-commercial purpose'? Recital 42 EUCD offers some guidance:

> the *non-commercial nature of the activity* in question should be determined by that activity as such. The *organisational structure* and the *means of funding* of the establishment concerned are not the decisive factors in this respect.[44] (*Emphasis added*)

In other words, almost all courses are offered in exchange for some payment, but this should not be enough to disqualify them under the exception. Private teaching institutions as well as public ones may benefit from the exception, but perhaps subject to different (or no) compensation regimes depending – for instance – on the nature of the institution and the registration fees paid by their students, and on the particular nature of each teaching activity. In that sense, member countries have a lot of discretion.

More precisely, nothing is said in Art. 5(3)(a) as to who is allowed to perform the teaching use. Are only teachers covered or also students?[45] Can students reproduce and communicate works to other fellow students under the teaching exception, as long as it is done for teaching purposes? Once again, the EUCD silence favours it, but it remains an issue for national legislators.

2.4. 'For the sole purpose of illustration for teaching'

The core of the exception is '*purpose of illustration for teaching*'. At first glance, the word *illustration* seems to unnecessarily complicate the scope of the teaching exception. We all know what *teaching* is, but '*illustration for teaching*' is not self-evident. Some alternative language was discussed during the parliamentary proceedings: 'education, learning and research' and 'education, learning, research and for private purposes',[46] but they were all discarded in favour of the more familiar Art. 10(2) BC wording.

---

[43] As the US TEACH Act does, by limiting the exception to non-profit educational establishments; *See* § 110(2) US Copyright Act.

[44] *See* Recital 42 EUCD.

[45] The US TEACH Act does cover teaching uses done by students. *See* § 110(2)(A) US Copyright Act.

[46] *See* Report of the EP Committee on Legal Affairs and Citizens' Rights on the proposal for a European Parliament and Council Directive on the harmonization of certain aspects of copyright and related rights in the Information Society, of 28 Jan. 1999, A4-0026/1999, pp. 43 and 58 (Amendments 18 and 24, to Art. 5.3).

One may argue that '*illustration for teaching*' should be narrowly interpreted, so as to exempt only those uses that ornament or exemplify the teaching. But this would leave out precisely the teaching uses that are substantial – not merely illustrative – for teaching. Besides, nothing in the EUCD indicates that '*illustration for teaching*' is intended to be narrower in scope than 'for the purpose of education and teaching' (as in Recital 14) or 'educational . . . purposes' (as in Recital 34) or than 'education, learning and research' (as considered by the Parliament[47]). They were all deemed to be equal. In addition, despite not being binding, it may be helpful to revisit the conclusion drawn under the BC: that '*illustration for teaching*' was not intended to limit or reduce the '*educational*' purpose itself, but rather to help clarify the amount of work that could be used for teaching purposes.

Furthermore, it makes sense to assume that the teaching exception goes beyond the uses exempted as quotations (Art. 5(3)(d) EUCD); otherwise, there would be no need for it. *Teaching* includes the use of works as part of a lesson[48] (for instance, the teacher's explanations) or an exercise (that the teacher presents the student with), but also as a reading (proposed by the teacher) to write a paper, or to participate in a debate, or simply to study. The US Teach Act makes it clear: the work used must be 'directly related and of material assistance to the teaching content'.[49]

And this would clearly include the making of teaching anthologies (compilations) under the exception. In fact, in its 1997 Explanatory Memorandum, the Commission expressly mentioned the 'compilation of an anthology'[50] as an example of teaching uses that might fall under Art. 5(3)(a). Besides, in a digital context, any materials used as part of instruction end up being posted (compiled) somewhere (such as a bulletin board or an e-reserve webpage or a common storage disc), at least while the course is on; thus, forming a teaching anthology. For this reason, the neutral EU solution – like the BC solution – makes perfect sense. And, as we already concluded under Art. 10(2) BC, allowing teaching anthologies to be covered by this exception does not mean that all teaching anthologies *per se* will be exempted, only those that are used for teaching purposes and comply with the non-commercial requirement, as well as with the three-step test – and to the extent that they do so – will qualify.

---

47   *See* ibid.
48   Including any use that is necessary to prepare for the teaching.
49   *See* § 110(2)(B) US Copyright Act; And *see* S. Rep. No. 107-31 (2001), p. 11: not 'for the mere entertainment of the students or as unrelated background material'.
50   *See* EUCD Commission's Proposal, *op. cit. supra*, COM(97)628 final, p. 40.

2.5.   How can the three-step test further shape the teaching exception?

EU Member States being part of the Berne Convention (and the 1996 WCT) as well as the 1994 TRIPs Agreement, the EUCD did not miss the opportunity to incorporate the three-step test provision into EU law. Nevertheless, after setting an exhaustive list,[51] Art. 5(5) EUCD omits the first step ('certain special cases').

It may be discussed whether it is a mandate for governments to guide implementation of the exceptions, or rather a mandate for courts and parties (people) to guarantee their narrow interpretation,[52] as a final limitation acting directly on the enforcement (rather than on the adoption) of the listed exceptions.[53] Perhaps it is both. In fact, bearing in mind that the listed exceptions are not mandatory – save Art. 5(1) EUCD – and that Member States are not obliged to use the precise EUCD wording, the full three-step test will necessarily act as a guide not only for the interpretation but also for the implementation of these exceptions into national law.

We will now analyse how the three-step test may reshape the scope of the teaching exception:[54]

First step: certain special cases   According to Prof. Ricketson, the exception must be for a 'specific purpose' and 'there must be something "special" about this purpose . . . meaning that it is justified by some clear reason of public policy or some other exceptional circumstance'.[55] In addition, it implies that it should be 'precisely and narrowly determined'[56] (as opposed to broad or undetermined), 'finite and limited in scope'.[57]

---

51   The list of exceptions in Art. 5 EUCD form an exhaustive list; no other exceptions will be allowed in Member States' national law, except as allowed under Art. 5(3)(o) EUCD.

52   *See* Cohen Jehoram, Herman (2005), 'Restrictions on Copyright and their Abuse', *European Intellectual Property Review*, (10), 359–64, p. 364.

53   One may wonder whether, as a two-step test, Art. 5(5) EUCD will function as some sort of *fair use defence* (like sec. 107 US Copyright Act) that will end up distinguishing the exempted use (covered by a correct '2ST sanctioned' reading of a statutory exception) from an infringement (resulting from a wrong 'non-2ST sanctioned' interpretation).

54   For an analysis of the three-step test, *see* the WTO Panel Report (WT/DS160/R) of 15 June 2000 on sec. 110(5) of the US Copyright Act (available at www.wto.org, accessed 13 November 2006) which may provide some non-binding guidance.

55   *See* Ricketson, *op. cit. supra*, § 9.6, p. 482; *See* Ricketson and Ginsburg, *op. cit. supra*, § 13.12, p. 764.

56   *See* Ficsor, Mihály (2002), *The Law of Copyright and The Internet*, Oxford, Oxford University Press, # C10.03.

57   *See* Ricketson and Ginsburg, *op. cit. supra*, § 13.14, p. 767.

There is no doubt that the teaching exception in Art. 5(3)(a) EUCD complies with the first step, not only because of the clear public policy that justifies it,[58] but also because it is precisely determined and limited in scope. Furthermore, we should not forget that it follows from Art. 10(2) BC, which was twice sanctioned to pass the three-step test when the TRIPs and the WTO subjected all exceptions – new and existing – to it. In any case, 'use for the sole purpose of illustration for teaching' must be narrowly interpreted, so as to exclude any use that is not specifically intended for teaching (that is, not every act done within an educational context will amount to *teaching*).

Second step: do not conflict with the normal exploitation of the work   The WTO Panel accepted that 'normal exploitation' includes actual as well as new potential uses of the work[59] (otherwise, it would lead to a circular argument, where new forms of exploitation would never qualify as 'normal'), but it concluded that only those uses that would deprive the owner of significant or tangible commercial profits will 'conflict' with normal exploitation.[60] In short, not every use that may yield some economic gain qualifies as 'normal exploitation'; it should be something less than the full scope of the exclusive right,[61] and it will ultimately depend upon the kind of work in question.[62]

As a result, in order to make sure that the exempted teaching uses do not conflict with the normal exploitation of the works, the following may be necessary:

- *works primarily intended for teaching* should be excluded from the scope of the teaching exception;
- *technological protection measures* should be implemented to avoid further downstream uses of copies received and downloaded by students;[63]

---

[58]   Although the WTO Panel preferred to leave public policy out of the first step (according to them, 'certain' means clearly defined, not necessarily 'explicitly identified', so as to guarantee 'a sufficient degree of legal certainty'; 'special' means limited in its field of application or exceptional in its scope; and 'cases' could be described in terms of the beneficiaries of the exceptions, equipment used, types of works or by other factors), they acknowledged that the specific public policy behind the exception may be strategic to clear the first step. *See* WTO Panel Report, *op. cit. supra,* §§ 6.108–10, pp. 33–4.

[59]   *See* ibid. § 6.178, at 47.

[60]   *See* ibid. § 6.182, at 48.

[61]   *See* ibid. §§ 6.182–9, pp. 48–50.

[62]   *See* Ricketson, *op. cit. supra,* § 9.7, p. 483.

[63]   For instance, downloads are allowed under the teaching exception, they could be limited to one or two copies per student (and/or assuming that any possibility of making subsequent digital or printed copies should be disabled), or a time-frame for permanent downloads could be set (for instance, for as long as the course lasts). Of course, all TPM scan be circumvented by a skilled user, but their implementation may

- *passwords* and other *access control measures* are critical to ensure that only the students officially enrolled in the course will have access to the works.

Third step: do not unreasonably prejudice the author's legitimate interests
The WTO Panel interpreted 'prejudice' as any damage, harm or injury, whether economic or moral. However, what is reasonable or unreasonable can only be decided *in casu*, taking into account not only the actual prejudice caused to the author,[64] but also the public interest that justifies the exception.[65]

In other words, a strong public interest – such as education – can counterbalance the prejudice caused to the author (it can make it 'reasonable'), as long as it is a special case and does not conflict with the normal exploitation of the work (see *supra*).[66]

Similarly, so could *fair compensation* in favour of the author, a possibility that has always been accepted under the BC,[67] as well as the EUCD,[68] and for which recital 35 EUCD offers some guidance:

- When determining 'the form, arrangement, and level of such fair compensation', the following should be taken into account: 'the particular

---

already disincentivize an important number of downstream uses, thus avoiding unnecessary (and unreasonable) prejudice to the author (*see infra*).

[64]   *See* WTO Panel Report, *op. cit. supra*, § 6.229, p. 59.

[65]   *See* ibid. § 6.224, p. 58: The WTO Panel interpreted 'legitimate' '. . . from a legal positivist perspective, but . . . also . . . from a more normative perspective, in the context of calling for the protection of interests that are justifiable in the light of objectives that underlie the protection of exclusive rights'.

[66]   In fact, it has been suggested that 'normal exploitation' should be interpreted not only on the basis of the economic harm caused to the rightholders, but also taking into account its 'normative dimensions': considering other interests at stake, such as privacy, access to information, etc. See Ginsburg, J.C. (2001), 'Towards Supranational Copyright Law? The WTO Panel Decision and the Three-Step Test for Copyright Exceptions', *Revue Internationale du Droit d'Auteur* (RIDA), **187**, pp. 51–3.

[67]   *See* Ricketson, *op. cit. supra*, § 9.8, p. 484:

> *unreasonable prejudice to the legitimate interests of the author* may be avoided by the payment of remuneration under a compulsory license (although this would not, of course, 'cure' a use that conflicted with the normal exploitation of the work – by definition, the receipt of royalties under a compulsory license could not be regarded as a part of the normal exploitation of a work). (Emphasis added)

See also Ricketson and Ginsburg, *op. cit. supra*, § 13.25, p. 775.

[68]   *See* Recital 36 EUCD: 'The Member States may provide for fair compensation for rightholders also when applying the optional provisions on exceptions or limitations which do not require such compensation'. Furthermore, the EU Parliament proposed to subject Art. 5(3)(a) to fair compensation; *see* European Parliament Opinion (1st Reading) of 10 February 1999, A4/1999/26, OJ C150/171 (28.05.1999).

circumstances of each case ... the possible harm to the rightholders resulting from the act in question ... the degree of use of technological protection measures';
- No compensation is required when prejudice is minimal or when rightholders have already received payment in some other form.

Beyond that, Member States are free to establish and arrange for any fair compensation regimes. Therefore, bearing in mind that fair compensation could be required for some teaching uses, but not for others, a compensation regime for teaching uses should take into account, at least, the following:

- *the kind of teaching use*: for instance, use of works for comment or criticism in the course of instruction does not need to be compensated (after all, it amounts to a quotation), but use of a work as part of an exercise or an exam, or as selected reading to prepare for a paper or a debate, or as supplementary reading for a particular lesson or topic, etc. should be subject to different amounts of compensation;
- *the nature of the teaching institution*: for instance, a private for-profit school could pay a higher fee than a public school;
- and *the specific uses allowed*: a higher fee could apply for works that can be downloaded and retained by students than for works that are only streamed to students.

2.6.   The teaching exception and TPMs?

Once the protection of TPMs was settled, the task of ensuring their co-existence with the exceptions listed in Art. 5 proved to be one of the most political and controversial topics of the whole Directive. Put bluntly, the issue was whether TPMs should prevail over the exceptions or, on the contrary, whether the exceptions should prevail over TPMs. The Council[69] came up with a sophisticated so-called 'compromise' solution: Art. 6(4) EUCD.

Only an oracle could explain why some exceptions made it into Art. 6(4)(1) EUCD and others did not.[70] Luckily, the teaching exception is there, which

---

[69]   *See* the EU Council's Common Position no. 48/2000, of 28 September 2000, OJ C344/1 (01.12.2000); following the First reading by the Parliament A4/1999/26, OJ C150/171 (28.05.1999) and previous to the Commission's Amended Proposal (COM(99)250 final) OJ C180/6 (25.06.1999).

[70]   Casellati points out that the exceptions listed in Art. 6(4)(1) EUCD are those considered in the WCT Preamble (education, research and public access to information), and that the beneficiaries of these exceptions can somehow be 'identified'. *See* Casellati, Alvise (2001), 'The Evolution of Article 6.4 of the European Information Society Copyright Directive', *Columbia – VLA Journal of Law & the Arts*, **24** (43), 69, p. 379.

means that – failing any voluntary measures implemented by rightholders – Member States must guarantee its enforcement against TPMs. Yet, Art. 6(4)(1) EUCD remains to be proven effective, because, lacking any definition of what are the '*means of benefiting from that exception*', domestic laws tend to simply rely on courts and arbitration, which may turn out to be too slow and costly a mechanism to effectively enforce them.

Furthermore, the EUCD failed again when setting contracts to prevail over exceptions, for works obtained by means of '*interactive on-demand services*' (Art. 6(4)(4) EUCD). Considering that many works available to teaching institutions have been (and will more and more often be) contracted on-line, the scope of any teaching exception may be strongly reduced in practice: any measures set by the Government to benefit from it, will be *de facto* limited to off-line environments.[71]

In short, we will need to be vigilant on how exceptions remain effective against the implementation of TPMs and contractual terms. The statement (as made in Luxembourg and Belgium) that exceptions are mandatory is certainly a gesture in their favour, but even then, contracts and TPMs may end up prevailing.

2.7. Conclusion

Use of lawfully disclosed works, in full or in part, for teaching purposes, by making them available on-line so that they can be accessed and downloaded by registered students, may be exempted under Art. 5(3)(a) EUCD, provided:

- that works primarily intended for teaching are excluded,
- that the work is used only to the extent necessary for the teaching purpose,
- that reasonable efforts (including TPMs) are undertaken to restrict access to registered students and to prevent misuse or, at least, minimize downstream infringement,
- that authors are duly credited (including the source),
- and receive fair compensation – which will take into account the particular teaching use (not all teaching uses should be compensated and compensated equally), the nature of the educational establishment and/or programme, and the existence of technological protection measures implemented.

---

[71]   Furthermore, it is not unrealistic to expect that similar clauses may easily find a way into all sorts of database contracts (including those not contracted on-line) and that the teaching institution will be forced to 'take it or leave it'. In theory, the exception would ultimately prevail over any non-on-line contracted terms and TPMs, but the teaching institution will have to go to court to effectively enforce it.

- No distinction should be made, for purposes of eligibility, between public or private, for-profit or non-profit educational establishments: they should all benefit from the exception (provided the remaining conditions are met), albeit they should be subject to different compensation regimes.

The EUCD has set the ground rules; let's see what national legislators have done.

3.   Teaching exceptions in EU national laws

As we have seen, both the BC and the EUCD provide for open, flexible and technology-neutral exceptions for teaching uses. Unfortunately, none of them is mandatory and as we will see, national laws fail to take full advantage of the opportunity, with solutions far from homogeneous.

A survey of national laws[72] shows that although some sort of exception for teaching uses may be found in all European copyright laws, their scope and conditions vary widely and many of them clearly fail to cover on-line teaching uses.

Some states have opted for an almost *verbatim* implementation of the EUCD. This is the case for Belgium, France, Germany, Italy, Luxembourg, Portugal and the Netherlands. Their exceptions closely follow the EUCD pattern.[73]

They cover the rights of reproduction and communication to the public (some also refer to distribution), but except for non-EU Malta,[74] none of them cover *translations*. This is a fine example of the disastrous results that the EUCD *fragmented* structure (where only some exploitation rights are harmonized and the corresponding exceptions only refer to these rights) may have on national laws. It might have been expected that national legislators would have been alert, when implementing EUCD provisions, and would have introduced any amendments necessary to maintain balance – and consistency – within

---

[72]   *See* Annex for the list of national laws that have been considered in this work. *See* also Ernst, Silke and Haeusermann, Daniel M. (2006), 'EUCD Teaching Exceptions in selected E.U. Member States – A Rough Overview', 8 June 2006, www.fir.unisg.ch, accessed 13 November 2006.

[73]   A few (for instance, Luxembourg, Netherlands, or Spain) expressly require that the source and name of the author be indicated and that the work used for teaching had previously been lawfully divulged. But even when the law is silent, both requirements spring directly from the moral rights of attribution (at least, for the name of the author) and divulgation – where it exists – and should therefore be enforced for any uses covered under the teaching exception. Therefore, for space considerations, from now on we will skip any reference to the indication of source/name.

[74]   *See* Malta (Art. 9.1).

their copyright laws. The non-harmonized exclusive right of transformation proves they have not done so. It is regrettable that national laws have made no effort to address this issue when implementing EU exceptions and have preferred simply to 'replicate' the fragmented EUCD structure.[75]

Nothing is said about *digitization*, but since none of them limits the exception to works available in digital format, it should be concluded – as we did for the EUCD – that digitization, as long as it is considered a reproduction, is exempted.

These exceptions generally refer to purposes of '*illustration for teaching*' and although the exact wording may be slightly different,[76] the final outcome should be similar to that of Art. 5(3)(1) EUCD: any use that is necessary to deliver the instruction. Ultimately, the exceptions are limited to 'the extent justified by the non-commercial purpose to be achieved' and the three-step test. Therefore, in general terms, these exceptions are designed to exempt on-line teaching uses.

However, some specific language, especially concerning the nature and quantity of works as well as the kind of institutions that may benefit from the exception, may complicate the scenario. Only Luxembourg and the Netherlands remain silent – following the EUCD approach – as to the amount of work that may be used.[77] The others add new language to expressly limit the exception to 'fragments' or 'parts' of works,[78] or even set specific amounts

---

[75]   As for the transformation right, implementation of the EUCD has unnecessarily and unjustifiably reduced the scope of some existing exceptions. For instance, before the EUCD implementation, the teaching exception in Luxembourg Art. 13(2) referred generally to 'use' for teaching purposes and closely followed the language of Art. 10(2) BC; The post-EUCD exception only refers to reproduction and communication to the public (distribution and translations having been left out).

[76]   France (Art. L122-5(3)(e)) refers to 'illustration in the course of teaching (instruction) . . . excluding any ludic or recreational activity' and Belgium (Art. 22.1) requires that 'it takes place within the context of the normal activities of the establishment'. Also the Slovak Republic Art. 28(1) has somehow adopted the EUCD language (exempting reproduction, distribution and communication to the public), but only 'for teaching purposes in school' which may be read as internal use in physical facilities only.

[77]   *See* Luxembourg (Art. 10.2); Netherlands (Art. 16.1); also Malta (Art. 9.1). Luxembourg (Art. 10.1) and the Netherlands (Art. 16.1) expressly require that the exempted use be 'according to good practices' or 'in conformity with what may be reasonably accepted in accordance with social custom'. Depending on how we read it, this may be nothing new under the three-step test or it may well add an additional requirement to those of the three-step test; *See* Ernst and Haeusermann, *op. cit. supra.* # 5.3.2.

[78]   Italy (Art. 70.1) limits the exception to 'fragments or parts of a work'; France (Art. L122–5(3)(e)) to 'fragments of works' ; Portugal (Art. 75.2) to 'parts of a published work'.

for specific works.[79] Further specific wording limits the exception to 'only for the participants in a course'[80] or requires that the public be 'composed mostly of pupils, students, teachers',[81] or expressly excludes works primarily intended for education.[82]

As we saw, some of this language[83] may amount to a concrete expression of the EUCD requirements, and especially of the three-step test. Besides, some limitation as to the amount and nature of works used, as well as to number of copies made, is already implied under the requirement that the work be used only 'to the extent required/justified by the . . . purpose'. However, such restrictions *ab initio* may reduce the scope of the exception. Courts will have room for interpretation but, in general, it remains to be seen how this additional language will affect the scope of the teaching exception under each law. Let's hope that the ECJ comes up (sooner rather than later) with some guidance, so that national courts can harmonize their positions and fill the gap between the specific language of their national exceptions.

The more visible and structured differences among these national teaching exceptions concern the kind of institutions that may benefit from them. Instead of the EUCD eligibility clause, based on the 'non-commercial purpose' of the teaching use, a few legislators have chosen different formulas. For instance, Germany refers to 'in schools and universities (higher education institutions)' and 'in non-commercial institutions of further education and of professional training'.[84] In Belgium, teaching uses are covered under two separate exceptions: one for reproduction (including digital formats) and another for communication to the public (including through digital networks), which is limited to establishments 'officially recognized or organized – for that purpose – by public authorities'.[85] Public

---

[79]   *See* Germany (Art. 52a) 'small parts of a published work, short works or isolated contributions to newspapers or periodicals'; Belgium (Art. 22(1)4ter) distinguishes between 'the fragmentary or full reproduction of articles or of works of art' and 'the reproduction of short fragments of other works'). Interestingly enough, though, the same distinction does not exist for communication to the public (Art. 22(1)4quater: 'the communication of works . . . for purposes of illustration for teaching').

[80]   *See* Germany (Art. 52a).

[81]   *See* France (Art. L122–5(3)(e)).

[82]   *See* Germany (Art. 52a) and France (Art. L122–5(3)(e)). In addition, Germany excludes movies, for a two-year period following their release.

[83]   For instance, the exclusion of works primarily intended for education.

[84]   *See* Germany (Art. 52a and Art. 137(k), respectively). Notice that the first group of institutions (schools and universities) may be for-profit or non-profit, while the second group (professional training and continuing education) is limited to non-for-profit institutions. Interestingly, due to the heavy pressure and criticism received during parliamentary proceedings, this exception will expire at the end of 2006.

[85]   *See* Belgium (Art. 22.1).

schools and universities will be clear beneficiaries, but it remains to be seen whether a private institution qualifies as an 'officially recognized establishment'. Belgian law further requires that teaching uses be conducted 'solely by means of closed transmission networks of the establishment', which, in principle, does not seem to require that the network be accessible only within the premises of the educational establishment.[86] Finally, in Portugal, only 'institutions which are not aimed at obtaining a direct or indirect economic or commercial advantage'[87] can benefit from the exception, thus clearly disregarding the EUCD intent and the specific explanation in Recital 42 EUCD (*see supra*).

Another area of dissimilarities is compensation. Belgium, France, Germany and the Netherlands establish remuneration in favour of the authors.[88] Luxembourg, Portugal and Italy remain silent;[89] one may only wonder whether the absence of any fair compensation will clear the three-step test.

Before we move on, we should mention the case of Spain, which shows how, despite using the original ingredients of Art. 5(3)(a) EUCD, the result will most likely fail to cover on-line teaching. The new Art. 32.2 covers the acts of reproduction, distribution and communication to the public of works (textbooks and university treatises being expressly excluded), for the purposes of 'illustration of the teaching activities' by 'teachers of official education' 'in the classroom'. One may argue that students on an on-line course may qualify as a 'classroom', but the legislative history suggests that only physical class-

---

[86]   *See* Belgium (Art. 22.1). A different interpretation would severely limit the scope of the Belgian teaching exception and virtually cast out on-line teaching from its coverage. A comparison with the language used in Art. 5(3)(n) EUCD 'communication or making available . . . by dedicated terminals on the premises of establishments', which has been transposed by Art. 22(1)(9) as 'by means of dedicated terminals accessible within the premises of these establishments' (*au moyen de terminaux spéciaux accessibles dans les locaux de ces établissements*), clearly supports the first interpretation.

[87]   *See* Portugal (Art. 75.2).

[88]   The specific regimes are not defined by law, but left for government regulation. Except for France (Art. L122–5(3)(e)): it will be a 'remuneration negotiated on a forfeit basis'.

[89]   According to the explanatory memorandum accompanying the EUCD implementation bill (No. 5128 of 14 May 2003), Luxembourg refused to establish a system of levies on recording supports and equipment, and acknowledged that *fair compensation* – as required by the EUCD – does not necessarily amount to *remuneration* and that 'alternative more balanced means of compensation should be explored'. Perhaps educational institutions and collecting societies (or copyright owners) may agree on some compensation regime for works used for teaching purposes. As for the Portuguese and Italian free teaching exceptions, they may ultimately pass the three-step test since only parts of works are allowed (especially in Portugal where only non-profit institutions are covered).

rooms were intended to be covered.[90] This new exception will add up to the two teaching exceptions that already existed and remain untouched: the quotation exception[91] and a specific exception for teaching purposes that only applies to databases.[92] One may well wonder why the legislator did not simply expand the database teaching exception to cover all kind of works. Ironically, under the current three-layered regime of teaching exceptions (none of which, by the way, establishes fair compensation), the old open-ended quotation exception will remain fundamental to covering on-line teaching.[93] In short, quite a useless implementation of Art. 5(3)(a) EUCD.

The second group of domestic teaching exceptions are those of Austria, Greece, Ireland and the UK. They *fail to cover on-line teaching* because they only cover reproduction, and usually refer to photocopying[94] or, when communication to the public is envisioned, the exception is limited to *live* performances (plays, recitals or performances in front of a real audience).[95]

---

[90]   During the parliamentary debate, alternative wording was proposed by all political groups (except for the Socialist Party of Government – which introduced the bill), to use language closer to Art. 5(3)(a) EUCD and, specifically, to delete both references highlighted above. All eight amendments proposed aimed at ensuring that the new exception would cover all types of education and also on-line teaching, as well as all sorts of uses in the course of instruction (including uses by students, not only teachers). Unfortunately, none of them succeeded. *See* Amendments in the Senate, BOCG, Senado, Serie II, no. 53 of 21 April 2006, pp. 21–58; and Amendments in the House of Representatives, BOCG, Congreso, Serie A, no. 44-10 of 30 November 2005, pp. 29–96.

[91]   *See* Spain (Art. 32.1): 'use by way of quotation or for analysis, comment or critical assessment . . . made for teaching or research purposes and to the extent justified by the purpose of the use'. As interpreted by courts, this exception covers two different kinds of uses: quotations (*stricto sensu*) and uses for analysis, comment or critical assessment (which easily fit teaching purposes).

[92]   *See* Spain (Art. 34.2(b)): 'use for purposes of illustration for teaching or scientific research, as long as it is used to the extent justified by the non-commercial purpose to be achieved and the source is always indicated'. This exception was introduced by Law 5/1998 of 6 March 1998, implementing Directive 96/9/EC of 11 March 1996, on the legal protection of databases (OJ L77/1996, 27.03.1996).

[93]   It imposes no limitation as to public or private institutions or as to classrooms, covers any use (therefore, reproduction, distribution, communication to the public, as well as translation), and allows for the use of any kinds of works (including textbooks and university treatises) 'to the extent justified by the purpose of the use' (therefore, in full or in part).

[94]   *See* Austria (Art. 42.6) and the UK (sec. 32). In addition to sec. 32, photocopying for teaching purposes is governed by sec. 36; and the making of teaching anthologies is very precisely dealt with under sec. 33.

[95]   This is the case of Ireland (the exception for purposes of instruction or examination which only covers the making of copies (sec. 53) and the exception to allow performing, playing or showing works in the course of activities of an educational estab-

In addition, it is worth mentioning that Switzerland and Liechtenstein[96] provide for a teaching exception only as a variety of private use, and their language seems to be limited to the context of *live* teaching; while Poland only exempts the making of teaching compilations.[97]

The last group is formed by the Nordic countries where teaching uses are subject to remunerated *extended collective licences*.[98] These licences used to exempt only the reproduction of published works (or the making of copies of audio and video recordings of school performances) for 'educational purposes' and failed to include communication to the public (or when they did so, covered live public performances that took place in the school). This is all about to change: extended collective licences for educational institutions are soon expected to cover digital uses. For instance, in Denmark the extended collective licence managed by COPY-DAN already covers scanning, printing, storage, e-mail transmission, upload in a password-protected intranet and download, in all kinds of educational institutions (schools – at all levels – universities, etc.), in exchange for a fixed amount per student, per year. Inherited from the reprographic licences, they only allow using of a maximum of 20% or 30 pages of a work, whichever is less.

This short survey shows that significant differences exist in national laws and that no harmonization should be expected to result from the EUCD. In addition, it remains to be seen how national courts will apply the three-step test to further shape the scope of the exempted uses *in casu*.

---

lishment (sec. 55) is clearly limited to live performances) and, most likely, of Greece, which provides for two separate exceptions covering 'reproduction' for 'teaching or examination purposes' (Art. 21) and 'public performance and display of works' (Art. 27), wording such as 'at the educational establishment' (Art. 21) and to 'the audience is composed of' (Art. 27) favours a restrictive – physical premises only – construction.

[96]   Switzerland (Art. 19(1)): 'Published works may be used for private purposes; Private use shall mean: . . . (b) any use of a work by a teacher and his pupils for teaching purposes' and Liechtenstein (Art. 22(1)): '. . . (b) any use of a work by a teacher for teaching in class'. These exempted uses are subject to equitable remuneration. Switzerland is currently revising its law under the 1996 WIPO Treaties, so both laws may soon change.

[97]   Poland (Art. 29(2)): 'for teaching and scientific purposes, to insert short disclosed works or fragments of more extensive works in manuals and collections of selected pieces'. Lithuania (Art. 22(1)) and Slovenia (Art. 50(3)) only cover reproductions 'for teaching and research' and 'for internal use in educational . . . institutions', respectively. And, on the opposite side, the Czech Republic (Art. 35(3)) covers any 'use' but only of 'a work created by a pupil or a student', 'for the internal use of the school or educational institution'.

[98]   And they all expressly allow for the making of teaching compilations (of small parts of works) under a remunerated (extended collective licensing) exception.

4. Quotations under Art. 10(1) BC and Art. 5(3)(d) EUCD

In addition to the exceptions for teaching purposes, both the Berne Convention and the EUCD provide for an exception for quotations. The quotation exception remains fundamental for teaching uses: it can complement a narrow (or non-existent) teaching exception and help draw the boundaries of the teaching exception (any teaching uses beyond a simple quotation).

The quotation exception was first introduced in the BC at the Rome Conference of 1928 'for the purposes of criticism, polemical discussion or teaching' and received its current wording at Stockholm:

> It shall be permissible to make quotations from a work which has already been lawfully available to the public, provided that their making is compatible with fair practice, and their extent does not exceed that justified by the purpose, including quotations from newspaper articles and periodicals in the form of press summaries.[99]

The EUCD uses similar terms, when allowing Member States to exempt:

> Quotations for purposes such as criticism or review, provided that they relate to a work or other subject matter which has already been lawfully made available to the public, that, unless this turns out to be impossible, the source, including the author's name, is indicated, and that their use is in accordance with fair practice, and to the extent required by the specific purpose.[100]

Both exceptions are open (in terms of purposes covered[101] and eligibility[102]), flexible (as to extent[103] and nature of works[104]) as well as technologi-

---

[99] *See* Art. 10(1) BC.

[100] *See* Art. 5(3)(d) EUCD.

[101] '[S]cientific, critical, informatory or educational purposes' were dropped from Art. 10(1) BC simply because it was thought that no list of purposes could hope to be exhaustive; See Ricketson, *op. cit. supra*, § 9.22 n. 3; See Ricketson and Ginsburg, *op. cit. supra*, § 13.41, p. 786. Similarly, the wording such as in Art. 5(3)(d) EUCD confirms that criticism and review are not the only legitimate purposes of quotation; quotations may be made for any other purposes, such as teaching.

[102] Since nothing is said as to who may benefit from it, both teachers and students may quote somebody else's work (for instance, use it for purposes such as criticism or review) in the course of a teaching activity, whether within public or private, profit or non-profit institutions.

[103] The concept of *quotation* already implies some limitation as to extent, but a work could be quoted in its entirety if 'the specific purpose' requires it and provided that it was done 'in accordance with fair practice'.

[104] The exception applies to all kind of works, provided they have been 'lawfully made available to the public.'

cally neutral (as to means of exploitation[105]), and are only limited on two accounts: 'fair practice' and 'the extent required by the specific purpose'. No compensation applies and, for the time being no national law requires it, either.

But, leaving aside their open, neutral and flexible scope, what sets them apart is the mandatory nature of Art. 10(1) BC, which the EUCD has completely disregarded. Since they are very similar in scope, no major inconsistencies in their interpretation and application should be expected *a priori*. However, domestic law quotation exceptions tend to be less generous than those of the BC and EUCD.[106] This may pose some interesting and difficult legal issues concerning the direct applicability of Art. 10(1) BC to limit the protection of foreign authors' rights in Berne countries, even within the EU States.

Are Berne countries obliged to exempt quotations, at least (*ex* Art. 5(3) BC[107]) in relation to foreign Berne Union works? Or should the principle of *minimum protection* allow Member States to derogate any restriction (such as a mandatory exception) envisioned in the BC? The debate is largely theoretical, but the answer is clear:

> if national legislation purports to grant protection to Union authors in such cases [*where the BC restricts or excludes protection*] this must be contrary to the Convention. Given the existence of article 19 [*stating the principle of minimum protection*], it would be desirable if these instances of 'maximum protection' were also given express recognition in the Convention, but the absence of such recognition should not affect this conclusion.[108]

Therefore, when protecting foreign Berne Union authors and works, Member States are obliged to allow any uses exempted as quotations under

---

[105]   Since it is not restricted to any specific rights or means of exploitation, it may cover any quotations made as part of any teaching activity, including within a digital networked environment.

[106]   Some countries have opted for a broad quotation exception that is not limited to any specific purposes (for instance, Luxembourg Art. 10(1), Italy Art. 70(1), and the Nordic countries), but many others refer to specific purposes – among them, teaching or education (for instance, France Art. L122–5(3)(a), Belgium Art. 21(1), Spain Art. 32(1), Luxembourg Art. 10(1), Italy Art. 70(1)). Furthermore, some quotation exceptions limit its extent depending on the nature of the work or even exclude certain kinds of works, such as is the case in France and Spain: *see* Lucas, André (1994), *Traité de la Propriété Littéraire & Artistique,* Paris, Litec, p. 311; And *see* Pérez de Ontiveros Baquero, Carmen (1997), 'Comentario al art.32', in Bercovitz, Rodrigo (ed.) *Comentarios a la Ley de Propriedad Intelectual*, Madrid, Tecnos, 607, pp. 610–11.

[107]   The BC does not apply to the protection of works/authors in their countries of origin.

[108]   *See* Ricketson, *op. cit. supra,* §§ 12.17–18; *See* Ricketson and Ginsburg, *op. cit. supra,* §§ 6.110–11.

Art. 10(1) BC. As a corollary, any national quotation exception that is more restrictive than Art. 10(1) BC would only be applicable to purely domestic scenarios of copyright protection; while any domestic quotation exception broader in scope than is exempted under Art. 10(1) BC should still apply to foreign works and authors, as a result of the BC principle of national treatment (Art. 5(1) BC). Unfortunately, this principle of compulsory minimum protection under the BC seems to be widely 'forgotten' by Member States. The EUCD failure to make the quotation exception mandatory for EU Members (which, beyond the EU principles, are still bound by the BC obligations towards each other) is clear evidence.

Then, within the EU context, to what extent should the mandatory BC exception apply when protecting EU works within EU States? Art. 20 BC allows Berne countries to 'enter into special agreements among themselves, in so far as such agreements grant to authors more extensive rights than those granted by the Convention, or contain other provisions not contrary to this Convention.' However, the purpose of this provision is to act as a barrier to any lowering of protection between Member States,[109] that is, to enforce the principle of minimum protection of Art. 19 BC. Therefore, if – as we concluded earlier – the BC sets a *maximum protection* and the quotation exception is part of that ceiling, Art. 20 BC should not be read against it.

On the other hand, it is true that EU Member States must eliminate any conventional obligations among them that are incompatible with EU obligations, but this is not a question of incompatibility, (after all, the EUCD is not obliging Member States to disregard the quotation exception – thus conflicting with Art. 10(1) BC) but rather of overlap: the EUCD *allows* Member States to provide for a quotation exception, while the BC *obliges* Member States to provide for it, at least as far as non-national authors/works. In short, since the BC obligation to exempt quotations remains effective among EU States, one can only regret that the EUCD missed an opportunity to formally integrate such a prior common obligation into the EU *acquis*. Of course, this failure does not derogate the mandatory nature of the quotation exception within the Berne Union members, but may unnecessarily make things more complicated.

5. Conclusions

Both the BC and the EUCD provide for flexible and technology-neutral exceptions for teaching purposes that are clearly intended to cover distance and on-line teaching. However, most national legislators have failed to take full advantage of such opportunities.

---

109   *See* Ricketson and Ginsburg, *op. cit. supra*, § 6.130.

Significant differences exist in EU national laws, jeopardizing any harmonizing goal. Very few countries have chosen to implement Art. 5(3)(a) EUCD as it is, so as to take full advantage of its flexibility. Others have implemented it but added specific language – as to the amount and nature of works that can be used and as to the kind of schools and universities that may benefit from them – strongly reducing the scope of exempted teaching uses. The remaining national laws keep differentiating between on-line teaching and face-to-face teaching.

Yet, several powerful reasons justify the BC and EUCD open and flexible approach in favour of all forms of education (whether face-to-face, distance or on-line teaching). On the one hand, the public interest that justifies copyright exceptions for teaching purposes is the same regardless of the means used to conduct that teaching. We should not forget that digital formats will be far too common (and valuable) for them to be treated differently; the distinction between face-to-face and on-line teaching will soon be obsolete.[110] On the other hand, education is severely constrained in a world where copyright owners have a right to *refuse permission* or to unilaterally set the conditions for their works to be used for teaching purposes. Authors should not have the power to control what is taught.[111]

Of course, copyright owners, collecting societies and educational institutions should have a lot to say when negotiating the conditions for teaching uses (including on-line teaching uses). But before they do so, the needs of education and access to culture must be guaranteed against authors' exclusive rights. It is a question of strict public policy and, as such, it can be addressed only by legislators – as guarantors of the public interest – within our copyright laws.

Education deserves more effective exceptions than those existing today in national laws and the EU scenario shows that this can only be attempted at a supranational level: the BC or, at least, the EUCD. As a result, in order to guarantee a clear balance between both public and private interests at stake, the teaching exception of Art. 10(2) BC or, at least, that of Art. 5(3)(a) EUCD should be mandatory for Member States: a mandatory exception for

---

[110]   *See* US Copyright Office (1999), 'Report on Copyright and Digital Distance Education', lcweb.loc.gov/copyright/docs/de_rprt.pdf, accessed 13 November 2006, p. 10: 'The concept of distance education may become obsolete, as distance and classroom education merge'.

[111]   *See* Gasaway, Laura (2001), 'Impasse: Distance Learning and Copyright', *Ohio State Law Journal*, **62**, 783, p. 815.

There is also a serious concern about academic freedom and the control that content providers can exert by whether and to what extent they allow their content to be used in distance education courses. The power to refuse to license or to offer terms that an educational institution cannot afford or cannot accept is the power to control what is taught in courses.

teaching purposes (or as a statutory compulsory licence), that would allow for unauthorized – albeit duly compensated – use of pre-existing works for teaching purposes. This would set the groundwork for a level playing field for on-line teaching to lawfully evolve and excel. Is it too late to hope for it?

As the EU playing field stands today, the different options taken by national legislators will likely result in a fragmentation of the internal market, which may ultimately become an impediment to the development of on-line teaching within the EU.[112] Education is extremely sensitive, being fundamental for the development of the EU internal market.[113] A Directive aimed at ensuring the freedom of the internal market (including the free circulation of services) and compliance of intellectual property within the Information Society[114] should not have missed such a strategic opportunity for the development of European culture and society.

Annex: Selection of national laws consulted

Austria: Federal Law on Copyright in Works of Literature and Art and on Related Rights of April 1936 (No. 111/1936), as last amended by Law of 6 June 2003. *Belgium*: Law on Copyright and Neighbouring Rights of 30 June 1994, as last amended by Law of 22 May 2005. *Denmark*: Consolidated Copyright Act of 2003 (No. 164 of 12 March 2003). *Finland*: Copyright Act Law No. 404 of 8 July 1961, as last amended by Law No. 821 of 14 October 2005. *France*: Law on the Intellectual Property Code of 1 July 1992 (No. 92–597), as last amended by Law No. 2006-961 of 3 August 2006. *Germany*: Law on Copyright and Neighbouring Rights of 9 September 1965, as last amended by Law of 10 September 2003. *Greece*: Law on Copyright, Related Rights and Cultural Matters of March 1993 (No. 2121/1993), as last amended by Law No. 3057/2002. *Ireland*: Copyright Act of 2000; *see* also, The Copyright and Related Rights Regulations 2004 (No. 16/2004). *Italy*: Law for the Protection of Copyright and Neighbouring Rights No. 633 of 22 April 1941, as last amended by Decree No. 68/2003. *Luxembourg*: Law on Copyright of 29 March 1972, as last amended by Law of 18 April 2004. *Netherlands*: Copyright Act of 23 September 1912, as amended by Law of 27

---

112   *See* Recital 6 EUCD: 'Significant legal differences and uncertainties in protection may hinder economies of scale for new products and services containing copyright and related rights'.

113   *See* the EU Commission Communication to the European Council, *Working together for Growth and Jobs; A New Start for the Lisbon Strategy*, of 2 February 2005 (COM(2005)24) and the *Bologna Declaration on the European space for higher education*, of 19 June 1999 (crue.upm.es/eurec/, accessed 13 November 2006).

114   *See* Recital 3 EUCD.

October 1972, and last amended by Law of 6 July 2004. *Portugal*: Code of Copyright and Related Rights, Law No. 45/85 of 17 September 1985, as last amended by Decree-Law No. 50/2004 of 24 August 2004. *Spain*: Consolidated Text of the Law on Intellectual Property approved by Royal Legislative Decree 1/1996 of 12 April 1996, as last amended by Law 23/2006 of 7 July 2006. *Sweden*: Act on Copyright in Literary and Artistic Works, Law No. 729 of 30 December 1960, as last amended by Law of 1 July 2005. *United Kingdom*: Copyright, Designs and Patents Act of 1988 (Ch.48) of 15 November 1988; *see* also The Copyright and Related Rights Regulations 2003 (No. 2498/2003). *Czech Republic*: Copyright Act No. 121/2000 of 7 April 2000. *Hungary*: Act No. LXXVI of 1999 on Copyright, amended on 1 May 2004. *Latvia*: Copyright Law of 11 May 2000. *Lithuania*: Law on Copyright and Related Rights No. IX-1355, of 5 March 2003. *Malta*: Copyright Act XIII-2000 (chapter 415), as amended by Acts VI-2001 and IX-2003. *Poland*: Law No. 83 of 4 February 1994, on Copyright and Neighbouring Rights. *Slovak Republic*: Copyright Act No. 618/2003 of 4 December 2003. *Slovak Republic*: Copyright Act No. 618/2003 of 4 December 2003. *Republic of Slovenia*: Copyright and Related Rights Act of 1995 (No. 21/95), as amended in 2001 (No. 9/01) and in April 2004 (No. 43/04). *Norway*: Act Relating to Copyright in Literary, Scientific and Artistic Works No. 2 of 12 May 1961, as last amended by Law of 17 June 2005. *Iceland*: Copyright Act No. 73 of 12 May 1972, as last amended by Act No. 60 of 19 May 2000. *Liechtenstein*: Law of 19 May 1999 on Copyright and Neighbouring Rights. Implementation of the EUCD is still pending in Iceland and Liechtenstein. *Switzerland*: Federal Law on Copyright and Neighbouring Rights of 9 October 1992, as amended by Law of 17 June 2006.

16 Development of law in Asia: divergence versus convergence. Copyright piracy and the prosecution of copyright offences and the adjudication of IP cases: is there a need for a special IP court in Malaysia?

Ida Madieha bt. Abdul Ghani Azmi[1]

Introduction

The TRIPS Agreement has brought about the harmonization of substantive intellectual property laws in WTO member countries, Asia included. Malaysia,[2] being a developing country, amended all its intellectual property (IP) laws and introduced new rights to comply with the Agreement in late 1999. To that extent, the degree of divergence between member countries on substantive IP rights has been substantially reduced. However, in certain instances, divergence still exists. One such area is the adjudication of intellectual property cases. In some countries, such as Indonesia and Thailand, special IP courts have been established to provide standardized procedure for the hearing of IP disputes. This is despite the fact that the TRIPS Agreement explicitly does not mandate for the establishment of such special courts. In Malaysia, the increasing backlog of IP cases before the courts has pushed the Government to introduce a specialized IP court.

This chapter attempts to investigate the problems of piracy in Malaysia and examines the actual problem of prosecuting IP offences in Malaysia. It explores all the legislative mechanisms available in Malaysia to assist the enforcement authorities in their effort to stamp out piracy. The important provisions of these statutes will be examined in determining their effectiveness. Understandably, a discussion of this nature would not be complete without looking at the actual number of cases.

A cursory comparison is done with practice in other countries, such

---

[1]   Professor of Law, International Islamic University Malaysia.
[2]   For this, statistics supplied by both the Malaysian Motion Pictures Association and the Enforcement Division of the Ministry of Domestic Trade and Consumer Affairs will be used to illustrate some of the points discussed herein.

as Thailand and Indonesia, to determine whether divergence in terms of prosecution of IP cases exists or not. This is relevant as divergence in court practices in the adjudication of IP offences would bring about legal uncertainty in Asia. Lastly, the chapter concludes by looking at whether the setting up of a special IP court in Malaysia is really needed and, to a certain extent, useful in bringing about greater convergence with respect to the treatment of IP cases in Asia.

But first, we need to understand the reality of copyright piracy in these countries.

1. Copyright piracy in Malaysia

1.1. Copyright piracy in Malaysia: a game of numbers!
America is currently negotiating a Free Trade Agreement with Malaysia and one item on its wish-list in the IP chapter is effective enforcement of intellectual property rights (IPR). This initiative underscores the success that the Malaysian enforcement team has had in its crackdown on piracy. From the statistics, the first quarter of 2006 witnessed a total number of 6,341 raids with 1.5 million units of discs worth RM 51.3 million seized. 350,000 of these discs destined for overseas markets were seized in airports around the country. The Recording Industry Association of Malaysia has also taken measures by suing shopping malls that allow their premises to be used to sell pirated CDs and VCDs.

In the recent United States Trade Representative (USTR) 'Special 301' Report, the rate of piracy per motion picture is 50%, for records and music the rate is 52%, 63% for business software, 91% for entertainment software and 10% for books. The total losses due to piracy in 2004 are USD 188.4 million.[3]

This is a huge reduction of the figures cited in 2001. Yet the success is hardly appreciated by the US government as in the recent USTR Report Malaysia is still listed on the watch list. From that Report, three Asian countries have been listed on the watch list; Indonesia in the priority watch list and Malaysia and Thailand in the watch list.[4]

What is the reason for this? Since 2003, Malaysia has been the biggest exporter of pirate DVDs to the UK within the Asia-Pacific region. From 2003

---

[3]   The USTR, 2005, 'Special 301', *Decisions on Intellectual Property, IIPA's 2004 Estimated Trade Losses Due to Copyright Piracy (in millions of U.S. Dollars) and Piracy Levels in Country* (IIPA, 2005).

[4]   A position Thailand has retained since 1994. See Edward J. Kelly and Hassana Chira-alphakul, Thailand: IP Developments, Tike & Gibbins International Ltd, April 2002.

and 2004, it was reported that UK customs seized 1 693 767 pirated DVD imports from Malaysia.[5] Whilst on production, from a report prepared by Motion Pictures Association, Malaysia has 126 production lines which are capable of producing more than 441 million discs per year. This number is three times the official number of 38 licensed factories in Malaysia. The actual number of illegal factories is not known, though it is estimated by the authorities to be not less than 20 based on the number of CDs and VDs found in the market without an SID Code. In 2006, the first quarter of the year had already witnessed six raids on factories, of which four were on licensed factories. From newspaper reports, big players behind the operation are being hauled before the courts.[6]

How has this turnaround been achieved? This chapter explores the various legislative efforts in stepping up copyright enforcement.

1.2.   Of bullets and ammunition: legal weapons against piracy

At present, copyright law is not the sole law that is being used to curb piracy. The enforcement agency has been assisted with a number of related legislations, particularly:

(i)   Optical Discs Act 2000 (Act 606)
(ii)   Trade Descriptions Act 1972 (Act 87)
(iii)   Trade Descriptions (Original Label) Order 2002
(iv)   Anti-Money Laundering Act 2001 (Act 613)
(v)   Film Censorship Act 2002 (Act 620)
(vi)   Printing Presses and Publications Act 1984 (Act 301)
(vii)   Price Control Act 1946 (Act 121)

All of these laws have been used by the enforcement authorities as legal weapons to fight piracy. It would have been thought that copyright law would be the key legislation that the enforcement authorities would refer to. However, this is not the case. From the 2002 statistics, a total of 1743 cases were prosecuted under the Trade Description Act 1976, 8799 cases were compounded under the Price Control laws, 749 cases were prosecuted under the Film (Censorship) Act 1981, 614 cases were dealt with under other government agencies' laws, including the Customs Act 1967 and the bye-laws of the local authorities and five cases were dealt with under the Optical Discs

---

5   MPA, 'Organized Crime & Motion Picture Piracy', *Asia/Pacific Report*, November 2005.
6   *New Straits Times*, Thursday, 20 April 2006.

Table 16.1 Copyright cases: 2000 statistics

Trade Description Act	1743
Price Control Laws	8799
Film (Censorship) Act 1981	749
Other government agencies laws including the Customs Act 1967 and the bye-laws of the local authorities	614
Optical Discs Act 2000	5

Act 2000.[7] Table 16.1 shows the relative reliance on copyright as a means to fight piracy.

A brief exposition of the relevant legislation is discussed below.

1.2.1. The Optical Discs Act 2000 (Act 606)   A special task force was set up in 1999 to oversee the running of optical discs operation, which, was identified as the main source of piracy. This Committee was responsible for the introduction of the Optical Discs Act 2000 and the Trade Description (Original Label) Order 2002. The role of optical discs legislation is to supervise and monitor legitimate replication operations through the giving out of licences and conducting routine inspections to ensure compliance. Under the Act, the manufacturer is mandated to cause each optical disc manufactured by him to be marked with the manufacturer's code assigned to him.[8]

The main criticism against the Act is that whilst it regulates the manufacturing of optical discs, it does not actually illegalize the burning of copyright materials onto CDs and DVDs. The potency of the Act in the war against piracy is, thus, questionable!

1.2.2. The Anti-Money Laundering Act 2001 (Act 613)   As piracy in Malaysia operates through organized criminal networks, such operations can fall within the domain of the Anti-Money Laundering law that targets criminal syndicates. Under section 3 of the Act, offences committed under section 41 of the Copyright Act and section 4[9] and section 21[10] of the Optical Discs Act 2000 (Act 606) are considered to be serious offences. In combating a serious offence of this nature, the competent authority and the relevant

---

7   International Federation of the Phonographic Industry (IFPI), 2002, Special 301 Report, cited in Jagjit Singh, 'Prosecution of Copyright Infringements: Section 42 Issues' [2002] 4 *MLJ* xvi.
8   Section 19(1) of the Optical Discs Act 2000.
9   Relating to the offence of manufacturing without a valid licence
10   Relating to the offence of applying false manufacturer's code.

enforcement agency could co-ordinate and co-operate with any other enforcement agency inside and outside the country.[11]

1.2.3   Trade Descriptions Act 1972 (Act 87) and Trade Descriptions (Original Label) Order 2002   A trade description order is often sought to support an action against counterfeit trade marked goods. As a result of the recommendation of the Special Task Force on Piracy in 1999, the Trade Descriptions (Original Label) Order 2002 was passed under the aegis of the Act. This Order took effect from 15 January 2003. The purpose of the Order is to ease identification of original goods by requiring the affixing of an original label bearing the national emblem, serial number, the words 'original' or 'tulen', the words 'KPDN' and 'HEP', the logo of the Ministry of Domestic Trade and Consumer Affairs and security features on original goods. The label, which costs 20 cents per sticker, adds an additional cost to the original goods. As a consequence, it has been questioned whether the imposition of the 'original label' requirement would be offending the TRIPS Agreement and the Paris Convention's obligation to confer copyright without any formality.

Any person who offers for sale or supply goods without the 'original label' or those who falsely affix an 'original label' to non-original goods would be committing an offence under the Order. Though the insistence on the affixing of 'original label' is meant to assist the identification of original copies, there were claims that the 'original labels' have fallen into the wrong hands and that fake copies of the 'original labels' are being sold to others. Whether these allegations are true or not could not be substantiated.

1.2.4.   Printing Presses and Publications Act 1984 (Act 301)   The Printing Presses and Publications Act 1984 Act has been used primarily to target 'smut' materials that are being sold widely in Malaysia through pirate CDs and DVDs. The Act makes it an offence for anybody to print any publication[12] or document which is obscene or otherwise against public decency.[13] Due to this, those in possession of a 'prohibited publication'[14] can be liable to a fine not exceeding RM 5,000,[15] whilst those who print, import, produce, reproduce, publish, sell, issue, circulate, offer for sale, distribute, or have in their

---

[11]   Section 29(3) of the Anti-Money Laundering Act 2000.

[12]   The term 'publication' has been defined broadly to include audio recordings.

[13]   Section 4(1)(a) of the Act.

[14]   Section 2 of the Act defines the term 'prohibited publication' to mean any publication which has been prohibited under subsection (1) of section 1 and includes any copy, reproduction, extract or any translation, precis or paraphrase thereof.

[15]   Section 8(1) of the Act.

possession any such printed publication can be liable to imprisonment for a term not exceeding three years or to a fine not exceeding RM 20 000 or both.[16]

In Malaysia, there are strict rules relating to content that apply to all forms of media. The strict observance of content rules by the authorities induces an increase in interest in 'smut' materials which are available on the black market and this explains why the majority of the pirated DVDs and VDs are 'pornographic in nature'.

1.2.5 Film Censorship Act 2002 (Act 620) Related to this, the Film Censorship Act 2002 is another powerful weapon that can be used against pornographic audiovisuals. Section 5 of the Act makes it an offence for anybody to possess, have in their custody, own, circulate, exhibit, distribute, display, manufacture, produce, sell or hire, any film-publicity material which is obscene or is otherwise against public decency. Any person found to offend this section is liable to a fine not exceeding RM 10 000 and not more than RM 50 000 or to imprisonment for a term not exceeding five years or to both.[17]

1.2.6. The Copyright Act 1987 The Copyright Act 1987 is the core Act from which the power of the enforcement officers is derived. The main section that relates to copyright offence is section 41; this makes it an offence to:

(a) make for sale or hire any infringing copy;

(b) sell, let for hire or by way of trade, expose or offer for sale or hire any infringing copy;

(c) distribute infringing copies;

(d) possess, otherwise than for his private and domestic use, any infringing copy;

(e) exhibit in public any infringing copy by way of trade;

(f) import into Malaysia, otherwise than for his private and domestic use, an infringing copy;

(g) make or have in his possession any contrivance used or intended to be used for the purposes of making infringing copies;

(h) circumvent or cause the circumvention of any effective technological measures;

(i) remove or alter any electronic rights management information without authority; or

(j) distribute, import for distribution or communicate to the public, without authority, works or copies of works in respect of which electronic rights management information has been removed or altered without authority.

---

[16] Section 8(2) of the Act.

[17] Section 5(2) of the Act.

From the above list, it would appear that almost all conceivable forms of abuse of copyright are being criminalized. However, as would appear from the statistics given by the Enforcement Division of the Ministry of Domestic Trade and Consumer Affairs, a large proportion of these actions are for possession and only a handful for export and manufacturing. Many question the wisdom of the Enforcement Division in their tendency to charge the offenders for distribution rather than possession. It could also be that from past experience, it is relatively easier to book offenders for distribution rather than possession or other charges, due to the more stringent burden of proof required by the courts for these latter offences.

1.2.7   Supplying, offering to supply or distributing infringing goods through the Internet   Internet sites showcasing infringing goods for sale are mushrooming in Malaysia. The intensity of raids that is taking place in Malaysia is forcing the peddlers to vary their strategy. From the traditional displaying of CDs and VCDs in 'pasar malam', on the roadside, in small and cramped shops or even in big shopping malls, the peddlers are now resorting to using children to peddle these goods or displaying only empty covers of the titles to avoid being caught with substantial copies and being slapped with hefty fines! The internet is also fast becoming a popular 'store' for showcasing pirated goods!

It might be questioned whether displaying the titles of movies or sound recordings on the internet is deemed to be an 'offer for sale' as far as section 41 is concerned. However, this is clearly the case as the venue in which such an offer takes place is irrelevant. However, the main problem with such distribution systems is that when a raid takes place, not a single physical infringing copy can be found on the premises. The best evidence rule practised by the courts means that in all instances hard evidence is required to prove a case. There is, thus, a need for a change of mindset not only among enforcement officers but also among the lawyers and judges involved if these offenders are to be severely punished. Otherwise, it will be quite easy for the offenders to evade from liability.

1.2.8   Possession   Past experience shows that the court has applied the same standard of 'possession' as in drug cases. The notion is that the prosecution needs to prove that the offender knows that the copies are infringing ones, just as in drug cases. Understandably, the main element of the two offences is the same, i.e. possession. However, a core distinction can be drawn between possession of drugs and that of copyright. The rationale behind the cautious approach for drugs is that it is punishable with capital punishment which is not the case with a copyright offence.

Moreover, the Act excuses the possession of three or fewer copies of pirated goods for personal use. This explains why some peddlers only display empty packages or just a list of titles in order to enjoy the privilege of personal use!

1.2.9   Export of pirated goods   Previously, it was reported that large-scale exports of factory-manufactured pirated optical discs are shipped from Malaysia. The escalation of cross-border smuggling calls into question the effectiveness of our surveillance at the border. The power to restrain and confiscate infringing copies at the border falls under the jurisdiction of the customs authorities with the incorporation of the border measure provisions in 2000. To take advantage of this administrative measure the copyright owner or his agent would need to have details of the consignment and its route, which is often difficult in most cases. It is for this reason that this administrative measure is rarely invoked in practice. In most instances, the custom authorities rely on the 'ex officio' powers granted under the Act to enable them to conduct raids on suspicious shipments. In fact, most pirated goods have been confiscated under this power rather than upon the request of the copyright owner.

The crux of the dissatisfaction is that exporting of infringing copies[18] has not been made an offence under the Act in contrast to importing. If Malaysia is fast becoming the source of exports of pirated goods, the suggestion is that exporting should equally be criminalized under the Act.

It has been pointed out that if the cross-border movement of pirated products were to be treated like the smuggling of drugs, interdiction of pirated goods could be further intensified. For this purpose, section 135 of the Customs Act, which relates to the penalty for various smuggling offences, would need to be amended to incorporate copyright-infringing goods.[19]

1.2.10.   Caning the offenders: how strong could it be?   From the promulgation of the 1983 Act till now, several amendments have taken place to provide for more stringent penalties. The Amendment Act 775 introduced further measures for enforcement authorities. It enables the enforcement authority to enter and inspect vehicles, not only buildings, under warrant.[20] It allows goods that are

---

[18]   'Infringing copy' means any reproduction of any work eligible for copyright under the Copyright Act 1987, the making of which constitutes an infringement of the copyright in the work or, in the case of any article imported into Malaysia without the consent or licence of the owner of the copyright, the making of which was carried out without the consent of the owner of the copyright.

[19]   See paras (j) and (x) of the section that deals with the conveyance, removal, deposition, or dealing with prohibited goods and the possession of prohibited goods in the baggage of passengers of carriers.

[20]   Section 44 of the Act.

intended to be used or capable of being used for infringing purposes to be seized. These goods must, however, be produced before the Magistrate and be kept in the custody of the Controller or Assistant Controller.[21] In a move to stop others from challenging the validity of search warrants on technical grounds, section 49 was clarified to the effect that any warrant is admissible notwithstanding defects. Statutory affidavits are often being abused. To eliminate such practices, section 48(e) was inserted to provide liability for false statements.

To make the penalty more severe, the amount of fines imposed was increased in 2003. Previously, for offences under section 41(a)–(f), the amount of fines that could be imposed might not exceed RM 10 000 for each infringing copy and RM 20 000 for repeat offences. The maximum fine that can be imposed is per infringing copy and not per title. That hardly justifies the small amount of fines collected from the cases. For example, in 2001, there were two cases in which the fines imposed were a mere RM 750! The total amount of fines does not correlate with the actual value of the goods confiscated! One possible justification is that as the provision underlines the maximum penalty, the judges tend to impose the lowest possible fine. The result is as soon as the peddlers are back in the street, they continue with their business as if nothing had happened! And only to recover their losses within days of business!

Perhaps, due to this disconcerting practice, in 2003, the fines have been imposed amounting to not less than RM 2000 and not more than RM 20 000 for each infringing copy and for repeat offences to a fine of not less than RM 4000 and not more than RM 40 000. The rationale for the amendment is to specify both the minimum and maximum amounts of fines for each infringing copy. The judge would then have to impose at least the minimum fine which would be RM 2000. Perhaps this is a reason why we can see an increase in the collection of fines to RM 7 945 150.00 in 2004![22] In 2006, the highest penalty imposed by the courts was recorded to be RM 7.3 million or three years' imprisonment. In another case in Sarawak an accused was fined RM 3.8 million and sentenced to jail for six months.

In a move to tighten investigative powers, the legislator introduced the power to arrest without warrant in 2003. The Assistant Controller, who would be spearheading the raids, would be empowered to arrest any person without warrant that he reasonably believes has committed or is attempting to commit any seizable offence under the Act. The only requirement is that the Assistant Controller is required to take the person to the nearest police station to be dealt with according to the normal procedure of police arrest. As a result of the amendment, a total of 1573 suspects have been remanded and many have subsequently been charged.

---

[21]   Section 44(2) of the Act.
[22]   Piracy Statistics, Ministry of Domestic Trade and Consumer Affairs.

1.2.11. Proving ownership and statutory affidavit   Section 42 of the Act was incorporated to enable a copyright owner to prove ownership of copyright by way of affidavit or statutory declaration stating that at the time specified, copyright subsists in the work and that he is the owner of the copyright in the work. The introduction of section 42 is to ease the burden of proving owner-ship by the copyright owner and shifts the burden to prove otherwise to the defence. However, in one decided case, it was found that despite such an affi-davit or statutory declaration, the prosecution would have to prove subsistence and ownership of copyright in the work. In *Public Prosecutor v KTA (Sarawak) Sdn Bhd*,[23] Rhodzariah Bujang J discharged and acquitted an accused for failure to prove beyond reasonable doubt that copyright subsisted in the alleged infringing copies of the software.

The difficulty of appreciating that section 42 is a departure from existing practices that require best evidence resulted in some High Court judges ruling that the agent that administers the statutory affidavit be required to produce the authorization document in writing. If this is not done, the statutory declaration would not be admissible in court. This was the tenor of the decision made by Suriyadi J in *Solid Gold Publishers Sdn Bhd v Chan Wee He and Ors*.[24] Suriyadi J found that the non-production of an authorization document would not qualify the contents of the relevant affidavit to be prima-facie proof of the facts contained therein. The lack of an authorization document may raise suspicion as to whether he was properly authorized to make the statutory declaration and hence was ruled to be inadmissible.[25]

These two judgments have defeated the basic reason behind the introduc-tion of section 42. Abdul Malik Ishak J, in a recent decision *Rock Records (M) Sdn Bhd v Audio One Entertainment Sdn Bhd*,[26] set the record straight. On the contention by the defence that the statutory declaration was not admissible as no authorization document was attached, he evinced that:

> It is quite apparent that section 42 of the Copyright Act 1987 prescribes the manner of proving copyright subsistence and ownership of works. It provides that an affi-davit or statutory declaration to be made by the copyright owner or persons shall be admissible in any proceedings as prima facie evidence of the facts contained therein. It is quite obvious that section 42 of the Copyright Act 1987 was enacted to

---

[23]   Judgment dated 11 November 2002 with Criminal Case Nos SC-63-21-97-I, SC-63-23-97-I, SC-63-24-97-II, SC-63-25-97-I, SC-63-26-97-II, SC-63-27-97-I, SC-63-28-97-II, SC-63-29-97-I, SC-63-30-97-II.

[24]   [1998] 1 MLJ 276.

[25]   *Solid Gold Publishers Sdn Bhd v Orang-orang yang tidak dikenali yang kononnya berniaga sebagai Shenton Video Centre (Terengganu) Sdn. Bhd & Anor*, [1998] 5 MLJ 122.

[26]   [2005] 1 CLJ 200.

facilitate and ease the process of proving copyright ownership. It is a concession of a sort. It circumvents the requirement of having to produce supporting documentary evidence which may have been antiquated and voluminous. Section 42 of the Copyright Act 1987 places the burden on the infringer to dispute and challenge the prima facie evidence adduced by the copyright owner.

Having taken that stand, the learned judge then concluded that the onus was on the defence to refute the claim of ownership by bringing in evidence to the contrary. A bare denial was not sufficient to dislodge or rebut the prima-facie evidence adduced in the plaintiff's affidavits and the statutory declarations. As to the judgment made in *Solid Gold v Chan Wee Ho*,[27] Abdul Malik J found the decision to be wrongly made. He pointed out that the provisions in the Evidence Act 1950 governing primary and secondary documentary evidence had no application to affidavit as made clear in section 2 of the Evidence Act 1950. Furthermore, there is no need to produce true copies of the authorization letter nor exhibits of the copyright work by virtue of O.41 r.11(1) of the Rules of the High Court. He opined that even if there were an irregularity, it would be curable. The plaintiff could be asked to produce original copies before the court to support his case. But the most important thing is that justice should not be dispensed with only on a technical matter.[28]

Whilst, Abdul Malik's decision on section 42 has helped to eliminate certain areas of uncertainty in the law, there remain many unresolved issues. For example, the prevailing view among the enforcement agencies is that it is mandatory for a copyright owner to appear before the court to substantiate the ownership of the work. It is hard to understand the logic behind this ruling as it is entirely impractical and illogical to expect a foreign copyright owner to fly in to testify before the court on the issue of ownership of copyright in a clear-cut piracy case!

This leads on to another impractical practice of requiring the deponent of the statutory document to appear before the court to confirm the content of the document. The insistence on calling the maker of the document to attend trial has resulted in a lot of hardship for the prosecution.

From a clear construction of section 42, copies of the original copyright work should be annexed thereto. As these goods may be in the form of CDs, VCDs or DVDs, there might be a problem in attaching them with the affidavit. One suggestion is to allow reproductions of the subject matter, such as photographs of the DVDs, be attached to the affidavit in place of the 'true copy' in order to overcome the practical difficulty of annexing the original goods.

Section 42 also uses the words 'at the time specified therein', which leads to the question whether it refers to the time of the raid or the date when the affidavit

---

[27] Op. cit.
[28] At pp. 221 and 222.

was sworn. The uncertainty of this provision may give rise to different interpretations, which may implicate the admissibility of the affidavit in the actual trial.

In comparison, in Hong Kong, a statutory declaration of ownership is admissible in any proceedings without further proof as made clear in section 121 of the Copyright Ordinance.[29] It is then for the defendant to dispute the claim of ownership. The deponent is not mandated to give evidence before the court unless the defendant has satisfied the court that the subsistence or ownership of the copyright is genuinely at issue.[30]

From the foregoing discussion, it would appear that though some provisions have been introduced to strengthen efforts to reduce piracy, nevertheless, due to uncertainty over the interpretation of the provision, many offenders escape prosecution on technical grounds. This is somewhat disconcerting as it is already difficult to accumulate enough evidence to charge offenders. Giving them the benefit of the loophole would only provide further avenues for them to escape liability!

1.3.   From raids to the courts

From a summary of raid reports from the Motion Picture Association (MPA), in 2005, a total of 1740 raids were conducted by the Enforcement Division of the Ministry of Domestic Trade and Consumer Affairs upon the initiation of the MPA. The total amount of seizures was 6 038 350 items consisting of VCDs, Games, CDR and Software, CDs and DVDs with a staggering number of 3 750 251 for DVDs. Several other implements and contrivances used in the offence have also been seized, amounting to six for VCD line, three for DVD line, one for Mastering line, 41 vehicles, 35 televisions and eight factories.[31]

Yet the official figures from the Ministry of Domestic Trade and Consumer Affairs are even more staggering. In the first quarter of 2006 alone, a total of 6341 raids and seizure of goods amounting to RM 51.3 have been recorded. In 2005, the number of raids conducted countrywide by the Ministry came to 38 022, with total goods seized amounting to RM 100 367 107.00! This is four times the value of goods seized in 2004, which amounted to RM 29 216 528.00 or 2003, when the figure was RM 45 665 038. Table 16.2 shows the number of raids and the amount of goods seized from the anti-piracy campaign organized by the government.

As the pirates are now moving to the internet as an avenue for the distribution of infringing goods, the number of raids against internet proprietor has increased. In 2005, a total of eight actions were initiated for internet supply of pirated goods. The biggest concern is retail sales where a total of 1123 actions

---

29   Cap 528.
30   Section 121(8)(b) of the Copyright Ordinance.
31   Statistics from Motion Picture Association – Kuala Lumpur.

Table 16.2   Piracy statistics

Year	Search/ raids	No. of cases	No. of arrests	No. of seized items	Value of seizure (RM)
2006*	788	241	117	224 940	36 650 245.00
2005	38 022	3780	710	4 781 040	100 367 107.00
2004	25 508	4400	524	6 081 045	29 216 528.00
2003	30 970	9504	124	4 575 101	45 665 038

Note: *Until 10 February 2006.

Source: Ministry of Domestic Trade and Consumer Affairs.

have been registered against them, followed by export with a total of 526, warehouse (75) and factory (8).

Despite the high number of raids all over the country, the amount of follow-up legal action is considerably smaller. From 1999 till August 2005, there were about 740 cases scheduled for trial. This is out of 3350 cases where action was taken, which means that less than 20% of cases are followed by a court trial. Of these, in only 171 cases did the accused plead guilty and a total of four cases were actually won and 15 acquitted.

The small number of cases that proceeded to trial can be rationalized by the view that nearly half of them are still under investigation; i.e. a total of 1581. This illustrates the difficulty the prosecution is facing in proving copyright cases. But this is increasing. It can be seen that the number of prosecutions in 2005 had increased by 24%. In 2005 alone, 91 cases were before the courts, 121 were pending and 598 were under investigation.

Fines imposed under the Act are considerably higher and this has been made more severe through several successive amendments. For example, for each offence of possession, the accused may be liable to a fine of RM 10 000 for each infringing copy. However, the amount actually imposed on offenders was considerably lower. From the statistics, the total amount of fines imposed for the 175 cases amounted to RM 8 898 474.00. This is because the amount of fine was considered to be the maximum penalty which the court could impose.[32]

Which kinds of copyright offences are more prevalent in Malaysia? From official statistics from 1999 to 31 December 2004, out of a total of 2627 cases where action was taken, a total of 2140 were for distribution, 13 for manufacturing and 474 for export. The number of cases involving distribution shows a

---

[32]   See Appendix A at the end of this chapter for a summary of the number of actions taken against piracy and the actual number of cases before the court.

Table 16.3   Cases against licensed factories

Year	No. of cases	No. of machines seized	No. of machines sealed	Value of machines seized (RMk)
2001	–	–	–	
2002	6	7	7	13.6
2003	1	–	1	3.7
2004	1	–	1	0.5
2005	–	–	–	–
2006	2	4	5	29
Total	10	11	14	46.8

Source: Ministry of Domestic Trade and Consumer Affairs.

concentration in big cities such as the Klang Valley (542), Shah Alam (225), Johore Bahru (176), Penang (153) Kuala Kubu Bahru (138), Kajang (125), Taiping (80), Kota Kinabalu (74), N. Sembilan (73), Kucing (42) and Malacca (42). This can be explained by the fact that most raids are conducted in big towns, leaving small towns as relatively safe havens for pirate copies. But no more! One classic example is Kota Bharu, a city in the most northerly state neighbouring the Thai border. From 1999 to 2002, there were no recorded cases. In 2003, a total of 10 cases were recorded and this shot up to 25 in 2004! In Kelantan, only two towns were involved. Besides Kota Bharu, the other town is Kuala Krai, which recorded only three cases in 2004 and none before that. For Kuala Terenganu, only three towns were recorded; Kuala Terengganu, Kemaman and Besut! All three towns recorded a very small number of cases, with Besut recording none.

As for manufacturing, the highest number of cases is recorded in Klang Valley (four), Shah Alam (two) and Kajang (two) with Pulau Pinang, Sepang and Kuala Selangor recording a total of one each. From these raids, the number of machines seized came up to 14 with a total value of RM 46.8 million. The usage of expensive and sophisticated equipment supports the belief that piracy is being controlled by organized crime. The number of illegal factories has been recorded as 29 with a total of 49 machines being seized with a total value of RM 91.9 million! Table 16.3 shows a break-down of cases reported to the Ministry of Domestic Trade and Consumer Affairs.

With regard to exports the highest number is recorded in Sepang with a total of 462 cases.

2.   Piracy in Indonesia and Thailand

2.1   The war against copyright piracy in Indonesia

The main criminal provision for copyright offences in Indonesia is Article 72 of the Law of the Republic of Indonesia (No. 19 year 2002). Fines range from one million rupiahs to 5 billion rupiahs depending on the nature of the offence:

(i)   for the offence of publication and reproduction of a copyright work, the punishment would be imprisonment of at least one month and/ or a fine of at least 1 million rupiahs or imprisonment of at most seven years and/or a fine of at most 5 billion rupiahs;

(ii)   for the offence of broadcasts, exhibits, distribution, or sales to the public, the punishment would be imprisonment of at most five years and/or a fine of at most 5 million rupiahs;

(iii)   for the offence of deliberate use and reproduction of a computer program for commercial purposes, the punishment would be at most five years and/or a fine of at most 500 million rupiahs;

(iv)   for the offence of reproduction and re-broadcast of broadcast work, the punishment would be imprisonment of at most two years and/or a fine of at most 150 million rupiahs;

(v)   for the offence against moral rights, the punishment would be imprisonment of at most two years and/or a fine of at most 150 million rupiahs;

(vi)   for an offence against technological protection measures, the punishment would be imprisonment of at most two years and/or a fine of at most 150 million rupiahs;

(vii)   for an offence against the Optical Discs law the punishment would be imprisonment of at most five years and/or a fine of at most 1.5 billion rupiahs.

From reports, it would seem that the effort to stamp out piracy in Indonesia has suffered the same fate as in Malaysia.[33] The number of raids is not commensurate with the number of total prosecutions of offences. Quite a number of cases are still under police investigation. Weaknesses in prosecution skills and preservation of evidence have exacerbated the problem further.[34]

To that extent, the Indonesian government has entrusted the task of resolving copyright disputes to the Commercial Court, which was initially established

---

[33]   Nicholas Redfearn, 'Indonesia's Progress in Enforcement', *Managing Intellectual Property*, July/August 2001, 29.

[34]   For this see a report prepared by Rouse & Co International, 2006, 'Indonesia – A Study of a Developing Country's Implementation of an Effective IPR Protection System', available at http://www.iprights.com.

to handle bankruptcy cases.[35] Any appeal against the decision of the Commercial Court would be submitted directly to the Supreme Court.[36] The main advantage of having such specialized courts is that a 90 day time-frame has been laid down for the settlement of IPR cases.[37]

To stamp out optical discs piracy, the Optical Discs law was passed in 2004.[38] Estimated losses from optical discs piracy in Indonesia have been as staggering as 92 per cent.[39] Backed by an enforcement initiative from the industry, the enforcement authorities have conducted a major crackdown on piracy hot spots in Indonesia.[40] The Optical Discs law requires producers to register their production facilities, maintain and report production records, and be subject to frequent supervision by the authorities. Under the law, valid optical discs must bear a government-approved source identification code.[41] As with other optical discs laws, offending the regulations would incur criminal punishment of imprisonment of not more than five years or a fine not exceeding 1.5 million rupiah.[42]

2.2. Piracy in Thailand

Piracy in Thailand is as stubborn as it is in its neighbouring country Malaysia. The supply and production of imitation goods is assisted by a cheap labour force. Thai workers who are renowned for their skill in traditional handiwork assist in the production of high quality imitation products.

---

[35]   From reports, five such Commercial Courts have special jurisdiction over intellectual property: Central Jakarta Commercial Court (Jakarta Capital Province); Semarang Commercial Court (Central Java Province); Surabaya Commercial Court (Eastern Java Province); Medan Commercial Court (Northern Sumatra Province) and: Makasar Commercial Court (Southern Sulawesi Province).

[36]   See Adriani Nurdin, 'Challenges Faced by Non-specialised Judicial Systems in Indonesia', paper delivered at the EU – Symposium on IP enforcement by Specialized Courts, Challenges and Recent Developments in IPR, Bangkok, 1–2 December 2005.

[37]   Adolf Panggabean and Erna L. Kusoy, 'Trade Mark System Strives to be Taken Seriously', *Managing IP*, Nov 2002, p. 78.

[38]   Signed on 5 October 2004 and went into effect on 18 April 2005.

[39]   '1.25 Million Pirated Optical Discs Seized in Raid on Jakarta Burner Lab', Report by Motion Picture Association, 1 December 2005. See also the IIPA report and 2006 Special 301 Report, Indonesia, available at http://www.iipa.com/rbc/2006/2006SPEC301INDONESIA.pdf.

[40]   'Asia-Wide Movie Piracy Crackdown Nets 5.7 Million Pirate Discs, 807 Arrests', Report by the Motion Picture Association, 9 February 2006.

[41]   See 'Taking Action: How Countries are Fighting IPR Crime', available at http://usinfo.state.gov/products/pubs/intelprp/action.htm.

[42]   Despite reservations made by the IIPA on the weaknesses of the Regulations, see also the IIPA report and 2006 Special 301 Report, Indonesia, available at http://www.iipa.com/rbc/2006/2006SPEC301INDONESIA.pdf.

The Thai Copyright Law criminalizes copyright infringement and provides for fines and imprisonment in such cases. The penalty provisions of the Thai Copyright Act 1994 are sections 69–77.

(i)   Section 69 provides for the punishment of someone who infringes copyright and performance right. The punishment would be a fine of between 20 000 and 200 000 baht.

(ii)   Section 70 provides for the punishment for someone who infringes section 31 to be liable to a fine of 10 000 to 100 000 baht. If the violation is committed for commercial purposes, the offender would be liable to imprisonment of three months to two years or a fine of 50 000 to 400 000 baht, or both.

(iii)   Section 75 provides that all infringing copies should be the property of the copyright owner and articles used for the committing of the offence are forfeited.

(iv)   Section 76 provides for one half of the fine imposed on the copyright offender to be payable to the copyright owner.[43]

Effective remedies are conferred upon the copyright owner, including confiscation of infringing goods and injunctions. The unique feature of Thai copyright law is that 50% of the fines levied by the court against the infringer are payable to the copyright owner.

The optical discs and internet piracy that now plagues Malaysia and Indonesia is equally felt in Thailand. In a 2002 report, at least 100 known plants for optical media with over 200 known manufacturing lines and mastering machines are known to exist in Thailand. These plants have the capacity to produce over 1 billion discs every year, making Thailand a leading source of pirated content.[44] It is no wonder that Thailand promulgated its Optical Discs Law in 2005.[45] This Act puts into place the same system as in Malaysia, i.e. production of optical discs is only possible under licence from the Government.[46] Legitimate optical discs are to carry a source identification

---

[43]   For a general discussion see 'Copyright Protection in Thailand', available at http://www.ipthailand.org/Static/GeneralIP.aspx; http://www.tillekeandgibbins.com/Publications/Articles/ip_registration/copy_th.htm.

[44]   See Edward J. Kelly and Hassana Chira-alphakul, Thailand: IP Developments, Tilke & Gibbins International Ltd, April 2002.

[45]   Optical Disc Production Act B.E. 2548 (2005), Enacted on 22 May 2005.

[46]   I.e. through notification to the competent official before starting production (section 5). Notification by the producer must at a minimum include details of the names and address of the producer, the factory, machine and other items as determined by the Director General (section 6).

code that identifies the producer and the copyright owner.[47] Producers that offend the obligation would be liable to a penalty of imprisonment for a term not exceeding one year or a fine not exceeding 200 000 baht or both imprisonment and fine. Worse still for those who imitate the source identification code, which would usually be the case for fakes, the punishment would be imprisonment for a term from six months up to five years and a fine from 100 to 1 million baht. The sophistication with which piracy operates in Thailand compels the government to consider taking measures under the Anti Money Laundering Act which falls under the Thai Anti-Money laundering Office.[48]

The modus operandi of enforcement against fakes is similar to other parts of the world. Enforcement authorities are given the powers to investigate, search premises and arrest suspected parties and seize goods as evidence and ultimately prosecute the offender before the court.[49]

A specialist IP court was established by royal decree on 1 December 1997. This Central Intellectual Property and International Trade Court hears both civil and criminal IP cases. Any appeal from this court would be heard by the Supreme Court. The court ensures the speedy resolution of IP disputes and litigation involving IP offences as a case is heard until it is fully resolved without an adjournment. Since its inception, the court has heard around 4,000 cases each year, most of them actually criminal cases.[50]

2.3 Convergence or divergence?

One cannot dismiss the common social and cultural factors behind the thriving piracy in Malaysia, Indonesia and Thailand. Patronizing pirated and counterfeit products is never seen as socially or culturally unacceptable, fostering support for backyard and mass production of pirated goods. The price gap between original and pirated goods only helps to further boost demand for such goods and thwart efforts to reduce piracy.[51] Intellectual property is still largely seen as a foreign product as in terms of numbers, the majority of intellectual property registered in these countries is owned by foreigners. It does not help that while governments in these countries have launched massive

---

47   Section 8 of the Optical Disc Production Act B.E. 2548 (2005).
48   Though in July 2004, the Council of State rejected the inclusion of IPR crimes as a predicate offence, citing concerns that IPR violations are 'commercial disputes', Hassana Chira-alphakul and Edward J. Kelly, 'Online Fake Goods Sales Hit by Enforcement Action', *Asia Law*, March 2004, 53.
49   Ibid.
50   Ralph Cunnigham, 'Thailand – Interview Judged to Perfection', *Managing Intellectual Property*, available at http://www.managingip.com.
51   See Assafa Endeshaw (2005), 'Intellectual Property Enforcement in Asia: A Reality Check', 13 International Journal of Law and Information Technology 378.

campaigns against piracy by conducting country-wide raids, open public apathy towards pirated goods simply undermines this.

It does not help that pressure to stem piracy and introduce stronger ammunition against piracy has largely come from external sources, especially the United States and European Union. This could not but be presented as unwarranted political intervention in domestic policy. The significant amount of public resources deployed to reduce losses resulting from piracy, which are essentially private losses, is a major diversion of resources that could be used to strengthen the domestic economy. It is no wonder that, to some, the fight against piracy is seen as a measure that benefits foreign interests the most. Unless and until piracy is culturally and socially seen as a menace in these three countries, no amount of aggressive legislative schemes to facilitate enforcement efforts will do the trick.

Despite there being a variety of legal actions that can be taken against piracy, the problems are far from being resolved. The modus operandi of raids and law enforcement by government agencies are similar, with common evidentiary and manpower problems. There have been complaints that there is no co-ordinated enforcement by various government agencies. Raids are conducted sporadically, they are not consistent and they do not attack the root of the problem. The high number of raids is not followed by effective prosecution of cases. On this note, there is a clear need to be more creative in the prosecution of copyright offences and to treat them differently from other criminal cases, especially possession of drugs.

But this is no longer the case in Malaysia. With rigorous enforcement by the authorities on 'hot spots' in Malaysia the number of open malls that thrive on pirated goods have dwindled. The enforcement authorities have adopted a multi-prong strategy:

(i)   continuous surveillance at hot spots;
(ii)   enhancing intelligence unit;
(iii) establishment of export unit in April 2005;
(vi)   two high tech scanners at KLIA and Penang Airport by MAS Cargo.

From this initiative, a total of 362 162 units of pirated goods amounting to RM 3777.752 have been seized, some of a shipment destined for South America, Africa and Asia. Open premises sales have dropped from 2386 in 2001 to about 505 by the end of 2005. Enforcement has also managed to intercept export activities at the exit point.

To beef up the manpower needed to carry out this task, the Malaysian government has recently endorsed the recruitment of 754 new enforcement officers. The government has also stepped up enforcement at the border. The initiative is the culmination of a recommendation to set up a Special Task

Force in April 1999 to combat piracy. This task force, chaired by the Minister of Domestic Trade and Consumer Affairs, is made up of representatives from the Royal Police, Customs, Local Authorities, Multimedia Commission and Chemistry Department. A forensic lab was established in 2003 with the co-operation of the Chemistry Department to assist in identifying the source of pirated CDs. The Ministry is also planning to criminalize shopping malls and owners of buildings that allow their premises to be used to sell or distribute pirated CDs and VCDs on their premises.

Copyright law alone is no longer a potent weapon against piracy. In all these countries, optical discs laws have been introduced to stem optical discs piracy. In Malaysia, more than one set of laws is being used in the war against piracy.

Effective remedies should be granted to copyright owners and severe punishment must be imposed on offenders. In Thailand, injunctions were introduced to permanently enjoin the offender from repeating the offence. Infringing goods are confiscated and harsh punishments are meted out, especially for repeat offenders. The willingness of the judiciary to explore newer forms of remedies demonstrates how serious is their commitment to address piracy.

3.   Adjudication of IP Disputes: the role of IP Courts

3.1.   Postscript: is there a need for a special IP court?
In all these countries, it has been alleged that prosecution remains the weak link in the enforcement chain and the judicial process remains slow. Prosecution of IP offences has been made more difficult by a lack of understanding of basic IP concepts and evidentiary rules. The problems could be resolved with more training of the judiciary, prosecutors and others involved in the prosecution. With the increasing sophistication of piracy, and high quality imitations, it is clear that enforcement officers require rigorous and continuous training to keep up with them. Such steps have been taken in Malaysia and are now producing results. A piracy rate of 88% in 2001 has now gone down drastically to 50%. The government has also recently announced the allocation of RM 745 million for the enforcement of IP.

A more difficult problem is the effective adjudication of IP cases through the courts. In Thailand, this has been improved with the establishment of specialized international trade and intellectual property courts. The idea is that since intellectual property rights are essentially private interests, having specialized IP courts will encourage right owners to use lawyers to protect their rights and reduce the burden of enforcement on the government.[52] In

---

[52]   In the words of Vichai Ariyanuntaka, in Ralph Cunnigham, 'Thailand – Interview Judged to Perfection', *Managing Intellectual Property*, available at

Indonesia, the move to vest the Commercial Courts with special jurisdictions over IP matters has helped to speed up the prosecution of cases, especially with the time cap imposed on the resolution of cases.

The advantages of specialized IP courts are numerous. In a study conducted by the International Bar Association Intellectual Property and Entertainment Committee, the lack of IP expertise has been identified as a major problem in the enforcement of IP rights.[53] The survey further reports that a specialized IP court model that is effective in one jurisdiction may not work in another. Factors such as local customs and practices, IP case loads, number of judges, budgetary concerns and local procedural issues, among others, have contributed to the existence of different types of specialized IP courts being established thus far. The Thai Central Intellectual Property and International Trade Court is an excellent example in which a local judicial system was improvised to provide speedy resolution of disputes.

In Malaysia, when the Ministry of Domestic Trade and Consumer Affairs first mooted the idea of setting up a special IP court, there were divergent reactions. The Bar Council and the Malaysian Intellectual Property Association (MIPA) fully supported the initiative. Both Associations call for the setting up of a court that is not only efficient but also works in tandem with the existing court. The specialized court is not to be a deviation from the existing court system. The IP court would also need to have its own rules and procedures, especially simpler rules and procedures. The need to have specialized judges is even more apparent with the increasing complexity of intellectual property cases. They cited several reasons for IP cases piling up in the courts: unfamiliarity of the judiciary with IP matters and the increasing number of appeals on technical aspects. It is felt that if session court judges were to specialize in IP, this might reduce appeal to the High Court. All of these problems could be resolved with the setting up of a specialized IP court.

Creating an independent IP Court of equal status to the existing High Courts would not be possible unless amendments to Article 121 of the Federal Constitution are effected. The main umbrella act that governs the jurisdiction of courts in Malaysia, i.e. the Courts of Judicature Act, would have to be revamped. All the IP legislations that vest civil and criminal jurisdiction over IP offences and disputes would have to be revisited. The core issue that needs to be given attention is the traditional division of jurisdiction between civil and criminal cases and the jurisdiction of courts in Malaysia. Most IP criminal

---

http://www.managingip.com. See also his work on TRIPS and the Specialized Intellectual Property Court in Thailand, available on the internet.

[53]   International Bar Association Intellectual Property and Entertainment Committee, International Survey of Specialised Intellectual Property Courts and Tribunals, London, February 2005.

cases under the Copyright Act 1987 and Trade Descriptions Act 1972 are heard before subordinate courts whilst civil disputes are typically dealt with at the High Court because of the injunctive relief and the amount of damages sought. All these distinctions would have to be considered in lieu of a specialized IP court. If a simpler working procedure for IP cases is required for this proposed specialized court, there must be an in-depth study of existing rules on courts and evidence and suggested ways in which this can be done. In addition, all those involved in the prosecution would need to be retrained in the new procedural rules.

There are other sections of the Malaysian community that are of the view that Malaysia does not need a specialized IP court as the IP case load[54] may not be enough to substantiate such a set-up. All that is required is to have courts that are dedicated to IP, which means that these courts would give priority of hearing to IP cases. In Malaysia, the government has already designated one of the KL Session Courts to hear intellectual property matters. Secondly, at the High Court, civil disputes over copyright cases are heard in the commercial division and many judges have handed down sound decisions that reflect a good command of the subject matter, thus questioning the need to have a specialized IP court. Thirdly, any feasibility study would have to take into account the relatively small number of judiciary officers in Malaysia. Currently, Malaysia has about 200 judges at the higher courts, 130 session court judges and 139 magistrates. In comparison, Germany has a total of 20,000 judges and therefore could afford to have specialized courts. Fourthly, the perceived increase in the backlog of IP cases before the subordinate courts would have to be seen as part of the overall increase in the total number of cases before these courts. From a newspaper report, in 2005, 1 041 564 criminal cases are before the Magistrate court, 12 412 criminal cases before the Sessions Court and 3 809 before the High Courts.[55] Undoubtedly, the need to clear cases that concern national interests and public security, such as drug cases, would prevail before IP cases that involve private interests. The first hurdle that needs to be resolved is why IP and not other matters? Fifthly, if a specialized IP court were to be set up, there would then be a corresponding need for appeal from this court to be heard by a specialized Appeal Court and Federal Court. This would require the setting of a special IP Division at both

---

54   From the case statistics of the Central Intellectual Property and International Trade Court, the number of criminal cases heard before the court has increased from 148 in 1997 to 4219 in 2005.

55   *New Straits Times*, 11 July 2006. This issue has been raised by Teo Bong Kwan, at the WIPO National Seminar on the Role of the Intellectual Property Courts in Enforcement of Intellectual Property Rights, Island of Langkawi, 18 and 19 July 2006.

the Appeal Court and the Federal Court. Lastly, it has also been pointed out that countries that have specialized IP courts are mainly from civil law jurisdictions and not common law jurisdictions.

Despite the above reservations, the government officially launched the IP Courts on 17 July 2007. The set up of the IP Courts are in tandem with the existing hierarchy of courts; with specialized IP Sessions Courts handling criminal cases and IP High Courts handling civil cases, thus bypassing the need to amend the Federal Constitution. The new courts comprises of fifteen Special IP Sessions Courts and six special High Courts that sit as special designated courts in states with the most number of IP infringements – Kuala Lumpur, Selangor, Johor, Perak, Sabah and Sarawak. The government has also appointed new judges and court personnel to hear IP disputes to relieve the problem of backlog in cases before the courts. As part of its capacity building programmes, the government has also allocated a generous sum for the training of prosecutors, legal officers and members of the judiciary on intellectual property law. With this approach, it would appear that the Malaysian government is really showing a serious commitment towards eliminating piracy and stemming IP infringement in Malaysia.[56]

---

[56]   See the Star online, Setting up IP Courts shows commitment, says Shafie, Wednesday 18 July 2007 available at http://thestar.com.my/news/story.asp?file*/ 2007/7/18/nation/18333876&sec=nation.

Appendix A

Table 16.A1 Cases brought against copyright offences

Year	Total no. of cases	In investigation	Mention	Trial	Plea guilty	Win	Fine	Acquitted and discharged	Discharged not amounting to acquittal	NFA
1999	113	10	0	0	5	1	36,250.00	8	21	72
2000	167	42	0	6	15	2	284,524.00	4	43	48
2001	379	172	4	15	14	1	59,650.00	4	87	45
2002	310	188	8	17	14	0	96,300.00	0	27	31
2003	715	473	21	74	30	0	262,700.00	1	13	81
2004	943	448	84	206	65	0	7,945,150.00	1	21	92

Source: Ministry of Domestic Trade and Consumer Affairs.

17 Alternative dispute resolution – a remedy for soothing tensions between technological measures and exceptions?

Brigitte Lindner[1]

Introduction

The interface of technological measures and exceptions has been the centre of attraction for legislators, scholars and commentators alike. Different solutions have been adopted in Europe and elsewhere for reconciling the sensitive relationship between technological measures and exceptions. This contribution examines more closely one of the ways chosen by legislators for achieving that goal, namely the recourse to alternative dispute resolution mechanisms for mitigating disputes between right holders and beneficiaries of exceptions.[2]

As a first step we will define the notion of alternative dispute resolution (hereinafter referred to as 'ADR') for the purposes of the present discussion. In the following, we will assess whether ADR could indeed be a suitable tool for solving disputes in the field of technological measures and exceptions. Finally, we will look more closely at the specific ways in which national legislators have accommodated alternative dispute resolution mechanisms for dealing with cases in this particular field. Where legislators have gone other ways, e.g. by referring such disputes to the courts or calling for government intervention, we shall assess whether the possibility of taking recourse to alternative dispute resolution mechanisms remains open. However, before tackling all these questions, it is certainly legitimate to ask why the problem has arisen at all.

1. Background

1.1. The technological scenario

The latest electronic copying and transmission techniques present a great challenge to the exploitation of literary and artistic works. Works cannot only be

---

[1]   Rechtsanwältin, Registered European Lawyer, Serle Court, Lincoln's Inn, London.
[2]   A choice which was welcomed at least by part of the legal doctrine, see for instance: von Lewinski, (2004a), at 849; Braun (2003), at 502.

reproduced and transmitted in a few seconds without any loss in quality, they can also be easily manipulated and used for the creation of a new work. Thus, new technology not only enhances the way creative works may be enjoyed, but also changes the role of the user from a more passive consumer to that of an active player in the production and distribution chain. The development of activities on the internet over the last decade demonstrates well that the new technological environment has not only benefited creators and their contributors by allowing them to engage in innovative forms of exploitation packaged in new business models. The internet also gave its users a great feeling of freedom to watch, read, hear and share with others at their leisure materials that could be found on the worldwide web. Thus, the new technological scenario also bears within itself the potential for abuse, a danger which may be met by relying on the very technology itself,[3] especially by employing technological measures in various forms of digital rights management to administer the exploitation of works.

While technological measures may thus appear to be the answer to the challenges posed by new copying and transmission techniques, they are not uncontroversial. On the one hand, technological measures are a necessary tool for allowing the secure use of works so that creators, authors, publishers and producers alike may authorise the use and receive a fair reward for the exploitation of their creations in that changed technological environment.[4] Thus it does not come as a surprise that the international legislator recognised the significance and the potential of technological measures by granting them specific protection in the WIPO Treaties of 1996.[5]

On the other hand, technological measures, and in particular digital rights management, have been criticised as an unwelcome privatisation of law threatening traditional copyright landmarks, affecting users' rights to privacy and controlling information and materials in the public domain.[6] Moreover, users and consumers developed a fear of a 'digital lock-up' which would prevent them from enjoying and consuming works at their leisure in the same way as they used to in an analogue scenario.[7]

---

[3]   In the words of Charles Clark: 'The answer to the machine is in the machine', (1996), 139–45.

[4]   Marks and Turnbull (2000), 198; Akester and Akester (2006), at 165.

[5]   Article 11 WIPO Copyright Treaty (WCT); Article 18 WIPO Performances and Phonograms Treaty (WPPT) – see Ricketson and Ginsburg (2006), at 15.02; Ficsor (2002), para. C.11.01; Reinbothe and von Lewinski (2002), Article 11 note 11/12.

[6]   Ottolia (2004), at 494 and 521.

[7]   Cohen (1999), 236; See also Ginsburg and Besek (2002), Session IB: The Market for Works of Authorship and the Problem of Digital Lock-Up, pp. 70–108; Dusollier (1999), at 293.

Nevertheless, the benefits of this new scenario must not be overlooked: those who fear a digital lock-up forget that works are created in the first instance for consumption and enjoyment by the public: the changed technological environment may not only encourage innovative forms of exploitation which facilitate access and enhance distribution of creative works, it may also pave the way towards 'authorial entrepreneurship'.[8] Ultimately, the success of the new exploitation scenario depends on the careful balancing of the public and the private interest.

1.2. Answers by legislators to the technological and legal challenge

Legislators who have addressed the relationship between technological measures and exceptions when implementing the WIPO Treaties have approached the issue differently, some of them more complex and far-reaching than others. Since it would exceed the purpose of this contribution to examine all of them, we will just briefly illustrate the main options.

For instance, the Australian legislator created a system of exceptions to the prohibition of supplying circumvention technology and services where the device or service is used for a permitted purpose.[9]

The US legislator adopted a three-pronged approach in the Digital Millennium Copyright Act of 1998[10] with a view to balancing the new protection of technological measures and the principle of fair use: first of all, as far as circumvention of technological measures is concerned, the US legislation only prohibits the circumvention of access controls and not that of copy controls.[11] Secondly, the US legislator created exceptions to the protection of access controls for the purposes of law enforcement, intelligence and other governmental activities.[12] Other exceptions are made for the benefit of non-profit libraries, archives and educational institutions as well as for the purposes of reverse engineering, encryption research, security testing, the protection of minors and personal privacy.[13] Finally, the DMCA created an administrative rule-making procedure by the Librarian of Congress upon recommendation of the Register of Copyrights in consultation with the Assistant Secretary of Commerce for Communications and Information with a

---

[8]   Ricketson and Ginsburg (2006), p. 982 at para. 15.24.

[9]   Sec. 116A(3) and (4) Australian Copyright Act as amended by the Copyright Amendment (Digital Agenda) Act 2000, No. 110. For further details see: Aplin (2001), p. 565 at 574.

[10]   The Digital Millennium Copyright Act of 1998, Public Law No. 105-304, 112 Stat. 2860 (28 October 1998) referred to as 'DMCA'.

[11]   Sec. 1201(a)(1)(A) DMCA.

[12]   Sec. 1201(e) DMCA.

[13]   See Sec. 1201(d) and (f)–(j) DMCA.

view to evaluating the impact of the prohibition against the act of circumvent-ing access-controls.[14]

By providing exceptions to the protection of technological measures as under the Australian system or by introducing a procedure before a govern-mental institution as in the US, the Australian and US systems would appear to offer fewer opportunities for recourse to ADR than other systems.[15]

The softer approach adopted by the European legislator in Article 6.4 of the EC Copyright Directive certainly represents an encouragement to take recourse to ADR.[16] Unlike in Australia or in the US, the system in the European Union does not provide for exceptions to the protection of techno-logical measures, but is built upon the idea of reaching consensus between right holders and users. The European approach attracted criticism from a number of commentators as highly unusual and unclear[17] or as overambitious, badly drafted and compromise-ridden.[18] This being said, the European approach is perhaps the most pragmatic since it gives technological measures at least a chance to survive. This distinguishes the European system from those which provide for exceptions to the protection of technological measures. While in comparison with other legislative solutions the European approach may thus be somewhat unusual, it is certainly well-suited to solving the deli-cate relationship between the interests of right holders in protecting their intel-lectual property and the longing of users to be able to continuously rely on limitations and exceptions: the approach simply consists in encouraging right owners to take voluntary measures, including the conclusion of agreements with other parties concerned, in order to accommodate exceptions and tech-nological measures. This is where the idea of alternative dispute resolution comes into play: the emphasis on consensus makes the system prone to more flexible ways of resolving disputes. It is thus not astonishing that the European legislator expressly encourages right holders and users in Recital 46 of the EC Copyright Directive to take recourse to mediation.

Already at the stage of negotiating voluntary measures, the guiding assis-tance of, for instance, a mediator may be beneficial for reaching an agreement. Where right owners do not voluntarily take appropriate measures, the

---

14   Sec. 1201(a)(1)(B)–(E) DMCA.
15   For a comparison of the US and Australian system: Fitzpatrick (2000), 214; for a comparison of the US and EU system: Foged (2002), 525.
16   Directive 2001/29/EC of the European Parliament and of the Council of 22 May 2001 on the harmonisation of certain aspects of copyright and related rights in the information society, OJ L 167 of 22 June 2001, p. 10, hereinafter referred to as the 'Copyright Directive'.
17   Hart (2002), 58 at 63.
18   Hugenholtz (2000), 499.

Directive obliges Member States to put beneficiaries into a position to make use of certain public interest exceptions.[19] In the case of private copying, this is not compulsory but optional, i.e. Member States are not obliged to provide for such measures, but where they decide to do so, they must comply with a number of additional conditions as set forth in Article 6.4.2 EC Copyright Directive.[20] Finally, most importantly, the obligation does not exist where works are made available to the public on agreed contractual terms in such a way that members of the public may access them from a place and at a time individually chosen by them (Article 6.4.4 EC Copyright Directive).

The focus on voluntary measures in the Directive raises the question whether the national legislator should equally take a soft approach when deciding on the measures to be adopted once negotiations between right owners and beneficiaries of exceptions have failed. There are no signs that the national legislator would be obliged to do so since the Directive leaves the choice of the appropriate measures to the individual Member State, but it may nonetheless be useful. This must have been a feeling shared by a considerable number of national legislators in Europe who made provision in their national laws for various forms of alternative dispute resolution to solve problems regarding the interface of technological measures and exceptions. The remaining Member States have either given priority to the courts or favoured some kind of government intervention, with some Member States leaving the issue completely open. This does not however mean that recourse to alternative dispute resolution would be totally excluded. Certain forms of alternative dispute resolution might still be useful as a first step to try and solve the problem without having recourse in the first instance to the legal mechanism provided for in the law as a result of the implementation of Article 6.4 EC Copyright Directive.

2.   Alternative dispute resolution – general remarks

2.1.   What is ADR?

ADR is a portmanteau term which covers various alternatives to ordinary court procedures for solving disputes with the involvement and assistance of a

---

[19]   Under the condition that the beneficiary has legal access to the protected work and only to the extent necessary to benefit from the exception – see Article 6.4.1 EC Copyright Directive.

[20]   The obligation applies unless reproduction for private use has already been made possible by right holders to the extent necessary to benefit from the exception or limitation concerned and in accordance with the private copying exception under the Directive and the three-step test, without preventing right holders from adopting adequate measures regarding the number of reproductions in accordance with these provisions (see Article 6.4.2 EC Copyright Directive).

neutral and impartial third party. There is no generally admitted definition of ADR.[21] The common denominator of all forms of ADR is that, compared with traditional court litigation, ADR is unconventional and flexible and hence leaves room for more innovative forms of dispute settlement. Its problem-solving atmosphere may also invite a greater preparedness of the parties to work towards a compromise. Although one might at first sight assume that these alternative forms of dispute resolution refer to procedures outside the ordinary courts, there is a growing tendency to link alternative dispute resolution mechanisms to court proceedings in some way or another, for instance by making them a prerequisite for bringing a claim before the court or by providing for an interruption of a pending procedure where this might be beneficial for reaching a settlement on a disputed matter.[22] This fact, which is recognised in the European Commission's Green Paper on alternative dispute resolution in civil and commercial law,[23] has been confirmed by the Proposal for a Directive on mediation in civil and commercial matters, which expressly provides that a court can invite parties to use mediation in order to settle the dispute.[24] The proposed Directive also calls for ensuring a sound relationship between mediation and judicial proceedings. It is also reflected in the Council of Europe's Recommendation on mediation in civil matters, which states that mediation may take place within or outside court procedures.[25] A prominent example in national law for building ADR into a court procedure is § 278 of the German Civil Procedure Code, which requires that a mediation procedure (*Güteversuch*) be conducted by the court before the actual hearing can begin. In the United Kingdom, lawyers are under an obligation to conduct litigation cost-effectively. Where this principle is not respected, this may have consequences on the costs of the case and may result in a wasted cost order.[26] For instance, in *Dunnett v Railtrack* the court refused costs to the successful party when it declined to mediate.[27] Hence, trial lawyers would appear to be under an obligation to mediate where this has

---

21 Mackie et al. (2000), 9.

22 Brown and Marriott (1999), para 2-013.

23 Green Paper on alternative dispute resolution in civil and commercial law of 19 April 2002, COM(2002) 196 final.

24 Proposal for a Directive of the European Parliament and of the Council on certain aspects of mediation in civil and commercial matters of 22 October 2004, COM(2004) 718 final.

25 Recommendation Rec (2002)10 of the Committee of Ministers to Member States on mediation in civil matters as adopted by the Committee on 18 September 2002.

26 Newman (1999), 21/22.

27 *Dunnett v Railtrack* [2002] EWCA Civ 302; see also *Halsey v Milton Keynes General NHS Trust* [2004] EWCA Civ 576.

been suggested by the court, if uncomfortable cost consequences are to be avoided.

While it may be laudable to encourage litigating parties to take recourse to ADR, one may nonetheless raise the question whether this is not a contradiction in itself since ADR can only be successfully employed if the parties are co-operative and show support for that particular way of dispute settlement. Where they are forced by law or the courts to mediate, conciliate or arbitrate, but have no willingness to do so, this may be a waste of time, money and effort since the case will ultimately have to be decided by the courts.

Various forms of ADR exist:[28] mediation and conciliation are the forms most commonly used in national law and practice. Mediation and conciliation involve a third-party neutral whose role it is to help the parties reach consensus. Depending on the role given to the mediator by the parties, the third-party neutral may either guide the parties through the negotiation process (mediation) or provide a non-binding evaluation of the situation together with a settlement proposal, which the parties may or not accept (conciliation). Other forms of ADR, such as expert determination, neutral evaluation or neutral fact finding give the third-party neutral a more determining role and hence come close to adjudication: in the case of a neutral evaluation, the third-party neutral provides a non-binding assessment of the case which the parties can accept. Neutral fact finding leads to an equally non-binding assessment and may be of help where some complex technical issues are at stake. The neutral expert will examine the facts of the case and produce a non-binding evaluation of the merits. By contrast, an expert determination goes much further: here, an independent expert is used to decide the issue.

As far as arbitration is concerned, there is some disagreement as to how it should be precisely classified: whereas some consider arbitration as a form of alternative dispute resolution,[29] others exclude it from its scope for the reason that arbitration is more rigid than other forms of ADR, such as mediation or conciliation, and lies in the hands of third-party neutrals who act akin to a tribunal and issue a binding decision.[30] However, for the purposes of the present analysis, all procedures taking place outside the normal court setting, including arbitration, shall be considered as forms of ADR.

Mediation and arbitration may also be combined in a so-called med-arb

---

[28] For an in-depth overview of the various forms see Brown and Marriott (1999), para. 2-026.

[29] So for instance the WIPO Arbitration and Mediation Centre, pp. 4–5. See also Brown and Marriott (1999), para. 2-002 with regard to the significance of arbitration for the history of ADR.

[30] Lambert (2003), at 410; Commission Green Paper on alternative dispute resolution in civil and commercial law of 19 April 2002, COM(2002) 196 final, p. 6.

procedure. Where the mediation fails in such a case, the mediator converts automatically into an arbitrator and can render a legally binding decision.[31]

An ADR procedure may be run either independently by third-party neutral(s) together with the parties as an ad hoc procedure or with the assistance of an institution. There are now several institutions in existence which promote ADR in the intellectual property field or offer relevant services. For instance, the World Intellectual Property Organisation maintains an Arbitration and Mediation Centre which provides specialised intellectual property ADR services at the international level. The Centre offers rules and neutrals for mediation, arbitration, expedited arbitration and a med-arb procedure.[32] In the UK, following a larger campaign by the Department of Constitutional Affairs to encourage recourse to ADR, the UK Intellectual Property Office launched a mediation service for dealing with IP disputes.[33] Finally, the Chartered Institute of Arbitrators also maintains an IP & Electronic Media Panel with panellists who combine a qualification in one or more ADR disciplines with experience in IP and electronic media issues.[34]

2.2. Reasons for ADR

Alternative dispute resolution has become fashionable in virtually all areas of law. The reasons for this development are well-known and are perhaps best summarised in Recital 6 of the proposed EC Directive on mediation in civil and commercial matters:

> Mediation can provide a cost-efficient and quick extra-judicial resolution of disputes in civil and commercial matters through processes tailored to the needs of the parties. Settlement agreements reached through mediation are more likely to be enforced voluntarily and are more likely to preserve an amicable and sustainable relationship between the parties. These benefits become even more pronounced in situations displaying cross-border elements.

Thus, ADR is usually considered faster, more cost-efficient and less complex than the usual court proceeding. In addition, ADR gives the parties a larger amount of autonomy: they may select the most suitable decision-maker for their particular dispute which may be a distinct advantage where complex technical issues are at stake. Parties may also choose the applicable law, the language and place of the proceedings. The confidentiality of the procedure is

---

[31]   Mackie et al. (2000), 51.

[32]   For details see http://www.wipo.int/amc/en/ (accessed 29 August 2006).

[33]   Further information may be found at the UK Intellectual Property Office's website at: http://www.ipo.gov.uk/press/press-release/press-release-2006/press-release-20060403.htm (accessed 15 September 2007).

[34]   For details see http://www.idrs.ltd.uk (accessed 15 September 2007).

an added benefit, particularly where technology and trade secrets are at stake. In the case of arbitration, the finality of awards may be of importance to some parties: arbitral awards may not usually be appealed, yet they are enforceable like court judgments where the United Nations Convention for the Recognition and Enforcement of Foreign Arbitral Awards of 1958 (the so-called New York Convention) applies. Conversely, where the parties are not interested in a binding decision, but prefer to use the process as an experiment for negotiation, mediation which usually is without prejudice may also be beneficial. Finally, ADR is well suited for international, cross-border litigation, since it is possible to solve problems in several jurisdictions in one procedure.

Yet, there are instances where ADR may be less suitable, for instance where a public legal precedent is required or where the parties are less co-operative such as in the case of infringements of intellectual property rights. The latter is perhaps the reason why ADR has so far been of less interest in the field of copyright and related rights.[35] While according to WIPO's caseload summary, some of the 66 requests for mediation concerned also copyright issues, of the 85 requests for arbitration none related specifically to copyright, the closest being disputes regarding software licences or arts marketing agreements.[36]

Would this not suggest that ADR may be of only limited interest for disputes regarding the interface of technological measures and exceptions? The situation in this particular field may be different since the European legislator not only proposed a consensus-based model which would accommodate ADR-type dispute resolution, but also expressly encourages recourse to mediation in disputes between copyright owners and users.

Finally, it must be borne in mind that Article 6.4 of the Copyright Directive concerns in the first place exceptions that are in the public interest. Copyright owners and beneficiaries of those exceptions, such as schools, universities, libraries, archives, museums and similar institutions have traditionally negotiated the use of copyright works together with right owners, even within the scope of an exception. It is therefore not surprising that particularly in this field national legislators have opted for ADR as a means to settle the dispute.

3.   ADR and the interface of technological measures and exceptions

As mentioned at the beginning, a larger number of those EC Member States which expressly implemented Article 6.4 EC Copyright Directive in their national law opted for ADR as a means of solving disputes relating to the

---

[35]   Lambert (2003), at 410.
[36]   WIPO Caseload Summary accessible at http://www.wipo.int/amc/en/center/caseload.html (accessed 15 September 2007).

interface of technological measures and exceptions. For the purposes of the present analysis, two phases may be distinguished: the first phase concerns the – more or less – voluntary making available of the necessary means for benefiting from an exception; the second phase follows in case of a failure to accommodate an exception in the framework of a technological measure, i.e. where the right holder has not taken up the chance given to him to make available the necessary means in the above first phase.

As regards the first phase, right holders are either under a strict legal obligation to provide the necessary means or are encouraged by the legislator to negotiate voluntarily with beneficiaries of exceptions measures which would accommodate a particular exception. Apart from more or less general statements encouraging or obliging right holders to make available voluntarily those necessary means for benefiting from an exception where users have gained lawful access to the work or other protected subject-matter in question, the Member States have not specifically regulated this first phase. Thus, in the course of this first phase, the parties would not appear to be prevented by law from calling upon the assistance of a mediator for sailing smoothly through the negotiation process in cases where this could prove useful.

The second phase begins when either the negotiations between the parties have failed or the right holder does not follow a legal obligation to make available the necessary means for benefiting from an exception. Where legislators have implemented Article 6.4 EC Copyright Directive by providing for a specific, more detailed so-called intervention mechanism, these rules concern mainly this second phase.[37] In this context it is interesting to note that in those cases where legislators opted for ADR, right holders are usually encouraged by law to negotiate voluntary measures during the first phase. By contrast, where the procedure in the second phase allows the user to go straight to the courts, this is often matched by a strict obligation to make the necessary means directly available to the beneficiary, sometimes without any reference to voluntary agreements, presumably in order to give users an enforceable claim. Consequently, where a legislator chooses a soft approach for the second phase, this is in general matched by a softer approach in the first phase as well.

In the following, we will first of all examine more closely those national laws which accommodated ADR in the implementation legislation. Since not all EC Member States opted for ADR as an intervention mechanism, we will thereafter assess whether ADR may still play a role in the remaining cases.

---

[37]   Intervention mechanism refers to a means which would allow a beneficiary to make use of an exception in a case where technological measures have been applied to a work, such as ADR, a court procedure or government intervention.

3.1.   Copyright laws with ADR as a means of solving disputes regarding the interface of technological measures and exceptions

An increasing number of national legislators in Europe favour alternative dispute resolution for settling disputes arising out of scenarios addressed by Article 6.4 EC Copyright Directive. This being said, the forms chosen by legislators vary a great deal. While the respective laws often refer to mediation,[38] conciliation[39] or arbitration,[40] this does not necessarily mean that these procedures would always reflect the traditional forms of ADR as outlined in section 2 of this analysis. In countries like Latvia, for instance, the parties are free to decide whether to embark on a mediation procedure, but recourse to the courts is left open from the outset and at any stage of the mediation procedure. In the Latvian system, the parties may also choose the mediator(s) who will determine the procedure and can make proposals which the parties may accept. In other countries, the parties are forced into a procedure before a specialised body, such as the Standing Committee on Copyright at the Office of the President of the Council of Ministers in Italy. What varies most between the various models adopted at national level is the degree of autonomy left to the parties.

In view of the floating use of ADR terminology by national legislators, it is not an easy task to allocate the procedures chosen to the different types of ADR as mentioned and defined in section 2. In the following review of the various models, a distinction is made between mediation- and arbitration-based forms as well as ADR-type procedures before special institutions.

3.1.1.   Mediation   A mediation procedure may be found in the national copyright laws of the Baltic States, Greece, Hungary and Slovenia. In the absence of an English translation of the most recent amendments to the Hungarian copyright law, we will concentrate in the following on the Baltic States, Greece and Slovenia.

THE BALTIC STATES   The three Baltic States, i.e. Estonia, Latvia and Lithuania, have all encouraged a solution of disputes on the basis of mediation. Before being able to take recourse to mediation, the laws of all three countries require the parties in the first phase to make an attempt to reach voluntary agreements with regard to the use of a work in the framework of a specific exception.[41]

---

38   Estonia, Greece, Hungary, Latvia, Lithuania and Slovenia.

39   Italy.

40   Portugal.

41   Article 80³ (4) with Article 87 of the Estonian Copyright Act 11 November 1992 as amended with effect from 29 October 2004 with regard to certain public interest exceptions and private copying; Article 18(4) of the Latvian Copyright Law as

Where the negotiations fail, the path to a mediation procedure lies open. The three Baltic States have taken different approaches in this respect.

As already indicated, the procedure provided for under Latvian Copyright Law[42] is probably the closest to that of a classical mediation leaving the parties with a high degree of autonomy. In fact, the parties are not forced to refer the dispute to a mediator. Mediation is optional; the case could just as well be brought before an ordinary court.[43] Where the parties opt for mediation, they must involve the Ministry of Culture. The mediator is appointed by the parties unless they cannot agree on a suitable candidate, in which case the mediator will be designated by the Ministry of Culture upon request. The Law does not contain onerous rules on procedure:[44] it simply states that where one of the parties has submitted a written proposal, this will form the basis of the mediation. Otherwise, the mediator may formulate proposals himself, in which case the procedure would be closer to conciliation. The proposal may be accepted or rejected by the parties, but the legal consequences of rejecting or accepting the proposal remain unclear since they are not addressed in the Law: presumably, the way to the courts remains open in both cases as a result of the provisions contained in Article 67^3 (4) Copyright Law. In order to maintain the confidentiality of the mediation procedure, the mediator is not entitled to disclose intelligence and information obtained during the mediation process. Consequently, it may be held that the Latvian legislator has actively encouraged recourse to a traditional mediation or conciliation procedure when implementing the provisions of Article 6.4 EC Copyright Directive.

The Lithuanian mediation procedure is similar to that of Latvia, but is institutionalised at the Council of Copyright and Related Rights (hereinafter referred to as the 'Copyright Council').[45] The Copyright Council is a public institution whose 14 members are appointed by representatives of right holders, users and the government for a period of two years. The members must be experts in copyright and/or related rights.[46] Although not expressly stated in the Law, it would appear that the parties are obliged to mediate under the auspices of the Copyright Council before the case can be referred to the ordinary courts. It is the task of the mediator to guide the parties through the negotiation

---

amended last on 22 April 2004 with regard to certain public interest exceptions only; Article 75(4) of the Lithuanian Law on Copyright and Related Rights as amended last on 5 March 2003 with regard to both public interest exceptions and private copying.

[42]   Articles 67^1–67^3 Latvian Copyright Law.

[43]   Article 18(5) with Article 67^3 (4) Latvian Copyright Law.

[44]   See Article 67^3 Latvian Copyright Law.

[45]   Rudimentary provisions are contained in Article 75(4) of the Lithuanian Copyright Law which will be supplemented by Implementing Regulations.

[46]   For details regarding the Copyright Council see Article 72 of the Lithuanian Copyright Law.

process and to present proposals. Where the parties accept the proposals, i.e. do not disagree within one month from the presentation of the proposal, the matter is considered as settled. It would appear that once the matter is settled by an agreement, it can no longer be brought before the courts. If the proposal is not accepted, the dispute continues before the Vilnius regional court. Since the mediation which is outlined in Article 75(4) Lithuanian Copyright Law will be supplemented by Regulations, it is difficult to predict whether and to what extent party autonomy will subsist.

The response given by the Estonian legislator to problems arising out of the interface of technological measures and exceptions is more similar to that of the Lithuanian than the Latvian example and is hence closer to a conciliation than a mediation: in the case of a failure of the negotiations, the beneficiary of certain public interest exceptions and the private copying exception may apply to the Copyright Committee whose task it is to assist the parties in finding an agreement. The Copyright Committee is an expert committee formed at the Ministry of Culture. Its members are appointed by the Government for a period of five years. Where a party has referred a matter to the Committee, the parties are required to enter into negotiations with the help of the Committee. The negotiations must be conducted in good faith and must not be prevented or hindered without valid justification. The Committee can also make proposals which the parties may accept or reject within a period of three months from the receipt of such proposals.[47] Where the proposal is rejected, the parties may call upon the courts to settle the matter. It is worth noting that the proposal does not only produce effects between the parties to the dispute. Where an interested person disagrees with a decision made by the Committee, such person can also take recourse to the courts concerning the same matter.[48]

In conclusion, only the Latvian legislator would appear to have opted for mediation in the traditional sense as a solution for disputes on the interface between technological measures and exceptions. By contrast, in Lithuania and Estonia it seems that the law does not leave the parties the choice whether or not to resort to mediation, but obliges them to apply to the Lithuanian Copyright Council or the Estonian Copyright Committee in the case of a dispute. Moreover, the parties are not in a position to choose the mediator since the members of the Copyright Council or the Copyright Committee are appointed by the government. The procedures in Estonia and Lithuania can hence at best be characterised as ADR-based with the closest form being conciliation. Does this now mean that they are less efficient than the classic mediation in Latvia? Since there is not as yet much practical experience with

---

47   Article 87(1)^2 Estonian Copyright Act.
48   Article 87(2) Estonian Copyright Act.

mediation in this field generally, and in the Baltic States in particular, it is difficult to give a definite answer. The least which can be said is that the expertise of the members of both the Copyright Council and the Copyright Committee in the area of copyright and related rights may render the procedure perhaps more attractive for the resolution of disputes concerning copyright and technology issues than a procedure before the ordinary courts.

GREECE   In line with the provisions in Article 6.4.1 EC Copyright Directive, Greek copyright law also requires parties to adopt voluntary measures or to reach agreements for accommodating certain public interest exceptions in the framework of technological measures.[49]

Where this cannot be achieved, the parties may request the involvement of one or more mediators to be chosen from the list set up by the Copyright Organisation. The Copyright Organisation is established under the jurisdiction of the Ministry of Culture with the overall goal of protecting copyright and related rights.[50] There are no further rules on procedure, save for the clarification that mediators may make recommendations to the parties. Hence the procedure is closer to conciliation than mediation. If such recommendations are not accepted, the dispute will be resolved by the Court of Appeal of Athens which acts as first and last instance court. It would thus appear that the Greek legislator made provision for a larger degree of party autonomy by leaving the choice of mediators to the parties and the determination of the procedure to the mediators. The procedure is thus similar to the Latvian example, although it would appear that the parties do not have a choice whether to resort to the courts or to mediation in the first instance.

SLOVENIA   Slovenian Copyright Law requires right owners to make available the necessary measures for enforcing certain public interest exceptions as well as the private copying exception.[51] Where right owners fail to do so, the other party may request a mediation of the dispute. This appears to be again a classical mediation[52] as in the case of the Latvian example. The regulations provided for in the Law are scarce. This being said, further implementing regulations in the form of a decree dealing also with the procedure are to be provided. For the time being, the mediator is to be chosen from a list of mediators appointed by the Slovenian government. The mediator shall guide the parties through the negotiation. The mediator may also make proposals to the

---

49   For details see Article 66A(5) Greek Copyright Law (Law 2121/1993), introduced by Article 81 No. 11 of Law 3057/2002 implementing the Copyright Directive.
50   For details see Article 69 Greek Copyright Law.
51   Article 166c(1) and (3) Copyright Law of Slovenia as amended up to 2004.
52   For details see Article 163 Copyright Law.

parties for the settlement of the dispute and hence act as a conciliator. The competent authority provides administrative support to the mediator.

3.1.2. Arbitration

As a matter of principle, Portuguese law encourages the negotiation and the application of voluntary measures and agreements in the field of technological measures and exceptions. This is highly important since Portuguese law also obliges right holders to deposit with the General Authority of Cultural Activities (*Inspecção Geral das Actividades Culturais* – IGAC) measures which would allow beneficiaries to make use of certain public interest exceptions as well as the private copying exception. In cases where it is evident that a beneficiary cannot make use of an exception, he may hence request from the IGAC to be provided with such measures.[53]

Any disputes regarding the interface between technological measures and exceptions must be dealt with by the Mediation and Arbitration Commission of the Ministry of Culture.[54] Hence arbitration is compulsory, but it is not final like traditional arbitration procedures, since the decisions of the Arbitration and Mediation Commission may be appealed to the Tribunal da Relação. In cases of urgency, the decision of the Commission must be rendered within three months. The general provisions regarding arbitration apply to the procedure before the Arbitration Commission.[55] The Arbitration Commission has seven members who must be lawyers and represent the various interests involved, including those of consumers. The members are appointed by the Prime Minister for a period of four years. The Arbitration Commission receives technical and administrative support from the Copyright Office at the Ministry of Culture. Hence the arbitrators cannot be freely chosen by the parties.

In conclusion, while the procedure may be called 'arbitration', it is not a classic case of arbitration since it is neither voluntary nor final nor does it give the parties the authority to appoint the arbitrators for their dispute. Nonetheless, in view of the specific expertise of the members of the Arbitration and Mediation Commission, such 'arbitration' may still be preferable to a procedure before the ordinary courts in cases involving complex copyright and technical issues.

3.1.3. ADR-type procedures before special institutions   Some national legislators entrusted a specialised institution, such as the Standing

---

[53]   See Article 221(1)–(3) Portuguese Code of Copyright and Related Rights as amended last in 2004.

[54]   Article 221(4) of the Portuguese Code with Articles 28–34 of Law no. 83/2001 of 3 August 2001.

[55]   Article 34 of Law no. 83/2001.

Committee[56] in Italy or the Regulatory Authority for Technological Measures[57] in France, with the resolution of disputes regarding the interface of technological measures and exceptions. The procedures are neither typical mediation nor arbitration, but fall somewhere in between. As we will see in the following, the degree of party autonomy varies considerably in the different procedures.

In Italy, right holders and beneficiaries of specified public interest exceptions and, to a certain extent, the private copy exception, are encouraged to enter into negotiations in order to allow the exercise of such exceptions.[58] Where no agreement can be reached, a procedure may be initiated by either party before the Standing Committee on Copyright in order to carry out a 'mandatory attempt' at dispute resolution.[59] The Standing Committee is established at the Office of the Council of Ministers and may be convened in general assembly or in special commissions which are set up on a case by case basis. In the case of the mandatory attempt for resolving disputes regarding the interface of technological measures and exceptions, the special Commission is composed of three members who must all be copyright experts designated by the President of the Council of Ministers. The applicant may make a proposal which the respondent may either accept or reject. Where objections are made by the respondent, an attempt at settlement is scheduled by the special Commission. Where a settlement is reached between the parties with the help of the Commission, a statement will be prepared and signed by the parties and the chairman of the Commission. The statement is immediately enforceable. Where no agreement is reached, the Commission will make a proposal for settlement. If the proposal is rejected by the parties, the procedure will continue before the ordinary courts.

Thus, the procedure in Italy in the second phase contains several layers: first, the parties may mediate over their own proposal with the help of the special Commission. This would be a case of traditional mediation giving guidance towards the adoption of a proposal. If that proposal is not successful, the special Commission may formulate a proposal which is immediately enforceable if it is accepted. If however the Commission's proposal is also rejected, the procedure will continue before the courts. Hence the procedure before the Commission stands somewhere between conciliation and arbitration: on the one hand, the Commission can render a final, immediately

---

56   *Comitato consultativo permanente per il diritto di autore.*
57   *Autorité de régulation des mesures techniques.*
58   Article 71 *quinquies* (2) and (4)1 of Law no. 633 for the Protection of Copyright and Related Rights of 22 April 1941 as amended last by Legislative Decree no. 68 of 9 April 2003.
59   Article 71 *quinquies* (4) with 194 *bis* of the Italian Copyright Law.

enforceable decision like an arbitral board, but only where the proposal is accepted by the parties. Otherwise, the Commission can only guide the parties through the negotiation process and in case of a failure in both layers refer the matter to the courts.

It is also worth noting that the Italian system contains a significant exception to the general principle of confidentiality in ADR procedures since the Law allows for the minutes of the mandatory attempt at settlement to be communicated to the court so that the costs of the proceedings can be determined by taking into account the behaviour of the parties during the attempt of settlement.[60] The Italian system nonetheless leaves a certain degree of autonomy by giving the parties the possibility of submitting their own settlement proposals for negotiation with the help of the Commission. This being said, the parties are however not in a position to influence the composition of the Commission. As in most other cases discussed in this part, it may however still be an advantage that a specialised body rather than an ordinary court will deal with these rather complex issues.

In France, the implementing legislation makes provision for the establishment of a so-called independent Regulatory Authority for Technological Measures whose task it is to observe the effects of the deployment of technological measures.[61] The Authority is to determine the conditions of exercise of certain public interest exceptions and may fix the minimum number of copies which must be available under the private copying exception.[62] The powers of the future Regulatory Authority in this context have been addressed in a decision of the *Conseil Constitutionnel* which may function as guidelines for exercising the Authority's tasks.[63] The decision also confirms that, in accordance with European law, the right holders must be given an opportunity to provide voluntary measures for reconciling technological measures and exceptions which, at first, was not clearly provided for in the implementation legislation. Thus, the *Conseil Constitutionnel* has instituted a first phase for the conclusion of agreement and voluntary measures.

The French Authority is also competent to solve disputes regarding the interface of technological measures and exceptions. It is the task of the

---

[60]   Article 194 *bis* (6) Italian Copyright Law as amended by Legislative Decree no. 68 of 9 April 2003.

[61]   Article L. 331-17 Code de la Propriété Intellectuelle (CPI) as introduced by Law no. 2006-961 of 1 August 2006 on Copyright and Related Rights in the Information Society.

[62]   Article L.331-8 CPI.

[63]   Decision no. 2006-540 DC of 27 July 2006 – Law on Copyright and Related Rights in the Information Society accessible at: http://www.conseil-constitutionnel.fr/decision/2006/2006540/index.htm (accessed 15 September 2007).

Authority to aim at achieving a settlement between the parties in a conciliation procedure.[64] Where the conciliation is successful, the minutes are enforceable and will be registered with the clerk of the first instance court. Where no conciliation can be achieved within two months from the application, the Regulatory Authority will render a decision. The decision may be appealed to the Court of Appeal in Paris. Hence there is a similarity of the procedure before the Italian Standing Committee and the French Authority: in both cases, the special institution exercises mediation functions at first and may make a proposal. The procedure differs however where the proposal is rejected: in such a case, the powers of the French Authority are much wider than those of the Italian Standing Committee since the Regulatory Authority is empowered to render a decision. By contrast, the Italian Standing Committee does not have powers to render a decision in the case of a disagreement of the parties with a proposal; here the matter can only be resolved by a decision of the ordinary courts.

3.2. National copyright laws without provisions on ADR as a means for solving disputes regarding technological measures and exceptions

As already indicated in the Introduction, some legislators have gone in different directions to solve disputes regarding the interface of technological measures and exceptions. In fact, some national laws remain silent on the issue.[65] For example, the Austrian legislator decided against the introduction of a so-called intervention mechanism while hoping for the adoption of voluntary measures by right holders themselves. A report to the Austrian Parliament by the Federal Minister of Justice which was released in July 2004 proves that this hope was not in vain. The report concluded that no legislative measures were needed for the time being and that it was sufficient to continuously monitor the situation.[66] Since the Directive requires a reaction of the national legislator only where the first phase remains unsuccessful, i.e. where no voluntary measures are in place, this is a perfectly legitimate practice.[67] This being said, some national legislators saw a need to refer disputes on the interface of technological measures and exceptions directly to the courts. Others took the view

---

[64]   Article L.331-15 CPI.

[65]   This is for instance the case for Austria, Poland and Slovakia.

[66]   Bericht der Bundesministerin für Justiz im Einvernehmen mit dem Bundesministerium für soziale Sicherheit, Generationen und Konsumentenschutz an den Nationalrat betreffend die Nutzung freier Werknutzungen of 1 July 2004, accessible online at: http://www.justiz.gv.at/_cms_upload/_docs/bericht_freie_werknutzung.pdf (accessed 15 September 2007).

[67]   See Walter, Michel (2004), at 68–9; von Lewinski, Silke in Walter (2001), 159, for the view that given the uncertainties of technical development and developing usage in this area, the legislator must wait until a practical need for such legislation has become apparent; Gasser and Girsberger (2005), pp. 170–1.

that the situation could be best helped with an intervention by the government. In essence, the situation can be described as follows:

3.2.1. Court cases before ordinary courts   A number of national laws expressly provide that beneficiaries of certain specified exceptions may apply directly to the court in cases where the right holder does not make available the necessary means for benefiting from such exceptions.[68]

One example of such a system is the German implementation of the EC Copyright Directive. The German legislator introduced an intervention mechanism which is three-fold:[69] court cases may first of all be initiated by an individual user to benefit from a public interest exception. Moreover, a kind of class action may be brought by an association of beneficiaries. And finally, an administrative procedure resulting in an administrative fine may also take place, whereby it is to date not entirely clear what the relationship of the three different procedures would be.

It is interesting to note that during the legislative process of implementing the EC Copyright Directive in Germany, there were repeated calls for an ADR-based intervention mechanism.[70] This is not at all surprising since there are various precedents for ADR-based solutions in German copyright law, such as conciliation within the framework of copyright contracts or arbitration with regard to disputes concerning tariffs fixed by collecting societies. Nonetheless, the legislator decided expressly against an ADR-type procedure since it was feared that this would render the enforcement of exceptions under the Law meaningless.[71]

This does not however mean that ADR would not play any role at all in this field in Germany. First of all, following an example from the copyright

---

[68]   See for example: Belgium: Article 87 *bis* § 1 of Law on Copyright and Related Rights as amended last by Law of 22 May 2005; Ireland: Court procedure before the High Court (Reg. 5(3) SI no. 16 of 2004 – European Communities (Copyright and Related Rights) Regulations 2004); Luxembourg: Article 71 *quinquies* (2) with Article 81 of the Law of 18 April 2004 modifying the Law of 18 April 2001 on Copyright, Related Rights and Databases; Malta: Sec. 42(2)(a) of the Maltese Copyright Law of 2000 as amended last by Law IX of 2003 obliges right holders to accommodate exceptions where technological measures are applied. In the absence of any express provisions it is assumed that the general provision in Section 43 of the Law, i.e. a procedure before the civil court, applies. Spain: Article 161 (2) of Law no. 23/2006 of 7 July 2006; Sweden: Article 52f Copyright Act as amended up to 2005.

[69]   §§ 95b (2) and 111a German Law on Authors' Rights, §§ 2a, 3a German Law on Injunctions. See also von Lewinski, Silke (2004b), at 33–7.

[70]   See for instance Position Paper of the German Forum der Rechteinhaber, accessible online at http://www.urheberrecht.org/topic/Info-RiLi (accessed 15 September 2007).

[71]   Government draft for a Law governing Copyright in the Information Society of 31 July 2002, published in Schulze (2002), p. 1614.

contracts law, § 95b Copyright Law contains a presumption to the effect that a measure is sufficient for complying with the legal obligation to make available a necessary means if it corresponds to an agreement concluded to this effect between associations of right holders and users. The first phase is hence of the greatest importance in avoiding possible disputes in the second phase. Thus, a successful outcome of the negotiation process in the first phase becomes even more vital. Moreover, as already indicated, the German Civil Procedure Code (§ 278) requires that a conciliation procedure be conducted before the actual hearing can begin. But even before a procedure has reached the courts, ADR may be of interest since nothing in the copyright law would prevent the parties referring a dispute to arbitration or mediation. It is commonly accepted that the courts are reserved for those disputes which could not be amicably resolved.[72] Thus, even though the intervention mechanism in German law seems to be rather strong and court-based, there is nonetheless room left for ADR-type procedures.

3.2.2. Procedures before specialised courts In Denmark, the legislator expressly encourages right holders to provide voluntary measures which include agreements with beneficiaries of public interest exceptions.[73] Hence there should be room for mediation during this first phase of negotiation.[74] Where no voluntary measures are provided or negotiations fail, the Copyright Licence Tribunal may, upon request, order a right holder to make such means available. If the right holder does not comply with the order within a period of four weeks from the decision, the user is even entitled to circumvent the technological measure.[75] The situation is made worse for the right holder since the decisions of the Copyright Licence Tribunal may not be appealed.[76] Hence the right holder has every interest to reach a solution amicably in the first phase and ADR could be a valuable asset in achieving that goal.

3.2.3. Government intervention At least two Member States of the European Union opted for government intervention when they implemented Article 6.4 of the EC Copyright Directive in national law: the Netherlands have not as yet introduced specific provisions, but the implementing law provides that government orders may establish the rules for accommodating

---

[72] Wild, Gisela in Schricker (2006), § 104 note 2; Dreier and Schulze (2006), § 104, note 15.
[73] Schønning (2004), at 97.
[74] Sec. 75d (2) Consolidated Act on Copyright 2003.
[75] Sec. 75d (1) Consolidated Act on Copyright 2003.
[76] Sec. 47(1) Consolidated Act on Copyright 2003.

exceptions where technological measures are applied to a work.[77] Presumably, this rule will only come into play where right owners do not provide voluntary measures or conclude agreements with beneficiaries of exceptions. Hence, alternative dispute resolution mechanisms are of importance in the first phase. Government orders will only be established if there is no agreement in place. Consequently, the assistance of a mediator who guides the parties through the negotiation process could be very helpful.

In the United Kingdom, the beneficiary of an exception may issue a notice of complaint to the Secretary of State in cases where a technological measure applied to a work prevents that person from carrying out a permitted act. This applies to a large catalogue of public interest exceptions as well as to the private copying exception in the form of the time-shifting exception.[78] Following the notice, the Secretary of State must investigate whether there are any voluntary measures in place.[79] Where the Secretary of State takes the view that this is not the case, he can give directions for complying with the obligation which is actionable before the courts in case of a breach.[80] As in the case of the Netherlands, a government intervention will only be required in cases where voluntary measures are not in place. Hence yet again ADR could be important in the first phase.

Conclusions

A number of conclusions can be drawn from the foregoing considerations:

ADR as a means to solve disputes regarding technological measures and exceptions may be encountered primarily in the European Union. The reason is that the system provided for in Article 6.4 EC Copyright Directive leaves more room for alternative methods to solve disputes than other solutions, for instance clear-cut exceptions to the protection provided for under the law, such as in Australia. This being said, the ways chosen by national legislators within the European Union to accommodate exceptions within the framework of technological measures vary a great deal. As a result, apart from general encouragement for consensus-based solutions, there is no harmonised approach in the European Union as to how this balance may be achieved in practice.

ADR in the classical sense, whether mediation, arbitration or any other

---

[77]   Article 29a(4) Copyright Act of 1912 as amended last in 2005, Article 19(3) Related Rights Act of 1993 as amended last in 2005.
[78]   Sec. 296ZE(1) SI 2003 no. 2498 – The Copyright and Related Rights Regulations 2003. For more details see Seville (2004), at 209–11.
[79]   Sec. 296ZE(2)–(3) SI 2003 no. 2498 – The Copyright and Related Rights Regulations 2003.
[80]   Sec. 296ZE(6)SI 2003 no. 2498 – The Copyright and Related Rights Regulations 2003.

form, only applies in a few cases, first and foremost in Latvia and Slovenia. In the remaining cases, even though the legislator may have described the procedures as ADR, they mostly differ from normal court procedures insofar as the proceedings take place before a specialised body instead of an ordinary court. Otherwise, the parties have on average not much more autonomy than in the case of a court procedure, particularly where provision has been made for solving the dispute by binding decision of a third-party neutral.

This being said, where a legislator has entrusted the ordinary courts or a government institution with the resolution of a dispute in the field of technological measures and exceptions, ADR can still be relevant. The help of a mediator can be useful for negotiating a voluntary agreement which would avoid the need to call upon a court or a government institution altogether.

In conclusion, there is a good chance that ADR may be increasingly relevant for disputes in the copyright field which involve complex technical issues, as is the case in the field of the interplay between technological measures and exceptions.

Bibliography

Legislation
With the exception of the most recent laws in Spain and France, the text of the national laws referred to in the text can be accessed at UNESCO's Collection of National Copyright Laws at http://portal.unesco.org/culture/en/ev.php-URL_ID=12313&URL_DO=DO_TOPIC&URL_SECTION=201.html (accessed 18 August 2006).

France   Law no. 2006-961 of 1 August 2006 governing copyright and related rights in the information society was published in the *Journal Officiel de la République Française* of 3 August 2006, pp. 11529–45.

Spain   Law no. 23/2006 of 7 July 2006 modifying and consolidating the Law on Intellectual Property was published in the *Boletín Oficial del Estado* on 8 July 2006, pp. 25561–72.

Textbooks and articles
Akester, P. and R. Akester (2006), 'Digital Rights Management in the 21st Century', *European Intellectual Property Review*, **28** (3), 159–68.
Aplin, Tanya (2001), 'Contemplating Australia's Digital Future', *European Intellectual Property Review*, **23** (12), 565–75.
Braun, Nora (2003), 'The Interface between the Protection of Technological Measures and the Exercise of Exceptions to Copyright and Related Rights: Comparing the Situation in the United States and the European Community', *European Intellectual Property Review*, **25** (11), 496–503.
Brown, Henry J. and Arthur L. Marriott (1999), *ADR Principles and Practice*, London: Sweet & Maxwell.
Clark, Charles (1996), 'The Answer to the Machine is in the Machine', in Bernt Hugenholtz (ed.), *The Future of Copyright in the Digital Environment*, The Hague: Kluwer Law International, pp. 139–45.
Cohen, Julie (1999), 'WIPO Copyright Treaty Implementation in the United States: Will Fair Use Survive', *European Intellectual Property Review*, **21** (5), 236–47.

Dreier, Thomas and Gernot Schulze (2006), *Urheberrecht, Kommentar*, 2nd edition, Munich: C.H. Beck.

Dusollier, Séverine (1999), 'Electrifying the Fence: The Legal Protection of Technological Measures for Protecting Copyright', *European Intellectual Property Review*, **21** (6), 285–97.

Ficsor, Mihaly (2002), *The Law of Copyright and the Internet*, Oxford: Oxford University Press.

Fitzpatrick, S. (2000), 'Copyright Imbalance: US and Australian Responses to the WIPO Digital Copyright Treaty', *European Intellectual Property Review*, **22** (5), 214–28.

Foged, Therese, (2002), 'U.S. and E.U. Anti-Circumvention Legislation: Preserving the Public's Privileges in the Digital Age?', *European Intellectual Property Review*, **24** (11), 525–42.

Gasser, Urs and Girsberger, Michael, (2005) 'Transposing the EU Copyright Directive: A Genie Stuck in the Bottle?', in B. Graber, M. Girsberger, C. Govoni and M. Nenova (eds), *Digital Rights Management: The End of Collecting Societies?*, Berne: Staempfli/Juris Publishing/Bruylant/A.N. Sakkoulas, pp. 149–81.

Ginsburg, Jane C. and J. Besek (eds) (2002), *Proceedings of the ALAI Congress, June 13–17, 2001, New York*, New York: published for ALAI-USA, Inc. by Kernochan Center for Law Media and the Arts, Columbia University School of Law.

Hart, Michael (2002), 'The Copyright in the Information Society Directive: An Overview', *European Intellectual Property Review*, **24** (2), 58–64.

Hugenholtz, Bernt (2000), 'Why the Copyright Directive is Unimportant, and Possibly Invalid', *European Intellectual Property Review*, **22** (11), 499–502.

Lambert, John (2003), 'IP Litigation after Woolf Revisited', *European Intellectual Property Review*, **25** (9), 406–18.

Lewinski, Silke von (2004a), 'Rights Management Information and Technical Protection Measures as Implemented in EC Member States', *International Review of Intellectual Property and Competition Law*, **7**, 844–9.

Lewinski, Silke von (2004b), 'The Implementation of the Information Society Directive into German law', *Revue Internationale du Droit d'Auteur*, **202**, 11–41.

Mackie, Karl J. and D. Miles, W. Marsh and T. Allen (2000), *The ADR Practice Guide*, London: Butterworths.

Marks, Dean S. and B.H. Turnbull (2000), 'Technical Protection Measures: The Intersection of Technology, Law and Commercial Licenses', *European Intellectual Property Review*, **22** (5), 198–213.

Newman, P. (1999), *Alternative Dispute Resolution*, Welwyn Garden City: CLT.

Ottolia, Andrea (2004), 'Preserving Users' Rights in DRM', *International Review of Intellectual Property and Competition Law*, **5**, 491–521.

Reinbothe, Jörg and S. von Lewinski (2002), *The WIPO Treaties 1996*, London: Butterworths.

Ricketson, Sam and J.C. Ginsburg, (2006), *International Copyright and Neighbouring Rights: The Berne Convention and Beyond,* Oxford: Oxford University Press.

Schønning, Peter (2004), 'Implementation of the Directive on Copyright in the Information Society', *Revue Internationale du Droit d'Auteur*, **202**, 81–105.

Schricker, Gerhard (2006), *Urheberrecht*, 3rd edition, Munich: C.H. Beck.

Schulze, Marcel (2002), *Materialien zum Urheberrechtsgesetz*, vol. 3, Munich/Berlin: Luchterhand/Wolters Kluwer Deutschland.

Seville, Catherine (2004), 'The United Kingdom's Implementation of the Copyright Directive', *Revue Internationale du Droit d'Auteur*, **202**, 185–221.

Walter, Michel (ed.) (2001), *Europäisches Urheberrecht*, Vienna/New York: Springer.

Walter, Michel (2004) 'The Implementation of the Information Society Directive in Austria, The Copyright Amendment 2003', *Revue Internationale du Droit d'Auteur*, **202**, 43–79.

WIPO Arbitration and Mediation Centre (ed.), *Dispute Resolution for the 21st Century*, WIPO Publication No, 779(E).

18 Qualitative effects of copyright policies
Antoon Quaedvlieg[1]

Introduction

The instrumental approach of copyright is increasingly popular. Copyright should promote the 'progress of science and the arts'. Growing attention to the social gain to be achieved by exclusive rights is justified and refreshing, even if it would be an erroneous reduction of the role of copyright if the instrumental side were to be over-emphasised to the detriment of the goal of justice it also serves.

Copyright is understood to promote science and the arts by stimulating the production of works and by creating conditions for optimal public access to those works. But does it also have a role to play in improving the quality and diversity of cultural and informational production (hereafter: informational production)?

Although from a purely instrumental perspective, a vocation to improve the quality of informational production would be the most heroic mission one could think of for copyright – and a proven failure to do so its deepest shame – the question is seldom asked. This is hardly surprising, as there are obvious grounds for opposing a quality-enhancing function of copyright:

1. Despite its instrumental *rationale*, copyright remains a private law institution. It creates property, not policy. It serves as a neutral basis for exploiting a work. The incentive to make excellent works should come from individual inspiration and public appreciation, not from the law.
2. If there is a policy aspect to copyright, it is primarily market regulation. Copyright's goal is to create a neutral regime offering both equitable protection for authors and a fair competitive environment for the information industry. The conditions for this protection should be non-discriminatory. A copyright which pursues goals of quality which are highly subjective cannot be a neutral regulation for fair competition.
3. 'Quality control' by copyright means government interference in a market which, more than any other, should be free of it, the market of free information.

Let us question the indisputable.

[1]   Professor of Law, Faculty of Law, Radboud University Nijmegen, The Netherlands.

Autonomy of the right holder versus public policy in copyright

The legal balance between property and access
It is certainly regarded as an old-fashioned approach to consider copyright as merely a private property resulting from natural law. In a contemporary perspective, copyright is an instrument which provides certain powers to the right holder but which also limits these privileges in some respects, in order to comply with the rights and interests of third parties and society as a whole. The freedom of authors and right holders to forbid the use of the material is restricted. Various interests may serve as a basis for limitations and exceptions in copyright law. Lucie Guibault distinguishes in this regard interests serving the protection of constitutional rights (freedom of expression, right to privacy), the regulation of industry practice and competition, the dissemination of knowledge, and market failure considerations.[2] Of course, a mixture of these can – and in many cases will – be at stake, as illustrated by recital 2 of the Cable and Satellite Directive,[3] which calls for the abolition of (copyright) obstacles to trans-frontier broadcasts as a way of pursuing political, economic, social, cultural and legal objectives.

Most limitations on the exercise of the exclusive right can be found in copyright law itself. But in some cases, the right holder is limited in the exercise of his rights, not on the basis of the exceptions contained in the Copyright Act but on 'external' legal principles or concepts. Rules of competition law and/or abuse of monopoly may interfere. In some member states, the exercise of copyright can be examined directly in the light of the freedom of expression guaranteed under art. 10 European Convention of Human Rights (ECHR).[4]

---

2   Lucie M.C.R. Guibault, *Copyrights and Contracts: An Analysis of the Contractual Overridability of Limitations on Copyright*, Deventer: Kluwer Law International, 2002.

3   Council Directive 93/83/EEC of 27 September 1993 on the coordination of certain rules concerning copyright and rights related to copyright applicable to satellite broadcasting and cable retransmission, OJ L 248/15 of 6.10.93.

4   Herman Cohen Jehoram, 'Copyright and Freedom of Expression, Abuse of Rights and Standard Chicanery: American and Dutch Appoaches', *EIPR*, 2004, 275 ff.; Christophe Geiger, *Droit d'auteur et droit du public à l'information, Approche de droit comparé*, Paris: Litec, 2004; *idem*, 'Die Schranken des Urheberrechts im Lichte der Grundrechte', in Reto M. Hilty and Alexander Peukert (eds), *Interessenausgleich im Urheberrecht*, Baden-Baden, Nomos 2004, pp. 143 ff.; *idem*, ' "Constitutionalising" Intellectual Property Law? The Influence of Fundamental Rights on Intellectual Property in the European Union', *IIC*, 4/2006, pp. 371 ff.; J. Griffiths and U. Suthersanen (eds), *Copyright and Free Speech: Comparative and International Analyses*, Oxford: Oxford University Press, 2005; P. Bernt Hugenholtz, 'Copyright and Freedom of Expression in Europe', in Rochelle Cooper Dreyfuss, Diane Leenheer Zimmerman and Harry First (eds), *Expanding the Boundaries of Intellectual Property*,

Furthermore, it cannot be excluded that the exercise of an intellectual property right could hurt the freedom to pursue a trade or profession, although the European Court of Justice (ECJ) seems reluctant to accept this in all but extreme circumstances: the intellectual property right would have to constitute a disproportionate and intolerable interference with the freedom of trade and profession, impairing the very substance of the rights guaranteed.[5]

However, the copyright republic is not without paradoxes. Alongside the majority of 'normal' citizens, whose rights are subject to as many obligations in terms of limitations and exceptions, lives a sovereign supplier of interactive on-demand services. Recent copyright legislation contains rules which show quite some resemblance to the primitive 'absolute right' which was thought to have been overtaken by evolution. For it is difficult to see where the limits of power are for a European author publishing on-line on agreed contractual terms. According to Directive 2001/29/EC on the harmonisation of copyright in the information society (hereafter: Infosoc), such an author disposes of a strong reproduction right (art. 2), only limited by the modest exception of art. 5, para. 1 for certain temporary reproductions which have no independent economic significance. He has a right of communication to the public, including the right of making available to the public. He finds – at least in the Directive – no bar against contracting-out[6] all the legal exceptions a user might possibly want to invoke except the one mentioned above. He is free to create a technological defensive wall around the work, which the user is not allowed to circumvent (art. 6). And he is not subject to the obligation to make available, to the beneficiary of an exception or limitation, the means of benefiting from it (art. 6, para. 4, first and fourth sentences). It cannot be denied: this author rules as a feudal sovereign over his property. In positive law, the *droit sacré et inviolable* is back.

It is intriguing however, that at the same time, large areas of copyright are subject to the opposite development: exercise of the right is increasingly subject to external directives and/or control, especially where it concerns collective administration of copyright. Let us take as an example the Satellite and Cable Directive 93/83/EEC. Article 9, para. 1 of this Directive provides

---

Oxford: Oxford University Press, 2001; P. Torremans (ed.), *Copyright and Human Rights: Freedom of Expression – Intellectual Property – Privacy*, Deventer: Kluwer, 2004; Strowel and Tulkens (eds), *Droit d'auteur et liberté d'expression*, Brussels: Larcier, 2006.

  5   ECJ, 28 April 1998, Case C-200/96, Metronome Musik/Music Point Hokamp, no. 21 ff.

  6   Lucie M.C.R. Guibault, 'Contracts and Copyright Exemptions', in P. Bernt Hugenholtz (ed.), *Copyright and Electronic Commerce, Legal Aspects of Electronic Copyright Management*, The Hague, London and Boston: Kluwer Law International, 2000, pp. 125–63.

that member states shall ensure that the right of copyright owners and holders of related rights to grant or refuse authorisation to a cable operator for a
cable retransmission may be exercised only through a collecting society.
Along with other examples which can be found in national laws, this is an
extended collective licence: where the right holder has not transferred the
management of his rights to a collecting society, the collecting society which
manages rights of the same category shall be deemed to be mandated to
manage his rights. The Directive promotes the smooth operation of contractual arrangements by additional measures. Article 11 obliges member states
to ensure that the parties to the agreement may call upon the assistance of
mediators. Article 12 contains a measure to ensure that negotiations are
conducted in good faith and are not prevented or hindered without valid justification. Recital 34 specifies that negotiations must take place within the
framework of general or specific national rules with regard to competition
law or the prevention or abuse of monopolies. The tendency however to bring
collecting societies under more scrutiny by the authorities is of a general
nature. A system of competition has been forced upon the musical collecting
societies.[7] Moreover, collecting societies are expected to consider the general
interest in their policy.[8]

There are more such examples. Article 5 of the Rental and Lending
Directive makes it possible for member states to derogate from the exclusive
public lending right, provided at least that authors obtain remuneration for
such lending. Article 5, para. 2(a), (b) and (c) introduces exceptions concerning reprography, private copying and reproductions of broadcasts made by
social institutions, subject to the condition of fair compensation to right holders. All these measures imply the intervention of collective management
bodies which will have to take into account the interests of all parties
involved.

As a consequence, where one might have expected to find a unitary
approach to copyright as an exclusive right limited by certain exceptions, a
dichotomy becomes visible: certain modes of exploitation are almost

---

7   Commission Recommendation 2005/737/EC of 18 May 2005 on Collective
Cross-border Management of Copyright and Related Rights for Legitimate Online
Music Services, OJ L 276/54 of 21.10.2005. Study on a Community Initiative on the
Cross-Border Collective Management of Copyright, Commission Staff Working
Document, 7 July 2005. Also see P.B. Hugenholtz, 'Is concurrentie tussen rechtenor-
ganisaties wenselijk?', *AMI*, 2003, 203; Martin Kretschmer, 'The Failure of Property
Rules in Collective Administration: Rethinking Copyright Societies as Regulatory
Instruments', *EIPR*, 2002, 126.

8   Evangelos-Panayotis Liaskos, *La gestion collective des droits d'auteurs dans
la perspective du droit communautaire*, Athens and Brussels: Sakkoulas/Bruylant,
2004, V., p. 349.

completely free of interference; others are more restricted or even heavily monitored. Can this be explained?

Control as a basis for property
As from the nineteenth century, the exclusive right in a work of authorship has been perceived as the property of an immaterial good, on which the law granted an intellectual property right, limited by exceptions and/or a restricted definition of the powers granted to the author. This may have concealed the fact that even if the balance between right holders and users is ultimately of a legal nature, establishing this balance was greatly helped by certain given *physical* conditions.

A public performance of the work demanded important and expensive physical facilities, for example the use of a theatre or stadium. It is likely that the general conditions of access for the audience regularly contain rules which conflict with certain exceptions in favour of that audience in copyright law, but no one seems ever to have bothered about this. In the case of museums, however, some authors have raised questions in the light of the public function (and funding) of these institutions. But in general, there seems to be a large degree of acceptance that a maximum degree of control – which is the case when someone is the owner of the facilities – has influenced the copyright balance in favour of the right holder.

As to reproduction of the work, private reproduction was, especially in the analogue world, beyond the control of the right owner. It was not considered as part of the exclusive right. But for a long time, because of inherent physical impediments, private activities could hardly become of any commercial significance. Reproduction on a larger scale and/or of a good quality depended on the availability of facilities which were simply beyond the reach of most people, so that this part of the balance was not hard for right holders to accept.

Conversely, the exclusive right was allowed to dominate in the *commercial* environment. This 'commercial property' was, however, again accompanied by the practical possibility of exercising control. Reproduction, distribution and communication to the public on a commercially relevant scale could, through the size of facilities demanded and the small number of such facilities that were available, relatively easily be monitored by the right holders. But the necessity of using these physical facilities also helped to keep effective control in a legal sense. It made it possible to combat infringements by holding liable the entities which provided the means for it.

Of course, property and control are not fixed notions in this respect. The case of libraries reveals their ambiguity: in the Netherlands, libraries had, until the 1970s, been conceived as a case in which the property right of the library as physical owner of the book had priority over copyright claims. But as libraries developed into large-scale public institutions, it was nevertheless felt that they trod on the commercial property of the right holders and that a remuneration was justified.

This traditional balance of property and control was disturbed when technical developments gradually made it possible to make more and better copies of the work of authorship. The public began to copy more substantial amounts. Control for the industry became harder. Recourse was taken to levies on devices and/or empty information supports, as indirect measures to repair the damage and restore some grip on the 'in house' copyright activities of private people and businesses. When digital techniques finally became available, a frontal conflict developed between the private sphere of the users and the commercial property of the right holders. Physical conditions could no longer help to create an equilibrium. In fact, it was the first time that the work really became a fully immaterial commodity, as illustrated by John Perry Barlow's telling phrase 'selling wine without bottles'.[9] The natural balance had now to be repaired by a system of *legal* concepts: a delicate operation, and uneasy to perform as the development and introduction of digital techniques advanced at dazzling speed and diverse legal interests clashed passionately with each other. How has this been done? What is the compass of the law?

A definitive answer to this question is clearly impossible, as the new legal balance in copyright is not framed according to a master plan of predetermined general principles. Rather, specific solutions are elaborated for specific problems. Such solutions can to varying degrees be based on the status quo, the pressure of interest groups, the new conditions and opportunities of the internet, and political preferences.

And yet it is striking how far, at a very general level, property and control still appear to play an important role in establishing the new balance. Let us – at random – take some striking features of the emerging copyright regime for the digital world. Firstly, as already stated, the provider of interactive on-demand services is spoiled by a very protective regime, which leaves him almost total freedom as to the conditions under which information is provided to the customer. The property idea is pushed to the maximum, the policy is reduced to supporting the property. But how new is this really? In many respects, the online provider can be compared to the owner of the physical stadium or theatre in the analogue world, who also provided additional services and who was also inclined to restrict the informational rights of users.

Secondly, providers of peer to peer (P2P) software like KaZaA and Grokster initially seemed to escape liability for copyright infringement, but

---

[9]   John Perry Barlow, 'Selling Wine without Bottles: The Economy of Mind on the Global Net', in P. Bernt Hugenholtz (ed.), *The Future of Copyright in a Digital Environment*, Deventer: Kluwer Information Law Series no. 4, 1996, pp. 169 ff.

now find themselves ever more exposed under the doctrine of contributory and vicarious infringement. Despite the fact that in many legal systems, an action can be brought against private people who engage in downloading and/or file-sharing, the music industry does not seem to intend a large-scale offensive against the public. The focus of legal attention is on the question of how *commercial* property can be maintained in the most efficient manner against other *commercial* players, who 'launch' the facilities at the root of the massive infringement. This implies that, in the first place, an evolution of the law is required to allow the elimination of commercially inspired actions by entities which make available filesharing software more or less clearly intended to promote illegal use of protected material.[10] As evidenced by various court decisions, this evolution is presently taking place.

Thirdly, we see a shift in the possibilities of control reflected in legislatures' preferences over which instruments should be provided to maintain the exclusive right in the sphere of private copying. Private copying is done outside the commercial space. It often concerns the reproduction of privately owned supports with privately owned devices. Neither the original copy, nor the reproduction, is the property of the right holder. Nevertheless, it remains the case that private copying on a massive scale undermines the essence of his pecuniary right: it threatens the commercial interests, and therefore the 'commercial property', of the right holder. This damage to the exclusive right will in some way have to be repaired. In the past this has been pursued by imposing levies. To a certain extent, an analogy cannot be denied between such levies and the instruments of contributory and vicarious liability which are presently being developed in order to hold liable commercial actors who take advantage of P2P filesharing software. The entrepreneur who benefits from activities allowing the massive use of protected material is brought in one way or another under the reach of the exclusive right. But levies are an increasingly imprecise instrument. Digital supports can be used for many purposes, which in many cases will not involve use which is relevant under the copyright law. Levies therefore become a claim for payments without a minimum of exactitude. Thus, it can no longer pretend that it fulfils a function of control which is necessary to justify the copyright claim. The European Commission shows a clear aversion to new levies, in favour of the use of more

---

[10]   Cf. on peer to peer filesharing, Thomas Hays, 'The Evolution and Decentralisation of Secondary Liability for Infringements of Copyright-protected Works (part 1)', *EIPR*, 2006, 617; Patricia Akester and Francesco Lima, 'Copyright and P2P – Law, Economics and Patterns of Evolution', *EIPR*, 2006, 576; G. Spindler and M. Leistner, 'Secondary Copyright Infringement – New Perspectives in Germany and Europe', *IIC*, 2006, L.A. Heymann, 'Inducement as Contributory Copyright Infringement: MGM/Grokster', *IIC*, 2006, 31.

precise instruments like digital rights management. DRM is an instrument which allows for maximum control. It is preferred, *although* the combination of DRM and technical protection measures limit users' rights to an absolute minimum.[11] This is another sign that concerns which in the context of some modes of exploitation are prominently observed, can apparently shrink almost to non-existence in the context of other exploitations, in fields where right holders maintain maximum control.

Policy in collective administration
Individual control by and a 'property attitude' on the part of the right holder can create a strong copyright position. But in certain situations of *mass use*, individual control and/or individual licensing can be impossible or undesirable. It is considered that collective mechanisms are to be preferred above individual control. At this point, copyright uses escape the property approach. Where individual licensing is banned, prices will be fixed at a collective level. Other conditions of use will have to be determined as well. It is not the individual work which is at stake, but 'trade in commercial activities' involving anonymous masses of such works, owned by multiple right holders. At the same moment that the logic of property loosens its grip, other interests may raise the stakes. Claims to facilitate mass use may be based on arguments of public education, the realisation of an internal market, the regulation of competition, or vaguer concepts like an easy flow of information in general. In this context, the rights and obligations of each of the parties are no longer founded on a property-oriented approach. It is policy which takes the lead.

When one looks at the whole, the impression is that both options, individually controlled property and collectively managed interests, arise in different situations. In rudimentary form, this dichotomy has always existed in copyright. In the digital environment, however, the contrast becomes sharper. It is now time to turn to our main question, whether models of exploitation can have a stimulating effect on quality and whether extreme differences in models of exploitation could cause, in the respective markets affected, asymmetrical effects as to the quality-enhancing function which is one of copyright's rationales.

---

11   Kamiel Koelman, *Auteursrecht en technische voorzieningen. Juridische en rechtseconomische aspecten van de bescherming van technische voorzieningen, SDU,* 2003; Kamiel J. Koelman and Natali Helberger, 'Protection of Technological Measures', in P. Bernt Hugenholtz (ed.), *Copyright and Electronic Commerce, Legal Aspects of Electronic Copyright Management,* The Hague, London and Boston: Kluwer Law International, 2000, 165–227; P. Akester and R. Akester, 'Digital Rights Management in the 21st Century', *EIPR,* 2006, 159; Maciej Barszewski, 'International Framework for Legal Protection of Digital Rights Management Systems', *EIPR,* 2005, 165.

Quality in regulated markets

So far, the conclusion is that two expoitation models exist under copyright which, in the digital environment, drift further apart. The legal system in place makes it possible to exploit works either in a highly autonomous way – by offering online information services – or in collective ways in which copyright is gradually being devaluated from a property right to just one aspect of the public interest, which has to be observed among others. Copyright no longer secures a privileged position vis-à-vis these other social interests. Ultimately, one could imagine property being reduced to a legal technicality: a private law label which permits the place of copyright to be identified in the system of property law, insofar as this is useful for correctly performing assignments and other transactions or for bringing actions in law against infringement. The exclusive right of the author (or his successors in title) has no special 'rank'.

Differences between the two models of exploitation are inevitable, but also justified, insofar as they each have their own background and their own logic. Nevertheless, in the end both of these models will have to comply with the rationales of copyright. One of these rationales is to promote the progress of science and the arts. One of the main ways to realise this progress is, no doubt, to secure sufficient access for the public to copyright-protected material. Another question is whether a different way of exploitation might entail a different level of incentive for right holders to enhance *quality*. Could the two regimes lead to asymmetrical results as to quality? Is either the autonomous or the 'policed' way of exploitation the most helpful to stimulate diversity, fantasy and innovation?

Although the autonomous approach to property is probably rather modest in its objectives as to stimulating quality – it aims at no more than the creation of a competitive environment with fair conditions for creative and informational industry – its concept could very well help to promote the quality of the content. Access to the information is exclusive and often relatively expensive. Customers will demand quality. Of an enterprise providing *services*, customers usually expect genuine attention to quality. In sectors where high profits can be realised, competition will probably be tough, and the quality of the content which is offered will be one of the most obvious aspects to compete on.

In sectors which are subjected to collective management of rights, a balance of interests is strived for. This means that users' interests occupy an important place. But when users' interests are considered, they often seem to be perceived in the first place as an interest in easy *access*, not always as an interest in the highest possible quality. The material must be available at a reasonable price. Collective management primarily serves as a mere 'means of legal transport' of the information to the user. As such, this is a perfectly neutral function. In markets where other quality-enhancing functions exist, it would be entirely redundant, and probably undesirable, for collective management to fulfil a function other than to bring this material within the reach of as many users as possible.

Yet there could be cases in which the conditions of a certain market create a tendency towards serving the average taste. Certain kinds of works depend for their promotion on broadcasting, and broadcasting services tend, under pressure from the commercial stations, to serve the average taste. It is conceivable that at current market mechanisms are at work which mean that a maximum is reached in the quality of music which pleases everyone, but conditions are not as easy for music which is beyond the grasp of the majority. Where the market itself is not conducive to creating quality, perfect collective management could unintentionally add to that effect. If music of a sufficient quality is available in abundance and for very reasonable prices, it might further complicate the market entry of 'special' products. This in turn raises the question whether there might not after all be reasons to reserve part of the proceeds of collective management organisations for cultural ends, namely, whether there might be grounds to assume that such subsidies would serve to (and are needed to) repair a market flaw, elsewhere in the commercial chain, which impairs competition in quality.[12]

Let us for a moment accept the hypothesis that there might be room and reason to think about a more active quality policy in the field of collective management. The way to realise this would be another question. It would have to be an approach within the logic and conditions of collective management. This means that there is no reason to try and copy quality-enhancing mechanisms which may be found in the free market. This 're-engineering' of the free market is sometimes attempted by the courts in cases where the law imposes, directly or indirectly, a compulsory licence in return for fair compensation. The amount of compensation is then based on the amount which it is believed would be paid under a reasonable licence fee. But however well argued, a reasonable price is difficult to establish in law. And to be provocative, the intention of the legislature and the judges reveals all too clearly that the remuneration must not be *too* high. However, it is perfectly reasonable to ask whether, in a genuinely free market, the licence fee could not be quite high where a clearing agency offers licences which guarantee smooth and simple acquisition of all the desired rights. By the way, it has not been contended here that the free market is the panacea in enhancing quality. Concentration of rights in the hands of too few market players and undervaluation of the creativity

---

[12]   The collective societies themselves stress the social and cultural impact of their policies. Buma Stemra, *Music in Europe: Sound or Silence? Study of Domestic Music Repertoire and the Impact of Cultural Policies of Collecting Societies in the EU 25*, Utrecht: Capgemini, 2004.

factor – the individual author – can here pose as much threat to the quality of informational production.

Perhaps there is no reason to worry about the quality of cultural and informational production under various exploitation models. Indeed, an impressive amount of excellent material is produced. However, we all know that quality is in some situations under threat. If we engage in copyright policy, and if we take copyright's rationale seriously, it would not be consistent to consider the many different interests concerned, but to ignore this very important one.

19 Questioning the principles of territoriality: the determination of territorial mechanisms of commercialisation

Paul Torremans[1]

Introduction

Under the broad heading of 'Questioning the principles of territoriality' this chapter looks at the determination of territorial mechanisms of commercialisation.

Territoriality is a concept that is often misunderstood, but that is often used to explain somewhat odd aspects and implications of copyright. These implications are then seen as inevitable, because of the omnipresence in copyright of that concept of territoriality. One of my favourite examples is the idea that the court of the domicile of the defendant cannot deal with a claim concerning the infringement of a foreign copyright. This is based on a fundamental misunderstanding of the concept of territoriality and the negative consequences of the idea, i.e. that multiple cases need to be brought in multiple jurisdictions, are seen as inevitable because of the presence in copyright law of this concept of territoriality.

A definition of territoriality

There is therefore a need to set the scene by defining the concept of territoriality. The international legal framework does not use the concept and does not offer a definition. The Berne Convention, the TRIPs Agreement and the WIPO Treaties, to name just three, are based on the concept or their implementation inevitably leads to it, depending on the view one takes, but they do not contain the term nor do they offer a definition of the concept. Let me therefore refer to one of the leading texts on copyright, at least as far as the UK is concerned. The editors of *Copinger and Skone James on Copyright* refer in their subheading to the territorial nature of rights when they discuss the concept of territoriality. In their words:

[1]   Professor of Intellectual Property Law, School of Law, University of Nottingham and Professor of Private International Law, Faculty of Law, University of Ghent. This chapter is based on a paper delivered at the Association Littéraire et Artistique Internationale (ALAI) Congress 2005 in Paris.

As a rule, copyright and related rights are granted with respect to a particular territory only and give protection to nationals of that territory alone; protection and the possibility of enforcing rights stops at the national borders except in so far as protection is extended outside the territory by bilateral or multinational treaties with other countries. The protection of works of foreign origin within the territory will also depend on such treaties.[2]

The starting point is therefore not even limited to copyright. It is indeed a generally accepted principle that the legislative powers of the legislature are limited to the territory of the state concerned. Copyright is an immaterial right that is created by the legislature and its territorial scope is therefore logically limited to the territory of the state concerned. And as an immaterial right it is in essence a negative right, for example the right to stop others from reproducing the work or from communicating it to the public, such an immaterial negative right needs an enforcement mechanism to come into practice and that mechanism necessarily has to have the same territorial scope as the right itself. If I have the exclusive right to make copies of the work in the UK, for example, then I will also be able to enforce that right against anyone who makes copies in the UK. *A contrario*, UK copyright will not extend to any territory outside the UK and I will therefore also be unable to enforce my UK copyright when copies of the work are made abroad.

The element that is more specific to copyright is that the right is normally only granted to nationals of the state concerned. This element is not at the core of the concept of territoriality, but it works neatly together with the core idea of territoriality when copyright attempts to overcome national borders. Indeed, what one does find in the international legal framework is the principle of national treatment.[3] That obliges foreigners to be treated as nationals when it comes to copyright. The result of the implementation of this principle is not only that the limitation of copyright to nationals is overcome, but also that the state's own nationals are granted reciprocal national copyrights abroad. Again these reciprocally granted national copyrights will have a territorial scope.

Territoriality and its implications for the commercialisation of
copyright works

What territoriality really means is that the international legal framework has failed to create anything that could be named an international copyright nor has a full-scale harmonisation of national copyright laws been achieved. Despite a certain level of harmonisation national copyright systems continue

---

2   K. Garnett, J. Rayner James and G. Davies (eds), *Copinger and Skone James on Copyright*, Sweet & Maxwell (14th edn, 1999), at 16.
3   See Article 5.1 Berne Convention and Article 3 TRIPS Agreement.

therefore to exist and national treatment has been introduced as a solution to grant the rightholder copyright protection at a global level, despite the absence of a proper global or international copyright. This solution needs to avoid overlaps between the various national rights concerned and this is where the principle of territoriality fits in, as it limits the scope of national rights to the national territory of each state.

The international exploitation of a copyright-protected work thus necessarily means the exploitation of the work under the legal cover of this patchwork of national copyrights. The national nature of the rights and the co-existence of neatly separated national rights obviously opens up opportunities for territorial mechanisms of commercialisation. One can easily separate the rights in different states and exploit them separately. By granting for example a licence under one national copyright law, one makes sure that the licensee has no rights in relation to the copyright work outside the territory of the state concerned. Carrying out any of the licensed activities outside that territory will therefore still be an infringement, whether for the licensee or for those holding the rights in other third territories. One can therefore adapt the conditions of the exploitation of the copyright work to the commercial circumstances that prevail in each market.

The territorial nature of copyright and the fact that commercialisation in more than one country through a licensee or assignee necessarily involves more than one national copyright does not however mean that any copyright litigation necessarily has to be brought on a country by country basis, each time in relation to the national right concerned. The territorial nature of the right has an impact on the scope of the right, i.e. the right stops at the border, but not inevitably on the issue of jurisdiction. The latter issue is left entirely to the private international law of the court before which the claimant wishes to bring the case.[4] The territorial nature of the right means that the place where the infringement takes place necessarily corresponds to the territory for which the national right was granted, but apart from that factual consequence the legislator remains free to allow cases on the infringement of foreign copyrights to be brought before its domestic courts if for example the defendant is domiciled locally. The same conclusion applies in relation to choice of law.[5] Territoriality does not necessarily determine the applicable law. In terms of international exploitation and commercialisation one needs in the first place to distinguish between issues that relate to the right as such, for example, existence and scope, and contractual issues. In relation to the latter there is no

---

[4]   See J.J. Fawcett and P. Torremans, *Intellectual Property and Private International Law*, Clarendon Press (1998).

[5]   Ibid.

reason to distinguish copyright contracts from any other type of contract. The general contract choice of law rules therefore apply to copyright contracts and in general the parties are free to chose the applicable law. That law applies to the contract, irrespective of whether it covers one or several national territories and one or several national copyrights, but it only applies to the contractual relationship between the parties. The right the contract deals with cannot be affected by the law applicable to the contract and the latter can for example only transfer the right with the scope it has in a certain country. The scope of the right and other issues concerning the right itself are subject to another choice of law rule. And on this point national treatment, which as we have seen is linked to territoriality, arguably has an impact. The easiest way to guarantee national treatment for foreign authors is to apply the law of the place for which protection is sought, i.e. the domestic law, to issues relating to the right. All authors and all works, be they national or foreign, are then subject to the same law. There may well be scope for exceptions to this rule, for instance in relation to authorship and first ownership,[6] but it is clear that territoriality indirectly has an impact on this point.

A lot more could be said on the principle of territoriality, but it is hoped that this introduction has clarified sufficiently what it means and what it does not mean for our current purposes. Let me therefore now turn to the territorial mechanisms of commercialisation which I was asked to analyse in the context of the increased tendency to question the principles of territoriality. I would like to distinguish in this respect between two types of commercialisation. There are obviously on the one hand those traditional forms of commercialisation that involve the transfer and distribution of hard copies of the work, such as CDs, books, paintings etc., but on the other hand of increasing importance are the various forms of commercialisation involving the electronic transfer of copyright works without hard copies being involved. Allow me to address the latter forms of commercialisation first.

Commercialisation of electronic copies of a copyright work
In this scenario one is necessarily concerned with mere electronic copies of the work, without the presence of a hard copy on any kind of material carrier. In practice this kind of commercialisation takes place on the internet. One may assume that any such commercialisation is by nature global in scope as a result of the borderless nature of the internet. Even if it is, this does not solve all problems, as copyright in the works that are being commercialised is by nature territorial in scope. Copyright permission therefore needs to be obtained in

---

[6] See P. Torremans, 'Authorship, Ownership and Works Created by Employees: Which law applies?', *EIPR* 220–24 (2005).

every single jurisdiction for every commercialisation that is, again on a terri-torial national basis, not covered by an exemption. This may not be a major problem if all the rights in every single country are owned by the same person, but this is by no means guaranteed. In the absence of uniform harmonised rules on authorship and initial ownership, the rights may from the start be granted to different persons in different countries and additionally rights may have been transferred by contract in some countries. Rights that have in one or more countries been granted on an exclusive basis to another commercial entity may also cause problems. And there is also the problem that most collecting societies and licensing bodies operate originally on a territorial national basis. It is therefore not entirely straightforward to be able to obtain a global licence from a single collecting society or licensing body. But this kind of problem is not at the heart of this chapter. After all we are concerned with territorial mechanisms of commercialisation. We are therefore to explore what would happen if one tried to depart from the global scope of commercialisa-tion of copyright works in electronic format on the internet.

As a rightholder I could indeed decide to license or assign my rights for a certain territory only. Such a territory may be composed of one or more coun-tries. Any exploitation by the licensee or assignee outside the contractual area will then remain an infringement and the rightholder may be inclined to enforce the remaining rights, as it may either wish to commercialise the work itself outside the contractual area or to enter into other contractual arrange-ments in this respect. It should be added from the outset that the territorial separation which the rightholder attempts to impose is not by definition based on unacceptable reasons. It may make commercial sense to use a different local licensee or assignee with specific local knowledge and reputation in different territories. Local market conditions may also impose a different marketing strategy and a different pricing strategy in different territories. One could for example think of language-related software and dictionaries which, for the reasons set out above, one may wish to deal with in a different way in Spanish and Latin American markets. Different pricing structures may also make commercial sense from a certain point of view when one markets music or software in different parts of the world.

The key question is therefore whether the licensee or assignee can limit its commercialisation to the contractual territory whilst still using the internet as a marketplace for that commercialisation. In terms of reproduction rights, uploading the copyright work may not be very problematic. But the question needs to be asked whether the licensee or assignee is entitled to upload the work on a server that is located outside the contractual territory, for instance, through the use of the services of a foreign service provider that will host the site of the licensee or assignee. It is submitted that such an authorisation cannot be taken for granted and that a specific contractual authorisation may well be required. Additionally, the reproduction right may also be infringed when the work is downloaded by customers of the licensee or assignee if this is done outside the contractual territory. Discussion over where the copy is made has not yet yielded a conclusive answer, but the majority view seems to be that the place of downloading is involved.[7] And if one could argue that the licensee or assignee is not involved in primary infringement of the reproduction right through the downloading activities of its customers, the argument that they are communicating the work to the public outside the contractual territory retains its value.

There may also be infringement through authorisation. On the one hand there is the narrow definition of authorisation that is derived from the *Amstrad* case.[8] From this point of view, authorisation requires the implied or express grant of a right to do a certain infringing act and to do so on one's own account or on the account of the person granting permission to do the act. On the other hand there is also a wider definition that has attracted support. According to this, it is sufficient to demonstrate that someone sanctioned or approved a certain infringing act being done by a third person to demonstrate that there is authorisation of the infringing act. Even countenancing such an infringing act could be sufficient to prove authorisation. There is no certainty on this point, but downloading from a website that fails to even indicate the territorial restrictions on the website owner's licence or assignment may be seen as an infringing act that has been authorised by the website owner. The latter may therefore infringe through authorising that act.

What measures can the licensee or assignee take to avoid liability? There may be situations where use of certain language can assist. A licensee or assignee for the Netherlands and Belgium may make all material and information on its website available only in Dutch. That would *de facto* render the material useless for customers outside the contractual territory, even if expatriates, nationals of former Dutch or Belgian colonial possessions or certain German or Afrikaans speakers may use the website. Imperfect as this factual tool is, it is not of any use when the language that is used is spoken by large numbers of people in different parts of the world. French, English, Spanish come to mind as easy examples.

The use of a disclaimer may be a more appropriate tool. The website could mention specifically that its owner's rights are limited to a certain territory and that it does not target other territories. It may not stop customers from other territories from accessing the material on the website, but at least it does not

---

[7]   See J.J. Fawcett and P. Torremans, *Intellectual Property and Private International Law*, Clarendon Press (1998).

[8]   *CBS v Amstrad* [1988] AC 1013 (House of Lords).

actively solicit their custom. A specific notice that prohibits downloading from outside the contractual territory may be required though, for instance to rule out liability on grounds of authorisation. But even that does not stand in the way of transactions through the website with customers outside the contractual territory. The website owner could additionally require identification from its customers and refuse to deal with those customers that provide internet or e-mail addresses outside the contractual territory. But then, the accuracy of the information provided cannot be guaranteed by the website operator.

What emerges is a picture of a potential defendant who is at best able to provide a best efforts defence. The website owner or operator can demonstrate that it tried very hard to restrict the scope of its dealings with the copyright work to the contractual territory, but it cannot offer watertight guarantees. The problem with this situation is that one relies on subjective factors, whereas copyright and copyright exemptions and defences to infringement rely on objective factors. The defendant may therefore not be able to escape liability. That is, unless one accepts that the licensor or assignor must implicitly have licensed the licensee or assignee for these spill-over effects which cannot be avoided altogether. The fact that the technology on which the internet is based does not allow these spill-overs to be avoided entirely without engaging in unduly complex procedures is a strong argument in favour of the idea that reasonable contracting parties must have included such an implicit licence.[9] Once more though this cannot be the perfect solution, as many copyright laws around the world require any such licence or assignment to be in writing. It is therefore better to suggest that the parties to the contract include such a spill-over or best efforts provision in the contract. This should not be seen as undue interference from the licensor or assignor with the way of commercialisation, but rather as a provision that provides legal certainty for the parties and especially for the licensee or assignee.

Lessons may perhaps also be learned from trade mark law and the way in which it deals with the use of trade marks on the internet. Trade marks are indeed also territorial rights and exploitation on the internet is also somehow global. The argument has therefore been put forward that any use of a trade mark on the internet is necessarily the use of the trade mark in every single jurisdiction, even in those jurisdictions where others hold the rights to the same mark. Maybe substantive trade mark law limits the impact of this argument through the rule that infringement presupposes use in the course of trade of the mark. Without such use, even if applicable in theory, the various trade mark laws will not result in liability for infringement. The impact in practice

---

[9]   See in a somewhat different context, P. Torremans, *Holyoak and Torremans Intellectual Property Law*, Oxford University Press (4th edn, 2005), at 547.

of the application of several trade mark laws may therefore be limited. Early cases did not take this approach on board. I am thinking of cases such as *Payline* in France, *Fender Musikinstrumente* in Germany, but later cases such as *1-800 Flowers* and *Euromarket v Peters* in the UK clearly established it. The *Payline* decision of 1996 concerned the conflicting use of the indication 'Payline' in Germany and France. While the plaintiff's sign 'Payline' was registered in France, the German defendant had a similar sign for identical services registered in Germany. As the defendant's website was also accessible in France, the plaintiff sued for infringement of its French trade mark. The French court[10] found the accessibility of the defendant's website in France sufficient to affirm jurisdiction (and infringement). The French courts ordered worldwide cessation of use. The subsequent German *Fender Musikinstrumente* decision concerned the offer of goods on the internet that if sold in Germany would have been considered infringing. Without even questioning if the defendant intended any sales in Germany, thereby 'purposefully availing himself of the forum', the court found it sufficient for a trade mark infringement that the offer was accessible in Germany.[11] These decisions therefore equate accessibility with use for the purposes of trade mark infringement.

Where interactivity has arisen in cases in the UK, it has been relevant to the question of *use*. *1-800 Flowers Inc v Phonenames Ltd*[12] concerned an appeal against a decision to register the trade mark 800 FLOWERS in class 35 for flowers and floral products. The question was whether the defendant had *used*, or had the *intention to use* the trade mark in the UK for the purposes of registration. The applicant had argued that the trade mark had been used in the UK by its use on a website. The court considered that merely because an internet website could be accessed from anywhere in the world, that of itself did not mean that it should be regarded as having been used everywhere in the world. *Use*, for trade mark purposes, depended on all the circumstances of a particular case, particularly the intention of the owner of the website and the understanding that a person using the internet would gain from reading the website. On the facts of this case, the applicant's use of the mark on its website did not sufficiently constitute evidence of the requisite intention to use the mark in the United Kingdom. The second UK case, *Euromarket Designs Inc v Peters*[13]

---

[10] Tribunal de Grand d'Instance de Nanterre, interim injunction of 13 October 1996, reported by T. Bettinger and D. Thum, 'Territorial Trade Mark Rights in the Global Village – International Jurisdiction, Choice of Law and Substantive Law for Trade Mark Disputes on the Internet', 31 *IIC* 166 (2000).

[11] Stuttgart High Court, 13 October 1997, *GRUR Int.* 1997, 806 – *Fender-Musikinstrumente.*

[12] [2000] ETMR 369, 1999 WL 1578359 (Ch D), [2000] FSR 697.

[13] High Ct Ch D No. HC 1999 No. 04494, 25 July 2000.

concerned alleged acts of infringement of a registered trade mark in the UK by the use of a sign by the defendant on a website emanating from Ireland. An American company had a UK and CTM for 'Crate & Barrel' in class 21. The defendant, Peters, runs a store in Dublin called 'Crate & Barrel'. The defendants advertised their shop in Dublin on a website. It was alleged that two kinds of goods sold in the Irish store, a hurricane lamp and a beaded coaster, fell within the specification of the pursuer's trade mark. The question again turned on whether the sign 'Crate & Barrel' on the defendant's website had been *used* in the UK. The court considered that an apt analogy was to consider peering down a telescope towards Dublin, and being invited to visit the shop in Dublin. This would not amount to use in the UK. This was different from other internet selling activities, such as those carried out by Amazon.com, who had gone out actively seeking worldwide custom. In those circumstances, a sign would be 'used' on a website.[14] But how would this work in relation to copyright? One could argue that the circumstances of the case can demonstrate that the website operator or owner did not intend to use the copyright work in the course of trade in certain jurisdictions, e.g. through adding a disclaimer or by turning down requests identified by means of a foreign e-mail. One can then indeed see the parallelisms with trade mark law. However, in doing so one overlooks one major obstacle. Copyright law does not require 'use in the course of trade' for there to be copyright infringement. The simple act of reproduction or communication to the public suffices and is equivalent to the use of an identical or similar mark. The additional concept that such use must be use in the course of trade is not present in copyright law. One might think of a creative use of the fair use concept to bridge the gap, but again that means that one already accepts that there is infringing use of the work and most copyright laws do not even have such a broad fair use concept. So in order to make this solution work one would need a redefinition of the concept of reproduction or communication to the public to include these more subjective factors. This will be anything but straightforward.

Competition law

Up to now we have been primarily concerned with the question of how territorial commercialisation systems can be put in place in an internet context. Now we turn to the question of whether competition law allows such a territorial approach. We will look at it from a European perspective under Article 81 EC Treaty. This is also a nice opportunity to bridge the gap between electronic and hard copy commercialisation, as the same rules apply to both forms of exploitation.

---

14 Torremans, *Holyoak and Torremans Intellectual Property Law*, at 400.

Agreements related to copyright may restrict competition and thus fall within the scope of Article 81. Such infringing agreements will involve an improper or abusive exercise of copyright, as confirmed by the Court of Justice in the *Coditel (No 2)* case.[15] Or in the words of the Court:

> Although copyright in a film and the right deriving from it, namely that of exhibiting the film, are not as such subject to the prohibitions contained in Article 81, the exercise of those rights may, none the less, come within the said prohibitions where there are economic or legal circumstances the effect of which is to restrict film distribution to an appreciable degree or to distort competition on the cinematographic market, regard being had to the specific characteristics of that market.[16]

It cannot be said that many cases have arisen in this area, but the practice of the Commission shows that its approach is similar to its approach in patent licence cases. For example no-challenge clauses, royalty clauses which were extended to non-protected goods or works, non-competition clauses which were to continue after the expiry date of the agreement, an exclusive grant back clause,[17] export bans[18] and attempts to guarantee absolute exclusivity[19] were disputed by the Commission and the relevant agreements modified at the Commission's request so that no formal decisions were issued. In *Coditel II* the Court considered whether an agreement whereby the owner of copyright in a film granted the exclusive right to exhibit that film within the territory of a member state for a fixed period could infringe Article 81(1). The Court confirmed that certain ways in which a copyright is exercised can fall foul of Article 81(1). In that case however, the Court held that the mere fact that the owner of a copyright in a film had granted to a licensee the exclusive right to show that film in a particular territory was not sufficient for the agreement automatically to be prohibited under Article 81(1).

Intellectual property contracts are dealt with by the EU Commission by way of a block exemption. Traditionally though copyright contracts have been excluded, mainly because they are seen to have an additional cultural element. The new block exemption[20] that came into force in 2004 still excludes copyright from its scope, but it does deal with software agreements. This inclusion

---

[15]   Case 262/81 *Coditel SA v Ciné Vog Films SA* [1982] ECR 3381 and [1983] 1 CMLR 49.

[16]   Ibid.

[17]   *Neilsen-Hordell/Reichmark*, 12th Annual Report on Competition Policy, points 88–89.

[18]   *Re Ernest Benn Ltd*, 9th Annual Report on Competition Policy.

[19]   *Knoll/Hille-Form*, 13th Annual Report on Competition Policy, points 142–6.

[20]   Commission Regulation (EC) 772/2004 on the application of Article 81(3) to certain categories of technology transfer agreements (2004) OJ L123/11.

can probably be explained by the very nature of software programs, which constitute a separate category, arguably the only one in copyright concerned with technology transfer. Contrary to other copyright works, software programs are above all, like technical inventions, created for utilitarian purposes and industrial applications. The special nature of software programs when compared with other literary and artistic works can also be seen in the legal system applicable to them. Changes such as the reduction in moral rights protection and the absence of a private copying exception bring them very close to patent law. The inclusion of software agreements in the scope of the block exemption and the continued exclusion agreements related to other copyright works seems as a result a little bit less of an oddity.

Software agreements
Let me summarise here the approach taken by the block exemption. Article 2 contains the main principle. Transfer of technology agreements between two undertakings permitting the production of contract products are in the application of Article 81(3) exempted from the application of Article 81(1) in as far as any of their provisions fall within the scope of the latter article. Two restrictions are to be noted immediately. The block exemption only exempts agreements between two undertakings. Agreements between more than two undertakings fall outside the scope of the block exemption and will require an individual exemption. Secondly, the exemption will only apply for as long as the intellectual property right in the licensed technology has not expired, lapsed or been declared invalid.

One of the main innovations in the new block exemption is the fact that the exemption provided for in Article 2 is linked to market-share thresholds.[21] In this respect a distinction needs to be made between competing and non-competing undertakings. Competing undertakings are undertakings that compete with one another either in the relevant technology or in the relevant product market, by licensing out competing technologies which are regarded as interchangeable or substitutable for the licensed technology by the licensees or by being active in the relevant product and geographic markets in which the contract product is sold (or could realistically be expected to undertake the necessary investment to enter that market). The relevant product market includes products which are regarded as interchangeable or substitutable for the contract products by buyers.[22]

Where the undertakings that are party to the agreement are competing undertakings the exemption will only apply on condition that their combined

---

[21]   Article 3 of Regulation 772/2004.
[22]   Article 1(j) of Regulation 772/2004.

market share on the affected relevant technology and product market does not exceed 20%.[23] Where the undertakings that are party to the agreement are not competing undertakings the exemption will only apply on condition that the market share of each of the parties does not exceed 30% on the affected relevant technology and product market.[24]

The market share of a party in the relevant technology market is determined in terms of the presence of the licensed technology in the relevant product market and the licensor's market share in the relevant market for the contract products is deemed to include both the licensor's market share and that of its licensees.[25] However, the main problems with market shares are on the one hand the way in which they are to be calculated and on the other hand the fact that they vary. In other words, companies may meet the requirements set out in Article 3 at the conclusion of their agreement, but they may exceed permitted market-share levels at a later date. The block exemption deals with these problems in Article 8. The basis for the calculation of market shares will be market sales value data and only if these are not available can estimates based on other reliable market information be used. The data used will refer to the preceding calendar year.[26] If market share goes above the 20% threshold the exemption will continue to apply for another two calendar years following the calendar year in which the 20% threshold was first exceeded. In relation to the 30% threshold, that extension will last for three calendar years.[27]

It is however self-evident that the market-share mechanism is not sufficient to weed out any agreement that may seriously harm levels of competition. The block exemption therefore rules out its own application to agreements that have certain undesirable objects. Once more a distinction is made between agreements between competing undertakings and agreements between undertakings that are not competing.[28]

Let us deal with agreements between competing undertakings first. The exemption does not apply to agreements between competing undertakings that have either directly or indirectly, in isolation or in combination with other factors under the control of the parties, one of the following four goals as their object.

First, an agreement should not have as its object the restriction of a party's ability to determine its prices when selling products to third parties.[29]

---

23   Article 3(1) of Regulation 772/2004.
24   Article 3(2) of Regulation 772/2004.
25   Article 3(3) of Regulation 772/2004.
26   Article 8(1) of Regulation 772/2004.
27   Article 8(2) of Regulation 772/2004.
28   Article 4 of Regulation 772/2004.
29   Article 4(1)(a) of Regulation 772/2004.

Secondly, an agreement cannot in principle have as its object the limitation of output. However, it is acceptable to set limitations on the output of contract products by the licensee in non-reciprocal agreements or to impose limitations on one of the licensees in reciprocal agreements.[30]

Thirdly, an agreement cannot in principle have the allocation of markets or customers as its object.[31] This exclusion in principle is however subject to seven exceptions. Field of use restrictions can be imposed on the licensee, as can a restriction to one or more product markets.[32] In non-reciprocal agreements such field of use restrictions can be imposed on both licensor and licensee and restrictions can also be placed on either party in terms of product markets or in terms of territories exclusively reserved for the other party.[33] The licence can also be exclusive in nature, i.e. the licensor can agree not to appoint another licensee in a particular territory.[34] Similarly, in a non-reciprocal agreement the licensor and/or the licensee can agree not to engage in active and/or passive sales into the exclusive territory or to the exclusive customer group reserved to the other party.[35] And again in a non-reciprocal agreement active sales by the licensee into the exclusive territory or to the exclusive customer group allocated by the licensor to another licensee can also be ruled out on condition that the other licensee was not a competing undertaking of the licensor at the time of the conclusion of its own licence.[36] Any licensee can also be obliged only to produce the contract products for its own use, as long as the licensee is not restricted in selling the contract goods actively or passively as spare parts for its own products.[37] The final exception allows the imposition on the licensee in a non-reciprocal agreement of an obligation to produce the contract goods only for a particular customer if the licence was granted in order to create an alternative source of supply for that customer.[38]

Fourthly, an agreement should not have as its object the restriction of the licensee's ability to exploit its own technology or to restrict the ability of any of the parties to carry out research and development activities, unless that restriction is necessary to prevent the disclosure of licensed know-how to third parties.[39]

---

[30]   Article 4(1)(b) of Regulation 772/2004. The terms reciprocal and non-reciprocal agreements are defined in Articles 1(c) and 1(d) respectively.
[31]   Article 4(1)(c) of Regulation 772/2004.
[32]   Article 4(1)(c)(i) of Regulation 772/2004.
[33]   Article 4(1)(c)(ii) of Regulation 772/2004.
[34]   Article 4(1)(c)(iii) of Regulation 772/2004.
[35]   Article 4(1)(c)(iv) of Regulation 772/2004.
[36]   Article 4(1)(c)(v) of Regulation 772/2004.
[37]   Article 4(1)(c)(vi) of Regulation 772/2004.
[38]   Article 4(1)(c)(vii) of Regulation 772/2004.
[39]   Article 4(1)(d) of Regulation 772/2004.

We now turn to agreements between not competing parties. The exemption does not apply to agreements between non-competing undertakings that have either directly or indirectly, in isolation or in combination with other factors under the control of the parties, one of the following three goals as their object.[40]

First, such an agreement should not have as its object the restriction of the ability of any party to determine its own prices when selling to third parties. It is however permitted to set a maximum or a recommended sale price as long as in practice this does not amount to a fixed or minimum sale price.[41]

Secondly, there should not be a restriction on the territory into which or the customers to whom the licensee may passively sell the contract products. This restriction is however subject to six exceptions. A territory or customer group can be reserved exclusively for the licensor.[42] And the same can be done for a licensee for the first two years during which that licensee is selling the contract products in a territory or to a customer group.[43] Any licensee can also be obliged only to produce the contract products for its own use, as long as the licensee is not restricted in selling the contract goods actively or passively as spare parts for its own products.[44] Another exception allows the imposition on the licensee in a non-reciprocal agreement of an obligation to produce the contract goods only for a particular customer if the licence was granted in order to create an alternative source of supply for that customer.[45] A licensee that operates at the wholesale level can be restricted from selling to end-users[46] and the final exception allows a restriction on sales to unauthorised distributors by members of an exclusive distribution system.[47]

Thirdly, a licensee that is a member of a selective distribution system and that operates at retail level should not be restricted in terms of active or passive sales to end-users, without prejudice to the possibility of prohibiting a member of such a system from operating out of an unauthorised place of establishment.[48]

Finally, the rules for non-competing undertakings will continue to apply on this point for the life of the agreement if non-competing undertakings become competing undertakings at a later stage unless the agreement is amended in any material aspect.[49]

---

40   Article 4(2) of Regulation 772/2004.
41   Article 4(2)(a) of Regulation 772/2004.
42   Article 4(2)(b)(i) of Regulation 772/2004.
43   Article 4(2)(b)(ii) of Regulation 772/2004.
44   Article 4(2)(b)(iii) of Regulation 772/2004.
45   Article 4(2)(b)(iv) of Regulation 772/2004.
46   Article 4(2)(b)(v) of Regulation 772/2004.
47   Article 4(2)(b)(vi) of Regulation 772/2004.
48   Article 4(2)(c) of Regulation 772/2004.
49   Article 4(3) of Regulation 772/2004.

Up to now we have dealt with restrictions that exclude an agreement altogether from the scope of the block exemption. Now we turn to restrictions that are not themselves covered by the exemption. But their presence does not take the whole agreement outside the scope of the block exemption. According to Article 5 the exemption does not apply to the following obligations in technology transfer agreements:

(a)   any direct or indirect obligation on the licensee to grant an exclusive licence to the licensor or to a third party designated by the licensor in respect of its own severable improvements to or its own new applications of the licensed technology;

(b)   any direct or indirect obligation on the licensee to assign, in whole or in part, to the licensor or to a third party designated by the licensor, rights to its own severable improvements to or its own new applications of the licensed technology;

(c)   any direct or indirect obligation on the licensee not to challenge the validity of intellectual property rights which the licensor holds in the common market, without prejudice to the possibility of providing for termination of the technology transfer agreement in the event that the licensee challenges the validity of one or more of the licensed intellectual property rights.[50]

And

Where the undertakings party to the agreement are not competing undertakings, the exemption provided for in Article 2 shall not apply to any direct or indirect obligation limiting the licensee's ability to exploit its own technology or limiting the ability of any of the parties to the agreement to carry out research and development, unless such latter restriction is indispensable to prevent the disclosure of the licensed know-how to third parties.[51]

Other copyright works
It is submitted that the approach taken in the block exemption to software contracts may not be entirely irrelevant in relation to other copyright works. I have already demonstrated above that the Commission extrapolates its approach to other intellectual property right to copyright and it is therefore likely that other rather utilitarian copyright works, such as for example databases, may well in terms of the agreements concerning them be treated in a manner that is very similar to that one contained in the block exemption.

The standard artistic works and the non-utilitarian concern that is associated with them may benefit from a more lenient treatment. It is often more difficult to see how in the absence of an exclusive right on ideas and other

---

[50]   Article 5(1) of Regulation 772/2004.
[51]   Article 5(2) of Regulation 772/2004.

ways of expressing the same idea there will be a significant impact on competition. The additional non-utilitarian concerns that are taken into account may also well bring the contract within the scope of the exemption provided in Article 85(3). For instance, content specifically targeted at local markets and local language versions or translations may well be benefits to consumers that can only be achieved under conditions of exclusivity, whilst not entirely eliminating competition in the relevant market. Let me just briefly repeat here the four conditions which the exemption imposes in terms of Article 85(3) EC Treaty:

> The provisions of paragraph 1 may, however, be declared inapplicable in the case of:
>
> (a) any agreement or category of agreements between undertakings;
> (b) any decision or category of decisions by associations of undertakings;
> (c) any concerted practice or category of concerted practices;
>
> which contributes to improving the production or distribution of goods or to promoting technical or economic progress, while allowing consumers a fair share of the resulting benefit, and which does not:
>
> (a) impose on the undertakings concerned restrictions which are not indispensable to the attainment of these objectives;
> (b) afford such undertakings the possibility of eliminating competition in respect of a substantial part of the products in question.

However, the combination of territorial restrictions and exclusivity will affect competition and for any such combination in a contract there needs to be a pro-competitive justification that outweighs the restrictions on competition. The *Coditel II* case demonstrated this just under a quarter of a century ago.

Commercialisation of hard copies of copyright works

In these cases another problem arises for a territorial commercialisation approach. Apart from the competition law issues highlighted above, the first sale or exhaustion doctrine may overrule a strictly territorial approach set up by contract. In Europe there is a well-developed exhaustion doctrine that applies to goods that were first marketed inside the European Economic Area (EEA).[52] We will first review this policy before turning to the situation in the US.

---

[52] In its recent decision in case C-16/03, *Peak Holding AB v Axolin-Elinor AB* ([2005] OJ C19/3) the Court of Justice clarified the concept of putting the goods on the market with the consent of the proprietor. In this case the proprietor had imported the goods into the EEA and had offered them for sale in its own shops, but it had not actually sold them. The Court held that the goods had not been put on the market with the consent of the proprietor of the mark in the absence of a first sale of the goods. However, such a first sale does take place when the goods are sold to another operator in the EEA even if the contract prohibits resale in the EEA.

The oldest EU case in which the exhaustion doctrine was applied was a case relating to records. In *Deutsche Grammophon v Metro*[53] the Court was faced with the following issue. Deutsche Grammophon sold the same records in Germany and in France, but its French subsidiary, Polydor, could only charge a lower price due to market conditions. Metro bought the records in France for resale in Germany at a price below the price Deutsche Grammophon charged. Deutsche Grammophon invoked its copyright[54] in the records to stop this practice. The Court ruled that Deutsche Grammophon had exhausted its copyright in the records by putting them on the market in France with its consent and could not oppose the importation of the records by Metro.[55]

This approach was confirmed in the *Musik-Vertrieb Membran v GEMA* case.[56] Once again records and cassettes were being imported into Germany after they had been put on the market in another member state with the consent of the copyright owner. The German collecting society GEMA tried to rely on the German copyright in the works to levy the difference between the low royalty that had been paid abroad and the higher German royalty. The Court reiterated that by putting the records and cassettes on the market with its consent the owner of the copyright had exhausted all copyright in them. They could as a result not rely on any copyright to prevent the importation, nor could they rely on it to charge an additional royalty. In the Court's view, the copyright owner who markets its works in member states where the royalties are low has to abide by that decision and accept the consequences of it. The approach sounds identical to that taken in the patent case of *Merck v Stephar*.[57] The case law of the Court has now also been reflected in the information society Directive.[58] Article 4(2) stipulates that

> the distribution right shall not be exhausted within the Community in respect of the original or copies of the work, except where the first sale or other transfer of ownership in the Community of that object is made by the rightholder or with his consent.

---

[53]   Case 78/70 *Deutsche Grammophon GmbH v Metro-SB-Grossmarkte GmbH & Co KG* [1971] ECR 487, [1971] CMLR 631.

[54]   For the purposes of our discussion of the case we can assume that the German exclusive distribution right is akin to copyright.

[55]   Case 78/70 *Deutsche Grammophon GmbH v Metro-SB-Grossmarkte GmbH & Co KG* [1971] ECR 487 at 500.

[56]   Joined cases 55 and 57/80 *Musik-Vertrieb Membran v GEMA* [1981] ECR 147, [1981] 2 CMLR 44; see also case 58/80 *Dansk Supermarked A/S v Imerco A/S* [1981] ECR 181, [1981] 3 CMLR 590.

[57]   Case 187/80 *Merck & Co Inc v Stephar BV* [1981] ECR 2063.

[58]   Directive 2001/29/EC of the European Parliament and the Council on the harmonisation of certain aspects of copyright and related rights in the information society [2001] OJ L167/10.

In *Warner Bros v Christiaensen*[59] a difficult problem arose. Video cassettes which were put on the market in both the UK and Denmark were being imported from the UK into Denmark. It is clear that the plaintiff could not rely on its Danish copyright to stop the importation of the video cassettes, as this only requires a normal application of the dictum in the two previous cases. The problem arose because Danish law granted a rental right to the author or the producer, while such a right did not exist in the UK and Christiaensen imported the cassettes to hire them out afterwards. Christiaensen argued that the rights in the cassettes had been exhausted because they had been marketed in the UK with the consent of the owner, but the Court rejected this argument. Indeed the rental right has to be treated as a separate right and as it did not exist in the UK, it could not have been exhausted.[60] Warner Bros could invoke the Danish rental right to stop Christiaensen hiring out the video cassettes.[61] It is easier to understand why the rental right should be treated as a separate right by looking at the consequences of not doing so. That would effectively have rendered the rental right worthless, as it would have been exhausted by sale in a member state where the right is not known. As we discussed in relation to patents, Articles 28 and 30 are construed in such a way that they must leave the existence of the right and a certain exercise untouched as any other interpretation would render them senseless. The approach taken by the Court must thus be correct.

The *Warner Bros* case[62] shows clearly that there are many facets to the essential function of copyright and especially to the specific subject-matter of copyright. The rental right point was clearly a separate aspect within the latter. This should not come as a surprise. Copyright is a broad right that protects a wide variety of products. It may in each case, broadly speaking, be the aim to protect the author and the subsequent rightholders because it is felt that their creative efforts deserve encouragement and protection, but the exact way in which this is put into practice by including different aspects within the specific subject-matter of copyright is not always as easy to determine as it is with the narrower patent right. While it can be understood that rental as a separate way in which the work is exploited may have been entitled to be promoted to a separate aspect of the specific subject-matter, one should not construe the latter too broadly either. The *Dior* case[63] illustrates this point. Dior had

---

[59]   Case 158/86 *Warner Bros Inc v Christiansen* [1988] ECR 2605.
[60]   See M. Henry, 'Rental and Duration Directives: Issues Arising from Current EC Reforms', 12 *EIPR* 437 at 439 (1993).
[61]   Ibid.
[62]   Case 158/86 *Warner Bros v Christiaansen* [1988] ECR 2605, [1990] 3 CMLR 684.
[63]   Case C-337/95 *Parfums Christian Dior SA v Evora BV* [1998] RPC 166.

exhausted all copyrights in the box in which it sold its perfume bottles by putting the perfumes, in the box, on the market for the first time. This is normal copyright exhaustion and the reward for the copyright in the design of the boxes is seen as being included in the sales price of the perfume. Any further use of the copyright in the design of the boxes would therefore go beyond the specific subject-matter of copyright in this case. A problem arose because the parallel importer wanted to reproduce the design of the boxes in its publicity. Printing a photograph of the boxes to advertise the fact that the perfume is now available at a lower price from certain outlets certainly involves copying. Could Dior stop this on the basis of its copyright? The Court of Justice ruled that it could not. The exhaustion of the copyright by putting the product on the market exhausted all rights. Reprinting for publicity purposes is clearly not a separate aspect of the specific subject-matter of the right; it is part of the main aspect of copyright. It could rather be argued that the parallel importer which has the right to import the perfume bottles which Dior put on the market in another member state must also have the right to advertise these products. Otherwise the consumer will not be informed and in the absence of real sales the whole system of parallel import will *de facto* collapse. Any use of copyright to stop advertising of the products would therefore be a use to block parallel imports of legitimately acquired products. This cannot be part of the essential function of copyright. It must be an abusive use of the right. It must therefore be treated as falling outside the specific subject-matter of the right and the right must be treated as having been exhausted for this purpose.[64]

It is therefore clear that the exhaustion doctrine will seriously restrict any territorial commercialisation system, especially as it cannot be overruled by contract.

Under US law the position is very similar, as the Supreme Court made clear in 1998 when the Court decided *Quality King Distributors, Inc v L'Anza Research International, Inc.*[65] In making its ruling, the Court reversed a Ninth Circuit decision that upheld the right under Section 602(a) of the Copyright Act to block the importation of grey market goods, even if the goods were first distributed and sold abroad.

In reversing the Ninth Circuit decision, the Court held that although Section 602(a) sets forth the right to bar unauthorised importation, that section is subject to the 'first sale' doctrine since the goods in question were first sold

---

64   See also I. Stamatoudi, 'From Drugs to Spirits and from Boxes to Publicity: Decided and Undecided Issues in Relation to Trade Mark and Copyright Exhaustion', IPQ [1999] 95.

65   *Quality King Distributors, Inc, Petitioner v L'Anza Research International, Inc*, No. 96-1470, 523 US 135 (1998).

abroad and then later re-imported into the US. The first-sale doctrine, which establishes a defence to alleged copyright violations, provides that once an item is first sold in commerce, the manufacturer or copyright owner cannot control the further resale of the item.

L'Anza made hair-care products which were primarily sold in hair salons. They were sold at higher prices than comparable types of goods sold in drug stores. They were distributed exclusively in hair salons in the US under licensing agreements. However, L'Anza exported products abroad at prices that were much lower than their products sold in the US. Because of the lower pricing abroad, there was an economic incentive to re-import the L'Anza products into the US and market them in discount stores.

L'Anza sued the discount merchants who had purchased the imported (but US-made) products, claiming the importation of goods bearing copyrighted labels violated Section 602(a) of the Copyright Act. Section 602(a) provides that unauthorised importation is an infringement of the exclusive right of distribution under Section 106 of the Copyright Act. In making its ruling the Court noted that although Section 602(a) does not expressly state that it is subject to the first sale doctrine, Section 106 is subject to the rule. Therefore, the Supreme Court reasoned that goods which are first sold abroad and re-imported are subject to the doctrine.

A concurring opinion of Justice Ginsburg makes clear that the decision does not apply at all to goods manufactured outside the US and imported into the US under exclusive licensing arrangements. This re-enforces the point made by Justice Stevens when he noted that 'section 602(a) applies to a category of copies that are neither piratical nor lawfully made under this title'. This category applies to copyrighted products lawfully made under the copyright law of a country outside of the United States. Thus, Section 602(a) allows American copyright owners to bring infringement actions against foreign distributors who produce materials under the copyright laws of a country outside of the United States. The first sale doctrine would apply (only) to copyright materials made under the Copyright Act of the United States.

Performance copyrights
This category is concerned with plays and films and their performance. Even in the absence of hard copies the exhaustion doctrine may apply and limit a territorial commercialisation approach. It is also clear that this category includes both traditional formats and digital electronic formats involving online technology.

The exploitation of these works takes place through public exhibitions which can be repeated an indefinite number of times. It is like rendering a service and the whole area has more links with the free movement of services provided for in Article 49 of the Treaty of Rome than with the free movement of goods. This implies that this category of rights should be treated differently.

The Court was confronted with this problem in the *Coditel* case.[66] This case made the French film *Le Boucher*, the copyright in which was owned by the French company, Les Films la Boétie, famous. A seven-year exclusive licence to exhibit the film in Belgium had been given to Ciné Vog. One of the clauses of the licence stipulated that Ciné Vog could only allow the film to be broadcast on Belgian television 40 months after its first cinema showing. A different exclusive licensee was appointed for Germany and that licence contract did not restrict the showing of the film on television. The film was shown on German television before it could have been shown on Belgian television and the Belgian cable company Coditel picked up the German signal and retransmitted it on its cable network. This required the authorisation of the Belgian licensee under Belgian copyright law because it was held to be a communication to the public. Because no authorisation had been applied for and because they feared loss of revenue because the Belgian television stations would be less interested in acquiring the right to broadcast a film that many of their viewers had already seen in the German version, Ciné Vog sued Coditel for infringement of copyright. Coditel based its defence *inter alia* on the freedom to provide services and argued that as the film had been shown with the consent of the owner of the copyright all copyright in it had been exhausted.

The problem with the free movement of services provision of the Treaty, however, is that it does not provide for an exception for intellectual property. This did not prevent Advocate-General Warner suggesting that Article 30 applied by analogy in this context. The Court must have agreed with this suggestion because it ruled that:

> Whilst Article 49 of the Treaty prohibits restrictions upon the freedom to provide services, it does not hereby encompass limits upon the exercise of certain economic activities which have their origin in the application of national legislation for the protection of intellectual property, save where such application constitutes a means of arbitrary discrimination or a disguised restriction on trade between member states. Such would be the case if that application enabled parties to create artificial barriers to trade between member states.[67]

In a next step the specific subject-matter of the performing right in a film was defined as the right of authorities to forbid each and every performance of the film, including the right for it to be televised. As the retransmission of the film by Coditel amounted to a new performance, the performing right in the

---

[66]   Case 62/79 *Coditel SA v Ciné Vog Films SA* [1980] ECR 881, [1981] 2 CMLR 362.

[67]   Case 62/79 *Coditel SA v Ciné Vog Films SA* [1980] ECR 881 at 903.

film had not been exhausted and Ciné Vog could rely on it. The restriction on the showing of the film which Ciné Vog claimed was necessary in order to guarantee it the benefit of the essence of the exclusive performing right. The remaining issue was whether the practice of having one exclusive licensee per member state was an example of the artificial barriers to trade to which the Court objected. The Court did not see it as such an example and accepted that such an approach was objectively justifiable because at that time all television services were organised on the basis of a national legal broadcasting monopoly.[68] Its conclusion was

> . . . that the provisions of the Treaty relating to the freedom to provide services did not preclude an assignee of the performing right in a cinematographic film in a member state from relying upon his right to prohibit the exhibition of that film in that State, without its authority, by means of cable diffusion if the film so exhibited is picked up and transmitted after being broadcast in another member state by a third party with the consent of the original owner of the right.[69]

In a digital online environment similar situations arise. Works are for example delivered online whenever the user needs them, for example through access to a database. Concepts such as communication to the public and making the work available to the public carry with them an element of services being provided rather than a material copy of the work being provided to the user. The information society Directive[70] takes this into account and stipulates in its Article 3(3) that the communication to the public right and the making available to the public right will 'not be exhausted by any act of communication to the public or making available to the public as set out in this Article'. In this respect EU law leaves more options open for a territorial commercialisation approach.

Conclusion

The aim of this chapter was to question the principles of territoriality and more particularly the determination of territorial mechanisms of commercialisation.

Its first obvious finding is that the commercialisation of copyright works on

---

[68] Arguably this is no longer the case now that Directive 93/83 on copyright and neighbouring rights relating to satellite broadcasting and cable retransmission has been adopted ((1993) OJ L248/15, see supra). For example Article 7(3) on co-production agreements shows that licences may have to be granted on a Community scale, thereby excluding territorial licensing. See Ph. Kern, 'The EC "Common Position" on Copyright Applicable to Satellite Broadcasting and Cable Retransmission', 8 *EIPR* [1993] 276 at 280.

[69] Case 62/79 *Coditel SA v Ciné Vog Films SA* [1980] ECR 881 at 904.

[70] Directive 2001/29/EC of the European Parliament and the Council on the harmonisation of certain aspects of copyright and related rights in the information society [2001] OJ L167/10.

the internet in electronic format creates significant difficulties when it comes to drafting agreements that put in place such a territorial mechanism of commercialisation and to implementing it. Secondly, whether one deals with electronic or hard copies, competition law imposes restrictions on any such territorial approach, especially when combined with exclusivity and in relation to more utilitarian copyright works. Perhaps though the potential impact of the first sale or exhaustion doctrine is even more significant than the impact of competition law. Competition law concerns can also be taken into account more easily when drafting agreements. It is on the other hand virtually impossible to address first sale or exhaustion concerns by contract. Overall, therefore, serious questions must be asked about the strength in practice of the principle of territoriality when it comes to setting up territorial mechanisms of commercialisation on the basis of this principle.

20 A broadcasters' treaty?*

Tom Rivers[1]

The primary purpose of this chapter is to describe the course of the negotiations which have taken place under the aegis of the World Intellectual Property Organisation (WIPO) on the subject of how best to protect broadcasters at an international level. This process, still unfinished, has taken a long time and has been at times contentious; lately, it has appeared that some governments and a number of 'civil society' non-governmental organisations (NGOs) doubt whether intellectual property protection is the right way to deal with the problems of broadcasters. Is this because protection for broadcasters is specially problematic or because the attitude to intellectual property more generally has shifted?

Describing what has happened may provide answers to this kind of question and of necessity will highlight specific issues which have emerged: the beneficiaries of protection, the extent of the substantive rights, the use of technological protection measures.

The Introduction is intended to give the reader some necessary background and a summary account of the process. There follows a more detailed account of how the work of the committee developed, the content of the governments' proposals, and the debate between the different points of view.

The Conclusion offers an assessment of the future prospects for work at WIPO on the broadcasters' treaty and other issues.

Introduction

In March 1998 the General Assembly of WIPO agreed a recommendation in the budget for the coming biennium to set up a number of Standing Committees: these would replace the existing ad hoc committees of experts. The Standing Committee on Copyright and Related Rights (SCCR) was one of the new committees thus established. It had the general remit to harmonise WIPO activities for protecting copyright and related rights. When the committee met in November 1998 its first working document was a memorandum from the WIPO International Bureau. This recommended that the

---

*   This chapter is affectionately dedicated to the memory of Tony Scapilatti, Andrés Lerena and Moira Burnett.
[1]   Intellectual Property Consultant, London.

committee should give priority to consideration of the Protocol concerning audiovisual performances,[2] and that the protection of non-original databases and the rights of broadcasting organisations should also be on the committee's agenda.

The underlying implication of the Bureau's memorandum was that this aspect of WIPO's activities, protecting copyright and related rights, was to be achieved by treaty-making. In the nature of things treaty-making cannot be an everyday activity, so WIPO's emphasis calls for some explanation. To do so, it is necessary to go back to an earlier period in WIPO's history. In its origins[3] the organisation existed as an agency responsible for the purely administrative oversight of the treaties relating to intellectual (and industrial) property. The scope of its responsibilities were extended in the Convention which in 1967 gave the agency its present identity as the World Intellectual Property Organisation.[4] The Convention set out as a prime objective for WIPO 'to promote the protection of intellectual property',[5] and 'intellectual property' itself was defined[6] as including literary, artistic and scientific works and performances of performers, phonograms and broadcasts; in other words the objects of protection of the Berne and Rome Conventions. In describing its functions the Convention stated that WIPO should 'promote the development of measures to facilitate the efficient protection of intellectual property throughout the world'.[7] When WIPO became a specialised agency of the United Nations[8] the text of the agreement between the two organisations referred to WIPO as being responsible for taking appropriate action '*inter alia* for promoting creative intellectual activity'[9] and omitted any explicit mention of the protection of intellectual property.

In the years that followed, although it was recognised that there were areas where the Berne Convention might stand in need of clarification and expansion, there was little sign that WIPO or its Member States envisaged treaty-making as a viable solution. Undoubtedly, this was in part because the

---

2   What was at that stage referred to as the Protocol and later became a proposed treaty represented unfinished business from the 1996 Diplomatic Conference.

3   The establishment in 1893 of the United International Bureaux for the protection of intellectual property (usually known as BIRPI), amalgamating the two bureaux responsible for administering the Paris and the Berne Conventions.

4   Convention Establishing the World Intellectual Property Organisation, signed at Stockholm 14 July 1967.

5   Art 3 ibid.

6   Art 2(viii) ibid.

7   Art 4(1) ibid.

8   By an Agreement dated 17 December 1974 between the United Nations and WIPO.

9   Art 1 Recognition ibid.

Convention itself imposed a requirement of unanimity in order to revise any substantive provision.[10]

The impetus to establish the original ad hoc Committee of Experts came indeed from the record industry not from governments or WIPO.[11] The subject of inquiry for the committee was whether phonograms might be regarded as falling within the category of works protected by the Berne Convention, with the implication that the desired result could be achieved by means of a protocol to the Berne Convention. Whilst it was decided fairly quickly that the answer to that question was in the negative, instead of the committee taking the view that its work was at an end, it was agreed that work should continue in two parallel ad hoc Committees of Experts, one examining possible revisions to the Berne Convention and the other examining a possible instrument to update the rights of performers and phonogram producers. Although some experts made the point that it would be logical to include broadcasters, the third group of beneficiaries of the Rome Convention, within the scope of work on such an instrument, this argument was not pressed, and broadcasters themselves did nothing to press their own case. This reticence on the part of broadcasters may have been because in their assessment the work of the Committees of Experts showed little sign of making headway.

The Clinton administration changed everything. It committed itself wholeheartedly to a 'digital agenda', seeing a borderless world, where the traditional nation-based legal weapons for fighting piracy would become as outdated as the cavalry when faced with tanks, meant that there was an imperative need for multilateral solutions and a new legal order. In something under two years the Committees of Experts had recommended and the Member States of WIPO in General Assembly had agreed to convene a Diplomatic Conference in December 1996.

The 'internet treaties'[12] represented a remarkable achievement, but it is important to remember that the 1996 Diplomatic Conference was not an unqualified success. The original intention had been to adopt three instruments: one updating the Berne Convention, one updating the rights of performers and phonogram producers, and one providing protection for databases. What many thought of as a key element in the WIPO Copyright Treaty,

---

[10] Art 27(3) Paris Revision of Berne Convention 24 July 1971 as amended 2 October 1979.

[11] But since US domestic legislation treated phonograms as copyright works of which performers and producers were the joint authors (and the US was not a Rome Contracting State) it may be reasonable to suppose that the US was sympathetic to this initiative.

[12] The WIPO Copyright Treaty (WCT) and the WIPO Performances and Phonograms Treaty (WPPT).

the updated reproduction right, fell by the wayside, a victim of sustained lobbying from the telecommunications industry and equipment manufacturers. Audiovisual performances were removed from the scope of the WIPO Peformances and Phonograms Treaty. The possible database treaty disappeared off the agenda of the Diplomatic Conference in the first few days. Nonetheless, the relative success in 1996 provided a model of how such treaty-making was to be done: the issue was put on the agenda of the committee of experts, Member States of WIPO submitted proposals in treaty language, in due course when the committee judged that things were sufficiently mature a recommendation was made to the General Assembly, which would decide on the convening of a Diplomatic Conference preceded by the drafting of a Basic Proposal. The model failed to function in the case of the Diplomatic Conference in December 2000 on audiovisual performances, but optimists argued that the breakdown was on a single (irreconcilable) difference between the US and the EC,[13] while pessimists took this as demonstrating the vulnerability of the process.

At the time of writing the SCCR has held 15 sessions, each three to five days in length, the last in September 2006. The General Assembly has had the protection of broadcasting organisations on its agenda in three successive years, 2004, 2005 and 2006. The conclusions adopted at the end of the fifteenth session of the SCCR envisaged one further special session of the committee in January 2007, in conjunction with the meeting of a preparatory committee to make arrangements for a diplomatic conference on broadcasters' rights to be convened in July 2007. The General Assembly, however, at its meeting in September–October 2006 introduced substantial modifications to that timetable and process: instead of one special session the General Assembly decided there should be two such sessions, the first in January 2007 and the second, in conjunction with the meeting of a preparatory committee, in June 2007; the date for the diplomatic conference was moved back from July to November/December 2007 and its convening was made conditional on the SCCR having in the course of the two special sessions agreed on and finalised a signal-based approach, the objectives, specific scope and object of protection with a view to submitting to the Diplomatic Conference a revised basic proposal.[14]

In the press release which WIPO put out after the January special session Mr Michael Keplinger,[15] the new Deputy Director General, was quoted as

---

13   A difference which seven years later shows no sign of being resolved.
14   §107 p. 38 Report of 33rd (16th Extraordinary) Session WIPO General Assembly, 25 September to 3 October 2006, WO/GA/33/10.
15   Previously head of US delegation. He replaced Mrs Rita Hayes as Deputy Director General at the end of 2006.

saying that Member States had 'demonstrated political will to conclude the negotiations'.[16] A rather different assessment was provided in *IP Watch* which quoted unnamed WIPO officials as judging the outcome 'unclear'.[17] The Revised Draft Basic Proposal,[18] prepared by the Chairman of the SCCR, Mr Jukka Liedes, in cooperation with the WIPO Secretariat for consideration by the committee at its 15th session, was a document over 100 pages long, characterised by one delegate[19] as inconsistent and full of ambiguities and by another[20] as an insecure basis for a diplomatic conference. It was apparent that unless agreement could be reached on a substantially shorter text, which in turn implied a willingness on the part of the major players to make concessions at the second Special Session in June, there was unlikely to be consensus on calling a Diplomatic Conference.

Why should it have taken so long to achieve so little? Or to look at the same question in a different perspective: why were WIPO and its Member States, to say nothing of the 50 or more NGOs which regularly attended the SCCR, willing to invest so much time, effort and money for such a paltry return? It is time to turn to a more detailed examination of the process.

The work of the committee

Preparation for the first session: the existing framework of rights
For the first session of the SCCR in November 1998 the International Bureau made available a memorandum on the existing international, regional and national legislation dealing with the protection of broadcasting organisations.[21] The memorandum included the submissions made by broadcasters at the two symposia organised by WIPO on modernising the international protection of broadcasting organisations.[22] At an international level, the Bureau referred to three instruments

International instruments

ROME CONVENTION   This requires Contracting States to provide certain minimum rights for broadcasting organisations. The rights in question are rights to

---

[16]   WIPO Press Release 473, 22 January 2007.
[17]   William New, 'Questions Loom for WIPO Broadcasting Negotiation', *IP Watch*, 23 January 2007.
[18]   SCCR/15/2, 31 July 2006.
[19]   Mr S.K. Arora, head of delegation, India.
[20]   Mr Jule Sigall, US delegation.
[21]   SCCR/1/3.
[22]   Report of the Manila symposium, WIPO Publication 57.

authorise or prohibit rebroadcasting by wireless means, fixation, and the reproduction of fixations,[23] of their broadcasts, and the communication to the public of television broadcasts but only in places to which the public is admitted on payment of an entrance fee (and Contracting States may determine the conditions under which this right is exercised).[24] The minimum term of protection is 20 years. A Contracting State may provide for exceptions to the minimum rights to cover private use, reporting of current events, and use for teaching or scientific research; it may also provide for the same kind of limitations as it provides in respect of the copyright in literary and artistic works.[25]

TRIPS   The minimum rights specified are the right to prohibit the following acts when undertaken without the authorisation of the broadcasting organisation: fixation of their broadcasts, reproduction of such fixations, rebroadcasting of their broadcasts by wireless means, and the communication to the public of television broadcasts.[26] However, where Member States do not grant such rights to broadcasting organisations, they shall provide owners of copyright in the subject matter of broadcasts with the possibility of preventing the specified acts subject to the provisions of Berne.[27] The minimum term of protection is 20 years, as in the Rome Convention. Member States may provide for the same exceptions and limitations as are permitted by Rome.

SATELLITES CONVENTION[28]   The Convention requires Contracting States to take adequate measures to prevent any distributor for whom the signal is not intended from distributing a programme-carrying signal originated by the national of another Contracting State or from another Contracting State. The Convention applies to satellite distribution of content; it does not apply to satellite transmissions intended for reception by the public, that is, broadcasts;

---

[23]   The reproduction right only covers reproductions of unauthorised fixations and reproductions of fixations where the fixation falls within a permitted exception or limitation but the reproduction does not.

[24]   Art 13 Rome Convention.

[25]   Art 15 Rome Convention. The further exception, which covers ephemeral fixations made by a broadcasting organisation by means of its own facilities and for its own broadcasts, is of course an exception exclusively in favour of broadcasting organisations rather than an exception capable of being made use of by third parties in relation to broadcasts.

[26]   Art 14(3) TRIPS.

[27]   It is unclear whether this is to be interpreted as meaning that Member States are obliged to provide the specified rights for broadcasting organisations in respect of those broadcasts which cannot be protected under Berne because the subject matter is in the public domain.

[28]   Adopted Brussels 1974, entered into force 1979.

nor does it apply to derived signals taken from signals already distributed, that is, retransmission of broadcasts.

The Bureau's memorandum describes the following regional instruments:

Regional instruments

EU DIRECTIVES[29]   Broadcasting organisations have the exclusive rights to authorise or prohibit fixation, reproduction (direct or indirect) of fixations, distribution by way of sale of copies of fixations, rebroadcasting, and communication to the public of their broadcasts in places where an entrance fee is paid. Cable distributors that originate their cablecasts, as opposed to retransmitting the broadcasts of others, have the same rights as broadcasters in respect of fixations, and the distribution and reproduction of fixations. Broadcasting includes satellite transmissions intended for reception by the public. Member States may provide for limitations to the rights of broadcasting organisations which correspond with those in the Rome Convention.[30] The retransmission by cable of broadcasts from another country should take place on the basis of contractual agreements between copyright owners, holders of related rights and cable operators. The term of protection is 50 years after the first (*sic*) transmission[31] of a broadcast.

COUNCIL OF EUROPE   Although the European Agreement of 1 July 1961 on the protection of television broadcasts only binds six countries[32] it has some significance because it antedates the Rome Convention by several months and has a wider scope than the Convention. It provides for protection for broadcasts when they are diffused by wire, in addition to protecting broadcasts (as Rome does) against retransmission by another broadcaster. It also gives broadcasting organisations an unrestricted right to authorise or prohibit reproductions of fixations.

---

[29]   Directive 92/100 (rental and lending), Directive 93/83 (cable and satellite), Directive 93/98 (term of protection).
[30]   It should be remembered that the International Bureau's memorandum dates from 1998 and so antedates the Information Society Directive 2001/29 of 22 May 2001. This widened the reproduction right and introduced a making available right for broadcasting organisations as well as extending the provisions in the WIPO treaties on technological protection measures and rights management information to broadcasting organisations.
[31]   And see now Recital 18 of Directive 2006/116 of 12 December 2006 where this misapprehension is perpetuated. The concept of a second or further transmission only makes sense with reference to the content of the transmission.
[32]   Denmark, France, Germany, Norway, Sweden and the United Kingdom.

CARTAGENA AGREEMENT   This Agreement between Bolivia, Colombia, Ecuador, Peru and Venezuela dates from 17 December 1993. Broadcasting organisations have the rights to authorise or prohibit retransmission of their broadcasts by any means or process, fixation, and reproduction of fixations. Retransmission is defined as relaying a signal or programme from another source by the distribution of signs, sounds or images by wireless, wire, cable, optic fibre or other medium. The minimum term of protection is 50 years. The exceptions and limitations correspond to those in the Rome Convention.

NAFTA   The parties to the North American Free Trade Agreement (NAFTA) are the United States, Canada and Mexico. The agreement is dated 8 December 1993. It mandates the imposition of criminal sanctions against the manufacture, sale or making available of unauthorised decoders for decrypting encrypted satellite television programmes. Parties must also give those with an interest in the content of the broadcasts standing to bring civil proceedings to prevent such activities. Additionally, a person who in the course of commerce receives or further distributes unencoded signals which have been decrypted without the lawful distributor's authority attracts civil liability.

The Bureau examined the protection given to broadcasting organisations in national legislation.

National legislation   According to the Bureau there were (in 1998) 67 countries which gave broadcasting organisations specific 'related rights' protection. These included Argentina, Brazil, Chile, China, India, Japan, the Russian Federation, Switzerland and Turkey. A further 36 countries, including Australia, Ireland, New Zealand and the United Kingdom, granted protection under copyright. US copyright does not treat broadcasts as protectable works, but if a fixation of the contents of a broadcast is made simultaneously with the transmission, then the broadcaster obtains copyright protection for all copyrightable subject matter that is transmitted.[33]

The Bureau drew attention to the technological developments in the field of satellite and cable distribution which meant that there were gaps in the protection provided by the Rome Convention. According to the Bureau 'most of the legislation examined include the rights granted under Art 13(a) to (c) of the Rome Convention'.[34] Some countries have chosen to follow the Rome provisions closely, but others go beyond Rome in granting an unrestricted right of

---

[33]   In addition, as the US made clear in one of its interventions in the SCCR, broadcasters have under the Communications Act a strong retransmission right.
[34]   §43, p. 12 SCCR/1/3.

reproduction. These latter include Australia, Brazil, Cameroon, Chile, China, Republic of Korea and Turkey. The Bureau noted other examples of rights being granted that went beyond the Convention minima: 33 countries, including the US, gave broadcasting organisations the right to issue copies of broadcasts to the public, and the majority of countries granted a 50 year term of protection with a few granting an even longer term.[35]

In the final section of its report[36] the Bureau set out the rights which the broadcasting organisations themselves, at the WIPO symposia in Manila in 1997 and Cancun in 1998, considered as constituting a modern level of protection. These were the exclusive rights to authorise or prohibit the following: simultaneous or deferred rebroadcasting by satellite or any other means; simultaneous or deferred retransmission by cable; making available to the public by any means including interactive transmissions; fixation (including photographs off screen); transmission of cable programmes; decoding of encrypted signals; importation and distribution of fixations or copies made without authorisation. The broadcasting organisations also drew attention to the need to protect the pre-broadcast signal and proposed a right of remuneration for private copying of broadcasts. At the Cancun symposium the list was enlarged by the addition of exclusive rights of communication to the public[37] and of authorising the rental of copies made from fixations.

The governments' proposals

To facilitate the SCCR's discussions at its 10th session in November 2003 the WIPO Secretariat distributed a document[38] comparing, article by article, the alternative proposals put forward by governments up to 15 September 2003. There had been four previous such comparative documents,[39] but the one distributed at the 10th session was to be the last; the committee, in its conclusions at the end of the session, decided that the Chairman and the Secretariat should prepare a consolidated text for the committee's 11th session in June 2004, the consolidated text to be available at the beginning of April 2004. Singapore submitted a treaty-language proposal in December 2003 which as it has turned out was the last full-dress proposal to be received.

---

[35]   Brazil grants a 70 year term.
[36]   'Questions raised concerning future international norms on the protection of broadcasting organizations' §§58–61 pp 15–16 SCCR/1/3.
[37]   'communication to the public' is here used in the same sense as in Art 13(d) of the Rome Convention as meaning the right to authorise public performance rather than the broad sense adopted in Art 8 of the WCT.
[38]   SCCR/10/3 15 September 2003.
[39]   SCCR/5/5 (proposals received up to 30 April 2001). SCCR/7/9 (proposals received up to 6 May 2002), SCCR/8/5 (proposals up to 16 Sept 2002), SCCR/9/5 (proposals up to 15 April 2003).

Using the Secretariat's document is a convenient way to structure an analysis of the divergencies and convergences which emerge from the formal proposals. However, it needs to be borne in mind that delegations which submitted formal proposals also expressed themselves in their interventions during the sessions, sometimes adding important nuances to what was on paper, and that those, the majority, which did not commit themselves to formal proposals, could nonetheless wield considerable influence by taking an active part in the discussion in session. There is a further distinction to be drawn here: a delegation which made a treaty-language proposal was inevitably indicating a degree of commitment to the updating of broadcasters' rights; those delegations which were sceptical about, or actively opposed, the objective generally had to express their scepticism or opposition by what they said in session; Brazil and Chile indeed found a way round this difficulty by submitting proposals[40] for the inclusion of articles which, arguably, had no place in a broadcasters' treaty. One should also not neglect the part played by the NGOs in, to some degree, influencing the agenda.

Before analysing the content of any of the proposals, it is worth enumerating which governments had submitted proposals by the cut-off of 15 September 2003. There were by that date 13 treaty-language proposals before the committee. They had been submitted by the following Members:

Switzerland – submitted by 31 March 1999
Mexico – submitted by 31 March 1999
Cameroon – submitted 18 May 1999
Argentina – submitted 29 July 1999
Tanzania – submitted 24 August 1999
Japan – submitted 25 April 2001
European Community – submitted 3 October 2001, addendum 24 June
   2003
Ukraine – submitted 9 October 2001
Eastern Republic of Uruguay – submitted 17 April 2002
Honduras – submitted 28 August 2002
Kenya – submitted 1 May 2003
US – submitted 21 October 2002, revised 1 May 2003
Egypt – submitted 24 June 2003

As well as these proposals, the committee received submissions in 1999 from regional round tables of Central European and Baltic states, of certain African states, and of certain states of Asia and the Pacific. The agreed statements range

---

[40]   SCCR/13/3Corr – Brazil, SCCR/13/4 – Chile.

Table 20.1 Analysis of overlap of membership of Rome and WPPT for countries which made treaty-language proposals up to June 2003

Countries making proposals	Region	Membership of Rome	Membership of WPPT	Signature of WPPT
Switzerland	Europe	Yes	No	Yes
Mexico	Central America	Yes	Yes	
Cameroon	Africa	No	No	No
Argentina	Latin America	Yes	Yes	
Tanzania	Africa	No	No	No
Japan	Asia	Yes	Yes	
European Community	Europe	25/27 of the Member States	No	Yes
Ukraine	Europe	Yes	Yes	
E. Republic of Uruguay	Latin America	Yes	No	Yes
Honduras	Central America	Yes	Yes	
Kenya	Africa	No	No	Yes
US	North America	No	Yes	
Egypt	North Africa	No	No	No

from the acknowledgement by the Central European and Baltic states of the case for updating broadcasters' rights because of the 'need to fight piracy',[41] and the 'general support' from the African states,[42] to the guarded statement that there was 'a need to study the possibility of updating' broadcasters' rights coupled with the declaration that 'At the same time, the interests of the developing and the least developed countries should be a primary concern' from the Asia-Pacific states.[43]

As Table 20.1 shows, five countries that made proposals were not members of Rome: Cameroon, Tanzania, Kenya, Egypt and the US. Three out of the five had also not signed the WPPT: Cameroon, Tanzania and Egypt. As for the other two, Kenya had signed the WPPT, and the US had brought it into force. The other eight countries were all members of Rome and had either already brought the WPPT into force (five of them) or had signed the instrument (the other three).

Another purely quantitative way of categorising these 13 proposals is to

---

[41] SCCR/2/10 Rev.
[42] SCCR/3/2.
[43] SCCR/3/6.

look at the length and the number of articles in a given proposal. On this yard-stick the proposals fall into two categories: short and full length, with four categorised as short and nine as full length.

The four short proposals are from Mexico, Cameroon, Tanzania and the Ukraine:

- *Mexico*   one page long, with no proposal for treaty text;
- *Cameroon*   four pages long: no treaty text as such but a number of suggestions – the pre-broadcast signal should be protected, there should be a 50 year term, exceptions and limitations should be based on Rome Art 15, and Art 6 Rome should define points of attachment, seven terms need definition but none is given;
- *Tanzania*   one page, no treaty text, general statement in support of modernising protection for broadcasters, the instrument should be a treaty; and
- *Ukraine*   three page proposal for a treaty with seven articles drawn from the WPPT, but without any substantive rights or definitions.

The proposals by Mexico and Cameroon both adopt by reference the list of substantive rights put forward by the regional broadcasting organisations at the WIPO symposia in Manila and Cancun. Domestic legislation as described in the Mexican proposal provides for a 25 year term of protection, whereas the broadcasters' proposals called for a 50 year term; it is unclear whether Mexico would support the longer term.

The remaining nine proposals may all be categorised as full length, though there are still variations in length, depending on whether a proposal includes text for the Administrative and Final Clauses, covering, for example, provisions for an Assembly, WIPO's responsibilities for administering the treaty, and when the treaty should enter into force. The EC, the US and Egypt all include Administrative and Final Clauses in one form or another, while Uruguay simply adopts the EC's text on Administrative and Final Clauses and Switzerland the WPPT's.

As one would expect there are important differences in substance between proposals, but there is also considerable overlap when one examines those provisions which provide what may be described as the armature of the proposals.

All nine proposals follow the equivalent WPPT provisions[44] on the following matters:

---

44   WPPT Arts 17(1), 19, 20 and 23.

- *Term* – 50 years
- *Rights management information*
- *No formalities*
- *Effective enforcement*

Eight of the nine also follow WPPT on technological measures. Switzerland has an additional article[45] which deals specifically with the provision of legal remedies against fraudulent decoding of encrypted broadcasts. Argentina addresses the same issue by adding specific obligations[46] relating to protection against unauthorised decryption to the general obligations taken from WPPT.

The WPPT allows Contracting Parties to make reservations[47] in accordance with its provision dealing with the right to limit the application of the right to a single equitable remuneration for the use of commercial phonograms. The WPPT also allows Contracting Parties, which are otherwise required to apply Berne Art 18,[48] to limit the application in time[49] of performers' moral rights. Six of the nine proposals exclude reservations: Switzerland, Japan, the EC, Uruguay, Honduras and Kenya. Argentina's proposal lacks any provision on reservations. The US follows Rome in allowing Contracting Parties by declaration to limit the application of the 'public rendition' right[50] and provides that if such a declaration has been made by one Contracting Party, other Contracting Parties are not obliged to grant public rendition rights to broadcasting organisations which have their headquarters in the Contracting Party that has made the declaration. Accordingly, the US allows reservations in respect of the public rendition provision but not otherwise. Egypt, whose proposal generally follows the US, has the same provisions. Eight of the nine proposals on application in time adopt Art 18 of Berne without qualification. The Argentinian proposal makes an exception to the general Berne rule in respect of rights acquired in a Contracting State before the entry into force of the instrument in that Contracting State.

---

[45] Art 14 Swiss proposal SCCR/2/5 p. 13.

[46] Art 8 Argentine proposal SCCR/3/4 p. 5.

[47] WPPT Art 21 Reservations and Art 15(3) Right to Remuneration.

[48] The general rule in Berne Art 18(1) is that the Convention applies to all works which at the date the Convention comes into force are still protected in their country of origin.

[49] WPPT Art 22(2).

[50] This right is more usually characterised as a 'communication to the public' right. In the context in which this latter term is used in Rome and in proposals on broadcasters' rights it has a much narrower scope than in Art 8 WCT. In the UK the term would be 'public performance'. The term 'public rendition' is defined in the US Proposal Art 2(h) p. 4 SCCR/9/4 Rev.

Three other provisions are treated in similar ways in all or most of the nine proposals. These are:

- Art 1 Relation to other Conventions (non-prejudice)
- Beneficiaries/points of attachment
- Eligibility

Five proposals use the same language for Art 1 as is used in the WPPT. They are Japan, the EC, Uruguay, Honduras and Kenya. The Swiss proposal inserts an initial paragraph declaring the instrument to be a protocol under the WPPT. Argentina adds a paragraph that the instrument leaves unaffected any copyright in the content of broadcasts. The US and Egypt substitute for the first paragraph of the WPPT text, which is a declaration that nothing in the new instrument derogates from obligations under Rome, a much broader declaration that refers to Berne, TRIPS, WCT, WPPT and the Brussels Satellites Convention as well as Rome.

All nine proposals deal with points of attachment in a way that conforms closely to the equivalent Rome provision;[51] the latter sets out two criteria, either of which if satisfied will entitle the beneficiaries to protection – that the beneficiary has its headquarters in a Contracting State other than the Contracting State where protection is sought or that the protected transmission has been transmitted from a transmitter in a Contracting State other than the Contracting State where protection is sought. It is open to Contracting States to make a declaration restricting the obligation to protect broadcasts of broadcasters whose headquarters are in the same Contracting State as their transmitters.

Only the EC and Uruguay retain the possibility for Contracting States by declaration to restrict the scope of their obligations to beneficiaries with headquarters in the same Contracting State as their transmitters. Six of the other seven proposals require that the beneficiaries are protected if they meet either of the two criteria. Argentina's proposal requires that beneficiaries have their headquarters in a Contracting State other than the one where protection is sought *and* have their transmitters in another Contracting State, but there is no requirement that headquarters and transmitters be in the same Contracting State. Argentina also defines in this Article the point of attachment for a satellite broadcast.[52] The Kenyan proposal does the same. The US proposal not only defines points of attachment for satellite broadcasts but also

---

[51]   Art 6 Rome.

[52]   'the point at which the sounds or images, or images with sounds, or the representations thereof, intended for direct reception by the public are introduced, under the control and on the responsibility of the broadcasting organisation, into an unbroken chain of communication towards the satellite and from it down to earth.'

for cablecasts and webcasts. Egypt adopts the same approach as the US but excludes any reference to webcasts.

Seven of the proposals are described in their title as Treaties; two, the Swiss and the Argentinian, as Protocols, with the Swiss expressly referring to the instrument as a protocol 'under the WIPO Performances and Phonograms Treaty', implying that membership of the WPPT would be a pre-condition. However, in session the Swiss Delegation stated that it was 'open and flexible to discuss and envisage other solutions'.[53] The Argentinian proposal does not identify the prior instrument to which its proposal is to be a protocol, although logically it might be supposed that it would be the earlier related rights treaty, the WPPT. Its article on eligibility[54] states that any Member State of WIPO may become a party to the instrument. The US proposal, by contrast, is described as a treaty, but its provision on eligibility[55] excludes states unless they are party to the WCT and the WPPT. Egypt does not follow the US on this point, leaving membership open to any Member State of WIPO.[56]

There is no Preamble to the proposals of Switzerland, Argentina, Japan, Uruguay or Egypt. The proposals which include a Preamble draw in a recognisable way on the Preamble to the WPPT. The EC uses the most similar language but adds at the end of the fourth paragraph a reference to a need for broadcasting organisations 'to acknowledge the rights of authors and holders of related rights' in the content of their broadcasts. The Preamble to the proposal of Honduras although the language of the WPPT has been somewhat modified is probably closest to the previous instrument. The Kenyan and the US proposals add language taken from the broadcasters' proposals[57] which stresses the direct benefits to other rights owners of protecting the rights of broadcasters (the US also refers to cablecasting and webcasting organisations).

The remaining elements of the proposals, namely the object of protection, the definitions and the substantive rights, are where one might expect to find the most variation between proposals since even if there were consensus that the object of protection was the broadcasts of broadcasting organisations, there could still be different views on whether there was a need to define such organisations and if so how, and there would undoubtedly be room for different approaches, wide or narrow, to the specific rights.

The object of protection and definitions of broadcasting and broadcasting organisations   All nine of the full length proposals identify broadcasting

---

53   §98 p. 19 SCCR/3/11.
54   Art 15 SCCR/3/4.
55   Art 18 SCCR/9/4 Rev.
56   Art 18 SCCR/9/8 Rev.
57   SCCR/2/6 p. 3.

organisations as the beneficiaries of protection in respect of their broadcasts, the objects of protection. Five of the nine full length proposals dispense with a definition of a broadcasting organisation. These are Switzerland, Japan, the EC, Uruguay and Honduras. Switzerland also does without a definition of broadcasting but is the only proposal to do so. At the opposite end of the spectrum is the US, which provides definitions of broadcasting, but also cablecasting and (notoriously) webcasting, as well as of broadcasting organisations, cablecasting organisations and webcasting organisations, and which proposes that webcasts, in addition to broadcasts and cablecasts, should be objects of protection. Three other proposals provide definitions of broadcasting organisations. One of them, Egypt, uses the same language as the US and so defines cablecasting and cablecasting organisations as well as broadcasting and broadcasting organisations but deletes any reference to webcasting or webcasting organisations. Argentina defines broadcasting organisation and assimilates cable distributors to broadcasting organisations. Kenya chooses to define 'broadcast' rather than 'broadcasting', though the content of the definition focuses on the same elements. Its definition of 'broadcasting organisation' is fairly close to the US definition. The EC defines 'broadcasting' and that is the only definition which is offered. In a revised proposal submitted in June 2003 the EC added language to the definition which was intended to assimilate 'simulcasting' to broadcasting. This analysis may perhaps mislead the reader into thinking that the differences are more marked or clearcut than is the case. If one supposes, as seems probable, that all those intending to make a proposal took as a point of reference the definition of 'broadcasting' in the WPPT, one can immediately see that that definition, in the context of the broadcasters' own proposals, raises a number of issues. The WPPT definition reads:

> 'broadcasting' means the transmission by wireless means for public reception of sounds or of images and sounds or of the representations thereof; such transmissions by satellite is also 'broadcasting'; transmission of encrypted signals is 'broadcasting' where the means for decrypting are provided to the public by the broadcasting organisation or with its consent.

In the WPPT the operational purpose of the definition is to identify the circumstances in which a performer's exclusive right to authorise live performances bites[58] and in which the single equitable remuneration is payable.[59] In the broadcasters' treaty the operational purpose of the definition is to mark out the object of protection. The definition draws to the draftsman's attention a number of relevant considerations:

---

[58]   Art 6(i) WPPT.
[59]   Art 15 WPPT.

Should broadcasting be confined to 'wireless means'? The EC, Honduras and Kenya have 'by wire and wireless means' in their definitions of 'broadcasting' and intend thereby to bring cable distribution within the scope of protection. The US and Egypt achieve the same result by different means, as already described. The EC within its definition excludes 'mere retransmission', so making it clear that only cable origination is to be protected. Argentina separates 'broadcasting', which involves wireless transmission, from 'cable distribution' by wire, but its definition of 'broadcasting organisation', which refers to a body authorised by a Contracting Party, embraces authorised entities that 'engage(s) in cable distribution'. It would be logical to deduce that the intention is to protect broadcasts and cable distributed transmissions: the question whether mere retransmissions are protected is unanswered.

Should transmissions by satellite be treated as broadcasting so long as they are intended for reception by the public[60]? All the proposals make it clear that satellite broadcasts are objects of protection. Some proposals achieve this in the same way as the WPPT: by including satellite broadcasts in their definitions of broadcasting: this method is adopted by Argentina, the EC, Honduras, Kenya, the US and Egypt. The same countries also deal with satellite broadcasting within the provision that defines points of attachment. Switzerland, Japan and Uruguay simply include a reference to satellite broadcasts within the provision on points of attachment.

Should encrypted transmissions qualify for protection? Again, all proposals agree that encrypted signals which are intended for reception by the public – that is, where the means of decrypting are provided or authorised by the broadcaster – should be objects of protection, while adopting different techniques to achieve this result.

As already mentioned, only four of the nine proposals have a definition of 'broadcasting organisation': Argentina, Kenya, the US and Egypt. The Argentinian definition refers to the broadcasting organisation having been authorised by a Contracting Party. This aspect, the notion that broadcasting organisations are entities subject to regulatory oversight and control, attracted some support in session but has not survived into the latest text.[61] The other three definitions focus on something quite different: what it is that a broadcasting organisation does. The Kenyan speaks of an organisation that 'assembles

---

[60] Art 2(f) WPPT has 'public reception' rather than 'reception by the public'. The author has long argued that if the English text of Rome Art 3(f), where the expression 'public reception' first appears in a definition of broadcasting, is intended to convey the same sense as the French text, then 'reception by the public' would be correct. See now Art 5(a) p. 25 SCCR/15/2 Rev.

[61] See Commentary 5.05 p. 26 and Art 5(c) p. 27 SCCR/15/2 Rev.

the schedule of programs and transmits the sounds and images or both or representations thereof, in such a manner as to cause such sounds or images to be received by the public'.[62] The US definition[63] is along similar lines but identifies more criteria: the organisation must be a legal entity; it must take the initiative and have the responsibility for the first transmission to the public and for the assembly and scheduling of the content. These criteria define cable-casting organisations and webcasting organisations as well as broadcasting organisations. It is interesting that the Egyptian definition[64] follows the definition in the earlier US proposal[65] rather than the revised version. The earlier definition has two elements that were changed in the later version. In the earlier version the organisation could be a person or a legal entity and satisfied the definition by performing either or both of the two functions specified: that is, taking the initiative and having the responsibility for the first transmission and/or assembling and scheduling the content.[66]

Other definitions   Argentina, Japan, Kenya, the US and Egypt include definitions of terms other than broadcasting[67] and broadcasting organisation. All five define rebroadcasting (or 'retransmission' in Argentina's proposal). For Argentina, the US and Egypt rebroadcasting/retransmission means the simultaneous broadcasting by one broadcasting organisation of the broadcast of another broadcasting organisation: this is exactly the definition to be found in Rome.[68] The US adds definitions of cable retransmission and computer network retransmission which are the same definition as rebroadcasting *mutatis mutandis*. The Egyptian proposal includes the US definition of cable retransmission but excludes computer network retransmission. Japan and Kenya define the term rebroadcasting as covering simultaneous and deferred broadcasting.

Argentina, Japan and Kenya have definitions of 'communication to the public' or in the case of the US 'public rendition'. Argentina defines the term as 'making the broadcast . . . or a fixation thereof audible or visible in places accessible to the public'.[69] Japan has a wider definition, referring to 'the

---

62   Art 2(b) p. 3 SCCR/9/3.
63   Art 2(d) p. 3 SCCR/9/4 Rev.
64   Art 2(c) p. 3 SCCR/9/8.
65   Art 2(d) p. 3 SCCR/8/7.
66   Compare: 'References . . . to a person making a broadcast . . . are – (a) to the person transmitting the programme, if he has responsibility to any extent for its contents, and (b) to any person providing the programme who makes with the person transmitting it the arrangements necessary for its transmission' Section 6(3) UK Copyright, Designs & Patents Act 1988.
67   Kenya uses the term 'broadcast' rather than 'broadcasting', as noted earlier.
68   Art 2(g) Rome.
69   Art 2(f) p. 3 SCCR/3/4.

transmission to the public by any medium, otherwise than by broadcasting, of a broadcast' and adds that communication to the public 'includes making a broadcast audible or visible or audible and visible to the public'.[70] Kenya's definition is very close to Argentina's.[71] The US definition, which covers public rendition of a broadcast, cablecast and webcast, refers to making 'the transmission or a fixation thereof . . . audible or visible or audible and visible in places accessible to the public'.[72]

The substantive rights Tables 20.2 and 20.3 set out for comparative purposes the package of rights included in each of the nine full-length proposals. Table 20.2 covers six rights:

- Rebroadcasting;
- Retransmission by cable;
- Retransmission over computer networks;
- Fixation;
- Public performance, ie making audible and/or visible in public;
- Reproduction (of authorised fixations), ie where the fixation but not the reproduction has been authorised.

Table 20.3 covers three possible rights which some of the proposals treat as exclusive, others as 'rights to prohibit'; as to the pre-broadcast signal, the protection of which is the fourth item on the list, those proposals which include it suggest that Contracting States should provide 'adequate and effective legal protection', which does not impose a requirement to give broadcasters a private proprietary right at all. The four are as follows:

- Distribution;
- Making available;
- Decoding;
- Protection of the pre-broadcast signal.

The content of the two tables derives in large part from the text put forward by the broadcasting organisations at the WIPO symposia and later circulated to the SCCR by the International Bureau.[73] In the broadcasters' texts ten substantive rights are identified,[74] but they are not the same as the ten in the

---

[70]   Art 2 (c) p. 3 SCCR/5/4.
[71]   Art 2 (d) p. 3 SCCR/9/3 Rev.
[72]   Art 2(h) p. 4 SCCR/9/4 Rev.
[73]   pp 8–16 SCCR/2/6.
[74]   See above, p. 491.

government proposals, and it is worth dwelling on the differences and considering why they arose.

The right to authorise or prohibit the simultaneous or deferred retransmission by wire or wireless means of a cablecast or webcast or a fixation of either is absent from the broadcasters' list of rights. That is because the objects of protection in the broadcasters' text, naturally enough, are the broadcasts of broadcasting organisations.

What is more interesting is why the broadcasters themselves did not propose any protection for simulcasts[75] (that is, internet transmissions of their broadcasts transmitted by broadcasting organisations at the same time as the broadcasts). The simple answer seems to be that simulcasting as an interesting possibility had not caught on with broadcasters at the time of the WIPO symposia in 1997 and 1998, and so they were not alert to the need for protection. The growth in the use of simulcasting by broadcasters tracks their growing awareness of the importance of the internet to the age group between 16 and 25.

Similarly, the importance of the internet came into focus only gradually at WIPO. In its first intervention[76] the US delegation indicated that its government was 'studying the nature of activities akin to broadcasting in new media, including activities in the Internet'. But thereafter the interventions by the US in session were extremely restricted until its own proposal was submitted just before the eighth session in October 2002. That proposal included cablecasts and webcasts as distinct objects of protection and gave them retransmission and other rights *pari passu* with broadcasters. Although the proposal extended the scope of the treaty, because the US did not 'see any basis for limiting the treaty to traditional broadcasters',[77] it did not expressly refer to simulcasts. In the first proposal from the EC, in October 2001, a year before the US proposal, the EC had adopted a broad definition of broadcasting which included 'transmission by wire'[78] within the definition, but the proposal contained no reference to simulcasting or webcasting or to the internet except in the context of the 'making available' right. Then, in June 2003, in the session after the US had submitted its proposal, the EC submitted a revision to its definition of broadcasting, which assimilated simulcasts to broadcasts. Another 18 months went by before there was any reaction in session from broadcasters. At the

---

75   'simulcasts' and 'simulcasting' acquired a special sense as referring to internet transmissions in the context of the WIPO discussions. In ordinary broadcasting parlance if a transmission was being simulcast it meant that a programme was being delivered in parallel, for example on AM and FM frequencies simultaneously.

76   §96 p. 19 Report of third session SCCR/3/11.

77   §19 p. 6 Report of eighth session SCCR/8/9.

78   See above p. 499.

12th session in November 2004 the representative of the European Broadcasting Union finally said that European broadcasters were grateful to the EC for the inclusion of protection for broadcasters' simulcasts in the EC proposal.[79] Other than that intervention, no representative of any regional broadcasting organisation spoke in favour of the inclusion of webcasting/simulcasting. Similarly, there have not been any interventions by representatives of regional broadcasting organisations in favour of the inclusion of cablecasting: those speaking on behalf of broadcasters have not seen any need to stick up for cablecasters, whose own representatives have been rather conspicuous by their absence.[80] Webcasters on the other hand had eloquent advocacy from the representative of the Digital Media Association (DiMA) in the early days and, it was clear in the result, effective Congressional support in Washington in securing their inclusion in the US proposal. Again, broadcasters had little reason to get behind someone else's bandwagon. Quite the reverse, since it was abundantly clear in Geneva that there was no support in the committee for the US line that a modern treaty on broadcasting needed to include webcasting. Unfortunately for the broadcasters, the US also took the position that if webcasting fell by the wayside it would be unacceptable for simulcasting to remain in the text. A crucial turning point was the decision by the Chair at the 14th session in May 2006 to give priority to the discussion of the protection of traditional broadcasting and to defer discussion of webcasting and simulcasting until a later date. This was a decision accepted only with considerable reluctance by the US. As for the EC it entered a reservation that its acceptance was without prejudice to simulcasting being 'reintegrated into the main package'[81] at the appropriate moment. There was no elaboration in session as to when the moment might be appropriate, but at the least the statement seemed intended to serve notice that the EC would feel free to re-introduce simulcasting at a Diplomatic Conference.

Returning now to the substantive rights in the nine proposals, the two Tables show the following:

---

[79] §194 p. 31 SCCR/12/4.

[80] The Canadian Cable Telecommunications Association (CCTA), whose representative regularly attended sessions of the committee, demonstrates the point. CCTA has to date not made a single intervention in support of the rights of cablecasters in their (original) cablecasts. The CCTA's interest in the proceedings have to do with the fact that if a treaty was agreed and Canada acceded to it a provision giving U.S. broadcasters a cable retransmission right enforceable against Canadian cable companies would considerably increase the amounts payable by the cable companies. The Canadian delegate has proposed that a Contracting Party should be able, by way of a reservation, to exclude the obligation to protect free to air broadcasters against retransmission by cable of their broadcasts.

[81] §368 p. 92 SCCR/14/7 prov.

Table 20.2 Substantive rights

	Rebroadcasting simultaneous and deferred	Retransmission by cable simultaneous and deferred	Retransmission by computer networks	Fixation	Making audible and/or visible in public	Reproduction of authorised fixations
Switzerland	✓ Art 4 in any manner or form whatsoever	✓ Art 4 in any manner or form whatsoever	✓ Art 4 in any manner or form whatsoever	✓ Art 7 in whole or in part	✓ Art 5 in any manner or form	✓ Art 8 in any manner or form
Argentina	✓ Art 5(I and II)	? Art 5(III) covers simultaneous but no ref to deferred	✗	✓ Art 5(VII)	✓ Art 5(VII)	✓ Art 5(V)
Japan	✓ Art 5(i)	Art 5(i) does not expressly cover deferred retransmission	Art 5(i) refers to transmission by any medium otherwise than by broadcasting	✓ Art 5(ii) includes still photography of a television broadcast		✓ Art 6 in any manner or form
EC	✓ Art 6 simultaneous or based on fixations	✓ Art 6 simultaneous or based on fixations	✓ Art 6 EC interprets by wire or wireless means as covering internet	✓ Art 4	✓ Art 8 but only where entrance fee is paid	✓ Art 5 in any manner or form

Country					
Uruguay	✓Art 7 simultaneous or based on fixations	✓Art 7 simultaneous or based on fixations	?Art 7 uses EC by wire or wireless means – unclear whether internet is covered	✓Art 5	✓Art 9 as EC but suggest broader right	✓Art 6 in any manner or form
Honduras	✓Art 5	✓Art 5	✗	✓Art 5 including photographs from television signals	✓Art 5 against payment of an entrance fee	✓By any procedure or in any form
Kenya	✓Art 5(1)(f) simultaneous or subsequent	✓Art 5(1)(e) refers to 'transmission' whereas definition is of 'distribution'	✗The definition of cable distribution is probably too narrow	✓Art 5(1)(a) other than for private purposes	✓Art 5(1)(d)	✓Art 5(1)(b)
US	✓Simultaneous Art 5(a) deferred Art 5(d) (all rights also cover cablecasts and webcasts)	✓Simultaneous Art 5(c) deferred Art 5(d)	✓Simultaneous Art 5(b) deferred Art 5(d)	✓Art 5(e)	✓Art 5(g)(i) against payment of an entrance fee	✗Art 5(f) covers unauthorised reproductions as Rome Art 13 Art 6(b) has right to prohibit
Egypt	✓Simultaneous Art 5(a) deferred Art 5(b) (all rights also cover cablecasts)	✗Art 5(b) only covers deferred transmission	✗Art 5(b) covers deferred transmission by means of a computer network	✓Art 5(c)	✓Art 5(e)(i) against payment of an entrance fee	✗Art 5(d) only covers unauthorised reproductions as Rome Art 13

Table 20.3   Further substantive rights

	Distribution of physical copies	Making available/ on-demand right	Decoding	Protection of pre-broadcast signal
Switzerland	✓Art 9	✓Art 10	✓Art 6	✗
Argentina	✗	✓Art 5 VIII	✓Art 5 VI	✗
Japan	✗	✓Art 7	✗	✗
EC	✓Art 9	✓Art 7	✗	✓Art 10 adequate legal protection
Uruguay	✓Art 10	✓Art 8	✓Art 11	✓Art 12 adequate legal protection
Honduras	✓Art 5	✓Art 5	✓Art 5	?Art 5 distribution by television
Kenya	✓Art 5(1)(g)	✓Art 5(1)(c)	✓Art 5(1)(h)	✓Art 5(2)
US	✗Art 6(c) right to prohibit	✗Art 6(a) right to prohibit	✗SCCR/8/7 provided protection deleted in SCCR/9/4 Rev	✓Art 7 adequate and effective protection
Egypt	✗Art 6(c) right to prohibit	✗Art 6(a) right to prohibit	✗	✓Art 7 adequate and effective legal protection

The proposal from Singapore[82]   Singapore's was the last full length proposal to be submitted. Like the US its proposal is a treaty, but only those WIPO members are eligible who are parties to the WCT and the WPPT.[83] The objects of protection[84] are broadcasts and cablecasts, as in the Egyptian proposal. Singapore is the only one of the full length proposals to propose a 20 year term

---

[82]   SCCR/11/2 submitted 26 December 2003.
[83]   Art 20 ibid.
[84]   Art 3 ibid.

of protection[85] as in Rome rather than the 50 year term in WPPT. Singapore follows the WPPT with its provisions on limitations and exceptions,[86] technological measures,[87] formalities,[88] reservations,[89] application in time,[90] and enforcement.[91] The definitions of broadcasting organisation and cablecasting organisation[92] stipulate that these must be legal entities and must take the initiative and have responsibility for the first transmission as well as assembling and scheduling the contents. There are five exclusive rights: simultaneous and deferred rebroadcasting; fixation; reproduction of unauthorised fixations, simultaneous and deferred cable retransmission, and public performance in places where an entrance fee is payable.[93] There is a requirement that Contracting Parties provide adequate legal protection and effective legal remedies to prevent unauthorised exploitation of signal prior to broadcast.[94] There is no protection for simulcasts, nor any protection in respect of the exploitation of broadcasts over the internet (the making available right is absent and so is a retransmission right that applies to the internet).

Working towards a Draft Basic Proposal   At the end of the 10th Session in November 2003 the committee took the decision to ask the Chair and the Secretariat to prepare a Consolidated Text for consideration at the following session in June 2004. As noted above, Singapore submitted its proposal at the end of December 2003; after that no further full length proposals were received. Brazil and Chile submitted proposals in November 2005; these were short and focussed on specific concerns about access to knowledge, cultural diversity and the development agenda; similarly, short proposals from Colombia and Peru were submitted in March and April 2006. The Colombian proposal contained a clause to be added to the provision on technological measures. The Peruvian submission was a more general commentary on the development dimension and the importance of not hurrying to convene a diplomatic conference.

The implication of the decision at the 10th session was that the process had reached a stage where the relevant issues were on the table in the proposals

---

85   Art 12 ibid.
86   Art 11 ibid.
87   Art 13 ibid.
88   Art 14 ibid.
89   Art 15 ibid.
90   Art 16 ibid.
91   Art 17 ibid.
92   Art 2 ibid.
93   Arts 5, 6, 7, 8 and 9 ibid.
94   Art 10 ibid.

made in the preceding sessions, and that the committee could now start to work towards a text which would provide the basis for negotiation at a Diplomatic Conference: a Draft Basic Proposal. The task of capturing the committee's deliberations in a way that helped to clarify its direction of travel fell largely to the Chair. As a matter of procedure any decision on the convening of a diplomatic conference is taken by the General Assembly on the recommendation of the SCCR. As already mentioned,[95] the General Assembly has already taken up the question of broadcasters' rights in three successive years. The exact sequence of recommendation and decision has been as follows:

1. In June 2004 the SCCR's conclusions at its 11th session included a recommendation to the General Assembly to consider the possibility of convening at an appropriate time a diplomatic conference. Responding to this recommendation and the discussion at the General Assembly itself, the General Assembly requested the SCCR to accelerate its work on the protection of broadcasting organisations with a view to approving the convening of a diplomatic conference by the WIPO General Assembly in 2005.[96]

2. The 12th session of the committee, held in the month after the General Assembly, proved to be so contentious that no consensus could be reached. The Chair issued his own conclusions, envisaging the holding of regional consultations but without any statement about when the committee would next meet nor any recommendation to the General Assembly.

3. No meeting of the SCCR was called before the General Assembly meeting the following year. Although many delegations in the discussion of the item at the General Assembly supported the convening of a diplomatic conference at an appropriate time or, specifically, in 2006,[97] others expressed concerns. Iran on behalf of the Asian Group suggested that two additional meetings would be necessary in 2006. Brazil on behalf of a group of Latin American and other countries[98] supported the need for two

---

95   See p. 486.
96   §56 p. 12 WO/GA/31/15 27 September–5 October 2004.
97   Ecuador, the Czech Republic on behalf of the Group of Central European and Baltic States, Switzerland on behalf of the members of Group B, Moldova on behalf of the Central Asian, Caucasus and Eastern European Group, the United Kingdom on behalf of the EC, El Salvador, Antigua and Barbuda on behalf of the Caribbean Delegations, Trinidad and Tobago, Kenya on behalf of the 14 African States that met in Nairobi in May 2005, Benin on behalf of the least developed countries, Mexico, Nicaragua, Colombia, Jamaica, Norway, New Zealand, Japan, the US and China.
98   Argentina, Bolivia, Cuba, Dominican Republic, Ecuador, Iran, Peru, Sierra Leone, South Africa, Tanzania and Venezuela.

additional meetings and expressed the view that more work was needed before the convening of a diplomatic conference could be agreed to. India urged the General Assembly not to rush to convene a diplomatic conference and said that India had asked UNESCO to ensure that the objectives of promotion of freedom of expression and universal access to information and knowledge were not hindered by the proposed treaty provisions.[99] The decision of the General Assembly was that two additional meetings of the SCCR should be scheduled to accelerate discussions. These meetings should 'aim to agree and finalize a Basic Proposal . . . to enable the 2006 WIPO General Assembly to recommend the convening of a Diplomatic Conference in December 2006, or at an appropriate date in 2007'.[100]

4. The 14th session of the committee was in May 2006. At this meeting what has been described earlier as a crucial turning point[101] was reached, when the US accepted the Chair's decision to remove webcasting and simulcasting from the committee's agenda and to confine the draft basic proposal to traditional broadcasting. The committee's conclusions endorsed the Chair's decision and described the aim of the 15th session as being to agree and finalise a basic proposal for a treaty in order to enable the 2006 General Assembly to recommend the convening of a diplomatic conference in December 2006 or an appropriate date in 2007.

5. The conclusions of the 15th session and of the General Assembly have already been described.[102]

6. Much of the time of the first special session in January 2007 was spent in informal discussions between the Member States, which were not minuted. There was no public indication that positions had altered or that there had been any appreciable movement towards consensus.

Changing the climate   In the interest of coherence the preceding narrative has to a large extent kept in the foreground the content of the proposals which WIPO Members tabled. As already noted[103] this inevitably does less than justice to those WIPO Members such as India, Brazil, Chile, South Africa, which had reservations about the process or the proposed treaty. Such an account also ignores the role of the NGOs. But probably the right place to start is with a general observation about the system of intellectual property protection and the climate of opinion. The internet treaties of 1996[104] were agreed at

---

99   §66 p. 14 WO/GA/32/13.
100 §85 p. 16 ibid.
101 See above p. 503.
102 See above p. 486.
103 See above p. 492.
104 See above p. 485.

a time when the atmosphere so far as the system of intellectual property protection was concerned was still relatively benign. However, the treaty implementation process, particularly in the US, began to create a community of opposition whose issues, broadly speaking, were focussed on keeping the internet free from regulation: this spread across to worries about the way in which access to public domain material and its use in the internet environment might be constrained by technological measures. Opponents of the broadcaster treaty transposed these same issues across to the discussion about broadcasters' rights.

There were changes at WIPO itself. In the mid-1990s WIPO was still led by Director-General Arpad Bogsch, who could without much exaggeration be said to have invented WIPO. Bogsch was whole-hearted in his advocacy of intellectual property protection and WIPO's role as a propagator of model legislation. With his departure and the appointment of Kamil Idris WIPO became more susceptible to other possible conceptions of its mission. In the summer of 2004 Brazil and Argentina began to gather support for a proposal to shift WIPO's focus. The group of 12 countries that signed the document launched by Brazil and Argentina became known as the Friends of Development. The other signatories apart from Brazil and Argentina were Bolivia, Cuba, the Dominican Republic, Ecuador, Iran, Kenya, Sierra Leone, South Africa, Tanzania and Venezuela. The group called for the establishment of a Development Agenda for WIPO and specifically stated:

> Intellectual property protection cannot be seen as an end in itself, nor can the harmonization of intellectual property laws leading to higher protection standards in all countries, irrespective of their levels of development.[105]

On the broadcaster treaty the group took the following position:

> The potential development implications of several of the provisions of the proposed Treaty on the Protection of Broadcasting Organizations that the Standing Committee on Copyright and related Rights is currently discussing should be examined, taking into consideration the interests of consumers and the public at large.[106]

The implications of the group's demand that the interests of consumers and the public at large should be taken into consideration were amplified later in the text as follows:

> WIPO should foster the active participation of public interest non-governmental organizations in its subsidiary bodies to ensure that in IP norm-setting a proper

---

[105]   p. 2 WO/GA/31/11.
[106]   p. 3 ibid.

balance is struck between the producers and users of technological knowledge, in a manner that fully services the public interest.[107]

At the 2004 General Assembly which called for the Standing Committee to accelerate its work on the protection of broadcasting organisations the Assembly also agreed to convene inter-sessional intergovernmental meetings to examine the Friends of Development proposal for the establishment of a development agenda. As was acknowledged in the proposal, if the new emphasis on development was accepted it would mean amending the Convention which established WIPO.[108] The implications for the broadcaster treaty discussions were less clearcut. The proposal from the Friends of Development was (and remains at the time of writing) simply a proposal. The most visible sign of a change in WIPO's approach to its mission has been the increase in the number of public interest or 'civil society' NGOs which have been granted full accreditation or ad hoc observer status to attend the SCCR and the General Assembly. This can be seen by analysing the record of attendance in the reports of the committee's meetings.

Participation by NGOs in the work of the SCCR From 1998 when the committee was set up until the seventh session in May 2002 most of the NGOs which came to Geneva (38 came to the seventh session) came as representatives of rights holders: for example, the International Confederation of Societies of Authors and Composers (CISAC), the Association of European Performers Organisations (AEPO), the International Federation of Film Producers Associations (FIAPF); add to that the NGOs, fluctuating between nine and twelve, which represented the various regional broadcasting organisations; and a small number of organisations which either have a professional or academic interest, as does the Max Planck Institute (MPI) or the International Literary and Artistic Association (ALAI) or which represent a relevant industry, such as the Japan Electronics and Information Technology Industries Association (JEITA). The only NGO at the seventh session which did not fit into one or other of these categories was the World Blind Union (WBU). Over the following five sessions the number of NGOs increased, going from 38 to 55 at the 12th session in November 2004 and then falling back somewhat to 48 at the 15th session in September 2006. A significant number of the NGOs who began to come to the Standing Committee over this four year period were 'public interest' organisations whose active participation was being solicited by the Friends of Development: Civil Society

---

[107] p. 5 ibid.
[108] See p. 539.

Coalition (CSC), Electronic Frontier Foundation (EFF), IP Justice, Union for the Public Domain (UPD), Public Knowledge, Creative Commons International (CCI), Open Knowledge Foundation (OKF). A number of other NGOs represented the interests of libraries and archives: Coordinating Council of Audiovisual Archives Associations (CCAAA), European Bureau of Library Information and Documentation Association (EBLIDA), International Federation of Library Associations and Institutions (IFLA). Others represented industries whose interests might be affected by a broadcasters' treaty: Computer and Communications Industry Association (CCIA), European Information and Communications Technology Industry Association (EICTA), the US Telecom Association. As it happens, the NGO which has played the most active and effective role in orchestrating and coordinating opposition to the broadcasters' treaty in its present form is the International Music Managers Forum (IMMF), which is not a public interest NGO and represents interests which are not directly affected by the proposed treaty.

Conclusion

What are the prospects for the second special session of the SCCR? A number of outcomes can be envisaged.

A failure to achieve consensus must be on the cards. The consequence of such a failure would be that there would be no diplomatic conference in 2007 and the General Assembly would have to consider the matter once again. It would be open to the US and the EC to seek a decision from the Assembly restoring webcasting and simulcasting to the agenda of the SCCR and to invite the General Assembly to assess at its next session in 2008, after a further two sessions of the SCCR, the possibility of convening a diplomatic conference sometime in 2009 covering traditional broadcasting and the new methods of distribution. It is a matter for speculation how the Friends of Development would react.

Another possibility is that some form of compromise is achieved. The attempt to reach a compromise is certainly likely to be attempted since that is the outcome which the WIPO process, much more genuinely multilateral now than in years past, enforces on participating governments. Compromise is enforced, that is, because the requirement of consensus is very stringent. In principle, a single negative voice denotes lack of consensus. A determined minority can delay progress almost indefinitely. The risk of trying to reach a compromise is that eventually all coherence disappears. A treaty from which all proprietary rights for broadcasters had been eliminated (the Brussels Satellites Convention model favoured by the IMMF) and which provided no remedy against unauthorised exploitation of broadcasts or simulcasts over the internet would be, in this writer's opinion, worse than useless.

Other issues could be regarded as candidates for the SCCR's agenda. There is the proposal from Chile for a treaty on limitations and exceptions. The audiovisual performers treaty remains obstinately on the back burner despite efforts behind the scenes by the Secretariat to persuade the interested parties that there is some possibility of movement. The effect of a failure by the committee to achieve agreement on a broadcaster treaty may be to restore the status quo ante the 1996 treaties: in other words, to move WIPO away from formal norm-setting.

Index